SCIENCE, TECHNOLOGY
AND EVERYDAY LIFE
1870–1950

SCIENCE, TECHNOLOGY AND EVERYDAY LIFE 1870–1950

Edited by Colin Chant

Contributors
· Richard Bessel · Franz-Josef Brüggemeier ·
· Noel Coley · James R. Moore · Gerrylynn K. Roberts ·
· Bernard Waites ·

Routledge

The Open University

Routledge in association with The Open University

First published in 1989 by
Routledge
11 New Fetter Lane, London EC4P 4EE
29 West 35th Street, New York 10001

British Library Cataloguing in Publication Data

Chant, Colin.
  Science, technology and everyday life, 1870–1950.
  1. Scientific knowledge. Sociological
  perspectives.
  I. Title.
  306′45

  Available
  ISBN 0–415–00037–8
  ISBN 0–415–03557–0 Pbk

This book forms part of an Open University course A282 *Science, Technology and Everyday
Life 1870–1950*. For information about this course please write to the Student Enquiries
Office, The Open University, PO Box 71, Walton Hall, Milton Keynes, MK7 6AG, UK.

This book is set in 10/11 point Times New Roman by Input Typesetting Ltd, London
Printed and bound in Great Britain at the University Press, Cambridge

CONTENTS

PREFACE

How has everyday life changed between the late-nineteenth and mid-twentieth century? How much of this change is due to innovations such as electric power, plastics, pharmaceuticals, reinforced-concrete construction, electric trains, motor cars, radio and cinema, processed food, modern surgery and sanitation, and mass-production techniques? And where do these 'marvels' of modern science-based technology come from? These are some of the questions debated by a group of historians of science and technology and social historians at the Open University (with the help of Franz Brüggemeier of the FernUniversität); the main result of their deliberations is this collection of essays, which forms the central text of a new undergraduate course. The volume is, however, self-contained by design, and its distinctive teaching purpose should present no barriers to the general reader.

The first two chapters raise some general issues in the study of science, technology and everyday life; the intermediate chapters take up some of these issues in specific areas of technological change, in the broadest sense of technology; some of the most over-arching issues, though, cannot be examined until the final two chapters, in which ensembles of technological innovation are considered in distinctive ways. Throughout, finer details of technological innovations have been limited to those that clearly bear on matters of social change.

As with any historical enterprise, but most perceptibly in one like this, which attempts to draw together research from a bewildering variety of historical disciplines and subdisciplines, much of the territory has been staked out in what may seem an arbitrary fashion. Chronological and geographical incisions in the seamless web of history are notoriously hard to rationalize. A convenient guiding concept for this collection is the 'Second Industrial Revolution' (see Hobsbawm, E. J., 1968, *Industry and Empire*, Weidenfeld and Nicolson; Landes, D. S., 1969, *The Unbound Prometheus*, Cambridge University Press), a term connoting change at more than one level: at the technological level, the introduction of new materials (organic chemicals, and bulk and alloy steels), new sources of power (the electric motor and internal combustion engine), new electrical communications media, and generally, the deliberate harnessing of scientific research to technological innovation; at the industrial and economic level, the proliferation of mass-production techniques based on innovations in machine tools and ever more precise interchangeability of parts; the spread of scientific management, as the old-style individual enterprise yielded to the joint-stock company and multi-unit business corporation; and at the social level, the emergence of a mass consumer society as everyday life grew ever more urban, and suburban, in the United States and Western Europe. The term is used advisedly, with the emphasis more on 'second' than on 'revolution'. We are talking here of a stage in the general process of industrialization, outmoding the main characteristics of the textile mills, ironworks and engineering works of the First Industrial Revolution: steam-driven plant, highly individual and authoritarian forms of ownership and management, and labour often sharply divided between the skilled few and the unskilled many. The term 'Second Industrial Revolution' is taken seriously enough to justify concentration on the main technological *innovations* connoted. To make their immense task manageable, the authors have said little about the undeniably persistent effects of First Industrial Revolution techniques based on coal, iron and steam (above all, the railways); similarly, innovations with roots in the chosen period, but social effects principally outside it, are largely passed over (television, nuclear power, computers, jet airliners).

The volume's emphasis on the United States and the United Kingdom reflects the background and expertise of the contributors. The prominence given to the United States is justifiable, nevertheless, in view of its striking contributions both as technological innovator, and as an exemplar of social change during the second stage of industrialization. But although two of the contributors are well-versed in German developments, none would deny that an ideal volume should have said more in addition about Western Europe as a whole. The final chapter attempts to redress any spatial imbalance in a rather different way.

A final word about the location of the collection on the present academic map. The contributors would situate their work in the *social history of technology*, currently less than a fledgling academic discipline, more of a set of aspirations shared by some practitioners of established historical studies. That some of these practitioners do not always agree in their characterization of the social origins and effects of modern science-based technology should be apparent to any discerning reader of this collection of essays. If there is a common programme yet in the social history of technology, it is surely this: to establish a domain integrating the best from present technology history (as practised, say, by specialists in business history, 'internalist' chroniclers of technological innovation, and general historians of industrialization and social change) while eschewing the worst (a view of technology that is either one-sided, purblind or superficial).

The authors wish to acknowledge their indebtedness to colleagues outside the Open University who have commented on drafts. Robert Fox has read all the chapters assiduously, but always as a constructive critic. Numerous helpful comments on specific chapters have come from David Brody, James Carey, E. J. T. Collins, Adrian Forty, Eric Monkkonen, Paul Weindling and Trevor Williams. It must be stressed, however, that responsibility for views expressed lies entirely with individual authors. The authors are also thankful to Open University colleagues for taking time from the production of other courses to help this project along, particularly Gaynor Arrowsmith, Tim Benton, David Goodman, Paul Lewis, Tony McGrew, Graham Martin, David Walker, Peter Zorkoczy and last but not least John Fauvel, among whose contributions was the source of the cover illustration. The authors have been particularly fortunate in the expertise, dedication and understanding provided by editor Kate Clements, media librarian Tony Coulson and designer Rob Williams; and in the administrative skills of Marilyn Ricci and Ruth McCracken, as well as in the shrewdness of their comments on the accessibility of drafts. Gratitude is also owed to almost all the Arts Faculty's secretaries, whose experience of a later technological 'revolution' might well inform another such volume.

Colin Chant
Milton Keynes, February 1988

1 EVERYDAY LIFE AND THE DYNAMICS OF TECHNOLOGICAL CHANGE

Section 1.1 by Bernard Waites; section 1.2 by Richard Bessel; section 1.3 by James R. Moore

**1.1
EVERYDAY LIFE:
A HISTORICAL
ANALYSIS, c.1870–1950**

This analysis of everyday life between 1870 and 1950 tries to describe some of the main changes in daily social experience which have come about with the evolution of the labour force and the growth of mass consumer markets. The illustrative material is drawn mainly from Britain; want of space and knowledge have precluded the more rigorously comparative treatment which the subject deserves. We may rightly question how typical the British experience has been, for certain features of her economy and social structure (most obviously, the absence of a peasantry and a very attenuated agricultural sector by 1900) have set her apart from other modern societies. She has also escaped the calamities of invasion, military defeat and dictatorship which at one time or another have overtaken France, Germany, Italy and Russia. Her population has never been forcibly moved *en masse*, nor threatened with genocide, nor subject to the brutal 'social engineering from above' exemplified by Stalin's collectivization of agriculture and industrialization. Equally, the British have experienced nothing like the voluntary mobility of American society in its westward expansion, nor have they been divided in the same way by sectional and ethnic loyalties. If this analysis seems insular – even parochial – to a Polish or a Polish-American reader, it is because it is largely about an insular, parochial society!

Yet, the stability and compactness of Britain does give the historian of everyday life a distinct advantage: it permits a type of generalization which would be inappropriate in the analysis of geographically dispersed social formations like the United States and the Soviet Union, and it allows one to set aside the question of the violent disruption of everyday experience by war, military defeat and revolution (a matter which Colin Chant returns to in chapter 12).

Some apology must be made for the doggedly empirical character of this analysis. It might seem difficult to be abstract about such a down-to-earth matter as 'everyday life', but, in fact, this is not just a commonplace phrase immediately understood by all. In social theory 'the everyday life world' is a quasi-technical term that figures in important debates about the relationship between human action and the constitution of society. These debates are too complex to summarize adequately here; they can crudely be resolved into diametrically opposed evaluations of everyday life. In one tradition, derived indirectly from the philosophical movement known as phenomenology, the 'everyday life world' is that social domain where intentional, autonomous human action expresses itself most fully. On the other hand, certain neo-Marxists, such as Henri Lefebvre and Herbert Marcuse, have argued that it is precisely in the 'everyday life' of advanced capitalist societies – with their commodity fetishism and constant gratification of false needs by 'pleasure industries' – that human potentials are most alienated. One tradition sees humankind as the creator of 'everyday life', the other as its creature.

These opposing evaluations occupy central positions in the conflict in our culture over the meaning of modernity. If they are not pursued here it is principally because of the detailed and concrete character of the subsequent essays in this volume.

So what do *we* mean by the phrase 'everyday life'? I think we use it to refer to clusters of recurrent, often routine experiences which we are confident would be recognized as commonplace in our society because others have experiences of a similar, if not identical, kind. I say 'clusters' because these experiences bunch around major themes of our life histories. Following an occupation is one such theme. Nearly all of us have to seek gainful employment on the labour market: much of our schooling is a preparation for work; most men, and a large number of women, spend the years between sixteen and sixty-five either in waged work or looking for a job; our entitlements to an income in retirement are acquired through the labour contract. The work experiences of everyday life are familiar to us even if we do not individually live them, for the simple routines of the factory, construction site or office are part of the common knowledge of our culture. People who do not follow or understand these routines don't, in some sense, fit into our society; hence our name for them. Finding an everyday partner and raising a family is a similar theme in our life histories, although one where social and moral change has, in the recent past, made the once uncommon experiences of divorce, re-marriage and single-parenthood quite commonplace. Closely related to this domestic theme is that of leisure, the recurrent experiences of which often take place at home, within the family. Summing it up, we are tempted to say: work, home, leisure – that's life!

We must immediately qualify this summary of 'everyday life' by acknowledging that everyday society (whether in its capitalist or socialist form) is complex and highly segmented. In contemporary Britain (as in all multi-racial western societies), daily experience is sharply differentiated by class, gender and ethnicity. The occupational hierarchy and the private ownership of capital form the main props of our class structure, while inheritance gives it continuity over time. Though work is our (more or less) common lot, people's occupations differ in the rewards they command, the authority and prestige attached to them, and their intrinsic interest. A tiny minority own such an unequal share of our society's material wealth that they do not, in any socially meaningful sense, follow an occupation at all. Many feminists would argue (persuasively in my view) that gender is a more basic source of differentiation. Biology reserves for women the labour of physically reproducing our society while their socially-determined occupational and career patterns mean they usually earn less than men, under their authority, in jobs of lower status. For ethnic minorities discrimination in the job and housing markets and humiliating encounters with the 'host' community are part of the routine of everyday life. These differences of class, gender and ethnicity do not segment our society in a straightforward, easily visualized way. There are exceptionally well-paid 'blue-collar' jobs and a few quite prestigious professions are ill rewarded. Many professionally-educated employees earn more than the owners of small and medium-sized businesses. There is in fact no conglomerate, societal experience of everyday life; rather a complex and changing variety of everyday lives.

In entering this qualification we are doing more than adding a caveat. Complex social differentiation, and a constant capacity for change both at the biographical and social levels, must jointly form a starting point for any historically-informed account of daily life in modern societies. Before the great break in history effected by industrialization and urbanization, material life for most consisted of daily routines which persisted with only slowly evolved modifications for several centuries. The technologies and practices of agriculture, food preservation and house building – which were the basis of pre-industrial civilization – changed very slowly during what Fernand Braudel has called *la longue durée* of the early modern period. The great mass of humanity lived under the constant threat of dearth and famine and the resources for innovation and experiment were so exiguous as to set up a profound tendency towards technological conservatism. True, the Western world went through its 'scientific revolution' and made fundamental advances in the technologies of clock-making, ocean navigation, artillery and printing in the early modern period, with far-reaching consequences for trade, diet, literacy and warfare. Yet before the evolution of new forms of social organiz-ation (notably, but not exclusively, the factory system) which could harness science and technology to large-scale production, daily material life was sustained and contained by a narrow array of techniques.

1.1.1
Industrialization and
urbanization

The dual process of industrialization and urbanization transformed daily experience. This accelerated during the founding years of Imperial Germany and in post-Civil War America, the two most rapidly modernizing societies of the later nineteenth century. There were eight German towns with 100,000 people or over in 1871; in 1910 there were forty-eight. These towns had less than 5 per cent of the population in 1871; in 1910 they had 21.3 per cent. 'This was the most extensive and rapid progress of urbanization yet seen in Europe, creating large new industrial cities out of mere villages, such as Geisen Kirchen and Bochum and ancient trading centres like Mannheim, Düsseldorf and Essen (Milward and Saul, 1977, p.45). Urban industrializ-ation affected French society much less precipitately; between 1850 and 1870, France's economic growth had been the most rapid in Europe, but after 1870 industrialization was retarded because of the traditionalism of its peasant agrarian sector, shortage of labour due to the low birth rate and the conserva-tive character of French family entrepreneurship. Despite periods of rapid growth between 1896 and 1913, and during the 1920s, France conserved substantial pockets of economic backwardness until the 1950s. So much so that when the sociologist Henri Lefebvre wrote an *Introduction to the Critique of Everyday Life* in 1946, he could still discern among the peasantry a 'natural or closed economy' in which everyday life practices (of thrift, the wife's role in the home, and so on) were quite different from those of the urban working classes (Lefebvre, 1971, p.38). In the 1890s Tsarist Russia underwent a spurt of state-sponsored industrial growth and by 1909 she was the fourth industrial power in the world, having overtaken France in indices of heavy industry – coal, iron and steel (Stone, 1983, p.197). But whereas French development maintained a comparatively stable balance between industrial and agrarian sectors, Russia's was marked by an unstable combination of an over-popu-lated, agriculturally primitive countryside and a geographically concentrated, heavy industrial sector. Russian enterprises were noted for their huge scale and their advanced technical nature, as well as the youth of the land-hungry peasants who worked in them. Italian industrialization in the 1890s and 1900s was, similarly, geographically concentrated around Turin and Milan, where the modern flair of Italian industrial design contrasted starkly with the impoverished backwardness of the south, the islands and, indeed, those parts of the north where a sharecropping peasantry stood in virtually feudal relation to their landlords. Finally it is worth adding to this catalogue of industrializing powers the Japanese empire, which began absorbing Western technique and technology from the 1850s, principally to resist better the threat of foreign armed intervention. From 1868 the restored Meiji regime set about creating an industrial state with sufficient success that its well-equipped navy and army were able to defeat Russia in 1904–05. When measured against its feudal isolation before 1854, the industrializing impetus under the Meiji regime was impressive enough, but it was the First World War which really forced the pace of Japanese industrial growth; steel output and electric power capacity both more than doubled between 1913 and 1920. Meanwhile, Japan had acquired some of the key institutions of the modern state, such as universal compulsory primary education (introduced in 1890, only nine years after a similar measure in France).

Not all industrialization took place in, or gave rise to, towns; sometimes – as in parts of Russia – it was cheaper for entrepreneurs to establish busi-nesses in the countryside because labour and transport costs were lower. But urbanization was the normal concomitant of industrialization because only with the social and geographic division of labour between town and country could the economies of scale, transport, marketing, and the maximum exploitation of human capital required by societal industrialization be achieved. Britain attained a degree of urbanization by the end of the nineteenth century which no other industrializing society approached because she had entered her Industrial Revolution without a peasantry, and when world agricultural prices fell in the 1870s she did nothing to protect native agriculture. Consequently, by 1911 only 8 per cent of her occupied population were farmers or farm labourers, as compared with 31 per cent in America. Despite the extremely rapid drift to the towns in Germany during the later 1890s and 1900s, over 28 per cent of her labour force was directly connected with agriculture in 1907, while in France the figure approached 40 per cent. The British 1851 census had been the first to reveal that over half the population was urban; not until the US 1920 census was a majority of Americans found to be town dwellers. Britain apart, migration from the countryside was the chief source of urban population growth before 1914; only in Britain did a majority of the population form a hereditary working class.

Movement from the countryside to the industrial town meant, for the male rural labourer, a loss of the seasonality of the agricultural year and an adjustment to 'industrial time'. Hours of work in factories, mines, building trades or transport were not necessarily longer, but they were more sharply demarcated from 'non-work', and more regular throughout the year. Many rural migrants brought skills which were easily adapted to mining, urban transport (still largely horse-drawn in 1914) and the construction industry, but in factory industries they were confined to unskilled tasks and machine-minding. The strength of craft unionism in Britain (and, to a lesser extent, America), the force of trade practices limiting the numbers of apprentices and reserving certain work for journeymen, the control exercised by the skilled worker over the labour process – all confronted the rural migrant with a barrier in his search for skilled, highly-paid work. For the Slav in Pittsburg's steel mills, the Pole in the Ruhr, ethnicity made the barrier more formidable. In the workshop-based, artisanal trades – such as coopering, working precious metals, cabinet making – which still accounted for a huge volume of industrial production, the exclusion of rural migrants was equally forceful; skill in these trades passed from father to son. Migrants were to be found, however, in the 'sweatshops' of the tailoring and other trades and in the 'putting out' trades (such as paper-flower making.) In New York's Lower East Side, whole families of Italian tenement dwellers were engaged in domestic work of this kind.

1.1.2
Women and the labour
market

The girl or single woman rural migrant could take up factory work as part of her move to the town, and evidence from Britain suggests that this was often preferred for its companionship, relatively high wages compared with other women's employment, and the sense of independence these brought women factory workers. But a more likely source of employment was domestic service. Throughout early twentieth-century Western Europe, women in manufacturing were concentrated in only three industries: clothing, textiles and, to a lesser extent, food processing, and of these only textiles was likely to offer factory employment (Stearns, 1975, p.28). Britain, with the world's largest textile industry, employed 654,000 women textile workers in 1911, and 1.4 million female indoor domestic servants.

Census data indicate that girls and women were a remarkably stable proportion of the labour force (in the conventional sense of those gainfully employed outside the home) from the late nineteenth to the mid-twentieth century. In Britain, just under 30 per cent of the labour force was female between 1901 and 1951, after which the proportion began to rise. In France, on the other hand, about 37 per cent of its labour force was female in the first half of the twentieth century, after which it declined perceptibly because of the contraction of the agricultural sector (Myrdal and Klein, 1968, p.46). America was an exception, for in the later nineteenth century a very small proportion of its labour force was female (15 per cent in 1870) and there was a steady increase from this low point. In all 'advanced' societies, married women were a tiny proportion of the labour force because, with the maturation of industrial economies, wives were excluded or withdrew from factory and workshop trades, 'domestic' systems of employment declined in importance, as did the number of independent businesses run by women, and the shrinking of the agricultural sector meant a loss of married women's work. From about 1870, the spatial division between home and work became more marked and married working-class women were increasingly expected to take on the social role of housewife in conformity with middle-class norms of domesticity (Oakley, 1974, p.32). The married woman's world became 'involuted' around the home. In Britain notions of respectability excluded a married woman from the pub, and though she might accompany her husband to the better type of music hall, the leisure opportunities for women (whatever their status) outside the home were meagre by comparison with those of men and boys. Britain, the world's first urban society, had developed a dense working-class culture by 1900: spectator and participant sport, small-stake gambling, the growth of hobbies, all gave substance and structure to working-class leisure, but it was overwhelmingly men's leisure. The social world of working-class husbands was solidary, of their wives individuated. Many were chronically lonely (Meacham, 1976, pp.48–49).

This domestic confinement of married women interlaced with a diffusion of methodical family-limitation from the professional middle classes to other social strata as couples came to see children as economic liabilities rather than assets. (See Banks, 1954, for the classic statement of the diffusionist argument.) Between the 1870s and about 1930 Britain went through the final phase of the 'demographic transition' characteristic of all maturing industrial societies. Before industrialization, these have had stable or slowly growing populations with fairly high birth and death rates. A population explosion has accompanied industrial take-off, but the maturation of the industrial economy has seen a return to a stable or slowly growing population with a low birth rate. In the 1860s in Britain, there were 5.7 live births per married woman; by the 1910s this had fallen to 2.9 and by the late 1920s to 2.19. In the 1860s, 63 per cent of all marriages produced five children or more; by 1925, only 12.3 per cent of marriages produced five or more children. The birth rate was sharply differentiated according to the husband's occupation: in the 1900s, women married into the professional strata bore 2.33 children, wives of salaried employees (mainly clerical workers) bore 2.37, those of unskilled manual labourers 4.45. In 1920–24, the corresponding figures were 1.75, 1.65 (white-collar workers were now limiting their families more than professionals) and 3.35. Curiously enough, marriage became more frequent as the birth rate fell: in 1931, when the birth rate was at its nadir, just under 43 per cent of the population was married as compared with under 35 per cent in 1871. This was not a result of the altering age structure in the population, but a real socio-moral change in everyday life. The proportion of singletons among men and women of marriageable age declined considerably, particularly in the first half of the twentieth century (Carr-Saunders *et al.*, 1958, chapter 1). America underwent a very similar change during approximately the same period (Degler, 1984, p.469).

The combined result of the exclusion of married women from the labour force, their involution around the home and smaller family size was to generalize a pattern of affective relationships which had originated, as an ideal and a set of social practices, among the urban middle classes.

Professional men, in particular, had been keenly sensitive of their position as sole family breadwinner, whose wives and children were entirely *dependent* on an income from fees or salaries. (Life and sickness insurance were devised to meet their special needs.) For professionals, the family was a consuming, not a productive, unit; wives were accountable for expenditure, not income. The culture of this milieu idealized marriage as companionate and a voluminous literature advised the wife on the management of home, servants and children. With the emergence of the modern urban working-class family, this ideal was propagated outwards through voluntary social workers among the poor – settlement workers, district nurses, and others concerned that the working-class wife should learn to manage the home with frugality and foresight. A great preoccupation of Frédéric Le Play in France, Seebohm Rowntree in Britain and Paul Kellogg in America was recording working-class family budgets. From the late nineteenth century to about 1950, the dominant social ideal of the modern housewife as a woman entirely dependent on a husband's income, as a consumer exclusively concerned with running a home and raising children, had a profound influence on social security legislation, employment practices, the retailing industry – not to mention the life experience of millions of women. The emergencies of two world wars, which culminated in Britain in the compulsory registration of women for national service during the Second, did not permanently dislodge this ideal. Rather, prolonged economic growth in the Western developed world in the 1950s and 1960s created new opportunities for married women on the labour market; legislative and moral change made divorce easier and more frequent; and a new feminist consciousness exposed the conventionality and oppressiveness of received notions of femininity.

**1.1.3
Structural changes**

Meanwhile, women in paid employment had taken part in the 'feminization' of large areas of clerical work, the distributive trades, and in the growth of 'lower professional' employment for women (schoolteaching, nursing) which amounted to a major structural change in the British workforce between 1911 and 1961: the evolution of white-blouse labour. Nothing is more striking in the British data than the stability of manual work as a proportion of the male labour force up to 1951: from 78.17 per cent in 1911 it fell to only 72.12 per cent (Routh, 1965, Table 1; Goldthorpe *et al.*, 1980, Table 2.3, give slightly lower figures but show the same stability over time). The contraction of men's manual work to just over half the male labour force has, largely, occurred *since* 1961. Before then clerical, administrative and professional occupations for men grew very slowly. Not so for women: only 3.3 per cent of women employees worked in clerical occupations in 1911, but in 1951, 20.41 per cent did so. The increase in lower professional employment was far less spectacular, but still significant: from 6.49 to 8.18 per cent. The growth of white-blouse labour 'compensated' for the decline of skilled manual work for women in textiles, dressmaking and other 'women's' industries: 24.78 per cent of women workers were classified as 'skilled manual' in 1911, only 12.75 per cent in 1951. Within the service industries, women were reshuffled from domestic service to catering and shopwork without significant change in the total involved.

In France, where the shortage of labour and the low birth rate encouraged women's work outside the home, the pattern of their employment changed in rather different ways. Between 1861 and 1906, at least 2.5 million were employed in agriculture while the numbers in manufacturing industry during this period grew from 1.38 million to 2.23 million. From 1906 to 1954, women were a diminishing part of the industrial labour force (declining to about 1.6 million or from 34 to 24 per cent of all those employed in manufacturing). Meanwhile, they increased their presence in the commercial occupations (rising from 39 to 44 per cent of those employed) and in the liberal professions and public services (where their numbers rose from 293,000 to 981,000). In agriculture – where many women were reckoned as employed but unpaid family helpers – their numbers fell much more rapidly in the first half of the twentieth century than did those of men. There were in the region of 3.3 million women in the agricultural labour force in 1906, and 1.8 million in 1954. A great deal of this decline occurred after the Second World War, with the rapid mechanization of agriculture, the consolidation of agricultural holdings and the migration of young workers from the countryside to better-paid urban jobs.

It is extremely difficult to evaluate the structural changes in women's work in Britain and elsewhere in terms of intrinsic interest. Generally speaking, only the routine clerical occupations were opened to white-blouse labour and most employers operated a 'marriage bar' which was an effective barrier to promotion and a career. There is some reason for thinking that the skilled manual occupations of weaving, dressmaking, and so on, offered more job satisfaction, but the cleanliness and sociability of office work carried greater cachet. Skilled manual women workers did not willingly leave their trades, and often returned to them when children had matured, but these trades failed to attract new, young workers who held them in low esteem. However, these structural changes certainly tended to increase the inequality of women's wages relative to men's up to the late 1950s: in 1911, the median annual male wage was £67, and the female £43 (64 per cent); in 1958 the male median was £570 and the female £270 (47 per cent), but by the latter date women were working fewer hours and accounted for more part-time workers. Within the same occupations, relativities tended to improve, although usually only slightly. The rule-of-thumb tendency was to fix women's wage rates at about half men's without reference to the skill required, on the assumption that this would suffice for a single person.

Though structural stability in the male labour force was its most salient feature, certain long-term trends (which have been more or less common to capitalist societies) testified to the dynamism of the economy. Chief among them was the substantial increase of employment in the tertiary or service sector. In 1911, domestic service was its largest constituent, but by 1960 this had shrunk to one-seventh of its former size while public administration, professional and financial services, catering and entertainment, the distributive trades, and transport and communications had all grown faster than the labour force as a whole. This growth was by no means even; the distributive trades, for example, expanded during the inter-war depression when unemployment drove workers out of manufacturing industries, but contracted during the 1940s when the war economy, and the export-led economic reconstruction, sucked workers into manufacturing industry. By 1968, just over half the total manpower in civil employment worked in the tertiary sector (Allen, 1970, p.8).

The growth of the tertiary sector in twentieth-century America has been so nearly identical that we can confidently assert that this is a characteristic of a certain kind of economy at a certain stage of development, rather than any national peculiarity. US employment in public administration grew by 163 per cent relative to population between 1910 and 1950, in finance, real estate and insurance by 103 per cent, in entertainment and recreations by 100 per cent, in professional and related services by 74 per cent. The tertiary 'industries' accounted for almost half the entire labour force in mid twentieth-century America (Wilensky and Lebeaux, 1965, p.94). The growth of this sector is to be expected in any prosperous economy where consumers spend an increasing proportion of their incomes on services rather than goods, and its comparatively more rapid growth in America can be taken as an index of greater prosperity and the higher labour productivity of her manufacturing industries.

What consequences has this structural change in the advanced societies had for everyday life in the modern world? One is that there has been a proliferation of work requiring purely symbolic skills, rather than the manual skills needed to handle materials extracted from nature on which the first industrial culture rested. It would be quite wrong to suggest that the artisans who built and worked the machinery of nineteenth-century industrialization were without symbolic skills, but these were inseparable from manual dexterity. Men with purely symbolic skills who were part of this industrial culture but did not physically work with natural material were few and far between. The type of worker I have in mind is the professional engineer, the designer or the draughtsman; between 1870 and 1950 their number grew about eighty times in America.

A second consequence is that there has been a proliferation of work in which face-to-face encounters with other people are part of the job of work, and not just of the social environment in which work takes place. Sales counter staff, bank tellers, managers of all kinds and social workers fall into this category. (In America, to give one example, the number of social workers rose from 5,000 in 1910 to 75,000 in 1950.) We often sense intuitively that societies become more anonymous as they 'modernize', and social theorists have sometimes argued that they become more 'anomic' or lacking in common norms and rules. The growth of work involving face-to-face encounters, and indeed of the service sector as a whole, should give us pause for thought about these notions. This whole area of economic activity seems to me to be suffused with, and *constituted* by common norms and rules. At the most basic level, these might be the norms and rules of speech: a coalminer, cotton-spinner or machinist can work in silence for the most part, but a sales clerk, insurance agent or social worker has to know and use the norms of speech as part of the job. (In ethnically divided societies, where one natural language is socially dominant over others, this can have a crucial bearing in deciding who does what in the service sector.) There are, of course, a host of other norms and rules operative in service industries: those governing credit worthiness when we become clients of banks and building societies, for example. We could well argue that all economic activity is in some way normatively regulated but the difference in the service sector seems to me that the norms are constitutive of its economic activity and social transactions, and of the work done.[1]

A third consequence (which is the last I will specify though there must be many more) is that the rather simple nexus of power and authority that subordinated the worker to his employer in the first industrial culture – and was the main nexus of power in that society – has been supplemented by a complex network of power/authority relationships in which people are, in their everyday lives, constantly enmeshed. Power, in this network, attaches itself to, and is often generated by symbolic skills and face-to-face encounters. Consider, for example the power and authority of the doctor whom, thanks to the growth of state welfare (or, in America, private medical insurance), ordinary people can consult in a much more routine way than was the case in 1900. Or the power and authority of the officials who staff our local and national social services. It may seem melodramatic to see power relationships in the buying and selling of services on the market, but is it straining language to say that bank and building-society managers, and insurance brokers are powerful people in the course of everyday life?

---

[1] For the difference between regulative and constitutive norms, compare the rule in chess that no player may take more than five minutes over one move, with the rule that the bishop moves diagonally across any number of vacant squares. Alter the second and we have a different game; alter the first, and we have the same game but differently regulated.

1.1.4
Persistence and
conservatism

The dominating facts in the evolution of the labour force of early industrializ-ation were the great movements into manufacturing and construction, and coalmining which fuelled this economic expansion. With the maturation of industrial economies, the rapid relative growth of manufacturing has deceler-ated, although it continued to grow absolutely, in most advanced societies, up to the 1970s. In America, the proportion of employed workers engaged in manufacture and construction peaked at about 32 per cent in the 1920s, and has since stabilized at rather less than this (with the exception of the Second World War). Britain sustained an exceptionally high proportion of its labour force in manufacturing, mining and construction in the first half of the twentieth century; from 46 per cent in 1911, it rose to over 49 per cent in 1951, although there was nothing like a steady growth, rather an erratic zig-zag through one war-related manufacturing boom, to the inter-war doldrums, recovery based on re-armament and house building in the later 1930s, and to another war-related manufacturing boom. Beneath these oscillations there have been certain underlying trends modifying the pattern of men's manual work. The great staples of nineteenth-century industry, coal and cotton, achieved their maximum size immediately before or (in the case of coal) immediately after the First World War, since when they have stagnated and declined. At their peak, these two industries had employed 2.6 million people, nearly 14 per cent of all occupied persons. In 1951, their combined labour force was still huge – 1.8 million – but was now only 8.2 per cent of occupied persons. Over the same period, engineering, motor vehicles and chemicals all made striking gains in the proportions of the labour force employed in them (engineering and shipbuilding combined, for example, rising from 4.9 to 8 per cent).

Behind these modifications in the occupational structure lay the rapid development, if not the origins, of science-based industries and of industries manufacturing quintessentially twentieth-century goods, such as radios and aeroplanes. As with the course of manufacturing overall, development in these spheres has been spasmodic. The First World War, in particular, gave a decided impetus to the science-based industries because of the need for import-substitution, and resulted in the government-sponsored cartelization of the chemicals industry. The aircraft industry scarcely existed before 1914; by the November 1918 Armistice, over 52,000 military planes had been manufactured. Wartime labour shortages, the demands of standardized manufacture and new fiscal inducements to capital investment led to the extensive electrification of factory plant. Many commentators in the 1920s were writing of a 'New Industrial Revolution', the dynamic elements of which (as they saw it) were the adoption of semi-automatic technology, standardization of production, more professional methods of cost accounting, scientific management, and the 'vertical' and 'horizontal' rationalization of industrial organization. As these commentators recognized, the 'Revolution' was new only in the sense of being new to Britain.

The analysis of the relationship between industrial development and the everyday world of men's work in Britain up to the 1950s should, in my view however, stress not novelty but persistence. Women and agricultural workers bore the brunt of occupational change. Industries which, like cotton and coal, suffered long-term decline, tended to do so by not attracting new workers to take the places of the retired (one consequence being the declining productivity of coal because of its ageing labour force). Coal and cotton were somewhat exceptional in that a man's occupation tied him to an industry whereas most tradesmen could follow their occupation in a number of indus-tries (electricians, for example, figure in every order of the 1951 industrial census). Yet even in industries employing a diversity of trades, such as shipbuilding and heavy engineering, there was a noticeable tendency for men to stick by an industry in which they had learnt a trade. During the depressions of 1921–23 and the early 1930s, the expulsive powers of unemployment in Britain's stricken industries worked very slowly. We can suggest a number of reasons why this was so: industrial development, particularly in the North of England, the Clyde Valley and South Wales, had been highly localized, so that occupational mobility within one town was restricted. When shipbuilding died in Jarrow, or cotton, coal and textile engineering declined in Burnley, there was little else for adult tradesmen to do without breaking ties of kin and community and leaving. Moreover, memory of the former prosperity of the depressed areas was fresh and kept alive by the facts of everyday life: both Burnley and Jarrow had remarkably high proportions of working-class home ownership in the 1920s.

The stress on persistence in the everyday world of men's work up to mid century might appear utterly inappropriate to a society which mobilized for total war, whose government conscripted men and women into civil (as well as military) occupations, enforced millions of changes of address, and 'commanded' the economy with an authority matched only by Soviet Russia. The momentous impact of mobilization on everyday life is unquestionable. But, though it is controversial to say so, one broad consequence of economic mobilization for war may have been to repair and conserve an outmoded industrial fabric, and to deflect certain trends in economic organization which had been evident during the recovery of the mid and later 1930s. There had then been indications of the 'Americanization' of British industry – particularly where it was new industry, as in outer London, Oxford or Bristol – with the introduction of assembly-line techniques, the concentration of production and ownership, new methods of training and personnel management, and 'open-shop' (or anti-union) policies. The war economy 'headed off' this incipient 'Americanization'. Changes in industrial organization and managerial practices – both heavily influenced by American example – were, after 1945, far more rapid in those countries that had suffered defeat: Germany, Italy and France.

Our sense of an unusual degree of persistence in the British labour force comes not only from the stability of the occupational structure over time, but also the stability of the reward structure. It is not just what men did when they took up manual work which changed surprisingly little; their pay – relative to other manual workers, professional incomes and the profits of capital – did not change much either. Wage earners undoubtedly became better off; the index of weekly wage earnings rose 5.8 times between 1911 and 1951, while the cost of living rose only 3.5 times. There was a substantial reduction of the average working week during the period as well, so real hourly earnings improved still more. But the society as a whole became much wealthier and the wage earners' share of this increasing wealth did not alter, except during and immediately after the two wars, when it rose slightly only to recede in the later 1920s and 1950s. The chief beneficiaries of the redistribution of national income have been the salariat. Within the wage-earning class, relativities between the skilled, semi-skilled and unskilled groups of workers were quite rigid, again with the exception of the wartime periods when government labour policies favoured national flat-rate increases to protect the less well paid from rises in the cost of living. In consequence, wage differentials narrowed between 1914 and 1920, and during the early 1940s. The relative improvements of unskilled men's wages during the First World War were extremely significant in bringing about a reduction of what Rowntree (and other sociologists) called 'primary poverty', the poverty, that is, which was due purely to the inadequacy of the labourer's wage to sustain the average family in minimal subsistence.

The long-term stability of economic relationships *within* the wage-earning class has had, it can be argued, a profound influence on workers' sense of deprivation relative to other classes and groups in society. What is remarkable about the working classes of Western societies (and Britain in particular) since the later nineteenth century is that their collective demands on regimes which have sustained great economic inequality have been so modest. This tolerance may well be explained by the fact that most people establish their sense of the justice and fairness of the social order by short-range comparisons of their own circumstances with those of people just above, and just below them, in the hierarchy of market rewards. While relativities remain stable, workers accept the economic differences of everyday life with comparative equanimity, and it is the disruption of these differences during periods of rapid wage and price inflation which most tends to excite a sense of economic grievance (Runciman, 1966).

The impression of persistence and conservatism within the everyday world of men's work is strengthened by comparing descriptions of workers' attitudes and values dating from the early and mid-twentieth century. At both periods, membership of the working class was looked upon as 'a life sentence'; though there was fairly extensive (albeit short range) inter-generational social mobility, once an adolescent had taken up a working-class 'career' he had little expectation of moving to a managerial, executive or even clerical post. At both periods, the working class was envisaged by workers and by social observers 'from above' as stratified by wage differences, skill and 'respectability'; at both periods, the three broad ranks or estates of the working class were the skilled, semi-skilled and unskilled. In 1950 it was recognized – as it had been in 1910 – that typically the working-class life sentence involved a cyclical movement through the working-class social hierarchy: family life followed a pattern of relative prosperity when the man and wife were still childless and both earning, leading to increasingly straitened circumstances when a man's wage had to support a wife and a growing family of dependent children, followed by the return of relative prosperity in the parent's early middle age when adolescents became wage-earners and supplemented the family income, and terminating in poverty in old age when the children had left the family home and the husband's earnings declined.

All this is not to deny the many changes in working-class life experience in the first half of the twentieth century: the incidence of primary poverty became much less frequent, workers' families typically came to live in much less insalubrious and overcrowded dwellings (principally because central and local government in Britain took on a major responsibility for the provision of working-class housing), child and maternal health improved; it is simply to assert that in the male manual labour market, and in the division of the society's income between wages, profits and salaries, certain fundamental relationships were very stable. Moreover, a certain structure of class feeling that had arisen on these relationships was equally enduring. In the early 1950s a Polish sociologist asserted:

> Workers often speak of themselves as 'we' and of others as 'they'. Who are 'we'? The average worker has only to look at a man to see whether he is one of them or not. He looks first at his hands, and when he sees strong horny hands, sometimes puffed up, and stained or greasy, he knows that he is one of 'us'. But if his hands are soft and obviously not used in his work, he belongs to the class of men from the office or shop, the men who are 'they'. (Zweig, 1952, pp.202–03)

This assertion was utterly commonplace when it was made, as were all Zweig's observations on class differences in dress, speech, fairness, and attitudes to promotion. What is remarkable is how close the assertion and observations were to those made in the 1900s by Edwardian social investigators.

1.1.5
Mass consumption

So far, our attention has been focused on men and women as participants in the labour force or producers. Clearly, however, a major feature of modernization in societies such as ours has been the emergence of mass consumption by ordinary people of goods and services not strictly required for subsistence. At the beginning of the period, between a quarter and a third of working-class families were too poor to feed, clothe and house themselves according to the minimum standards used by Charles Booth when projecting a 'poverty line'. Yet alongside this mass poverty existed large working-class consumer markets for the popular Sunday press, beer, tobacco, commercialized and 'standardized' entertainment (such as the music hall offered) and, by the 1880s, commercialized sport. After this date, consumer markets broadened with increasing real incomes and a growing diversity of goods (such as bicycles, ready-to-wear clothing, daily newspapers and comics, radios and motorbikes) which working-class families could afford.

One of the most salient features of the emergence of mass consumption was the marketing of 'leisure' and entertainment. The first of the modern entertainment industries, which both catered for and constructed a truly 'national' taste in leisure, was the music hall, a business concentrated by the 1890s in a small number of chains. Its social organization prefigured in many ways that of the most important of early twentieth-century leisure industries, the cinema. The technical evolution of silent films (discussed in chapter 7 by James Moore) was completed by about 1900 (in time to allow for faked newsreels of the Boer War) and an audience for short films was created initially by showing them as part of the music-hall programme. By 1910, purpose built cinemas were opening and within a year there were 94 in the county of London and substantial numbers in other major cities.

During the inter-war period, cinema-going established itself as the most socially pervasive of all leisure habits. Though the first audiences appear to have been predominantly working-class male adolescents, during the 1920s girls and women came to outnumber men among cinema-goers, and a middle-class audience was created by opening new, plush suburban cinemas during the 1930s. The habit was inexpensive (over 40 per cent of seats in 1934 cost 6d. or less), so within the means of the unemployed and the young. By 1939, 20 million tickets were being sold each week. Cinema audiences reached a peak in the late 1940s, by when 27 per cent of men, 35 per cent of women, 45 per cent of boys and 43 per cent of girls were reckoned to go to the cinema at least once a week (Rowntree and Lavers, 1951, pp.228–29).

Ascertaining the brute facts of cinema attendance is easy enough; assessing the significance people attached to the films they saw and the part they played in shaping perceptions of society is far more difficult. Undoubtedly, many films (such as the Valentino vehicles) were romantic, escapist fantasies which elicited an intense, but ephemeral identification with the star. For most, this kind of experience could be 'bracketed off' from everyday life. But other films, such as the immensely popular Gracie Fields comedies, invited a more complex response because they drew upon a 'common sense' and lore which circulated in popular milieux, reworked these meanings according to comic generic conventions and then projected them back to the audience. Since the messages of the films were always wrapped in a cheerful stoicism that invited folk to put up with the world as it is, several scholars have attributed a highly conservative influence to them, and the British cinema more generally (for example, Richards, 1984).

1.1.6
Capitalist production and
mass consumption

The view that the largest entertainment industry of our period drew upon and reinforced deeply conservative sentiments of the masses has some affinities with the neo-Marxist evaluation of 'everyday life' to which I alluded. In neo-Marxism – particularly that of the Frankfurt school – the growth of mass consumption and 'commoditized leisure' is intrinsically linked with the persistence of exploitative, unequal relations of production. It is the everyday life of consumption which – so the argument runs – induces a 'false consciousness' that happily tolerates the everyday life of capitalist production. In my view, this analysis greatly exaggerates the persuasive powers of the mass media, derogates the good sense of the lay actor and ignores the many other institutions that mediated between the individual and capitalist society. But in a fundamental respect the analysis is, I think, on the right lines for it considers production and consumption in everyday life holistically. It has only been by virtue of the extraordinary growth of the productive forces of capitalism since the 1870s (an expansion in which science-based technology has played a major role) that mass consumption has been made possible. Some of the essays that follow (such as Noel Coley's examination of the emergence of the new materials on which were based the modern ready-to-wear clothing industry) will examine this dual relationship in more detail.

**1.2
THE DYNAMICS OF
TECHNOLOGICAL
CHANGE:
HOW DO
TECHNOLOGIES
PREVAIL?**

Most people's rough comparisons of 'everyday life' in mid-twentieth century industrialized societies with conditions eighty years before probably would focus very largely upon the effects of technological change. Inhabitants of these societies came to live longer, produce more, travel faster, communicate at greater speeds and distances, and kill their fellow human beings with greater efficiency and in far greater numbers than could their counterparts in the middle of the nineteenth century. The 'modernization' of industrial society appears to have been in large measure synonymous with the march of technological 'progress'.

Of course, the changes affected people differently from place to place. For example, on the eve of the First World War, recorded rates of infant mortality in European Russia (at 245 per 1,000 births during the period 1907–1911) were more than twice as high as in England and Wales (116 per 1,000) and more than three times as high as in Sweden (76 per 1,000) (table in Gatrell, 1986, p.33). Londoners could travel on the world's first underground railway (the Metropolitan railway line between Paddington and Farringdon) in 1863; Muscovites did not get their underground palaces until the 1930s. In 1934 there were thirteen telephones per 100 people in the United States, but only five in the United Kingdom and just one in Spain (Williams, 1982, p.307). In 1926 there was one motor vehicle to roughly six inhabitants in the United States (the United States at that time had 19,954,347, or roughly 82 per cent, of the world's 24,538,090 motor vehicles), while in Britain the figure was one to 49, in France one to 54, in Germany one to 211, and in Czechoslovakia one to 787 (*Statistisches Jahrbuch 1928*, 'Internationale Übersichten', p.75). And, of course, not only national boundaries delineated the differentiated spread of technologies: urban/rural and class divides also were important.

Observations about the differential rates at which technological change permeated societies and affected people's everyday lives lead us to a number of questions: How are we to account for the differences? Why, for example, should certain technological innovations have made a greater or more rapid impact on the streets of New York than on the streets of Prague? What were the stimuli to technological developments? Why did some technologies prevail and not others? Did scientific and technological developments set the pace for social and political change, or were these developments largely a product of economic, social and political considerations? Or is this a false dichotomy? Where, indeed, did the impetus for technological developments (and, through that, for change in 'everyday life') come from: from the political realm, from (capitalist) economic considerations, from public policy and government intervention, from military needs, or from the internal logic of (inevitable?) technological 'progress'? And to what extent was technological change – and, perhaps more importantly, the ways in which it directly affected millions of people – shaped by the ideological framework within which it occurred: by, for example, ideas of 'progress', of the triumph of 'rationality'?

Such questions probably are impossible to answer precisely. It is very difficult to separate, for example, the extent to which the push for technological change has come from the market place or from state intervention and regulation. But clearly this is important in explaining why technological change occurred and spread more rapidly in some places and among some groups than others. Without a ready capital market, it may have been extremely difficult – even impossible – for inventors or businesses to develop and sell new products. Without substantial state investment, there may have been little possibility for some technologies to become widespread. Without the environment created by a strong state regulatory mechanism, it may not have been worthwhile to develop and market new products. Without a general level of wealth in a society, the consumer market may not have existed for the spread of technological innovations, no matter how worthy or revolutionary these might have been. And without a measure of social, economic and political stability, some scientific and technological initiatives may never have got beyond the drawing board.

These points are well illustrated by the early history of electric lighting. As everyone knows, Thomas Alva Edison – the 'Wizard of Menlo Park' – gave the world incandescent light. (For further discussion, see chapter 3.) But why have we heard of Edison? His was not the first electric light. At the time he set to work on electric lighting, in late 1877, considerable progress was being made with arc lighting (which had first been demonstrated by Sir Humphry Davy in 1808 and which involved light from an electric arc formed between two pieces of carbon, which were consumed in the process), a source of high-intensity light which is still in use today, for example in cinema projection. Indeed, in 1881 the German electrical engineer Werner Siemens decided not to take up a licence to manufacture the Edison lamp because he was convinced that arc lighting would dominate the market (Passer, 1953, p.80). Edison was not the only person to have been developing incandescent lighting at that time; a number of other people were working on an incandescent lamp, including J. W. Swan, who also played an important role in bringing electric lighting on to the market in Britain during the 1880s (Byatt, 1978, pp.14–16). But Edison's achievement was to have developed and marketed an entire *system* of electric lighting; as Matthew Josephson has noted, 'it involved not only technology but also sociology and economics' (Josephson, 1974, p.127).

Unlike arc lighting, which was wired in series (so that all the lamps wired up had to be turned on and off together) and gave an extremely bright light while emitting noxious gases, the incandescent lighting developed by Edison was independently controlled (that is, wired in parallel) and delivered much lower intensity light. Because of its harshness and the fumes it emitted, the main use of arc lighting had been the illumination of large public spaces, such as railway stations and streets; the main use of the incandescent light, as Edison saw it, was in the home. Thus, right from the beginning Edison was inspired as much by the vast potential market as by technological innovation, and he tailored the latter to suit the former. Seeing that the main competitor for supplying light in the home was gas, Edison aimed to construct an electric lighting system which could match the costs of gas lighting. He even made his lamps match the light of the ordinary gas jet: 16 candle power. Indeed, the economics of the gas industry and the costs of gas lighting to the domestic consumer were among his most intensive research at this time. His employees made careful studies of the use of gas in the district of Lower Manhattan in New York City where he chose to place his first central generating station, and surveyed gas consumers about whether they would switch to electric lighting if its price were the same as for gas.

It was the price of gas which therefore fixed the parameters within which Edison worked. And the importance of the fact that Edison's was a high-resistance system lay not just in that the necessary high-voltage transmission of current meant reduced energy loss in transmission; it also meant that relatively small amounts of expensive copper were needed. Essentially, Edison set to work to create a system of electric lighting the costs of which made it commercially attractive, and then devoted tremendous effort to marketing. This included getting a statement from the New York Board of Fire Underwriters that insurance rates for buildings connected to the Edison system would not be increased (provided the wiring was inspected), and offering to pay the costs of wiring a building until the consumer decided, after a trial period, to remain connected (Passer, 1953, pp.91–92).

All this cost a lot of money. It has been estimated that to develop and bring the Edison lighting system on to the market cost nearly half a million dollars – an enormous sum in the 1880s (Passer, 1953, pp.86–88). Just between 1878 and 1881 about $150,000 was spent on the experimental work alone. Clearly for Edison to succeed, he had to operate in an environment where the necessary capital was available, and where there was sufficient wealth to create the effective demand which could justify such a system commercially. These preconditions were present in 1880s America. Without them, the 'Wizard of Menlo Park' might well have tinkered in vain. With them, he became a rich man, and in the process a lot of people got electric lighting within their homes. (For further discussion of Edison's business practices, see chapter 7.)

It is also relevant that in the United States the price of gas – the chief competitor of incandescent lighting – was relatively high, 'manufactured by an inefficient, monopolistic industry with relatively high raw material costs' (Byatt, 1978, p.23). It was, for example, much higher than in Britain, where gas companies faced price controls and where municipalities had begun purchasing gasworks in the 1870s and consequently had reduced the gas price. As a result, particularly in the larger cities (where the greatest potential for electric lighting was located) the commercial possibilities for Edison's British counterparts were more limited. This no doubt was an important reason why electric lighting caught on relatively slowly in Britain: at the turn of the century 58.9 per cent of central-station lighting in America was provided by electricity, and 41.1 per cent by gas; in Britain the corresponding percentages were 6.1 and 93.9 (Byatt, 1978, pp.26–27).

Many of the market-related factors which influenced Edison in the 1880s were, by later standards, still at a relatively primitive stage. Subsequent decades witnessed a huge expansion of business, and with this a growth of corporate research, an institutionalization of innovation through research and development, and much more sophisticated marketing and advertising. These, in turn, gave new impulses to technological innovation, for by the end of our period the industrialized world was inhabited by corporate giants whose financial health and indeed survival depended upon developing new products and cultivating new markets for these products.

Whenever we examine the effects of technological innovation upon people's everyday lives, it is important to ask how and why these technologies got there. As the example of Edison's electric light demonstrated, a crucial element was formed by commercial considerations: the availability of capital, the relative costs of alternative technologies and products available on the market, the level of disposable income among the population. But we have not yet really mentioned the state, and its role in how technologies prevail. This, of course, varied tremendously according to time and place: the contribution of the state towards the introduction and spread of new technologies obviously was quite different in late nineteenth-century America from what it was in the Soviet Union during the 1930s. And there are a great many ways – some obvious and some less so – that the state figures in this story: whether through active investment, providing a regulatory framework, providing a system of law within which commercial interests might operate freely, or providing a stable environment generally.

Among the most widely discussed historical developments of the period 1870 to 1950 has been the growth of the state. The share of economic activity comprised by public expenditure, the areas where the state intervened directly in people's everyday lives, the size of the state bureaucracy, and the extent to which it regulated society, all grew tremendously in the industrial world during our period. This growth of the state went hand in hand with the development and, particularly, the spread of technological innovation. The state often invested heavily in new technologies. Perhaps the most obvious area of such expenditure was weapons technologies: probably the single most costly scientific research effort during the period we are discussing was the American 'Manhattan Project', which developed the first atomic bomb.

But the importance of the state in determining how technologies prevail is not limited to its active intervention in specific areas. No less important is the role of the state as regulator and guarantor of an environment in which technological innovation could develop. Often overlooked is the role of the state, particularly in its local manifestations, as regulator – setting standards for the ways in which technologies affect everyday lives. To take one example: in 1907 the municipal city administration of the eastern German city of Posen (today's Poznan in western Poland) published a comprehensive guide for its citizens of local laws and statutes which governed, among other things, the following: the disposal of human waste, the proper construction of cesspools, connection to the municipal sewerage system, the sale of gas by the municipal gasworks, connection to the city's water system, the supply of electricity from the municipal generating station, technical specifications for electrical systems connected to the municipal lighting works, and even the inspection of animals slaughtered at the municipal abattoir (*Bürgerbuch der Provinzial-Hauptstadt Posen*, 1907). Posen was no special case, although Germans perhaps were more enthusiastic than others about extending state involvement in the economy and regulating the activity of the citizenry; throughout the industrialized world, at national as well as local level, state regulation increased markedly during the late nineteenth and early twentieth centuries. Such regulations may not seem earth-shaking in and of themselves, but they did govern – and thus provide a framework for – the ways in which technologies affected people day to day.

One particularly good example of the importance of state involvement in shaping the parameters within which technological innovations spread is patent protection. Without reasonable assurance that inventions could be protected, that those who had invested their time and money developing some new process or product would possess the legal claim to benefit from it, the process of technological change might well have been severely inhibited. An effective state regulatory mechanism is necessary to protect the property rights – including rights over the disposal of technological invention and innovation – which provide the economic justification for the effort involved. The last third of the nineteenth century saw major steps taken in the field of patent law, the setting up of state patent offices and the legal registration and protection of inventions in many countries, and discussions (beginning in Vienna after the World Exposition of 1873) about the international protection of patents. In Germany, for example, the passing of the first Reich patent law, the 'Reichspatentgesetz' of 1877, was followed by an impressive use of the new legal framework: between 1877 and 1907 (during which time German industry took the lead in a number of highly technological fields, in particular chemicals and pharmaceuticals) roughly 195,000 patents were registered in Germany (Hoffmann, 1965, pp.264ff). In the United States, which had become the world's leading industrial power, more than 20,000 patents a year were being registered in the final years of the nineteenth century (Motteck, Becker and Schröter, 1975, p.49). Clearly the protection afforded by state regulation and patent offices made it more attractive for individuals and businesses to invest in new processes and products, and this served to stimulate the development and spread of technological innovation.

Lest we think that this was merely a facet of a great inevitable march of 'progress', we should be aware that the putting into place of patent law and patent offices was not without its opponents, and that the forms it took often were the subject of intense political discussion and lobbying. The relationship of the German pharmaceutical industry to the enactment of German patent law in the late nineteenth century is a case in point. Initially, there had been considerable opposition to patent protection within Germany. Many free-traders were convinced, as one group of economists put it in a declaration after a congress in Dresden in 1863, 'that patents governing inventions are harmful to the general welfare' (quoted in Fleischer, 1984, p.50). But as German industry grew in size and technological sophistication, the pro-patent lobby grew as well (led by Siemens, the co-founder of the Siemens und Halske concern and inventor of the dynamo). The 1877 Reich Patent Law was a culmination of many years of discussion, but for the pharmaceuticals industry it nevertheless left some things to be desired. Most importantly (unlike the French patent system, for example), it protected *processes* rather than *products*. Although this acted as an incentive to the establishment of large industrial laboratories which were a source of strength for German science-based industries, it also left German companies open to the competition of foreign (usually Swiss) firms which developed similar products using slightly different processes in order to avoid transgressing the patent laws. For this reason the German pharmaceuticals industry lobbied long and hard, and eventually successfully, to have the law changed. The new Reich Patent Law passed in 1892 conformed very largely to the wishes of this industry, and helped to provide a platform from which the German pharmaceuticals industry was able to capture a dominant position in the world market before the First World War (Fleischer, 1984, p.370). In contrast particularly with their British competitors, the German pharmaceutical concerns (some of which – for example, Hoechst, Bayer – were also among Germany's leading chemical companies) took advantage of a highly state-regulated home market to establish a high reputation for quality and innovation and achieve considerable commercial success.

Another important, and related, feature of state involvement in technological innovation has been the growth of the educational and research establishment. Between 1870 and 1950 the resources devoted by the state to universities and their research institutes grew massively. This was obviously important in the late nineteenth century, especially in Germany, where close links were established between the research institutes of universities and the newer 'technical high schools' (technical universities, of which there were nine by 1900) on the one hand, and industry on the other. Following the reforms of the early nineteenth-century, German universities no longer were devoted simply to training the next generation of civil servants but also to promoting scientific research. The first scientific laboratories had been established in the early nineteenth century (in chemistry, physiology, physics), but from the 1870s laboratories were established in such things as mineralogy, electrical technology and machine-building as well. Between 1865 and 1910 the total number of academic staff at German universities grew by 130 per cent and – what is more relevant to our discussion here – in medicine and the sciences by 188 per cent (table in Lundgreen, 1980,

p.106). The number of students grew even faster, and of particular significance is the fact that the number of 'Privatdozenten' (people qualified, and
indeed required if their qualifications are not to lapse, to teach at universities)
grew far faster than did the number of established chairs: the number of
'Privatdozenten' in medical and natural-science faculties increased between
1865 and 1910 by 304 per cent! This in turn led to a surplus of qualified
academic researchers, for whom there was insufficient place within the
universities and who often turned to industry (for example, the chemical and
pharmaceutical industries).

The success of German industry during the Imperial period in developing
and using new technological processes had much to do with a fortunate
combination of a willingness by industry to invest in research (beginning with
large laboratories of the heavy and chemicals industries in the 1860s), and a
commitment by the state to invest in research at universities and to train
generations of scientists and engineers who then found appointments in
industry. This was of crucial importance in the success of the German pharmaceuticals industry before the First World War. Not surprisingly, the
German research university, with its stress on technological education and
research, was the great example to educational reformers elsewhere.

Looking at the input of universities in the development and dissemination
of new technologies, it is instructive to make comparisons across state boundaries and to ask why this input appears to have been particularly important
in Germany. A few points stand out. To begin with, German universities
were financed essentially by the state: as they were directly subordinate
to ministries of education (which, for example, had final say on academic
appointments) their links with government were very close; their budgets
were paid largely by government; their staff were (and are) civil servants.
This is not to say that the state resources played no role in university funding
in Britain and America: the new red-brick universities in Britain received
support from local rates and the Land Grant and State Colleges in the United
States (which have developed into some of America's most famous state
universities) received support from individual state governments. (The land
grants themselves often gave these institutions a significant financial base.)
But scientific research in German universities was better funded around the
turn of the century: the emphasis on laboratory work was greater and facilities were better. Added to this was the fact that in many ways academic life
was freer in authoritarian Imperial Germany then in democratic America or
Britain. Students could – and were expected to – move from one university
to another in the course of their studies; and academic staff were not
restricted to teaching a fixed curriculum but could lecture on whatever subject
they chose, which often meant lecturing on their current research. Although
there were frequent complaints within Germany about the drawbacks of this
system (for example, a tendency of the universities to train people too
narrowly), an atmosphere particularly congenial to scientific advance was
created, and was one reason why Germany was able to take a lead in so
many aspects of the chemicals industry.

In America private universities filled the breach. Perhaps the best examples
of this were two universities which were modelled on the German system:
Johns Hopkins University, which opened in 1876 in Baltimore and was the
first American university to stress scientific research rather than undergraduate teaching; and the University of Chicago, which opened in 1892 and
benefited from massive contributions (ultimately roughly 30 million dollars)
from John D. Rockefeller. Britain, on the other hand, often has been seen
as the laggard with regard to training in engineering and applied science.
Frequent reference is made to such facts as that in 1872 there were more
university graduate research chemists in Munich than in all English universities together (Trebilcock, 1981, p.63); according to L. F. Haber, in his

standard work on the chemicals industry in the early twentieth century, 'only two places . . . were able to meet the needs of industrial chemists at the turn of the century': Manchester University and the Glasgow Technical College (Haber, 1971, p.41). However, the alleged failure of British scientific and technological education recently has been re-examined, with the suggestion that in many respects the British education system actually suited the country's requirements fairly well and that, if there was a failure in applying scientific research in Britain, the problem did not necessarily lie with the educational system (Bud and Roberts, 1984; Fox and Guagnini, 1986).

The state also figured directly in the promotion and spread of technological change. It built roads, extended railways, organized electricity grids, put municipal sewerage systems in place, developed and bought armaments. In some countries the state directly owned and operated many of the industries which brought new technological developments to the masses. For example, in Prussia virtually the entire railway network was in state hands by the 1880s; and by 1900 the same was true in most of the other German states (Treue, 1975, pp.218–19). In Russia as well the state was taking control of the railways during the 1880s, and began construction of that mammoth engineering project which transformed the eastern parts of the Tsarist Empire, the Trans-Siberian Railway (Gatrell, 1986, pp.173–75, 215–18). Public ownership of energy generating capacity grew rapidly during the late nineteenth and, particularly, the early twentieth centuries: in Germany, for example, there was a great push in this direction during the Weimar period, and by 1928 57.3 per cent of electricity generating capacity was in public hands, 28.9 per cent was in mixed public and private ownership and a mere 13.8 per cent was privately owned (Hughes, 1974, p.163). Even that bastion of private enterprise and relative latecomer to the era of state regulation, the United Kingdom, saw municipal involvement in local transport (tramways) and electricity supply (Byatt, 1978, pp.204–06).

It should be noted that public involvement did not necessarily spell 'progress': sometimes it even acted as a brake on technological development. For example, with regard to electricity supply, municipalities could be reluctant to lose their own municipal systems to a regional generating supply which would have proved more efficient. Another, classic example where state involvement inhibited technological development is the case of the early telephone network in the United Kingdom (see chapter 7). And in France (unlike in Germany) the infiltration of industrial concerns in the higher education system seems to have taken place as the central state began to withdraw support and moves were made towards a more devolved system in which local interests had greater say.

State sponsorship of technological development was particularly important during wartime. Both world wars were accompanied by vast increases in direct state involvement in the economy, in scientific research and industrial production. Thus, for example, the aircraft industry was virtually non-existent before 1914 but grew tremendously – in terms both of size and the technological sophistication of its products – during the First World War. In Britain the Great War, which heightened awareness of the technological deficiencies of British industry, stimulated the development in 1915 of the 'Department of Scientific and Industrial Research', to carry out scientific research into industrial problems and encourage private industry to do the same. Research establishments devoted themselves to war-related work, and the state became the major customer for a wide range of goods. For a short period, the state supplanted the market.

Nowhere was the hand of the state in promoting technological change more important than in the economic development of Soviet Russia. Right from the beginning the new rulers of Russia were committed to the systematic development of a nationwide electricity generating system. In February 1920 a 'Commission for Elaborating the Plan for the Governmental Electrification of Russia' was founded; and the Commission prepared a report, approved by the Eighth All-Russian Congress of Soviets in December 1920, constituting 'a carefully worked out, unified state plan for the restoration of all national economy on the basis of advanced technique – electrification', involving the construction of regional electricity generating stations and a grid system (Hughes, 1974, pp.158–59). This marked the beginning of large-scale economic planning in Soviet Russia, and pointed towards the gigantic projects undertaken during the 1930s as part of the first Five-Year Plans. Clearly this was to have a tremendous effect upon the lives of millions of Soviet citizens. But the significance of this for our discussion here has two other aspects. Firstly, it presents perhaps the most extreme example of state involvement in technological change during our period. And secondly, it suggests that explanations of technological change which stress just the technological imperative – or portray it as part of a grand inevitable march of progress – may be less than complete; for in this particular case, the urge to electrify Russia was due not just to a worship of technical progress and a desire to develop an industrial economy (both of which were important, to be sure), but also to a political commitment to centralize resources and economic decision making.

It is more than coincidental that interest in developing national electricity grids spread across the industrialized world during the inter-war period. (For further discussion of the development of electricity grids, especially in Britain, see chapter 3.) In terms of the available technology and of industrial needs, it was an idea whose time had come. Yet what actually came of this had a great deal to do with political concerns and constraints. The Stalinist command economy provided one (particularly brutal) way of settling the question of how technological innovations were to be introduced and paid for. The pragmatic reformism of Franklin Roosevelt's 'New Deal', which gave birth to the giant Tennessee Valley Authority, was another (see chapter 3). And the pluralist capitalism of Weimar Germany, and the fate of proposals for a national electricity grid therein, provided yet another. Following the First World War there was great interest in developing a unified system of supply in Germany; and in 1919 – in the immediate aftermath of the revolution – plans were drawn up and the legal framework created for such a system. But the law allowing for the socialization of electricity, passed in December 1919, was never implemented, and the large regional electricity supply systems were not joined into a single system. The particularist interests of the various German states (for Weimar Germany was a federal state) and different regions, and those with vested interests in the maintenance of the existing system defeated, at least temporarily, the march of progress. (These vested interests included owners of smaller, less efficient plants, who feared that their operations would be closed down in a unified national system, or major customers of the most efficient plants, who feared that their electricity rates would rise if their relatively cheap power sources were drawn in to a general system.) Concluding a discussion of attempts to form a national grid in Germany, Thomas Parke Hughes made an observation which is of general relevance to the discussion of technological innovation and its impact upon everyday life:

> The history of the effort to form a unified electric power system in Weimar Germany reinforces the commonplace assumption that technology is or can be a major force in history. However, it challenges another interpretation: instead of technology being an inexorable force bringing inevitable social change in existing societal structures, it may well be a force with identifiable implications which can be used by discerning radicals, liberals, conservatives, or reactionaries to fulfill political and economic programs. Tech-

nology may not be a deterministic force changing societal structures so much as a means used by men, consciously on unconsciously, to structure society. (Hughes, 1974, p.166)

This observation lies at the heart of the question, 'How do technologies prevail?' and the question of what forms the effects of technological change have upon everyday life. It is a reminder that the investigation of the impact of technology upon everyday life cannot ignore economics and politics or, for that matter, the cultural context within which technological innovations are introduced.

This was made quite clear during the mercifully short history of the Third Reich. For example, the Nazi regime promoted a cheap wireless receiver for the masses – the 'Volksempfänger' (people's wireless) – so that they would be able to tune in to what Goebbels had to tell them; it pressed the development of synthetic rubber and oil products because of its war plans; but it also invested heavily in motor transport and motorways, despite the fact that the military was sceptical about what they regarded as a waste of scarce resources (at a time when most soldiers and military supplies were transported by rail) and voiced open relief in August 1939 that the 'Volkswagen' (people's car) was not yet being mass produced (Ludwig, 1974, pp.323–24). Many of the images we have inherited of Nazi Germany – the propaganda extravaganzas of the Nürnberg Party Rallies, the autobahns, the motorized tank columns heading out for their wars of plunder – are closely bound up with a cult of technology and the apparent success of the Nazis in widespread application of technological innovation. And Hitler, who was keen to identify himself with the newest technology (and who, in 1932, had made a great popular impression by becoming the first major German politician to campaign via aeroplane), was well aware of the attractions of 'progress' – both for propaganda and for the pursuit of war.

But it was not just the Nazis who sought to identify themselves publically with technological progress. Mussolini and the Italian Fascists did the same; so did the Soviet Union and its admirers ('I've seen the future, and it works'); and so, in rather different political contexts, have political leaders in the western democracies. The cults of speed, efficiency, and technological 'progress' became international currency. This illustrates well the proposition that the 'advance' of technology has been as much an ideological construct as it is a social, political or economic one. Just as it is necessary to consider the economic and political context in which technologies have developed, it also is necessary to understand the ideological framework which has determined how technologies prevail and affect people's everyday lives.

1.3 IDEOLOGY Part of everyday life are people's ideas about the world, including their ideas or beliefs about science and technology. These ways of thinking belong to the wider cultural context of technological change and subsist in a reciprocal relationship to it. We have seen already in this chapter how the play of markets and the policies of the state determine in complex ways the technologies that develop and prevail within a given society. Further, comparative studies among societies suggest that technological change has no special logic or momentum of its own. But the economic and political shaping of technologies also takes place in a larger intellectual environment. Managers, engineers, market analysts, corporate executives and politicians generally share with other individuals in their culture certain values and assumptions about the desirability of technological change and its tendency or direction. These ideas or beliefs guide their economic and political decisions, which shape technological development, and are themselves in turn continuously affected by the technological changes that actually occur in society. Thus it makes sense to talk both about the impact of technology on everyday ideas about the world and about the influence of everyday ideas on technological change, although any real separation of the two would be artificial. We shall consider these subjects in the remainder of this chapter.

1.3.1
The interplay of
technology and ideology

To begin with, a word about the role of ideas in society – what sociologists call 'the problem of ideology'. The term 'ideology' has numerous definitions, most of them pejorative. An ideology is a system of interrelated ideas – not necessarily coherent ideas – which is commonly said to misrepresent reality. An idea or belief is said to be 'ideological' because it participates in an ideology that offers a subjective, over-simplified, partial, abnormal, distorted, unscientific, or just plain uncommonsensical, view of the world. One's idea of ideology may itself be regarded as an ideological idea, a false version of someone else's 'true' idea of ideology! Under these circumstances – all ideas of ideology being in principle ideological – it might be well to work with a definition of ideology that is less pejorative and restrictive. There is, for example, good reason to understand ideology simply as the view of the world from the standpoint of an interested party, whoever the party happens to be; and this is the sense in which we shall use the word. An *ideology* consists of the ideas or beliefs about the world shared by people with compatible social interests. A *dominant ideology* is one held by most of the people who shape a society's view of the world, and consequently one that is held by most people in that society, although it may represent the interests of only a fraction of them (Berger and Luckmann, 1967; Harris, 1968).

Ideology affects everyday life in many ways. Often, indeed, there is a clash of ideologies when people encounter interpretations of the world that differ from their own. The role of ideology can perhaps be seen most clearly in the categories by which people habitually interpret their activities and experiences, the *separations* they make among people and things. For instance, the concepts of 'family' and 'marriage' are used to set apart certain kinds of relationship; 'politics' and 'economics' are thought to refer to different arenas of public life; 'home' and 'work' are regarded as separate spheres of economic activity, the one based on kinship and paid with love, the other based on contract and paid with cash (Barnett and Silverman, 1979). The distinction made above between 'the impact of technology on everyday ideas about the world' and 'the influence of everyday ideas on technological change' is also no doubt an ideological one, but it has been introduced for strictly heuristic reasons. And having done this, we may now proceed to consider the role of ideology in technological change under these two aspects.

To put it compactly: technology gives rise to ideology in everyday life; ideology in everyday life serves to justify or 'legitimate' technology. The success with which scientists and engineers control the physical world changes the quality of people's lives and thereby alters their perceptions of space and time, health and disease, life and death – in short, the 'natural' order of things. This is the *ideological impact* of technology. At the same time, however, and in so far as everyday life is transformed, people's perception of technology also changes. They may come to believe, for example, that technology *per se* is a good thing, that more and more problems will be found to have technological solutions – in short, the more technology the better. This is the *ideological legitimation* of technology, and in advanced industrial societies it takes the form of what one critic has called the 'American Ideology' (Wilson, 1977).

Although indigenous to the professional-managerial class, the American Ideology has become the dominant view of technology in Western-capitalist and most state-socialist societies during the twentieth century. All problems, whether of nature, human nature, or culture, are seen as 'technical' problems capable of rational solution through the accumulation of objective knowledge, in the form of neutral or value-free observations and correlations, and the application of that knowledge in procedures arrived at by trial and error, the value of which is to be judged by how well they fulfil their appointed ends. These ends are ultimately linked with the maximization of society's productivity and the most economic use of its resources, so that technology, in the American Ideology, becomes 'instrumental rationality' incarnate, the tools of *technocracy*. According to technocratic reasoning, just as engineers know best how to design a bridge or fly an aeroplane, so other professional experts – statisticians, economists, sociologists, personnel managers – demonstrate through rational scientific procedures how best to order and conduct society's affairs.

What makes the American Ideology 'ideological' is the separation it creates between technology and values, between purely instrumental techniques on the one hand, and the human ends they are supposed to serve on the other. Without this distinction the ends and the means could get mixed up, technology would no longer appear neutral, and people might contest technological change on moral or political grounds rather than accept it automatically as a natural, progressive development. Indeed, the notion that technology is inherently progressive – that the history of technology charts the history of human progress – is a latent assumption of the American Ideology and quite possibly its linchpin. For if the assumption is true, and progress is interpreted in the conventional sense as change on the whole for the better, then the distinction between technology and human values looks weak. Any technology that promotes a better state of affairs may itself retain some positive value. But if the assumption is false, and technology results in change for the worse, then, *mutatis mutandis*, technology may also retain a negative value. The distinction between technology and human values again looks shaky and the American Ideology tends to collapse.

We shall consider the question of the neutrality of technology at greater length in the next chapter. It has been broached at this point in order to establish beforehand that the question does not arise from purely factual considerations but from an analysis of the role of ideology in technological change. To be fair, though, our analysis itself forms part of the ideological debate over the neutrality of technology and as such it is bound to appear controversial. The issue has been joined with our suggestion that a component-idea of the American Ideology, the belief in progress, may be its downfall. We shall have to look further at this legitimating idea and place it in a larger historical and political context if its real significance is to be understood. But first it will be useful to consider the other half of the technology-ideology dialectic: the ideological impact of technology. For if a given technology alters not just people's perception of it, but how they ordinarily view the world, and if this effect can be shown to be neither neutral nor accidental, then that technology, like the belief in progress, may offer scope for evaluating a dominant ideology of our time. Appropriately enough, one of the best examples of such a technology comes from American history.

1.3.2
The ideological impact of
the electric telegraph

The electric telegraph, a relatively simple and apparently innocuous technological system of batteries, wires, switches and electromagnets, spread its web over the continental United States during the middle decades of the nineteenth century. Messages could be sent faster than ever; events at a distance could be effected impersonally by means of an invisible, intangible force. This new technology was dominated almost from the start by America's first great industrial monopoly, Western Union, and its social repercussions were as various as they were extensive and profound.

'The telegraph', as James W. Carey explains in a recent study, 'was a new and distinctively different force of production that demanded a new body of law, economic theory, political arrangements, management techniques, organizational structures, and scientific rationales with which to justify and make effective the development of a privately owned and controlled monopolistic corporation'. In addition, as the telegraph transformed commercial and civil relationships, its effect on the popular imagination was to elicit religious or quasi-religious commentary, which Carey refers to as the 'rhetoric of the electric sublime'. Astonished at the new technology, bourgeois preachers and pundits wondered rhetorically with Samuel Morse, 'What hath God wrought?' They replied with equal fervour that the telegraph was the heaven-sent means of using the mysterious force in the sky, electricity, to transcend space and time, spread the Christian message farther and faster, and thereby bring about salvation, enlightenment, and the 'Brotherhood of Man'. Carey understands this religious legitimation of the new technology as 'a mediator – a progressively vanishing mediator – between middle-class aspiration and capitalist and, increasingly, imperial development' (Carey and Quirk, 1970; Carey, 1984, pp.306–09).

But ideological legitimation is typically overt, even when it is vague or just plain daft; the ideological impact of a new technology can be more subtle. It must be sought in people's changing perceptions in everyday life, in their altered beliefs and expectations, in their acceptance of a new order of relationships as something 'natural'. Carey suggests that the electric telegraph had just such an impact in nineteenth-century America: firstly, through its effects on language and journalism; secondly, in supplying the ground conditions for the development of modern imperialism; and thirdly, by altering the manner in which space and time were understood in ordinary human affairs. The first two of these points can be dealt with briefly; the third will need elaboration.

The electric telegraph snapped the tradition of partisan journalism by forcing the wire services to generate news that could be used by papers of any political stripe. 'News' became co-extensive with the telegraph network. To sell a story nationwide the wire services had to employ a standard format and a neutral or 'scientific' language, stripped of regional and colloquial elements. This spelled the demise of the traditional correspondent with his own political slant. Stringers now supplied the 'facts' efficiently, in the usual 'telegraphic' style, and editors reconstituted the standardized story at a central office for release along the wire. Thus, according to Carey, the origins of 'objectivity' as a journalistic concept may be sought 'in the necessity of stretching language in space over the long lines of Western Union' (pp.310–11).

Another ideological concept, 'imperialism', may also have owed much to electric telegraphy as one of its preconditions. The word itself entered the language in 1870, soon after America and England were linked by cable, and England with Africa and India. Telegraphy now made it possible to co-ordinate economic and military activities not only within a colony or across a continent, but round the globe. For the first time people could think of 'empire' as a geo-political system of centralized communication and control governed by a single set of policies. 'It was the cable and the telegraph, backed of course by sea power', writes Carey, 'that turned colonialism into imperialism' (p.312).

The third aspect of the electric telegraph's ideological impact was at once the most extensive and the least contested. 'Objectivity' in journalism and 'imperialism' in politics have remained topics of running debate, but the new assumptions about space and time to which the new technology gave rise crept into the practical consciousness of the nation and, after a brief period of adjustment, established a comfortable residence from which they have never been dislodged.

The telegraph marked the decisive separation of 'transportation' and 'communication', words that had once been synonymous. Messages could now move independently of geography and faster than means of transport. This meant the end of traditional commodity markets. Formerly the price of a commodity such as wheat would vary from city to city. Agents would buy cheap and sell dear by moving their wheat around in space. The telegraph put everyone in the same place for the purposes of trade. It made geography less important and, simultaneously, it shifted speculation from space to time. With the spatial uncertainty of prices eliminated, agents began to buy cheap and sell dear by trading 'futures' – August wheat against October, this year against next. In this sense 'the telegraph invented the future as a new zone of uncertainty and a new region of practical action', Carey explains. 'Time . . . was opened up to the forces of commerce' (pp.316,317).

One effect of this development can be seen in the adoption of 'standard time'. To enable markets and the railways that served them to co-ordinate their activities over the vast expanse of a continent, a grid of hourly time zones was superimposed upon the United States. On 18 November 1883 the changeover was flashed by telegraph from the east coast to the railway hub of Chicago. Innumerable communities across the country, each with its own 'local time', reacted with angry resentment. 'Standard time offended people with deeply held religious sentiments. It violated the actual physical working of the natural order and denied the presence of a divinely ordained nature' (p.321). But the protests did not avail, and within a few months the new conception of time had set its seal upon space, rapidly displacing older notions of rhythm and temporality.

Other effects of the telegraph's rearrangement of space and time were no less ideological: the separations that necessarily took place in commercial activity and the standardization of commodities that these required. Firstly, with the shift of speculation from space to time, markets were removed from their historical and geographical contexts and made abstract and universal. Their operation now seemed both more powerful and more mysterious, and just in proportion to their unresponsiveness to local conditions of supply and demand. Secondly, the commodities with which these markets dealt were divorced from their representations. Goods bought against the future did not change hands; only the receipts for them did. Thirdly – and most importantly for the ordinary consumer – the goods sold had to be graded in advance to lend themselves to futures trading, and this required that the actual commodities were mixed or diluted – even adulterated – in order to achieve an abstract standard. The status of the end-product as a commodity thus represented, according to Carey, 'the sundering of a real, direct relationship between buyer and seller', and concealed from the buyer 'the real conditions of production' (pp.317–18). The product itself and its by-products – wheat, flour and bread, let us say – might have originated anywhere, anytime, for all the ordinary consumer knew. They were deprived of any uniqueness, which, however, could be restored through skilful advertising.

We may seem to have left the nationwide web of wires, batteries and electromagnets far behind, but in fact it was just the *integrative* effects of the electric telegraph on practical consciousness – its diffusion of objective news and imperial policies through space, its co-ordination of economic activity through the reduction of relations between people and things to quantities in time – that enabled advertisers to conceive the possibility of a pervasive consumer culture in America. By the end of the nineteenth century advertisers saw themselves as a 'modernizing vanguard', educating a grateful nation in the ways of cleanliness, health and prosperity. They inveighed against old-fashioned, unhygienic practices such as buying loose goods from bins and barrels. They assailed the rural home-producer, arguing that 'packaged brand-name goods insured predictable quality and purity'. Their ideology of commercial consumption thus answered perfectly to the defect in the standardized, composite commodities thrown up in futures trading by courtesy of the electric telegraph. Only the illiterate, the superstitious and the backward, according to this ideology, would resist the advice of advertisers, for – thanks again in no small measure to the telegraph – in the lexicon of national advertising, uniformity and standardization had become 'symbols of progress' (Lears, 1983, p.364). And progress was then something in which no right-thinking American disbelieved.

1.3.3
The belief in progress as ideological limitation

Earlier we stressed that ideology and technological change subsist in a reciprocal relationship. Technology gives rise to ideology, ideology serves to legitimate technology, and so on. In the case of the electric telegraph we have seen that part of its ideological impact in America was, indeed, to give rise to an ideology that expressly legitimated it, a 'rhetoric of the electrical sublime'. The case is typical: the legitimation of a new technology forms part of its ideological impact. But it is also typical that a new technology acquires legitimation long before it exists. When the technology has been deployed it will not only acquire its proper ideological legitimation, as in the case of the electric telegraph; it will also feed and strengthen the legitimating idea that presided over its development. We have identified this legitimating idea as a latent assumption of the so-called American Ideology: the belief in progress.

The belief in progress comes in all shapes and sizes. Whether it is one of those unit-ideas that the philosopher A. O. Lovejoy once said 'enter into interstate commerce' may well be doubted, for since classical antiquity it has assumed widely contrasting forms. Progress has been regarded as material or moral, linear or spiral, partial or universal. It has been held to characterize some people or all people, some of the time or all of the time. It has been thought of as necessary or contingent, a historical fact or a human ideal. In the last 150 years the conviction that material and – with less certainty – moral progress is the ordinary and more-or-less inevitable long-term tendency of social change has generally prevailed among the middle classes of industrialized nations, at least until recent decades. To justify this belief appeal has usually been made to the development of the natural sciences and technology, which both underpinned the rise of industrial capitalism, with its proliferation of material goods, and furnished precedent for attempts to interpret history as subject to laws of progressive development. The *criterion* of progress has, however, changed from time to time.

The later nineteenth century was the heyday of belief in automatic progress. Saint-Simon, Comte, Darwin and Herbert Spencer were supposed to have justified the expectation of continuous evolutionary and industrial advance according to the criterion of *natural law*. When the English historian J. B. Bury seized the moment of disillusion following the First World War to publish his classic study, *The Idea of Progress* (1920), he called this belief a 'dogma'. Although himself a firm adherent of progress, Bury ventured that the belief may yet be superseded. Twelve years later, in 1932, the American 'progressive' historian Charles A. Beard took the occasion of the 'Century of Progress' exposition held at Chicago to launch the transatlantic edition of Bury's book. In his introduction he sought to brighten its outlook by considering the development of technology:

There is something intrinsic in technology which seems to promise it indefinite operation. First of all there is nothing final about it. The solution of one problem in technology nearly always opens up new problems for exploration . . . Then the passionate quest of mankind for physical comfort, security, health, and well-being generally is behind the exploratory organs of technology . . . At all events it has behind it man's insatiable curiosity which leads him to search the heavens with telescopes, dive to the bottom of the sea, and explore atomic worlds. Curiosity would have to die out in human nature before technology could become stagnant, stopping the progress of science and industry. (In Bury, 1932, p.xxiv)

Beard here suggests that the roots of progress are imbedded in human nature, to which technology gives expression. And he agrees with Bury in another context that 'progress' is an evaluative, human concept and, as such, can never become a scientific 'law' or technical 'fact' of history, although it remains a reasonable hope (pp.xxx–xxxi). This view of *humanity* as the criterion of progress represented the chastening of nineteenth-century expectations.

But despite the events of intervening decades, something like the old optimism has been revived. Hans Jonas, a German-American philosopher of technology, has argued that technology and progress can be so identified that the belief in progress loses its ideological character:

> Progress . . . is not just an ideological gloss on modern technology, and not at all a mere option offered by it, but an inherent drive which acts willy-nilly in the formal automatics of its *modus operandi* as it interacts with society . . . There *can* be indefinite progress because there *is* always something new and *better* to find . . . What makes it more than a sanguine belief . . . is an underlying and well-grounded, theoretical view of the nature of things and of human cognition, according to which they do not set a limit to novelty of discovery and invention. (Jonas, 1979, pp.35–36)

The words 'new and *better*' would appear to suggest that progress is an evaluative, and therefore an ideological, concept after all. But Jonas maintains that his usage is 'purely descriptive', although – strangely – he states it is not thereby 'neutral'. Technological change is the process of fitting means to ends. The process is circular, for new technologies 'suggest, create, even impose new ends, never before conceived, simply by offering their feasibility'. These ends are then fitted with means, and *better means* by turn, for realizing them, so that 'a later stage is always, in terms of technology itself, superior to the preceding stage . . . The internal motion of the system, left to itself and not interfered with, leads to ever "higher", not "lower" states of itself' (p.35). Such is 'the theoretical view of the nature of things and of human cognition' that would make *technology* the criterion of progress, not merely its agent.

One difficulty in Jonas's view is its assumption of 'autonomous technology', a subject to be discussed in the next chapter. Repeatedly he speaks of technology acting as if it possessed human qualities rather than just representing them. So far, he states, does technology 'dominate our lives' and 'establish *itself* as the transcendent end' of human conduct that it now appears 'Technology is destiny'. Another, closely related difficulty is Jonas's non-ideological understanding of progress. If technology is to be both autonomous and inherently progressive, then of course progress must be defined in purely technical rather than evaluative terms. It must be placed above human interests; it must be judged of by how well – quickly, efficiently, thoroughly, extensively – a job is done rather than by reference to whose interests are being served in the process. But it is hard to extrude human interests from technological assessments (consider Jonas's amazing suggestion of an 'ever more destructive atom bomb') and harder still to construct a 'theoretical view of the nature of things and of human cognition' that does so. This, then, may be why the American Ideology, which Jonas's 'theoretical view' clearly represents, conceals the belief in progress as a latent assumption: because it pertains to the realm of means, not ends. Progress is not considered to be an ideological *belief*, peculiar to human beings, but a technical *fact* of history.

**1.3.4
Political ideology and
technological progress**

Despite their differences over the criterion of progress, Jonas and Beard must be regarded as technological optimists; and it may be no coincidence that they and a disproportionate number of others like them during the last century have hailed from the United States (Segal, 1985). The fact, however, that Jonas was born in Germany and came to America as late as 1955 suggests that the belief in progress has not been simply an export smuggled into other industrialized nations under the guise of the American Ideology. The belief in progress has had diverse origins; it has also served as a component-idea in diverse political ideologies that have relied on science and technology to assert their dominion in the world.

In his *History of the Idea of Progress* (1980) Robert Nisbet surveys the tradition of nineteenth-century *liberalism* in a chapter entitled 'Progress as Freedom'. His account in the next chapter of the tradition to which another nineteenth-century ideology, *Marxism*, belonged, is entitled 'Progress as Power'. This dichotomy is in many ways unfortunate, for the liberal belief in progress sanctioned the acquisition of power – the exploitation of nature, the command of goods and services, the dominance of competitive markets, and the control of the labour process – quite as much as the Marxist belief in progress sanctioned a class struggle leading to a full historical realization of freedom. The family resemblance between liberal and Marxist views of progress could easily be pursued, but the analysis would run aground on the notion of technological progress. Marx's own attitude to technological progress was characteristically dialectical. Whereas liberalism heralded each new machine as a human triumph over nature and a fount of higher living standards on the whole, Marx viewed the same developments as inexorable steps in the class struggle, whereby owners subordinate producers through the implements of manufacture and achieve higher living standards for the few at the expense of the many (Mackenzie, 1984). Progress had been achieved, according to the canons of liberalism and Marxism alike. But for Marx it was progress towards revolution.

In the twentieth century, where Marxist revolutions are deemed to have occurred, the divergence between liberal and Marxist versions of technological progress has not been so marked. Lenin's famous definition of communism as 'Soviet rule plus electrification' acquires its significance in this respect. The post-revolutionary communist belief in progress sustained attitudes towards technology in everyday life for the most part indistinguishable from those of liberalism, or indeed the American Ideology. In the wake of the First World War, Europeans revived hope for their shattered economies by borrowing from America technocratic practices that would ensure renewed prosperity through industrial productivity. Lenin and his advisers followed the same path. They embraced 'Taylorism', 'Fordism' and rational planning techniques; they measured progress by the scope and rapidity of technological development (Maier, 1970; Bailes, 1978; Lampert, 1979). 'Like the establishment liberals of the last one hundred and fifty years', a later critic has reflected,

> . . . the ideologists of ruling communist parties combine elitist convictions with democratic rhetoric, voice undiminished confidence in the achievements they have made and expect still to make and are reticent or altogether silent about the human costs of progress. In both the establishment-liberal and ruling-communist pronouncements the ideology of progress supports the increasing bureaucratization of social life. (Meyer, 1982, p.77)

And this was written before Chernobyl. Much the same could be said of many non-communist socialists in the twentieth century, particularly the British Fabians, although their disillusionment came with the revelation of the dreadful human cost of progress in the Soviet Union under Joseph Stalin.

It would be wrong to leave the subject of progress and ideology without considering the very real, though equivocal, progressive impulse in *fascism*. Fascism looked backward even as it looked ahead. It was 'irrational', according to the last section: romantic and reactionary as well as modern and optimistic. In Nazi Germany progress was seen as the outcome of a collective striving of the national-racial spirit. In this sense the fascist belief in progress owed much both to the chosen-people concept of Judaeo-Christian eschatology – Hitler proposed to establish a 'Thousand-Year Reich' – and to nineteenth-century romantic evolutionism, which destined the highest races to master and lead humanity. At the same time, however, the collective striving that leads to progress was to be expressed, according to fascist ideology, through all the implements of modern civilization. Goebbels, the German propaganda minister, referred to this as 'steelly romanticism'. The national-racial spirit must find practical embodiment in the artefacts of the twentieth century – the Volkswagen, the autobahn, the V-2. The paradox of this view of technological progress has been aptly labelled 'reactionary modernism' in its German context (Herf, 1984, pp.195–96), but Italian fascism developed similar preoccupations at the same time. This can be seen perhaps most clearly in the Futurists, whose adulation of the machine as a source of eroticism, violence and death in their artistic works inevitably calls to mind the latter-day admirers of Rambo and SDI.

Marx deplored 'the poverty of philosophy' that did not set out to change the world. Recent authors have deplored 'the poverty of progress' as inspiration for technological changes in everyday life that are not sustainable on a world scale (Miles and Irvine, 1982). Their criticism applies to all traditional political ideologies alike. None has yet devised, or is likely to devise, a criterion of progress that takes account of human interests from a global standpoint. To the extent that the history of technology bears this out, the American Ideology, which exports progress as a mere technical fact, loses credibility and indeed becomes dangerous. It remains to be seen how the belief in progress will be accommodated to world-sustainable 'appropriate' technologies and their ideological legitimations. Whether or not these technologies prevail may ultimately depend on it.

REFERENCES Allen, G.C. (1970) *The Structure of British Industry*, Longman.

Bailes, K.E. (1978) *Technology and Society under Lenin and Stalin: Origins of the Soviet Technical Intelligentsia, 1917–1941*, Princeton University Press.

Banks, J.A. (1954) *Prosperity and Parenthood*, Routledge.

Barnett, S. and Silverman, M.G. (1979) *Ideology and Everyday Life: Anthropology, Neomarxist Thought, and the Problem of Ideology and the Social Whole*, University of Michigan Press.

Berger, P.L. and Luckmann, T. (1967) *The Social Construction of Reality: A Treatise in the Sociology of Knowledge*, Allen Lane.

Bud, R. and Roberts, G.K. (1984) *Science versus Practice. Chemistry in Victorian Britain*, Manchester University Press.

Bury, J.B. (1932) *The Idea of Progress: An Inquiry into Its Origin and Growth*, Macmillan.

Byatt, I.C.R. (1978) *The British Electrical Industry 1875–1914. The Economic Returns of a New Technology*, Oxford University Press.

Carey, J.W. (1984) 'Technology and ideology: the case of the telegraph', *Prospects: The Annual of American Cultural Studies*, 9, pp.303–25.

Carey, J.W. and Quirk, J.J. (1970) 'The mythos of the electronic revolution', *American Scholar*, 39, pp.329–41, 395–424.

Carr-Saunders, A., Caradog Jones, D. and Moser, C.A. (1980) *A Survey of Social Conditions in England and Wales*, Oxford University Press.

Degler, C. (1984 edn.) *Out of Our Past*, Harper.

Fleischer, A. (1984) *Patentgesetzgebung und chemisch-pharamzeutische Industrie im deutschen Kaiserreich (1871–1918)*, Deutscher Apotheker Verlag.

Fox, R. and Guagnini, A. (1986) 'The flexible university: some historical reflexions on the analysis of education and the modern British economy', *Social Studies in Science*, Vol. XVI, No. 3.

Gatrell, P. (1986) *The Tsarist Economy 1850–1917*, Batsford.

Goldthorpe, J.H., Llewellyn, C. and Payne, C. (1980) *Social Mobility and Class Structure in Modern Britain*, Oxford University Press.

Haber, L.F. (1971) *The Chemical Industry 1900–1930. International Growth and Technological Change*, Oxford University Press.

Harris, N. (1968) *Beliefs in Society: The Problem of Ideology*, C.A. Watts.

Herf, J. (1984) *Reactionary Modernism: Technology, Culture, and Politics in Weimar and the Third Reich*, Cambridge University Press.

Hoffmann, W. G. (1965) *Das Wachstum der deutschen Wirtschaft seit der Mitte des 19. Jahrhunderts*, Springer.

Hughes, T.P. (1974) 'Technology as a force for change in history: the effort to form a unified electric power system in Weimar Germany' in Mommsen, H., Petzina, D. and Weisbrod, B. (eds.) *Industrielles System und politische Entwicklung in der Weimarer Republik*, Droste Verlag.

Jonas, H. (1979) 'Toward a philosophy of technology', *Hastings Center Report*, 9, pp.34–43.

Josephson, M. (1974) 'The invention of the electric light' in Scientific American, *Scientific Technology and Social Change*, Freeman.

Lampert, N. (1979) *The Technical Intelligentsia and the Soviet State: A Study of Soviet Managers and Technicians, 1928–1935*, Macmillan.

Lears, T.J.J. (1983) 'Some versions of fantasy: toward a cultural history of American advertising, 1880–1930', *Prospects: The Annual of American Cultural Studies*, 8, pp.349–62.

Lefebvre, H. (1971) *Everyday Life in the Modern World*, Allen Lane.

Ludwig, K. (1974) *Technik und Ingenieure im Dritten Reich*, Droste.

Lundgreen, P. (1980) *Sozialgeschichte der deutschen Schule im Überblick. Teil I: 1770–1918*, Vandenhoeck & Ruprecht.

Mackenzie, D. (1984) 'Marx and the machine', *Technology and Culture*, 25, pp.473–502.

Maier, C.S. (1970) 'Between Taylorism and technocracy: European ideologies and the vision of industrial productivity in the 1920s', *Journal of Contemporary History*, 5, pp.27–61.

Meacham, S. (1976) *A Life Apart*, Thames and Hudson.

Meyer, A. G. (1982) 'The idea of progress in communist ideology' in Almond, G.A., Chodorow, M. and Pearce, R.H. (eds.) *Progress and Its Discontents*, University of California Press, pp.67–82.

Miles, I. and Irvine, J. (1982) *The Poverty of Progress: Changing Ways of Life in Industrial Societies*, Pergamon Press.

Milward, A.S. and Saul, S.B. (1977) *The Development of the Economies of Continental Europe, 1850–1914*, Allen & Unwin.

Motteck, H., Becker, W. and Schröter, A. (1975) *Wirtschaftsgeschichte Deutschlands. Ein Grundriß*, Vol. III, VEB Deutscher Verlag der Wissenschaften.

Myrdal, A. and Klein, V. (1968 edn.) *Women's Two Roles*, Routledge.

Nisbet, R. (1980) *History of the Idea of Progress*, Basic Books.

Oakley, A. (1974) *Housewife*, Allen Lane.

Passer, H.C. (1953) *The Electrical Manufacturers 1875–1900. A Study in Competition, Entrepreneurship, Technical Change, and Economic Growth*, Harvard University Press.

Bürgerbuch der Provinzial-Hauptstadt Posen (1907) Hofbuchdruckerei W. Decker & Co.

Richards, J. (1984) *The Age of the Dream Palace: Cinema and Society in Britain 1930–1939*, Routledge & Kegan Paul.

Routh, G. (1965) *Occupation and Pay in Great Britain, 1906–1960*, Cambridge University Press.

Rowntree, B.S. and Lavers, G.R. (1951) *English Life and Leisure. A Social Study*, Longman.

Runciman, W. G. (1966) *Relative Deprivation and Social Justice*, reprinted Penguin, 1972.

Segal, H.P. (1985) *Technological Utopianism in American Culture*, University of Chicago Press.

Statistisches Jahrbuch für das Deutsche Reich 1928, Verlag von Reimar Hobbing.

Stearns, P. N. (1975) *Lives of Labour*, Croom Helm.

Stone, N. (1983) *Europe Transformed 1878–1919*, Fontana.

Trebilcock, C. (1981) *The Industrialisation of the Continental Powers 1780–1914*, Longman.

Treue, W. (1975) *Gesellschaft, Wirtschaft und Technik Deutschlands im 19. Jarhundert*, Deutscher Taschenbuch Verlag.

Wilensky, W. and Lebeaux C. (1965 edn.) *Industrial Society and Social Welfare*, Free Press.

Williams, T.I. (1982) *A Short History of Twentieth-Century Technology, c. 1900–c.1950*, Oxford University Press.

Wilson, H. T. (1977) *The American Ideology: Science, Technology, and Organization as Modes of Rationality in Advanced Industrial Societies*, Routledge & Kegan Paul.

Zweig, F. (1952) *The British Worker*, Penguin.

2 SCIENCE AND TECHNOLOGY: PROBLEMS OF INTERPRETATION

Sections 2.1 and 2.2 by Colin Chant;
section 2.3 by James R. Moore

2.1 THE RELATIONS OF 'SCIENCE' AND 'TECHNOLOGY'

We began chapter 1 with an examination of the range of social phenomena covered by the term 'everyday life'. We might then have immersed ourselves in the theoretical problems of defining 'science' and 'technology', but chose instead to go straight to an empirical study of the conditions of technological innovation and diffusion, assuming, not unusually in such projects, that there would be a measure of agreement about what the objects of the study should be. If there were any doubts, these would presumably be dispelled by our choice of examples (electric lighting, organic chemicals, the electric telegraph) and, more comprehensively, by the structuring of the collection as a whole under its broad technological headings.

Another point to make about chapter 1 is that any differences that exist between science and technology were not presented as problematic. What holds for technology presumably also holds for the scientific discoveries of which so many innovations can be seen as the practical and profitable embodiment. As we have already noted, there is a solid empirical basis for this assumption. There has clearly been since around 1870 an increasingly deliberate fostering of scientific research in the expectation of useful applications, as at first large private corporations, and latterly governments, sought to preordain the unexpected economic, political and military dividends seen to accrue from electrical theory and organic chemistry. This trend, beginning with enhanced employment prospects of industrial scientists in industry and commerce, and leading by the turn of the century to the first major industrial research laboratories, has inspired ready references to 'scientific technology', 'science-based industry' and 'the scientific-technical revolution'. Indeed, it is one of the defining features of the so-called 'Second Industrial Revolution' that science, in the sense both of a general method of solving problems, and of a number of well-established bodies of natural knowledge, has been systematically applied to the processes of invention and innovation. It is on this point that this new stage of industrialization is most obviously contrasted with the First Industrial Revolution, the orthodox view on which is that the crucial innovations in textiles, steam engines and metals came about principally through the trial-and-error, rule-of-thumb efforts of craftsmen largely innocent of the contemporary state of scientific knowledge.

The distinction between the happy insight of the practical inventor, and the made-to-measure patent of the industrial research laboratory, has doubtless been overdrawn. But it will become clear from the substantive chapters of this volume that the great majority of the technological innovations selected as the most closely involved in social change can be portrayed as causally dependent, though with a greater or lesser time lag, on prior scientific advance. Thus advances in theoretical physics yielded the electric light, the electric motor, in its industrial and domestic applications, and the various forms of electric traction and electrical communications (chapters 3, 6 and 7). It almost goes without saying that chemical theory underpinned the production processes of the chemical industry, though special mention is made of the necessity of Staudinger's theoretical work for the rise of modern plastics (chapter 4). One of the fundamental differences between traditional wrought-iron manufacture and bulk-steel production was the transfer of control of the production process from craftsmen to technical personnel trained in the fast developing metallurgical sciences (chapter 5). Chemistry again bore practical fruits in its applications to photography, cinematography, agriculture and the analysis of food (chapters 7, 8 and 9). Moving to the life sciences and at the same time beyond any narrow equation of technology with machinery, the emergence of cell physiology and then the germ theory of disease lay behind the rise of a scientific medicine, and a more systematically scientific approach to problems of public health (chapters 9 and 10); evolutionary theory, biometrics and genetics are then shown to be among the conditions of certain social policies involving compulsory sterilization, immigration control and educational testing (chapter 11). Finally, the application of science as an exemplary method of problem solving, rather than as a distinctive body of theory, found expression in the attempt to rationalize manufacturing work practices and production processes through the techniques of scientific management (chapters 11 and 12).

The list above is not intended to be exhaustive, and may be biased towards instances of great lag between theory and application. If the relationship between science and technology were a prime focus of these studies, then examples of close reciprocity between the work of scientists and engineers could be used to skew the relationship the other way, especially in the second half of the period, when there is rather more goal-directed research being undertaken for military and industrial interests. The point to retain for the purposes of this theoretical discussion is that these science/technology relations do not compel us to accept the conflation 'scientific technology'. They are in fact compatible with two contrasting sets of views on these relations. One, embraced by most commentators in the period of all political persuasions, as well as by most currently practising scientists and orthodox specialists in science studies, has it that basic science is a human activity of a different order from technology; it develops largely through the dynamic of its own progressive revelation of the workings of nature, rather than by any stimulus of useful applications which it happens to throw off. The other, very strongly identified with the revisionist tendency of recent Western Marxism, sees science and technology as being much of a piece; they have both become institutionalized in mature capitalist societies, and are instrumental in the increasing 'rationalization' of all aspects of life in those societies. This rationalization is, however, no more than a covert, or less openly exploitative, means of class domination (see sections 1.3 and 2.2).

There are of course many intermediate positions on both the distance between the scientific and technological communities, and the extent to which the activities of either are determined by, or reflective of, social interests. It would constitute too large a digression in a work such as this to pursue these issues through the appropriate disciplines of science and technology studies; but we should nevertheless ponder some of the implications of the two extremes already presented, as these implications have a bearing on one of our central concerns, the causal relations of technology and social change. Our concern in this section will be with the first extreme, or 'dichotomy' view. This is not as such a theory about the relations of science, technology and society, in the way that the second extreme manifestly is, though in fact, as we shall see, it may implicitly uphold a technological-determinist view of those relations. It is on that count intrinsically relevant to our discussion, but it is also worth discussing before the second extreme, or 'identity' view, because it challenges what the second extreme often simply presupposes: the growing interdependence, and even identity, of science and technology.

The first extreme puts a gulf between science and technology, and one main way in which science and technology have been sharply differentiated is by the attribution to one or the other of a definitive ultimate goal. Thus, for example, the ultimate goal of the scientific enterprise is posited as the better *understanding* of the natural world, or the extension of our *knowledge* of it; the definitive aim of technology, on the other hand, is the *exploitation* of the world's natural resources in the *interests* of the human race, or some portion of it, or more prosaically, 'the *making* or *using* of artifacts' (Mitcham, 1980). Science, however practical its methods and instruments, is essentially an *intellectual*, *truth-seeking* endeavour. In assessing the value of scientific work, for example, Tombaugh's discovery of Pluto, or Einstein's general theory of relativity, or the Piltdown Man hoax, we should ask questions of the following kind: Is it true or genuine? Does it fit the facts? Does it increase our knowledge of the natural world? Does it increase our understanding of it by accommodating more facts within a coherent explanatory framework? Technology, however much it may sometimes rely on a scientific under-standing of natural processes in order to turn them to human advantages, is an essentially *practical*, *problem-solving* enterprise. In the evaluation of a technological innovation, such as wireless telegraphy, assembly-line manufac-turing or the electric automobile, an entirely different sort of question is appropriate: Does it work? Is it any use? Can it be made more efficient? And, in many instances, is it profitable?

No one model of the relations of science, technology and society is entailed by this standard science/technology dichotomy, but it is certainly compatible with the simplest, so-called *linear-sequential* models of technical innovation (Layton, 1977), in which technology sits in the middle, picking up spin-offs of pure scientific research, and tailoring them to the demands of the public and private sectors of the economy. Not, of course, that all technology is even now the application of basic scientific research; but even where it is, it is not the concern of the disinterested, truth-seeking scientist that there may be benefits (or otherwise) in the applications, say, of the discovery of X-rays, nuclear fission or the inert gases. Science is on this account an indepen-dent variable, developing largely by way of its own internal intellectual dynamic; technology is a dependent variable, pushed by scientific discovery, and/or pulled by public and private need.

A typical expression of this dichotomy of goals from the period, using an appropriately contemporary (if rather static) simile, comes from an essay by the director of the Engineering and Industrial Research Division of the American National Research Council:

> Modern research may be classed into two main divisions; the first 'pure science', – 'academic' or 'abstract' research; the second 'applied', – 'tech-nical' or 'industrial' research. The distinction is one of motive. Pure science research is fundamental; applied research is consequential. The one reveals the forces of nature; the other controls them. The one is the foundation; the other the superstructure.
>
> I have likened modern industry, in terms of research, to a towering skyscraper, the foundations securely anchored in the bedrock of 'pure science', the framework of steel girders, strong flexible sinews of 'applied science' or 'industrial research' and the stones and mortar the solid practical knowledge of experience – the technology of industry. (Holland, 1928, p.313)

We shall look first at the 'science' section of the standard dichotomy. The exalted view of science as the noble and disinterested pursuit of truth, as intrinsically worthy of study irrespective of any theological edification or commercial profit which might accrue from it, was promoted by the majority of nineteenth-century scientists, ambitious as they were for enhanced social status, greater financial rewards and a proper place for science in the educational curriculum. To a large extent, the philosophical buttressing of their conception of science and its relation to technology and society came from the various forms of *positivism* springing from Comte's *Course of Posi-*

tive Philosophy (1830–42). Characteristic of the more buccaneering variants of positivism were (1) an *inductivist* commitment to observation and experiment as the alpha and omega of scientific method and the guarantors of scientific truth; (2) the systematic purging of science of all vestiges of 'metaphysics' (the ridding of notions like 'atoms', 'forces' and 'purposes', which were not actually present in our sensory experience, but only inferred from it); (3) a sharp distinction between the objective realm of hard facts, and the subjective world of values, science being exclusively about the former; (4) the bold assertion that science is an exemplary form of knowledge, setting rigorous standards for all other fields of inquiry. (Positivism is discussed again in chapter 11.)

But the positivist foundation of the dichotomy view has been subject to erosion, pretty well from the start of our period. In the late nineteenth century, the belligerent, Comtean conception of positive science as a progression beyond religious and metaphysical explanations of the world, gave way to a more modest positivist portrayal of science as no more than an economical way of ordering our experiences, with no hope or promise of access to the realm of spiritual values, or to the world of things as they really are, independent of human perceptions. On this interpretation of science, associated above all with Ernst Mach (1838–1916), it was as much the limitation as the rigour of scientific method that was highlighted; this emphasis persisted in the early twentieth century in various *instrumentalist* philosophies of science, in which the idea of the truth or falsity of scientific theories was explicitly discarded, and what was valued in its place was the capacity of any scientific theory or model to *predict*. Thus some of the questions previously confined to technological innovations might now be asked of a scientific model: Does it work? Can it be made more productive?

The positivist ideal of the disinterested, truth-seeking scientist has met more fundamental criticism from philosophers, historians and sociologists of science during the last half-century. One of the most influential critics has been Karl Popper, who was close to the last notable group of positivists, the Vienna Circle of the 1920s and 1930s. Although he shared the wish of these 'logical positivists' to establish a line of demarcation between the genuinely scientific and the non-scientific, he rejected their choice of empirical *verification* as the deciding criterion. Popper repudiated on the one hand the logical positivists' implicitly *inductivist* route to scientific truth (positivist tenet 1 above), and on the other, the instrumentalists' ditching of the notion of truth and falsity in science. What for Popper made a theory or hypothesis scientific was not its method of verification, nor its origin in observation and experiment (it need not originate in this way), but its capacity to be *refuted* or falsified (a test which he argued Marxist theories signally failed). Scientific theories or conjectures could never be verified, only confirmed, by any one experiment or observation, but they could thereby be refuted. Adherence to scientific theories was therefore provisional, and science progressed by the ceaseless attempt to refute those theories currently accepted.

Popper's combined aversion to Marxism and falsificationist conception of science must have been nourished simultaneously by his experiences of inter-war Central European social and political life, and his close acquaintance with leading protagonists in the early twentieth-century revolution in physical theory (Popper, 1976). Others without his impetus have found his portrayal of the scientist as arch-sceptic equally as idealized as its positivist forerunner. His foremost critic has been the American historian of science, Thomas S. Kuhn, whose book *The Structure of Scientific Revolutions* (1962) presents a model of scientific change quite at odds with Popper's depiction of self-critical scientists constantly engaged in the refutation of each other's conjectures. Kuhn's model has it that periods of 'normal science' or problem-solving within a universally accepted theoretical framework or 'paradigm', alternate with times of 'crises' and 'revolution', when the prevailing paradigm is challenged and eventually supplanted by another. Kuhn's normal science is characterized by a tenacious defence of the accepted framework: any apparent anomalies which cannot be explained by *ad hoc* modifications of accepted theories are simply ignored, until such time as their accumulated weight precipitates a crisis.

Although both Popper and Kuhn have in different ways undermined the positivist view of science as the progressive unfolding of truth, neither subscribes to its diametric opposite, the belief that scientific 'truth' is relative only to the culture in which scientists practise. Popper's intention is to demarcate genuine, objective science from 'pseudo-science'; Kuhn continues to believe that authenticated knowledge accumulates even through paradigmatic shifts. Nevertheless, their respective works have stimulated a prolonged debate over the objectivity of science, in the course of which a number of contemporary sociologists and social historians of science have taken seriously the possibility that not only the institutions and practices of science, but also its intellectual content, are culturally or socially determined.

Such a view is associated, for example, with the 'strong programme in the sociology of knowledge' supported by a group of British sociologists of science at the University of Edinburgh. The strong programme calls for causal accounts of the relations of scientific beliefs to their social contexts which will be impartial as to the truth or falsity of such beliefs. The truth of scientific theories is not thereby ruled out, but deemed irrelevant to any explanation of their origins and acceptance (Bloor, 1976). The targets of this approach are traditional sociology of science, which has generally presupposed that scientific methodology offers a peculiarly reliable route to objective knowledge of the natural world, and has consequently directed its attention to the social institutions and behavioural norms which ensure the proper observance of the methodological canons; and mainstream sociology of knowledge (or perhaps better, 'accepted beliefs'), which has on similar grounds exempted scientific knowledge from social causation, except where social and cultural biases have manifestly resulted in *erroneous* conclusions. The Edinburgh School's insistence on a 'symmetrical' account of scientific beliefs, whether currently accepted or rejected, does not of itself entail a relativist theory of knowledge, though relativism has in fact been advanced by one of the leading proponents of the strong programme, Barry Barnes. One of his main arguments is the lack of any clear fact/theory boundary in science, even in what are apparently straightforward observation statements (a position the plausibility of which rests partly on relativity theory's counter-intuitive implications for space and time); once it is accepted that apparently incontrovertible scientific 'facts' incorporate some theory about the natural world (be it even so simple as the existence of 'light'), then it is at least arguable that a full explanation of the origins of scientific knowledge must include the transmission of such theories by the socialization process, and cultural constraints affecting choice between alternative theories (Barnes, 1974).

The starting-point of this Cook's tour of changing conceptions of the relations of science with technology and society was the historical grounding of the linear-sequential model in positivist philosophy of science. We have seen that critics of positivism have gone so far as to draw mainstream science into the domain of sociology of knowledge. But we need not go so far in establishing a social context for scientific practice. There are alternative ways of reconstructing science, other than as a privileged form of knowledge; it may, for example, be viewed less as a set of *results* than as an *activity* carried out by a community of researchers practising the techniques of a certain kind of craftsman (Ravetz, 1971) – an analogy with obvious potential for dissolving the science/technology dichotomy. But to establish a social-historical context for the scientific theories bound up with the technological developments discussed in this volume would be a daunting task in itself. It is not one that the authors of the substantive essays have taken on, their concerns being more immediately with the economic, political and social conditions under which technologies (whether 'scientific' or not) come to be bound up with changes in everyday life. One of these conditions is undoubtedly in this period the institutionalization of scientific research; but this assertion may not be enough to deflect the criticism that the authors do not aspire to a fully-fledged social history of a 'scientific' technology. The point of this discussion is therefore in part apologetic. The authors readily own up to the limitations unavoidable in such a project, but most would disclaim the apparent assent to linear-sequential causal models suggested in the way science tends to intrude without cause into the various narratives which follow.

The main point of the discussion thus far, however, has been to question part of the theoretical justification of the linear-sequential model: the conception of science as an autonomously evolving, privileged domain of natural knowledge. We next turn our attention to another assumption of the linear-sequential model: its characterization of technology as 'applied science'. The equation of technology with applied science is again open to criticism, though clear thinking about the issues is hindered by the profound ambiguity of the term 'technology'. The ambiguity stems partly from the absence in English of a distinction made in the other major European languages: for example, in French, *la technique* is a general term, referring to artefacts and the means of producing them, whereas *la technologie*, much less frequently used, is closer to the original nineteenth-century sense of 'technology': 'the study of the industrial arts'. In current usage, the English word does the work of both, a confusing sign of a historical shift from the original meaning to the increasingly widespread popular equation of technology with the artefacts themselves, a 'machinery' or 'hardware' definition of technology. Some writers have in consequence proposed a distinction, following Mumford (1934), between 'technics' or 'techniques', and 'technology'. Freeman (1977), for example, defines 'techniques' as 'the methods employed to produce and distribute commodities and services', and 'technology' as 'a body of knowledge about techniques'; whereas for Cardwell (1972), the distinction emerges from a process of historical development, 'technics' having *evolved* into 'technology', defined simply as 'technics based on science'.

The proposed technics/technology distinction has yet to find its way into much academic, let alone popular, discourse, even though it offers a way of tidying up some of the present confusion, and perhaps further a way of relating that confusion to the central historical relations of this volume. For if technics is identified with products and processes, this leaves technology as a form of knowledge. We have already considered the theoretical objections to any conception of science as an exemplary or culturally autonomous kind of knowledge, and the consequent blurring of the science/technology dichotomy. The dichotomy would surely collapse if it could be demonstrated that both science and technology were culturally bound, and even partly related, kinds of knowledge. In fact, the idea that science and technology are different kinds of knowing is far from new, and a version of technology as knowledge comes across in the popular notion of technical competence as 'know-how'. But the elevation of this kind of practical knowledge to rank with well-founded scientific statements meets with objections which most philosophers would regard as obvious. As Mitcham (1980) points out, 'knowing' how to achieve technical goals is following *prescribed* rules for action, and argument over them is likely to be about their efficiency; scientific knowledge, on the other hand, purports to *describe* reality, and choice between scientific theories is made on the grounds that one is more accurate than the other. We need only yield to the force of Mitcham's argument if we accept the interpretation of scientific knowledge presupposed, and as we have already seen, there are alternative approaches, such as the instrumentalist, which would distinguish less sharply between practical and theoretical knowledge.

An argument which is less dependent on preferences in the theory of knowledge appeals to the existence at the heart of technology of bodies of systematic knowledge and substantive theories which employ exactly the same methods and techniques as the natural sciences: for example, the 'engineering sciences', such as aerodynamics and materials science, which consist of the experimental applications of scientific theories to real or nearly real situations. There are other instances of such 'technological sciences' in medicine and agriculture, and their existence has prompted some scholars to stress the primacy of thought and ideas in technological activity. In an article entitled 'Technology as Knowledge', Edwin Layton propounds a view of technology as 'a spectrum, with ideas at one end and techniques and things at the other, with design as a middle term' and criticizes models of the science-technology relationship which look at only one end of the technological spectrum (Layton, 1974, pp.37–38).

The detection of intellectual activity at the heart of the technological endeavour has led Cardwell (1972) to appeal for a history of technology conceived as 'an autonomous study related to the history of science, the history of ideas, and to philosophy generally' (p.224). But the conception of technology as knowledge hardly commits us to the autonomy of technology, or the belief that it develops largely under its own momentum. As we have seen, there is a case for relating the knowledge-content of science to its social context, irrespective of its capacity for truth or falsity, and much the same can be argued for technological knowledge. Layton insists that the ideas of technologists must be seen in the context of a community of technologists and of the relations of that community to other social agencies: 'paradoxically, a concern for knowledge serves to emphasize the importance of social history for the history of technology' (Layton, 1974, p.41).

One upshot of the foregoing discussions of science and technology is that they can plausibly be constructed as distinct, but nevertheless compatible and indeed overlapping, activities. The science/technology dichotomy is therefore, at least in theory, undermined, and so, to that extent, is the linear-sequential model of technological innovation which incorporates it. The point, however, remains largely theoretical, and in sore need of historical substantiation. An example of the scholarship required is Cardwell's demonstration of the origins of the physical theory of thermodynamics in the practical development of heat engines (Cardwell, 1971), thereby reversing the causality assumed to obtain between pure scientific research and technological application in the linear-sequential model. Cardwell's contribution is one of a number of attempts to revise what might be caricatured as the received historical view of the relations of Western science and technology. On this view, protoscientific speculation about the natural world ('natural philosophy') was divorced from the practice of the useful arts by the social divisions of feudal society, a divorce that persisted until the late Middle Ages. From the early seventeenth century, intellectual reformers like Francis Bacon and René Descartes perceived how the union of scholastic theory and craft technique promised human mastery over nature, and infinite material benefits. The immediate fruit of this union was a science based on experiment rather than speculation; untutored craft skills and rule-of-thumb techniques were sufficient for the mechanical innovations of the First Industrial Revolution, but science's true potential for practical applications began to be realized in the second half of the nineteenth century in the electrical and chemical industries.

The received historical view has been challenged on many of its particulars, such as the mooted origin of experimental science in craft techniques, or the supposed independence from natural science of eighteenth-century technology. More relevant to our purposes are (1) the general lessons that the relations of science and technology are dynamic, and that therefore no absolute ahistorical model of these relations can realistically be expected; and (2) the equation of technology with applied science implied in the later particulars – an equation that is increasingly resisted. Layton (1971) sees science and technology as different communities, each with its own goals and value systems. He identifies a 'scientific revolution in technology' in the nineteenth century, resulting in the emergence of a new technologist with a college education, professional organization and technical literature modelled on science. The two communities share many of the same values, but are like 'mirror-image' twins in that among the technologists there is a reversal of the priority accorded in science to theoretical over practical work. The relationship is 'symmetric' in that there is a two-way flow of information between the two communities.

A similar picture is presented by Derek de Solla Price (1982), who agrees with Layton that in the normal course of events, new science comes from old science, and new technology from old technology. (See sections 3.4.3 and 3.7 for the importance of technological momentum in the electrical industry.) Cases of the direct practical application of science, such as penicillin and the transistor, are unrepresentative, however compelling. 'Inventions do not hang like fruits on a scientific tree' (pp.169–70). Technology is not applied science, but rather science and technology are parallel structures in a symbiotic, weakly interacting relationship. Ultimately, they depend on each other: science without technology would become sterile, technology without science moribund.

The models of Layton and Price are incompatible with the linear-sequential portrayal of technology as 'applied science' and also incorporate a view of science some steps removed from the old positivist ideal. But there is still in the distance between the communities something of the first 'extreme' or sharp dichotomy between science and technology. There is also some ambivalence about the relations of these communities with society: Layton welcomes investigation of the social context, whereas Price's position is explicitly antagonistic, and may therefore be seen implicitly to uphold a one-way view of the causal relations of technological and social change. (We do not set out systematically to evaluate these models in the substantive essays, though there may be enough correspondences established between pure science and technological innovation to unhinge Price's model of weakly interacting parallel structures, at least for the period 1870–1950.)

There is evidently little consensus even in Western liberal scholarship about the relations of science, technology and society. This methodological confusion reflects the immaturity of the disciplines of technology studies, to be sure; and the very fact that the fields of history, philosophy and sociology of science have been by comparison so intensively cultivated is a further reflection of the science community's greater social cachet, and sense of its own intellectual superiority. Revised views of science's primacy over technology need only be taken as indicative of growing self-esteem among the community of technologists; such revisions as Price's can therefore readily be seen as consistent with a broadly *unilinear* causal model, in which an independently evolving body of theory (whether scientific or technological) constitutes a mysterious intellectual motor of social change. A model such as this remains highly suggestive of technological determinism, discussed in the next section. We can at least see at this point in the development of the discussion that any convincing advocacy, or indeed rebuttal, of technological determinism presupposes (1) a firm hold on the historical slippery terms 'science' and 'technology', and (2) a resolution of the difficulties in either establishing, or denying, a formative social context for whatever it is they are held to represent!

We have, at this point, arrived at two quite divergent interim conclusions: (1) that any simple unilinear portrayal of the relations of science, technology and society is up against some substantial contemporary historiographical objections; and (2) that some recent revisions of this simple picture may still incorporate the spirit of technological determinism. It is high time we looked closely at this term and the positions to which it has been applied. Consideration of the second extreme identified at the beginning of this section forms a natural part of this scrutiny, since many of its representatives trace their ideas to the writings of Marx, and Marx's 'historical materialism', as we shall see, was sometimes held up in our period as the definitively technological-determinist interpretation of history.

2.2 TECHNOLOGICAL DETERMINISM

The concept of 'technological determinism', almost as such, has already been invoked in the quotation from Thomas Parke Hughes near the end of section 1.2. Hughes's stance underlines the point that 'technological determinism' is one of those labels ('reductionism' is another) which is usually attached to certain sets of ideas by sceptical or hostile commentators, rather than by their authors. Partly for this reason exemplary definitions of the term are lacking, though much of the difficulty also stems from inherent ambiguities. We have already seen that 'technology' can vary enormously in its range of meaning and application, and much the same point can be made about 'determinism'. In philosophy, determinism is generally taken to be the position that every event has a natural cause, or is the (in principle) predictable outcome of the operation of natural laws – a position frequently associated with the morally notorious rejection of free will or freedom of choice as illusory. It is difficult at first glance to invest *technological* determinism with quite this cosmic significance, if nothing more is intended than that technology (whatever this may cover) is the most important or the decisive factor in explaining general historical change; though as we shall see, the question of human autonomy is paramount. To get the discussion under way, let us agree that the following propositions are entailed if any account of the relations of science, technology and society is covered by the term 'technological determinism':

1 all social and cultural change is ultimately dependent on technological change;

2 all technological change is ultimately independent of social and cultural change.

This is clearly more of a semantic test than an exhaustive definition, but you will note that the unilinear model referred to at the end of the previous section passes this test with flying colours. It matters not that technology may be increasingly seen as dependent on natural-scientific theories, provided that the development of the theoretical content of natural science is itself judged to be an autonomous process. The criterion that technological change is ultimately independent of social and cultural change is still thereby satisfied.

Who then can we pick out as a technological determinist? Identification is neither straightforward nor uncontroversial. MacKenzie and Wajcman (1985) instance, among others, prophets of the 'microelectronic revolution', pioneers of industrial sociology, propagandists of the 'post-industrial society' and the 'scientific-technological revolution'; all of these manifest an uncritical acceptance of recent developments in industrial automation and the use of computers, and concentrate on their effects on the workplace, and on worker-manager relations, as well as on broader social relationships. There is undoubtedly in this sort of writing a blindness to the possible social and cultural origins of technological change, a blindness that is arguably consistent with technological determinism; more, however, as an uncritical assumption than as a self-conscious theoretical standpoint. Langdon Winner (1977, p.74) also complains of 'uncriticized quasideterministic assumptions' in much contemporary literature on 'technology assessment' and 'alternative futures'.

Such assumptions abound in our period. They are, as we have seen, latent in the American Ideology (section 1.3). Specific instances emerge in later chapters; for example, the promotion of electric appliances in the home (chapter 3), and the lauding of the wonders of the new communications media (chapter 7). But to deepen the discussion, we need to consider rarer instances where writers have consciously developed a position on the relations of technological, social and cultural change, and where their reflections have some bearing on the question of technological determinism.

As we saw above, among the implicit technological determinists were pioneers of industrial sociology, many of whom, according to MacKenzie and Wajcman, were 'influenced by a reading of Karl Marx which saw him as a technological determinist' (p.69), what has been dubbed a 'technicist' interpretation. Marx (1818–83) is an obvious figure on whom to dwell, above all because of the nature, profundity and influence of his social philosophy, and specifically because his analysis of capitalist production constitutes an intellectual threshold to our period. The three volumes of *Capital* (1865–79) span the notional starting date of our period, recapitulate the revolution in the economic base associated with factory production, and in conjunction with the other writings of Marx and his collaborator, Friedrich Engels, are controversially prophetic about the second main phase of industrialization with which we are concerned.

Marx's 'materialist conception of history' (subsequently known as 'historical materialism') posited a sequence of historical events in accordance with which changes in the 'forces of production' determined the 'social relations of production'; these in their turn decided all social relations, in particular the divisions of social classes; finally, this characteristic social configuration found its reflection in the ideas or theoretical products of a society (religion, politics, philosophy, and so on). Marx thus distinguished the economic foundation of society from its dependent legal and political superstructure, intrinsic to which were specific attitudes, values and ways of thinking. This emphasis in historical explanation is commonly classified as 'economic determinism', but if changes in the economic base depend upon changes in the 'forces of production', and if 'forces of production' is Marx's term for technology, then it would seem to follow that historical materialism is indeed a 'technological interpretation of history' (Hansen, 1921).

The identification of the productive forces with technology is only one of the problematic features of this technicist reading of Marx. It might be objected that when Marx talked of the 'productive forces of capital' he meant not merely the material means of production, but also the division of labour, the factory mode of organization, and the harnessing of science and natural power sources. But as we saw in the previous section, it is only an impoverished 'hardware' conception of technology which excludes these wider considerations, and to insist on it in this context is to make a straw man of Marx's supposed technological determinism.

David McLellan, a British non-Marxist authority on the life and works of Marx, warns against illicitly generalizing certain statements and 'crediting' Marx with a theory of technological determinism (McLellan, 1980, p.137), but we can hardly avoid that risk in such a brief survey. There are several passages from Marx's writings implying a determining role for productive

forces in history: among the most frequently quoted are those from a relatively early publication, *The Poverty of Philosophy* (1847):

> What is society, whatever its form may be? The product of men's reciprocal
> action. Are men free to choose this or that form of society for themselves?
> By no means. Assume a particular state of development in the productive
> forces of man and you will get a particular form of commerce and consump-
> tion. Assume particular stages of development in production, commerce
> and consumption and you will have a corresponding social constitution, a
> corresponding organisation of the family, of orders or of classes, in a word,
> a corresponding civil society. Assume a particular civil society and you will
> get particular political conditions which are only the official expression of
> civil society . . .
>
> It is superfluous to add that men are not free to choose their *productive
> forces* – which are the basis of all their history – for every productive force
> is an acquired force, the product of former activity. The productive forces
> are therefore the result of practical human energy; but this energy is itself
> conditioned by the circumstances in which men find themselves, by the
> productive forces already acquired, by the social form which exists before
> they do, which they do not create, which is the product of the preceding
> generation . . .
>
> Social relations are intimately bound up with productive forces. In
> acquiring new productive forces men change their mode of production,
> and in changing their mode of production, their manner of making a living,
> they change all their social relations. The windmill gives you society with
> the feudal lord; the steam mill, society with the industrial capitalist.
> (McLellan, 1980, pp.141–42, 40.)

We should clearly pause before accepting a few extracts from one work as
representative of Marx's position; but it is evident that at this stage in the
development of his ideas Marx saw productive forces as the basis of all
human history, and minimized the role of human choice in determining their
development. Such a downgrading of human autonomy is certainly suggestive
of determinism, though even if this were accepted, whether it would be
technological determinism is still open to doubt: there is a hint in the second
paragraph that the social forms created initially by productive forces go on
to play a part in stimulating technological change. If so, the requirement that
technological change be independent of social change would not be met.
This point is insisted upon by Donald MacKenzie (1984), who argues that
both in *Capital*, and in the historical record, changes in social relations paved
the way for the mechanization of manufacture.

How else has Marx been exculpated from the charge of technological
determinism? McLellan doubts whether the scheme of historical materialism
was intended by Marx as a strictly causal theory; he also insists like
MacKenzie that the 'instruments of production' cannot be isolated from their
social context (McLellan, 1980, p.137). The two are in fact 'dialectically'
related, which is to say that they are different, partly contradictory, aspects
of the same objective reality. (In Marxist thought, it is the 'dialectical'
resolution of internal contradictions which leads to change: thus the central
contradiction of capitalism which dooms it to extinction is that which exists
between the increasingly social and concentrated nature of the relations
of production, and the private and individual character of ownership and
accumulation.) The same point is urged by David Noble (1979, p.xix): forces
of production and social relations are different aspects of the single process
of 'social production', and just as changes in *productive forces* bring about a
transformation of the social activity of production, changes in *social relations*

make possible further development of the forces of production. There is thus a *reciprocal* relationship and not a linear causality. Noble goes on to portray technology as an essentially human and social process inescapably reflecting the contours of the social order producing and sustaining it:

> And like any human enterprise, it does not simply proceed automatically, but rather contains a subjective element which drives it, and assumes the particular forms given it by the most powerful and forceful people in society, in struggle with others. The development of technology, and thus the social development it implies, is as much determined by the breadth of vision that informs it, and the particular notions of social order to which it is bound, as by the mechanical relations between things and the physical laws of nature. Like all others, this historical enterprise always contains a range of possibilities as well as necessities, possibilities seized upon by particular people, for particular purposes, according to particular conceptions of social destiny. (Noble, 1979, p.xxii)

Noble's reading of Marx is evidently a long way from technological determinism. In no sense is technology depicted as an independent variable, and the emphasis on the 'subjective element' is closer to determinism's opposite, *voluntarism*, the view that human volitions can be decisive in history. Interpretations like Noble's are, it should be stressed, among the most recent in a long process of extending and revising Marx's thought in witting and unwitting response to historical developments since his death. Marx himself undoubtedly and inevitably was more impressed and optimistic about the potential of science and technology than many modern critics in our nuclear and microelectronic age. Marx's collaborator Engels survived him, and went on to elaborate Marxism as a 'scientific' enterprise, laying bare the deterministic laws of historical change. Engels' systematization of Marx's thought was taken up by Lenin and adapted to the contingencies of the Russian situation, and the set formulae of Marxism-Leninism emerged after the Russian Revolution, including the rigid division between economic base and ideological superstructure. Technological determinism had obvious ideological utility for a system that has always placed a higher premium on massive investment in technology than on human autonomy. Among followers of Marx in the West during our period, a 'technicist' reading of Marx reflected a faith in the liberating potential of scientific technology, buttressed by a belief that any current ills associated with it resulted from its *misuse* under capitalism, rather than from any inherent repressive properties. So we find the Irish scientist J.D. Bernal writing on the eve of the Second World War:

> [Science] is the chief agent of change in society; at first, unconsciously as technical change, paving the way to economic and social changes, and, latterly, as a more conscious and direct motive for social change itself . . . Science will come to be recognized as the chief factor in fundamental social change. The economic and industrial system keeps civilization going. The steady process of technical improvement provides for a regular increase in the extent and commodity of life. Science should provide a continuous series of unpredictable radical changes in the techniques themselves. (Bernal, 1939, pp.383, 415)

The Bernalist faith in the ideological neutrality of technology wilted, at any rate among Western radicals, in the face of the nuclear arms race and the Vietnam War. At the same time as the positivist idealization of science has been under siege, historical and sociological writings savouring of technological determinism have been increasingly stigmatized. It is in this changed intellectual climate that the second extreme, or 'identity', view mentioned at the beginning of the previous section has found expression. On this view, the autonomy of science, and it is claimed, of technology too, is a mystification; in reality, science and technology in tandem have become one of the most powerful instruments of class domination under advanced capitalism. The technological determinism implicit in the linear-sequential view can now be shown for what it is: a rationalization of transnational corporations' interest in market innovations, and of the military-industrial complex's appetite for capital expenditure.

Ironically, this line of reasoning has reintroduced the spectre of techno-logical determinism in another shape. This is largely by way of revisions of the Marxian legacy, but even in classical Marxism the notion of technological determinism may well capture something of the experience of those most directly affected by the transformation of the forces of production. In Marxian theory, technology may be seen as the outcome of a dialectical encounter between human action and nature, affording the prospect of full human self-realization in communal activity; but under the capitalist system of production, this desirable state of affairs is impossible, because factory workers become *alienated* in more senses than one: alienated from their own labour, now a commodity to be sold on the market; alienated from the end product with which their increasingly divided labour becomes ever more indirectly associated; and alienated from their tools and work processes, which now serve to control their lives like some alien force. The fullest discussion of alienation is found in an early writing, the *Economic and Philosophical Manuscripts* (1844):

> The *alienation* of the worker from his product means not only that his labour becomes an object, assumes an *external* existence, but that it exists independently, *outside himself*, and alien to him, and that it stands opposed to him as an autonomous power. The life which he has given to the object sets itself against him as an alien and hostile force. (Bottomore, 1963, pp.122–23)

In *Capital* Marx likens the factory to 'a lifeless mechanism independent of the workman, who becomes its mere living appendage'. From the point of view of the factory workers, then, technological determinism is real enough, for their entire way of life is governed by a mechanical system over which they exercise no control. Winner is right to point out that this is not as such a theory of autonomous technology, since these inhuman means of production are in fact controlled by a group of humans, albeit a small minority of factory owners; moreover, the absence of control by the majority is an impermanent feature, as the prospect of revolutionary change brings with it the prospect of the liberation of the toiling masses from technological bondage.

The question of technological determinism emerges again, with relevance to our period, in the way that Marx's concept of alienated labour has been revised by recent writers, less hopeful than Marx that humanity could regain control of technology. Herbert Marcuse, for example, was struck by the fact that Marx's central contradiction between capitalism's social relations and forces of production had failed so far to materialize in open class warfare. Though influenced by a 'humanist' (rather than 'technicist') reading of Marx based on his early writings, Marcuse attributed this failure to the sheer power and even beneficence of modern technology, and its part in a growing 'fetishism of commodities':

> Our society distinguishes itself by conquering the centrifugal social forces with Technology rather than Terror, on the dual basis of an overwhelming

efficiency and an increased standard of living . . . The people recognise
themselves in their commodities; they find their soul in their automobile,
hi-fi set, split-level home, kitchen equipment. The very mechanism which
ties the individual to his society has changed, and social control is anchored
in the new needs which it has produced. (Marcuse, 1964, pp.x, 21–22)

Marcuse subscribed to a 'totalitarian' account of advanced society according
to which cohesion is achieved not by terror (as in Hitler's Germany and
Stalin's Russia) but by mass consumption and the 'pleasure' industries. The
technology of the cinema, radio and television and so on, had served to
institute new, more effective, and more pleasant forms of social control and
social cohesion than that achieved by the Gestapo or NKVD. Pleasure had
been de-sublimated and made available only in the form of commodities.
Certain forms of pleasure and culture have the potential of making us aware
of forms of life which transcend the given state of affairs. Great art, for
example, can suggest human values that are 'higher' than or transcend those
that routinely inform the present. The totalitarian tendencies of advanced
societies, Marcuse believed, blocked this potential. Art is confined to an
élitist high culture and its values are construed as purely aesthetic, except
for its exchange value which has been grotesquely inflated by the art market.
Meanwhile, mass culture – the culture of everyday life – affords pleasures
which simply conform their consumers to the society dominated by technological rationality; they reconcile the people to the present.

  The modern technological order therefore succeeds in containing the opposition of its exploited workers by creating in them needs and desires which
it alone can satisfy; but it also dissipates the object of class antagonism by
transforming the mighty capitalist boss into a corporate bureaucrat (Marcuse,
1964, pp.31–32). In this way autonomous technology re-emerges; as Winner
puts it, 'The privileged position of an élite or ruling class is not proof that it
steers the mechanism but only that it has a comfortable seat for the ride'
(Winner, 1977, p.41).

  During the 1960s Marcuse became the best-known representative of the
'critical theory', or critique of advanced capitalism, identified with the Frankfurt Institute for Social Research co-founded in 1923 by Max Horkheimer.
The revisionist Marxism of Horkheimer, T.W. Adorno and Marcuse has
been further extended by Jürgen Habermas, who was once a junior colleague
at the Institute. According to Habermas, many of the doctrines and categories
of orthodox Marxism need to be reworked to accommodate the increasing
importance of scientific technology under advanced capitalism. Science itself
can no longer be regarded as a superstructural ideological reflection of underlying changes in the technological and economic base. The growing fusion
of science and technology means that science itself has become a productive
force; indeed scientific technology is now a greater source of economic value
than labour. This state of affairs is associated on the economic and political
level with larger, monopolistic industrial forms and increasing state intervention, and at the social and ideological level by a spreading of the cloak
of 'technological rationality' over areas of everyday life in which autonomous
personal interaction formerly prevailed. The peculiar significance of scientific
technology in advanced capitalist societies is dual: (1) as the leading
productive force it provides the material basis of political power, and (2) it
also furnishes the concepts of the technocratic ideology which legitimates the
exercise of that power. So complete is this circle that Habermas is led to
question the liberating Marxian assumption that growth in the productive
forces eventually disrupts the existing framework of social relations.

  How near does this despairing critique of the self-replicating power of
advanced capitalism come to technological determinism? Habermas, fortunately, is at his least impenetrable on this point:

It is true that social interests still determine the direction, functions, and pace of technical progress. But these interests define the social system so much as a whole that they coincide with the interest in maintaining the system. *As such* the private form of capital utilization and a distribution mechanism for social rewards that guarantees the loyalty of the masses are removed from discussion. The quasi-autonomous progress of science and technology then appears as an independent variable on which the most important single system variable, namely economic growth, depends. Thus arises a perspective in which the development of the social system *seems* to be determined by the logic of scientific-technical progress. The immanent law of this progress seems to produce objective exigencies, which must be obeyed by any politics oriented toward functional needs. But when this semblance has taken root effectively, then propaganda can refer to the role of technology and science in order to explain and legitimate why in modern societies the process of democratic decision-making about practical problems loses its function and 'must' be replaced by plebiscitary decisions about alternative sets of leaders of administrative personnel. (Habermas, 1971, p.105)

Strictly speaking, neither Marcuse nor Habermas's views amount to techno-logical determinism, since the necessary autonomy accorded to scientific technology is a mystification, an ideological construct. They do, however, present scientific technology as by now the main determining force in history, and reluctantly conclude that there appears to be very little that can be done to alter this. The practical difference between our two extremes on the relations of science, technology and society seems to be the degree of enthusiasm with which the various proponents greet the power of science and technology to determine our everyday lives.

Thus far we have only considered explicit theorizing on the causal relations of technology and social change within the Marxist tradition. To illustrate his theme of 'technics-out-of-control', Winner also presents us with an array of largely American non-Marxist historians, anthropologists, social theorists and scientists who have, in one way or another, upheld the bracketing of an inevitable and self-sustaining process of scientific and technological advance with the unending prospect of far-reaching social change. There is often in this writing at least an implicit subscription to linear-sequential models of technical innovation and the associated 'dichotomy' view of the relations of science and technology. One figure in Winner's book looms even larger than Marx, is not a Marxist, but nevertheless presents an uncompromising statement of the 'identity' view. The prominence of this figure, Jacques Ellul, in Winner's book is testimony to the considerable vogue for this French professor of jurisprudence on American college campuses during the heady years of the late 1960s and early 70s.

Ellul's most influential work, *The Technological Society*, has more bearing on our period than the timing of his American heyday suggests, as the original French version was published in 1954. Ellul recounts how he accepted Marx's *Capital* on reading it as a young man, but soon opted for 'faith in Jesus Christ', while retaining Marx's 'method' of seeing political, economic and social problems (Winner, 1977, p.349, n.50). It is therefore perhaps less paradoxical, given this element in his intellectual development, that a religious conservative like Ellul should share with a revolutionary socialist like Marcuse a vision of modern society repressed by an irresistible and pervasive technological rationality. For Marcuse, though, technology is a refined instrument of capitalist domination, whereas for Ellul, the totalitarian nature of modern technology is inherent in it, and transcends political systems. For this reason, Ellul appears rather more pessimistic than Marcuse about human autonomy. In *One-Dimensional Man*, Marcuse leaves open the possibility, though with little conviction, that modern technology will not always manage to contain the inherent contradiction of capitalist production; Ellul's effective equation of technology with sin or Mammon, and of the rise of technological rationality since the eighteenth century with a second Fall of Man, lead him to an even greater estimate of the power of technology and the impotence of human action in the face of it.

The first striking feature of Ellul's *The Technological Society* is its very broad definition of technology, or *la technique*, as '*the totality of methods rationally arrived at and having absolute efficiency* (for a given stage of development) in *every* field of human activity' (Ellul, 1965, p.1, original emphasis). Thus we find references to educational theory, political propaganda and advertising as examples of 'human techniques'. It also follows from this definition that the distinction between science and technology is obsolete, modern science being yet another instance of technique.

Ellul goes on in a 'characterology of technique' to enumerate its main characteristics. Among these are *rationality*, the elimination of spontaneity and personal creativity by the application of analytical and logical methods; *artificiality*, the subordination and destruction of nature; *automatism*, the effective elimination of choice when efficiency becomes the sole criterion of value; and most directly of relevance to the issue of technological determinism, *self-augmentation* and *autonomy*. Technology is self-augmenting, not because it no longer needs human intervention, but because modern society is so geared towards technical progress that the work of thousands of technicians guarantees it. There is therefore now no need for geniuses like Newton; if the time is ripe for a discovery or invention, someone, or more than one, will succeed. The empirical basis of this claim is the frequency of simultaneous discoveries or inventions (for example, the inventors working on the incandescent filament lamp in the 1870s – see section 3.2.2), and also the fact that technological advance is largely a matter of the accretion of a host of minor improvements, or the synthesis of existing inventions. In the extracts that follow, Ellul summarizes his view of the inexorable advance of technique, and characterizes its autonomy:

> What is it that determines this progression today? We can no longer argue that it is an economic or a social condition, or education, or any other human factor. Essentially, the preceding technical situation alone is determinative. When a given technical discovery occurs, it has followed almost of necessity certain other discoveries. Human intervention in this succession appears only as an incidental cause, and no one man can do this by himself. But anyone who is sufficiently up-to-date technically can make a valid discovery which rationally follows its predecessors and rationally heralds what is to follow . . .

> . . . technique is autonomous with respect to economics and politics. We have already seen that, at the present, neither economic nor political evolution conditions technical progress. Its progress is likewise independent of the social situation. The converse is actually the case, a point I shall develop at length. Technique elicits and conditions social, political, and economic change. It is the prime mover of all the rest, in spite of any appearance to the contrary and in spite of human pride, which pretends that man's philosophical theories are still determining influences and man's political regimes decisive factors in technical evolution. (Ellul, 1965, pp.90, 133)

The foregoing extracts would seem to be quintessential technological determinism, though there are some qualifications to be made. In the first place, for Ellul the autonomous and self-augmenting nature of technique is a distinctly modern phenomenon dating from the eighteenth century, and arose out of a conjunction of favourable circumstances, only one of which was the state of technological development – the others being population growth, a favourable economic climate, and the emergence of a sufficiently 'plastic' social configuration open to the propagation of technique (Ellul, 1965, pp.59–60). Thus Ellul is no absolute technological determinist: society has not always been a reflection of technology, as it is for 'technicist' readers of Marx. Ellul might therefore be dubbed a 'progressive' technological determinist. Nor does he deny human free will; he only denies that its effects are discernible at the level of general sociological analysis (p.xxvi). Inevitable progress is also for Ellul a feature of the *ensemble* of techniques, not of any one particular technique, which may encounter temporary barriers in its development (p.90). We might distinguish here an increasingly general electrification of all aspects of everyday life, from localized lags or setbacks such as the persistence of gas-lighting in Britain (section 3.3.1), the failure of Ferranti's scheme (section 3.3.2), or French cultural resistance to electrical appliances (section 3.5.2). In conclusion, for Ellul the rift which the 'technical phenomenon' has brought about between human beings and nature is irreversible: 'Enclosed within his artificial creation, man finds that there is "no exit"; that he cannot pierce the shell of technology to find again the ancient milieu to which he was adapted for hundreds of thousands of years' (p.428).

What objections may be levelled at Ellul's thesis, and at technological determinism in general? We have already noted some semantic problems, and although Ellul's all-embracing definition of 'technique' is a welcome advance on hardware definitions, the very breadth suggests some begging of the question in his claims for its universality. Furthermore, if, as it sometimes looks, technique is virtually synonymous with rationality, its inevitability appears less startling. Ellul almost seems to be arguing that 'irrational opposition to rational (technical) solutions is possible, but most people will always prefer the rational to the irrational'. This is probably to go too far in reducing the shock value of Ellul's position, since as we have seen, technological rationality is opposed not so much to irrationality as to human creativity and spontaneity. Thus a second, and more substantial, objection to technological determinism in general is the assertion of the real *efficacy* of human choice, against positions like Ellul's and Marcuse's, according to which modern scientific technology severely circumscribes free will. Historians can contribute by investigating areas in which individual action and human choices may be set against any notion of irresistible technique: consumer preference and environmentalist opposition are two obvious categories, equivocal instances being protest against the National Grid route (section 3.4.4), and the reception of brown bread and baked beans (chapter 8). But the issue is not settled simply by placing human choices on the historical record. Both Ellul and Marcuse argue strongly that human desires and choices in modern technological society are the *creation* of technique, and that it is precisely through the stimulation of new material wants and needs, notably by advertising, that technique maintains its ascendancy and sustains its drive. Consider here Edison's use of publicity, and later the selling of domestic appliances (sections 3.3.1 and 3.5.1). As Winner puts it, 'A need becomes a need in substantial part because a megatechnical system external to the person needed that need to be needed' (Winner, 1977, p.248).

A third broad front on which Ellul and all alleged technological determinists can be assailed is their isolation of technology as the one, or the main, determinant of historical change. Ellul himself has conceded that a multifactoral explanation is necessary to account for the *emergence* of the 'technical phenomenon'. As the essays in this volume show, a variety of factors other than the prior state of technology need to be invoked to explain both the adoption and the diffusion of the key innovations in our period (see in

particular section 1.2 and chapters 3,5,6 and 11). Even a *philosophical* determinist might baulk at the isolation of scientific technology as the fundamental
causal agent. Why in the acrobats' wheel of reciprocal causality should the
scientific-technological, rather than the social, economic, political, demographic or ideological, be singled out as really keeping the thing rolling? As
we shall see, it is one thing to demonstrate that technological change is a
necessary condition of changes in everyday life, quite another to show that
it is *sufficient*. The problem here, as Winner warns, is to chart a course
between a 'Scylla of cross reductionism' and a 'Charybdis of wild, multifactoral confusion' (Winner, 1977, p.176).

The fourth main objection to Ellul and company is directed at the second
presupposition of technological determinism put forward at the start of this
section: in short, the autonomy of scientific technology. There is a great deal
of evidence in the body of this volume establishing social, political and
economic contexts for scientific-technological innovations. Indeed a case can
even be made for the social and political content of certain technological
designs (sections 2.3 and 3.5.2; MacKenzie and Wajcman, 1985). All of this
evidence reveals a logical flaw in technological determinism, but it does not
necessarily reduce its emotive power. For it is one thing to *establish*, for
example, the growing interdependence in our period of the technical
community, government and administration, and the 'military-industrial
complex'; it is quite another to open up the possibility of intervention in
these relationships, and in consequence to exorcize the spectre of 'technics-
out-of-control'.

Throughout the period covered by this collection of essays technological
determinism has attracted people with diverse estimations and expectations of
science and technology: some with a naive belief in some future technological
heaven on earth, and some motivated to protect the freedom of industry to
innovate in the face of a cumulative penalty of environmental hazard; others
with a persisting faith in the power of technology to liberate the mass of
humanity, despite its present abuse, and others still who equate technology
with man's ineradicable depravity. In Winner's words, the doctrine of technological determinism can easily become 'a swamp of intellectual muddles'
(Winner, 1977, p.74). Not least of such muddles is the meaning of the term.
Adopt a simple hardware definition of technology, and you conjure up sci-
fi visions of Frankenstein's monster, and a world to come in which human
beings are eclipsed by the thinking machines they create. Replace it with a
conception of technology that recognizes it as an essentially human and social
activity, and interpret determinism in a way that does not subject all human
actions to an iron causality, and you may then have a way of capturing the
undoubtedly major determining or shaping role of scientific technology in
modern everyday life. Even here, there is a price: either technological determinism collapses, as the autonomy of technology is effectively ceded; or else
it starts to empty of meaning, as it verges towards the remarkable insight
that 'vital areas of human activity have important effects in other areas of
human activity'. Perhaps there is a position in between which is not so
easy to knock down. As Winner argues, refuting technological determinism
requires more than 'a vague multifactoralism and a glib reassertion of the
voluntarist position' (Winner, 1977, p.77).

So far, this chapter has shown that the business of clarifying the causal
relations of science, technology and everyday life is fraught with semantic
indecision. There are also inescapable limits to what can be resolved here,
partly because of the unavoidably restricted aims of this volume, and partly
because of the sheer generality of some of the positions discussed in this
section. As we saw, any complete historical examination of the linear-sequential model would require some investigation of the social context of the
scientific discoveries on which so many of our technical innovations partly

depend, and this cannot be undertaken systematically in a study of this length. Another limitation stems from the quite defensible decision to divide the bulk of the volume into particular areas of technology. This means that strong claims for the determining role of particular innovations, or related sets of innovations, can readily be tested, either by pointing out their social, economic and political context, or by bringing to light variable social effects associated with the same technology, or yet again by identifying social changes not connected with technical innovation (see in particular chapters 3, 5 and 6). This quite reasonably multifactoralist strategy may be inappropriate to the criticism of scenarios like those of Habermas or Ellul. The nearest we come to discussing the causal role of a technocratic consciousness is in chapters 11 and 12, with their much broader technological canvas. There is, however, at present a yawning gap between the abstractness of such general philosophical positions, and the present incomplete findings of social historians of science and technology. We hope that these essays will do a little more than merely reflect that gap.

2.3
IS TECHNOLOGY
NEUTRAL?

So far in this chapter we have explained that the interpretation of science and technology, both in their mutual relations and in their relations with society, has been a matter of controversy. The sheer variety of interpretations we have canvassed should not, however, be allowed to obscure the very real prospect that critical scholarship has achieved a more authentic or satisfactory understanding of the science-technology-society complex than was current a generation ago. The old positivist ideal of science as disinterested enquiry leading to a progressive unfolding of truth has been shown to bear little resemblance to what scientists actually do and achieve. The traditional linear-sequential view of technology as mediator between pure research and social needs – applying scientific truth in response to practical demands – now appears to overlook both the social shaping of 'pure' research and the techno-logical shaping of social needs themselves. The more recent unilinear view that technology, far from merely shaping social needs, in fact dominates and determines society as an autonomous force can be shown to be either irrefutable, and therefore uninteresting, or simply a brash over-generalization of the uncontentious statement that technological change is the precondition for many other changes in everyday life. Above all, it has become clear through our earlier discussions that both 'science' and 'technology' refer to a range of human activities which, as such, are socially and historically imbedded. Each enterprise can be understood as knowledge-productive, whether of knowing *how* or knowing *that*. Each achieves practical as well as theoretical results that are vital to the structures and research traditions of the other. Their broadest common ground is the society in which they subsist.

It remains therefore to consider how science and technology are actually imbedded in society. Given that science does not consist of disinterested truthseeking and that technology is not socially autonomous, we shall address this problem by raising the question of 'neutrality'. What would it mean for science and technology to be neutral, or non-partisan, in their social relations? How can this view be contested? In what sense can a technology be said to embody social values?

The question of the neutrality of science and technology has been broached repeatedly in the foregoing pages. Earlier in this chapter, for example, it arose in an exposition of the relativist critique of scientific 'objectivity' as defended by the post-positivists Popper and Kuhn. In chapter 1 the neutrality of technology was signalled as a problematic assumption of the so-called 'American Ideology'. What became evident in these contexts is that the question of neutrality has been debated in ways that would suggest the existence of vested interests in the outcome. In other words, the answer to the question of the neutrality of science and technology cannot apparently itself be regarded with neutrality. The entire debate is ideological, in the sense in which we have used the word.

The neutrality of science now finds fewer defenders than formerly, even among practising scientists. However the term may be construed, a strong empirical case has been mounted that neither the institutions, nor the practitioners, nor even the theories of science, can be regarded as 'neutral' with respect to their historic social contexts (Shapin, 1982). Moreover, the philosopher Max Black has argued on logical grounds alone that the assertion of neutrality may be misguided.

> If science really has no intrinsic tendency to further human welfare rather than to increase human misery, the case for massive and indiscriminate support of science may well appear problematic. Even if the human usefulness of science can be grounded in its *indirect* bearings upon welfare and happiness, it is natural for a firm believer in the neutrality thesis to have serious qualms about the value of science. (In Lipscombe and Williams, 1979, p.44)

But in fact few such believers do. The same point, as we shall see, can be made with reference to the neutrality of technology.

Turning then to this aspect of the debate, from one standpoint – roughly that of the American Ideology – it goes without saying that people who *use* technology may not be neutral. Indeed, it often happens that their choice of the *ends* (goals, objectives) of innovation is dictated consciously or unconsciously by moral and political imperatives. But neither the technological *means* (machines, devices, processes) nor the technicians responsible for their design, construction and deployment are to be implicated in this choice or in the ends actually achieved. If things go awry, the wrong ends may have been sought ('bad policy'), or the means – the technology – may have been *abused* ('bad management'). And conversely if things go right. These are matters of political concern, where value judgements must be made. More typically, the problem is that the means available are not sufficiently sophisticated to achieve the chosen ends, and this calls for new and better means to be developed as a matter of technical priority. Here, however, as in other circumstances, the technology itself and the technicians who develop and deploy it are non-partisan. The realm of means is neutral.

In reply, critics such as the science journalist David Dickson have branded this account a 'myth'. Like other technological myths – the romance of commercial power in imperial Britain, the mystique of heavy industry in Bolshevik Russia – the myth of the neutrality of technology is a substitute for authentic historical understanding. It conceals the material genesis of events and obscures their real interconnections, much as the creation myths do in the Old Testament. But there is a method in the mythology, and Dickson (1986, p.26) suggests whose it is: 'The myth . . . legitimates the contemporary social function of technology by attempting to take it out of the realm of political debate. We cease to question the nature of the institutionalised structure of technology and the way in which it has developed historically; we accept both as natural, or rather as inevitable.' And this is good news for politicians, whose agenda is already cluttered, for entrepreneurs, whose aim is to make money with minimal political interference, and for engineers, who just want to get on with their job.

But politicians, entrepreneurs and engineers share other interests besides the avoidance of disruptive challenges. In most industrialized societies they are mutually committed to promoting a positive image for 'research and development' – institutionalized innovation – as the bulwark of economic growth and political stability. Here, according to Dickson, the myth of the neutrality of technology also serves them well by legitimating the 'R & D' process as the 'objective, technical response' to given circumstances.

> The legitimation can be expressed in terms of 'increased efficiency' (e.g. the introduction of assembly-line production techniques), as the 'technical' solutions to social needs (e.g. the development of a new transport system), as the economic 'rationalisation' of outdated techniques (e.g. the introduction of automatic telephone systems), or even as the need to maintain a competitive position in a world market (e.g. Concorde). Whatever the terms used, they attempt to imply an objective rationality to the process of technological innovation that presents any particular innovation as being the 'logical' response to a given objectively defined situation. (Dickson, 1986, p.26)

Dickson argues that this neutralist rhetoric is merely a fig-leaf to cover naked value judgements. Any application of abstract knowledge to practical tasks is already a 'politically determined process'. And in industrialized capitalist economies technological innovation serves directly or indirectly to maintain and reinforce the position of the dominant entrepreneurial class.

Thus, Dickson observes, technological innovation has been used 'directly to increase supervision and tighten control' over labour (factory-based construction methods in the building industry); it has been used as 'a means of introducing stability into a work situation by displacing militant factions of the workforce' (containerization of ports); it has been used to 'achieve an apparent improvement in the work situation and hence a removal of possible sources of conflict' (teamwork production methods in the automotive industry); and, finally, it has been used variously as 'a threat to blackmail sections of the workforce into particular tasks'. Under these circumstances, Dickson concludes, the entire process of technological innovation is politically fraught. From start to finish, from conception to execution to evaluation, the advisers and the devisers of technology serve concrete power interests. Means and ends alike are imbedded in the process. Neutrality is impossible.

It is all very interesting to deal with technology at this level of abstraction – the conventional case for the neutrality of technology can do so as well. But Dickson's argument must be refined much further if its evident radicalism is to appeal directly to most people's experience of technology in everyday life. In the paragraphs above, 'technological innovation', rather than 'technology', was the dominant theme. Dickson considers technological innovation to be a political process; he understands technology as a 'cross-section of the process of technological innovation' in the way that the photograph of a football match provides a static description of the state of play at a particular instant (p.22). On this account technology becomes a structured 'social institution', much as the players and implements visible in the photograph constitute a particular kind of game. Technological *artefacts* remain imbedded in their social relations; they can no more be regarded in isolation, as a heterogeneous collection of machines, tools, and other things people usually think of as 'technology', than the football, the goal posts, and the playing field in the photograph can be seen as an aggregation of miscellaneous objects. The artefacts not only owe their existence to human action, but acquire any meaning and value they possess from their individual social relations and by reference to the wider social movements in which they participate.

This, again, may be an admirable view of technology, but it is very broad. At best it only provides a framework within which to begin to analyse the neutrality or otherwise of particular artefacts. For discrete objects are what most people regard as 'technology' in everyday life: typewriters, torque wrenches, traction engines, and so on. Dickson may well be right to contend that 'a society's technology can never be isolated from its power structure' (p.22), but to make his case at least plausible it is necessary to explain how particular technologies do not subsist in social isolation. Their design and introduction must be shown to be contingent in at least some respects on critical social pressures as well as on discoveries or decisions that may appear to be purely technical. In recent years the challenge to analyse the non-neutrality of technology at this level of particularity has been taken up. Following the lead given by researchers who have sought to undermine the neutrality of so-called scientific facts, historians and sociologists have begun to analyse the 'social construction' of technological artefacts. Although many of these scholars do not approach the problem from a radical perspective, their accounts seem almost as far removed from the conventional, neutralist interpretation of technology as anything Dickson has written.

Consider, for example, the work of two sociologists of technology who have analysed the early development of an artefact that has remained a part of everyday life for over a century: the bicycle. Trevor Pinch and Wiebe Bijker (1984) have proposed a 'multi-directional' evolutionary model to suggest how the modern 'safety' bicycle, with low wheels, indirect rear-wheel drive, and pneumatic tyres, emerged in 1898 after some twenty years of complex conflicts and negotiations. According to this model, the safety bicycle did not appear suddenly in isolation; it was developed from the 'Penny Farthing' by 'selective' social pressures on 'variant' designs for two-wheeled conveyance that existed in the 1870s (Figure 2.1). Each of these bicyclic artefacts was contested or championed by different social groups. Each group – an institution, organization or association of organized or unorganized individuals – was characterized by a homogeneous interpretation of the artefact: that is, a set of meanings that expressed a range of problems to be connected legitimately with it.

Figure 2.1 The development of the Penny Farthing bicycle (after Pinch and Bijker, 1984, p.418, fig.7). Neither all the artefacts, social groups, problems and solutions, nor all their interconnections are shown, as this would complicate the diagram uselessly.

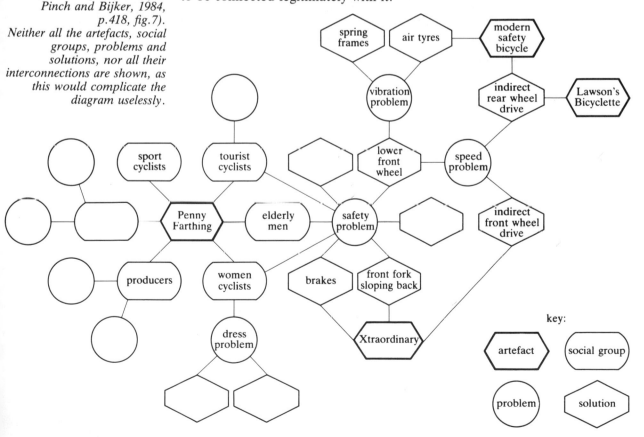

Figure 2.2
Typical 'Ordinary' high wheel
bicycle, 1870. Front wheel
sizes varied from 40 to
60 inches, the 'Penny' of the
'Penny Farthing'. (From
A. Sharp, 1896, Bicycles and
Tricycles, *Longman)*

Figure 2.3
Lawson 'Bicyclette', 1879.
(From A. Sharp, 1896,
Bicycles and Tricycles,
Longman)

Figure 2.4
Prototype of Rover 'safety
bicycle' built in 1884. (From
A. Sharp, 1896, Bicycles and
Tricycles, *Longman)*

Thus anti-cyclists, who had blanket objections, condemned bicycles out-of-hand. Women cyclists favoured safe designs that were compatible with their cumbersome garments. Young sportsmen preferred the original, high-wheeled Penny Farthing with its allure of speed and danger. Each of the problems connected with each artefact by each social group was held to have various solutions, and so the opportunities for conflict multiplied again. Different design preferences were based on differing perceptions of the relevant problems for each design and on the adequacy of available solutions. Was speed or safety to be the paramount factor? Could safety be achieved on a fast, high-wheeled bicycle or did it require a slower, low-wheeled design such as 'Lawson's Bicyclette' or the 'Extraordinary'? Were groups of women and elderly men to be excluded from cycling if the high-wheelers prevailed? In negotiating these differences the social groups subjected the variant artefacts to selective pressures which, in turn, elicited further variants and led eventually to the 'stabilization' of particular designs.

Pinch and Bijker stress this point: the 'interpretive flexibility' of an artefact is seen not only in the range of problems associated with it but in the designs it may undergo. 'There is not just one possible way, or one best way, of designing an artefact' (p.421). The design that wins out is neither 'natural' nor inevitable; it depends entirely on contingent circumstances, including the reinterpretation of *other* artefacts with which the original design may be modified. The safety bicycle itself consisted of a number of such artefacts that had been reinterpreted in the light of particular problems and pressures. One of these was the tyre.

If a low-wheeled bicycle with solid rubber tyres were adopted in the interests of safety, the problem of vibration became acute. Small wheels rode rough surfaces more closely than large wheels; cyclists suffered accordingly. Some engineers saw the pneumatic tyre as the solution to this problem, often in conjunction with a sprung frame. Other engineers argued that the pneumatic tyre made low-wheeled bicycles unsafe because of 'side-slipping' when under-inflated. The general public chimed in that the 'sausage tyre' was in any event unaesthetic, while sporting cyclists sped past, oblivious on their high-wheelers. Various attempts were made to resolve the question, but 'closure', as Pinch and Bijker call it, did not occur until 'the problem with respect to which the artefact should have the meaning of a solution' was redefined (p.428). When racing tests had shown that the pneumatic tyre could in fact be regarded as a solution to the problem of speed, rather than vibration, in low-wheeled bicycles, the public, the sportsmen, and eventually the engineers, were convinced. Now anyone would be able to cycle as fast as possible without undue risk to life and limb. With the resolution of the additional problem of an indirect rear-wheel drive, the stabilization of the modern safety bicycle was complete.

The social constructivist approach to the early development of the bicycle is of course suggestive rather than definitive. Pinch and Bijker derived their model empirically from a series of case studies; they intended its function to be 'primarily heuristic' (p.419). So far, however, does it represent an advance on radical generalizations about the non-neutrality of technology that at least one critic of Dickson's persuasion has felt moved to address its deficiencies in a constructive way. Stewart Russell, a researcher on technology policy, argues (1986, p.335) that under the apparently neutral guise of an evolutionary model, Pinch and Bijker have in fact assumed an 'essentially pluralist view' of society. Variant designs seem to appear naturally and spontaneously; selective pressures seem to emanate from isolated social groups effectively equal in power; stabilization seems to occur through a kind of political consensus. 'We may ask how a choice was made between several different configurations of bicycle frame, but not why these were the only possibilities presented to cyclists' (p.333). We may ask about the identity of groups that negotiated the choice but not about their differential access to technical information and the design process, about their conscious or unconscious misrepresentation of the real interests actuating them or, indeed, about groups in society capable of securing their interests without participating in the debate. In short, the evolutionary model is both circular and reductionistic. It proves only what it assumes, and this by reducing complex phenomena to its own simplistic categories.

The problem, according to Russell, is that Pinch and Bijker lack 'an adequate model of the basic social structures which provide the contexts of technological development'. He himself opts for the 'established framework . . . provided by a broad current of radical social analysis' (pp.331–32, 338). Since artefacts are designed and introduced for purposes closely linked with social interests, and since these interests are differentiated, conflictive and unequally represented, the meaning of artefacts – the nature of their non-neutrality – depends entirely on the social context in which they are, or could be, designed and introduced. Thus there are 'fundamental differences' in the social relations shaping a bicycle, a machine tool, a military aircraft, and a domestic appliance, just as there are fundamental differences in the social relations that obtain on a highway, in a factory, in the armed forces, and in the home. The non-neutrality of each artefact must be judged initially in its primary social context, then in any other contexts it may inhabit. 'As we move away from participants and contexts which fit neatly into the fundamental categories of Marxist analysis – classes and class fractions, in economic relations in the spheres of production and exchange – so', Russell acknowledges, 'the analysis gets more complex, with a wider range of groups and different types of interaction between them. The extent to which we can derive the interests and power of groups a priori from our social model is increasingly restricted, and the dangers of circularity and reductionism in our explanation grow' (p.340).

This is a needful caveat. And Pinch and Bijker have replied with a challenge (1986, p.354): 'Russell and his colleagues . . . need to show us how their elaborate theoretical structures can be used to explain the development of particular technologies. The analysis in terms of social groups may be too simplistic for most technology, but it does at least provide a useful starting point.' Which is undeniable. The evolutionary model may describe the development of simple technologies in relatively undifferentiated societies – hand tools in a subsistence economy, for example. At a low level of abstraction it may even account for more sophisticated technologies in relatively undifferentiated contexts under industrial capitalism – bicycle design, say, within a single Victorian workshop. Beyond these applications, however, the model remains merely suggestive, and something like the nuances of Russell's radical analysis must be brought to bear in analysing the non-neutrality of particular artefacts.

'Non-neutrality with respect to what?' it may still be asked. For to claim that an artefact is non-neutral in its social relations leaves open the question of how precisely the non-neutrality is manifested. Dickson, as we have seen, does not deal with particular artefacts but takes a radical non-neutralist line on the political process of innovation in which, he argues, they are imbedded. And the evolutionary model of Pinch and Bijker, which does suggest how particular artefacts are socially constructed, no more pronounces on their neutrality than it takes sides among the pressure groups that, according to the model, promote technological development. Thus the sense in which an artefact may be said to be non-neutral has yet to be explained.

In fact, at least two senses are apparent from the growing literature on technology and society. The first and weaker sense is somewhat equivocal: artefacts may be regarded as non-neutral with respect to their *effects*. Bicycles set people dangerously in motion. The risk of injury, both for cyclists and pedestrians, in a society that permits the development of the bicycle is significantly greater than it would otherwise be. Therefore the bicycle itself is a hazard and non-neutral: it is predisposed against social well-being. Now this rough-and-ready argument may seem simplistic and unappealing, although it should be recognized that, in form at least, it sometimes appears rather more congenially in debates over other human hazards such as television and nuclear power. The point, however, is that even if this weaker sense of non-neutrality were argued with great sophistication, conventional technophiles could easily invoke the means-ends dichotomy to establish that the non-neutrality lies in the *abuse* of the artefact rather than in the artefact – the means – itself. Bicycles are neither good nor bad; it all depends on how they are used. If the ends are ill chosen (getting from A to B at breakneck speed) or unforeseen (running over a pedestrian), the 'human factor' is to blame.

It can easily be pointed out, in turn, that this counter-argument is double-edged. Technophiles cannot legitimately claim that a technology – artefact-and-architect – is neutral only when it stands accused of wrongdoing. They must also resist the temptation to credit the technology for any good it may achieve. In other words, there can be no such person as a techno*phile*, strictly speaking. Philandering with technology is illicit. Rather it would be more nearly consistent for defenders of neutrality to doubt whether technology has any real value at all. 'Progress', considered as an evaluative concept, should have nothing whatever to do with mere material artefacts. Progress is just what people who use material artefacts well bring about.

Put in this way, the neutralist argument begins to sound untenable. It cuts straight across everyday perceptions of progress (which are not unproblematic) and contradicts what most people mean when they say, 'Thank God for my pacemaker!' or 'What would I do without my washing machine?' It is not God or the cardiologist, the charlady or themselves, they really intend to praise. The point of the rejoinder should, however, be clear. When people ask of an artefact 'Is it any good?', they do not usually mean just 'Does it produce good effects?' They also want to know whether the artefact is good in itself, aesthetically and operationally. Is it good to look at, to handle, to use? And what is it good *for*? Does it do what it is supposed to do? Their demand, in other words, is to know whether or in what ways the artefact is non-neutral with respect to its *design*. This is the second sense of neutrality. That it carries social and political weight will be apparent from the simple fact that it is people who must ask these questions. People by no means always agree on what is aesthetically and operationally good about a particular design. Nor are they indifferent about whether it suits themselves. Thus, in asking of an artefact 'Is it any good?', they also imply 'Whose good does it serve? Whose interests does it promote?' The value of the artefact may well have a moral dimension.

The technophiles, however, still have a comeback, even granting the untenability of their neutralist argument as phrased above. What about the transfer of technology into contexts where its supposed non-neutrality is no longer apparent? After all, 'mass production' has been imported from capitalist into communist economies, where it acquires a very different meaning. Or consider again the humble bicycle, which has been introduced throughout the world without appreciable social effects. If either of these technologies were inherently non-neutral, one would expect them to reproduce their constitutive values wherever they have become imbedded, and to affect social relationships accordingly. The fact that they have not done so – that communism with mass production is still communism, that Hong Kong, Peking and New Delhi remain vast overcrowded cities, bicycles or no – suggests strongly that the non-neutrality of technology is relative to its social context – how it is used or abused – rather than to its design.

There are several points to be considered here, leaving aside the element of technological determinism in the argument. Firstly, it is by no means certain that mass production in communist economies or bicycles worldwide have not had effects in keeping with their original design, even if large-scale social changes have not been detected. Secondly, the transfer of technologies such as mass production and the bicycle may often be accompanied by slight modifications that effectively reconstitute their design and thus alter the nature of their non-neutrality. Both these points suggest that the non-neutrality of technology may be assessed in various ways, at more than one level of social reality. Discrimination is needed. At one extreme whole societies may be affected, at the other merely individuals. The Colt revolver, designed as an instrument of killing, has contributed decisively to America's 'gun culture'; the diffusion of right-handed tools and tableware across the world has had negligible cultural effects but has frustrated left-handed users everywhere.

The last point to emerge from the argument that technological transfer implies technological neutrality must be an acknowledgement that artefacts have more than one history. This was assumed in the account of Russell's rejoinder to Pinch and Bijker given above. The primary history of an artefact reveals its non-neutrality in the social context where it was *designed*. The secondary history of the same artefact reveals its social significance in contexts where it has been *introduced*. The primary history gives the purpose that the artefact was originally intended to serve. The secondary history gives the purposes with which the artefact has subsequently been invested. An artefact may thus have many uses – a plutonium warhead makes a dandy door-stop – but just because it is an artefact rather than a natural object it has at least one main purpose, and that purpose, for which it was designed, is built-in. The cultural anthropologist makes no mistake about it. A hand-axe or an arrowhead is not a stone. A tool or a weapon is known by the end it serves, which does not vanish irretrievably with the decease of its user. The end is embodied in the means just as surely as those who fashioned the means chose the end or pursued it as prescribed. The means may indeed become plural: the tool or weapon may acquire a further history in which it functions for good or ill. But it possesses at least one original history in which its non-neutrality exists by design.

This is by no means a new interpretation or even necessarily a radical one, although in denying the neutrality of technology we propose, in effect, that through it ideology may become a material force in society. The view applies equally to ancient implements and to modern tools, weapons and everyday artefacts, which even now are becoming the primary sources for new inter-disciplinary studies of material culture, ethnography and industrial archae-ology (Mackenzie and Wajcman, 1985). We shall consider some of these artefacts in the following chapters, together with other technologies and the social relations in which they have been imbedded.

REFERENCES Barnes, B. (1974) *Scientific Knowledge and Sociological Theory*, Routledge & Kegan Paul.

Bernal, J.D. (1939) *The Social Function of Science*, Routledge.

Bloor, D. (1976) *Knowledge and Social Imagery*, Routledge & Kegan Paul.

Bottomore, T. (ed.) (1963) *Karl Marx: The Early Writings*, Watts.

Cardwell, D.S.L. (1971) *From Watt to Clausius: The Rise of Thermodynamics in the Industrial Age*, Heinemann Educational.

Cardwell, D.S.L. (1972) *Technology, Science and History*, Heinemann Educational.

Dickson, D. (1986) 'Technology and the construction of social reality' in Levidow, L. (ed.) *Radical Science Essays*, Free Association Books, pp.15–37.

Ellul, J. (1965) *The Technological Society*, Jonathan Cape.

Freeman, C. (1977) 'Economics of research and development' in Spiegel-Rösing, I. and Price, D.J. de S. (eds.) op.cit., pp.223–75.

Habermas, J. (1971) *Toward a Rational Society: Student Protest, Science and Politics*, Heinemann.

Hansen, A.H. (1921) 'The technological interpretation of history', *Quarterly Journal of Economics*, 36, pp.72–83.

Holland, M. (1928) 'Research, science and invention' in Wile, F.W. (ed.) *A Century of Industrial Progress*, Doubleday, Doran.

Kuhn, T.S. (1962) *The Structure of Scientific Revolutions*, University of Chicago Press.

Layton, E.T., Jr. (1971) 'Mirror-image twins: the communities of science and technology in 19th century America', *Technology and Culture*, 12, pp.562–80.

Layton, E.T., Jr. (1974) 'Technology as knowledge', *Technology and Culture*, 15, pp.31–41.

Layton, E.T., Jr. (1977) 'Conditions of technological development' in Spiegel-Rösing, I. and Price, D.J. de S. (eds.), op.cit., pp.197–222.

Lipscombe, J. and Williams, B. (1979) *Are Science and Technology Neutral?*, Butterworth.

MacKenzie, D. (1984) 'Marx and the machine', *Technology and Culture*, 25, pp.473–502.

MacKenzie, D. and Wajcman, J. (eds.) (1985) *The Social Shaping of Technology: How the Refrigerator Got its Hum*, Open University Press.

McLellan, D. (1980) *The Thought of Karl Marx: An Introduction*, second edition, Macmillan.

Marcuse, H. (1964) *One-Dimensional Man: Studies in the Ideology of Advanced Industrial Society*, Routledge & Kegan Paul.

Mitcham, C. (1980) 'Philosophy of technology' in Durbin, P.T. (ed.) *A Guide to the Culture of Science, Technology and Medicine*, Free Press, pp.282–363.

Mumford, L. (1934) *Technics and Civilization*, Routledge.

Noble, D. (1979) *America by Design: Science, Technology and The Rise of Corporate Capitalism*, Oxford University Press.

Pinch, T.J. and Bijker, W.E. (1984) 'The social construction of facts and artefacts: or, how the sociology of science and the sociology of technology might benefit each other', *Social Studies of Science*, 14, pp.399–441.

Pinch, T.J. and Bijker, W.E. (1986) 'Science, relativism, and the new sociology of technology: reply to Russell', *Social Studies of Science*, 16, pp.347–60.

Popper, K. (1976) *Unended Quest*, Fontana.

Price, D.J. de S. (1982) 'The parallel structures of science and technology' in Barnes, B. and Edge, D. (eds.) *Science in Context: Readings in the Sociology of Science*, Open University Press, pp.164–76.

Ravetz, J.R. (1971) *Scientific Knowledge and its Social Problems*, Oxford University Press.

Russell, S. (1986) 'The social construction of artefacts: a response to Pinch and Bijker', *Social Studies of Science*, 16, pp.331–46.

Shapin, S. (1982) 'History of science and its sociological reconstructions', *History of Science*, 20, pp.157–211.

Spiegel-Rösing, I. and Price, D.J. de S. (eds.) (1977) *Science, Technology and Society: A Cross-Disciplinary Perspective*, Sage.

Winner, L. (1977) *Autonomous Technology: Technics-out-of-control as a Theme in Political Thought*, MIT Press.

3 ELECTRIFICATION

Gerrylynn K. Roberts

> The day must come when electricity will be for everyone, as the waters of the rivers and the wind of heaven. It should not merely be supplied, but lavished, that men may use it at their will, as the air they breathe. (Émile Zola, *Travail*, 1901; quoted on a wall plaque at the Electrical Association for Women in London, until it folded in December 1986)

From the perspective of our own times, this statement of 1901 has the look of a prophecy fulfilled. Although it is not 'free' like the air we breathe, electricity undeniably permeates the everyday life of members of industrialized societies – at home and at work. People may use it at their will; provided that they are connected up, it requires only the flick of a switch. Loss of supply by accident, such as the famous blackout of the north-eastern United States (including New York City) in the autumn of 1965, or other means, such as the British power workers' strike of 1971 or the coal miners' strike of 1973, can severely disrupt whole societies, very much like a collective loss of breath.

Although the phenomena of current electricity had been investigated by scientists from the turn of the nineteenth century, in 1901 electricity was arguably part of the experience of the public at large only in connection with telegraphy, which had been developed from the 1840s. Some may have enjoyed the use of the inexpensive domestic products of electroplating, or the decorative products of electrotyping. Further, those familiar with certain major cities would have experienced electrical street lighting, the lighting of some public buildings and factories and perhaps electric traction in improved urban transportation systems, all from the 1880s onwards. Residents of certain parts of the United Kingdom and Germany might have travelled on electrified railways. Seamen would have known the effects of electric arc light from lighthouses around the UK coast. Another urban, mainly business-related, development of the 1880s and 1890s was the telephone. On the domestic level, electricity had been known for some twenty years, but it was a luxury, effectively available only to the very wealthy, and even then mainly only for lighting. In industry, the substitution of the electric motor for steam or human power had started slowly during the 1890s.

By 1901, many of the other inventions which subsequently were also to feature in the electrical transformation of everyday life predicted by Zola had already been made. Edison patented a non-electrical version of his phonograph in 1877. An early cinematographic performance had been given in 1895 in France. An electric fan was available from 1889 and portable electric fires date from a similar time. On the domestic front, an electric iron was on sale by 1891 in London, New York and Berlin. Electric cookers and a range of other kitchen appliances were available to the enthusiastic and well-off, if not the practical, cook from the 1890s. Small and reasonably reliable electric motors were on sale in the United States for fitting to already purchased human-powered appliances, such as treadle-operated sewing machines, from the turn of the century. 1901 itself is, by some accounts, the year of the invention of the domestic vacuum cleaner; and the year when Marconi claimed the first successful transatlantic wireless transmission.

Indeed, in one sense, Zola was right. Apart from short-term fluctuations, demand for and the supply of electricity increased steadily in Europe and America. It is all too easy, however, to read from such figures that this growth was inevitable, justifying the 'must' in Zola's prediction, made in the

Figure 3.1 Margaret Fairclough's School of Cookery, Black and White *12 January 1895. (Reproduced by permission of Chatto and Windus from Caroline Davidson (1986) A Woman's Work is Never Done: A History of Housework in the British Isles 1650–1950)*

midst of what proved to be a boom period in the industry around the turn of the twentieth century (Byatt, 1968, p.244). Why and how electricity came to be so all pervasive in Britain and the United States will be our concern here. In part, the story is, of course, one of the fruitful application of scientific and engineering expertise in steady technical innovation of increasing complexity. Clearly no electrical industry would have been possible without such developments, but they did not occur independently. Alone, they cannot explain the rise of an electrical industry, nor its particular shape and components, in which personalities, entrepreneurial skills, commercial, legislative and administrative considerations as well as broader ideological, economic, political and social circumstances were all involved. In this essay, in order to begin to understand some of these complexities, we shall look briefly at the impact of the adoption of the electric motor in industry and concentrate on the spread of domestic electricity.

Figure 3.2
Electricity generated by public utilities in Germany 1880–1940. (Data from Rudolf von Miller 'Ein halbjahrhundert Deutsche stromversorgung aus Offentlichen Elektrizitätswerken' Technikgeschichte *25, 1936, p.112 by permission of the author)*

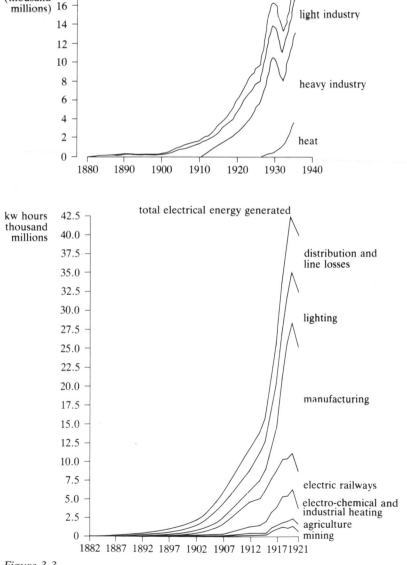

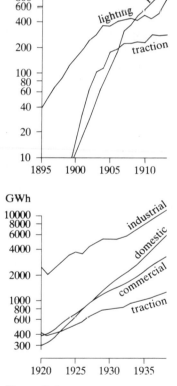

Figure 3.4
The growth of electricity sales in the United Kingdom, 1895–1913 (data from I.C.R. Byatt 'The British Electrical Industry, 1875–1914', DPhil thesis Oxford University, 1962) and 1920–1938. Reproduced by permission of Macmillan from Leslie Hannah, 1979, Electricity before Nationalisation: A Study of the Development of the Electricity Supply Industry in Britain to 1948)

Figure 3.3
Electricity generated by utilities in the United States 1882–1921. (From Electrical World *80, 1922, p.546)*

3.1
ELECTRICAL
DEVELOPMENT TO 1870

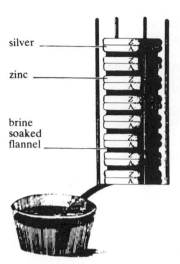

silver

zinc

brine
soaked
flannel

*Figure 3.5
An early electric battery.
When the bottom and the top
of the pile were linked by
wire, electric current was
produced. (Photo: Ronan
Picture Library)*

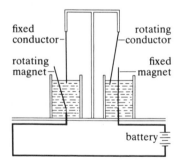

fixed
conductor

rotating
conductor

rotating
magnet

fixed
magnet

battery

*Figure 3.6
Diagram of Faraday's
apparatus for producing
rotation by electromagnets.
On the left a magnet floating
in mercury and tied at the
bottom of the vessel rotates
around the fixed current-
carrying wire. On the right the
conductor is free to move and
it rotates around the fixed
magnet. (Reproduced by
permission of Peter Peregrinus
Ltd from Brian Bowers,
1982,* A History of Electric
Light and Power)

Zola's simile (which of course should not be looked to for technical accuracy, but as a contemporary view on the 'promise' of this technology) breaks down when we consider the properties of electricity. For, unlike air, it is not 'naturally' available for use; its utility depends upon its artificial production. It is the conditions of that production that have mediated its relationship with everyday life. There are, of course, widely occurring natural electrical phenomena such as lightning. Static electricity artificially produced by friction was studied in the eighteenth century and led to the discovery of current electricity and a means for its artificial production, the first electric battery, in 1800. This new phenomenon caused great excitement in the scientific world of its day; current electricity and its effects became, virtually immediately, the subject of intense study internationally.

One focus of investigation, dating from 1819–20, was the relationship between the phenomena of the relatively recently discovered electric current and those of magnetism, which had been known for centuries. Battery-generated electricity was seen to have a magnetic effect. Michael Faraday (1791–1867) experimented with such phenomena at the Royal Institution in London. In 1821 Faraday used electricity to produce mechanical rotation; that is he converted electrical energy into mechanical energy and demonstrated the principle of the electric motor, later, of course, a cornerstone of the electrical industry. In the following year, Faraday noted as a task for the future, producing the opposite effect, 'Convert magnetism into electricity'. In 1831, he demonstrated electromagnetic induction, using the system illustrated schematically in Figure 3.7. This experiment only produced a current momentarily, at each instant of connection and disconnection of the coil [A] to the battery.

Later the same year, Faraday succeeded in generating a continuous electric current by rotating a copper disk between the poles of a powerful permanent magnet. Faraday had converted the mechanical energy needed for turning the disk into electrical energy by rotating the disk through what would later be called a magnetic field. This was the principle of the dynamo or generator, another subsequent cornerstone of the electrical industry (Figure 3.8).

Faraday's interest at this point was theoretical. He postulated that a magnet had lines of force surrounding it, and that it was the cutting of these lines by a conductor (the copper disk in the example in the margin) that generated the current. The more lines of force that were cut, as in the case of a strong electromagnet, the greater the current. These ideas were not taken up on the practical side for almost forty years, after their mathematization in the early 1860s. However, various generators were built following empirically the model of rotating a magnet and a conductor relative to each other.

A French scientific instrument maker made, in 1832, a practical device shown schematically in Figure 3.9. Generators on this principle produced what we call alternating current (AC), the direction of flow of the current altered as the position of the poles of the magnet altered. The chemical battery, the then familiar source of current, gave direct current (DC); the current flowed in only one direction. Subsequently, this technical distinction arising initially from the different modes of production of electricity would be of considerable importance in the establishment of electrical systems.

Technical developments in the means of generating electricity occurred in fairly specific contexts in relation to actual or projected applications for which there was a demand. For example, in the 1840s, in Britain, a steam engine was attached to a hefty magneto-electric generator to produce electricity for electroplating at a Birmingham firm. Considerable development work was done on magneto-electric machines in relation to telegraphy. Generators of this type were also used from the 1850s and 1860s for arc lighting in a few lighthouses in France and Britain. In all these cases, the use of battery-generated electricity was an established technique, so it was a matter of

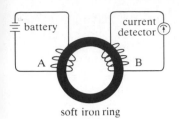

battery   current detector

A   B

soft iron ring

Figure 3.7
Production of a momentary electric current. Faraday wound two coils of wire, (A) and (B), on opposite sides of a soft iron ring. He connected coil (B) to a device for detecting electric current. From the principle of Oersted's work, he knew that the wire of coil (A) would have magnetic effect when a current was passed through it from a battery: coil (A) was a powerful electromagnet. The question was whether this would produce a consequent electrical effect in coil (B). At the moment of connection and disconnection of (A) to the battery, the device connected to (B) did register an effect.

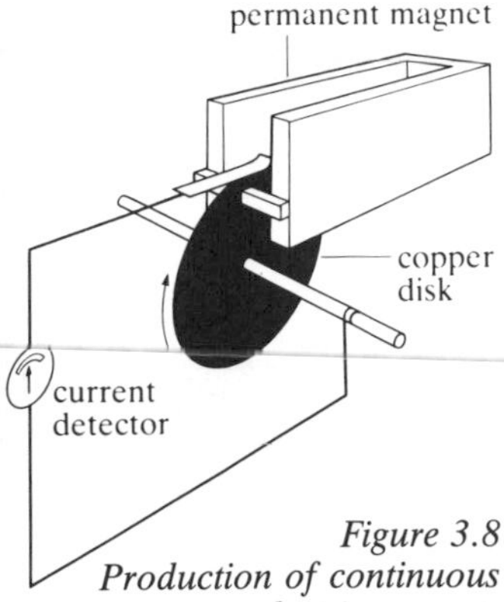

permanent magnet

copper disk

current detector

Figure 3.8
Production of continuous electric current.

substituting electricity produced in a different way, for which there had to be some fairly potent justification in relation to cost or convenience. It is important to note that the distinction between mechanically generated electricity and that produced by the chemical battery was that the former was generated at its point of use at the time it was required.

Work to meet this level of demand in the contexts of electroplating and arc lighting led to some improvements in both elements of magneto-electric design during the late 1860s and early 1870s, which would later facilitate the large-scale production of electricity. In the first place, much more powerful electromagnets replaced the permanent magnets of earlier designs, making possible larger currents from smaller machines. Secondly, some fundamental alterations in coil (armature) design were devised, so that the more intense lines of magnetic force of the electromagnet would be cut more efficiently. This ability to produce electric current on a large scale altered the perspectives of those working in the industry and, on the technical side, stimulated further work on electric lighting.

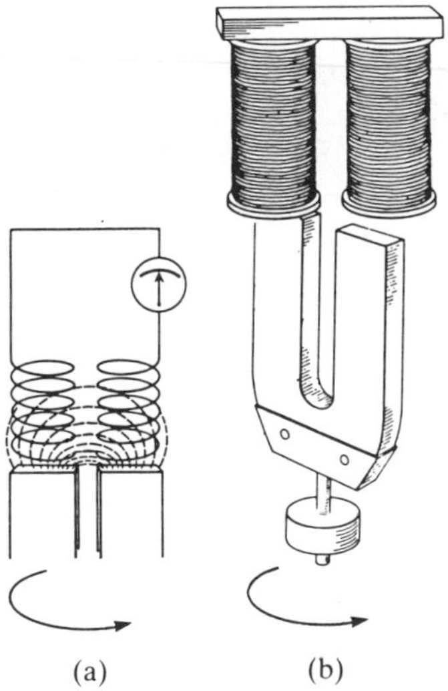

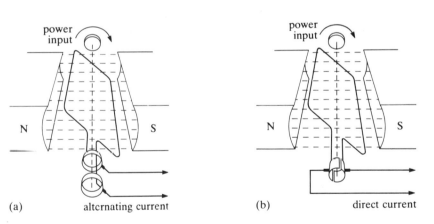

(a)   (b)

(a)   alternating current   (b)   direct current

power input   power input

N   S   N   S

Figure 3.9
Principle of Pixii's generator 1832. This generator had a permanent horseshoe magnet rotated by hand beneath two stationary coils wound on bobbins (b). Its shortcoming was that, because of the manner of winding, only a small part of each coil was cut perpendicularly by the lines of force of the rotating magnetic field (a). (Adapted from Scientific American, *May 1961, p.113)*

Figure 3.10
Principles of Alternating Current (AC) and Direct Current (DC). (a) Alternating Current. A loop of wire (armature) is rotated so as to cut the lines of force between magnetic poles. A current – clockwise in this case – is induced in the loop, which is connected to brass slip rings, and the current is led to the external circuit by two brushes. The current alternates because it reverses directions as the two sides of the loop cut the magnetic field first in one direction and then in the other. (b) Direct Current. This is made by substituting a commutator for slip rings. The commutator, a ring divided into two segments, switches the sides of the loop from brush to brush so that current flowing through each brush always goes in the same direction.

(Adapted from illustrations by James Egleson from Harold I. Sharlin, 'From Faraday to the Dynamo', Scientific American, *May 1961. Copyright © 1988 by Scientific American Inc. All rights reserved)*

3.2
ELECTRIC LIGHTING –
THE EARLY
ELECTRICAL
INDUSTRY

3.2.1
Arc light

The important point about the improved generators was that they made possible not only the production of more electric current, but a more constant current more cheaply. Among the earliest lines of development with public impact were transportation, discussed in chapter 6, and arc lighting. As individual installations, arc lights had been used in lighthouses from the 1850s, where the requirement for intense and reliable light justified the expense and size of the installations. Cheaper electricity made it possible to contemplate competing with already well established gas light for lighting urban streets in the expanding cities, as well as public buildings and open spaces. There was a consequent flurry of technical development in arc-lamp design during the 1870s to make the lamps themselves reliable and easy to maintain.

In the United States an arc-lighting system was demonstrated at the Philadelphia Centennial Exhibition of 1876. From 1877, that city's polytechnic, the Franklin Institute, organized a series of trials of lamps and generators from around the world, an innovation in technological decision making, and decided in favour of the system of a young American chemist, C.F. Brush (Passer, 1953, pp.14–21). In 1878, he installed arc lighting in a prominent Philadelphia department store. Brush's development work made it possible to link the high-current consuming arc lamps in series so that several could be driven by a single, centrally located high-voltage generator. By 1881, there were Brush central stations in New York, Philadelphia and Boston, among other American cities.

Brush showed financial as well as technical acumen, developing a licensing mechanism for his system and a sales policy including quite substantial periods of free demonstration to havering city authorities. The Brush case was based on the argument that, for lighting city streets, arc lighting was superior in quality and cheaper than gas lighting. His six-months' free demonstration of 22 arc lights replacing 500 gas lamps along 20 blocks of Broadway in 1881 resulted in a cost saving of 20 per cent. In the context in which he developed his system, the urban United States, he was right: electricity could be highly competitive. By the turn of the century, almost 400,000 arc lights were in service there (Passer, 1953, p.70).

By 1878, arc lighting was well established in the streets of Paris. In England, the cost benefits in relation to gas lighting were less clear because of the pricing structure of gas (Byatt, 1979, p.3); but various of the London vestries did introduce it, using French devices, from 1878. R.E.B. Crompton, an English pioneer of arc lighting, promoted his wares with a steam-driven portable system at fairs and exhibitions. He would then hire the system out for public construction work and entertainments. In Sheffield, on 14 October 1878, a highly publicized showpiece football match was played under arc lights (Bowers, 1982, p.108). According to Byatt (1979, p.22), by 1890 there were only 700 arc lamps lighting British streets. Falling electricity prices by the late 1890s allowed further development and another 20,000 arc lamps were installed over the decade to 1907, still a very small number.

With the possibility of extending the hours of construction work on the one hand, and access to the popular sport of football on the other, we begin to see some of the unique implications for everyday life of electricity. For these were activities which existing gas networks could not service. However, for urban indoor applications, such as theatres, factories and railway stations, competition with gas had to be faced. Arc lamps reputedly gave a whiter, more intense light with the advantages of not raising the ambient temperature or requiring ventilation. However, it was thought to be harsh and it flickered, so comparative cost was a deciding factor between gas light and arc lighting.

3.2.2
Incandescent light

From the 1880s, arc lighting competed not only with gas, but also with another form of electric lighting – incandescent light. Although it too could, and did, provide street lighting, the target market for the incandescent light was internal light in smaller-scale spaces, for which it was generally conceded that arc lamps were too harsh. Here, too, gas light already had the market and it was a matter of selling electric light as a superior product at no extra cost. In addition, the sale of incandescent light could also be targeted at areas for which open-flame light was considered too hazardous, in certain sorts of manufactures and libraries for instance.

As was the case with the electric arc, the phenomenon of incandescence, that a current flowing through a wire could heat it to the point of glowing, was known from the early days of experimentation with the chemical battery, and was explored experimentally from time to time. No practical incandescent lamp was developed however until after the cheapening of electricity supplies in the early 1870s, and the demonstration in 1875 of a means for evacuating the air from glass bulbs with the Sprengel mercury pump (developed in 1865). This was essential, for in the presence of air, the substances used for the incandescent element would be too readily consumed, giving the lamps an impractically short life. In the 1870s, several inventors were working on incandescent filament lamps independently along distinct lines. In late 1878/early 1879 both Thomas Alva Edison (1847–1931) of the United States and Joseph Swan (1828–1914) of Newcastle, England were successful. In the event, their lamps were similar, but the commercial conceptions of the two men, operating in completely different economic, technical and social contexts, were quite distinct. Swan saw his lamp as symbiotic with existing arc-lighting systems, as a way of extending them. Though building his own manufacturing company, he sought the collaboration of arc-lighting suppliers, whose generating and other equipment he made use of and who would, in turn, then give their own customers the choice of a suitable lamp for particular circumstances. R.E.B. Crompton, for example, actually became chief engineer to Swan's company. He installed a number of mixed systems in places such as railway stations and the new Law Courts in London.

Edison did not aim to complement the market of the arc-lighting industry, but to tackle the market of the gas industry across the board. That is, rather than generating electricity at its point of use, which made it prohibitively expensive for the small consumer, he envisaged the central generation of electricity and its distribution on demand to the consumer. Edison studied the technology and economics of the gas industry intensively, for if his objective was to be achieved, it was essential that the cost to his consumers be no higher than that of gas. The insight which enabled him to proceed along these lines was a solution to what was known in contemporary scientific circles as the problem of the subdivision of light. If light was to be available on demand, it had to be possible for large numbers of individual lamps to be switched on and off as required. For the circumstances in which arc lights were used, the fact that they were grouped in smallish numbers, were connected in series and all went on together was advantageous. Such a system was not suitable for domestic use. Parallel rather than series connection would make his envisaged system possible.

Essential to Edison's success was his detailed working out with colleagues from the first principles of electrical science that a lamp of a particular technical design would achieve his aims. Every practical detail of his system followed from this decision. And, since his was a totally new system, he and his team designed each detail of every component. Edison's development was financed from the start by a group of wealthy backers who knew him

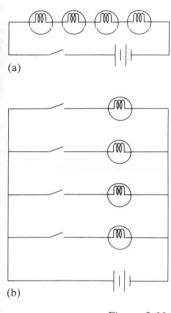

(a)

(b)

Figure 3.11
Series circuit and parallel circuit. (a) A series circuit requires that a number of electric lights (circles) be turned on or off at the same time by a single switch. (b) The parallel circuit, which was adopted by Edison, makes it possible to turn lights on or off one at a time. (Illustration adapted from Emi Kasai from Matthew Josephson 'The invention of the electric light', Scientific American, *November 1959. Copyright*

from previous projects. Publicity was central to his scheme, as was the establishment of a number of companies for manufacturing the various components. His productivity and that of his group was prodigious, extending not only to details of generating electricity supply, but to its transmission and distribution as well. The famous Pearl Street Station, Edison's first central generating plant, was important as a technical proving ground. During its construction over the period 1880-82, Edison applied for 156 patents. It was a record period of invention and innovation even for him.

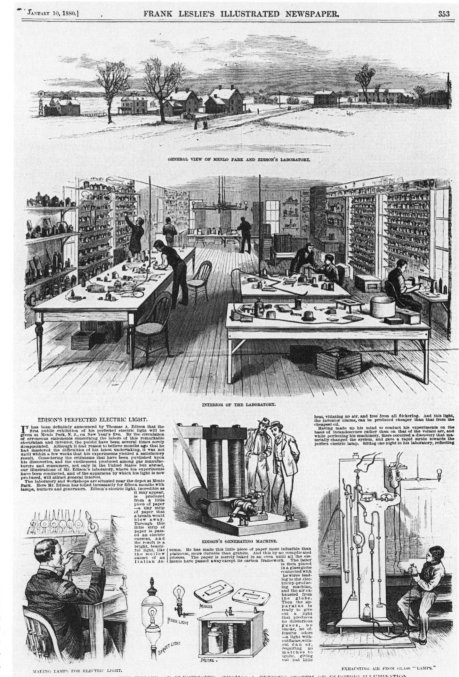

*Figure 3.12
Creation of the Edison system, Menlo Park. (From* Leslie's Weekly, *10 January 1880, reproduced by courtesy of Edison National Historic Site, West Orange, New Jersey)*

3.3
ELECTRICITY SUPPLY
TO 1914

3.3.1
The spread of Edison's
system

Edison's Pearl Street Station in the highly public and prosperous heart of New York's financial district began to supply subscribers over about a square mile in September 1882. According to Hughes (1983, pp.43–46), Pearl Street was never commercially viable in its early years, but was kept going at a secret loss because of its importance to Edison as a showpiece. By 1888, at which time Pearl Street supplied 65,000 lamps, there were Edison systems supplying roughly 400,000 lamps in cities from the East Coast to the Midwestern United States, as well as in Milan and Berlin, and a failed venture in London.

Along with selling central station supply systems to companies that would produce and themselves sell electricity for lighting, Edison also sold isolated lighting plants, typically to firms that needed to produce their own electric light for particular purposes (Passer, 1953, pp.112–18). Isolated lighting plants were installed in firms such as textile mills, furniture factories and printworks, for which the quality of electric light provided superior discrimination between colours and textures. In firms generally, incandescent light made it possible for workmen to have their individual tasks specifically illuminated (impossible with arc light and reputedly unpleasantly hot and smelly with gas), and there were reports of consequent increases in productivity. Firms such as flour mills and chemical factories, which found open-flame light hazardous, also installed incandescent light. Salesmen of incandescent systems could quote substantial savings on fire insurance rates. That saving and the fact that existing steam plant and engineering personnel could be used in many instances made incandescent installations financially attractive. Other installations tended to go into buildings such as theatres, banks and hotels where the quality of light available and the ease of its control were part of the service provided by the establishment. So, as early as the 1880s, electricity began to affect the everyday lives of some workers, but it was hardly a mass phenomenon.

Edison deliberately sought the spread of his system abroad, using international exhibitions to great effect with elaborate displays at the Paris Exhibition in 1881 and the London Exhibition of 1882, held at Crystal Palace. Interestingly, these were, already by this date, specialist electrical exhibitions. The Paris Exhibition has been given direct credit for stimulating visiting German engineers and industrialists, together with financiers, to establish an Edison-type system in Berlin where the first central station opened in 1884. There, electricity was seen as a luxury development, available to the wealthy, and it was promoted as such. In 1886, theatres, banks and restaurants accounted for almost two-thirds of the load, with domestic demand being only 1 per cent and industrial demand 2 per cent.

In April 1882, the impact of the Crystal Palace Exhibition was deliberately followed up by the formal opening of an Edison central station at Holborn Viaduct in London, even before the opening of Pearl Street. Indeed, Passer (1953, p.90) suggests that Holborn Viaduct served as a full-scale test of Edison's central-station design. But it was also a London showpiece, aimed at providing a springboard to the English market. It was hoped that Holborn, like Pearl Street, would reach a general market by deliberately pricing its product to be competitive with gas light, but this proved not to be viable given London gas prices. The rash of options taken on Edison franchises in other parts of England in 1882 was never exercised and the Holborn Viaduct venture folded in 1886.

There has been considerable debate among historians about the role of legislation in determining the rate and nature of electrical development in England. In New York City and in Berlin, it was local legislative and political circumstances that had to be dealt with by prospective electricity suppliers (Hughes, 1983, p.78). In England, national legislation (the Electricity Supply Act of 1882) created conditions which had the effect of favouring enterprises undertaken by local authorities, rather than private companies. The former were already major suppliers of gas and therefore had competing interests at stake. It is also argued that they were less likely than private enterprise to take risks (with ratepayers money) in unproven industries. To some extent, the stiffer conditions of the 1882 Act were ameliorated by further legislation in 1888.

Certainly English contemporaries pointed to the effect of legislation. However, generally gloomy British economic conditions at the time should not be overlooked, nor should the pricing structure, efficiency and resilience of the gas industry itself (Byatt, 1979, p.23; Hannah, 1979, p.9). For example, the Welsbach mantle for gas lamps, which came into general use in the 1890s, essentially gave gas light the same visual properties as incandescent electric light. The legislation did not, however, impede a number of small-scale local electricity supply developments in London, in cases where prestigious electric light could be sold at a price covering costs to wealthy consumers. This kept the industry before certain sections of the public and helped to develop a core of innovative problem-solving engineering expertise.

3.3.2 AC electricity supply

Edison's vision of the large-scale supply central station proved to be the direction taken, but not on the basis of his technological system. Edison's system rested on the generation of direct current (DC) electricity and its distribution in a densely populated, fairly compact urban area. However, given the technology of the time, there were design limits to the capacity of DC generating systems (Hannah, 1979, p.10). The possibility of expanding demand required being able to cheapen supplies by larger capacity stations reaching wider areas. However it was expensive to distribute DC electricity over wide areas as there were considerable losses of energy in transmission. Seen as a problem at the time, long-distance transmission was tackled in various ways by Edison and others within a DC context. Others investigated approaches using alternating current. AC electricity could be transmitted at high voltages over long distances, then converted to safer lower voltages by transformers for distribution to points of use.

Indeed, in Britain and elsewhere AC systems were developed at the same time as DC systems. Important pioneering work was done on transformer design in Britain by Parisians L. Gaulard and J.D. Gibbs, who perceived that the device created by Faraday some fifty years previously was a possible key to the problem of AC transmission. In 1883, they lit five widely spaced stations around London's Metropolitan Railway Company's Circle Line. In 1884, they moved their efforts abroad, installing for exhibition purposes a lighting circuit extending for some fifty miles around Turin. Over the following two years, they set up permanent installations in France, Italy and Germany. Having been seen at the Turin Exhibition, their transformer design underwent considerable development work by the Austro-Hungarian electrical manufacturers Ganz & Company, who installed roughly seventy AC central stations supplying over 100,000 lamps around Europe by 1890. The Turin Exhibition was also the source of the US Westinghouse firm's introduction to the Gaulard and Gibbs transformer which, after modification, served as the basis of a successful system. By 1890, there were some 300 Westinghouse Electrical Company central stations supplying electricity to half a million lamps.

Perhaps Gaulard and Gibbs' most famous installation was that put into the Grosvenor Art Gallery in New Bond Street in London in 1885. At first confined to lighting the high society gallery itself, this was initially the wealthy owner's enthusiastic project for providing viewing conditions which would not damage the paintings. He had been persuaded to install incandescent lighting by a nephew who had seen Edison's display at the Paris Exhibition of 1881. The effect was evidently so impressive that Gaulard and Gibbs were

*Figure 3.13
Welsbach mantle. (Photo:
Science Museum, London)*

called in to extend the supply to neighbouring properties, distributing it across the roof-tops to avoid legislative problems about digging up the streets for such purposes. As the load increased, however, their system could not cope and S.Z. de Ferranti (1864–1930) was called in as chief engineer in 1886. Though young, he was already an independent manufacturer of electrical equipment, some of which was used at the Gallery, and had had considerable experience of electrical installations. By 1888, the Grosvenor Gallery station was supplying some 34,000 lamps.

Ferranti, however, had even larger scale ideas. In 1887 his London Electric Supply Company (which subsumed the Grosvenor Gallery) proposed a great technological leap, that of siting a massive power station on the Thames, at Deptford in south-east London, which would supply a large area of the city covering several local authorities with current for up to 2 million lamps. The scale of the project was technically and administratively unprecedented, but it attracted venture capital from those who had been personally and successfully associated with Ferranti in the Grosvenor Gallery expansion, rather like Edison. Also like Edison, with whom he was compared by contemporaries, Ferranti himself undertook the design of every component of this enterprise. Having decided on the principle of AC transmission at an unprecedentedly high 10,000 volts to local substation transformers for distribution, the design of the entire system, including the building in which it was housed, followed.

Construction started in 1888, and late in 1890, electricity was transmitted to London. Historians have tended to be sympathetic towards Ferranti's aims and some of what can now be seen as the more far-sighted aspects of his scheme. Its concept of universal, rather than local and specific, generation subsequently came into standard use. Similarly, his choosing an out-of-town riverside site for ease of transport of raw materials and access to cooling water became good practice. It also avoided the problem of the nuisance created for neighbours by the operation of heavy mechanical generating plant. (Grosvenor Gallery had had complaints about vibrations.) Indeed, in this Ferranti was following examples set by London gas companies. However, in relation to the technical, social, legislative and economic circumstances of its own day, the project failed. Ferranti left the London Electric Supply Company in 1891.

In technical terms, in relation to sound contemporary engineering practice, Ferranti did not allow adequate development time for the enterprise. Furthermore, not only were the components of his system untested, but the scale was such that component failure could lead to a major disruption of supply. Alas for Ferranti, this happened, spectacularly, resulting in a loss of three-quarters of his customers. Ferranti's reliance on huge reciprocating steam engines, of dimensions never before tried (physically some five times larger than standard), was unwise. Furthermore, unlike Edison's, his market was uncertain. Though by 1891, London led Europe in the number of incandescent lamps supplied by central stations, Ferranti's prediction of lighting demand proved to be extremely optimistic (Byatt, 1979, p.103). Subsequently it was the markets of traction and power that such large-scale enterprises would be aimed at. And unlike the cases of Edison, Ganz & Company and Westinghouse, partly because it marked such a departure from standard practice, there was no onward market at the time for the equipment that he was developing. Profits were completely dependent on the sale of electricity for lighting purposes, rather than on the sale of generating equipment which was central to the finances of other companies.

Ferranti himself, with some reason, attributed the failure of the scheme to legislative and administrative barriers. In 1889, the Board of Trade ruled that local authorities should have priority in offering supply, but that private developments should not be impeded where local authorities did not intend to proceed. Furthermore, a second supplier would be allowed in a particular area where it offered the opposite type of electricity – AC where there was a DC company or vice versa. These provisions were settled on in relation to the inconclusive state of the AC-DC debate and patterns of consumption of the time. However, the effect on an enterprise like Ferranti's was to restrict the area which it would be allowed to supply, thereby undermining its concept as a capital-intensive, large-scale, wide area supplier. Under such provisions, small-scale central stations using non-uniform systems proliferated. The number operating in Britain grew from twenty-six in 1888 to fifty-four by 1891, of which seventeen were in London run by seven supply companies (Bowers, 1982, p.158). By 1903, almost every British town with a population greater than 100,000 had at least one central station supplying electricity for lighting (Byatt, 1979, p.25).

3.3.3
AC versus DC

The debate between proponents of AC and DC systems during the late 1880s and early 1890s was intense, referred to even in its own time as 'the battle of the systems'. This 'battle' was conducted on a number of levels, generally on a scientific, technical and economic basis, but also on an emotive level aimed at the public gallery. In the AC-DC controversy, public safety became a battle ground. In a bizarre incident, taking advantage of the State of New York's concern to find a method of execution more humane than hanging, the Edison interests in 1888 went so far as to encourage the adoption of electrocution by AC as the new means. They fostered and publicized the installation of an AC electrocution system by their main rival, Westinghouse, and gave considerable publicity to the first electric execution in 1890. If AC could be used deliberately in this context, how could it be safe enough for use in everyday life? Such arguments tended to concentrate on the question of the safety of the higher AC voltages, ignoring the fact that a number of longstanding DC arc lighting systems used voltages as high as the AC voltages of the time.

Indeed at the turn of the 1890s, there was no clear general technical or economic advantage for either system. AC was technically superior and cheaper for long-distance transmission, and therefore was particularly suitable for bringing electricity to a dispersed clientele. However, there were operational problems working against such cost savings. Eventually, these would be solved, but in the 1890s, they limited AC's ability to compete. In compact, densely populated cities which used electricity mainly for lighting, DC retained a cost edge, partly because it was the 'established' technology, the teething problems of which had been solved through operational experience. Given these circumstances, the battle was not 'won' by either of the systems in the nineteenth century. Rather, a *modus vivendi* was established with the development at this time of rotary converters, devices for cross-linking between the two systems, so that they could co-exist more or less harmoniously.

The City of Frankfurt am Main, for example, resolved its dilemma over what sort of system to install by holding an electrical exhibition in 1891, allowing the proponents of AC to demonstrate their capabilities. A newly built hydroelectric plant powering a cement works some 175 kilometres away in Lauffen was linked with the Frankfurt Exhibition to power a brilliant lighting display and an artificial waterfall. This was the first demonstration of transmission over such a long distance and it showed how rurally derived energy, given the co-operation of imperial and local governments over rights of way, might provide power for 'remote' industrial cities. A striking feature of the set-up was the high efficiency of the energy conversion. Furthermore, the waterfall pump was driven by a new type of motor, the AC polyphase induction motor.

The development of an effective AC motor proved in fact to be the key to the eventual success of AC systems because, as demands for electricity

*Figure 3.14
Waterfall and incandescent
lamps at Frankfurt powered
by a natural waterfall at
Lauffen 175 kilometres away.
(From* Offizielle Feste Zeitung
. . . Frankfurt am Main, 1891,
*p.828. Photo: Stadtarchiv
Frankfurt am Main)*

increased beyond that for lighting, to include traction and the stationary electric motor, the case for large-scale central generation of AC and its universal distribution for whatever purpose became stronger. Experience with electric traction in the late 1880s indicated that the DC motor (effectively a generator working in reverse) was well suited to the demands of urban transport with the irregular stresses of acceleration and braking. However, the DC motor was prone to sparking and tended to give off heat which made it unsuitable for many industrial and domestic uses. Furthermore, its commutator, a crucial moving part, was likely to require frequent replacement. The AC motor, which ran at constant speed, became the standard industrial motor.

It is generally recognized that the first patentable polyphase induction motor was that announced to the public in 1888 by Nicola Tesla, who was working on contract to Westinghouse at the time. Tesla eliminated the commutator from his motor design, producing a rotating magnetic field from alternating currents flowing in fixed coils. Independent alternating currents fed to suitably oriented electromagnetic coils produced a rotational force on any conductor placed between them. With the development of this motor, the battle between AC and DC on the technical side began to even out.

Westinghouse successfully outbid a complacent and over-confident Edison company, which failed to anticipate competition, for the lighting contract for some 250,000 lamps at the 1893 Chicago World's Fair. As well as providing the lighting, Westinghouse's own stand displayed its AC energy transmission system. For the first time, the concept of universal supply was explained to the public. With an integrated system of transformers and rotary converters, the same AC supply was used to drive various DC and AC motors with distinct requirements, as well as the lighting system. For example, a 500-volt DC railway motor was run from one converter, while an electroplating plant was run from another converter, which itself was driven at a different frequency from the first. Effectively, the Westinghouse display demonstrated the great flexibility of the universal system which could deliver direct current at any voltage and alternating current of any voltage and any frequency, for lighting and for power. Perhaps the most significant feature of this demonstration was that it showed how existing distribution systems could be incorporated in the universal system without making expensive plant redundant.

The biggest coup, however, for AC generation and Westinghouse's universal system was the Niagara Falls project. From the middle of the nineteenth century, there were proposals to harness the vast and exceptionally even power available from the Niagara River as it gathered water from four of the Great Lakes and dropped some 200 feet over the famous Falls into the fifth lake. In 1890, something like a fifth of the population of the United States lived within 400 miles of the Falls, and the industrial city of Buffalo, a quarter of a million strong, was only twenty miles away. So long as mechanical methods of transmitting power had to be used over long distances, the power of the Falls could only be utilized on a local scale. However, the costs of harnessing such power were such that it could not be economical just for local use. Development plans were further complicated by the Falls being declared a conservation area from 1885.

In 1889, the Cataract Construction Company was created, with New York City finance behind it, to bring the power of the Falls to Buffalo. After consultation with a galaxy of international scientific and engineering experts, and with the example of the Frankfurt Exhibition of 1891 in mind, an electrical system was decided upon. There remained the question of which sort of electricity. Buffalo already had, according to Hughes (1983, p.125), a central station 'with seven steam engines of several makes and fifteen generators of seven different types supplying five different kinds of customers, or loads, on separate circuits'. These requirements would have to continue to be met. When, in 1892, a Swiss-made water turbine was chosen to drive the generators, the balance tipped in favour of AC. The commutation problems for DC output from that turbine would have been considerable (Passer, 1953, p.287). Transmission began in 1896, by which time consumption at the rapidly expanding industrial complex at Niagara exceeded the amount sent to Buffalo. By 1897, local industrial consumption was three times that of Buffalo and 90 per cent of local consumption was for electrochemical firms, a factor not anticipated when the project was planned (Passer, 1953, pp.293–94).

The electrically-dependent methods for the products of the firms above were all quite new, developed in the late 1880s and early 1890s. Carborundum, a synthetic substitute for natural emery, was a new material, discovered only in 1891. It outperformed emery as an abrasive for glass and metal polishing by a factor of three or four (see chapter 5). The Pittsburgh Reduction Company made aluminium by a method developed simultaneously in the 1880s in France and the United States, which made that previously recalcitrant material available relatively cheaply for general industrial use. The Carbide Company made a long-known product, calcium carbide, cheaply available by means of an electric furnace developed from the 1880s (see chapter 4). Similarly, the Mathieson Alkali Company manufactured a long-used and essential industrial product, caustic soda, by electrolytic means developed from the 1880s. Such processes all used electricity directly in production and deliberately located at Niagara so as to have a cheap hydroelectric supply.

Although the Niagara Falls project was not a unique hydroelectric scheme, as there were significant contemporary developments in the Alps and in Scandinavia, it is a milestone in the history of electrification and was understood as such at the time. Financially, it marked investment on an unprecedented scale in high technology, a perception of a role for innovation in the economy. Furthermore, the initiative for the project did not come from electrical manufacturers or inventors, but rather from financiers who drew on appropriate expertise for its execution. On the technical and organiz-

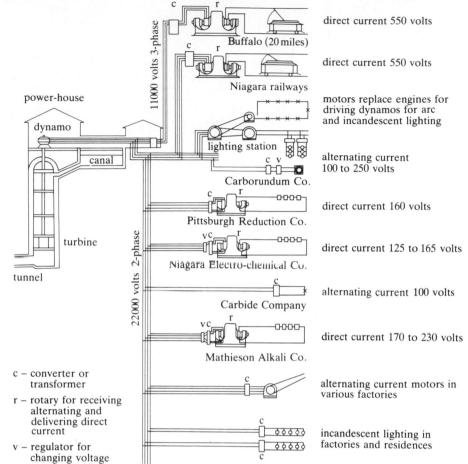

direct current 550 volts

Buffalo (20 miles)

direct current 550 volts

Niagara railways

motors replace engines for
driving dynamos for arc
and incandescent lighting

lighting station

alternating current
100 to 250 volts

Carborundum Co.

direct current 160 volts

Pittsburgh Reduction Co.

direct current 125 to 165 volts

Niagara Electro-chemical Co.

alternating current 100 volts

Carbide Company

direct current 170 to 230 volts

Mathieson Alkali Co.

alternating current motors in
various factories

incandescent lighting in
factories and residences

11000 volts 3-phase

power-house

dynamo

canal

turbine

tunnel

22000 volts 2-phase

*Figure 3.15
Niagara (universal) system:
diagram of circuits. (From
E.A. Adams,* Niagara Power,
*1927, Niagara Falls Power
Company, Vol.2, p.251.
Photo: Local History Dept,
Niagara Falls, New York,
Public Library)*

c – converter or
    transformer
r – rotary for receiving
    alternating and
    delivering direct
    current
v – regulator for
    changing voltage

ational side, it established a strong precedent for the universal system based
on long-distance AC transmission as the way forward for electrification.

In addition to the Niagara Falls project's striking demonstration of the
efficacy and potential of AC transmission, there was a further roughly
contemporary development on the technical side that would give AC transmission the possibility of being more generally available. The Niagara project
was, of course, hydroelectric, based on water power driving a water turbine.
However, water power on a suitable scale was not universally available; for
the most part, central generating stations were driven by reciprocating steam
engines. Ferranti's Deptford experience had shown the problems inherent in
attempting to increase the amount of electricity generated by scaling-up
existing reciprocating engine technology. Within the limitations of the relatively slow-moving reciprocating engine, more electricity could only be produced by having more installations which meant a higher cost per unit of
electricity generated. Furthermore, the vibrations produced by reciprocating
engines made them unsuitable for installation in many areas. As one London
cleric put it in 1891:

> Alas, the Electric Railway is doing us terrible damage by three engines
> fixed, 400 horsepower each, just against wall of girls' house [of an
> orphanage]. They intend putting 3 more, and already they cause the houses
> to vibrate like ships at sea. I fear the law will give us no real remedy. I
> pray about it, and God can do more than courts. (Quoted in Bowers,
> 1982, pp.167–68)

Figure 3.16
1,000 kilowatt Willans-Parsons steam turbine opened for examination. 'In principle a steam turbine is simplicity itself. It is a pinwheel driven by high-pressure steam rather than by air. Basically it consists of a rotor from which project several rows of closely spaced buckets, or blades. Between each row of moving blades, there is a row of fixed blades that project inward from a circumferential housing. The fixed blades are carefully shaped to direct the flow of steam against the moving blades at an angle and a velocity that will maximize the conversion of the steam's heat energy into the kinetic energy of rotary motion' (Hossli, 1969, p.159). (From James Weir French, 1908, Modern Power Generators. Steam, Electric and Internal Combustion and their Application to Present-day Requirements, *London, Gresham Publishing Co., p.115*)

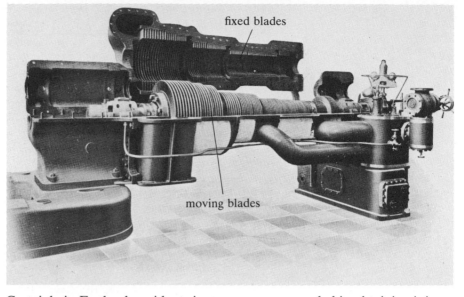

Certainly in England, residents in some areas succeeded in obtaining injunctions against supply undertakings to ameliorate the effects of electricity on this particular aspect of everyday life.

In fact, the development of the steam turbine solved both the problem of size and speed limitation and the problem of vibration. The type of steam turbine that came to be at the centre of the generation of electricity was developed by the English scientist and engineer, Charles Parsons (1854–1931). He constructed his first turbogenerator in 1884. By 1895, over 400 Parson's turbines were operating in a combination of central and isolated generating plants.

The steam turbine quickly became the norm, coupled with alternating current. Given an increasing demand for electricity, that pairing proved the cheapest way to fulfil it. Not only were they cheaper to manufacture, turbogenerator sets proved cheaper to run and incurred only about a fifth of the maintenance costs of engine type generators. Thus, according to Bowers (1982, p.169), in principle, the technical developments that were to predominate in power-station design until the end of our period were in place in 1903. Changes from then onwards were the result of small refinements in plant leading to increasing generating capacity and decreasing coal consumption.

3.3.4 Consolidation

In relation to use, this combination of developments making possible greater and cheaper supplies of electricity carried implications for both suppliers and consumers of electricity. Large quantities of electricity could only be produced cheaply by large central plants if there were adequate demand for it. The logic of this technical situation was, on the one hand, that lighting requirements should no longer dominate electrical thinking and, on the other, that small-scale, localized generation could not continue to be economical. Cheaper electricity could only be provided by such large central plants if they supplied a range of customers who had different requirements spread over the day. It made no economic sense, for example, to have expensive plant lie idle during the day, serving only an evening lighting load. A mixture of loads (lighting, traction and industrial and later domestic) and the consequent ability to balance requirements over twenty-four hours came to be seen in some quarters as the new ideal. This would maximize the average use of plant while still meeting peak demands.

In Britain and Germany, as in the United States, the turn of the century was a period of electrical expansion and consolidation (see Figures 3.2–3.4). Between 1897 and 1904 the sale of electricity for lighting British towns increased by a factor of 10. By this time however, lighting was only part of the demand. Byatt (1979, pp.27–28) indicates that by 1907 public supply sales of electricity in Germany and Britain were about the same with 42 per cent being sold for lighting in Germany and 43 per cent in Britain. The other major user of electricity in the early years of the twentieth century was electric transport. The choice of electric power for certain types of transport in relation to the technical, economic and social circumstances of urbanizing industrial societies is discussed in chapter 6, where its significance for everyday life is explored.

Although the demand for electricity for traction was substantial, it did not always serve to spread the load on central power stations, as it had done at Niagara Falls. In Britain, for example, in 1907, half of the electricity used by tramways and over 90 per cent of that used by electric railways was generated at installations owned by the various transport companies themselves, rather than purchased from electricity undertakings. This was partly for technical and financial reasons; previously existing lighting stations could not necessarily be altered to take on a tramway load. New pricing structures needed to be established as traction was uneconomic if its electricity was costed on the same basis as that for luxury lighting. Furthermore, there were political difficulties caused by the complications of mixed private and municipal ownership of both tramways and lighting installations.

Of more immediate significance for the industry was the effect of the requirements of electric traction on the manufacturing side. Profits from the manufacture of electric lamps had been the mainstay of the industry. Electric traction meant diversification and also provided an active commercial context which stimulated further work on electric motors. The promotion of the industrial electric motor was to become the key to the exploitation of cheap electricity generated on the universal system from the turn of the century and to the subsequent direction and nature of electrification generally.

**3.4
ELECTRICITY IN
INDUSTRY**

**3.4.1
The scale of electrification**

During the 1890s, there was a thirty-fold increase in the use of electric power in US industry. By 1900, electric power accounted for about 55 per cent of US industrial power, with roughly one-third of that supplied by central stations (Passer, 1953, p.343). The US Bureau of the Census said in 1905, 'The use of electric motors is now so general that it is difficult to name any industry, manufacturing or otherwise, to which this modern mechanism has not been applied' (quoted in DuBoff, 1967, p.509). The Bureau reported that, over the previous five years, most new American shops and factories had chosen electric drive.

In France, where long-distance transmission had been tried as early as 1885, the amount of electricity consumed increased six-fold during the period 1900 to 1913, growing by an annual 11 per cent. By the latter date, more than 20 per cent of the power of all French steam engines (the number of which was also growing) was used to generate electricity (Caron, 1979, p.300). Coal-fired stations driving reciprocating engines tended to be located in northern France where there was reasonable access to coal supplies. There had also been important hydroelectric developments in the mountainous areas of the south which compensated somewhat for France's problem of limited coal resources. In such regions there were complementary electrochemical and electrometallurgical developments, much as at Niagara Falls. French electricity supply too was fragmented during this period. Even the hydroelectric stations did not transmit over particularly long distances, though they accounted for roughly 40 per cent of French electricity by 1930 (Hammond, 1958).

In Britain, the first polyphase AC power station (the new standard) was built in 1900 in London and the second in 1901 to serve industrial Newcastle. From about the same time, the price of electric motors began to fall, dropping by more than 50 per cent between 1901 and 1905, and motor sales began to increase in the United Kingdom. By 1907, when lighting accounted for some 43 per cent of the British load, about 10 per cent of industrial power was electrical. Five years later, the figure was 25 per cent and, by 1924, roughly 50 per cent. The period also saw a transition from most industrial electricity being generated on the premises to being purchased from supply undertakings.

The degree of electrification varied from industry to industry. In 1907, something like 70 per cent of all British industrial power was used by the mining, textiles and iron and steel industries, but only 5 per cent of mining and textile power was electric and 8 per cent in the iron and steel industry. In engineering however, 40 per cent of the machinery was electrically driven, but this industry accounted for only a small percentage of the total power used. By 1924, when mining and textiles still consumed a quarter of the total power, only 40 per cent of mining power was electrical, and 25 per cent of textile power. However, the engineering industry was 90 per cent electrically driven by this time.

Table 3.1 British electrification (based on Byatt's analysis of Census of Production figures, 1979, pp.74–76)

Industry	Date	% Electrified		% National power
		Own	Bought	
Mining	1907	4	0.2	29
	1912	14	5	30
	1924	26	13	27
Textiles	1907	4	2	24
	1912	5	3	24
	1924	15	11	19
Iron & Steel	1907	6	2	19
	1912	15	7	20
	1924	21	24	19
Engineering*	1907	21	21	7
	1912	31	36	8
	1924	19	68	13
Building**	1907	4	3	5
	1912	14	6	3
	1924	17	33	4
Food etc	1907	7	8	5
	1912	11	17	4
	1924	13	46	4
Chemicals* Non-ferrous metals	1907	12	7	4
	1912	14	17	4
	1924	22	43	5
Other	1907	8	14	7
	1912	12	22	7
	1924	18	24	8

*   General and electrical, marine, shipbuilding, tools, vehicles
** Construction and materials

Available data are such that fine international comparisons are difficult to make (Wilson, 1976, p.160). However, some broad national differences do emerge. British and US engineering became electrified at a similar rate. But in mining, textiles and iron and steel, the US percentage of electrification in 1907 was higher: 20 per cent versus 4 per cent in mining, 25 per cent versus 8 per cent in iron and steel, 19 per cent versus 5 per cent in textiles. However, in terms of overall power use, textiles was a less important sector in the United States, accounting for only 9 per cent (DuBoff, 1967, p.516).

Germany too was 'more electrified' than Britain during the early years of the century. Large-scale, wide-area AC supplies were developed there early in the twentieth century (Landes, 1969, p.286). Already by 1907, when Britain and Germany had similar lighting loads, German industry was roughly 20 to 24 per cent electrified, while British industry was roughly 10 per cent electrified, although German industry used less power overall. Engineering was electrified to a similar extent in Germany and Britain. As power users, mining and textiles were less important in Germany than in Britain (31 per cent versus 54 per cent). However, Germany's smaller mining industry had more electric motors than Britain's and its textile industry, which was half the size of Britain's, had as many electric motors. The German iron and steel industry was more than 19 per cent electrified, and the German chemical industry was more electrified than its British counterpart. Such differences were probably due to differing industrial structures generally rather than to any technical 'forwardness' or 'backwardness' in the particular national electrical industries (Byatt, 1979, pp.81–82; Wilson, 1976, pp.53, 192–93).

3.4.2
The effect of electrification

There is then ample evidence about the extent to which industry electrified in the early twentieth century. However, rather less documentation is available to help explore the questions of why particular industries chose electric power and how that choice affected everyday working lives.

> Although electric power in industry was quantitatively more important than in traction or in lighting, there is less hard information available about its advantages, compared with traditional methods. Turning power in industry had a vast variety of applications from looms and lathes to coal cutters, and from steel-rolling mills to cranes. In each case, the relative advantages of electricity differed, and the information necessary for a detailed examination of the multitudinous applications of electricity would involve an inquiry into production methods that is no longer possible. Contemporary investigations into the costs and benefits of electric driving, if made, were generally not published . . . (Byatt, 1979, p.83)

DuBoff (1967, p.510) argues from American evidence that the main reason for manufacturers to adopt electric power was some expectation of cost savings, initially material and subsequently capital as well. From the point of view of comparative power costs, which British users tended to emphasize in their calculations, Byatt points to a number of circumstances in which electricity was seen to be cheaper than steam power. Electricity proved cheaper where power was required in relatively small amounts at scattered points around a works. The elimination of shafting and belting made possible by using electricity in such circumstances was quickly seen as an advantage. Shafting itself was expensive and a notorious cause of loss of power in transmission. The small electric motor was cheaper to install, run and maintain than the small steam engine. Furthermore, once freed of the locational constraints of belting and shafting, factories' workflows could be rearranged. The design of traditional mill structure, developed in relation to the new power requirements of the eighteenth century, needed no longer to predominate. This freeing of buildings from the design requirements of steam made possible the use of lighter and cheaper steel and concrete structures for industrial premises (Nelson, 1980, p.11; see chapter 5).

Electrification also meant greater geographical freedom as access to coal and water need no longer be important to individual firms for power supply purposes. Furthermore, electricity made possible more accurate measurement of what real power costs were for running particular pieces of machinery, leading potentially to their obsolescence. Where the inefficiencies were found to be in the steam engines themselves, this analysis sometimes led to the substitution of more efficient steam engines rather than electrification. However, overall, the trend was towards employing electric power (DuBoff, 1967, p.512).

Electric power also proved advantageous where connection to a central supply by shafting impeded mechanical operations, such as the use of overhead travelling cranes. Indeed, with steam, operations requiring variable speeds or frequent starting and stopping had to use expensive and inefficient gear and clutch mechanisms to run off central shafting. Electricity's adaptability and mobility made it attractive in factories where several different types of power were needed for different purposes. In factories which had previously been steam driven, some operations were powered for the first time. Not surprisingly, Westinghouse cited changes at its own East Pittsburgh works. 'Not only [were there] great economies over the steam engine, but an entire list of operations under one roof that steam could never serve' (DuBoff, 1967, p.514). The list included warehousing, a machine shop, a carpentry and cabinet shop, a blacksmith, and press and punch shops, powered by fifty-three electric motors. Thus, electrification brought a new relationship between previously unpowered traditional shop processes and factory processes, enabling a new economic effectiveness for the former (Landes, 1969, p.288). Furthermore, where power requirements were small, the electric motor made it possible to substitute mechanical for human power in isolated enterprises where power had never been contemplated, such as home sewing, dentistry and in the jeweller's shop. Electric power also tended to be advantageous in circumstances where power was used only intermittently. The electric motor needed no attendant and could be powered up quickly and easily when required, using less fuel over all and avoiding the overheads of maintaining coal stocks and continually running shafting.

The difference in power costs alone was of relatively minor importance in the longer term (Byatt, 1979, p.85; Wilson, 1976, chapter 3). More significant was the increase in productivity it made possible. This, rather than potential power cost savings, tended to be the argument advanced for factory electrification in America. An important American showpiece was the electrification of the US Government Printing Office in 1895. A much quoted 1901 government survey argued that output there had increased by almost 30 per cent because of the reorganization made possible by electrification, more than justifying the capital outlay (DuBoff, 1967, p.513). More accurate running of machinery became possible, with greater control over starting and stopping and speeds of operation than centrally determined shafting speeds would have allowed. According to Nelson (1975, pp.21–23 and 1980, p.11), one important result of the impact of electrification on factory arrangement, materials handling and machine control was a revolution in the factory system, facilitating, among other things, greater managerial control along scientific management lines. Indeed, DuBoff argues that the overhaul of manufacturing processes made possible by electrification was important for the development of systems of mass production. He points out that the US automobile industry, dominated by Ford, was 70 per cent electrically powered by 1919, when the overall electrification level of US industry was of the order of 30 per cent. The amount of power used by the automobile industry had increased some seven-fold during the decade to 1919 (DuBoff, 1967, p.513). These issues are discussed further in chapter 11 on social and human engineering.

A British electrical pioneer, R.E.B. Crompton, predicted a complete industrial restructuring based on the small electric motor.

> England in the future, instead of being spoilt by densely populated industrial centres, might be covered with cottages . . . the population would be more evenly spread over the kingdom. The factory hands, instead of having to work under shafting in factories, should be able by the electrical transmission of power to carry on industrial pursuits in their own cottage homes. (Quoted in Bowers, 1978a, p.296)

His German contemporary, electrical manufacturer Werner Siemens, had expressed similar sentiments in 1878: 'The electric motor will in course of time produce a complete revolution in our conditions of work, in favour of small-scale industry' (quoted in DuBoff, 1967, p.518). Though these predictions proved wide of the mark as concentration became a dominant trend in twentieth-century industry, electricity did at the same time make many smaller-scale operations viable, not just in the case of smaller industries but in the case of bigger industries working in small units, such as clothing, machine tools and printing.

> Electrification ushered in a period of 'efficiency', soon to become a watchword for the drastic reorganization in manufacturing techniques that began after the turn of the century. Cost cutting became possible over much larger ranges of output than under steam. Subdivision and mobility of power offered a much wider array of labour, material, and capital equipment combinations, from work-shop, domestic-type activities, reacting to irregular patterns of demand and supply often found in local markets, to factories sometimes surpassing the 'monster mills' of the Victorian era. Subdivision in turn meant greater diffusion of power needed to support a decentralized, less capital intensive structure of industry. Smaller plants earned a new lease of life since most of them could now afford equipment commensurate with their operations. (DuBoff, 1967, p.518)

3.4.3 Electrification in particular industries

The reasons for adopting electric power, its suitability, and its effect, varied from industry to industry. The impact of the application of electric power in the steel industry is mentioned in chapter 5. In the early years of the twentieth century, it was used in that industry both for electric furnaces, and for powering machinery to handle the materials through various stages of manufacture. The furnaces were the biggest power consumers, both the electric arc furnace, which produced high-grade steel of accurately known composition, and the induction furnace, used to produce relatively small quantities of high quality alloys with special properties. A desire to produce materials of a particular sort actually required electricity. Though the furnaces used more power, it was the electrification of the materials handling processes and of the rolling mills that had the biggest impact on the everyday life of the workforce leading to a redistribution of responsibilities. Electrification of this aspect of steel works led to higher precision work and a greater degree of automation.

In the case of the British engineering industry, electric driving became cost competitive with steam when the price of motors began to fall in the early years of the twentieth century. Electricity proved attractive because of the intermittent nature of the demand for power in many engineering enterprises. One estimate in 1905 suggested that, for a typical electrically driven engineering works, generating capacity of about 50 to 60 per cent of the total power of the machines to be used would be adequate. There is anecdotal evidence indicating significant increases in output as a consequence of electrification. According to Byatt, shipbuilders electrified particularly readily.

Given its range of tasks, the shipbuilding industry had scattered and variable power requirements which electricity was well suited to meet. Tyneside shipyards adopted electric power particularly readily, but it was not solely a matter of adopting a new form of power. Electrification took place along with a general alteration of working systems from the late 1890s, which included a broad move to more power use for drilling and riveting of metal ships. In this reorganization, electricity was not the only source of power employed. Compressed air, despite complexities in distribution, was also a contender. Tyneside, however, was one of the first areas in the United Kingdom in which electricity was rationalized on a large-scale basis with supplying industry as a major goal. In this context of new working processes, electricity could therefore be extremely competitive.

As in the case of shipbuilding, an important feature of the use of electricity in the machine tools industry generally was that it made possible a system of (more or less) portable individually driven tools for heavy work. Although the early electrically powered tools were quite bulky by later standards of portability, the potential of being able to move tools to tasks and the implications of that for altering working practices were clearly recognized (Wagoner, 1966, p.11). Technical development effort was put into increasing portability and performance. The first British electric drill, made by Wolf in 1914, weighed in at 23.5 pounds. By 1925, five and a half pound drills capable of turning at much faster speeds were available, powered by the new 'universal motor' with a high power to weight ratio, which could be run off either AC or DC supplies (Bowers, 1978b, p.1089). Other major features of change in machine shops were improvements in materials handling and the ability to use power intermittently.

Electric motors were not generally installed as integral parts of individual machine tools until after the First World War. In the earlier applications, electric motors were installed to power groups of machines transmitting the drive via shafts and belts. The initial main difference from previous practice then was that the machines were driven in smaller groups with shorter lengths of shafting, allowing more flexibility in their use. With demand in the 1920s for increased operating speeds to cope with the properties of new materials, there was a move to individually fitted motors (unit drive). Wagoner (1966, p.12) argues that once certain tools were electrified, a momentum of technological development was created leading to further innovations in the industry. In particular, he mentions the magnetic chuck, which made certain very awkward operations feasible, and the development of devices for controlling the performance of machines with great precision. According to Wagoner (p.34), this latter aspect led to a gradual reduction in the skill required of machine operators, and also contributed to the transformation of factory practice by scientific management.

For the textiles industry, as the figures in Table 3.1 show, conversion to electricity was not necessarily a particularly attractive option. This was partly because power engineering was already very highly developed in both the British and US textiles industries. New mills in the southern United States employed electric power after the building of a successful hydroelectrically-driven mill in 1894 in Columbia, South Carolina, where other methods had proved unsuitable (Passer, 1953, pp.303–05), but well-established northern mills cautiously calculated the costs of changing. Electrification is an area which needs to be examined when considering the much-debated question of British managerial conservatism. Ancillary branches of the textiles industry, such as bleaching and printing which needed scattered and intermittent power, did begin to find electricity worthwhile. However, although electrical engineers argued that electricity could run mill machinery at more even speeds, hence improving output by something like 4 per cent in weaving and 8 per cent in spinning through limiting thread breakage, often little incentive was found to electrify in an industry traditionally so well engineered.

> Probably in no other branch of industry, considered as a whole, will there be found such well-designed and carefully built engines and such smooth running shafting as is the case of cotton mills . . . until the adoption of electrical transmission of power in recent years [in other trades] . . . the cotton mill was infinitely better equipped as regards its power installation than was the average engineering shop or shipyard. (F.S.A. Matthews 'Lancashire mills and electric driving', Supplement to the *Electrical Review*, 1908, quoted in Byatt, 1979, p.90)

Byatt argues that, for the traditional spinning and weaving mills, electricity came rather late. The last great boom in cotton textiles was in 1905–08, just as large-scale electrification was becoming feasible.

Mining was early identified by engineers as an area in which electric power would be valuable. Already in 1877, the German Siemens firm was in contact with the head of the Prussian State Mines and began a research programme on the application of electricity to mining. Quite apart from power uses, electric lighting was seen to have considerable potential underground. Fixed lighting became steadily more common underground from the 1880s for lighting roadways. It was some fifty years, however, before portable electric lamps became the predominant type of safety lamp in British coal mines. Their use increased from 5 per cent of all portable lamps in 1913, to 28 per cent in 1920, to being the main form of lamp used by 1930.

Because of the nature of the industry, the power requirements in mines were scattered and intermittent. It was the portability and flexibility of electricity and its freedom from belting and shafting that made it attractive in this context. In the case of mining, it was not so much a question of new applications of power, but of the substitution of electricity as a preferred form of power in existing applications, not only for steam but for compressed air as well. There were genuine fears about its introduction because of the fire risks of sparking motors below ground, and the implications of a power breakdown for crucial ventilation and lifting mechanisms (Byatt, 1979, p.92). Many of the safety and productivity changes in nineteenth-century mining predated the introduction of electricity. However, by the turn of the twentieth century, electricity was widely used underground to power pumping and winding, but less so for haulage. Most collieries generated their own electricity.

According to Buxton (1978, p.109), the most spectacular application of electricity was to the motors of mechanical cutters and drills which made it possible to tackle previously uncommercial seams. Mechanical cutters and drills were developed from the 1850s, often powered by compressed air. Electric power was applied to such devices from the 1880s, but compressed air remained the major form of power until the early twentieth century. However, mechanical cutters were taken up in varying degrees. By 1900 in the United Kingdom, only 2 to 3 per cent of output was machine cut. At about that time, approximately one-third of the cutters used was electrically powered. The figure for mechanically-cut output was nearer 20 per cent in the United States at the same date. However, the number of electrically driven UK coal cutters grew rapidly from 145 in 1902 to 1,000 to 2,000 in 1912 (Byatt, 1979, p.93). In general, US geological conditions in mining areas were more uniform and more suited to mechanical techniques than British ones. In Britain, their adoption was quickest in thin, difficult to work seams, where manual cutting brought out the coal in an unsaleable form (Buxton, 1978, pp.109–15). Otherwise, conditions were so varied that, in a highly profitable era for coal with good supplies of labour and equipment

that still posed some technical problems, decisions about funding mechanization were finely judged. Byatt (1979, p.93) points to A.J. Taylor's argument
that mechanization in the coal industry was closely related to labour costs;
as they began to rise from 1906, investment in mechanization became more
common. In the case of mining too, Byatt indicates that electrification was
complementary to other innovations in mining practice, such as different
underground layouts facilitating mechanical haulage. On the other hand,
Tyneside electricity suppliers noted a marked difference between the uptake
of electricity by engineers and that by coal owners, attributing it to the fact
that most colliery managers were ex-pitmen, trained by local practice, rather
than engineers (Byatt, 1979, p.94).

Figure 3.17
Taverdon electric drilling
apparatus for mines.
(Electrical World 1885
courtesy of IEEE)

However, even with this relatively limited degree of mechanization, British
coal output rose by some 70 per cent between 1890 and 1913, reaching a
never to be repeated peak in that year. And this occurred in a context of
increasing production internationally. The period between the wars marked
an abrupt change, both nationally and internationally. 'The misfortune of
the British coal industry was that a stagnating level of world demand, together
with an absolute decline in domestic demand, occurred at a time when
the productive potential of international coalmining was increasing rapidly'
(Buxton, 1979, p.54). It was at this point, in the 1920s, that mechanization
of coal cutting and underground haulage, though increasing, began to lag
significantly behind that on the continent. Output per man-shift, however,
remained higher than in some highly mechanized continental mining areas
because of superior coal-winning conditions in Britain. Buxton discounts
mechanization as the main feature in Britain's relative position in coal
production between the wars, stressing instead adverse market conditions.
Electrification was important for the coal industry in this context as electricity
increasingly came to provide an alternative source of power. Furthermore,
though that power was still derived mainly from coal between the wars, its
production became increasingly efficient. A state-of-the-art power station in
1903 burnt 2 kilograms of coal for every unit of electricity produced; one
opened just after the First World War used 1 kilogram for the same amount
of electricity; and by 1930, the latest technology required only 0.6 kilogram
per unit of electricity (Bowers, 1978b, p.1071).

3.4.4
Rationalization and
economies of scale

In whatever area it was used, much electricity before 1914 was generated directly by users rather than in central power stations. This was the case not only in Britain, with its legislative complexities, but also in countries such as Germany and the United States which already had some large-scale supply schemes. As late as 1912, some 60 per cent of the electric motors in mining and manufacturing used specially generated electricity, though 50 per cent of UK central-station electricity was by then being used for power. This situation developed when there was little potential for economies of scale.

> But as the economies of central generation increased and transmission costs fell, the minimum efficient area for a supply station rose and some interconnection [between existing local suppliers] became desirable. Also, as electricity came to be used more widely, different loads with different peaking characteristics developed. The more appliances in use, even if the same kind, the less likely it is that they will all be used simultaneously; diversity of demand in an interconnected network can save a great deal of generating capacity for a given aggregate power of appliances. (Byatt, 1979, p.96)

In the United States, Germany and Britain, the case for economies of scale and rationalization was most persuasively made by the experience of the First World War when electric power and the products of the electrical industry were heavily used. To deal with wartime exigencies, some large-scale supply projects were promoted in the United States and Germany along with interconnection of existing generating capacity, which was the path followed in Britain. But the issue of 'rationalization' at the national level was socially and politically contentious in all three countries, when the wartime legacy of increased electrical capacity had to be sorted out in the context of peacetime industrial programmes.

In the United States, the debate was seen as striking at the very foundations of its private enterprise economy; the concern was that initiative in the area of power supply should not pass to the planning and control of federal government. The upshot was that regional interconnection and large-scale development schemes proceeded there, but on the basis of planned local commercial collaboration and sharing of supplies to service diverse loads, not on the basis of national considerations. In Germany, where a high percentage of the electrical utilities were owned by some mixture of the separate states or various other levels of government plus private enterprise, the vested interests were different, but nonetheless similarly against proposals for nationally imposed rationalization. As Hughes put it:

> Manifestly, numerous persons with political and economic power in the Weimar Republic foresaw the changes that a unified electrical system would bring and they opposed these changes on the grounds of their personal or corporate interests. The technology of unified electricity supply systems was by no means a neutral technology. The dice were loaded in favor of Reich authority and a national economy. (Hughes, 1983, p.319)

In Britain, during the war, various government committees with a strong consultant engineering input proposed post-war rationalization schemes, using the often-voiced pro-technology argument that the future prosperity (indeed superiority) of British industry depended on the maximum exploitation of electric power, feasible only with centrally organized supplies. Wartime rationalization had increased electrical output over 100 per cent with only a 39 per cent increase in central generating capacity (Bowers, 1978a, p.287). In peacetime, however, successful undertakings saw less reason to cede their autonomy by co-operating. Legislation of 1919, resulting from these deliberations, did little more than set up a mechanism to aid voluntary rationalization schemes. Given the strength of the desire for autonomy in a situation where 642 undertakings (some AC, some DC, some both) supplied electricity at seven different frequencies and forty-four different voltages, the voluntary line proved ineffective in practice.

As post-war industrial performance deteriorated, successive governments reinvestigated questions of energy supply. The Conservative-appointed Weir Committee reported in 1925, recommending nationally co-ordinated rationalization by means of the construction of what became the National Grid. Leslie Hannah comments that, in order to state a simple and clear case, the Weir Committee argued beyond the available evidence about Britain's electrical 'backwardness' and the potential savings of national interconnection (1979, pp.92–93). It appears, however, that electricity was already so well established as a symbol of progress and modernity, that the identification of Britain's industrial future with it was compelling, even if that implied a major policy shift towards direct government involvement in industry. The Weir Committee recognized that the issue was not primarily technical. Given co-operation, the incompatibilities were resolvable within existing technical knowledge. Rather, the issue was political. With this in view, its

> . . . key proposal was that the existing undertakings should retain control not only of distribution but also of the construction and operation of power-stations. However, the coordination of new power-station planning and the control of power-station operation within the framework of a newly constructed national 'gridiron' of high voltage transmission lines was to be the responsibility of a new state-financed body, to be called the Central Electricity Board . . . [It] would buy electricity from selected stations and would plan the installation of new power-station capacity in conjunction with existing undertakings; it would resell electricity to undertakings wholesale and at cost price (after allowing for the costs of constructing and operating the 'gridiron'). (Hannah, 1979, pp.93–94)

The non-selected stations would be closed down.

Legislation in 1926 enacted the Committee's proposals, after winning over the support of key bodies such as the Federation of British Industries and the Institution of Electrical Engineers, with considerable Labour as well as Conservative support. Apparently, state intervention by means of a non-accountable body (and the subsidizing of electricity at the expense of gas) could be justified in the belief that it would rejuvenate industry generally. The original grid, organized as a set of interconnected regions (rather than as a single national entity), was constructed in stages between 1927 and 1933 and went into commercial operation in 1935. Perhaps the most immediate impact of the grid upon everyday life was its literal march across the nation: 26,265 pylons averaging 70 to 80 feet in height, but sometimes much taller, made a dramatic impact on many areas of the countryside. And not without opposition and consternation. Articulate Sussex residents, for example, protested vigorously about the spoilage of the South Downs by the proposed route of the grid. A highly publicized inquiry was held in 1929 at which the environmental and civic case was put by bodies such as the Council for the Preservation of Rural England, the Sussex Downsmen, the Sussex Archaeological Society, the Central Landowners' Association and several vociferous local authorities. Rural amenity was seen as being sacrificed for urban/industrial gain. The promise of consequent rapid rural electrification was seen as neither likely to be fulfilled, nor desirable by the mainly upper-middle and middle-class protesters. The fact that the scheme had been decided by a central authority without local consultation was especially repugnant.

KEY

132kV CIRCUITS ———

POWER STATIONS & SUBSTATIONS ON THE ROUTE OF THE 132kV SYSTEM   o

*Figure 3.18
National Grid at its inception
1933. Adapted from CEB's
annual report 1932.
(Reproduced by permission of
Macmillan from Leslie
Hannah, 1979,* Electricity
before Nationalisation: A
Study of the Development of
the Electricity Supply
Industry in Britain to 1948)

*Figure 3.19
'The old order changeth,
yielding place to the new'.
Illustration from* General
Electric Review *at the time of
the first national grid
1927–33.*

The protest had little chance of succeeding (Luckin and Moseley, 1985). The centralist Minister of Transport, Herbert Morrison, under whose aegis the CEB came, was adamant that an alternative route (or the proposed alternative of underground lines) would make the grid uneconomically expensive. Britain's recovery, in a climate of unemployment, had priority, and supporting it was a social and moral (and political) duty. In strongly emotive terms, the pro-pylon lobby accused its opponents of being privileged beneficiaries of rural amenity who objected to benefiting less favoured urban working-class contemporaries with cheaper electricity. Environmentalism was equated with recidivist nostalgia. Other pylon advocates argued that pylons were disliked mainly because they were unfamiliar; they would soon become as assimilated into the landscape as railway lines. Some defenders spoke quite positively about seeing beauty in engineering; considerable design effort was put into them.

If the more optimistic projections of the likely impact of the grid on British industry were not fully realized, the increasing supply of electricity and its reduction in price made the electrical engineering industry itself a strong sector of the British economy and an important source of overall growth in the inter-war years (Catterall, 1979). British consumption of electricity rose by 70 per cent over the period 1929–35, whereas world consumption rose by 20 per cent in that time. But Britain was starting from a lower baseline, having produced less electricity in 1929 than Canada, France, Germany, Japan or Italy and ten times less than the United States. Between that year and 1935, employment in the British electrical engineering industry increased by 90 per cent so that, by 1938, it accounted for 5 per cent of manufacturing employment and more than 3 per cent of UK gross output. Ironically, though some politicians initially supported the grid so that industry might be dispersed more 'equitably' around the country, the industrial development consequent on more available electricity supplies tended to concentrate in the south-east, especially around London.

It was there that the electrical consumer goods industry flourished. For once the case for economies of scale had been established, effort was concentrated on creating new markets for electricity which would spread the load, making generating costs even cheaper and in turn making electricity cheaper and more attractive to the consumer. The home was one such vast market.

**3.5
DOMESTIC
ELECTRICITY**

By any measure, the figures for domestic electrification over the period from 1920 to 1950 are striking, as are the national differences. Given that British generating capacity increased six-fold over the period 1920 to 1950 and that thirteen times more electricity was sold (Bowers, 1978a, p.290), the table below shows how important the volume of domestic consumption was to the electrical industry.

Table 3.2 Percentage of total electricity sales made to different classes of consumer in Britain (Bowers, 1978a, p.291)

	1920	1940	1950–51
Industrial	69%	57%	49%
Commercial	11%	12%	14%
Farming	–	0.3%	1%
Domestic	8%	26%	32%
Traction	11%	5%	3%
Street lights	1.3%	0.1%	0.9%

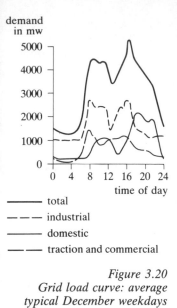

------- total

— — — industrial

——— domestic

— · — traction and commercial

*Figure 3.20
Grid load curve: average
typical December weekdays
1934–38. (Reproduced by
permission of Macmillan from
Leslie Hannah, 1979,
Electricity before
Nationalisation: A Study of
the Development of the
Electricity Supply Industry in
Britain to 1948)*

The average grid load curve from the early years of the National Grid (Figure 3.20) makes a different but related point. Not only was the volume of the domestic load important, but its characteristic of being heaviest when the industrial load was low meant that it made effective use of generating capacity in a large-scale system. The domestic market was therefore actively and successfully 'courted' by electricity undertakings and electrical manufacturers. In Britain, the 1930s was a period of especially rapid development.

Table 3.3 Percentage of homes with electricity supply

	In Britain (Hannah, 1979, p.188; *Bowers, 1978a, p.293)	In the USA (Cowan, 1983, pp.93–94)
1907		8%
1912		16%
1919	6%	
1920		34%
1921	12%*	
1931	32%*	
1938	65%	
1941		80%
1948	86%	

At the outset, domestic electricity was quite simply an expensive luxury, for lighting the homes of the wealthy. Gradually, however, large-scale generation and increased consumption allowed the price to drop so that electric lighting became the norm throughout the population. More significantly, from the 1930s onwards, the use of electrically heated and powered appliances began to make an impact on domestic lifestyles, of the middle classes in particular.

Table 3.4 Percentage of households owning particular electrical appliances

	In Britain, 1939 (PEP, 1947, p.246)	In the USA, 1941 (Cowan, 1983, p.94; *Busch, 1983, p.223)
Iron	85%	79%
Clothes washer (including boilers)	4.7%	52%
Refrigerator	2.6%	52%
Vacuum cleaner	30%	47%
Cooker	19.5%	8.2%* (1939)
Water heater	6.3%	–

Rather than concentrating on particular technological developments, this section will consider how and why the figures in the tables above came to be the case, and what they actually meant for everyday domestic life.

**3.5.1
The selling of electricity**

Initially, in Britain and in the United States, the spread of electricity for domestic purposes was mainly an urban phenomenon. Concentrated populations made for cost-effective distribution and the expanding middle classes provided a 'mass' market for the modern energy source. Placing ourselves in the position of middle-class inter-war householders in Britain, why should we have been attracted by electricity? We would have had well-developed, probably coal-based systems for heating our homes and the necessary water. We might even have enjoyed the amenity of a gas geyser for hot water on demand, would quite likely have read by gas lighting, and would possibly have eaten meals prepared on a gas cooker. Given the slowly falling number of servants and the increasing size of the middle classes, we might or might not have had domestic assistants. Until the 1930s, when houses began to be built ready-wired, converting to electricity would mean an expensive and disruptive installation process and running costs indisputably higher than those for equivalent coal or gas systems. And for what? It was possible to envisage all sorts of appliances, but until convenient and efficient ones were part of general experience, how could a householder evaluate their utility? Furthermore, using electricity, however simple it was supposed to be, would mean coming to grips with unfamiliar items of unproven safety. Arguments in favour of making the change must have been very appealing indeed.

The style of incentive pricing policies employed by Brush and Edison in the 1880s was one strategy followed by the supply industry. In addition to the supply installation and running costs, the expense of appliances was a recognized problem; a cooker could cost some £30 in the 1920s and a vacuum cleaner £20, at a time when professional and managerial salaries were of the order of £500 to £700 (Forty, 1986, p.194). Before the rationalization of the grid, appliance manufacturers had little incentive to lower costs. With the wide array of supply standards to be catered for, there was little advantage in bulk manufacture. Indeed, the array of standards was also a disincentive to mobile private purchasers who might not be able to move an expensive appliance. To get around the high costs, supply undertakings became major appliance purchasers, though they were prohibited by law from retailing them, and rented them out at preferential rates to their electricity customers. 'Free' rental periods were often thrown in as sweeteners to installation deals. The undertakings were also quick to exploit the possibilities of extended hire purchase facilities from the late 1920s.

In addition, recognizing that installation costs would be a significant barrier until they could be 'lost' in initial building costs, supply undertakings were often associated with estate-building plans. The period between the wars was a boom period for housing construction in Britain. Some 4 million homes were built over twenty years at prices and with government-manipulated credit facilities that put home ownership within the reach of many who would not have aspired to it previously. Almost a third of these homes was built by local authorities, providing a large and valuable market for the electrical industry. Supply undertakings competed fiercely, sometimes offering special terms for the electrification of these houses. From the 1930s, most new houses were wired during construction for electric power as well as electric lighting as a matter of course. Two-thirds of the houses built in 1935 were wired for power. Some builders even included appliances in the purchase price. The very existence of the wiring helped to create a demand for appliances. Once people had experience of electric lighting, they tended to explore appliances as well. Roughly three-quarters of domestic electricity sales were for non-lighting purposes by the late 1930s. Indeed, most of the increase in consumption and appliance purchasing was as a result of diversification of use by a minority of customers, rather than of the dramatic increase in the number of subscribers, the majority of whom only used electricity for lighting (Hannah, 1979, p.193).

Given the competition from gas, electricity was expensive in the 1920s and still not cheap in the 1930s. Price, then, would not be a sufficient incentive. Manufacturers made technical improvements, such as the introduction of thermostatic control of ovens, in order to keep up with the features offered by gas cookers. Indeed, gas and electrical appliance manufacturers continually bested each other with features offered to their respective consumers

(Busch, 1983). Furthermore, to provide the otherwise unfamiliar experience of domestic electricity, many undertakings opened showrooms with model kitchens staffed often by female salespeople. There, potential consumers could see demonstrations of appliances at work and try them out themselves. Many offered qualm-allaying lecture courses and programmes of cookery lessons. Many offered after-care support in the home. Sales devices such as these were practical, concrete, even obvious. It is perhaps still difficult to see why we, as prospective consumers, might have been attracted to electricity. However, what was being sold was not just an alternative form of energy, but an entire way of life based on an ideology of housework and woman's role in society.

The British Electrical Development Association

Taking the case of Britain, a useful starting point for understanding the nature of the sale of electricity is the establishment of the British Electrical Development Association (EDA) in 1919. It was founded by joint action of the British Electrical and Allied Manufacturers Association, the Incorporated Municipal Electrical Association, the Institution of Electrical Engineers (whose Heating and Cooking Committee instigated it), and the Cable Manufacturers Association. Thus its views may be taken as representative of the marketing philosophy of a large segment of the industry. Founded at a time when interconnection was a hot political issue, the EDA's brief was educational and propagandist, aimed at increasing use and boosting demand for electricity. In fact, some undertakings refused to support it on the grounds that they had supply and demand in balance in their own profitable firms. The EDA quickly identified women as key electrical consumers and directed much of its voluminous propaganda at them via articles and advertisements in women's magazines, its own quarterly journal (*Electrical House-Keeping*), and later radio and films.

The EDA advertisement dating from 1928, shown in Figure 3.21, stresses that electrical housekeeping is the *modern way*. The pictures are captioned and the text is explicit about the benefits of the appliances illustrated. Notice how all the 'benefits' of electricity point by implication to the disadvantages of the alternatives. Thus, the non-electric range does not give freedom of kitchen design because its position is constrained by the need for flues; nor is its temperature controllable (not an accurate statement for gas, and electric cookers did not have thermostats until 1933); the cook must be in constant attendance. An iron that has to be heated and reheated on a non-electric range ties a woman to the kitchen, demands a great deal of physical effort, tends to be dirtier and give unreliable temperature control. Cleaning carpets by beater can, at best, be done only infrequently; other cleaning methods such as sweeping merely shift the dirt from one place to another, leaving behind dangerous germs which can threaten the health of children. As for the open coal fire, it requires considerable effort to get going; it smokes and creates dirt and fumes; and it constrains room design. The issues are efficiency, ease and health, projected as the concerns of the inter-war housewife.

The Electrical Association for Women

The advertisement in Figure 3.21 appeared in *The Electrical Age for Women*, the journal published by the Electrical Association for Women (EAW), an organization self-consciously dedicated to articulating, and converting women to, a progressive ideology of housework, while encouraging them to take a hand in their own technical futures. We shall use the EAW to explore the way that electricity was projected on to that ideology. In some ways, the EAW had an internally contradictory brief. On one hand, it wished to release women from the drudgery of household work so that they could take a wider role in the community at large. The founders of the Association were women engineers who felt that lay-women's lack of technical understanding was a

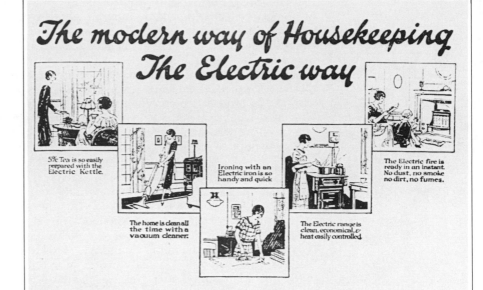

*Figure 3.21
The modern way of
housekeeping. The Electric
way. (Advertisement in*
Electrical Age for Women,
*Vol.1, 1926–30, p.445.
Reproduced by permission of
British Library Board)*

significant barrier to their liberation for wider responsibility. On the other hand, industry had identified women as consumers and the EAW wanted women to have a say in what they consumed. While formulating and conveying women's views on electrical matters to the male-dominated industry, it enhanced woman's role as houseworker, investing it with yet additional authority – this time, the authority of technical understanding. The EAW established a qualification in electrical housecraft to raise the status and competence of women working as demonstrators in the industry and it offered a similar curriculum to women who would use the skills in their own homes.

The EAW was founded in 1924 on the initiative of the Women's Engineering Society during the post-war and post-women's suffrage era of 'organizing'. The Women's Engineering Society, founded in 1919 by a group of women engineers, aimed to promote the study and practice of engineering among women and to facilitate the exchange of information about training, employment opportunities and working conditions. Its first secretary Caroline Haslett, who had trained as a secretary but then became apprenticed to the engineering firm for which she worked, represented the Society at the First World Power Conference, held in London in 1924. Here she met and was extremely impressed by the views of Lillian Gilbreth, an American efficiency expert who was engaged in bringing the principles of scientific management, developed in the factory environment (see chapter 11), to bear on the work processes of the home. Taking a somewhat different line from the long American domestic-science tradition of confirming women's role in the servantless home by dignifying housework through studying its scientific basis, Gilbreth argued that, despite its fragmentation and unpredictability, housework could be 'rationalized' and made more efficient, freeing women from unnecessary drudgery. Substituting electric power for human labour was part of this double-edged re-evaluation which gave housework high status, and the goal of ever higher standards while trying to minimize it.

Haslett and the Women's Engineering Society wished to promote such ideas, 'a new attitude of mind towards housework', among non-technical women, releasing them from drudgery by introducing them to electricity. The Electrical Association for Women was the result, with Caroline Haslett as its director for more than thirty years. The objects of the EAW were to promote the wider use of electricity in the service of women by collecting and distributing information on key areas of interest to them (home, hygiene, public welfare and housing, industrial and commercial life, transport and communication, agriculture and horticulture, smoke abatement) and, significantly, to provide a platform for women's voices to be heard. An especially important object was to promote electrical housecraft in schools. A projected by-product of the Association's activities was to give women, who would have new-found free time through the use of electricity, experience (through participation in its committees and activities) which would help them take an independent role in the wider world beyond the home. The EAW very quickly formed a branch structure in local areas, rather on the model of the Women's Institute (WI) which had been founded in 1915.

The first council included wide representation of women's groups and others with linked social concerns: the Garden City and Town Planning Association, the Smoke Abatement League, the National Housing and Town Planning Council, the Industrial Welfare Society, the Women's Local Government Society, the People's League of Health, the League of Skilled Housecraft, the Women's Sanitary Inspectors and Health Visitors' Association, the Association of Teachers of Domestic Subjects and the Good Housekeeping Institute. The electrical industry itself was represented by bodies such as the EDA, the Incorporated Municipal Electrical Association, and various London undertakings. (For the record, there were twenty-five women and seven men.) The EAW was formed in the midst of the debates over interconnection; the electrical industry gave more than moral support. Its financial backing through direct funding and provision of equipment kept the Association going. A succession of EDA officials were especially supportive.

A sample front cover from an issue of the EAW's journal, which started in 1926, gives the flavour of its concerns. It listed articles explaining how best to organize the use of particular appliances in domestic work processes; information on the progress of electricity in other countries; discussions of scientific management; descriptions of the technical and scientific basis of electricity generation and distribution; comparative evaluations of the costs of various fuels and hints on electrical economies; comments on local supplies and branch activities; discussions of electricity in industry; instructions for performing minor repairs; as well as the more traditional fare of ladies' magazines such as recipes. And, of course, the journal carried advertisements from the industry. The purpose of this consumer education was clear: to give women control over the technology they manipulated and confidence in its use through technical understanding.

The EAW did not merely propagandize; it was a very constructive body, running a series of campaigns. The very first was an important survey of women's views on the characteristics of cookers and other domestic appliances which was reported to the industry. It ran an outlet campaign, for encouraging provision of power outlets as well as lighting sockets in all new buildings, recognizing that increased electrical supplies and better appliances were useless without the infrastructure of power points. By surveying its members, it defined a Women's National Specification for Electrical Outlets, requiring a minimum of two outlets per room and three in the kitchen with due concern for safety and convenience of positioning. The Outlet campaign also called for standardized outlet and appliance types. A campaign for a more uniform tariff structure among the undertakings, so that consumers could calculate accurate comparative costings, was another activity. The EAW branches aided the EDA campaign for the all-electric home as implemented by electricity authorities all around the country. Through this and their interest in scientific management of the home, they promoted competitions on questions of lighting and kitchen design. It was not only middle-class housing that occupied their attention; the EAW was active in the inter-war years' campaign for improved working-class housing.

Exhorting women to even greater efforts of electrical efficiency and economy on the eve of the Second World War, Caroline Haslett reviewed its importance for women in a book called *Household Electricity*. If installed in a purpose-designed building at the time of construction, the capital costs of electricity could be covered by the savings on fireplaces and chimneys. So, she argued, cost was not an issue. Quite apart from any financial considerations, electricity would save women's labour and promote health. Its cleanliness meant that less redecoration was required. Electrical refrigeration made it possible to buy food in bulk and save on shopping time. Electricity gave women independence from outside help at the same time as freedom from drudgery. It would provide mothers with more time for their children, at the same time as it would make life possible for the working girl. A warm, comfortable, well-lit home would mean fewer doctors' and oculists' bills. It would ameliorate smoke-abatement problems leading to lower laundry bills and better health. Sun lamps, too, would promote better health. Importantly, electricity would free the woman's time, enabling her to take part in the community. The wireless would keep her up-to-date and sharpen her intellect. Indeed, Haslett argued, the improved mental health of women with all-electric homes deserved research.

3.5.2
The buying of electricity

Historians disagree about whether or not more domestic electricity might have been sold, but that a lot was bought in Britain and the United States is beyond dispute. Why did people make the change there, while in France, for example, they did not?

> The weaknesses on the side of supply [in the electrical industry of France] were compounded by those of demand, particularly among domestic consumers. It took a long time for the French householder to accustom himself to the desirability, even the necessity, of domestic appliances. In our period, he used his current only for lighting, plus usually a radio (though less frequently than in other countries), and often, but not always, an iron. The more costly appliances . . . were viewed as bourgeois luxuries, and even the bourgeoisie seems to have adopted them with reluctance.

One can even hear today Frenchmen who contend that the taste of refrigerated food is necessarily altered for the worse . . . In any event, the non-
electric way of life is in itself tied to a given pattern of social action and
relationships. Refrigeration is unnecessary if one shops every day, or even
several times a day . . . (Landes, 1969, p.438)

As we have seen by looking at the EAW, the electric way of life is also tied
to patterns of social action and relationships. Electricity was bought because
of the way in which it was perceived to interact with changes in these and
because it could be afforded.

The idea that electrical appliances would be substitute servants was a
potent one in the promotion of the electrical industry, and it has been
argued that they were instrumental in the decline in the number of servants.
However, in neither the United States nor Britain was this the case (Cowan,
1983 and Forty, 1986). In the United States in the 1920s, appliances tended
to be bought precisely by those homes that had servants anyway. The number
of servants did fall off, but for a variety of reasons, including the fact that
the traditional US source of fresh supplies – immigrants – dried up with the
imposition of quotas in the inter-war years (see chapter 11). In both countries,
fast-growing middle classes were simply unlikely to benefit from
proportionate growth in numbers of those willing to go into service. In other
words, there were large numbers of new people aspiring to a comfortable
lifestyle, but who would never have servants. In the United States, it became
respectable to 'do it yourself' with the aid of appliances. Housework was
reconstituted, not as a series of chores, but as an expression of the housewife's devotion to her family and womanly fulfilment (Cowan, 1983, p.177).
That appliances could be cast as substitute servants was a way of coping with
the fact that what the housewife was doing was formerly low status: the
actual work could be allocated to the appliances, as it had been allocated to
servants before (Forty, 1986, p.209; Sparke, 1987, pp.9–14).

The idea of efficiency was another potent one in the sales pitch. For the
good housekeeper was not a drudge, but a 'manager', who applied to her
workplace in the home the same criteria that male managers applied in their
sphere of work. It was a question of organizing the work processes of the
various domestic functions (Giedion, 1948, 512ff). In America particularly,
the process of rationalization, the object of which was to give the woman
full charge of her sphere, began in the late 1860s. However, it was mechanization that made it fully realizable; appliances, then, filled already made
niches in this ideology. Marshalling the best tools to do the job in efficiently
arranged rooms was an essential feature of what became 'technologized' as
household engineering in the scientific management movement as it
developed in the 1910s and 1920s. Electrical appliances could be seen as just
such tools, located in modern rational kitchens. In Germany the idea of
scientific management in the home was rapidly taken up both by women's
movements emphasizing the importance of the feminine domestic role and
those seeking feminine independence. They worked for improved housing
together with modernist architects/designers to whom the ideology of household engineering was attractive, particularly in the area of kitchen design,
the kitchen being the core of the home. So, in Germany the impetus for
domestic rationalization came from a rather different quarter (Sparke, 1987,
p.17; Bullock, 1984).

Along with managerial skills, electricity was projected as appealing to
creative skills. Released from the positional constraints and limiting characteristics of gas lighting as well as the necessity for a hearth, the woman could
exercise her talents as an interior decorator. An amazing variety of lamps
and lighting fixtures came on the market from the 1920s, which meant that
light really could be and was used decoratively rather than just functionally.

The Lamp that Lights the Way to Lighter Housework

HOUSEWORK is hard work—and the problem of help in the home is growing more and more acute. But there's a way to simplify both the work and the problem—a way surprisingly easy and inexpensive. And here it is

Electric servants can be depended on—to do the muscle part of the washing, ironing, cleaning and sewing. They will cool the house in summer and help heat the cold corners in winter. There are electrical servants to percolate your coffee, toast your bread and fry your eggs. There's a big, clean electrical servant that will do all your cooking—without matches, without soot, without coal, without argument—in a cool kitchen.

Don't go to the Employment Bureau. Go to your Lighting Company or leading Electric Shop to solve your servant problem.

Use all your Current—don't waste it

Your first economy is your purchase of Edison MAZDA Lamps. By using Edison MAZDAS in place of out-of-date carbons you will save enough current to operate several electrical appliances without increasing your electric bill. In this way Edison MAZDA Lamps are lighting the way to lighter housework.

Get them today—enough for every socket in your house. You'll see the difference in the light they give and you'll see the saving on your next month's bill.

EDISON LAMP WORKS
of General Electric Company
HARRISON, N.J.   *Agencies Everywhere*

Backed by MAZDA Service

*Figure 3.22
The lamp that lights the way
to lighter housework.
(Advertisement for Edison-
Swan lamps in McClure's,
1917. Reproduced by
courtesy of General Electric
Company Archives,
Schenectady)*

(Interestingly in Britain, the hearth retained its role as a central domestic symbol, even when it was no longer functionally necessary or efficient.)

You will have noticed the emphasis on health and hygiene in the section on selling electricity. Along with issues of household engineering, they became very important concerns in the early twentieth century, concerns that were entrusted to women. Already in the nineteenth century, sanitation had been a crucial part in public-health programmes' fight against disease, as were educational campaigns about personal hygiene, 'scientific' advice overlaid with moral prescription (Forty, 1986, pp.160–61). This is discussed in chapter 9. In the early years of the twentieth century, piped water finally entered the majority of homes in the United States and in Britain, where 80 per cent of households had piped supplies in 1951 (Davidson, 1986, p.32). Not only did this eliminate a gruelling domestic workload in the hauling of water; it also encouraged ever higher standards of cleanliness, standards that simply would not have been possible before. New forms of uncleanliness were even identified. The household germ, a 'discovery' of the 1920s, gave women grave cause for anxiety and added to their work as guardians of the family health (Cowan, 1976, p.14). So the fact that electricity was so clean in use, especially when compared with coal, was a strong selling point. It made less dirt in the first place and made thorough cleaning easier.

Finally, we need to consider the mechanisms for conveying these messages about appliances to the consumer. Ruth Cowan argues that advertising was an important link between technological developments and social changes (Cowan, 1976, pp.20–22; Cowan, 1983, 137–38). We have already seen some of the ways in which the EDA advertisements projected electricity as scientific, progressive, modern and elegant. American appliance companies, in particular, had considerable resources for promoting their products. Their campaigns were directed to the issues of the time. To take a simple example, advertisements in ladies' magazines for the period before the First World War show servants using the products; while post-war, work is done by the housewife (Strasser, 1982, pp.76–84). Some advertising was consciously aimed at 'the servant question', and may have contributed to it (Cowan, 1976, p.22). The lady in the EDA adverts certainly seemed to be doing her jobs with ease, and electricity gave her leisure as well.

Advertising could also set standards. The British General Electric Company's Miss Magnet (Figure 3.23) smiles happily (while ironing!) from the middle of her array of appliances which will secure her considerable advantages of comfort, convenience, economy and hygiene in this 'Ideal Home'. Electricity makes her jobs easy and pleasant and her environment warm, clean and smokeless. A persistent theme in advertising from the 1920s, a period from which the number and size of ladies' magazines began to grow, is housewife's guilt (Cowan, 1983, pp.187–88; Strasser, 1982, p.253). Cowan's content analysis of advertisements in the *Ladies Home Journal* found guilt, celebrity and social status to be the top three pitches made. The cleanliness of the home and consequent health of the family was a woman's responsibility – the implication being that the consequences of her failing to meet the high standards set would be embarrassing at least, and mortal at worst. Working-class women were not exempt. Figure 3.24, aimed at miners' wives during the Depression, was guilt with a vengeance. The purchase of appliances could scarcely have been within their reach.

Such tactics were not, of course, uniquely applied to electricity, but across the range of products aimed at the female consumer. Nor was advertising the only means of linking the advertiser and the consumer. Adrian Forty (*Objects of Desire*, 1986) argues for the key role of appliance design in this process. From the 1930s, when it became possible to think in terms of a 'mass' market for electricity, manufacturers began to consider questions of appearance. 'Modernity' and 'Efficiency' were concepts already stressed in

Figure 3.23
Miss Magnet's Ideal Home.
*(*Electrical Age for Women,
Vol.1, No.7, June 1928.
Reproduced by permission of
British Library Board)

the industry's propaganda, and these became the key design images. 'To symbolise these qualities, manufacturers and designers employed "modern" design, based on the "Art Deco" style, on the style of the European Modern Movement, or on features derived from automobile styling' (p.198). Interestingly, the design of gas and electric cookers converged so that they were hardly distinguishable.

Other features of our characterization of electrical housework were also conveyed to the consumer by design. Raymond Loewy's refrigerator design for Sears Roebuck (Figure 3.25) carries an image of hygiene and cleanliness. The pressed steel cabinet with its rounded corners, smooth bright white finish and concealed door mechanism is cleanliness itself. With such an appliance, the housewife would certainly be able to keep dirt under control because every speck would show. Design also played a role in guaranteeing modernity

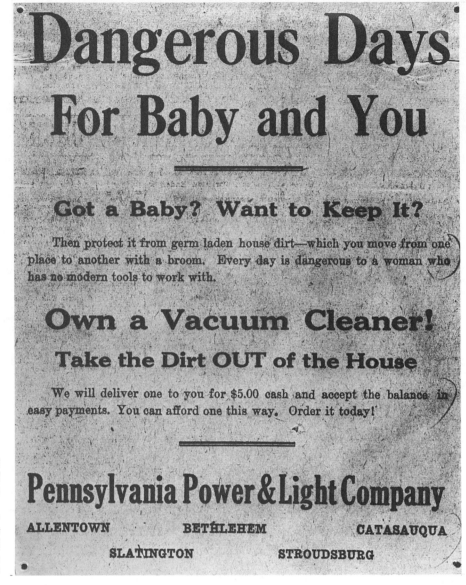

Figure 3.24
Dangerous days for Baby and
You. (Advertisement from
Shenandoah Miner's Weekly,
1930. Reproduced by courtesy
Pennsylvania Power and Light
Company, Allentown and
Pennsylvania Anthracite
Heritage Museum, Scranton)

and efficiency, while furthering the sale of appliances through artificially generated obsolescence. The vacuum cleaner and the iron provide instances of technical features remaining constant, while external styling features are changed to attract repeat purchases.

Design also helped to reinforce the concepts of household engineering. Industrial styling was employed to make domestic equipment look like efficient factory equipment, so that the factory-derived efficiency principles of scientific management would be seen to be applied in the home. 'The willingness of rational people to believe that appliances could remove work from the home was made possible only through a whole set of ideologies about housework, and to a large extent it was domestic appliance design that was responsible for making housework seem what it was said to be' (p.208).

3.5.3
The effects of
electrification

Any assessment of the effect of domestic electrification will depend on the point of view from which it is undertaken. As the tables at the beginning of section 3.5 indicate, from the perspective of the electricity supply industry,

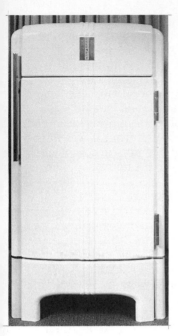

Figure 3.25
Cold Spot refrigerator 1939
styled by Raymond Loewy.
(Reproduced by courtesy of
Sears Merchandise Group,
Chicago)

the spread of domestic electricity did provide a significant new demand and was helpful in evening out the load. By the end of the 1930s, Britain was catching up internationally in consumption per head (Hannah, 1979, p.209); but it still lagged behind Germany in the percentage of homes wired for electricity and in industrial use. There were also regional variations in domestic provision with the homes of the northern urban poor and in rural areas being less well supplied than the more prosperous south and midlands. At the end of the inter-war period, similar patchiness characterized US supplies (Brown, 1980, p.x), although consumption of electricity in units per capita was greater there.

As for the appliance manufacturing branch of the electrical engineering industry, in Britain, despite the growth following the spread of the grid and the inter-war house building boom, it was not until the 1950s that mass consumption justified mass production (Corley, 1966, chapter 1). We have already noted Hannah's point that, up to the Second World War, increased consumption was a product of intensification of use by a minority of consumers rather than widespread purchasing of electrical appliances. Also, electricity is only part of the appliance story during the inter-war period. The gas industry in Britain and the United States remained extremely competitive. As in the case of the electrical industry, many of the appliances in use in the inter-war years existed already in rudimentary form in the nineteenth century. The 1893 Chicago World's Fair featured not only a model electric house, but also a model gas house (Strasser, 1982, p.73). By the 1920s, gas had generally conceded lighting to be the domain of the electrical industry, but the gas industry in both countries moved vigorously into cookers, space heating appliances (furnaces in the United States, fires in the United Kingdom), water heaters and refrigerators in the United States (Cowan, 1983; Strasser, 1982; MacKenzie, 1947, passim). In 1940, the number of gas cookers sold in the United States still outnumbered the number of electric cookers by roughly 4 to 1 (Busch, 1983, p.223). United Kingdom figures also indicate the dominance of gas. In Britain in 1939, about three-quarters of all families had gas cookers, while 19 per cent of households had electric cookers (Davidson, 1986, p. 69; see Table 3.4 above). In both cases, gas was cheaper for cooking. The gas industry used promotion techniques similar to those of the electrical industry, including building a set of showpiece all-gas council flats in London in the 1930s (MacKenzie, 1947, pp.36–37).

In relation to everyday life, the perspective of the consumer is perhaps of more interest than that of the electricity supply industry or the appliance manufacturers. The results of the process through which electricity became part of daily domestic life have been so profound, that it has been character- ized as an industrial revolution in the home. Together with the arrival of piped water, mains electricity and the spread of mains gas plus new materials brought a major transformation in domestic life. What was the impact of the new technology which promised so much to that person identified by the American household management expert turned market research advisor, Christine Frederick, as 'Mrs Consumer'? (Frederick, 1929) The titles of three recent books on technology and housework indicate the direction of historians' current views on that question: *Never Done: A History of Amer- ican Housework* (Strasser, 1982); *A Woman's Work is Never Done: A History of Housework in the British Isles, 1650–1950* (Davidson, 1986); and *More Work for Mother: The Ironies of Household Technology from the Open Hearth to the Microwave* (Cowan, 1983).

Though technology undoubtedly relieved women of the drudgery and sheer heavy labour of the type of housework that involved the carrying of water and fuel and the tending of fires for daily necessities, the amount of time devoted by women to housework in the United States and Britain remained remarkably constant right through the period of 'domestic industrialization' from the 1920s into the 1960s (Vanek, 1974; Bereano, Bose and Arnold, 1985). A range of interacting reasons has been advanced to explain this striking phenomenon. In economic terms Table 3.4 above indicates that, however important the number of appliances purchased was to the electrical industry in the inter-war years, very few households in Britain actually owned electrical appliances, apart from the electric iron, before 1940. The major expansion in appliance ownership there and in Europe did not take place until the 1950s and 1960s. Though appliance ownership was more widespread earlier in the United States, again apart from the electric iron, it was in the period of post-war prosperity that ownership of other appliances reached similar levels there. So we need to question just how much impact appliances could have made before 1950.

Also, there is the question of what the appliances could actually do. The level of iron purchases indicates that women found electric ironing, even before thermostatic control, genuinely preferable to heating and reheating the old flat irons on a hot stove, especially in the summer when the ironing burden would be heaviest. The iron was a relatively cheap appliance, and not very bulky, so it could easily be accommodated without domestic rearrangement. We also need to realize that, technically, it was possible for the iron, which drew relatively little current, to be used off lighting circuits which were cheaper to install and far more widespread than the heavier duty circuits required for appliances such as cookers and heaters. Indeed, some British supply undertakings in the 1930s were reluctant to encourage the use of electric heaters for (justifiable) fear of overshooting peak generating capacity. Vacuum cleaners were also popular, drew relatively little current and fairly early on reached a stage of genuine utility; and they were superior dust removers. In the case of laundry, the washing machine could only eliminate part, albeit a demanding part, of the labour involved. Until the advent of automatics, considerable manual intervention was required. Even the automatic was not necessarily a time-saver, although it restructured the home-laundry process by eliminating the need for a designated washing day; laundry could be scheduled to suit the housewife's convenience (Strasser, 1982, p. 268).

The broad grounds on which electrical appliances were sold – ease, efficiency and health – were similar in Britain and America, but Table 3.4 above shows that purchasing patterns were rather different. The iron and the vacuum cleaner were universally popular, but the electric cooker had greater market penetration in Britain and the washing machine and refrigerator in America. Differing degrees of affluence are, of course, part of the explanation, but so are differing levels of commercial activity and different practical concerns and social perceptions. British supply undertakings did not always pursue commercially optimal policies (Wilson, 1976, pp.103, 152 and 171) and the indigenous appliance industry tended to be on a small scale and fragmented. Foreign appliance firms were, in fact, quite important (Sparke, 1987, pp.25–36). In relation to a specific appliance, to take the case of the refrigerator, practical and marketing concerns were quite distinct in the two countries. The climate in many parts of the United States and the remoteness of, especially, rural dwellers from shops meant that chilled food storage was important. The electric refrigerator, vociferously marketed by competing appliance firms from the 1920s, was simply a modern replacement for the old-fashioned ice-box, already a standard feature of American homes (Sparke, 1987, pp.78–79).

Quite apart from what individual appliances might or might not help women to accomplish, it is necessary to consider the extent to which the aims of the scientific management of the home movement were actually achieveable. Several authors, including Lillian Gilbreth herself, have pointed out fundamental differences between factory work and housework; differences that make optimum scientific management of the home inherently unfeasible (Oakley, 1974; Berch, 1980; Arnold and Burr, 1985). For example, housework is performed in isolation on a very small scale by one person, who is both manager/administrator and worker; so the two functions cannot be separated to maximum effect. Furthermore, the houseworker can seldom concentrate on a single task, but will more likely be engaged in, or at least thinking about, several tasks at once. Nor are domestic tasks such that it is possible to define measurable, or repeatable, standards. When is cleaning really finished? A rational arrangement of time and domestic space for one task (cake baking tends to be the one most often cited) may not be suitable for other tasks; the arrangement of domestic space in relation to tasks involves compromise. And, the *coup de grâce*, even where tasks can be rationalized, there is no guarantee that the houseworker, particularly one who is also a carer of young children or the elderly, will have the freedom to execute them as planned. Indeed, as we noted in the discussion of electrical advertising, the emotional content of housework is high.

Having the right tools for the job – appliances in the case of the home – was an important part of the scientific management movement, but the tools themselves of course could not achieve 'efficiency'. Whatever their labour-saving potential, unless they were used in a labour-saving manner, no labour could be 'saved'. Underlying the above discussion has been the (correct) implication that houseworkers are in the main house*wives*, that is women. The domestic science and household engineering movements, while aiming to release women from the physical burdens of housework, reinforced the social concept discussed in chapter 1, that women's place was in the home. Cowan (1983) and others have argued that the ideology of housework has developed in such a way that the low status tasks of housework became reserved for unpaid women whose area of operation is their own home. The labour potentially 'saved' by appliances has been used to perform ever more tasks to ever higher standards – standards urged by the teachings of the domestic science movement and reinforced by advertising. Where the 'spring-clean' was once a major annual event when the carpets would be taken outside and beaten thoroughly, the ease of running the vacuum cleaner makes it possible to have a home that is always 'spring-clean', as the EDA had it. That is, carpets are cleaned more often. Similarly, rising standards of hygiene led to more frequent changes of bed and personal linen, and so more washing is done more often. Greater wealth and therefore greater appliance purchasing ability does not necessarily lead to less time spent on housework. Indeed, while appliances are often purchased for reasons of status, as symbols of wealth, the ownership of gadgets beyond the basics tends to create more tasks to be done (Bose, Bereano and Malloy, 1984).

What is most interesting is that women have accepted these responsibilities. Housework then becomes a question of attitudes rather than appliances. It is precisely middle-class women who can afford appliances who have gone back to home bread-baking. Bose, Bereano and Malloy (1984) argue that more than 'industrialization' in the home, it is revised social perceptions and organization that have led in very recent years to less time being spent on housework. A number of surveys have shown that women employed outside the home spend less time on housework than women with no outside occupation. This is not necessarily because they can afford to own more appliances, but because they budget their time and define their standards differently. Falling family size too has meant that, in one important labour-intensive area, there is less work to do. Evidently, television ownership has also been linked with fewer hours being spent on housework; domestic priorities are being rearranged (Bereano, Bose and Arnold, 1985, p.175).

Furthermore, in the 'pre-industrialized' home, many domestic tasks were done by people other than the housewife – husbands, children, servants, relatives living in, albeit mostly women. Broadly, the appliance industry was geared to maintain the ideology that woman's place was in the home. More and more tasks became reserved for the housewife alone. Cowan (1983) and Strasser (1982) point to the, in industrial terms, inefficiency of tasks being done countless times on a small scale by individual workers using individual appliances and note that such development was not inevitable. Commercial laundries, now largely displaced by home laundry facilities, were viable alternatives until the ideology of housework made it the housewife's personal responsibility to guarantee the cleanliness of her family. Similarly, commercial and co-operative food services were explored unsuccessfully in America in the 1920s and 1930s (Hayden, 1981). The ideology of women's role, among other social attitudes, ultimately worked against such developments.

3.6 RURAL ELECTRIFICATION

The discussion so far has stressed the urban, industrial context of electrification, and with good reason. In Britain and America, electricity supply developed in its early years through private enterprise and municipal initiative, where corporate or local profitability were prerequisites of survival. Put simply, in that context rural electrification was uneconomic. The overheads of getting supplies out to the countryside with a low density of users were such as to make the costs to consumers unaffordable in systems where each consumer had to pay the economic rate. Urban consumers were seldom keen to see their own costs rise in order to supply rural contemporaries. In Britain, the rapid programme of electrification in the inter-war years bypassed the farming community; only 12 per cent of British farms were electrified by 1939 (Hannah, 1979, p.192). In the mid-thirties, only about 10 per cent of US farms had electricity supply (Brown, 1980, p.16). Much was made there of public ownership developments elsewhere, in the Weimar Republic, France, Sweden, Finland, Denmark and Czechoslovakia (Brown, 1980, p.17). Canada too enjoyed a high level of rural electrification.

We have already noted that in the case of Britain, bringing electricity to rural areas was part of the brief of the government-created Central Electricity Board. Local pressure groups and bodies such as the EAW and WI were vocal advocates of rural electrification as an aid to the farm housewife. It was hoped that bringing modern amenities to the countryside would reverse the trend towards moving to the cities (Hannah, 1979, p.190). To seed non-village rural developments, the government financed various Rural Demonstration Schemes, aimed at showing the benefits of electricity to isolated farms. They were, in effect, a form of loan subsidy.

In the United States, too, a major motivation for rural electrification schemes was to make farm life attractive again in comparison to the temptations of the city (Brown, 1980, chapter 1). There, too, it was eventual federal government action, following political pressure from the poorer agricultural states, which brought electricity to rural areas. As in Britain, the First World War brought some measure of interconnection as well as some large-scale developments. In 1916, the US government, which was not yet in the war, authorized the vast Muscle Shoals scheme in the Tennessee River Valley in Alabama. The aim was to provide a hydroelectric plant which could provide cheap power for the production of nitrogen by the cyanamide process. Nitrogen, for which the United States relied on imports from Chile, was an essential ingredient in fertilizers and explosives. The war over, the plant was a political embarrassment to the government as wartime toleration of public investment in industry waned. The plant was put up for sale, and in 1921 Henry Ford bid for it. He saw a possibility of opening up the whole of the Tennessee Valley to development, with electric power as the driving force.

Ford's bid failed. He was opposed by a combination of interest groups with diverse and contradictory reasons for defeating the bid.

> The way in which these various advocates intended to exploit Muscle Shoals reflected not only different economic and political views but the different ways in which the technology of electric power could be developed. The [local private] utilities were agreeable to government ownership of the hydroelectric plant at Muscle Shoals, but they wanted the government to sell them the power wholesale for transmission and distribution to their customers; the Wall Street bankers and the well-established energy-intensive manufacturing industries like aluminum and carborundum had the twofold objective of opposing Ford's monopoly of Muscle Shoals power and favoring development of isolated industrial power sites along the Tennessee River; and the advocates of public utilities envisaged the coordinated development of power, agriculture, and industry. (Hughes, 1983, p.295)

In 1923, the power supply industry itself was instrumental in setting up a programme called the Committee on the Relation of Electricity to Agriculture. Aimed at broadening electrical service, the programme drew on the knowledge of state agricultural colleges and the American Farm Bureau Federation. The programme limped on for some ten years doing useful research and education on rural uses of electricity. It did manage to foster the establishment of some consumer-financed services, but the economics were such that profits were not encouraging. Experiments with co-operatives, a self-help avenue explored by some farming areas, had mixed fortunes.

The vast power resource at Muscle Shoals was used rather haphazardly and unsystematically until 1933 when another national emergency, the Depression, provided the context in which federal government initiatives would be tolerated again in the United States. As part of F.D. Roosevelt's efforts to solve the economic problems, the Tennessee Valley Authority was created and Muscle Shoals became a crucial part of a vast government energy supply system ranging eventually through six states. Seen alternatively as a monument to regional planning or as an example of creeping socialism, the TVA, which in the first instance provided many construction jobs, enabled the upgrading of the agriculture of an entire region, but not without some social dislocation and considerable incentive programmes relating to soil conservation. The device worked out by TVA authorities for getting supplies to farms was an extension of the co-operative concept, this time in partnership with government which sponsored low-cost financing.

Then in 1935, as part of FDR's New Deal, advocates of planned public power supply succeeded in having the Rural Electrification Administration established. The electrification of the countryside became a public responsibility. The co-operative became its basic unit and federal finance the key to development. Though a major departure in principle for private enterprise America, the REA worked because it served a market which private enterprise did not wish to tackle. At the same time, it was hardly centralist, working through local co-operatives and grass-roots concern. By 1953, American agriculture was essentially electrified (Brown, 1980, p.113). According to Brown, the main initial impact of rural electrification was on the farmhouse: the electric pumping of water, lighting, the electric iron and the radio transformed daily life in rural areas. In farm work electric lighting was, for a long while, the main application. However, the light portable motor was soon brought to bear on small-scale tasks. In some areas of the south, electrification made possible the transfer from cotton farming on exhausted soil to chicken farming. But however much it transformed rural life, electricity did not stop the exodus to the cities; instead, it made it possible for the remaining rural sector to keep pace (Brown, 1980, p.120).

3.7
DEVELOPMENTS TO
1950

Rather than to attempt comprehensive coverage, the approach in this chapter has been to treat the material selectively in order to bring out general themes about the relations between electrical technology and everyday life. Regrettably, certain important issues, such as the growth of electrical expertise and its integration in both trade union and education systems, have not been covered. At the outset of our period, the electrical industry was the pet project of a few enthusiastic inventors; but it soon became a showpiece of the new concept of research and development. Corporate investment in electrical research began to pay and engineers themselves gained a new authority in the community.

Table 3.5 summarizes the growth internationally in the generation of electricity to the end of our period. In 1949, hydroelectricity was dominant in a number of countries: 96 per cent of installed capacity in Canada, 94 per cent in Switzerland, 90 per cent in Italy, 80 per cent in Sweden (Bowers, 1978a, p.291). Hydroelectricity was also important in France. As had been the case in the First World War, wartime exigencies led to even further rationalization and concentration of electrical development. In Britain, a national voltage was finally established in 1945, and the electricity supply industry was taken into public ownership by the post-war Labour government in 1948. In Italy and France, electrification formed part of post-war industrial reconstruction programmes.

Table 3.5   Units of electricity generated per head

	1900	1910	1920	1925	1930	1940	1950
Great Britain	5.4	46	126	–	394	616	1295
United States	59	217	535	–	933	1366	2575
Germany	17	83	231	–	–	906	907*
France	–	26	90	–	408	493	782
Italy	4.3	37	109	–	252	418	441
Canada	–	–	670	–	1876	2873	3953
Soviet Union	–	–	–	19	–	283	480
Switzerland	–	–	721	–	1290	1887	2223
Norway	–	–	2000	–	2711	3073	5161
Sweden	–	144	439	–	833	1352	2582

(Based on data from Mitchell, 1981, Tables B1 and E27,   *BRD
and Mitchell, 1983, Tables B1 and E22)

Given the sheer scale of electrical enterprises from the very early days, it would be unwise to ignore the technical and economic momentum in the industry. As we have seen, technical change has, to a certain extent, generated further technical change; and economic considerations often guided technological decision-making. However, the industry exists in the context of broader social, political and ideological infrastructures, and the knowledge of this is essential to an understanding of its development.

REFERENCES

Arnold, E. and Burr, L. (1985) 'Housework and the appliance of science' in Faulkner, W. and Arnold, E. (eds.) op.cit.

Berch, B. (1980) 'Scientific management in the home: the empress's new clothes', *Journal of American Culture*, 3, pp.440–55.

Bereano, P., Bose, C. and Arnold, E. (1985) 'Kitchen technology and the liberation of women from housework' in Faulkner, W. and Arnold, E. (eds.) op.cit.

Bose, C., Bereano, P. and Malloy, M. (1984) 'Household technology and the social construction of housework', *Technology and Culture*, 25, pp.53–82.

Bowers, B. (1978a) 'Electricity' in Williams, T.I., *et al*. (eds.) op.cit., Vol.VI, pp.284–97.

Bowers, B. (1978b) 'The generation, distribution, and utilization of electricity' in Williams, T.I. *et al*. (eds.) op.cit., Vol.VII, pp.1068–90.

Bowers, B. (1982) *A History of Electric Light and Power*, Volume 3 of History of Technology Series, Peter Peregrinus.

Brown, D.C. (1980) *Electricity for Rural America: The Fight for the REA*, Contributions in Economics and Economic History, No.29, Greenwood Press.

Bullock, N. (1984) 'First the kitchen – then the facade', *Architectural Association Files*, No.6, pp.59–67, May.

Busch, J. (1983) 'Cooking competition: technology on the domestic market in the 1930s', *Technology and Culture*, 24, pp.222–45.

Buxton, N.K. (1978) *The Economic Development of the British Coal Industry, From Industrial Revolution to the Present Day*, Batsford.

Buxton, N.K. (1979) 'Coalmining' in Buxton, N.K. and Aldcroft, D.H. (eds.) op.cit., pp.48–77.

Buxton, N.K. and Aldcroft, D.H. (eds.) (1979) *British Industry Between the Wars, Instability and Industrial Development, 1919–1939*, Scolar Press.

Byatt, I.C.R. (1968) 'Electrical products' in Aldcroft, D.H. (ed.) *The Development of British Industry and Foreign Competition, 1875–1914: Studies in Industrial Enterprise*, Allen & Unwin, pp.238–73.

Byatt, I.C.R. (1979) *The British Electrical Industry, 1875–1914: The Economic Returns to a New Technology*, Clarendon Press.

Byers, A. (1981) *Centenary of Service: A History of Electricity in the Home*, The Electricity Council.

Caron, F. (1979) 'La croissance industrielle, secteurs et branches' in Braudel, F. *et al*., *Histoire Economique et Sociale de la France*, Vol.IV, *1880–1980*, Part I, Presses Universitaires de France, pp.285–314.

Catterall, R.E. (1979) 'Electrical engineering' in Buxton, N.K. and Aldcroft, D.H. (eds.) op.cit., pp.241–75.

Corley, T.A.B. (1966) *Domestic Electrical Appliances*, Cape.

Cowan, R.S. (1976) 'The "Industrial Revolution" in the home: household technology and social change in the 20th century', *Technology and Culture*, 17, pp.1–23.

Cowan, R.S. (1983) *More Work for Mother: The Ironies of Household Technology from the Open Hearth to the Microwave*, Basic Books.

Davidson, C. (1986) *A Woman's Work is Never Done: A History of Housework in the British Isles, 1650–1950*, Chatto & Windus.

DuBoff, R.B. (1967) 'The introduction of electrical power in American manufacturing', *Economic History Review*, 20, pp.509–18.

Faulkner, W. and Arnold, E. (eds.) (1985) *Smothered by Invention: Technology in Women's Lives*, Pluto Press.

Forty, A. (1986) *Objects of Desire: Design and Society, 1750–1980*, Thames and Hudson.

Frederick, C. (1929) *Selling Mrs Consumer*, Business Bourse.

Giedion, S. (1948) *Mechanization Takes Command: A Contribution to Anonymous History*, Oxford University Press; reprinted Norton, 1969.

Hammond, C. (1958) *Factors Affecting Economic Growth in France, 1913–1938*, University of Illinois PhD; reprinted Arno Press, Dissertations in European Economic History, 1981.

Hannah, L. (1979) *Electricity before Nationalisation: A Study of the Development of the Electricity Supply Industry in Britain to 1948*, Macmillan.

Haslett, C. (1939) *Household Electricity*, English Universities Press.

Hayden, D. (1981) *The Grand Domestic Revolution: A History of Feminist Designs for American Homes, Neighborhoods, and Cities*, MIT Press.

Hossli, W. (1969) 'Steam turbines' in Rochlin, G.I. (ed.) op.cit., pp.158–68.

Hughes, T.P. (1983) *Networks of Power: Electrification in Western Society, 1880–1930*, The Johns Hopkins University Press.

Josephson, M. (1959) 'The invention of electric light' in Rochlin, G. (ed.) op.cit., pp.127–37.

Landes, D.S. (1969) *The Unbound Prometheus: Technological Change and Industrial Development in Western Europe from 1750 to the Present*, Cambridge University Press.

Luckin, B. and Moseley, R. (1985) 'Attitudes towards technical change between the wars', unpublished typescript, pp.40–54.

MacKenzie, C. (1947) *The Vital Flame*, British Gas Council.

Mitchell, B.R. (1981) *European Historical Statistics 1750–1975*, Macmillan (second edition).

Mitchell, B.R. (1983) *International Historical Statistics: The Americas and Australasia*, Macmillan.

Nelson, D. (1975) *Managers and Workers: Origins of the New Factory System in the United States, 1880–1920*, University of Wisconsin Press.

Nelson, D. (1980) *Frederick W. Taylor and the Rise of Scientific Management*, University of Wisconsin Press.

Oakley, A. (1974) *Housewife*, Allen Lane.

Passer, H.C. (1953) *The Electrical Manufacturers, 1875–1900: A Study in Competition, Entrepreneurship, Technical Change and Economic Growth*, Harvard University Press.

Political and Economic Planning (1947) *The British Fuel and Power Industry*, PEP.

Rochlin, G.I. (ed.) (1974) *Scientific Technology and Social Change: Readings from Scientific American*, Scientific American.

Sharlin, H.I. (1961) 'From Faraday to the Dynamo' in Rochlin, G.I. (ed.) op.cit., pp.83–89.

Sparke, P. (1987) *Electrical Appliances*, Unwin Hyman.

Strasser, S. (1982) *Never Done: A History of American Housework*, Pantheon Books.

Vanek, J. (1974) 'Time spent in housework', *Scientific American*, 231, pp.116–20.

Wagoner, H.D. (1966) *The US Machine Tool Industry from 1900 to 1950*, MIT Press.

Williams, T.I., *et al.* (eds.) (1978) *A History of Technology*, Oxford University Press.

Wilson, D.A. (1976) 'The economic development of the electricity supply industry in Britain, 1919–1939', PhD dissertation, University of Bristol.

4 MATERIALS: PRODUCTS OF THE CHEMICAL INDUSTRIES

Noel Coley

While we are all familiar with materials such as concrete, steel, rubber and plastics, and with manufactured goods such as domestic appliances, decorating materials, textile fabrics and motor cars, most of us have only hazy notions about the extent to which chemicals, or chemical processes and controls, contribute to the making of these everyday things. Most manufactured goods depend at some stage in their production on the products of the chemical industries, and since the mid-nineteenth century the effects of chemical technology on society have been extremely wide. It can be argued that the use of new materials has improved the quality of life, that chemical products have helped to reduce the burden of manual labour and have increased the comfort, convenience and hygiene of our homes. They have improved our health and made more time available for leisure pursuits. Food, medicines, transport, fabrics and fashions, communications, hobbies, sports and many other facets of everyday life have all been affected. Consumer goods of all kinds and activities which were formerly the prerogative of the rich have been brought within the reach of working people by the introduction of new and cheaper products from the chemical industries. There is also the fast-growing pharmaceuticals industry supplying drugs, perfumes, toiletries and a wide range of fine chemicals.

But in addition to the manufacture of such consumer goods, since the early nineteenth century there has been a very large part of the chemical industries concerned with so-called heavy chemicals such as sulphuric acid, soda, pigments, organic solvents, fertilizers, explosives, and other products which are now manufactured on the scale of millions of tons per annum. As many of these products are sold within the chemical industries themselves or to other industries for use as intermediates in the manufacture of consumer goods, they are unfamiliar to most people. Nevertheless such primary chemical products are very important for the rest of industry, and throughout our period the production of such materials has grown rapidly and the chemical industries have become a most important part of the economy in all the industrialized countries.

Between the late nineteenth century and 1950, changes occurred in the activities of the chemical industries which brought them into more direct contact with individual consumers. New materials were invented, developed and manufactured by the chemical industries specifically for the retail market. This trend began with celluloid and the various types of artificial silk, but it grew rapidly with the introduction of plastics, new dyes, drugs and other compounds, especially after the Second World War. One objective of this essay is to consider the various ways in which these new materials were introduced. In the first place consumers, whether in other industries, the military or the general public, have demanded products with quite specific properties for particular purposes. Consequently the chemical industries have been concerned to supply materials which fulfil the given criteria as precisely as possible. Indeed, the success or otherwise of a new product may even be judged in terms of the extent to which its physical and chemical properties meet the requirements of potential users, rather than as a new material *per se*.

Take, for example, PVC (polyvinyl chloride), familiar to everyone as a substitute for leather and as an electrical insulator for wiring and cables.

PVC is one of the cheapest of the new polymers and has been produced worldwide since the 1940s on a very large scale indeed. A whole range of technical processes is involved in its manufacture, from the preparation of vinyl chloride itself, through its polymerization (that is, joining together many individual vinyl chloride molecules to form large polyvinyl chloride ones) and various methods of conversion into usable, attractive plastic materials. Each stage must be thoroughly worked out and the problems posed by the development of each process must be solved satisfactorily if the demands of the consumer are to be met. Many different grades of PVC plastics are made to meet a wide range of demands, and the variations between the different forms of PVC required for different purposes depend upon molecular weight, particle size and distribution, the proportion of added plasticizers and other similar technical factors. None of this is important to the consumer however. The problems of achieving materials with the required characteristics are solely the concern of the chemical manufacturer. What matters to the user of PVC is that the material is durable, non-toxic, a good electrical insulator, hard-wearing, fire-resistant, and so on, but above all that it is reasonably cheap. These are the criteria that the chemical manufacturer is required to fulfil, and it is a product with these properties that he sets out to supply.

While the response of the chemical manufacturer to consumer demand has been a powerful stimulus to the invention of new materials of all kinds, chemical research in universities and other academic institutions as well as research and development within the chemical industries themselves have also generated many ideas for new materials since the late nineteenth century. Important discoveries are sometimes made as a result of industrial research and new ideas proposed which may later lead to refinements to the original product or the manufacture of an entirely new product. Some of the best examples are found among polymers like polythene and the synthetic rubbers, or fibres such as nylon and terylene. The chemical manufacturer uses the results of research as an entrepreneur, capitalizing on the expertise of his company and profiting from his essential outlay on research and development. But once a new product has been developed to the point of sale, a market must be created, or an existing one expanded. We are therefore back again to the problem of demand. The new material must be brought to the attention of the public and promoted by advertising, which may make exaggerated claims to persuade prospective consumers that a near-perfect solution to some well-known problem has been achieved, and demand for the new product is thus created.

Sometimes a new material introduced for one purpose has made possible a quite different set of developments. Celluloid is one of the most striking examples of this. In 1862 Alexander Parkes introduced a new material called 'parkesine' as a cheap substitute for ivory and gutta-percha in buttons, combs, knife handles and so on. Parkesine was a form of cellulose nitrate (discovered as the high-explosive gun-cotton by Schonbein in 1845) which is highly inflammable, and therefore dangerous in many domestic situations. Celluloid, which is also very inflammable, was invented by a New York printer, John W. Hyatt, who in 1870 patented a process of treating parkesine with camphor. The product was first used for many of the same purposes as parkesine, for detachable collars and as a substitute for ivory in billiard balls. Later it became the essential material on which a new art form and leisure industry was to be based – the cinema. Still photography using cumbersome glass plates was itself quite new when the possibilities of celluloid film were first recognized. Celluloid was found to possess most of the physical and chemical properties necessary to enable it to replace glass as a support for the photographic emulsion, but it was also flexible and could be made in long reels on which a series of photographs could be taken which, when projected rapidly in sequence, would give the impression of movement. Without the existence of celluloid, or some comparable material, the motion-picture industry could not have developed. Similar arguments can be applied to the use of shellac, ebonite and xylonite for gramophone records. In each of these cases the technological development of a new material made possible developments in an entirely different field from that for which it had first been introduced.

4.1
PROGRESS AT A PRICE

In whatever ways a new material is first conceived or subsequently used, it is difficult to escape from the idea that 'progress' has been made. Indeed, the predominant view of chemical technology throughout our period was almost entirely optimistic. This view, that the chemical industries since the late nineteenth century have promoted rapid, beneficial progress, is encapsulated in the title of Alexander Findlay's book, *Chemistry in the Service of Man* (1916), which saw its seventh edition in 1947. It is also revealed in the following extract from the preface to a textbook of organic chemistry, the fifth edition of which was published in the same year:

> Since the last edition [only four years earlier in 1943] much that is significant in organic chemistry has happened. A new industry, the petroleum chemical industry, is now firmly established; synthetic rubber has been manufactured at the rate of approximately a million tons per annum; penicillin is no longer a chemical curiosity of unknown structure but is available in every chemist's shop; the sulphonamides have appeared under ever more potent forms; paludrine promises to be the most effective anti-malarial; and DDT has proved to be an insecticide of unparalleled value . . . (Schmidt and Rule, 1947)

Throughout the period, despite a strong reaction against science and technology in France *c.*1890–1900, the idea of progress resulting from scientific and technological advances was widely accepted, and public confidence in new products was often sought through advertising which used scientific, or pseudo-scientific ideas, and tended to create a direct, if sometimes spurious, link between science, technology and the needs of the consumer. This relied upon and reinforced a popular perception of science and technology as the engine of progress. On the domestic front, for example, new products for the laundry, household cleaning or home decorating were presented to the housewife or handyman with the backing of scientific research, while there were many proprietary medicines for which extravagant therapeutic claims were made on the basis of scientific or pseudo-scientific tests. By these subtle means a generally beneficent image of science and technology was projected, which in Britain at least was not seriously challenged until the 1960s.

There is however a negative side to the expansion of the chemical industries, for against the social benefits which they bring it should not be forgotten that chemical works of all kinds have always been responsible for large-scale environmental pollution. This problem is also mentioned in connection with medicine and public health (see chapter 9). Costs and benefits are perhaps more starkly opposed within the chemical industries than in most others. Take for instance the notorious alkali industry, which until the beginning of the twentieth century in Britain continued to use the wasteful and inefficient Leblanc process to manufacture alkali (washing-soda) from salt in enormous quantities. Already before 1870 the alkali industry had been challenged for causing serious pollution of the environment, first of the atmosphere and later of rivers and canals. The main offender was hydrogen chloride, a by-product of the process, which was at first discharged into the atmosphere as an acid cloud, blighting the area surrounding the works and killing all the green plants. Later the fumes were dissolved in water to form an acid effluent which was allowed to drain away untreated. From 1863, however, pollution caused by alkali works was regulated by the Alkali Acts and monitored by specially appointed Alkali Inspectors. But although the acid effluent problems proved amenable to control, it seemed that little could be done about the solid waste product of alkali manufacture (calcium sulphide), which formed noxious barren heaps of 'galigu', disfiguring the landscape around the alkali works in areas such as Tyneside. Yet with all its disadvantages the Leblanc process continued in use for the manufacture of soda, although with declining importance, into the 1920s, and the environmental pollution which it caused is therefore significant for much of our period.

The alkali industry offers a particularly marked example of environmental pollution, but other chemical processes also produce effluents which, despite the efforts of the chemical industries, find their way into the environment. A good example of this comes from the detergent industries. Until about 1930 the chief detergent was soap made from animal and vegetable fats. Unfortunately soap has the drawback that it produces an insoluble scum with hard water, and this was a particular problem for automatic washing machines which were becoming increasingly common from the 1930s, first in America and later in Britain and Europe. Alternative detergents which did not produce scum with hard water were required, and these were developed from the products of the petrochemicals industry. Their use on the domestic front was promoted (and still is) by ingenious advertising, but these detergents also find many uses in industry. Unfortunately, effluents from both industrial and domestic sources containing detergents began to find their way into rivers, lakes and the sea in such quantities as to cause serious effects to eco-systems. There were two aspects to the problem. First the increasing use of these detergents and second the fact that they resisted chemical breakdown in the environment. Now, while for economic reasons the detergent industries wished to increase the sales of these products, they were clearly under an obligation to modify their chemical composition so as to reduce their polluting effects. This was later achieved and now the sale of non-biodegradable detergents is banned in many countries of the world.

Obviously, the most favoured and cost-effective chemical processes are those in which the minimum amount of waste and pollution is caused and the maximum use made of the original raw materials. In any case, as this is an economic as well as a social and environmental issue, the chemical industries wishing to avoid undue criticism and censure annually devote considerable resources to solving the problems of their industrial effluents.

In addition to these pollution problems there is a large element of danger in any chemical process. Most of the substances used are toxic and many are highly inflammable, especially among organic materials. Moreover, most chemical processes involve the use of heated fluids (liquids, vapours or gases) under pressure, and this all tends to create working conditions which are both dangerous and deleterious to the health of the chemical workers. The dangers of working with chemical substances, while they are real enough, have often been ignored by the chemical workers themselves who most need to take precautions against coming into contact with poisonous or otherwise harmful substances. Chlorine, phosphorus, mercury, arsenic, lead and their compounds all took their toll of human health and life in the chemical and related industries before the dangers were realized and steps taken to control or avoid them. Thus, chlorine used in bleaching attacked the lungs, phosphorus used in making matches caused softening of the gums leading to a condition known as 'phosyjaw', while lead compounds caused colic and other digestive troubles; lead also accumulates in the bones.

Chemical works, exerting their effects over long periods of time, also pose a threat to the health and possibly even the lives of those who live in proximity to them. Of course, chemical workers and the people who live near to chemical works may not appear to suffer the adverse effects of prolonged exposure to chemical substances for many years. Steps to control all of these disadvantages have long been taken by the chemical industries, though often under compulsion since the necessary procedures are usually very costly and inevitably lead to higher operating costs which must be passed on to the consumer, reducing the competitiveness of the product. Within the chemical industries costs and benefits are sharply contrasted not only on the social and environmental level, but in economic terms as well, and the fine balance which is generally achieved between them poses many difficult problems both within the industries and for society in general.

For example, chemical products such as pesticides, food additives and drugs may be used for long periods with evident benefits before any adverse effects appear. Thus, some of the products developed by the chemical industries, and used extensively during our period, laid the foundations for problems which have only been recognized since the 1960s. The excessive use of insecticides like DDT, brought to notice in Rachel Carson's *Silent Spring* (1963), is one example, while the tragedy of thalidomide, the de-oxygenation of rivers and streams by synthetic detergents and the effects of highly toxic compounds such as dioxin are others. These and similar problems which have given cause for concern since the 1960s were largely unrecognized before 1950, but they serve to illustrate some aspects of the dark side of the cost-benefits nexus which appears to be inescapable in the continual search for better materials.

The chemical industries are complex; their products and effects are very diverse. A full survey would need to cover heavy chemicals like sulphuric acid and soda, pesticides, explosives, foodstuffs, fertilizers, drugs, cleaning and polishing preparations, glue, ink, perfumes and toiletries, fibres, fabrics and dyes, plastics . . . the list seems almost endless. Whole industries have grown up around the fabrication of materials from rubber, cellulose, coal-tar and petroleum, and the range of products was already very wide by 1950. It would clearly be impractical to attempt to cover so large a field within this essay and therefore I shall concentrate on three main areas in which new materials have been introduced during our period with significant and fairly obvious effects, namely, man-made fibres and fabrics, plastics and products like dyes, drugs and insecticides. In the period up to 1950 the last were derived mainly from coal-tar, but since the 1920s in America and after the Second World War in Britain, petroleum and natural gas have steadily displaced coal-tar as the major primary feedstock of the organic chemicals industry.

4.2
RAYON: THE FIRST
MAN-MADE FIBRE

In 1870 all fabrics were made of natural fibres such as cotton, wool, flax (linen), and silk. Clothes, furnishing fabrics and household linen available to most people were often heavy, difficult to keep clean and either white or dyed in rather drab colours, although by 1870, with the introduction of synthetic dyes following the discovery of mauveine by W.H.Perkin in 1856, new and brighter colours were beginning to appear. Of the natural fibres cotton continued to be among the most important commodities in international commerce. The United States produced between 50 and 60 per cent of all the commercial cotton grown in the world throughout most of our period, and in 1950 almost 89 per cent of world output was produced by only eight countries. Some of these, including the United States, used most of their output themselves, while others, such as Pakistan and Egypt, exported most of the cotton produced mainly to Britain. Between 1870 and the Great Depression of the mid-1920s the output of the cotton mills in Britain continued to increase, despite import tariffs on raw cotton which

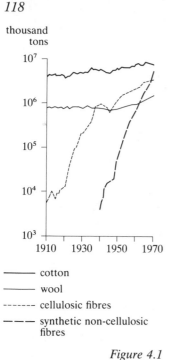

thousand
tons

—— cotton

—— wool

------- cellulosic fibres

— — synthetic non-cellulosic
fibres

*Figure 4.1
World production of natural
and man-made fibres 1910–70.
(Reproduced from B.G.
Reuben and M.L. Burstall
(1973)* The Chemical
Economy: A Guide to the
Technology and Economics
of the Chemical Industry, *by
permission of Longman
Group Ltd*

kept the price of cotton goods relatively high. Thereafter, as millions of low-paid and unemployed workers were unable to afford cotton goods, output dropped dramatically in response to the falling demand, and unemployment among textile workers rose.

Also in the 1920s certain countries, notably Germany and Japan, brought in government regulations requiring the use of the cheaper, man-made rayon in place of cotton. In other countries textile manufacturers replaced cotton with rayon for purely commercial reasons. Thus rayon or 'artificial silk', cheaper than cotton and much cheaper than natural silk, rapidly increased in importance from the 1920s. The demand for artificial silk was further stimulated by changes in women's fashions. As clothing became lighter and skirts shorter, there was a growing demand for neater, sheer 'silk' stockings and knitted rayon underwear. Already by 1913, 40 per cent of the British rayon output was being used in hosiery manufacture, while in America the proportion was even higher (reaching 70 per cent by 1915).

The idea of artificial silk is very old, but the first practical method for making it in quantity was introduced by Count Hilaire de Chardonnet, a French chemist, in the 1880s. The fibres made by Chardonnet consisted of cellulose nitrate, which is made by treating cotton or other cellulose materials with a mixture of nitric and sulphuric acid. Chardonnet found that by dissolving the resulting cellulose nitrate in a mixture of ether and alcohol he could produce a viscous solution called 'collodion', from which threads could be drawn out by forcing it through fine glass tubes to form filaments.

Unfortunately, as we have already noted, this material is highly inflammable, and Chardonnet set out to find ways of reducing its fire hazard. In 1884 the Société Anonyme pour la Fabrication de la Soie de Chardonnet was founded in Paris, and by 1900 80 per cent of all artificial silk was being made by this process. It was soon joined by three other methods. In each case the product was derived from cellulose but, as the different forms of artificial silk had distinctive properties and could be put to somewhat different uses, it was to become a very important commodity in the textile trades.

Before turning to these other forms of artificial silk, however, I should mention briefly two other developments, both of which involved cellulose nitrate and serve to illustrate some ramifications of the science and technology of new materials. In the 1880s Sir Joseph Swan was looking for a method of making a carbon filament for his newly invented electric lamp bulbs. He, too, used a viscous cellulose nitrate solution from which he obtained thin filaments of artificial silk. The material was exhibited at the Society of Chemical Industry in 1884, and a year later fabrics made from this material in the form of crocheted nets were shown at an exhibition in London. Swan used carbon filaments made from cellulose nitrate in some of his early electric lamps. These were not very successful however, as they gave a feeble light and had only a short life. It is ironic that the very same substance was used with more success by Baron Auer von Welsbach in his invention of the incandescent gas mantle, patented in 1893. The mantle was made of a loosely woven cotton fabric impregnated with a mixture of thorium and cerium salts in the shape of a large thimble, and collodion was chosen as the stiffener which enabled the mantle to be packaged for sale. This invention improved the efficiency of gas lighting and ensured continued competition between gas and electricity well into the twentieth century. The gas mantle was widely used in its inverted form in domestic and industrial gas lighting from about 1900.

Of the other processes for manufacturing artificial silk, the most important was undoubtedly the so-called 'viscose' process, patented by two British chemists (C.F. Cross and E.J. Bevan) in 1892, and developed into an important new industry by the long-established silk-weaving firm of Courtaulds Ltd. from 1905 in Britain and in America five years later. As artificial silk increased in popularity in the 1920s, Courtaulds also established viscose plants in France, Germany, Italy and Canada. In 1941 Courtaulds sold the American Viscose Corporation, but after the war they began viscose production in America again and also set up new interests in Australia and South Africa. World production therefore became (and has remained) very considerable – of the order of 1,000 million pounds (weight) per annum. Viscose rayon is regenerated cellulose made chiefly from wood pulp and is, therefore, unlike Chardonnet's rayon, not strictly a synthetic fibre. It is spun in continuous filaments which are stretched to twice their original length during the spinning process to give them greater strength. Before the First World War the properties of artificial silk were not very satisfactory; ordinary viscose does not compare well with cotton in its wearing properties even though both fibres are made from cellulose. This is because during manufacture some of the basic physical and chemical properties of the original cellulose are changed in ways that degrade the rayon. In particular its wet strength is low and it is therefore unsuitable for any purpose in which it might come into contact with water. When washed, early fabrics made from it lost their shape by stretching; sometimes they fell to pieces. Fabrics made from rayon were also liable to crease; even so rayon was used to produce special effects, for example, stripes in cotton dress materials and shirtings. Another disadvantage was that the continuous rayon filaments could not be worked on traditional textile machinery mixed with natural fibres. This problem was partially solved about 1920 by cutting the continuous rayon filaments into short lengths to form so-called 'staple fibres', comparable in length with the fibres of cotton and wool. Thereafter it was possible to work rayon on ordinary textile machinery, either alone or mixed with these natural fibres. Courtaulds began to spin this staple viscose fibre on cotton spinning machinery about 1925 and it was soon possible to produce a good staple yarn. Within four years world production of viscose from staple fibre reached about 3,000 tons, and with rising living standards in the inter-war years, production grew rapidly so that by 1938 world production had reached 485,000 tons. By this time much more staple was being produced than continuous filament yarn, and heavier fabrics traditionally made wholly from wool could be manufactured using rayon and wool mixtures.

Being relatively cheap and attractive, viscose was widely used for women's wear – hosiery, underwear and dress materials – and for many domestic purposes from curtains and furnishing fabrics to carpets. In the 1920s fashionable dresses first began to be manufactured using artificial silk on a large scale by factory methods in America. By the mid-1920s pretty, inexpensive, smart dresses which had the look and some of the glamour of real silk were being factory-made in large numbers, so that women of limited means could be in the fashion to a degree not previously possible. During the 1930s, however, manufacturers began to make thinner, weaker rayon materials in attempts to undercut their competitors. This short-sighted policy led to the manufacture of poor quality materials, which gave rayon a bad name as a cheap substitute for cotton until the problems were eventually overcome by the introduction of minimum standards of crease resistance, colour fastness and strength by the leading manufacturers. Rayon also brought a revolution to underwear. Pretty garments in a wide choice of colours became available at modest prices, replacing the traditional white cotton still prevalent among those who could not afford the fashionable but expensive silk or crêpe de Chine. To the professional seamstress in the trade this was a mixed blessing, because the new garments were being made cheaply in great numbers by unskilled labour. For the top end of the market, however, the appeal of handmade lingerie remained until the advent of nylon after the Second World War, and the relatively low prices which were often charged for such handmade garments indicate an army of poorly paid workers. Stockings,

*Figure 4.2
Advertisement for Enka
Rayon 1952. (American Enka
Corporation)*

which had been made mainly from wool or lisle (a fine cotton fabric) for the
ordinary woman with pure silk for the rich, were often black, or white for
summer wear. These materials were rapidly replaced by rayon from about
1922 and fawn, grey or flesh coloured stockings in artificial silk became
fashionable for all classes. From then on rayon dominated the stocking
market almost unchallenged until nylon appeared towards the end of the
Second World War.

    Another interesting and now commonplace product of the viscose process
is 'cellophane', the well-known transparent film used as a wrapping material.
To make this film the viscose solution is forced out into the coagulating bath
through a narrow slot about two metres wide, instead of through a number
of fine holes. The material is thus regenerated as a thin film which, after
being subjected to various treatments, is dried to a specified minimum
moisture content and wound into large rolls to be stored in warehouses

before sale. The main European producer of cellophane is a German firm, Kalle AG, first established in 1863 for the manufacture of dyestuffs. This firm, now a subsidiary of Hoechst, part of I.G. Farben, had to seek new products in 1925 when I.G. Farben gained control of German dyestuffs manufacture. Having moved into the production of cellophane film, Kalle set out to develop applications for the new product. While development chemists at the works explored potential new uses for cellophane, teams of representatives travelled all over Germany in attempts to popularize the new material, with the result that cellophane began to replace or supplement conventional paper packaging during the 1930s. Here we have an example of a company, forced by circumstances to develop a new product, deliberately setting out to create a market for that product by advertising and sales promotion.

Figure 4.3
One of the first cellophane spinning machines, Kalle, West Germany. (Courtesy of Hoechst UK Ltd)

In the field of new materials from the chemical industries, this is not an uncommon occurrence, although it is in marked contrast to the demand-led processes mentioned above. In this case chemical research followed by technical development leads to a new material with useful properties for which a demand must be created. The manufacturer therefore sets out to demonstrate the advantages of the product to potential customers. Fortunately for Kalle, cellophane proved successful and has remained an important retail packaging material for foods, cigarettes and many other goods. Its continued success has depended on its unsurpassed transparency and brilliance and also its suitability for use in automatic packaging machines. For the retailer as for the customer, the advantages of cellophane are its convenience and attractive appearance, as well as its contribution to improved hygiene, especially in the case of pre-packed foodstuffs. The essence of the self-service food shops which began to appear in the 1930s was that the customer could inspect and handle the food without contaminating it. For this, thin, tough, transparent wrapping materials like cellophane, and later cling film made from polythene, were essential.

Regenerated cellulose filaments can also be made by dissolving cellulose in an aqueous solution of ammonia with a copper salt, the cuprammonium process. The first use of this method dates from 1859 when cellulose dissolved in a cuprammonium solution was used for waterproofing and rot-proofing fabrics. In 1881 Sir William Crookes suggested the production of carbon filaments for electric light bulbs from cuprammonium cellulose solutions instead of the cellulose nitrate which was being explored by Swan about the same time. The first cuprammonium rayon was spun in Germany in 1891, but it was only ten years later, when the stretch-spinning process was introduced, that useful artificial silk could be made by this method. Very fine, strong yarn can be produced and its chief uses have been for stockings and underwear. Cuprammonium filaments are about the same thickness as natural silk and this gives fabric made from cuprammonium rayon a softer handle and better drape than standard viscose, and until the invention of nylon it was considered the best man-made substitute for natural silk. However, as silk is an expensive fibre used mainly for high-class garments, the demand for such a substitute has never been strong and the manufacture of cuprammonium rayon was not developed to the same extent as viscose. It has always remained a minor contributor to textile fabrics.

The fourth member of the group of artificial silk fibres, cellulose acetate, is not regenerated cellulose but, like Chardonnet's artificial silk, it is a cellulose compound, and its properties are therefore different from the other forms of rayon. Cellulose acetate was first prepared in 1869 using laboratory methods, but Cross and Bevan showed how it could be made on a production scale in 1894. It was found to dissolve in chloroform to give a viscose liquid from which filaments could be drawn out. However, the use of chloroform for such a purpose on an industrial scale was impractical because of its anaesthetic properties and the ease with which it is oxidized to the highly toxic gas 'phosgene'. In 1903 it was found that cellulose acetate would dissolve in acetone, a much less hazardous solvent which could be used on a large scale.

The first application to which this solution was put came in the First World War when aeroplanes had fabric-covered wings and fuselage. It was found that when coated with a solution of cellulose acetate in acetone, the fabric became taut and impervious to air, and all aeroplanes in the First World War were treated in this way. At the beginning of the war the cellulose acetate was manufactured in Switzerland by the Dreyfus brothers, but since their production was inadequate in quantity the British Government asked them to set up a factory in England at Spondon, near Derby. After the war there was little call for this material until about 1921, when Henry Dreyfus invented a method for converting the viscous solution into artificial silk. The new material, 'celanese', was water repellent, making it suitable for swimwear, but it also had a soft warm feel which ensured its success for lingerie, dressing gowns, dress materials, neckties and other items of dress. Another interesting application of cellulose acetate was for producing semi-stiff shirt collars by a process known as 'trubenizing'. In this process a layer of fabric containing cellulose acetate is sandwiched between two layers of cotton fabric and then pressed at a temperature just high enough to melt the cellulose acetate. This then produces a permanent stiffness in the collar which improves the appearance of the shirt. It also reduces the work involved in laundering the shirt collar.

All such applications have been dictated by the demands of fashion or convenience, but in addition cellulose acetate has also been used quite widely as an electric insulator, for injection mouldings or extrusion as a film and in household furnishings. In fact, there is a close connection between the properties and uses of the synthetic fibres and those of the plastics which we consider in the next section. Nylon, discovered in 1938 by W.H. Carothers, is a good example of this. Undoubtedly its most familiar use has been as a fine strong synthetic fibre for stockings, for which it largely replaced artificial silk after the Second World War, but nylon has also found many other applications as a plastics material.

Figure 4.4
Trubenized collar. (Courtesy of Double Two Ltd)

**4.3
PLASTICS, RESINS AND
POLYMERS**

The term 'plastics' is the generic name of an industry and its products adopted in the 1920s when the ready formability of these substances under heat and pressure was thought to be their most important feature. Plastics have commonly been thought of by the general public as cheap substitutes for natural materials such as wood, glass and metals. They are also frequently considered together as though they were a single group of substances with common properties. Both views are misconceived. Plastics themselves are by no means cheap but, as they generally have a low specific gravity, a given weight of plastics material provides a greater bulk than an equivalent weight of wood, glass or metal: consequently individual plastics items can be made in greater numbers and therefore more cheaply than similar objects made in traditional materials. Plastics are also far more than substitutes for other materials; each type of plastic has unique properties which make it specially suitable for particular purposes.

Plastics have become so common today that we need to stop and think about the many ways in which these manufactured materials have affected everyday life since Alexander Parkes first exhibited his parkesine in 1862. Although Parkes made large claims for his invention, there was still a long way to go before it could be successfully marketed commercially as celluloid and, as we have seen, this was not done by Parkes himself.

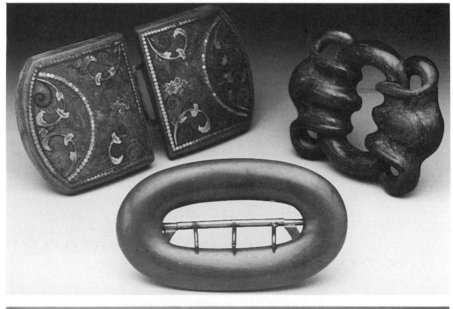

*Figure 4.5
Mouldings in parkesine
1861–68 by Alexander Parkes:
(top) two buckles and a
brooch; (bottom) two plaques.
(Photo: Shell UK Ltd.
Reproduced by permission of
the Plastics Historical Society,
Plastics and Rubber Institute,
London)*

Table 4.1   Production of some plastics materials in Britain during the Second World War showing the effects of wartime demands upon production. (Williams, 1972, p.184)

Type of material	Production 1941 (tons)	Production 1946 (tons)
Cellulose acetate	3,452	5,737
Celluloid	1,719	2,100
Perspex	1,463	3,949
PVC	–	5,471
Phenol-formaldehyde	13,521	25,221
Urea-formaldehyde	4,136	6,471
Total:	24,291	48,949

Compare these figures with the American output of similar materials amounting to 370,000 tons in 1947.

Nevertheless, celluloid was not the first plastics material to be used, although it was the first to be chemically manufactured. Before the 1860s shellac and casein, both derived from natural sources, were the most widely used plastic substances, and since they were important throughout our period we need to learn a little about them. Shellac comes from the secretion of a tropical beetle (*Coccus lacca*) common in India and Malaya, deposits of which are collected from the trees in which the beetles live, melted and formed into rods or sheets. It has been known since early times and was used by the ancient Egyptians and Chinese as a glue, for preserving wood, in decorating vases and as a polish. It is still widely used in varnishes, French polish and for making laminates with sheets of mica for insulation purposes, but its most important use between the 1880s and 1930s was for gramophone records. Indeed, until about 1933 all gramophone records were made using shellac. Thus it is evident that this natural plastic had a large part to play in bringing entertainment into the home during our period.

Casein is the oldest and commercially most important of the natural protein plastics which include bone, horn, hair and materials produced from agricultural products such as soya beans, corn, oats and wheat. Casein is made from skim-milk by the action of rennet; the whey is discarded and the curds are washed and dried to a powder which, when made into a dough with water, can be extruded into rods or sections and sheets. Hardened chemically using formaldehyde, it forms a bone-like material familiar as buttons on old dresses. The first patent for this material dates from 1885–86 in Germany and a later patent for a substance called 'galalith' was filed in 1897. In England casein was first manufactured in 1913 from milk supplied by Ireland and was therefore called 'erinoid'. It was used for making knitting needles, millions of which were required in the First World War for knitting woollen garments for the troops. Commercial production in the United States began in 1919 and the material was manufactured widely until 1940, latterly using milk from Argentina. Buttons, buckles, handles, poker chips, fountain pens, cigarette holders, paints, dressings for paper and the waterproof coating for playing cards were some of the main uses for this material. It has even been marketed as a fibre, but was too weak unless mixed with others like wool or viscose. When inflammable celluloid was in widespread use in the 1920s, casein was tried as a safer substitute, but its affinity for moisture and the fact that it warps and cracks in use made it unsatisfactory.

Another protein plastic was developed from soya beans by Henry Ford, who in the 1930s tried water-melons, carrots, cabbages and onions in his search for a protein plastic from which to mould an entire car body. By 1940 he had the complete set of dies for moulding the parts, and in October 1941 the first plastic motor car was unveiled, cheaper and lighter than steel, but with ten times the impact strength of the ordinary metal body. The new design consisted of fourteen plastic panels made from soya-bean fibre hardened with a phenolformaldehyde resin, formed in a press, set into shape by heat and pressure and fitted to a tubular steel frame. The use of soya beans for such a purpose gave hope to American agriculture and the idea also showed that plastics might be used for large mouldings. Unfortunately the new material, like casein, was found to absorb water and so it was not suitable as a car body and never went into production, although the concept of a moulded plastic car body was later developed using fibre-reinforced and glass-fibre materials.

Figure 4.6
Major body sub-assemblies,
Chevrolet Corvette 1953.
(Chevrolet Motor Division,
General Motors Corporation,
Detroit)

4.3.1
German contributions to the rise of the plastics industry

At the beginning of the twentieth century the importance of organic chemistry in industry was recognized, especially in Germany, and this stimulated the search for processes which would lead to new materials. It has often been the case that a new compound was discovered long before any use was found for it, and this was particularly true of the plastics industry. Many of the substances which became well known between 1870 and 1950 were first discovered earlier in nineteenth-century German organic chemistry laboratories, and were then virtually forgotten until the 1920s and 1930s (see Table 4.2). It must be remembered though, that the discovery of a new chemical compound is only the first small step on the road to a useful new material which can be manufactured on a commercial scale. In the plastics industry enormous effort and great ingenuity have been needed to convert newly discovered chemical compounds into effective and useful new materials. Nor is the development of a commercially viable plastics material merely a matter for the chemist. Contributions from other professions are also essential. The role of the engineer is perhaps obvious, as are those of the works manager and accountant. If the new material is to be widely used by the public, perhaps in everyday dress, it is essential to ensure that it is non-toxic and harmless. A new material which irritates the skin, for example, would clearly be unsuitable as a dress fabric. The research, testing and development necessary to ensure the safety of any new material will certainly be lengthy and may, or may not, in the end result in a commercially viable product. Strong commercial incentives are needed before a manufacturer will consider the cost justified. One important source of such incentives comes from advertising and the commercial promotion of new products. Another arises from the requirements of the armed forces, which provided plenty of stimulus in Germany, for example, when the rapidly developing armaments industries of the inter-war period made urgent demands for new materials.

In the 1920s and 1930s the German chemical industry extended its interests in the field of organic chemistry, both academic and technical. The aim was to make Germany self-sufficient by manufacturing synthetic materials from air, water, chalk and the products of coal-tar. Substitutes for leather, metals, rubber, wool, cotton and other materials, even butter, were manufactured from such unpromising sources and passed on to the public. In Britain, where the use of traditional materials remained common and 'cheap' substitutes were eschewed, it became fashionable to jibe at German 'ersatz' materials and ridicule the efforts of German chemists to replace imported natural materials with home-produced substitutes. Nevertheless many of these synthetic materials performed extremely well.

Germany entered the Second World War with a large synthetic rubber and plastics industry. The efforts of the inter-war years had laid the foundations of a vast industrial complex based on the highly reactive chemical acetylene, obtained from calcium carbide, made in powerful electric furnaces from limestone and coke. In 1944 carbide was being produced in Germany at the rate of 1.32 million metric tonnes per annum, and most of the acetylene obtained from this vast quantity of carbide was converted into polystyrene, vinyls and several forms of synthetic rubber. After the war, compounds formed during the 'cracking' of petroleum increasingly displaced acetylene as the starting-point for many of these products.

But, if the demands made by a state preparing for war were important for the development of the plastics and synthetic rubber industries, another equally important stimulus came from the theoretical work begun in the 1920s by Hermann Staudinger, professor of organic chemistry at Zürich, who introduced the concept of the macro-molecule in 1922. It had long been thought that complex organic substances like cellulose, starch or rubber consisted of numbers of smaller molecules held together by weak physical forces in groups or 'micelles', and it was to this idea that Staudinger turned his attention in the early 1920s. X-ray diffraction studies of stretched rubber suggested that the smaller molecules of which it was formed were not merely grouped loosely together, but were chemically linked in long chains of 2,000-3,000 units. Thus it seemed that rubber was made of giant molecules rather than loose aggregates of small ones. The idea met with strong opposition and Staudinger was to spend the rest of his active life in efforts to substantiate his theory. He steadily produced evidence in support of the idea against the opposing micelle theory until, by about 1940, he was able to gain acceptance for it. At Freiburg in Switzerland in that year the first Institute for Macro-molecular Chemistry was established and the first journal devoted to the subject appeared – sure signs of the arrival of the new discipline. In 1953 Staudinger was awarded the Nobel Prize for Chemistry in recognition of the important influence of his theoretical work on the industrial development of plastics. Certainly it was this work on the properties of substances made up of macro-molecules that stimulated the search for new plastics and the chemical modification of old ones.

4.3.2
Bakelite and other synthetic resins

About 1910 another important new plastic material was introduced, made from phenol, a product of coal-tar distillation, and formaldehyde under carefully controlled conditions of heat and pressure. Developed in America by Leo Baekeland and in England by James Swinburne, the new material, bakelite, was patented in 1906 and manufacture began soon afterwards. In 1928 the British and American interests were merged into a single company of which Swinburne was chairman until 1948, and during this time bakelite was used in so many everyday connections that the name became a household word. In the 1930s the phenolic resins probably found their commonest uses in the booming radio industry, where they were used for control knobs, valve sockets, insulating lacquers and even the complete cases for radio sets. Since the introduction of bakelite, plastics have brought attractive household objects, both decorative and useful, within the reach of most people.

Figure 4.7
Room setting for the Pierce Foundation, New York, 1933, showing all items made of plastics, including 'Vinylite windows' and walls. (Courtesy of Modern Plastics)

One disadvantage of the phenolformaldchyde resins was their unattractive dark brown colour which prevented them from taking on other pigments, and in 1928 a rival material developed by a British firm came on to the market. It was made from ureaformaldehyde resin, a substance first prepared in 1884. This material is water-white and could be used to make mouldings in white or pastel shades. In the following year a new design for the telephone was introduced, which soon began to replace the old black ebonite candlestick model dating from 1905 with the familiar handset known as Siemens' telephone. Millions of these were produced, especially for the American market, in black or brown bakelite and in cream, red, green or brown ureaformaldehyde, although for some years the coloured telephone was not very common. At the British Empire Exhibition at Wembley in 1924–25, a modified ureaformaldehyde was exhibited in which urea was replaced by thiourea (identical with urea, except that it contains sulphur instead of oxygen). The new materials were enthusiastically received, and by 1931 many products made from urea- and thiourea-formaldehyde resins were available throughout Europe. Working-class homes were soon filled with colourful

*Figure 4.8
Objects of ureaformaldehyde
mouldings, including:
'Bandalasta Ware' sandwich
box, beakers and plates from
a 'Coracle' picnic set, 1927–32,
'Rolinx' cigarette box,
armchair tray with spring-
loaded flaps, round box with
lady and dog moulded relief,
designed by Harry J. Earland
for Pignon Plastics Ltd, 1947,
'Beetleware' picnic cups and
plates, 'Acme' vacuum flask,
'Thermos' flask in wood-filled
urea, 'Quickmix' egg-flip
shakers, biscuit bucket, cotton
wool dispenser, sugar shaker,
'Velos' napkin rings, box with
moulded relief of Diana and
early salt and pepper pots of
'Beetle' resin. (Collections of
Sylvia Katz, Dr and Mrs
Nicholas Kemp. Photo: Fritz
Curzon)*

plastics mouldings in pastel shades of blue, pink, green and orange – picnic baskets, cruet sets, the outer cases of vacuum flasks, handles for hair brushes, combs, childrens' toys, snap fastenings for trinket boxes, a vast array of the trivia of everyday life. Nevertheless, there were some everyday uses to which these materials could not be put since they too had a serious drawback. They could not be used successfully where they were likely to come into contact with water because they tended to absorb it. Therefore plastics could not be used for the many domestic items which must be washed regularly, from picnic cups to draining boards; nor could they be used in hospitals. These resins were found to craze badly when used in such situations and became not only ugly, but unhygienic. The problem was solved about 1938 by the introduction of yet another new resin, melamine-formaldehyde, or more commonly just melamine. This has steadily replaced the older products.

While the ureaformaldehyde resins were not an unqualified success in the home, they turned out to be excellent bonding materials for plywood, still widely used in aircraft construction in the 1930s. In the First World War the standard glue for all-wood aeroplanes was made from casein, or animal albumin. This was dangerous at low temperature or high altitude because it would become brittle and the whole aircraft would fall apart. The development of glue using ureaformaldehyde resins in 1931 was a closely-guarded secret which enabled mass-production techniques for aircraft manufacture to be introduced. One product of these new methods was the De Haviland Mosquito fighter, constructed entirely of plywood, yet capable of flying at high altitudes and sub-zero temperatures. The Horsa glider, boats, pontoons, rafts and other military equipment also used the same materials.

The large-scale manufacture of other plastic materials was also developed as a result of military demands during the Second World War. Perspex (methyl methacrylate) had been discovered in 1877 by the German chemist Fittig, and was manufactured on a small scale in Germany from about 1928. At first it was used as an adhesive and in coatings, but it was converted into a mouldable rigid plastic material by two British chemists at ICI about 1934. Two years later transparent acrylic sheet was on the market with the trade names of 'perspex' in Britain and 'plexiglas' in Germany. Domestic uses such as cutlery handles, doorknobs, salad servers, bathroom fittings, costume jewellery and other similar items were introduced about 1937, but these were set aside until after the war during which the main use for perspex was in the transparent parts of military aircraft for which its shatter-proof properties made it ideal.

Two other plastic materials developed during the war have become, like bakelite, household names. They are polythene and nylon and both resulted from research based on Staudinger's ideas about macro-molecules. Polythene (polyethylene) was discovered in 1933 by two chemists at ICI while exploring the industrial potential of chemical synthesis under high pressure – a process first achieved on a large scale in Germany in 1913 for the manufacture of ammonia and nitric acid for explosives. By 1938 one ton of polythene had been made and full-scale production began in the following year with a fifty ton per year plant using ethylene from alcohol produced by fermentation. Polythene was first used as a covering for cables, but its properties as an electrical insulator were to prove invaluable during the war for the development of radar. In 1940 Du Pont and Union Carbide in America were licensed by ICI to manufacture polythene, and the American output soon exceeded that of Britain which by 1945 had risen to 1,000 tons per year. After the war ICI sought other outlets for polythene and by 1950 it was being used for toys, plastic bottles, washing-up bowls and luxury packaging. Production reached only 2,000 tons per year while it still depended on ethylene costing up to £250 per ton from fermentation alcohol, but in 1952 petroleum-based ethylene at about £90 per ton became available. This reduced the price of polythene immediately, and it continued to fall as production rose and new uses for the product were found. Today polythene is perhaps the most widely used of all plastics (annual production about 5,000,000 tons worldwide).

Just before the outbreak of the Second World War Du Pont in America announced the discovery by W.H. Carothers of a new synthetic fibre called Nylon 66, and by the end of 1938 this new material had made its appearance as bristles in Dr West's Miracle Tuft toothbrushes. Nylon enjoyed almost instant success as a fibre; in 1939 the first nylon stockings became available in America and within the year 64,000,000 pairs were sold. In 1941 nylon moulding powders were first made and it was shown that these could be used for making a wide range of strong, tough and chemically resistant objects. Its inertness to oils and fuels, its resistance to abrasion and low coefficient of friction enabled nylon to replace metals, particularly for small engineering components such as gears, cams, bushes and bearings, where shock resistance and the ability to run silently without lubrication are important.

Both polythene and nylon were discovered as a result of chemical research in industry, based on ideas from theoretical chemistry, notably those of Staudinger. In both cases scientific curiosity rather than consumer or technical demands led to the discoveries. Once their special properties became more widely known through advertising, consumer demand led to their manufacture on an industrial scale.

Table 4.2 shows that while many of the well-known plastics materials were discovered much earlier, they came into commercial production from the 1930s and were only important in Britain and America after the Second World War. Since that time plastics have enabled the working class to equip their homes with modern, hygienic, useful and attractive things which previously, handcrafted in fine woods, metals, glass, tortoiseshell, ivory and so on, they would not have been able to afford. Moreover, the introduction of easily cleaned kitchenware and surfaces made in polythene, formica and melamine, significantly reduced the domestic workload while increasing both the hygiene and attractiveness of the kitchen.

Table 4.2 Dates of discovery and first commercial production of major synthetic polymers

Product	Discovery	First commercial production			Firm responsible
		Britain	USA	Germany	
Phenol-formaldehyde	1891	1910	1909	1910	General Bakelite
Urea-formaldehyde	1884	1928	1929	1929	British Cyanide
Melamine-formaldehyde		1938	1939	1935	Henkel
Alkyd resins	1863	1929	1926	1927	General Electric
Epoxy resins	1891	1955	1948		Du Pont
Polyethylene (l.d.)	1933	1938	1941	1944	ICI
Polypropylene	1954	1959	1957	1957	Montecatini
Polystyrene	1835	1950	1933	1930	IG Farben
Polyvinyl chloride	1871	1942	1933	1931	IG Farben
Polyvinyl acetate	1911	1949	1928	1928	Union Carbide
Nylon	1932	1941	1940	1943	Du Pont
Terylene (Dacron)	1941	1949	1950		ICI
Polyacrylonitrile	1922	1959	1948	1952	Du Pont

(Source: extracted from Reuben and Burstall, 1973, p.31)

Unfortunately, the great versatility of plastics gave rise to one of their main problems. They so often replaced scarcer and more expensive natural materials that they came to be associated with the idea of cheapness. This was underlined by the fact that early plastics materials all too often showed faults in use. Plastic tableware became crazed and stained, colours faded, mouldings became distorted or cracked, and consequently plastics were often regarded as poor substitutes for the 'real thing' rather than as new materials in their own right. The connotation of 'cheap plastic' generally led to the idea that they were inferior; they were considered to be 'ersatz', and it took the plastics industry a long time to overcome this image and show that plastics have useful properties of their own, different from and sometimes superior to those of natural materials. In spite of this early adverse image, the role of plastics in everyday life was well established by 1950 as new improved materials and new methods of fabrication were developed. Until the end of the Second World War only small items could be made by injection moulding techniques; larger articles such as perspex cockpit covers for aircraft were made by heating sheets of the plastic materials to soften them and then shape them in specially designed presses. By 1950, however, methods had been developed for making large injection mouldings – items of kitchenware, chairs and tables, baths, dustbins and piping for gas mains, for example. These things brought plastics more prominently into everyday use and their success owes as much to the new techniques of fabrication as to the introduction of the new materials themselves.

**4.4
SOME SYNTHETIC
MATERIALS FROM
COAL-TAR**

Many of the most useful developments in the chemical industries since 1870 have been among the so-called organic compounds, that is, compounds of the element carbon, which all originate from natural sources in plants or animals. Some of these natural products, for example, flower perfumes, occur only in very small quantities, but by examining their chemical structures it has been possible to synthesize them and produce them on a much larger scale. Others, such as the alkaloids, for example, have been extracted in more or less pure forms or in low concentrations as tinctures from plants grown for medicinal purposes for centuries. Chemical synthesis makes it possible to produce them up to 100 per cent pure and so control their use in medicine more precisely. Yet other natural products have for centuries been extracted from plants and animals for use as dyes. These too have been synthesized and many other coloured compounds have been invented with structures related to the natural ones so that hundreds of thousands of such coloured compounds are now known of which about 4,000 are actually used as dyes. Most of this chemical activity has occurred since 1870.

The manufacture of dyes, drugs and perfumes developed from just about the least promising of all industrial waste materials, coal-tar. This black, smelly, sticky mess was produced in very large quantities by the gas industry throughout the period. In 1901, for example, world production of coal-tar was over 2.6 million tons, of which Britain alone produced more than 900,000 tons. Coal-tar was at first regarded simply as a nuisance for which there was no use and which had to be discarded. It was dumped, burned as a fuel to heat the retorts in the gasworks where more tar was being produced all the time. Small amounts were used to preserve timber or surface the roads – anything to get rid of it. Yet in Britain from the late nineteenth century to the end of the Second World War when it began to be superseded by petroleum, it was to be one of the principal raw materials for the organic chemicals industry. For this purpose coal-tar is first distilled to obtain organic compounds such as benzene, toluene, phenol, aniline, naphthalene and anthracene, each of which is an important starting point for the synthesis of dyes, drugs, perfumes, and other useful products.

4.4.1 Dyes   The first synthetic aniline dye (mauveine) was produced accidentally in 1856 by W.H. Perkin while engaged in efforts to synthesize quinine. Some thousands of synthetic colouring materials were later obtained starting from benzene, naphthalene or anthracene and produced in large quantities. Much of this work was done in Germany and as each new dye was patented to prevent its manufacture by others, the German dyestuffs industry expanded rapidly. In the present century many new types of dyes have been discovered or invented. Often these developments have been made necessary by the introduction of new synthetic fibres which cannot be dyed using the traditional methods. New dyes suitable for use with fibres such as nylon and terylene were therefore demanded and had to be invented by colour chemists. The relationships between chemical constitution and colour have been so thoroughly investigated that it has become possible to invent new dyes more or less to order. The variety of shades, and the brilliance and fastness of modern dyestuffs, has ensured a range of colours and designs in fabrics which could hardly have been imagined in 1870, and this too has had its effects on the quality of everyday life.

But the introduction of synthetic dyestuffs has had marked effects on the economies of some of the less advanced countries. Thus, at the beginning of our period the cultivation of plants for producing natural dyes was still a significant part of agriculture in certain parts of the world. Across Southern Europe and in Asia Minor, for example, large areas of land totalling some 300,000 to 400,000 acres were devoted to growing the madder plant. When the roots of this plant are fermented a substance called 'alizarin' is formed. This dyes cotton bright red (Turkey Red) and is one of the oldest dyestuffs for cotton goods. By the 1950s these madder fields had completely disappeared. Once the molecular structure of alizarin had been determined in 1869, it could be manufactured relatively easily from anthracene and the synthetic dyestuff could be sold for about one-twelfth the price of the natural product.

In India similar changes occurred in relation to indigo. This blue dye has been known for at least 3,000 years; in Europe woad, from which indigo was made, was cultivated well into the sixteenth century. Indian indigo is superior to the European variety, however, and from the sixteenth almost to the end of the nineteenth century, Indian indigo plantations controlled the world markets for this dyestuff. In 1897 for example, India produced over 8,000 tons of indigo with a market value of £4,000,000, but in that year German organic chemists brought synthetic indigotin, the chief constituent of natural indigo, on to the market in competition with the natural product from India, and during the ensuing half-century the quantity of synthetic indigo produced outstripped that of natural indigo. More than a million acres of land formerly devoted to indigo production were reclaimed and used for producing food.

Tyrian purple, another ancient dye, is secreted by certain species of marine snails found on the shores of the Mediterranean. The traditional dye has always been costly, mainly because of the enormous numbers of molluscs required to supply even very small amounts of it. In the first decade of the twentieth century Tyrian purple was shown to be a compound of indigo with bromine which could fairly easily be synthesized. The manufactured product is much cheaper than the natural one and again the introduction of this new synthetic material had major effects on some traditional industries.

4.4.2
Perfumes
Besides these developments in colour chemistry there have also been significant discoveries in other fields related to natural products, for example, the synthetic perfumes. The extraction of odoriferous principles from flowers and plants, either by distillation with steam or extraction with a solvent, has a very long history and until about 1875 this was the chief source of perfumes; synthetic perfumes were almost unknown. Very large quantities of plant material are required to extract usable amounts of the natural perfumes, which are consequently very expensive. The first synthetic perfume, coumarin, the odoriferous principle of sweet woodruff, was prepared by W.H. Perkin in 1868 from phenol, a constituent of coal-tar, and its synthesis was quickly followed by that of vanillin, a flavouring material formerly extracted from the pods of the vanilla orchid. To these early synthetic materials many more were soon added – oils of winter green and of bitter almonds, hawthorn blossom and lily of the valley.

Since the 1870s organic chemists have been able to determine the molecular structures of many of these substances and synthesize them mainly from the derivatives of coal-tar, so that passable imitations of the natural perfumes of the violet, rose, hyacinth, lilac, heliotrope and orange blossom can be made along with the flavours of apple, pear, pineapple and other fruits. The senses of smell and taste are very closely related and so it is not surprising to find that synthetic perfumes and flavours are made by similar methods from the same origins. In nature each of these perfumes is a subtle mixture of many compounds and, while the chemist and the perfumier copy nature as nearly as possible, synthetic perfumes are imitations which can never match the natural products precisely. There is therefore a difference between these new materials and the plastics discussed above. The new plastics had their own unique characteristics and were not intended merely as substitutes for natural materials, even though this is how they were often seen. Synthetic perfumes, on the other hand, can never be more than imperfect substitutes and are always likely to be regarded as inferior. Nevertheless, the introduction of these materials has led to a great extension of the use of perfumes in soaps, creams and other toiletries, and has given rise to keen competition among manufacturers to sell what are basically the same products.

4.4.3
Drugs
During the period between 1870 and 1950, the products of chemical research in the fields of drugs, anaesthetics, insecticides, germicides and so on, have also made significant changes in the practice and effectiveness of medicine. It was only in the early years of the twentieth century that the foundations of a true chemotherapy were laid. Paul Ehrlich, working at the Robert Koch

Institute in Berlin, observed that methylene blue, used for staining living tissues for microscopic examination, was absorbed selectively and to different extents. He had the idea of combatting diseases caused by protozoal parasites by using substances which would be absorbed into certain tissues and would be toxic for the parasites without causing any ill effects to the host organism. After many false starts he at length discovered an arsenic compound which he called salvarsan and which was used as a treatment for syphilis.

This was in 1912, and later the same compound was found to be effective against other diseases caused by parasites known as spirochaetes, especially the disfiguring disease of yaws. Seven years later in America another arsenic compound (tryparsamine) was found to be effective in treating the later stages of sleeping sickness, while in Germany a new drug was introduced for the early stages of the same disease. By means of these drugs some control over sleeping sickness was secured. Then in 1948 a new drug was introduced, which could be injected into cattle, horses and camels so that the disease would be less likely to be carried from these animals to people by its usual vector, the tsetse fly.

Malaria, another insect-borne disease, has been known as a killer since ancient times, and its life-cycle in people and mosquitoes was worked out by Manson, Ross and others between 1879 and 1900. The disease is said to affect 400–500 million people throughout the world and used to kill about 4 million annually. Quinine, an alkaloid obtained from the bark of the cinchona tree, was traditionally used to control the ravages of malaria, but when the Japanese invaded Java in 1942 the supply of this natural product was cut off, and the consequent predicament of the Allied armies led to the use of two synthetic drugs prepared by German chemists in the inter-war years. The best known of these, mepacrine, was supplied to British and Allied troops in Burma and the Far East packed between sheets of polythene to protect the tablets from moisture; it was an important factor in the war against the Japanese. In 1945 another drug, paludrine, was found to be even more effective both as a prophylactic (that is, preventive medicine) and as a control for malaria itself.

During the twentieth century the use of synthetic drugs has increased greatly. More than half the 440 substances described in the 1948 edition of the British Pharmacopoeia were synthetic products, resulting from chemical and medical research. Among all these new products the most spectacular results have been achieved by substances called antibiotics, of which the best known is undoubtedly penicillin. Discovered accidentally in 1929 by Sir Alexander Fleming, this substance was only isolated for large-scale production in 1940 by Sir Howard Florey at Oxford using a process which depends upon biosynthesis on moulds. It was developed in Britain and America and by D-Day, 1944, enough supplies for all the Allied forces were available. Penicillin enabled physicians and surgeons to control wound infections and gas gangrene which had previously been responsible for so many deaths, but it was also found effective for treating diphtheria, tetanus, boils, impetigo, syphilis and yaws.

4.4.4 Insecticides While these products of the fine chemicals industry have greatly assisted medical treatment, others have been used to improve public health by controlling insects. In part this has been stimulated by economic considerations, such as crop protection, but by destroying insect vectors the incidence of some serious human diseases has been reduced and in a few cases almost eliminated.

Several inorganic compounds containing arsenic or fluorine have long been used to control insect pests both on crops and in the human environment. Lead arsenate was first used against lice in 1892, while calcium arsenate was used to kill the cotton boll weevil and Paris green (copper aceto-arsenite) was used against the Colorado beetle. Sodium fluoride was also widely used to kill lice on animals. Mosquitoes were controlled by means of an extract of pyrethrum flowers, either as a powder or dissolved in kerosine. (The insecticidal properties of 'Flit' depend on the pyrethrins, for example.) At the beginning of the Second World War, however, a completely new insecticide, DDT (dichlorodiphenyltrichloroethane), was introduced and was to become so widely used that it caused ecological problems by the 1960s. First synthesized by an Austrian student in 1874, the insecticidal properties of DDT were discovered only in 1939 by a Swiss chemist, Paul Müller. The compound was manufactured in Britain and America in the early 1940s and was first used to control an outbreak of typhus in Naples in 1943 when one million civilians were disinfested of lice. A year earlier another powerful insecticide had been introduced. Called gammexane (hexachloro-cyclohexane), this too was an organo-chlorine compound as were aldrin and dieldrin introduced in the early 1950s. By using these powerful insecticides in carefully orchestrated campaigns, the insect carriers of some deadly human diseases such as malaria, yellow-fever, sleeping sickness, dysentery, typhus and bubonic plague were greatly reduced, while fruit-tree and other crop-destroying insects, especially locusts, were controlled. This apparently bright prospect led to almost indiscriminate use of these organo-chlorine compounds by farmers for obvious economic reasons. The immediate benefits were considerable. Crops were protected, the threat of famine seemed to recede, while the incidence of malaria and sleeping sickness was significantly reduced.

But in the 1940s and 1950s the disadvantages were still to be recognized. The destruction of so many insects led to marked ecological changes: for example, the numbers of some species of insectivorous birds were drastically reduced. Then DDT began to be detected in the bodies of birds, wild animals and fish, as well as in food crops, meat, milk and so on, and its potential effects on the human body were unknown. Other problems were also looming. Even by 1947 it had been observed that some insects were developing resistance to DDT: by forced selective breeding insect populations were becoming immune to the lethal effects of these organo-chlorine compounds. Clearly this could lead to the renewed spread of insect-borne diseases and the hunt for new insecticides had to be intensified. From about 1947 alternative types of insecticides have been sought and thousands of compounds, all highly toxic to insects, have been synthesized. Unfortunately, all but a very few are also highly poisonous to humans and animals. In any case, there could be no certainty that the use of new insecticides would not result in the repetition of a similar cycle of events. In this case it seems that the costs and benefits are so finely balanced as to constitute an almost insoluble problem.

**4.5
CONCLUSION**

Having considered briefly some of the many new products of the chemical industries in the period 1870–1950 we should be able to make tentative responses to at least some of the questions raised in chapters 1 and 2. First, you will recall that the question of where the impetus for scientific and technological change comes from was raised. For the chemical industries we have identified various influences ranging from consumer demand, the profit motive, military requirements, the demands of war, the economic survival of an industry with a product looking for markets, to pure scientific research and technical development. Usually more than one of these was involved, but in every case the objective was to invent new materials or develop old ones in order to solve problems or stimulate and satisfy demands. Then the question of why some technological developments occurred in certain places rather than others was raised. In the case of the chemical industries it seems clear that many different circumstances were usually involved. Thus, artificial silk manufacture flourished in Britain, in part, at least, because we already had an extensive and highly developed cotton textiles industry which was in some difficulties in the 1920s and 1930s. Coal-tar dyes, though closely related to the manufacture of textiles and first discovered in Britain in 1856, later developed in Germany partly because the study of organic chemistry and especially the training of chemists for industry was better organized there. In Britain, while there was plenty of chemical training available in the universities and technical institutions, it was not well integrated with the needs of industry. Moreover, the British chemical industry was geared towards the manufacture of inorganic materials, whereas in Germany the organic chemicals industry was further advanced and it was from the latter that so many of the new materials were derived.

Two of the materials we have mentioned, namely, celanese and polythene, were first brought into large-scale production for military purposes in wartime. After the war new uses were sought for these materials, either to ensure the economic survival of a company, or simply to make use of valuable production capacity. British celanese developed at Spondon in Derbyshire in the 1920s because that was where Dreyfus's cellulose acetate plant had been established during the First World War, while polythene was made almost exclusively in America and Britain up to 1955 because these countries had developed the manufacturing capacity for this material during the Second World War.

We have not paid much attention to the economics of the chemical industries, but clearly this is also an important determinant for the development of new products. The availability and cost of raw materials, for example, may make the introduction of new materials either necessary or economically desirable. In the examples we have considered, the rising cost of imported raw cotton contributed to the development of rayon in the early years of the twentieth century, while the increasing production of coal-tar by the gas industry throughout the period made it possible to manufacture relatively cheaply many organic compounds which could be substituted for more costly natural ones. Sometimes a new material made from an expensive raw material has been introduced on a limited scale because its properties justified its cost for particular purposes. Polythene made from ethylene derived from fermentation alcohol was an example of this, but when much cheaper ethylene from petroleum became available in the 1950s and the price of polythene fell, new uses were found for it ('cling film' for example) and the market in this new material expanded rapidly creating additional economies of scale.

Another economic problem which plagues chemical manufacturers arises from the unavoidable noxious by-products of their processes. This raises social and environmental issues, for what is done with these by-products cannot be allowed to depend entirely on the whim of the chemical manufacturer, whose first considerations would probably be economic. Without effective control of effluents, serious environmental pollution results and chemical manufacturers must be constrained by law to render waste products from their processes harmless. The cost of treating effluents is often significant when compared with other costs of chemical manufacture and therefore has great importance for the economic viability of any given process. On the other hand, if it proves feasible to convert the by-products of a process into saleable products, overall profitability will be increased; the economic effects of these considerations are clearly important.

Chemical manufacturers are always seeking new products and improvements or cheaper methods of making established ones. If they are to remain in business, considerable financial resources must be allotted to research and technical development. This adds further to the cost of the product. Another important issue related to research and development is that of the vexed question of patents. In view of our discussion of several new drugs, it is interesting that this issue was so important for the German dyestuffs and pharmaceuticals industries which fought for the idea that their *products* rather than their processes should be the subject of patents. The success of the German industries in bringing about this change stimulated research to discover new dyes and drugs. All of these different issues, as well as the actual operating costs of the process, must be taken into account in fixing a competitive price for the end-product.

All of this, of course, assumes the general desirability of the products of the chemical industries, while at the same time raising questions about the nature of 'progress'. In the developed economies of the West it is now difficult to imagine everyday life without many of the products discussed in this essay, despite the ecological problems caused by the activities of the chemical industries. While in the past mistakes have been made both in industrial processes and the use of the products, it ought to be possible to avoid the worst of these problems in future developments, especially those in underdeveloped countries of the Third World. Unfortunately so far this has not been done. Other motives have too often influenced developments and important questions about the ideological neutrality or otherwise of such technological 'advances' are inevitably raised. Too often multinational chemical companies have expanded in underdeveloped countries for purely economic reasons, especially the ready availability of cheap labour, while governments have used science and technology to achieve economic, political or military domination over weaker nations and each other. Science and technology have therefore become pawns in the international struggle for power. But such issues, vital as they are, fall outside the scope of this essay.

REFERENCES

Anon (1962) *Landmarks of the Plastics Industry, 1862–1962*, ICI.

Baümler, E. (1968) *A Century of Chemistry*, Econ Verlag.

Bradbury, F.G. and Dutton, B.G. (1972) *Chemical Industry: Social and Economic Aspects*, Butterworths.

Caglioti, L. (1983) *The Two Faces of Chemistry*, MIT Press.

Carson, R. (1963) *Silent Spring*, Hamish Hamilton.

Couzens, E.G. and Varley, V.E. (1968) *Plastics in the Modern World*, Pelican.

Findlay, A. (1916) *Chemistry in the Service of Man*, Longman, seventh edition, 1947.

Hardie, D.W.F. and Davidson Pratt, J. (1966) *A History of the Modern British Chemical Industry*, Pergamon Press.

Katz, S. (1978) *Plastics, Designs and Materials*, Studio Vista.

Moncrieff, R.W. (1969) *Man-made Fibres*, Heywood Books.

Reuben, B.G. and Burstall, M.L. (1973) *The Chemical Economy: A Guide to the Technology and Economics of the Chemical Industry*, Longman.

Schmidt, J. and Rule, H.G. (1926) *A Textbook of Organic Chemistry*, fifth edition, 1947.

Smith, R.B. (1985) *The Development of a Medicine*, Macmillan.

Taylor, F.S. (1952) *The Century of Science*, Heinemann.

Taylor, F.S. (1957) *A History of Industrial Chemistry*, Heinemann.

Tilden, W.A. (1917) *Chemical Discovery and Invention in the Twentieth Century*, Routledge.

Various authors (1937) *Technological Trends and National Policy*, US Government Printing Office.

Williams, T.I. (1972) *The Chemical Industry*, EP Publishing.

5 MATERIALS: STEEL AND CONCRETE

Colin Chant

This essay deals with what may loosely be termed 'inorganic' materials. It concentrates on steel and reinforced concrete which, of all new materials, have surely made the largest impact on the built environment since 1870, and to that extent have helped shape all major facets of everyday life. There will be space only to mention in passing other new building materials, such as asbestos sheet and plasterboard. In attending exclusively to steelmaking and steel-related products (it being steel that reinforces concrete), I have also passed by the non-ferrous metals. I only note here the rapid growth in aluminium output (see Table 5.1). The availability of a strong but light metal that enabled large aircraft to get off the ground is a matter of obviously growing everyday import during the twentieth century, although in our period arguably the most obvious social impact of aviation was extraordinary: the bombing of civilian targets in wartime (see section 6.3).

Table 5.1   World production of major non-ferrous metals and steel (tons)

	1875	1900	1950
Copper	130,000	525,000	2,523,000
Lead	320,000	850,000	1,674,000
Zinc	165,000	480,000	1,819,000
Tin	36,000	85,000	162,000
Nickel	500	8,000	183,000
Aluminium	–	7,300	1,566,000
Steel	1,800,000	28,000,000	191,000,000

(Dennis, 1963, p.127; Warren, 1975, p.19)

The place of steel in the everyday life of our period is at once more central, and more deeply rooted in the first phase of industrialization. Typically, the companies that produced wrought iron, the major structural material of the First Industrial Revolution, went on to manufacture its counterpart in the Second: bulk steel. In the first part of this essay I shall look at the effects of this technological transition on labour, above all in the United States, which grew to be the largest steel-producing nation. The emphasis then shifts from new processes of steelmaking and the everyday world of industrial work, to new products and their parts in an array of everyday contexts. I begin with high-speed tool steel and its relations with wider change in the labour process in mechanical engineering; I then look in rather more detail at the effects of the uses of structural steel in the built environment, and its close relative and rival, reinforced concrete. Needless to say, there were numerous other contexts in which new materials and everyday life met; some of the most important will be dealt with in subsequent chapters.

A number of issues discussed in chapters 1 and 2 are potentially relevant to these subjects: in this essay, I deal explicitly with changes in the nature of industrial work, and more generally with the question of causality. For example, was new steelmaking technology entirely responsible for concomitant industrial conflict? And did new building materials and techniques dictate a high-rise dystopia?

5.1
THE APOGEE OF
WROUGHT IRON

Iron was the foremost structural material of the First Industrial Revolution. Given Britain's lead in industrial technology, it is not too surprising that its iron industry's output in 1870 exceeded that of the rest of the world combined. This supremacy rested also on a favourable disposition of natural resources, and on transportation advantages. Thus, iron ore, and coking coal suitable for smelting it, as well as limestone for fluxing out impurities, were found in close proximity. Moreover, Britain was not only well endowed with inland waterways, but as a small island was well positioned to exploit foreign markets in the industrializing decades before railways, when it was still several times dearer to transport goods by land than by water. The very success of the British export trade guaranteed its own eventual end; for the wrought-iron rails on which the boom was founded helped overcome the land distances between coke and ore deposits which had hindered the development of industries abroad.

Keeping in mind that the British iron and steel industry would shortly be overtaken in output by its American and German competitors, let us survey briefly the labour process in the British ironworks dominating the first years of our period. The range of employment in the iron industry as a whole was extensive, reflecting the complexity of the mature ironworks, and the several stages and divergent paths from iron ore to finished metal product. Take as an example the largest mid-nineteenth-century ironworks in the world, at Dowlais near Merthyr Tydfil. In 1866, the company employed 8,500 workpeople; of these, about 4,000 laboured with picks and shovels in the company's mines and quarries, amassing the ironstone, coking coal and limestone to fill the throats of the blast furnaces. About a thousand others worked in ancillary occupations associated with the company's many steam engines, its internal railway and road networks, its various buildings (including church and schools), and its team of workhorses (Birch, 1967, pp.255–56).

The remaining 3,000 or more were directly or closely associated with the main flow of iron through the works. The principal nodes of activity were the blast furnaces and associated foundries; the puddling forges; and the rolling mills. In such enterprises there was a very small number of managers as such; rather, the company directly employed a few experienced forehands who were responsible for the quality and output of iron at each stage of the production process, and for the payment and training of a team of younger underhands, providing their successors in the hierarchies of ironworking. Because of their managerial responsibilities as subcontractors of labour, as well as their higher-than-average remuneration for manual work in industry, these skilled forehands were among the so-called aristocrats of nineteenth-century labour. As we shall see, their methods of work and social and economic status would shortly be undermined by nascent bulk-steelmaking techniques. To understand these developments, we need to look a little more closely at the main stages of ironmaking, though some of the technical niceties must be overlooked.

The first main category of skilled ironworkers were the furnace keepers. Their area of responsibility was the blast furnace, at the start of our period an awesome ironclad brick-built structure some sixty feet or more in height, inside which a continuous column of burning coke, iron ore and limestone descended against a forced blast of air. Several tons of smelted iron were regularly tapped at the furnace hearth, as well as waste slag. The metal had been parted from the oxygen in the ore by the carbon in the coke, but in the process some of the carbon was absorbed. This fraction of carbon (3–4 per cent) reduced the melting temperature of the iron (1535°C. for pure iron down to about 1140°C.), so that it literally poured out of the blast furnace along a system of channels in a large sand-bed, each main channel fancifully likened to a sow and its litter. The resultant solid bars are consequently

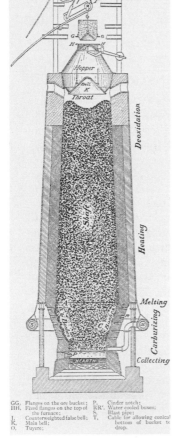

GG, Flanges on the ore bucket;   P,   Cinder notch;
HH, Fixed flanges on the top of   RR', Water cooled boxes;
     the furnace;   S,   Blast pipe;
I,   Counterweighted false bell;   T,   Cable for allowing conical
K,   Main bell;   bottom of bucket to
O,   Tuyere;   drop.

Figure 5.1
Section of Duquesne blast furnace. (From Encyclopaedia Britannica, *eleventh edition 1910–11, Cambridge University Press, Vol.14)*

finished wrought or bar iron
(sheets, bars, rails, plates, etc.)

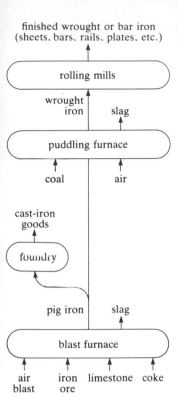

Figure 5.2
*Flow diagram showing
ironmaking.*

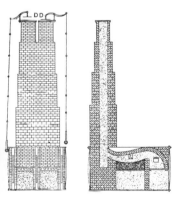

Figure 5.3
*Puddling furnace: external
view (left), vertical section
(right). (From* A History of
Technology, Vol.IV, *edited
by Charles Singer and others,
copyright Oxford University
Press, 1958)*

known as *pig iron*, though the generic name for this carbon-rich metal is *cast iron*. In this form, the iron could be taken to the foundry, relatively easily remelted, and poured into moulds specially crafted by the founders to obtain almost any shape of cast-iron product, endlessly repeated if need be.

Despite the economies of what was potentially a mass production process, no more than 30 per cent of overall pig-iron output found its way at this time into cast-iron goods. The uses of cast iron are restricted by its properties, for although very strong in compression it is brittle (thus a cast-iron bar can support a considerable weight along its length, as a column, but not across it, as a girder); nor can it be shaped by hammering or rolling, hot or cold. Before it can be rendered malleable in this way, the smelted iron must be refined: its carbon content must be drastically reduced. The competition between wrought iron and bulk steel in the 1870s and 1880s was about the most effective means of refining pig iron.

It may help at this point to use an otherwise inappropriate organic metaphor for ironmaking, seeing its roots in the coal and ironstone mines, and limestone quarries, with the blast furnace as the common trunk. The foundry is a lesser branch, the main branch being the puddling forge, the domain of the most numerous of the skilled ironworkers, the master puddlers, and the source of malleable or wrought iron. Here the pig iron was reheated in a number of small furnaces to oxidize out as much as possible of the carbon absorbed in the blast furnace. These coal-fired puddling furnaces, invented in the 1780s by Henry Cort, completed the transition from charcoal to coal in British ironmaking (a process beginning with coke-smelting). About the same time, steam engines began to replace water wheels for raising the air blast, lifting the hammers and turning the rolling mills. By these means, a rural scattering of separate furnaces and forges was transformed during the First Industrial Revolution into a highly concentrated industry at the coalfields.

Back at the blast furnaces, the keepers oversaw much repetitive, back-breaking work, as armies of unskilled labourers wheeled and shovelled mountains of raw materials and slag, and shifted tons of solid pig iron. But it is generally accepted that the most arduous work took place in the puddling forge under conditions of extreme temperature fluctuation (the forge being a roofed but otherwise open working space). This was not simply because of the need to work six batches of iron or 'heats' in a shift, but because each heat demanded in its 1½-hour course thirty minutes of strenuous stirring of the molten metal by the puddler and his underhand. This effort, moreover, intensified, for as the metal yielded its carbon content, consequently its melting temperature rose, and it would stiffen, resisting further manipulation.

After preliminary hammering and rolling, the wrought iron went to the rolling mill proper to be forced into a variety of saleable shapes: rails, bars, plates, sheet and so on. Each characteristic cross-section required its individual rolling mill, housing a pair of appropriate shaped rolls (Figure 5.4), and its own team of workers, again led by a skilled forehand, the master roller. Considerable manual labour was involved in feeding the mill with hot iron, catching it on the other side and returning it for another pass on the standard non-reversing mills of the period. Nevertheless the output of these steam-driven mangles of the wrought-iron trade far exceeded that of the puddling furnaces, five or six of which might be needed to feed one mill. There were in consequence far fewer rollers than puddlers, and rolling skills were more highly rewarded; this was a situation which often led to disunity among the ironworkers, of whom the puddlers were by far the most militant.

The militancy of the puddlers was certainly one element in the ironmasters' growing dissatisfaction with the puddling furnaces, which in technical and economic terms became a bottleneck in the wrought-iron trade. While the average annual output of the British blast furnace had risen from 1,500 tons

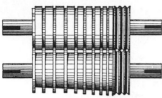

*Figure 5.4
Grooved rollers for bar-
making. (From* A History of
Technology, *Vol.IV, edited
by Charles Singer and others,
copyright Oxford University
Press, 1958)*

in 1805 to about 9,000 by 1870, the output of a puddling furnace was limited by the physical capacities of the puddlers, and remained at a maximum of 1,000 tons of wrought iron, the only significant improvement being a change in furnace lining which reduced the wastage of iron and improved the quality of the product. The only way to meet the accelerating demand for wrought iron was to construct yet more puddling furnaces and take on more puddlers. From about 1860 many attempts were made to mechanize the puddlers' manual exertions, without success; the least unsuccessful was the American Samuel Danks' rotary furnace, of which seventy-four were being built in 1872 in Britain, at a time when there were over 7,000 standard puddling furnaces (Carr and Taplin, 1962, pp.38, 57). It is significant that at this time demand was increasing for wrought-iron armour plating to match developments in artillery; and that the 1860s was a time of unprecedented industrial conflict in the British iron trade. In 1869, the Duke of Devonshire spoke to the British Iron and Steel Institute of 'constant and increasing difficulties in dealing with the puddlers' (Carr and Taplin, 1962, p.56). In the event, the means of solving these difficulties lay not with the mechanization of puddling, but with the opportunities for mechanization throughout the industry offered by the new bulk-steelmaking techniques.

5.2
THE ADVENT OF BULK STEEL

The British wrought-iron trade reached its zenith, in number of puddling furnaces and wrought-iron output, during the years 1870–75. As early as the 1850s and 1860s, new technologies were being developed which would transform the industry and bring into existence a range of new ferrous materials partly definitive of the so-called Second Industrial Revolution, and partly instrumental in the new manufacturing processes connoted by that term. It was some years before any of these materials were competitive in cost with wrought iron; but during the 1880s the puddling furnace gave way under the joint impact of two new bulk-steelmaking techniques: the Bessemer converter (1856) and the Siemens open-hearth furnace (1864–67).

The superiority of these methods lay in the fact that the charged metal was maintained in a molten state throughout. As we saw, the central fact which set the pace of the wrought-iron industry – the arduous and skilled nature of puddling – was bound up with the stiffening of the iron as its carbon content reduced. Moreover, the end-product as a result always incorporated rolled-out threads of slag, as it was impossible to expel the entire detritus of impurities from the pasty ball which was plucked from the furnace and delivered to the steam hammer and rolling mill. Hence the characteristic fibrous structure of wrought iron and, advantageously, its corrosion resistance and tensile strength (unlike cast iron, it resists stretching forces, but tends to buckle under compression). If, however, the metal remained in its molten state, complete separation from the slag would be possible affording a material of greater all-round strength. Moreover, furnaces of several tons' capacity could be constructed (the end-result of a 1½-hour 'heat' in a puddling furnace being four 'balls' of a hundredweight or so), and the molten refined metal cast into ingots, instead of being hammered into shape. The opportunities for reducing costs, including labour, were rich indeed.

The two new refining vessels employed distinctive means of raising the additional heat required to maintain decarburized iron in a molten state. Most striking and startling was the Bessemer converter, the action of which was literally based upon an upward blast of cold air through several tons of molten pig iron. But how could cold air raise the temperature of hot metal? Henry Bessemer's counterintuitive process (anticipated by the commercially unsuccessful Kentucky ironmaster William Kelly in 1851), worked because reactions between oxygen in the air blast, and carbon and silicon in the metal, give out heat (are exothermic), sufficient to keep the charge molten

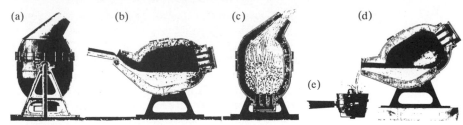

throughout the brief, violent blow of less than thirty minutes. From the ironmasters' point of view, the appeal of the new converter was that it acted without fuel. Moreover, far from requiring the constant incursions of troublesome puddlers, the process restricted intervention by the blowers to appropriate orientations of the vessel and control of the blow from a raised platform (the 'blower's pulpit').

Henry Bessemer (1813–98) was typical of the nineteenth-century generalist professional inventor, with a medley of patents to his name. His departure into ironmaking was stimulated by the Crimean War, a golden opportunity for him to turn his inventive flair to further profit by the devising of more powerful and effective artillery guns. It was the inability of existing guns to cope with his patented self-revolving shot which led him to seek a metal with the characteristics of wrought iron 'and yet capable of being run into a mould or ingot in a fluid condition' (Bessemer, 1905, p.138).

The open-hearth furnace was altogether subtler, more secret and unspectacular in its action than the Bessemer converter. Hidden beneath the bath of molten metal were firebrick regenerators, which recovered and stored the heat of waste gases resulting from the initial combustion of coal-gas fuel. Each regenerator in turn gave up its stored heat to supplement the heat derived directly from the fuel; in this way, the charge could be maintained in a molten state for hours on end (typically about fourteen), a marked contrast with the brief, volcanic climax of the Bessemer converter. The reaction could in consequence be controlled, and the chemical properties of the charge tested and adjusted as necessary. Thus the crucial skills were now those of trained analytical chemists who were employed in growing numbers in the steel industry, a reflection also of the recent emergence of a science of metals. We should note, though, that a degree of manual skill was still exercised by the melters, who charged and tapped the furnaces.

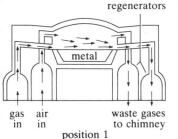

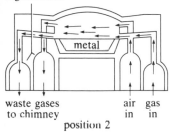

The main authors of the open-hearth process, Charles William Siemens (1823–83) and his younger brother Frederick (1826–1904), had an altogether firmer basis in scientific theory than Bessemer. Their elder brother Werner founded the Siemens-Halske electrical enterprise, and William himself was trained in science at Göttingen University. The two brothers emigrated to England in the 1840s, bringing with them a continental preoccupation with fuel economy foreign to British ironmasters luxuriating in cheap and accessible coal. William Siemens' express motivation was to discover more economical ways of extracting useful iron. He observed that 'the process of puddling, as practised at present, is extremely wasteful in iron and fuel, immensely laborious, and yielding a metal only imperfectly separated from its impurities' (Carr and Taplin, 1962, p.32).

During our period, the Bessemer and open-hearth processes co-existed, but in the long run, the fuel cost disadvantage of the open hearth was more than outweighed by its power (unlike the Bessemer converter) to digest considerable proportions of scrap iron and steel, as well as by its greater versatility as engineers increasingly demanded custom-made steels of precise composition. The Bessemer converter was at its relative peak when demand for steel rails predominated, but was gradually overtaken by the open hearth in all the leading producer countries during our period (in Britain this happened in 1894, in the United States in 1908, and after the First World War in Germany).

We should not overlook a further innovation of crucial significance for the worldwide diffusion of bulk-steelmaking technology. A problem which had threatened to kill the Bessemer converter at birth was its inability (unlike the puddling furnace) to refine pig iron extracted from ores with an appreciable phosphorus content. (Phosphorus renders iron and steel brittle.) It was soon realized that the phosphorus could be taken out in slag at these unprecedented temperatures, provided the conventional *acidic* siliceous furnace linings were replaced by a chemically *basic* material which would not react with the basic slag (bases by definition combine readily with acids). An appropriate material, calcined bricks of dolomite, was discovered in 1878 by Sidney Gilchrist Thomas (1850–85), assisted by a cousin, Percy Gilchrist, who was a trained analytical chemist. Thomas himself was an amateur; he was stimulated by a chemistry lecturer's casual remark during an evening class at Birkbeck College in London that anyone who could eliminate phosphorus in the Bessemer process would make a fortune. Basic linings were applicable both in Bessemer converters and open hearths, and their first commercial use in 1879 marks the point where all ores could be turned to the production of bulk steel. This was of particular significance on the European mainland, where ores were largely of medium to high phosphorus content; without the basic process, the growth of the German industry in particular would have been stunted by the need to import non-phosphoric Bessemer, or haematite, ores.

Before we consider the social ramifications of these briefly sketched innovations, a word about the novelty of the new steel products. They bore the generic name steel rather than iron, but steel had been produced since antiquity, albeit in small amounts and at considerable cost. At the start of our period, traditional steelmaking was a small, highly labour-intensive offshoot of the main branch of wrought-iron manufacture. There were two principal techniques practised in tool and cutlery centres like Sheffield. In *cementation* furnaces, wrought iron was effectively baked in a charcoal jacket; the absorbed carbon was then distributed throughout the metal by repeated breaking, piling and reheating. In *crucible* furnaces, a superior cast, slag-free steel was obtained by melting a few pounds of the carburized wrought iron in special clay crucibles. Although most of this steel went into small items, the near-simultaneous teeming of a multitude of crucibles could give a large ingot but at a commercially prohibitive cost.

We are in any case talking here of steel in its old, easily definable sense, of a ferrous material of carbon content (and incidentally melting temperature) between that of wrought iron and cast iron, and possessed of a happy blend of their respective qualities of malleability and hardness. But the immediate product of a Bessemer blow was not steel in that sense since, like wrought iron, it was an almost wholly decarburized metal. Effectively a slag-free version of wrought iron, but with greater all-round strength, it acquired the name and aura of steel, albeit somewhat controversially at the time. Quite soon, a distinction was made between *mild steels* and *carbon steels* of more traditional composition. The latter were as readily obtained in bulk by the addition after the Bessemer blow of cast-iron alloys, or with greater precision by the controlled cooking of the open hearth. One effect, therefore, of the new refining techniques was to confuse the previously tidy division between cast iron, steel and wrought iron. From the redrawn matrix of ferrous materials, mild steel should really be classed as a new material, not merely an old one available in bulk. Equally new were the fast-expanding range of custom-made *alloy steels* produced in bulk by the open hearth, and from the early years of the twentieth century with great purity by highly-mechanized electric furnaces.

**5.3
STEELMAKING AND
LABOUR**

The era of wrought iron and the world supremacy of the British industry were approximately coterminous. The yielding of this lead to the Americans was inevitable, once their own vast sources of metallurgical raw materials had been unlocked. That this took place as soon as 1890 is testimony to the extraordinary tenacity with which American companies exploited the new steelmaking technology. And nowhere else was this technology more dramatically brought to bear on the everyday world of the ironworker.

In 1870, world output of steel of all kinds was around 700,000 tons, little more than a tenth of wrought-iron production. A mere 69,000 tons were made in the United States, of which 38,000 were Bessemer, and a tiny 1,000 open hearth. By 1910, when the process of mechanizing the American industry was more or less complete, the corresponding figures were 26.1 million tons overall, 9.4 million Bessemer, and 16.5 million open hearth (Temin, 1964, pp.270–71). Essential to the American success story was a remarkable transportation network of railways and lake shipping connecting up the gargantuan ore bodies of Michigan and Minnesota in the Lake Superior region, and the coking-coal deposits of the Connellsville district of Western Pennsylvania. These raw materials converged upon the steelworks of the lower Great Lake ports, and above all on Pittsburgh, Pennsylvania, the centre of traditional steelmaking.

Equally necessary was the vast domestic appetite for metal, initially for the building of a transcontinental railway system, and latterly for the booming automobile industry; throughout the period, however, demand diversified, the interim leading consumer being the building and construction industry. The conditions for rapid growth also engendered cut-throat competition, and what David Brody has dubbed an 'economizing temper', or a ruthlessly rational attitude to the costs of steel production, whether plant or labour, an attitude that regularly startled visiting British steelmen.

In no one was this economizing temper so consistently displayed as in Andrew Carnegie, whose Pittsburgh company had grown into the largest factor in the American industry by the end of the nineteenth century, and who so upset and unnerved his competitors that in 1901 they connived with leading Wall Street financiers to buy him out. In the meantime Carnegie and his partners had assumed complete or virtual control of all the sources of raw materials and transportation systems they needed for the production of semi-finished steel, and taken every opportunity to mechanize the through-put of materials from the mine to the market. In so doing Carnegie reduced the traditional ironmaking craft unions to impotence, an achievement even more grandiose in conception than the philanthropic works of his retirement years.

The secret of Carnegie's success was his obsession with reducing costs (Wall, 1970, p.337). At all his plants costs and production figures were recorded daily, and managers held accountable. Existing plant was scrapped where any new investment might reduce the eventual price of rolled steel by a few cents, and certainly investment in plant took precedence over any sharing out of the rapidly growing profits. This remarkably austere approach to the business of iron and steelmaking was unprecedented, and enabled Carnegie to undercut his rivals' prices, run his mills full in periods of slump, and at such times buy up competing mills at knockdown cost.

With Carnegie in the market, his competitors were obliged to emulate his methods. But it would be wrong to continue in this heroic vein, as though this recently emigrated Scots-born weaver's son had singlehandedly turned the American iron and steel industry on its head. Carnegie was simply the most brilliant and most uncompromising exploiter of the new labour process opened up by the new steelmaking techniques. Previously, the pace of the iron industry had been set by the skills and manual capacities of the puddlers and rollers, on whose performance the quality of wrought iron depended. But the displacement of the puddling furnaces by the Bessemer converter and open hearth overturned the relations between man and machine, and enabled employers to mechanize and accelerate the entire journey from raw materials to markets in the ceaseless drive to increase productivity.

Some of the most striking examples of mechanization affected the transit of iron ore from the Lake Superior region by rail, lake and canal. The discovery of vast, rich and accessible deposits of ore in the Mesabi range in Minnesota in 1890 led later in that decade to their stripping by huge steam shovels in open pits, though already by the 1870s in the existing Michigan mines, hand picks and gunpowder were giving way to power drills and nitroglycerine. From the 1880s, iron- and then steel-hulled bulk lake carriers took on the business of transporting the ore down to the lower ports. Loading was easily mechanized once the orefields had been connected to the upper ports by rail, the ore being poured down chutes from rail cars. Unloading was a considerable labour-intensive bottleneck, as gravity no longer assisted. Steam-powered hoists were used as early as the 1860s, but the iron tubs still had to be filled by shovellers. The greatest impact on productivity was effected by the Hulett ore unloader at the beginning of the twentieth century: resembling a 'mechanical praying mantis' (Wright, 1969, p.153), it incorporated an electrically-powered clam-shell bucket which scooped the ore out of the carrier's hold, and deposited it in waiting rail cars. Following its introduction, fifteen times as much ore was unloaded per employee (Brody, 1960, p.29); in other words, there were fewer employees.

At the steelworks itself, blast-furnace output continued to soar. We saw that British furnaces were producing an annual average of 9,000 tons each in 1870; but by 1909, the American average was about 100,000 tons (Carr and Taplin, 1962, p.209). This was partly because the practical skills of the furnace keeper were increasingly over-ridden by scientific expertise; Carnegie, who was one of the first to appoint an analytical chemist to oversee blast-furnace operations, boasted: 'nine-tenths of the uncertainties of pig-iron making were dispelled under the burning sun of chemical knowledge' (Oliver, 1956, p.320). The rise was also made possible by constructing furnaces up to heights of 100 feet, with wider hearths and more powerful blowing engines. These new heights ruled out manual charging; powered skip hoists now raised the raw materials to the furnace throat. At the start of the twentieth century, the Uehling pig-casting machine made further inroads into the army of labourers: an endless chain of moulds received molten iron from a ladle, drawing the iron through a water tank or spray before dumping the solid bars, untouched by human hand, into a rail car. The American metallurgist H.M. Howe eulogized the machine as follows:

> Besides a great saving of labour, only partly offset by the cost of repairs, these machines have the great merit of making the management independent of a very troublesome set of labourers, the hand pig-breakers, who were not only absolutely indispensable for every cast and every day, because the pig iron must be removed promptly to make way for the next cast of iron, but very difficult to replace because of the great physical endurance which their work requires. (Howe, 1911, p.816)

Alternatively, metal was conveyed from blast furnace to Bessemer converter or open hearth in its molten state to avoid the expense of remelting solid pig iron. This was made possible by the Jones mixer, patented in 1888 by Captain William Jones, a prized Carnegie employee: the mixer was a giant heated reservoir sufficient in capacity to even out the variable composition of molten metal from a number of blast furnaces, an essential stage if reliable steel was to be obtained.

*Figure 5.7
Hoist at Lysaghts foundry,
Scunthorpe, manufactured by
Lilleshall Co. (Archives of
Museum of Iron, Ironbridge
Gorge Museum)*

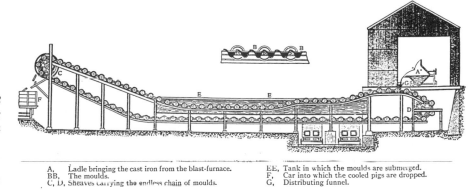

*Figure 5.8
Diagram of pig-casting
machine. (From
Encyclopaedia Britannica,
eleventh edition 1910–11,
Cambridge University Press,
Vol.14)*

A,	Ladle bringing the cast iron from the blast-furnace.	EE,	Tank in which the moulds are submerged.
BB,	The moulds.	F,	Car into which the cooled pigs are dropped.
C, D,	Sheaves carrying the endless chain of moulds.	G,	Distributing funnel.

The upshot of these changes was a twelve-fold increase in the productivity of men employed at the furnaces in little more than two decades after 1887. Further reductions in labour took place in the Bessemer and open-hearth departments: electric cranes were used to feed the converters and the electric Wellman charging machine empowered one man to charge a seventy-five ton open-hearth furnace in less than an hour, estimated at a thirty-five fold increase in productivity (Brody, 1960, p.30). The transition of refined metal to the rolling mills was speeded up by casting ingots directly on to waiting rail cars. Improvements to rolling-mill practice are too numerous to document

here, but the guiding principle was again the reduction of human intervention, and of reheating costs, the metal perhaps being passed both ways
through a set of rolls, or accelerated through a continuous train of rolling
mills. It was another Carnegie lieutenant, Alva Dinkey, who pioneered the
use of electricity to drive feed tables taking the metal to and from the rolling
mill, thereby displacing the rollers' hooks and tongs.

By some of the above means, the Carnegie Company was able by the
1890s to progress the smelted iron from blast furnace to rolled steel rail in
one 24-hour heat, a feat of integration and control which led one historian
to declare that 'continuous steel production marked the beginning of the
assembly line' (Oliver, 1956, p.329). Be that as it may, it surely marked the
end of the ironworkers' craft skills. In this period of the perfection of the
new steelmaking technology, there was a significant reduction in labour and
a very small rise in real wages overall, set against a massive rise in output
(a little over 3 million tons in 1887, compared with 26 million in 1910). At
Carnegie's Homestead Works, the biggest in the world with a steelmaking
capacity of 2 million tons, 2,900 men were needed to run the plant full in
1897, a drop of nearly a quarter since 1892. Compare this with the greater
numbers needed at the old wrought-iron giant Dowlais, with its capacity of
100,000 tons. In the twenty years after 1890 labour costs as a proportion of
the American industry's total manufacturing charges fell by nearly a third
from an already relatively low 22.5 per cent to 16.5 per cent: 'the proportional
reduction of labour cost was the principal achievement of the economizing
drive' (Brody, 1960, p.28).

Behind these bare figures lie notable changes in the social and economic
status of labour, and a remarkable shift in the balance of power between
labour and management. The effect of the new integrated steel technology
was to eliminate many unskilled tasks and also to reduce the level of highest
skills needed, as steelworkers increasingly became tenders of machines.
Mechanization resulted in an increasing proportion of semi-skilled workers,
28 per cent of all workers in a typical modern plant (Brody, 1960, p.40).

By 1910, the steelworkers' average annual wage of $697 was $46 higher
than the overall average in manufacturing industries; nevertheless, the twenty
years of high mechanization saw a real rise in incomes of only 3 per cent.
Behind these figures lay marked changes in differentials reflecting the relative
downgrading of the highest skills. In the early 1890s, a roller paid on output,
or 'tonnage', could earn seven times more than an unskilled labourer paid
on a daily rate unconnected with output. This disparity was partly a legacy
of the old subcontracting system of the iron trade, which in the United States
did not survive the 1880s; but it also measured the superior bargaining
position of the skilled steelworkers, making up less than 5 per cent of labour.
By 1900, however, this differential had narrowed to three times:

> Technological change saw the reduction of such wage spreads. In addition
> to changing the character of their work, the use of machinery . . . substan-
> tially weakened the bargaining position of the skilled workers. Since
> management did not attribute productivity increases to labour but to capital
> investment, tonnage rates were substantially reduced. Between 1889 and
> 1908, rates in certain positions declined 60% and 70% . . . (Hogan, 1971,
> Vol.2, pp.445–46)

There was little enough that the skilled steelworkers could do to remedy
their weakened position. The period of mechanization was notorious for a
series of strikes in the steel industry, the most sensational involving a pitched
battle between strikers and hired Pinkerton's guards on the Monongahela
river at Carnegie's Homestead Works in 1892. The upshot of these disputes

was the emasculation of the Amalgamated Association of Iron and Steel Workers, a craft union originating in 1875 among the skilled furnace keepers, puddlers and rollers of the old wrought-iron trade. Before the Homestead strike, the Association was probably the strongest organization in the American labour movement, and may have succeeded in organizing half the skilled workers in the steel industry; by 1914, its membership having dwindled to 6,500, it was judged by a contemporary observer to be tolerated by the employers only as an insurance against the emergence of a more effective organization (Brody, 1960, p.75). By 1910, US Steel (the giant billion-dollar corporation formed in 1901 after Carnegie was bought out) had become an open-shop corporation, after a final, protracted and unavailing strike in 1909; it remained so until 1937.

The old union had been undermined by the introduction of new technology, together with the employers' well-attested tactics of strikebreaking, espionage and blacklisting (Brody, 1960, pp.82–84, 251–55; Wall, 1970, p.579), as well as the union's own craft exclusiveness, which ruled out any concerted action with the unskilled workers. Crucially, craft skills were no longer at a premium, and it was now possible in the event of a dispute for the employers to bring in unskilled men and train them quite rapidly to operate the new machinery. Thus, at a time of massive immigration from Europe, large numbers of Slavic workers were taken on. This influx intensified the divisive rift between skilled and unskilled, the Anglo-Saxon skilled worker bitterly resenting the non-English-speaking unskilled 'hunkies'. The immigrants for their part were reluctant to get involved in any dispute which might mean a loss of earnings, and acquiesced in very low pay and a seven-day working week as a temporary hardship before their expected return to Europe.

The second half of our period saw some overall improvement in working conditions. This was partly because US Steel was nervous about antitrust legislation given its near-monopoly position, and hence responsive to public criticism of its policies. US Steel took the lead in welfare provision, its accident compensation plan and pensions programme representing 'a leaven of benevolence . . . bringing a measure of stability to the labor system' (Brody, 1960, p.147). Sunday work was conceded relatively early, but the twelve-hour shift was defended against increasingly hostile public opinion until the personal intervention of President Harding in 1923. Mechanization continued to undermine the Amalgamated Association; one of the last areas of craft skill was the tinplate and sheet-rolling trade, but in 1924 the American Rolling Mill Company perfected the widestrip continuous sheet mill, rendering many of these manual skills obsolete (Brody, 1960, p.278). The domination of the American labour movement by craft unions partly explains the extension into the 1930s of the so-called non-union era of the American steel industry. The end of this era cannot be attributed to any outstanding technical innovation, but to the changed economic and political conditions of the Great Depression. After substantial trading losses in the early 1930s, the steel companies were anxious to avoid labour confrontation; the influx of East European labour had been stemmed by immigration laws, and social divisions among workers had lessened over the years; but above all, New Deal legislation obliged employers to bargain with unions, and outlawed the repressive tactics which had doomed earlier strikes to failure. The non-union era in steel bears witness to the failure of a craft union to adapt to a changing labour process, and it was an industrial union, one representing all workers in the industry, the Steel Workers Organizing Committee, which stepped into the breach: 'mass-production unionism had to await a reordering of the established framework of American labor relations' (Brody, 1965, p.188).

The choice of topic, the mechanization of the American steel industry in the first half of our period, accentuates the determining role of new technology. Technical change was indeed decisive in this period of intense competition and expanding markets, but after about 1910, productivity stabilized, and the prospects of further economies through technical improvements diminished. Thereafter, economies resulted through the specialization of mills and rationalization of organization and distribution which giant corporations like US Steel were able to effect. Technology, therefore, was not the exclusive determinant of industrial change throughout the period; nor, to reinforce the point, did the same technology have identical results in other national contexts.

If we go back to our starting-point, the British wrought-iron trade, a rather different pattern can be discerned. Anxious to avoid the industrial strife of the 1860s, employers and union representatives in England thereafter formed conciliation boards to set wage rates, an early precedent for collective bargaining, and an indicator of generally pacific industrial relations and flourishing union activity in the industry during our period. In spite of some inter-union conflict the transition from wrought iron to steel was less traumatic than in the United States; indeed, the old subcontracting system persisted in the melting shops of many steelworks right up to the First World War. Even then it was replaced by a system of promotion controlled by the union, and based strictly on seniority; a system that preserved much of the élitism of subcontracting and similarly discouraged 'a sense of communality of interest between lower and senior grades from which trade-union strength is fostered' (Docherty, 1983, p.41).

Any proper comparison with the United States must take into account differences in union structure and history, ethnic composition of labour, employer attitudes, company size and the general political environment (Holt, 1977). One element of the comparison would be the British industry's lower investment in new technology, despite its early lead. Blast furnaces, Bessemer converters and open hearths were generally smaller and less productive, mechanization of the movement of materials less advanced, electrification and the utilization of basic linings delayed. The less rigorous exploitation of new technology in Britain helps to explain a less painful transition from the skilled, craft basis of wrought-iron manufacture, to the semi-skilled capital-intensive nature of bulk steelmaking. But this relatively low technological profile itself demands an explanation: indeed, historians have of late vigorously debated whether these investment decisions represented a failure of latter-day British entrepreneurs, or whether they were economically rational given the industry's markets, labour supply and access to raw materials. Whichever may be the case, technology is seen to be operating within characteristic social and economic constraints.

Doubtless the point could be further reinforced by looking at major industries on the European mainland. In Germany, as in America, large vertically-integrated steelmaking concerns quickly emerged, investing heavily in mechanization and large plant. Nevertheless, despite a notably harsh industrial regime, labour relations were on the whole as pacific as in Britain. Barrington Moore (1978, pp. 265–66) has compared the docility of the German steelworkers with the greater militancy of the miners, and attributed it to a technology and organization of work which created much greater divisions between workers. As we have seen, though, the same technology was associated with notable industrial conflict in the United States. It is more significant, perhaps, both that the supply of labour came more (as in Britain) from internal migration than was the case in the United States, and furthermore that industrialists and legislators recognized rather early the value of welfare provision in reconciling their workers to the rigours of steelmaking. Thus the virulently anti-socialist and anti-unionist armaments manufacturer, Alfred

Krupp, issued a *Generalregulativ* in 1872, binding his Essen workers to the firm in return for a paternalist package of company housing, health, accident and pension schemes (Manchester, 1969, pp.178–80).

It would be impossible in a short essay to establish a firm basis for comparison, but it should be clear that there are grounds for doubting any technological-determinist interpretation of the social impact of bulk-steelmaking technology. As we have seen, the same technology is associated with rather varying changes in industrial work practices in differing national contexts. Looking further back at the circumstances of the invention and adoption of these new techniques, circumstances including war, profit and the need to control labour, there are also grounds to doubt their autonomy and neutrality. Bulk steelmaking undoubtedly represented technological progress measured in terms of productivity and a range of valuable new products, but it was progress at the expense of craft skills and jobs (many of them admittedly unpleasant ones). For those in work, however, conditions in the long run improved as insurance programmes gave employers an incentive to reduce accidents and illness, shorter working hours compensated for the 'speed-up' of work brought by mechanization, and the less skilled were spared the exploitation practised by some of the old subcontractors.

**5.4
ALLOY STEELS**
The emphasis now shifts from the *processes* of steelmaking to the more diffuse effects in everyday life of its *products*. First, alloy steels, a class of materials the origins of which are almost entirely within our period. These are usually mixtures of steel and at least one of the non-ferrous metals, but the definition is somewhat arbitrary, as virtually all steel contains a fraction of metals like manganese. The point is that alloy steels contain enough of elements other than carbon to confer properties unavailable in carbon steels, such as unusual magnetic properties, extreme hardness, exceptional resistance to heat, wear or corrosion, and so on. As was noted before, bulk alloy steels were the province of the open-hearth furnace, whereas the old crucible process monopolized the manufacture of high-quality alloys in the first half of our period. The crucible furnaces, identified with the Sheffield area, continued in Britain up to 1950 and even beyond, but from the 1920s increasingly gave way to electric furnaces, in which the absence of fuel guaranteed freedom from contamination.

One of the first alloy steels, containing tungsten, was invented in 1868 at Coleford in the Forest of Dean by the skilled metallurgist Robert Forester Mushet (1811–91), and remained the prime material for metal cutting tools for the remainder of the century. From the late 1880s, steel companies exploited the hardness of nickel steels by manufacturing ever bigger shells and ever thicker and harder armour plate. A spin-off of this lethally spiralling trade was perhaps the most domestic of the new alloys, 'stainless steel', a corrosion-resistant high-chromium alloy. Its inventor Harry Brearley (1871–1948), of the Sheffield ordnance manufacturers Thomas Firth and Sons, discovered the property which made it so suitable for cutlery when testing it for rifle barrels in 1913.

Worth dwelling on in this section is the successor to Mushet's original tool steel, the so-called 'high-speed steel', containing a higher percentage of tungsten as well as chromium. This was developed in 1898 in association with J. Maunsel White by Frederick Winslow Taylor (1856–1915), now remembered principally as the originator of time-and-motion studies and scientific management. The new material was exceptionally heat-resistant, enabling cutting speeds of up to 500 feet per minute, more than three times the machining speed of tools in the 1890s, and more than ten times the speed of the first carbon-steel tools.

Existing machine tools were simply inadequate to exploit the potential of the material, and there ensued 'a complete revolution in the design and manufacture of machine tools during the early 1900s' (Carr and Taplin, 1962, p.554). The significance of this revolution in industrial work was its part in the general shift towards the breaking down and de-skilling of manufacturing processes, culminating in the assembly line. The assembly line was predicated upon exact interchangeability of parts, impossible without wholesale improvements in machine-tool design and materials. The turret lathe, milling machine and grinding machine brought the required precision of fit, at the same time reducing reliance on the individual judgement of the skilled engineer in both manufacture and assembly. An essential ingredient in this process of de-skilling was the substitution in the construction of machinery of steel for wrought iron, 'of a hard, smooth material, resistant to wear, for a comparatively soft metal, nervy in structure and irregular in abrasion' (Landes, 1969, p.299). High-speed steel as such can be seen as a significant accelerator in this complex set of developments, to be set alongside a new non-ferrous artificial grinding material, carborundum, first used in 1896, and harder than any known natural abrasive, excepting diamond.

It is difficult to see high-speed steel as an independent determinant in this flow of mutually reinforcing industrial changes, the more so when we consider its better-known discoverer, F.W. Taylor. In his own distinctive way, Taylor is as good an example as Carnegie of the rational, economizing temper of the period of high mechanization in the American steel industry. During the very period (at Midvale Steel in 1880s and at Bethlehem Steel in the 1890s) when he was engaged in methodical and painstaking experimental work on the optimum mix for a cutting alloy, he was also involved in the careful measurement of ironworkers' and lathe machinists' movements, and in the general analysis of the division of labour and the organization of work on the shop floor. As Landes (1969, pp.321–22) concludes: 'It is no coincidence that [Taylor] discovered high-speed steel . . . The point is that his search for an optimum pace of work led him to study and set standards of efficiency for every aspect of production.'

**5.5
STRUCTURAL STEELS**

The foregoing discussion of high-speed steel illustrates some of the difficulties in separating out the origins and impacts of new materials from the social-technological complex which they help to shape. Much the same problems arise when we turn our attention to the increasingly diverse range of products of the steel industry beyond the special engineering steels and alloys. In general, the twentieth century saw a sharply rising demand for *steel sheet*, not only for automobiles, but for domestic gadgets, notably the body shells of washing machines, refrigerators and cookers, and also for tinplate (tin-coated steel sheet) to cater for the booming tinned food market. New steel-making technology was a necessary ingredient in this market shift; but it was hardly the exclusive determinant of the social ramifications of automobiles, consumer durables or convenience foods. The aim of this section is to see whether such a case might be made for structural steels.

It is a broad truth that in the twentieth century, the automobile industry succeeded the railways as the main market for finished and semi-finished iron and steel products. But there was also an underlying theme of diversification of product. In the early 1880s, when Bessemer production was at its relative peak, more than 90 per cent of all rolled iron and steel in the United States was steel rails. Thereafter other sectors of output grew rapidly, notably: *plate and sheet* for shipbuilding, boilers, armour and tinplate; *wire* for nails, bridge cables, telegraph wire and barbed wire (an American invention of 1873 of vital importance for agriculture on the prairies, where wood was scarce); *tubes and pipes* for water supply and drainage, and for the gas and oil industries; *hoop* for barrels for the oil industry; and finally *structural steel* for the building and construction industry. We shall turn to this last industry in the remainder of the essay, and consider the extent to which new materials and associated production processes have transformed the built environment, and thereby helped shape everyday life.

The use of ferrous materials instead of, or in conjunction with, the established building materials of stone, wood, brick and glass, dates from the early decades of the First Industrial Revolution, when cast-iron bridges first appeared, and cast-iron columns were introduced in an attempt to make mills more fire-resistant. A striking everyday use of cast iron during the infancy of bulk steel was the large department store façade, common in large American cities from the mid-nineteenth century onwards. The two prime exponents of such buildings were the competitors James Bogardus (1800–74) and Daniel Badger (1806–84), Bogardus the more inventive, and Badger the more responsible for the characteristic appearance of up to six storeys of uniform rows of iron columns and spandrels imitating classical styles. Of greater structural significance were the interior cast-iron frames of these buildings: these carried much of the load usually supported in tall buildings by stout masonry walls, and went at least part of the way towards Bogardus' dream of a wholly cast-iron building.

What separates the pioneering efforts of Bogardus from the imposing slabs of the Manhattan skyline (in building rather than architectural terms) is precisely the fact that in his commercial buildings the metal frame was never fully load-bearing. In technical jargon, he failed to achieve full skeletal construction (no mere retrospective judgement, as this was his aim). The failure is significantly that of the materials. Large single beams were required: size was no problem with cast iron, but strength in tension was; wrought iron possessed the tensile strength, but because such small amounts issued from the puddling furnace, there were considerable problems in assembling a large enough mass to roll into the required length. Wrought-iron members in bridges, for example, were usually compounded of smaller elements bolted together. The availability of the massive cast ingot from the bulk-steelmaking processes was therefore of decisive importance in construction, though developments in rolling machinery were required before the great beams, joists and girders could be pressed into service. A key piece of equipment was the universal mill, in which an additional pair of rolls in the vertical plane supplemented the usual horizontal pair. First used at the start of our period for plate, it was adapted to the rolling of structural beams in 1877 by an Englishman, Henry Grey, though by now characteristically, it found application not in Britain but in Germany and the United States in the 1900s.

Again it was the Americans who were quickest to realize the full potential of the new structural steels, auspiciously in the construction of tall buildings. (The term 'skyscraper' was introduced in 1889, referring specifically to tall buildings in Chicago.) There was nothing new, of course, in having buildings of several storeys, nor in one of the prime stimuli for building high being escalating inner-city land values: hence the imposingly tall but narrow Victorian middle-class town house, built of traditional masonry and brick, and the working-class tenements of Liverpool, Glasgow and the capitals of Northern Europe. But the American skyscraper marked a discontinuity with the past, not simply because of the spectacular upward spurt of heights attained for commercial buildings, but because of the constructional revolution which facilitated this record-breaking and ostentatious drive.

The details of the corporate competition which spurred the architects of the 'cathedrals of commerce' in Chicago and New York need not concern us; more relevant to us are the economic and technical springboards of this near-literal take-off of the American building industry. The prime technical item in this development was the new load-bearing framework of steel

Figure 5.9
E.V. Haughwout & Co. store, 488–492 Broadway, New York, designed by J.P. Gaynor with ironwork by Daniel Badger. (Photo: Cervin Robinson for Historic American Buildings Survey, Library of Congress, Washington)

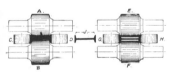

Figure 5.10
Grey's Mill for girder making. (From F.W. Harbord and J.W. Hall, sixth edition 1918, The Metallurgy of Steel. Vol II Mechanical Treatment, by J.W. Hall, Griffin)

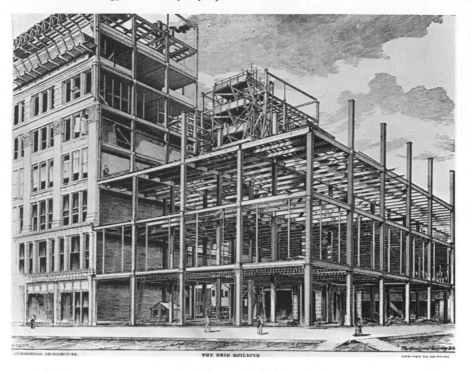

*Figure 5.11
Fair Store, Chicago, in
construction to show steel
framing. (From* Industrial
Chicago, Vol.II, *1891,
Goodspeed Publishing by
courtesy of Chicago Historical
Society)*

columns and girders; this could be raised to unprecedented heights without the widening at the base which set a practical limit to masonry walls, especially in the narrow plots of downtown New York and Chicago. It was the all-round strength of steel which enabled it not only to carry the weight of the roof, floors, walls and internal partitions, but also, given the appropriate bracing members, to withstand the buffeting of the wind, substantial at such heights, and moreover unpredictable where tall buildings jostled for scarce inner-city space.

The transfer of load from walls to steel skeleton reduced the function of the external wall to that of an infilling panel; and because both lightness and light became desiderata in the congested space of these American downtown areas, the chosen material came to be largely, or even wholly, sheet and plate glass, giving us in time the ubiquitous curtain-walled steel-and-glass office block of the mid-twentieth century. We should note also in passing the general change in the interior design of commercial and industrial buildings (for example, factories and warehouses) partly issuing from the all-steel load-bearing frame, and parallel developments in broad-span light steel roof trusses: internal work spaces could be much wider, now that architects and engineers could largely dispense with internal load-bearing columns, partition walls and brick arches. This was a development rich in antecedents and implications. It issued not only from technical conditions, but also from the need to maintain re-sale value with the minimum of industry-specific interior design, in a period of increasingly rapid obsolescence of plant and process, and changes in consumer demand. It tells us something too of increasing mechanization and supervision in office work, and of the increasing division of labour and flow of work in assembly-line manufacture.

Some of the points above apply as much, if not more, to the broad, open-plan, one- or two-storey commercial and industrial buildings made possible by steel framing, as well as to the tall buildings of the administrative metropolis. Returning to the latter, and their origins, we might at this point ponder over the load of historical causation which the preceding account appears to place on the new metal frame. First, we should note some of the contingencies

*Figure 5.12
New Turbine Hall, Berlin,
designed by Peter Behrens
1908–09 with wide-span steel
roof for overhead gantry and
window walls for increased
light. (Photo: AEG
Firmenarchiv, Frankfurt)*

which surround the inception of this structural innovation in the large cities of the United States. Rising site values stemming from the growing administrative activities of large companies had created the necessary economic conditions for building high in New York in the boom years following the end of the Civil War. From 1870, buildings in excess of five storeys were erected, but with the same mix of masonry load-bearing walls and partial interior iron-framing of the previous two decades; indeed, the design was if anything more conservative: 'the New York builders seldom trusted the iron frame that Bogardus saw rising to ten-mile heights' (Condit, 1960, p.43). It was not until the mid-1890s that Manhattan saw its first fully steel-framed skyscraper, an innovation which originated in Chicago, New York's Middle West commercial and financial rival. Ironically, Chicago had been reluctant to follow New York in the construction of cast-iron buildings; what few there were proved unable in 1871 to resist a calamitous fire fed by the preponderance of wooden buildings. The fire gutted the city's central area, and competition for prime inner-city sites intensified. The crisis was compounded by Chicago's unstable subsoil, which demanded that foundations and their supported structures be kept as light as possible.

Experiments in iron framing by the Chicago school of architects culminated in the controversial and epoch-making Home Insurance Building (1884–85) built by William le Baron Jenney (1832–1907). Originally a nine-storey building, the first six were framed with cast-iron columns and lintels, and wrought-iron beams, but during construction, Jenney gained permission to use for the remaining floors Bessemer steel beams manufactured by the Carnegie Steel Company. From 1890, fully steel-framed tall buildings proliferated in Chicago: not only office blocks, but apartment blocks, hotels and warehouses, thereby touching all facets of everyday life in that area.

We have seen, then, the importance of economics, geology and acts of God as well as technology, in the genesis of tall buildings; we should therefore take with more than a pinch of salt the ringing statement of the general history of technology: 'steel begat the skyscraper' (Derry and Williams, 1970, p.407). Even if we confine ourselves to technical antecedents, the skyscraper

Figure 5.14
Empire State Building, New York,
designed by Shreve, Lamb and
Harman, 1932. (Photo: Empire
State Building Co.)

Figure 5.13
Home Insurance Building,
Chicago, designed by William
Le Baron Jenney 1884–85,
before additions of 1891.
Demolished 1931. (Photo:
Chicago Historical Society)

has an assortment of competing parents, foremost among them the mechanical lift, without which the majority of the 102 storeys of the 'ultimate statement of verticality', the Empire State Building (1929–31), would have been strictly for the birds. The first safe lift (one with an automatic brake in the event of the rope's failure) was invented as early as 1852 by Elisha G. Otis (1811–61) and it helped to raise the heights of traditional buildings. This, however, was operated by a hydraulic motor; lifts fast enough for the new skyscrapers awaited the application of electric power in the late 1880s. The upwardly growing skyscraper was in any case increasingly dependent on a range of services apart from the lift, notably telephones, electric lighting, central heating, ventilation and water tanks for fire-fighting beyond the play of ground-based hoses.

**5.6
REINFORCED
CONCRETE**

Structural steel was a vital new material for the building of tall structures, but not the only one. At the outset another new material had literally a more fundamental role: the foundation of the Chicago Home Insurance Building was reinforced concrete. From the beginning of the twentieth century, this new material was to get out from beneath steel's heel, and rival it for the framing of large buildings. The term 'reinforced concrete' covers a variety of bonded aggregates (typically crushed stone and cement), strengthened by a ferrous material. The novelty of reinforced concrete lay in the mix of desirable properties achieved when existing materials were combined. Thus the all-round strength of steel was imitated by the combination of concrete's high compressive strength (like cast iron), and the compensating tensile strength of its initially wrought-iron, then steel, reinforcing bars, rods and wires. The first patents for concrete reinforced by iron rod or wire date from the mid-nineteenth century, and actually led to the construction of reinforced-concrete houses, one by W.B. Wilkinson in Newcastle upon Tyne about 1865, and another by William E. Ward at Port Chester, New York (1871–76).

It was only about 1880 that framing buildings with reinforced-concrete columns and beams became a practical proposition, once the stress characteristics of the new material were better understood, and more reliable cements developed. It was in France, Germany and Denmark that enthusiasm for the new material's potential was first kindled, at a time when European steel-making suffered from the problem of phosphoric ores. American engineers and architects were a little slower to use it, largely because of the advanced use of structural steel and, initially, a dependence on imports of cement from England. Eventually, American reinforced-concrete factories and grain silos would in their turn help inspire European modernist architecture (Banham, 1986). It is harder to explain British suspicion of the new material, a reaction which changed to little more than grudging acceptance in our period. Any analysis of this phenomenon would have to account for British resistance to modernist architecture, and also tackle the controversial problem of the reasons for the relative decline in British industrial performance.

Ideally, we should now explore in some depth the part played by reinforced concrete in shaping aspects of everyday life by looking at a representative sample of structures it helped create; but space is lacking and some general observations must suffice. At first, the upstart material supplemented structural steel in providing a light, fully load-bearing frame for tall buildings. But reinforced concrete had great versatility, which enabled it to outstrip steel and become one of the dominant construction materials. This growth paralleled the increasing independence of architects in their applications of reinforced concrete, for just as the first uses of cast and wrought iron mimicked the techniques of masons and carpenters, so the orthodoxies of structural steel limited the early applications of its hybrid offspring to the standard column and beam.

From the 1900s, engineers and architects began to see that reinforced concrete offered unique solutions to problems of construction. Apart from its evident strength, durability and cheapness, it had tremendous versatility because it could be moulded into virtually any shape of any required size. Structural units could therefore, with differing advantage, be either pre-cast or moulded on site. It was thus a material of unprecedented plasticity, and allowed extensive continuity of structure; the architect and engineer were thereby enabled to execute previously undreamt-of structures with combinations of newly invented slabs, shells and thin ribs, and more nearly than before to approach 'the organic ideal – that is, the structural form in which the distribution of material corresponds exactly to the distribution and kind of stress'. These technical achievements depended upon a precise, qualified understanding of the various tensile and shearing stresses acting upon the material. For this reason building in concrete was 'the most scientific of

Figure 5.15
Reinforced concrete framing.
Interior Jahrhunderthalle,
Breslau (now Wroclaw),
designed by Max Berg, 1913.
(Copyright Architectural
Association. Photograph by
F.R. Yerbury)

structural techniques' (Condit, 1961, p.152) and very much a technique of the Second Industrial Revolution.

The most palpable and diffuse impact of reinforced concrete as well as of the steel frame on everyday life has been their part in the transformation of the built environment through a range of public, commercial and industrial buildings and civil-engineering projects, often new in function as well as in structure: factories, warehouses, department stores, railway terminals, sports stadiums, hotels, theatres, apartment blocks, cinemas, bus garages, hospitals, power stations, aircraft hangars, highways, bridges and so forth. This impact has been partly aesthetic. Much of the beauty of the new materials for the engineer lies in their functional possibilities. This kind of elegance may be lost on the lay multitude, and has led to a dissociation of sensibilities between the designing professions and the building industry on one hand, and the public on the other. Lay impressions of concrete construction in our period have often resembled reactions to the new plastics: cheap and shoddy. Such impressions are far from groundless, especially in damp and cold climates; inferior concrete crumbles rapidly, and is permeable, so that staining can result when the reinforcing metal is corroded by moisture, and cracking if the trapped moisture freezes.

Aesthetic repudiation of reinforced concrete was to some extent a peculiarly British form of conservatism, and for most of the period an attitude shared by architects; thus quite late into the period virtually all concrete-framed buildings were disguised by a masonry shell (Collins, 1959, p.86). When steel framing was finally introduced in this country in 1904 with the construction of the Ritz Hotel in London, the external masonry walls were still made of load-bearing width and strength to comply with local bye-laws (Hudson, 1972, p.97). Steel frames continued thereafter to be preferred by architects and builders for multi-storey buildings throughout the inter-war period even when the cost advantage of reinforced concrete frames was clear (Bowley, 1966, pp.39–52). The exceptions in the thirties included blocks of flats designed by younger architects, and intended for letting to middle-class families. Steel framing and prefabricated concrete units were tried in a public project, the Quarry Hill Flats in Leeds; but the cost of each flat worked out at £630 in 1938, at a time when three-bedroomed brick-built houses could cost as little as £300 (Sutcliffe, 1974, pp.126–27).

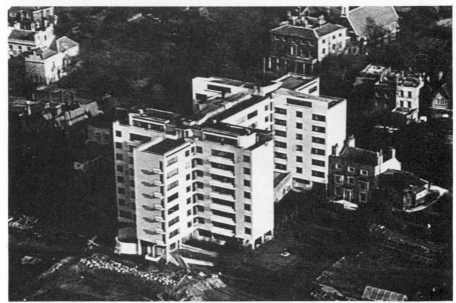

Figure 5.16
Highpoint I flats, Highgate,
London, 1933–35, designed
by Berthold Lubetkin and
Tecton. (Architectural
Review, *January 1936*)

Figure 5.17
Entrance archway, Quarry
Hill flats, Leeds, 1934–41,
designed by R.A.H. Livett.
(Photograph by Tim Benton)

5.7
BUILDING MATERIALS
AND HOUSING

The example of the Quarry Hill Flats raises the question of the impact on housing of new materials and construction techniques. The focus here will be largely on British developments. The difference between working-class housing in this country and elsewhere has been succinctly encapsulated as 'vertical slums abroad, horizontal slums in England' (Denby, 1944, p.27). We find outside England established patterns of multi-storey tenements providing cheap working-class housing well before the invention of skeletal framing. The introduction of steel frames, lifts and concrete construction in these areas served only to add a few storeys on occasions, and should not be associated with any radically new departures in the quality of working-class life. Although the unpopularity of blocks of flats was an English character-istic, the notorious technical and social problems sometimes associated with residential high-rise tower blocks belong everywhere to the period since 1950.

Despite British conservatism in our period, a transformation took place in the urban built environment, in no small measure as a result of new building materials and associated construction techniques. And yet the kind of struc-tural change which took effect in large public, commercial, industrial and recreational buildings seems scarcely to have encroached upon domestic life. The major gross change in housing patterns was the outward sprawl of suburbia. This is not to say that the housing stock retained its late nineteenth-century character. There was a general improvement in the size and internal fittings of working-class housing as building standards were made subject to government regulation and local authorities came to be the major sponsors.

Rising standards in working-class housing were one side of a convergence in the building stock. On the other side, middle-class houses shrank in size, a trend reflecting lessening incomes differentials, a reduction in the size of families (and considerable growth in their number), the scarcity of domestic servants, and the increasing amount of income and space devoted to the automobile. Given improved transportation links, continued horizontal growth of housing was practicable, and site values in consequence so low as to render uneconomic tall-framed residential buildings.

The overall reduction in the size of the average housing unit, itself to some considerable extent a product of industrial change, ironically tended to work against the introduction of parallel rationalizations and economies of scale in the building of houses. The business of construction remained to a large extent a handicraft operation, relying as ever on a mix of unskilled and skilled labour with relatively stable proportions of carpenters and joiners, bricklayers, plumbers, plasterers and slaters. The major occupational change was the virtual eclipse of the stonemason by the bricklayer. This labour-intensive business was not, however, completely immune from mechaniz-ation. On site, manual operations were speeded up by the introduction of small power plant, notably the diesel engine, and equipment such as concrete mixers and power drills. Prefabricated units and factory-made products were increasingly incorporated, especially fittings, but also standard doors and window frames and other items of joinery, and new sheet materials such as plasterboard, fibreboard, asbestos-cement sheet and plywood. However, such innovations were marginal, and a long way from the visionary designer's objective of a fully prefabricated house bringing with it dramatic reductions in site time and labour. Throughout the period, prefabricated housing was almost entirely a response to crisis conditions, notably rapid settlement at times of colonial and territorial expansion, and of remote mineral exploitation (Herbert, 1984).

The eclipse of the mason by the bricklayer reflects one major impact of industrialization on British housebuilding in our period, and one with notable implications for the texture of the built environment. In 1870, however rudimentary and insanitary the bulk of the housing stock, it could at least be said that much of it possessed the distinctive character of local stone and brick earth. The basis of brickmaking is any clay which can be readily moulded and hold its shape during firing; the composition of such materials is highly variable, and lends distinctive hues and shades to local bricks. Traditional brickmaking, not unlike traditional textile bleaching, was a remarkably lengthy process, with stages like weathering, air-drying and burning taking weeks and even months. From the 1880s, major savings in time and cost accrued from the exploitation of materials from the Lower Oxford Clay in the Peterborough, Bedford and North Buckinghamshire areas. These could be pressed and fired without any prior drying, and also contained their own carbonaceous fuel supply, thereby reducing by two-thirds the amount of coal required for the kilns (Hudson, 1972, p.34).

The new bricks became known as Flettons, after the site near Peterborough of their first manufacture. Large Fletton producers like the London Brick Company, formed in 1936, could now compete with small brickyards in local markets. Fletton producers made a third of all bricks in 1937, and only a third of the 3,500 yards operating at the beginning of the century were still in business in 1936 (Powell, 1980, p.122). The success of the Fletton industry has led to the growing homogenization of housing exteriors, but it is probably the major reason for the largely successful resistance to the use of new materials in the domestic sector during our period. Aesthetic preferences for traditional materials undoubtedly played their part; but equally beyond doubt is the decisiveness of cost, especially at a time when local authorities were increasingly footing the bill. The plain fact was that non-traditional houses, by and large, were more expensive.

It is instructive that in Britain, experiments in mass non-traditional housing (as opposed to individually designed, expensive upper-middle-class projects) were confined to the years immediately following each World War, when traditional building materials and skilled labour were in short supply. In the early 1920s, various systems using steel or concrete for framing or cladding were tried, but eventually they worked out more expensive than traditional methods.

The experiment following the Second World War was the more substantial. Problems similar to those of the 1920s of shortage of traditional materials and labour were intensified by extensive bomb damage to towns and cities. Over 100,000 temporary prefabricated bungalows ('prefabs') were built in the years 1945–48, and in some areas of Britain in the period 1945–55, between 40 and 50 per cent of local-authority housing provision was non-traditional (Bowley, 1966, pp.201, 203). The materials and methods used were similar to those in the first experiment; there were, however, innovatory uses of asbestos sheet and aluminium in the claddings of prefabricated bunga lows. Again, there was no lasting cost advantage, once traditional materials and labour had been re-established, and similarly, the appearance of the new buildings was uncongenial to most.

This section on new inorganic materials consequently ends on something of a downbeat. This is salutary, as it reinforces the point that there was nothing inevitable about the onward march of these products of the new scientific technology. On the contrary, it would appear that new building materials had almost to be forced by government decree via local authorities on an unwilling populace. High-rise dystopias were not, it appears, the inevitable outcome of steel frames and ferro-concrete; their emergence in recent decades has much to do with the exceptional contingencies of post-war reconstruction. This is not to gainsay the considerable impact on the built environment of new materials and building techniques, but the overall picture is somewhat confused:

. . . in general new methods and ideas which involved a manifest break with orthodoxy appear to have been regarded with ambivalence. Sometimes, where a sense of progressiveness was the aim or basic utilitarian considerations applied, innovations were thought to be appropriate; at other times, in housing and where a sense of dignity was sought, there was a strong attachment to that which was tried and proven, or which appeared to be so. International-style factories were juxtaposed with homely mock-traditional half-timbering and stained glass; bold cinemas, embellished with neon lighting and chromeplated tubes, contrasted oddly with heavy neo-classical town halls. (Powell, 1980, p.105)

REFERENCES   Banham, R. (1986) *A Concrete Atlantis: US Industrial Building and European Modern Architecture 1900–1925*, MIT Press.

Bessemer, H. (1905) *Autobiography*, Offices of Engineering.

Birch, A. (1967) *The Economic History of the British Iron and Steel Industry 1784–1879*, Frank Cass.

Bowley, M. (1960) *Innovations in Building Materials: An Economic Study*, Gerald Duckworth.

Bowley, M. (1966) *The British Building Industry: Four Studies in Response and Resistance to Change*, Cambridge University Press.

Brody, D. (1960) *Steelworkers in America: the Nonunion Era*, Harvard University Press.

Brody, D. (1965) *Labor in Crisis: the Steel Strike of 1919*, J.B. Lippincott.

Carr, J.C. and Taplin, W. (1962) *History of the British Steel Industry*, Harvard University Press.

Collins, P. (1959) *Concrete: the Vision of a New Architecture*, Faber and Faber.

Condit, C.W. (1960) *American Building Art: the Nineteenth Century*, Oxford University Press.

Condit, C.W. (1961) *American Building Art: The Twentieth Century*, Oxford University Press.

Denby, E. (1944) *Europe Re-Housed*, George Allen & Unwin.

Dennis, W.H. (1963) *A Hundred Years of Metallurgy*, Gerald Duckworth.

Derry, T.K. and Williams, T.I. (1970) *A Short History of Technology*, Oxford University Press.

Docherty, C. (1983) *Steel and Steelworkers: the Sons of Vulcan*, Heinemann.

Eggert, G.G. (1981) *Steelmakers and Labor Reform 1886–1923*, University of Pittsburgh Press.

Gintz, H. (1954) 'Effects of technological change on labour in selected sections of the iron and steel industries of Great Britain, the United States and Germany, 1901–1939', PhD thesis, University of London.

Herbert, G. (1984) *The Dream of the Factory-Made House: Walter Gropius and Konrad Wachsmann*, MIT Press.

Hogan, W.T. (1971) *Economic History of the Iron and Steel Industry in the United States*, 5 volumes, D.C. Heath.

Holt, J. (1977) 'Trade unionism in the British and United States steel industries, 1880–1914: a comparative study', *Labour History*, 18, pp.5–35.

Howe, H.M. (1911) 'Iron and steel', *Encyclopaedia Britannica*, 11th edition, Vol.XIV, pp.801–34.

Hudson, K. (1972) *Building Materials*, Longman.

Landes, D.S. (1969) *The Unbound Prometheus: Technological Change and Industrial Development from 1750 to the Present*, Cambridge University Press.

Manchester, W.R. (1969) *The Arms of Krupp, 1587–1968*, Michael Joseph.

Moore, B. (1978) *Injustice: The Social Bases of Obedience and Revolt*, Macmillan.

Oliver, J.W. (1956) *A History of American Technology*, Ronald Press.

Powell, C.G. (1980) *An Economic History of the British Building Industry 1815–1979*, Architectural Press.

Singer, C., et al. (1954–78) *A History of Technology*, 7 volumes, Oxford University Press.

Sutcliffe, A. (ed.) (1974) *Multi-Storey Living*, Croom Helm.

Temin, P. (1964) *Iron and Steel in Nineteenth-Century America*, MIT Press.

Wall, J.F. (1970) *Andrew Carnegie*, Oxford University Press.

Warren, K. (1975) *World Steel: An Economic Geography*, David & Charles.

Wright, R.I. (1969) *Freshwater Whales: A History of the American Shipbuilding Company and its Predecessors*, Kent State University Press.

6 TRANSPORT

Richard Bessel

> Pa said that as soon as he had the crops in, they would all go to town. Laura and Mary could go too. They were old enough now. They were very much excited, and next day they tried to play going to town. They could not do it very well, because they were not quite sure what a town was like. They knew there was a store in town, but they had never seen a store. (Wilder, 1956, p.91)

Thus Laura Ingalls Wilder, in one of her books describing her childhood in the American Midwest, recalled preparations for the first time she ever visited a town. The year was 1872. At the time she was five years old; her sister Mary was six. The town they were to visit was Pepin, Wisconsin, seven miles from the cabin in which the family lived. The trip to Pepin and back, in a wagon pulled by horses along a sandy road, took an entire day.

Extreme physical mobility is something which people in developed industrial societies now take for granted. But in fact it is a fairly new phenomenon. Until quite recently, most people travelled day-to-day on foot; most goods moved slowly with animal power; and the physical space within people's everyday reach was rather limited. Clearly, transport is an activity in which scientific and technological innovations have had great effects upon everyday life. In technological terms, the changes in popular modes of transport during the period between roughly 1870 and 1950 have involved a shift from human, animal and steam power to the use of electric power and then the widespread application of internal combustion engines driven by petroleum products. In economic terms, changes in transport technologies have helped to shape residential and working patterns. Machine-powered transport – at least in developed capitalist industrial societies – became available to large numbers of private individuals, able to get where they wanted to go in their *own* mechanically powered vehicle when they wanted to get there.

To be sure, major improvements in transport technology – the railways and international steam-maritime transport – had had considerable impact by the second half of the nineteenth century; but compared to what came later, the effects of this upon most people's *everyday* lives were small. By 1870 the railways had changed the landscape in most major industrial nations, first and foremost in Britain. Certainly the effects of the railways – although their importance for economic development has been questioned by economic historians – were profound: they compelled the standardization of time and timekeeping, helped create national markets both for labour and produce (and newspapers), and allowed fast travel over long distances to an extent never before imaginable. It was a sign of the times when in the summer of 1851 the London and North Western Railway brought 775,000 people to London on five-shillings excursion tickets to see the Great Exhibition, or when 20,000 people were able to converge upon Chelmsford on a single day for the Royal Agricultural Society's show in July 1856 (Bagwell, 1974, pp.121, 127–28). And the effect of improved international maritime transport was scarcely less great: during the nineteenth century millions of Europeans were borne across the Atlantic to North America.

The revolution in transport was not just a matter of lengths of railway track laid or numbers of passengers carried; it also led to fundamental changes in the ways in which people in industrialized countries perceived the world around them. The standardization of timekeeping is only one aspect of this. With the diffusion of the steamship, telegraph and – most importantly

– the railway in the nineteenth century, there was what one historian of the railways has regarded as a fundamental restructuring of the capitalist world on the basis of modern means of transport: 'The pre-industrial relationships of location and space to time no longer were valid' (Schievelbusch, 1979, p.171). The new means of transport extended 'civilization'; limitations imposed by space and distance were redefined; communication, circulation and movement came to be regarded as coterminous with 'progress'.

However, in the late nineteenth century most people still did most of their moving about on foot. Cities, even in the industrialized world, still were essentially walking cities until the last third of the nineteenth century; most people walked to and from work, and the use of the new, modern means of transport generally was reserved for the occasional trip across country. In 1870 the built-up area of Kingston-upon-Hull, which held 121,000 inhabitants at that time, was only about two square miles; most people lived within walking distance of their work (McKay, 1976, pp.7–8). Most of the new building in Liverpool and Birmingham between 1830 and 1870 was within about two miles from the city centre. Urban growth until the last third of the nineteenth century often meant packing more people into a given space rather than a vast increase in the physical size of the city. For example, the population of Lille grew from 59,000 in 1804 to 100,000 in 1860 as the city became a leading industrial centre in northern France; yet John McKay has noted that 'all this increase was crowded into the already inhabited area within the city walls, an area of less than three square kilometers' (McKay, 1976, p.7). Even in America, where mechanized urban transport systems developed particularly rapidly and where there was space for the physical expansion of cities, the 'walking city' remained the reality for most urban dwellers until rather recently. Indeed, it has been calculated that as late as 1914 'the typical American averaged about 1,640 miles of total travel per year, and nearly 1,300 [that is, about 3.5 miles/day] of this was accounted for by walking. In other words, he travelled only about 340 miles per year with the aid of horse, cycle or mechanical means' (Aldcroft, 1976, p.217). Half a century later his counterpart travelled on average thirty times as much – a fact which suggests that, in terms of the effects of new transport technology upon people's everyday lives, the real revolution has taken place not so much in the nineteenth century as in the twentieth.

Yet in many ways, the 1870s mark a convenient watershed in transport development – even with regard to that greatest of all nineteenth-century transport innovations, the railway. In many of the early industrial nations – Britain, France, Belgium, Germany – the basic outlines of the railway system already were in place by 1870. The last third of the nineteenth century saw the filling in of railway networks, the building of branch lines, their technological improvement, and vast increases in traffic. In Germany, for example, the greatest expansion of the railway network took place in 1870–75, during the speculative boom which followed the Franco-Prussian War (Treue, 1975, p.218). In France, the length of railway lines roughly trebled between 1879 and 1914 (Weber, 1976, p.205). In Britain – the pioneer of railway development – railway passenger traffic was roughly four times in 1910 what it had been in 1870 (Bagwell, 1974, p.109); in Germany, passenger traffic on the railways in 1913 was more than nine times the 1870 figure, and goods traffic in 1913 was more than ten times what it had been in 1870 (Hohorst, Kocka and Ritter, 1978, p.82). The changes registered in some urban centres were even more striking: for example, in Greater Berlin the number of railway journeys (largely by people using the connections between suburban areas and Berlin proper) grew from 13 million in 1866 to 1,235 million in 1913; during that same period the population of the region grew from roughly 700,000 to 4 million, while Berlin became one of the world's leading industrial cities (Treue, 1975, p.218).

But the transport changes which came about during the last third of the nineteenth century were a matter not just of quantity: they also affected the quality of everyday life. In his *Peasants into Frenchmen*, Eugen Weber has stressed the importance of the development of the railway and road networks: 'Roads that permitted carts, roads reinforced by railroads, would be an emancipation as important as political revolution, probably more important' (Weber, 1976, p.208). New roads and railway branch lines opened up the French countryside to outside influences, to 'civilization', to new possibilities for marketing agricultural produce, to new consumption patterns. Similarly, a historian of Imperial Germany has observed:

> If the years preceding unification [that is, before 1870] had been the era of main-line building, the period which followed was marked by a crucial if less spectacular consolidation through the construction of local branch lines. This not only locked the countryside more closely into the market economy; it also facilitated movement in and out of the village. The railway carried the occupants of the village to new jobs in the town, like the 200 commuters (*Einpendler*) who, in 1900, travelled daily into the growing Swabian market town of Ebingen from the rural hinterland. The railway similarly carried peasants into the towns on occasional Sunday outings, as well as on more hallowed enterprises like pilgrimages and the annual excursion of the Brown Cow Insurance Society. (Blackbourn, 1984, pp.53–54)

New means of transport carried national 'culture' as well as commodities, and did much to break down local and regional differences in custom and language. Mechanical means of transport – chiefly the railway – brought the industrial world into contact with the majority of the population of industrializing countries who did not live in the new manufacturing centres. Despite the stress that has been placed on the rapid industrialization of Britain, the United States and some European countries during the nineteenth century, it is worth remembering that at the start of our period a large proportion of the people in 'industrial societies' lived lives not all that different from their 'pre-industrial' forebears.

**6.1
URBAN TRANSPORT
AND ELECTRIC
TRACTION**

In his study of the impact of railways on Victorian cities, John Kellett demonstrates how limited was the extent to which the railways sparked suburban development in the nineteenth century. Of the cities he examined (Birmingham, Glasgow, Liverpool, London and Manchester), only in the capital did large numbers of people go into work from suburban communities by rail, and in London this commuter traffic grew only towards the end of the century (Kellett, 1969, pp.354–82). Railway building tended to follow, rather than precede, suburban development. The effects of other forms of transport were even more limited. Urban transport systems, such as they were, had consisted either of horse-drawn omnibuses (the first of which appeared in the western French city of Nantes in 1826) or, later, horse-drawn tramways, which began to spread in the United States during the 1850s and in Britain and Europe in the 1860s and 1870s. The horse-drawn omnibuses moved little faster than people on foot, and their clientele was limited largely to the better off; horse-drawn tramways (street railways) moved somewhat more quickly, used horsepower more efficiently, and could carry greater loads more smoothly (something particularly important in the United States because of the rather primitive condition of the roads in American cities). But as Donald Olson has noted in his study of Victorian London, 'we must keep in mind that the Victorians, like every generation before them but unlike ours, walked' (Olson, 1979, p.298). It was not until the end of the century that things really began to change.

The last third of the nineteenth century saw a veritable tramway boom in Britain and Western Europe. The first tramway in Britain – which opened in Birkenhead in 1860 – was in fact promoted by an aptly named young American, George Francis Train. Train also backed the first experimental horse-drawn tramway lines in London in 1861, which, however, were ordered to be closed within a year because the rails, which were raised above street level, endangered other traffic. It was not until the late 1860s that a real tram mania began, with Berlin (1865), Hamburg (1866), Liverpool (1868) and Stuttgart (1868), and spreading to many French, German and British cities during the 1870s (McKay, 1976, pp.15–17). At the end of the 1870s there were 321 miles of tramway in the United Kingdom (Bagwell, 1974, p.154). Generally these new transport networks were privately built and operated on public thoroughfares, publicly regulated, and quite profitable. In Britain, for example, the Tramways Act of 1870 allowed local authorities or private interests to build tramways, but local authorities could not operate the lines – although they could, after twenty-one years, purchase them compulsorily. (These provisions acted as a disincentive for British operators to switch to electric traction in the 1880s, since their leases were coming to an end and it was uncertain whether new heavy capital outlay would pay.)

The numbers of people carried by tramways grew as new lower fares came within the reach of working-class urban dwellers: in Britain tramways carried 416.5 million passengers in 1886, more than a million a day; in Germany in 1887 nearly as many passengers were carried on the tramways as on the railway network (245.7 millions as against 295.8 millions); in Holland the number of tramway passengers in 1886 (83.9 millions) exceeded that of passengers on the railways (66.4 millions) (McKay, 1976, p.22). But even so, most people still walked when they had to get somewhere; indeed, urban congestion was often such that walking proved faster. Even in Berlin, where the tramway had made an early appearance and the network was quite extensive, in 1895 the average Berliner made only seventy-seven tramway rides per year. In Leipzig the comparable figure was fifty-two; in Vienna in 1893 it was only forty. And although the horse-drawn streetcar certainly was an improvement on the omnibus, problems remained: speed was no more than moderate. Horses had difficulty negotiating hills or starting from dead stops, and often double teams of horses were needed for hills. The costs of maintaining horses were considerable; with five to seven horses required per tram car and with a horse's working life limited to about four to five years, the animals accounted for roughly half of operating expenses. Illness among the horses could put the system out of commission, as in 1872 when the 'Great Epizootic' – a respiratory and lymphatic disease – killed thousands of horses in cities in the eastern United States and paralysed public transport, or about sixteen years later when the services of the Keighley Tramways Company were suspended for two months because its horses got pink-eye.

Figure 6.1
Street scene in New York before the rise of the motor car: a dead horse lies by the road. Removing dead animals and clearing up after live ones was a major task for city administrations. (Motor Vehicle Manufacturers Association of the United States Inc., Detroit)

And animal droppings posed a continual health hazard (McKay, 1976, pp.25–26; Hilton, 1969, p.124). An appreciation of the congestion and smells on Oxford Street, Broadway, the Champs Élysées or Unter den Linden one hundred years ago should dampen any attempt to romanticize city life before the roads were inundated by mechanical contraptions.

The real breakthrough in urban transport in the late nineteenth century, the effective mechanical alternative to horsepower, was electric traction. A number of alternatives – steam street railways, cable cars – met with some success. In particular, cable cars proved quite successful in the United States, where streets (frequently laid out in grid patterns) often were quite straight and thus well suited to cables. Cable systems worked with an endless cable, driven by a stationary engine, slotted in the ground between the rails; starting and stopping was by means of a 'grabber' which could be hooked onto or unhooked from the cable by a motorman. The greatest success was in San Francisco, which with its grid street pattern and steep hills was ideally suited to the cable car, which remains in operation today. But although it could move people at least half as fast again as the horse car, the cable car was extremely expensive to install, had difficulty negotiating curves (which had to be taken at the same speed as all other parts of the line), and was inefficient in its use of energy. And if the cable broke the entire system stopped.

Electric traction, by contrast, proved more energy-efficient, more flexible and cheaper – and thus created the basis for a new system of public transport. First applied successfully with an electric tramway by Werner von Siemens at the Berlin Industrial Exhibition in 1879 and then on the streets of Lichterfelde (a well-to-do suburb south-west of Berlin, where Siemens opened a 2.5 kilometre line to fare-paying passengers), electric traction made possible clean, efficient, rapid mechanical forms of transport capable of carrying the masses. It liberated transport companies from the problems (and costs) of horses, and made the streets of cities in Europe and North America smell much better. But what did it consist of, and what were the technologies it employed?

Basically, electric traction means moving a vehicle with an electric motor. Electric motors had already been developed by the middle of the nineteenth century and applied experimentally to railways and paddlewheel boats. However, electric motors remained an unpractical power source. The problem was the current: primary batteries, the only source of current then available, were extremely heavy and expensive, much more expensive than steam. This changed fundamentally in the 1870s, with the development of the dynamo. By providing a cheap source of electric current, the dynamo enabled electricity to play major roles in the everyday lives of millions of people – not least in opening up the possibilities for electric lighting. It was not long before people grasped its revolutionary potential for transport: that a dynamo could convert the mechanical energy of a steam engine into electricity, which then could be distributed from a single point throughout a transport system and then be reconverted by a motor (a dynamo operating in reverse) into mechanical energy to drive a tram.

This meant that a motor had to be mounted on the vehicle itself, and a reliable means found to get the current to the vehicle wherever it happened to be. Siemens solved this problem on his small exhibition tram in 1879 with a stationary generator and an isolated third (central) rail to carry the current to the motor on the car, and used the wheels and running rails to transmit the current back to the generator and thus complete the circuit. On his line in Lichterfelde, Siemens simply used one of the running rails to transmit the current from the dynamo and the other running rail to return it. But live rails on the streets brought new problems: shocks to horses and people. High voltages were required on long lines, because of losses at lower potential.

Therefore if the shocks were not to be so large as to endanger life, tram lines had to be kept short; otherwise they could not be used on public thoroughfares. In an attempt to overcome the hazards posed by live rails, Siemens looked to overhead cables: experimental systems with overhead cables were presented in 1881 at the Paris Exhibition and on the streets of Charlottenburg (to the west of Berlin), and in 1884 the Frankfurt/Main-Offenbach Tramway became the first public transport system to use overhead cables. Thus a system was developed which essentially powers the world's electric railways today – some (such as the London Underground, British Rail's Southern Region, the Berlin S-Bahn and the New York City 'subway') using a third rail to carry current to the train, and some (most European tram systems and most electric railways) using overhead cables.

Although they had been discovered and developed in Europe, these new systems had their greatest effect during the late-nineteenth century in the United States. The first American commercial street railway started in Cleveland, Ohio, in mid-1884, but it was not an immediate success. Technical problems with a system involving the current being carried by wire conductors laid underground in a wooden conduit between the rails plagued the venture and undermined its financial health. The breakthrough came with the efforts of Frank Sprague, a young American naval officer (a graduate of the American Naval Academy at Annapolis) who had the good fortune to be stationed in Europe in the early 1880s. Sprague had been secretary of an award jury at the Electrical Exhibition at London's Crystal Palace in 1882, and worked for a short time for Thomas Edison upon returning to the United States. Edison showed rather little interest in Sprague's work on electrical motors, and in 1884 Sprague set up on his own developing electric motors (which actually were built and recommended to the public by Edison). Sprague's first customers were industrial users of his motors, but soon he was concentrating on electric traction. After an unfortunate experiment with a third-rail system for an elevated railway in New York (when a fuse blew during the demonstration, frightening one of the potential main financial backers, the railway tycoon Jay Gould, who panicked and jumped from the train), Sprague concentrated on street railways with overhead conductors.

Success came in Richmond, Virginia. In 1887 Sprague won a contract to equip a new streetcar company in the one-time capital of the Confederacy. The primitive nature of the city's streets (hilly and unpaved) made animal traction difficult and expensive. In designing the Richmond system, Sprague introduced a number of important innovations, which made electric traction a practical and profitable proposition. By substituting carbon for metallic brushes on the commutator, he solved the problem of sparks flying; and by designing a universal swivelling, under-running trolley wheel (hence the name 'trolley' for streetcar in America) to pick up the current from a single overhead copper-wire conductor attached to poles (with the current returning via the rails), Sprague made the overhead method of transmitting current much more reliable. Although poor building work meant that Sprague lost money on his Richmond contract, the Richmond system – with twelve miles of track and forty cars, it was the largest electric street railway in the world – set the new American standard and opened up a vast new market.

In the mid-1890s Sprague added another significant development: 'multiple-unit control', which allowed the operator of the first car of a multi-car train to control all the motors of all the cars. This meant that trains could be lengthened or shortened as traffic required; all the cars could have their own electric drive, instead of cars with motors pulling cars without, and all could be controlled by a single motorman. Sprague's multiple-unit system was demonstrated experimentally in 1897, and soon thereafter the South Side Elevated Railway in Chicago converted from steam to Sprague's new system (Cudahy, 1979, pp.21–22).

The last major technological change which should be mentioned was not a product of Sprague's inventiveness. Sprague's motors used direct current, but during the 1890s there began a switch to alternating current, not only in the transport field but in the electrical industry generally. Long-distance transmission of AC current had been demonstrated in Frankfurt/Main in 1891, and the AC induction motor had been invented in the United States three years before. The reasons why the switch occurred were clearly economic: AC could be generated at high voltages, which meant lower energy losses and lower costs.

Thus was introduced what George W. Hilton has described as 'one of the most rapidly accepted innovations in the history of technology' (Hilton, 1969, p.126). The Richmond system opened in February 1988. By July 1890 one-sixth of America's street railways, 914 of 5,783 miles, had been electrified. Steam and cable systems, with 524 and 283 miles respectively, had been overtaken. By the end of 1893 the amount of street-railway track had more than doubled, to 12,200 miles, and three-fifths were electrified; ten years later there were about 30,000 miles of street-railway track in America, 98 per cent electrified (McKay, 1976, pp.50–51). Within this short space of time, roughly two billion dollars – a vast amount of money at that time – had been invested in America's electric street railways (Hilton, 1969, p.125). In Europe Germany took the lead, with 102 kilometres of electrified street-railway line in 1893 and 3,692 ten years later; in 1895 23 per cent of Germany's street-railway lines had been electrified, and by 1902 nearly all were. (The German firm Siemens und Halske also developed a significant innovation: discarding Sprague's trolley wheel, the Siemens system used a broad sprung bow to contact the overhead cable. Unlike the trolley, the bow could slide across the cable, which lessened the chances of its jumping the overhead wire.) Britain lagged roughly ten years behind America and Germany; in part because British street-railway companies were not allowed to speculate in real estate and thereby profit on their own expansion: only 38 per cent of Britain's street railways had been electrified by 1902. However, in the years before the First World War electric traction spread throughout the United Kingdom as well. Sprague's system, as the historian of European streetcar systems, John P. McKay, has observed, 'brought about a revolution in urban transport, a revolution that spread to Europe and around the world' (McKay, 1976, p.51).

But why did it spread so quickly? To begin with, the rapid spread of electric traction would not have been possible without the prior existence of a fairly well-developed electrical industry which could supply the equipment, and of the capital available to finance it. A main reason for its subsequent success was that it provided a vastly superior service to animal-powered urban transport systems: it was faster (at least 25–50 per cent faster, even in the narrower, congested streets of European cities), more reliable, cleaner, cheaper, more comfortable, less affected by bad weather (if necessary, electric snow-ploughs could clear the tracks), could ascend hills better, and could carry many more passengers (partly because the trams moved faster, partly because electrically-powered cars could be larger and trailer cars could be attached). But probably the most important reason electric traction spread with such astonishing speed was that it proved extremely profitable for the operators, not least because of the economies of scale with a system which could be powered from a single generating station. To quote John McKay once again:

The owners and managers of first American and then European horse tramways generally adopted overhead electric traction for the same reason that privately owned, capitalist industry generally adopts technological innovations: anticipated greater profits. In the simplest terms, these decision-makers concluded that this type of electric traction would cut their per unit operating costs markedly and also substantially increase total revenues. The result would then be a large increase in profits. In the best of circumstances, the result might even equal the reported 200 per cent gain in net income reported in 1889 for one line in Boston, Mass., which, as the *Street Railway Journal* rhapsodized [in 1889], 'is something marvelous'. (McKay, 1976, p.51)

Lower operating costs meant the promise of higher profits alongside lower fares, which in turn stimulated demand. In Germany, for example, the introduction of electric traction around the turn of the century was accompanied by a lowering of fares – often by more than 10 per cent – at a time when the length of the average journey was increasing (Desai, 1969, p.94). Lower fares and greater speed meant that people could travel further to and from work. Public transport also was brought to urban areas where, because of steep hills, it had been impossible to run horse-drawn trams previously – as, for example, in the Ukrainian capital of Kiev (the first city in the Russian Empire to get electric streetcars) or the western German industrial town of Remscheid (which had the steepest gradients in Europe). New markets for urban transport were created and, with the increased capacities of the new technology, satisfied. Passenger numbers skyrocketed. For example, in Britain the number of passengers carried annually on tramways rose from 151 millions in 1879 (before the advent of electric traction) to 759 millions in 1896, 2,907 millions in 1910 and 3,426 millions on the eve of the First World War – at which time nearly twice as many tram journeys as train journeys were made in the country which had given the world its first railways (McKay, 1976, p.60; Bagwell, 1974, p.155).

Electric traction was not limited to the streets. It also was used with urban railways which enjoyed their own exclusive rights of way. Indeed, both Siemens and Sprague originally conceived of the use of electric traction for elevated urban railways, which travelled above the congested streets of the major cities. Although the electric tram became much more widespread – because it required less capital to build and operate and because it could be used economically in small and medium as well as large cities – electric elevated, underground and suburban railways soon followed.

The world's first underground railway, London's Metropolitan from Paddington to Farringdon Street which was opened in January 1863, had been powered initially by steam locomotive, which caused considerable problems of pollution in tunnels and consequent discomfort to passengers. The District Railway opened its line along the Victoria Embankment in 1871, and the Inner Circle – today's Circle Line – was completed in 1884. The Metropolitan and the District Railways were not electrified until 1905, in large measure because of the competitive pressure coming from the newer electric underground tube lines. The early elevated urban railway lines in America – in Manhattan in 1870, in Brooklyn in 1885 – were also first powered by steam engines; Manhattan's elevated lines were fully electrified in 1903, Brooklyn's in 1900. The first underground railway to use electric traction was the tube line between Waterloo Station and the Bank, opened in December 1890 and operated by the City and South London Railway; this was soon followed by the tube line which became the Central London Railway between Shepherd's Bush and the Bank. This tube line was proposed in 1890, the building was started in 1896, and it was opened in the summer of 1900. (Britain's other early underground line, in Glasgow, was opened as a cable line in 1896; it was converted to electric traction in 1935.) In the New World as well electric traction went underground in the most densely built-up large cities: an underground tramway line opened in Boston in 1897;

Figure 6.2
Traffic in Boston in 1907. All the vehicles are horse-drawn except the streetcar. The structure in the middle of the square is the entrance to the underground ('subway') station in Haymarket Square. Boston built the first underground railway in the United States, for streetcars to travel through the congested downtown area. (Reproduced from Ray D. Appelgate (1979) Trolleys and Streetcars on American Postcards *by permission of Dover Publications Inc.)*

the first 'subway' line in New York City opened its doors to the public in 1904; and in Philadelphia an underground/elevated line was completed in 1908. So too on the Continent. In Berlin, for example, Werner von Siemens was able in 1897 to organize a 'Society for Electrical Elevated and Underground Railways in Berlin' to build an east-west electric railway line to the south of the city centre, partly elevated and partly underground, which opened in 1902.

The building of these underground railways required enormous engineering effort and large amounts of capital – and therefore the promise of large enough numbers of passengers to make the projects pay. The Central London Railway is a case in point. Raising the money for this immense project involved share flotations authorized by Acts of Parliament, and shareholders were attracted from France, Germany, Austria and the United States as well as from within Britain. Altogether, the line between Shepherd's Bush and Bank cost £3,725,000 to build – an enormous sum in those days. It required a lot of passengers paying the 2*d* fare to make this a commercial proposition; in 1901, its first full year of operation, the line carried roughly 41 million passengers – or more than 110,000 per day. Building New York's first underground line, which ran the length of Manhattan, involved setting up a municipal 'Rapid Transit Commission' to finance construction at a cost of nearly $38,000,000. (The New York line was then leased to a private operator which ran the 'subway'.)

Two consequences of the fact that such large sums were required to build urban transport systems should be noted. First, their planning and financing became a major undertaking, often involving international concerns. In London, for example, Americans were deeply involved: after the completion of the Central London Railway, the building of the tube lines was carried out by a company (Underground Electric Railways of London Ltd.) headed by Charles Yerkes, who had played a leading role in developing Chicago's elevated railway system. Thus, during the first decade of the twentieth century, London's underground-railway construction was organized by an American, financed by American banks, supplied with American rolling stock and motors and, finally, was managed by an American. Secondly, as the size and scope of the projects grew, so did the role of the state. We have noted already that the New York municipal government was directly involved in building the first subway line, even though it was operated privately; in the 1920s, however, the New York City government went a step further and began work on its own 'Independent' underground-railway system, which it

Figure 6.3
Two elevated railway lines
cross near downtown
Brooklyn, New York, with a
streetcar in the foreground.
The picture comes from a
postcard dated 1913.
(Reproduced from Ray D.
Appelgate (1979) Trolleys and
Streetcars on American
Postcards *by permission of*
Dover Publications Inc.)

operated as well. Throughout Europe municipal governments ran urban transport companies; public transport became 'public' in a new sense.

It is hardly coincidental that the building of elevated and underground urban railways flourished during the last decades of the nineteenth century and the first decades of the twentieth. One reason for this is that technological developments (electric traction and so forth) had reached a stage which made such urban railways possible. Another, no less important, reason is that these decades saw the peak of tremendous urban growth in the western industrialized world. Industrial growth and commercial expansion created new employment opportunities and drew millions of people to the great cities of Germany, Britain, France, Russia, the United States – something that was disrupted by the First World War. Urban residential densities (for example, in the tenements of Manhattan or in the 'rental barracks' of Berlin) reached all-time peaks. This meant that not only the requisite technology but also the potential demand (large numbers of people within a relatively small space) necessary to justify the investment were there. This can be seen clearly from the example of Chicago – where multiple-unit electric traction was first introduced on the city's elevated railways in 1897, and which was perhaps the fastest growing city in the world in the last decades of the nineteenth century. Between 1880 and 1890 Chicago's population doubled, to 1.1 million; by 1900 its population had reached 1.8 million; and by 1910 it stood at nearly 2.2 million, with nearly one million people living within four miles of the city centre, or 'Loop' of elevated railway tracks. Between 1892 and 1906 more than eighty miles of elevated railway were built and the mileage of the city's street railways doubled; and rides per capita in the city rose from 164 in 1890 to 215 in 1900, 253 in 1905 and 320 in 1910 (Barrett, 1983, p.15). Similar increases in rides per capita were registered in other American, British and German cities, as more people used public transport more often. Despite the enormous investment required, building new urban rail-transport systems was profitable.

It also seems hardly accidental that the beginning of the decline of travel on public transport, at least in the United States, coincided not only with the growth of private car ownership but with declines in inner-city population. To remain with the example of Chicago: between 1920 and 1934 the population of the thirty-six square miles of central Chicago declined by 211,000. Yet at the same time the population of the city as a whole was still growing and that of Chicago's suburbs was growing faster still (Barrett, 1983, p.210). This was a reflection of growing private car ownership and changed urban growth patterns. These new patterns made it much more difficult to serve residential areas adequately with public transport (particularly with fixed-rail transport) than was the case when urban growth had tended to follow Chicago's railway lines radiating from the city centre. This in turn undermined the profitability of electric traction and thus the prospects for the future building of street, elevated or underground lines without state subsidy.

The development of mass transport networks, especially around the turn of the century, changed the face of cities in the industrialized world, and greatly altered the ways in which millions of people lived in industrialized countries. People became more mobile than ever before, not just on special occasions but every day. In 1910 electric tramways carried roughly seven times as many people in Austria-Hungary, France, Germany and Britain as horse-drawn streetcars had done in 1886, and per capita usage among urban dwellers rose by a factor of four (McKay, 1976, pp.81, 240). And this change was not just quantitative but also qualitative. In support of his assertion that the spread of electric streetcars in the decades before the First World War constituted a 'revolution in urban public transportation', John McKay has drawn certain parallels with the industrial revolution in that both constituted a 'revolutionary, once-and-for-all change':

> I would argue that the change from animate-powered transport of the age of walking cities and horse-drawn vehicles, including tramways, to inanimate, mechanized, mass-produced, and mass-oriented urban public transportation has occurred only once. For Europe that once was with electric streetcars. Thereafter urban public transportation has evolved with buses, high-speed trains, express subways, etc., or even declined where the harmful consequences of basing urban civilization upon the private automobile have been grossly underestimated, as in the United States. But it has not been revolutionized. (McKay, 1976, p.241)

The new transport technology also changed the urban environment. The diffusion of the new transport technology allowed the spread of urban development far beyond the narrow confines of the walking city. 'Streetcar suburbs' (the phrase of Sam Bass Warner, 1962, from his pioneering study of Boston in the last three decades of the nineteenth century) grew up around the old urban centres; new juxtapositions of residential and industrial areas became possible; many people, living far from their places of employment, now rode to work rather than walked.

This also changed the urban housing market and affected the level of rents – as the author of the most detailed analysis of real wages in Imperial Germany, Ashok Desai, has pointed out:

> The explanation of the failure of rents to fall in 1875–80 [a period of economic depression, when wages and other prices fell] is probably that owing to the inadequate means of transport, the limits of expansion had been reached in many towns, and the differential advantage of old houses [which were closer to town centres and work places] was large; further, the newer a building, the less favourable its location, and the higher the differential rent of old houses over it. Hence the building of houses with substantially lower servicing charges had little effect on rents of old houses [. . .].

With the advent of the electric tram, however, the differential advantage of old houses crumbled, and their rents became more responsive to rents of new houses (Desai, 1969, p.65).

But the most striking changes were those that occurred at what had been the limits of urban development. New areas around major cities were 'colonized', as builders and speculators took advantage of the building of new transport links which made it possible to live in new residential areas far from one's work.

Perhaps the best examples are provided by the London tube lines. The function of the underground lines built during the early twentieth century in London – in particular the Northern and Piccadilly Lines – was different from that of the very first lines (Circle and Central). Whereas the latter were built to facilitate travel around Central London, the former were designed to bring people from their homes in well-to-do outlying residential communities to their work in the metropolis' financial and commercial centres. Thus Golders Green was largely open country before the Northern Line was extended there in 1907, but soon afterwards it developed into a dormitory community for London. Similar examples may be found in the United States. Thus Harlem, in northern Manhattan, was a rather genteel middle-class white community before 1904, when the opening of the first 'subway' line (connecting Harlem with the Wall Street area) led to a wave of speculative residential building, which soon came to be inhabited by blacks hitherto squeezed into neighbourhoods further south. In London this development accelerated during the inter-war period, when the Southern Railway began to be electrified, underground lines were extended (the Northern Line to Edgware in 1924 and the Piccadilly Line to Cockfosters in 1933), and the bus network linked new neighbourhoods with new train stations. In 1934 housebuilding in Greater London reached a peak with 72,700 units, and between 1921 and 1937 roughly 1.4 million people moved to Outer London (Burnett, 1980, p.252).

But before assuming that the development of urban electric transport forms an unambiguous example of a grand march of progress and the revolutionary transformation of residential and work patterns, some caveats should be noted. Technology did not always prevail rapidly; other things were important, as we can see from this description of developments in late nineteenth-century Detroit by Oliver Zunz:

> It is clear that the street-railway companies had not fulfilled their outspoken claim, echoed by a Detroit real-estate publication of 1892,
>
> that rapid transit had solved the problem of city life. It is fast abolishing the horrors of the crowded tenements. It is shortening the hours of labor. It makes the poor a land owner. It is doing more to put down socialism, in this country at least, than all other things combined.
>
> Such claims and the advertisements for a few well-located subdivisions must not obscure the basic fact that the street-railway companies, primarily motivated by profit, had largely neglected the working-class sections of Detroit.
>
> Street railways did not play a major part in Detroit's expansion during the last two decades of the nineteenth century, when the city grew and expanded its housing from 1.5 miles past city hall to the fringes beyond 3 miles from city hall. At least half of the city did without the street railways. In the west, white-collar Americans had been provided with transportation to their subdivisions as they opened. In the east, working-class immigrants could not count on it. If Detroit in 1880 was a profoundly divided city, it remained so as it grew, and technological change did not cut across social cleavages but rather adapted to them. (Zunz, 1982, p.125)

It is worth considering whether the ways in which new transport technology was introduced were so very different elsewhere, for example in London, where outlying northern and western boroughs were well served by tube lines very early, but where Hackney still lacks an underground station.

The heyday of electrified urban transport systems, in particular of streetcar systems, proved rather short. Although the growth of urban electric rail transport lines was extremely rapid, their decline followed quickly after their rise. The main reason was the motor car. As with the rise of electric-streetcar systems, America led the way with their fall. Problems began to appear during the First World War. Henry Ford's Model T, which transformed motoring from an expensive hobby of the rich into something within the reach of millions of Americans, had already been in production for nearly a decade when the United States entered the war. By 1915, increasingly widespread car ownership had begun to be reflected in a decline in the traffic carried by some street railways. Motorized buses on rubber wheels also started to attract passengers, although buses were common earlier in London and Paris than in the great American cities – with the exception of New York, where buses were introduced on Fifth Avenue in 1905 because the city government would not allow rails to be laid on this prestigious thoroughfare. Wartime inflation raised the costs of the streetcar operators, and it proved difficult with rigid fares structures to keep pace. By 1920 the automobile was used for half the journeys made by Americans, and in 1924 the number of passengers carried on American tramways declined. Of course streetcars remained an important means of urban transport for a few years yet (more than half of the people who used public transport in American cities in the mid-1930s used trams), but their days as an important means of mass transport were numbered. (The only American cities which retain them are Boston and Philadelphia, and in both cases the streetcars go underground in the city centre.)

6.2 INTERNAL COMBUSTION AND THE RISE OF THE MOTOR CAR

As a social device as well as a technological one, the motor car differed fundamentally from the electric tram, the underground line and the main-line train in a number of important respects – and these differences provided the basis for far-reaching changes in the ways in which new transport technologies affected people's everyday lives. Firstly, it is flexible: the route it follows is not fixed by rail. Secondly, it carries its own fuel supply, and can be turned on and off quickly and easily. And thirdly, it provides individual – not collective or communal – mechanically powered transport. As such, it has given considerable freedom to those who have had access to it: no longer dependent upon where railway or street railway companies chose to build their lines and no longer regimented by the tyranny of the timetable, car owners could go where they wanted when they wanted, in privacy, provided the roads were available (and not too congested). Although for a time in the early twentieth century electricity (from batteries carried on the vehicle) seemed to offer a promising source of power for individual motor cars, the power source eventually implemented was, as we all know, the internal combustion engine.

In 1876 Nicolaus August Otto, a German, developed a successful internal combustion gas engine. Internal combustion was not new, however. Indeed, the first internal combustion engine was the gun – which works with short explosive bursts of energy. The problem was how to put the energy to work with a smooth flow of power. In 1860 the Frenchman Étienne Lenoir had built an internal combustion engine which aroused considerable excitement at the time, with some journals confidently predicting that the development of Lenoir's engine meant the end of the age of steam (Bryant, 1974, p.109). Yet Lenoir's engine failed to live up to these high hopes. It was a two-stroke engine – similar in operation to steam engines – which drew in air and gas for the first stroke and ignited it with an electric spark in the second. And it had a host of problems: it overheated badly; it required large amounts of oil and cooling water; and it was not notably more efficient than the steam engine it was designed to replace. The result was that most Lenoir engines soon were scrapped or converted to steam.

While a travelling salesman in the Rhineland, Otto had begun by experimenting with a model of a Lenoir engine, and his invention marked a far-reaching improvement on its predecessor. It was the first four-stroke engine, which worked quite differently from the familiar steam engine. By compressing a controlled mixture of gas and air (petrol was still considered too dangerous to use as a fuel in such an engine), which then was ignited, Otto developed an engine three to four times more efficient than contemporary steam engines. Instead of the Lenoir two-stroke process, in Otto's engine one complete cycle involved four strokes of the piston: (1) downwards, to draw in the fuel and air mixture through a valve near the top of the cylinder, (2) upwards, to compress the mixture, then after ignition (3) the power stroke downwards, and (4) upwards to expel the burnt gases through another valve. Otto's engine proved to be a tremendous commercial success, and his Gasmotorenfabrik at Deutz (near Cologne) became the world's largest manufacturer of internal combustion engines.

Otto's engines were stationary and extremely heavy. The first Otto engines weighed roughly one ton per horsepower! But a concept had been developed which, with lighter engines using liquid fuel, eventually would provide power plants for millions of motor cars. The world's first petrol-driven motor cars made their appearance in Germany in 1885; and it was one of Otto's associates, Gottlieb Daimler (who became technical director of the Otto engine factory), who put the Otto engine on wheels in Stuttgart. In the same year Karl Benz, who had a gas-motor factory in Mannheim, also took to the roads in a petrol-driven vehicle. For Daimler, the adaptation of the Otto engine to a 'horseless carriage' was just one use among many – he also used the engine to power boats, farm equipment, machinery and generators. Benz, on the other hand, focused upon the motor car, and developed a series of inventions which were crucial to its development. The car that Benz wheeled out in Mannheim was a three-wheel vehicle which had electric ignition, a water cooling system, a differential gear and carburettor. Soon afterward Benz invented the steering system involving a fixed front axle with steerable stub axles, and in 1899 a gear box for changing speeds. The shape of the modern motor car, however, owes much to René Panhard and Émile Levassor, who produced Daimler engines under licence and began building cars in France in 1891. The cars which emerged from the firm of Panhard et Levassor had rear-wheel drive; the engine was at the front of the car and the radiator in front of the engine, while the gearbox was located in the centre of the car, between the engine and the rear wheels.

Cars came to the United States and Britain a bit later. The first motor car in America was the 'gas buggy' driven by the Duryea Brothers in Springfield, Massachusetts, in 1893. Other American engineers developing petrol cars at this time were Ransom E. Olds, whose 'Oldsmobile' became the first car to be sold in large numbers in the United States, and Henry Ford, then chief engineer for the Edison Illuminating Company in Detroit, who built his first car in 1896. The first cars to appear on British roads were imports from France, and the first British prototypes appeared in 1896 – the year in which Parliament did away with the requirement, as laid down in the 1878 Highways and Locomotives Act, that any mechanical vehicle using public roads had to be preceded by a man on foot and should not exceed four miles per hour.

The new machine caught on remarkably quickly, in part because it met an easily identifiable need and in part because the technologies involved in its manufacture were such as to allow many entrepreneurs to jump on the motorized bandwagon. Many of these early car manufacturers had been bicycle or coach builders, for whom the transition to motor-car manufacture was not all that great. By the turn of the century there were already 600

Figure 6.4
Pioneer of the motor car: Gottlieb Daimler rides in his motorized carriage in 1887, with his son Adolf at the wheel. (Daimler-Benz AG Archives)

Figure 6.5
Pioneer of the motor car: Karl Friedrich Benz (right) in the third variation of his first motor vehicle, in 1888. (Daimler-Benz AG Archives)

different makes of car in France (the world's leading producer, accounting for half of the world total of 52,000 cars in 1903), 60 in the United States, 110 in Britain, and 80 in Germany (Pettifer and Turner, 1984, p.13; Montagu, 1986, p.44). Yet the car business was risky: for example, of the 220 car-building firms which had set up in Britain by 1905, 80 already had gone out of business (Plowden, 1971, p.60). Typically the numbers of cars built by any one manufacturer were quite small, often no more than a handful of cars in a year. In the United States, for example, the total production of motor cars in 1900 was 4,192: 1,575 were electric cars, 1,681 were steam-driven and a mere 936 were petrol-driven (*America's Highways*, 1976, p.54).

These early cars were large, heavy, individually crafted and, therefore, very expensive. Not surprisingly, in its first years this new means of transport was limited to the very wealthy: in Britain during the early 1900s cars cost upwards of £1,500 (Plowden, 1971, p.44) – a vast sum at a time when few male workers could hope to earn as much as £2 per week – and in the United States they cost between $3,000 and $12,000, at a time when labourers could expect to earn $1 per day (*America's Highways*, 1976, p.54). What is more, making a journey in one of these new contraptions could be quite an adventure. There was virtually no repair service should the car break down, and in the event of difficulties drivers had to see to the problem themselves; running out of fuel could mean a long walk to a paint shop to get some more (the first modern petrol station did not appear until 1913, in the United States); dusty roads were extremely unpleasant for passengers exposed to the elements; after a rainstorm getting bogged down in mud was a constant threat; and blowouts and punctures were both frequent and difficult to repair. In 1902, in an article entitled 'The caprices of the petrol motor', C.S. Rolls advised motorists: 'Don't go out even for a short run without a complete equipment of tools, spare parts, petrol and repair outfit, or you may be back late' (quoted in Barker, 1985, p.10). The condition of the roads in most countries was hardly conducive to pleasant motoring, and the new motor cars made matters worse. As William Plowden noted, in his book on *The Motor Car and Politics 1896–1970*, during the early years of motoring 'dust *was* the road, broken down by heavy vehicles and flung into the air by the faster light ones' (Plowden, 1971, p.64). That was in Britain, and in the United States – where at the beginning of the twentieth century less than 10 per cent of the roads were paved with anything at all – the condition of most roads was far worse than in Britain or Western Europe. There was considerable public concern about the damage that the large and heavy new cars were causing to the existing road networks, and about the money it would cost to make the necessary repairs; not surprisingly there were loud calls to restrict where and at what speed cars could be driven.

Thus while the early cars certainly fascinated many people, they also frightened and repelled many others and aroused considerable antipathy – in part because they were so expensive and therefore essentially the play-things of the rich. Particular hostility developed in the countryside. For example, the *Newcastle Daily Chronicle* reported in August 1905 a public denunciation of motor cars at an agricultural show, in which one speaker was recorded as speaking of cars as follows:

> They were a hideous sort of thing, and the occupants were generally dressed up in a manner more representing monkeys than anything else. They travelled along at what they considered their legal rate – he supposed 20 mph – killing and maiming men, women and children, and driving everyone else from the roads with their hideous noise and wretched dust. Still farmers were obliged to contribute largely towards the cost of main-taining the roads, which these hideous things did so much to destroy. (Quoted in Plowden, 1971, p.65)

In the United States, where most surfaced roads built around the turn of the century were urban roads paid for through the taxes of urban dwellers, rural hostility was no less sharp. The rural population tended to regard car drivers as intruders from the city. Some observers even perceived a political threat arising from the animosity towards cars and their wealthy drivers, arousing 'dangerous class feeling' and spreading sympathy for socialism (Pettifer and Turner, 1984, p.43). Probably the most extreme expression of antipathy towards the motor car came from one canton in Switzerland, which in 1900 prohibited 'the driving with automobiles' on all its roads – a prohibition that remained in force until 1925! (Glaser, 1986, p.17).

From about 1905 the shape of the motor industry, and the market for its products, began to change. The numbers of cars produced and sold grew enormously, and the United States overtook France to become far and away the world's largest producer and market for the motor car. This coincided with the advent of the motor car in the countryside, in particular the American countryside. The first cars tended to be found in the cities, which was one of the reasons why they often were greeted with such hostility in the countryside. Rural roads and the problems of repair and maintenance in the countryside posed enormous obstacles; and the concentration of cars in cities was one important reason for the early popularity in America of electric cars, which were easier to start than petrol-driven vehicles (the starter motor was not introduced until 1912) but which had a limited range. The car which, more than any other, changed this picture was Henry Ford's Model T, not least because, with its high ground clearance, it could be driven on awful roads and thus brought motoring to the American countryside.

Henry Ford, working in Detroit, Michigan, introduced several important innovations in motor-car production. Using newly available vanadium alloy steel and other alloys, Ford designed the Model T as a lighter and smaller car than his previous models; unlike the previous Model N, the engine of the Model T consisted of a single-cast block; cheaper pressed steel was used wherever possible instead of cast steel (for example, for the crankcase and transmission case); Ford organized the mass production of components for this new model, and his engineers re-arranged production operations and employed single-purpose machinery to the limit (that is, machines were designed not for general purposes but to produce a specific part for assembly on to this particular model); and faced with tremendous demand for his car and the challenge of producing the unprecedented total of 200,000 cars in a single year, in 1913 he introduced a moving assembly line. Here mass-produced components were put together to produce motor cars far more rapidly, economically and efficiently than hitherto had seemed possible (although, it should be noted, at the cost of extremely high rates of labour turnover). Indeed, from 1909 Ford produced only the Model T; all the different versions of his motor vehicle, from runabout to delivery van, had the same chassis. As a result of his new production methods, Ford was able to lower the price of his car, which opened up a new mass market and ultimately brought motoring within the reach of millions of people. When Ford introduced the Model T in 1908, its price was $850; in 1909 Ford sold 12,295 Model Ts at a price of $950; in 1914 he sold 260,720 for $490; two years later the price was $360 and sales were 577,036 (Hounshell, 1984, p.224). In 1920 half of the roughly 8 million cars on American roads were Model Ts. In 1923 annual production of Model T cars and vans peaked at 2 million, and in 1924 the price of the car reached a low of $295. By the time its production was halted finally, in 1927, 15 million Model T Fords had been sold – a record which stood until finally surpassed by the Volkswagen Beetle in the 1970s.

During the 1920s, however, Ford was overtaken as America's – and the world's – largest motor manufacturer by General Motors. The American car

*Figure 6.6
Model Ts line the main street
in Shamrock, Oklahoma,
during the oil boom in 1914.
(Wyatt Collection, Western
History Collections, University
of Oklahoma Library,
Norman)*

market was changing, as more and more people already had cars (and looked to trade them for something better) and as rough rural roads (for which the Model T had been ideal) were being paved. In 1921 Ford accounted for more than half the American car market; five years later his share was less than a third; and in 1927, when Ford stopped production to switch from the Model T to the new Model A, this slumped to less than a sixth. Ford had been successful by producing a single model, with improvements over the years, ever more cheaply; in David Hounshell's words, 'the Model T was as much an idea as it was an automobile . . . the idea was an unchanging car for the masses' (Hounshell, 1984, p.275). The successful strategy of General Motors during the 1920s offered a marked contrast, which involved heavy advertising expenditure and aimed at selling rather more expensive cars which changed year by year. (General Motors introduced annual model changes in 1923.) Eventually other car makers – even Ford – were compelled to follow suit, not just in the United States but, during he 1930s, in Britain as well.

The architects of the new strategy were Alfred P. Sloan Junior, the president of General Motors, and William Knudsen, a former Ford employee (directing assembly operations in factories outside Detroit) who had left the Ford Motor Company because of disagreements with Henry Ford. Knudsen came to head the Chevrolet Division of General Motors, and deliberately chose neither to imitate the methods of his former boss nor to compete with the Model T directly on price. Instead he opted for constant styling changes, abandoned the Ford idea of 'single-purpose manufacture', and designed the production line for the Chevrolet to facilitate smooth model changeovers, that is, with machines that were not single purpose, for use on only a single model. (The use of single-purpose machines made any fundamental change at the Ford factory cause major disruption, as happened when the Model A replaced the Model T.) In 1927, when the final nail was driven into the coffin of the Model T, General Motors sold more than a million Chevrolets. Whereas the Ford strategy had been ideally suited to bringing private motoring to millions of people who never had owned a car before, the new General Motors strategy was suited to a market where people had second-hand cars to sell, and could be tempted (often with credit facilities, through the General Motors Acceptance Corporation) to 'trade up' (that is, buy a higher priced car) when they came round to purchasing a new car. His own success (and inflexibility) and the resulting maturity of the American car market, paved the way for Ford's eclipse. Finally Ford was compelled to adapt his marketing strategies to the new and more mature market for motor cars: with the ending of Model T production and its replacement by the

Model A in 1927, and then the introduction of the Ford V8 in 1931, the establishment of credit sales through Ford's Universal Credit Corporation, extensive nationwide advertizing campaigns, and a move towards periodic model changes in the 1930s.

The rise of the Ford Motor Company was the single most important component of the spectacular growth of the American automobile industry in the early years of the twentieth century. In 1905 only about 25,000 motor cars were produced in the United States; five years later annual production was 187,000 units; by 1913 the Americans were producing nearly half a million cars annually (as against 32,000 in Britain); and in 1915 American car production stood at 969,930 (*America's Highways*, 1976, p.56ff; Plowden, 1971, p.107). After the First World War, America dominated the world's motor-car industry. In 1922, 12.5 million cars were registered in the United States – four-fifths of the world total of 15.5 millions (Barker, 1985, p.3). But from the middle of the 1920s – the time when the term 'mass production' became widely used in the United States – General Motors was making the running. The company did not succeed simply by producing huge numbers of a single model, but through a carefully planned programme of design change instituted on a regular basis without upsetting production and which constantly raised the interest and expectations of the buying public. The concept of the Model T – 'the single-purpose manufacture of a single-car model with single-purpose machinery' (Hounshell, 1984, p.329) – ultimately proved to be a dead end.

During the 1920s car sales boomed, spurred on by falling prices and the introduction of payment by instalment – part of the credit boom which crashed in 1929. In 1921, 1.6 million new motor vehicles were sold in the United States; in 1923 the figure was 4 million; and in 1929 the total stood at 5.3 million, at which time 471,000 people were employed in the American motor-vehicle industry and were producing roughly ten times as many cars as the entire rest of the world (*America's Highways*, 1976, p.115; Pettifer and Turner, 1984, p.83). (However, the Depression had a savage effect upon the American car industry; annual output slumped to 1.9 million vehicles in 1932 and did not again reach the 1929 total until after the Second World War.) At the beginning of 1930 more than 23 million cars and over 3 million goods vehicles, or one motor vehicle for every 4.6 inhabitants, were registered in the United States. This level of car ownership would not be matched in Britain, with its lower personal income levels, until the mid-1960s. Indeed, America remained the home of more than half the world's cars until well after the Second World War. Motoring had reached the American masses, and the rest of the world (with the exception perhaps of Canada, Australia and New Zealand) was left far behind.

Not only was the difference between the United States and other major industrial countries with regard to car ownership very great, both in terms of the total number of motor vehicles registered and in terms of motor vehicles per capita, but also the nature of the motor-vehicle population was different. Whereas in France 28 per cent, in the United Kingdom 23 per cent, and in Belgium nearly 35 per cent of all motor vehicles were goods vehicles, in the United States the figure was a mere 12.7 per cent. Even though the United States led the world in the number of goods vehicles on its roads, individual private motoring had grown to such an extent that seven-eighths of all motor vehicles on American highways were private cars.

Perhaps even more important, with reference to changes in everyday life, is that widespread car ownership gave people a freedom to move about which they never had had before. People had much greater choice about where they could live, work, shop or spend their leisure time. Urban housing markets altered, as new suburban areas became accessible by car for large numbers of people. Urban centres which had developed first as compact

THIS   FREEDOM

FOR a thousand years we Englishmen have fought for our freedom. Our home is our castle; the highway winds unbarred. Every river is musical with memories; every green field, every beacon hill, is rich with the dust of those who fought for "This Freedom."

Have you spied the purple iris blossoming along the river bank? Have you glimpsed a bit of heaven whilst "picnicing" by the scented pinewood? The wind's on the heath, brother; the highway is calling; there's laughter and deep breath and restful life over there on the hills. Freedom is waiting you at the bang of your front door.

"Is it possible," you ask, "that this freedom can be mine?" Once you ask that question a Jowett is beginning to drive up to your door. For sixteen years the Jowett Car has been bestowing "This Freedom" on grateful folk, at a price you can easily afford. Freedom! at less than you pay for the humdrum, crowded railway train. Read on, and you will ride on —Brother of the Broad High Way! THIS FREEDOM IS YOURS

Figure 6.7
The motor car: the key to freedom. Advertisement for Jowett cars. (Photo: Graham Turner)

Table 6.1   Numbers of motor vehicles registered, 1 January 1930

		Population per	
	Cars	Goods vehicles	Motor vehicles
Belgium	93,475	49,861	56
France	930,160	366,007	32
Germany*	501,254	157,432	97
Italy	188,978	52,485	172
Japan	52,769	31,711	735
Netherlands**	71,751	40,577	70
Poland	30,258	6,738	822
Sweden	101,655	34,591	45
United Kingdom***	1,157,344	348,441	31
United States	23,128,250	3,373,193	4.6

*   1 July 1930, excluding the Saarland
**   1 July 1930
*** 30 September 1930

Source: *Statistisches Jahrbuch für das Deutsche Reich 1930* ('Internationale Übersichten')
(Berlin, 1930), p.73; *Statistisches Jahrbuch für das Deutsche Reich 1931* ('Internationale
Übersichten') (Berlin, 1931), p.78.

walking cities, to which were added strips of residential development along
major roads carrying streetcar lines, now began to see the areas between the
rail-transport lines filled in with housing. A – perhaps surprising – example
of this is Los Angeles, which generally is held up as the archetypal city built
for the automobile. In fact the basic shape of Los Angeles was determined
largely by the fixed-rail transport systems of the pre-car era, especially the
very efficient system of electric trams which criss-crossed the region. The
car, later aided by the city's famous freeways, permitted the filling in of
residential areas between the linear developments which had been built along
rail and tram lines. This actually *increased* the residential density of the city!

During the 1920s a sizeable minority of Americans began to drive their
private cars to their place of work: according to studies made in 1928, in
Baltimore, Maryland (which had a very good tram system), 8 per cent of
industrial workers got to work in a car; in Milwaukee, Wisconsin, the figure
for industrial workers was 12 per cent; and in Washington DC it was more
than 20 per cent (Barrett, 1983, pp.161–62). At the same time, during the
second half of the 1920s, travel on American public transport systems began
to decline – a sign that motor cars were beginning to influence the travel of
large numbers of people. The extent of the changes during the inter-war
period is suggested by studies done of the ways people went to and from
work in Chicago, summarized by Paul Barrett:

> Studies done by the CSL [Chicago Surface Lines] at the beginning of
> World War II revealed that both transportation and residence patterns
> had changed dramatically since 1916 and 1926. In 1916, 79.2 per cent of
> workers in a southeast side steel plant had lived within walking distance
> of their jobs. By 1941, 27.4 per cent walked to work, 34.9 per cent used
> streetcars, and 35.2 per cent rode in automobiles. At one major stockyards
> plant, a 1942 survey showed that only 7.8 per cent of the workers walked
> to work, while 28.8 per cent drove and 62.5 per cent used mass transit. In
> 1916 the proportion of presumed walkers in the same general area had
> been between 30 and 47 per cent . . . The preference for the automobile
> was evident, rational and destined to grow. (Barrett, 1983, p.210)

These figures indicate not only vastly altered residential patterns; they also indicate that, during the period discussed, the car did not so much replace transport (trams, elevated railways and the like) as it replaced walking.

Even more than in the cities, where there were alternative means of public transport, the motor car greatly affected life in the countryside. With better roads and access to motor cars, the rural population – and rural society generally – became far less isolated than it had been. Regional trading and shopping centres were able to draw customers on a regular basis from a much wider area, and the larger regional trading centres grew at the expense of the smaller ones. Thus the author of a 1930 study of 'Farm trade centers in Minnesota, 1905–29' noted:

> Families that once lived in the area of one or two centers were thrown into the area of several dozens of centers. An increase in the possibilities of travel to the trade center from 4 miles to 15 miles increased the area of the trade community from 50 square miles to 706 square miles. (Quoted in Fuguitt, 1978, p.344)

Shopping was no longer so geographically restricted, and the nature of modern retailing began to change correspondingly.

The coming of widespread car ownership changed more than just spatial relationships. After the First World War in the United States the motor car ceased to be regarded as a luxury and came to be seen increasingly as a necessity. Rising purchasing power, cheaper car prices, and the advent of the closed (and therefore all-weather) car in 1923, fundamentally changed the character and appreciation of private-car ownership. Thus a newspaper in the prairie state of Nebraska noted during the post-war depression in 1921 that 'not only would the men do without harvesters rather than lose their cars, but the women would yield up their very chewing-gum. Yea, more than that, their pretty clothes' (quoted in Barker, 1985, p.11). In their famous studies of 'Middletown' (Muncie, Indiana) during the 1920s and 1930s, Robert and Helen Lynd observed that the arrival of the car had affected almost every facet of everyday life in Middle America (Lynd and Lynd, 1929 and 1937). The Lynds found 'since about 1920, the automobile has come increasingly to occupy a place among Middletown's "musts" close to food, clothing and shelter' (Lynd and Lynd, 1937, pp.266–67). As a result, consumption patterns altered, as credit facilities brought car ownership within reach of wider circles and people frequently devoted one quarter of their income to their new motorized transport. Sales of clothing sometimes suffered as a consequence, and people often were more prepared to spend money on a motor car than to invest in indoor plumbing. During the savage depression which was heralded by the 1929 stock-market crash, the importance of car ownership became even more sharply apparent. Both in 'Middletown' and in the United States as a whole, although new car sales slumped, neither the total number of car registrations nor the sales of petrol fell appreciably. (In fact, the tax on motor fuel was one of the few taxes actually to yield *increased* revenue during the early 1930s – *America's Highways*, 1976, p.124.) According to the Lynds, 'Car ownership, in Middletown was one of the most depression-proof elements of the city's life in the years following 1929 – far less vulnerable, apparently, than marriages, divorces, new babies, clothing, jewelry, and most other measurable things both large and small' (Lynd and Lynd, 1937, pp.266–67). Respectable businessmen were scandalized 'that some people on relief still manage to operate their cars', and trade-union organizers bemoaned the fact that 'many Middletown workers were more interested in figuring out how to get a couple of gallons of gas for their cars than they were in labor's effort to organize':

> While some workers lost their cars in the depression, the local sentiment, as heard over and over again, is that 'People give up everything in the world but their car'. According to a local banker, 'The depression hasn't changed materially the value Middletown people set on home ownership, but *that's* not their primary desire, as the automobile always comes first.' (Lynd and Lynd, 1937, p.265)

Whatever economic difficulties people faced, they desperately tried to keep their cars.

They also managed to use their cars to kill and maim one another in increasing numbers. During the inter-war period driving habits left a lot to be desired, and accidents were far more frequent relative to the number of cars on the road than they are today. In the United States 10,723 people were killed in highway accidents in 1918; by 1924 the figure had almost doubled, reaching nearly 20,000; in 1929 the figure stood at 31,215, nearly three times the 1918 total; and in 1941 it reached 39,969 – a figure not exceeded until 1957! (*America's Highways*, 1976, pp.115, 127, 149.) In Britain roughly 120,000 people were killed on the roads between 1918 and 1939 and another million and a half were injured; the annual number of British traffic fatalities during the mid-1930s, in excess of 6,500 per year, was higher than in the mid-1960s (Bagwell, 1974, pp.233–35). In Germany as well traffic fatalities rose rapidly during the inter-war period, despite the relatively low levels of car ownership: in 1926, 2,379 people died in car and motor-cycle accidents; in 1930 the figure stood at 5,867; and in 1936 it had reached 7,738 (*Statistisches Jahrbuch*, 1928, pp.54–55; *Statistisches Jahrbuch*, 1938, pp.64–65). (Of this last figure, 5,438 died in car accidents and 2,200 in motor-cycle accidents; nearly 79 per cent of the car fatalities and over 87 per cent of the motor-cycle fatalities were male!) Small wonder that Hitler complained in his speech at the 1939 Berlin International Automobile Exhibition that in six years motor traffic claimed more German lives than had the Franco-Prussian War (quoted in Glaser, 1986, pp.35–36).

The effects of the motor-car industry upon the American economy as a whole were no less impressive than its social effects. As we have noted, on the eve of the depression the American motor-vehicle industry directly employed nearly half a million people. Garages employed many more. The growth of car ownership changed the nature of the oil industry, as world consumption of petroleum spirit suitable for the motor car grew from 9 million gallons in 1903 to 34 million gallons in 1909, 119 million gallons in 1914, 199 million gallons in 1919 and 4,200 million gallons after the Second World War in 1948 (Barker, 1985, p.10). As W.W. Rostow noted in his famous treatise on *The Stages of Economic Growth*, on the eve of the Second

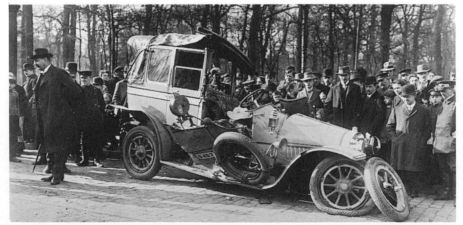

*Figure 6.8
The dark side of motorization: an accident in Berlin in March 1913, in which five people died and two more were seriously injured. (Ullstein Bilderdienst, Berlin)*

World War, in 1938, the American automobile industry consumed '51 per cent of [America's] strip production; 34 per cent of steel bars; 41 per cent of steel sheets; 53 per cent of malleable iron; 54 per cent of alloy steel; 69 per cent of plate glass; 29 per cent of nickel; 25 per cent of lead; 40 per cent of mohair . . . and 80 per cent of rubber' (Rostow, 1971, p.199). One can see how Rostow could regard the mass motorization which took place first in the United States and later in other industrial countries as a key element of his model of economic development culminating in 'the era of high mass-consumption'. This is how he characterized the 1920s:

> The United States took to the wheels. This was quite truly the age of the mass automobile. With the automobile the United States began a vast inner migration into newly constructed single-family houses in the suburbs . . . Automobiles, single-family houses, roads, household durables, mass markets in higher-grade foods – these tell a good deal of the story of the transformation of American society in the 1920s, a transformation which supported the boom of the 1920s and which altered the whole style of a continent's life, down to its courting habits. (Rostow, 1971, p.77)

Motorization also directly affected public-transport systems. Not only did it lead to a decline as people began to abandon the trams for their cars; it led as well to the introduction and widespread use of petrol-driven buses. The advantages of such buses over electric-traction systems were marked, especially for smaller communities. Buses were far more flexible; their routes could be altered easily and quickly to satisfy demand, and the mechanical breakdown of one vehicle did not hold up all other vehicles behind it; and they did not require the large capital expenditure necessary to build and maintain street railways, elevated or underground lines. Until the late 1920s, however, petrol-driven buses remained far less attractive than trams: they were relatively slow to load and too small to compete effectively with the electric trams. However, in the late 1920s new, larger and more robust buses appeared which matched the capacities of trams but did not have the drawbacks. Although electric-traction companies and political interests in the United States worked to delay the widespread introduction of buses on the streets (electric traction meant more jobs than buses), and although trackless trolley buses provided an intermediate stage in many British and American cities, the petrol-powered bus was ultimately to replace the electric tram almost entirely in Britain and in the United States.

Of course, motor vehicles need roads. Without a decent road network, the spread of motor cars was bound to remain circumscribed. As noted above, before the advent of the motor car, roads in most countries were in poor condition. Few were equipped to handle motorized traffic, fewer were paved, and the new heavy motor vehicles inflicted severe damage on the existing road network. And, perhaps paradoxically, roads in the United States – where mass motorization first became a reality – tended to be worse than those in Western Europe. (France had probably the best, and best maintained, roads in the world in the early twentieth century.) The older macadam and gravel roads could not stand up to the wear caused by ever larger numbers of motor vehicles, whose pneumatic tyres tended to suck stones out of the road surface, thus destroying it. During the early years of the twentieth century considerable energy was put into developing new road-building techniques, to produce roads which could bear the burden of motorized vehicles. Since the 1870s hot-laid asphalt roads had appeared in both European and American cities, but this was regarded as too costly for the thousands of miles of country roads. The problem was to find a cheap way of building tough, dust-free roads. Around the turn of the century experiments were made with both steel and brick trackways; Portland-cement concrete was used, and the possibility of using slag as a road-building material was investigated; another idea was the sprinkling of crude oil on roads, which settled dust and killed weeds, and which 'it is claimed by some . . . will make a surface impervious to water, and consequently comparatively free from frost and mud' (quoted in *America's Highways*, 1976, p.67). But as traffic increased concern shifted from preventing dust to preserving the road, and the construction method which proved the best was the use of bitumen to bind roads: bituminous tar or asphalt surfaces which could bear up under the weight of increasing motorized road traffic were placed over macadam, slag or gravel bases. Even so, most roads were not hard-surfaced before the First World War: in the United States, although the mileage of hard-surfaced roads was increasing rapidly during the first years of the twentieth century, by 1914 only 10.5 per cent (257,291 miles) of the 2,445,760 miles of rural road were surfaced with anything other than dirt, and a mere 32,180 miles (1.3 per cent of the total) had dust-free surfaces (bituminous macadam, brick, concrete) (*America's Highways*, 1976, p.89).

Road building on a massive scale meant massive expenditure, and that spelled increased state involvement. The arrival of the motor car meant that a vast amount of money had to be generated to pay for the building and maintenance of thousands of miles of road, which were subjected to increasing wear and tear. In the United States, for example, yearly expenditure on roads rose from $79.62 millions in 1904 to $240.26 millions ten years later (*America's Highways*, 1976, p.89). And the question of who should bear the brunt of the costs (for what still was a minority interest) was, understandably, a contentious political issue. In Britain this gave birth to the 'Road Fund' announced by Lloyd George in his Budget speech of April 1909, which made the roads system self-financing and, therefore, expenditure on it politically acceptable. The increased motor taxation (motor-vehicle tax and tax on petrol) was to be spent specifically on roads; the Exchequer, according to Lloyd George, 'shall derive no advantage'. As William Plowden noted, 'tar replaced dust at the expense not of the ratepayers, but of the motorists' (Plowden, 1971, p.95). In the United States the problem was compounded by the myriad of different authorities in a federal governmental system, which placed huge obstacles in the way of creating a unified highway network. Road building in America was essentially a local and state affair, paid for by the issue of road and bridge bonds. However, a wide range of interests (including the American Automobile Association, the Post Office, agricultural producers concerned about the costs of getting produce to the nearest rail station, and the construction industry) pressed for the Federal government to help finance road building. During the last years of the nineteenth century and the first years of the twentieth, the first, tiny amounts of aid by the Federal government to states and counties for road building was aimed at developing a system of the rural free delivery of post – one of the most notable steps towards lifting the isolation of rural America. A major change came with the passing by Congress of the Federal Aid Road Act in July 1916. This allocated, for the first time, comparatively large amounts of Federal money ($25,000,000 per year) for aid to the states for their road-building programmes. Furthermore, it stipulated that after 1920 each had to have a State Highway Department to administer the aid and supervise highway planning, construction and maintenance (in 1914 about half the states had a highway department, but by the end of 1917 they all did), while it left the building and maintenance in the hands of the states (that is, neither the counties within the states nor the Federal government).

During the First World War, however, there were other priorities in most combatant countries: production of motor vehicles for civilian use was curtailed or suspended, as was much work on road-building projects; private motoring was discouraged; and the building materials used for roads as well as labour were in short supply. The effects of the neglect of road maintenance during the war were, particularly in the United States, compounded by a vast increase in heavy-goods traffic on the roads. America's entry into the war was followed by a Federal government takeover of the railways, massive shortages of rail cars, and delays in the movement of goods (most of which were moved by rail). The production of heavy-goods vehicles in the United States was not restricted in wartime – quite the opposite. As a result, the numbers of non-military trucks on America's roads increased by roughly 60 per cent (roughly 326,000 to 525,000) between 1917 and 1918.

One important consequence of these developments – blockages on the rail network and a vast increase in the number of goods vehicles on the road – was the birth of the American 'trucking' industry. Before the First World War goods generally had been transported by rail for long distances and by horse-drawn wagons for short distances, local deliveries and distribution from the railway terminals. And goods transport on the roads was rather slower to be motorized than passenger transport. (One illustration of this is the fact that on the eve of the First World War, 88 per cent of goods vehicles in London were horse-drawn, whereas 90 per cent of London's passenger vehicles were motorized – Barker, 1985, pp.7–8.) In America the war saw the creation of new road freight delivery services. For the first time large quantities of heavy goods were moved over long distances – sometimes hundreds of miles – by road, and the savings in time, money and paperwork were often considerable. Goods generally spent much less time waiting to be conveyed (rail cars spend far more time at terminals than actually moving); transporting goods in company-owned vehicles cut down on paperwork; less expense was necessary to box and crate goods which previously would have had to be extremely well protected to survive a rail journey. The positive experiences of motorized freight transport during 1917 and 1918 'permanently changed the shipping habits of American industry. In a matter of a few months, the railroads lost millions of tons of freight business by default – business they were destined never to recover' (*America's Highways*, 1976, p.99). However, the increased loads left many roads in need of considerable repair after the war.

The real boom in highway construction came after the First World War. The damage done to American highways by heavy-goods vehicles and the mobilization of interests urging massive new road-building projects created pressure for the improvement of the road network. In 1919 the President of the American Association of State Highway Officials, A.R. Hirst, asserted (in response to criticism that the states had not been active enough in improving the road network after the war):

Never, I believe, since the days of early railroad development have the American people been so determined to change instantly their means of transport and not even then were they so willing to pay the cost, provided they could get the results.

What are the results they are now demanding and what are some of the problems that grow from these demands?

They are expecting the States which had no highway organizations three or even two years ago, which had done no preliminary work and in some of which hardly a mile of rural highway had ever been built, to create an organization full sprung from the earth . . . and to build instantly hundreds of miles of modern roads costing millions upon millions of dollars. In the older States in the highway game, better prepared with organizations and contractors, and with some knowledge of materials and construction conditions, they are asking us to double, triple, or quadruple our annual output of roads. (Quoted in *America's Highways*, 1976, p.104)

During the 1920s, as car ownership increased, so did the pressure for better roads both in the countryside and in the increasingly congested cities. As Paul Barrett pointed out in his recent study of private and public transport in Chicago during the first three decades of the twentieth century, 'motorists, unlike transit-bound non-drivers, could take their business – and their homes – elsewhere if the city did not accommodate them' (Barrett, 1983, p.141).

As pressure for road building in America grew so did the role of the Federal government. For one thing, it distributed war-surplus materials – in particular motor vehicles and explosives – to state highway departments. At the end of the First World War the US Army owned more motor trucks than any other organization in the world, and in June 1919 the US Bureau of Public Roads allocated over 20,000 of them to the states; and altogether more than 20,000 tonnes of explosives – of great importance in road building – was distributed to the states. No less important was financial aid for highway building, which was notably increased during the early 1920s (as prices fell from their post-war inflationary heights), enabling state highway departments to undertake many important highway projects. According to Thomas MacDonald, the Chief of the Bureau of Public Roads, who looked approvingly at the 10,247 miles of American highway built with federal aid in 1922:

> Merely to say that this year has added 10,000 miles to the previously existing mileage conveys no adequate sense of the far-reaching effects of the work that is being done. The 10,000 miles completed represent something more than the equivalent of three transcontinental roads. They are not transcontinental roads. They are not even connected roads, though as the work continues they will be connected; but each separate project is to some community a new opportunity, a means of bettering, in some respects, the economic and social status of the community, and together they form the links which, eventually united, will constitute a new means of transportation, no less important to the country as a whole than that offered by the railroads. (Quoted in *America's Highways*, 1976, p.113)

The hyperbole was not misplaced. The 1920s saw a vast increase in car ownership and road building; and even the depressed 1930s saw car ownership increase and the continued building of new highways, partly as a result of Federally-subsidized road-building projects used to provide jobs for some of the millions of unemployed.

There was also increased interest taken in traffic patterns, as American cities and states devoted considerable effort to counting traffic, and the post-war decade saw the first well-researched 'transportation surveys' analysing car ownership, traffic patterns and driver behaviour. In 1924 Maine (which began systematically counting traffic in 1916) used a state-wide traffic survey to plan the development of its highway system, and Illinois' Cook County (Chicago) did the same in 1924 and the State of Ohio in 1925; in 1927 the first comprehensive regional road transport planning was presented in Ohio – the Cleveland Regional Area Traffic Survey, which was funded partly by the US Bureau of Public Roads and which produced a ten-year road-improvement plan. For the first time, social-scientific planning techniques were applied in a systematic way to the problems of regional transport, of determining the framework within which new means of transport would shape people's everyday lives. The scientific management and application of technological innovation appeared to be the key to 'progress'.

The 1920s also saw the first examples of a new type of highway, with limited access. The first example of this was the Bronx River Parkway, in wealthy suburban Westchester County to the north of New York City, which was opened in 1923. Planned in 1917, the Bronx River Parkway was intended as a recreational highway connecting the parks in the northern reaches of New York City with the city's water reservoirs further to the north, part of the Bronx River Commission's schemes to save the Bronx River from the polluting effects of tips and land fills. Completed at a cost of $15,000,000 for fifteen miles, the road was built in a long, landscaped parkland along the river; great effort was made to preserve and enhance the landscape – and the only trees chopped down were those actually growing where the road itself was to be; and all commercial traffic was excluded. The new road proved extremely popular, so much so that a 'Westchester County Park Commission' was established to build more parkways – now planned primarily for suburban commuting. The new roads helped to finance themselves by opening up new areas to suburban development which then provided increased tax revenue, and by the Second World War many miles of parkways had been built in the New York City region. (The high cost of this new form of road building limited it largely to New York and, to a lesser extent, Washington, DC.) They were financed also with tolls: the great success in this regard came with the Merritt Parkway, which was opened in 1938 and connected southern Connecticut with the parkways in Westchester County. When the Connecticut state government began to look round in 1939 for ways to finance the extension of the parkway northwards to the state capital at Hartford, it was decided to impose a 10-cent toll on cars using the Merritt Parkway. The result was a tremendous financial success which was soon imitated.

Two other noteworthy American road-building projects were undertaken during this period: the first of the famous Los Angeles Freeways (opened in 1940 as the Arroyo Seco Parkway, later renamed the Pasadena Freeway), and the Pennsylvania Turnpike, designed to traverse the Appalachian mountain range and planned from the outset to be financed through tolls (although it also benefited from Federal funding, through the Public Works Administration and the Reconstruction Finance Corporation). Building work on the 160-mile highway in Pennsylvania, which used the right-of-way of an abandoned railway, began in November 1938 and was completed a little less than two years later. Modelled on the German autobahns, the Pennsylvania Turnpike – with its two-lane divided carriageways, controlled access, and absence of steep gradients – became the prototype for future highways in the land of the motor car.

The growth of the American motor-car industry, private-car ownership and the building of the American highway network raise a number of important questions about the ways in which technology and technological innovations come to affect people's everyday lives. Before 1950, the United States was far and away the world's most motorized country. On the eve of the Second World War the American motor-car industry was producing many more cars than the rest of the world put together, and the American population was driving far more cars than all the rest of the world's population. In the United States in 1935 the density of car ownership was more than four times that in France or the United Kingdom, and more than twelve times the density of car ownership in the home of the autobahn, Nazi Germany. Why? Why should the United States have taken such an overwhelming lead in the motorization race, particularly when the requisite technology was developed in Europe? How are we to explain the fact that the widespread dissemination of motor-transport technology took place so much earlier in the United States than in those countries (in particular, France and Germany) where the technology of motor transport initially was much more advanced?

One reason was America's size and wealth. Real incomes were far higher in the United States than they were in Europe, and the American home market was enormous. In 1911 an agent for American cars in Britain saw this clearly when he observed:

The sale of cheap cars can never be as large in England as it is in the United States. The same class of people that would find it difficult to pay $650 (about £135, and roughly the cost of a Model T at the time) for a car in the United States find it difficult to lay aside half that sum here. (Quoted in Barker and Savage, 1976, p.142)

In 1913, when Ford began producing his Model T on an assembly line at the Highland Park plant in Detroit, there was not sufficient purchasing power to justify an equivalent development in Britain or any other country. During the 1920s American wages were sufficiently high for skilled workers to afford a Model T Ford – which in 1924 cost a mere $295, a sum which a skilled worker in the steel industry at that time could expect to earn in less than three months. This created the potential for a mass market, which in turn made possible immense economies of scale; and it was these economies of scale which allowed Ford to succeed so famously in providing millions of Americans with their first car. In Britain even the small £100 cars which appeared in the 1930s (when Morris began Britain's first assembly-line car production) were far more expensive for British buyers than American cars were for higher-paid Americans. In Germany, where the extent of motorization during the 1920s was particularly low, and where a rather large number of motor manufacturers were producing a relatively small number of cars, prices were far higher than in Britain or the United States (and wages were lower).

A related point was that economies of scale and the concentration of most of the American market on a few models meant that the unit costs of American car manufacturers were often much lower than those of their counterparts elsewhere. To compare with Britain: in 1935, 2.86 cars were produced in Britain for each car worker; in the United States the figure was 8.76 per annum. Productivity per head in the United Kingdom car-components industry (important because components bought from outside suppliers comprised an especially large proportion of the value of British cars) was roughly half that in the United States (Rhys, 1972, pp.13–14). Thus a larger, wealthier American market allowed economies of scale and efficiencies of production, which in turn allowed the making of products which were, both relatively and absolutely, cheaper than elsewhere and thus stimulated demand further. This enabled the American car industry to dominate world motor-vehicle production to an extraordinary degree until well after the Second World War.

Another important condition governing the extent and character of popular motorization was formed by the tax structure and financial conditions generally. Here Germany, with its surprisingly low level of motorization before the Nazis came to power, is an interesting case in point. The German car industry (with the possible exception of Adam Opel AG, which re-tooled almost completely between 1924 and 1928 and introduced an American-style assembly line) was quite inefficient by international standards during the 1920s and therefore incapable of producing cars within reach of the budgets of most Germans. (The cheapest 4-horsepower Opel cost roughly twice as much as a 20-horsepower Model T, in a country where people earned much less than in America – Glaser, 1986, pp.30–31.) It also faced a number of further obstacles, even before the economic crisis knocked the bottom out of the car market. German roads were rather poor and Weimar governments did not make great efforts to repair or extend them; the German railway network was dense and efficient, and received considerable government funding for improvements during the 1920s: taxes on cars, regarded as a luxury, were quite heavy; and the economic difficulties during wartime and the continued and accelerating inflation afterwards destroyed much of the personal savings which possibly could have been directed towards private car purchases. The annual costs of running a car before the Nazis began their mass motorization campaign could equal the new purchase price. The tremendous growth of the German motor-vehicle industry during the 1930s was sparked by the reversal of many of these phenomena: the Nazi government put a tremendous amount of money into building and improving the road network (especially with the vast autobahn project, begun in 1933 and resulting in 3,000 kilometres of completed motorway by the time the Second World War began); with the decline of unemployment, many more people found it possible to save up for a car; and major tax concessions were introduced in order to stimulate car buying – on 10 April 1933 motor tax was abolished for new cars.

In Britain as well, tax structures played an important role in shaping the car market. From 1910 British car tax was calculated on the basis of horse-power, and would continue to be until after the Second World War. The greater the horsepower, the greater the tax, on a sliding scale; and in 1920 the scale was re-drafted to slide much more steeply (with increases of £1 per horsepower), which for the owners of some medium- to large-engined cars meant an increase in tax liability of three to four times (Plowden, 1971, pp.167–69). The result was a concentration by the British motor industry on small-engined, light cars. Whereas in 1927 only one-quarter of new car registrations in Britain were of cars of 10 horsepower or less, this figure rose to one-third in 1929 and between 1933 and 1938 it stood at three-fifths; sales of cars with 10 horsepower or less were three times as high in 1937 as they had been in 1929 (Miller and Church, 1979, pp.191–92). This had both advantages and drawbacks. On the plus side, it was an important reason why British car sales were not so savagely affected by the Depression as they might have been, and it meant that British car manufacturers catered for lower-income buyers to an extent unparalleled in Europe; 95 per cent of new-owner car sales in Britain during the 1930s were of cars of up to 10 horsepower. This also afforded British manufacturers some measure of protection against foreign (especially American) competition at home (although imports of small Italian Fiats and German Opels rose substantially during the 1930s). However, it made British cars less attractive in some foreign markets, where larger, more robust and powerful vehicles were better suited – especially in countries with poor roads.

In the discussion of the spread of motorization, connections often are made between the spread of cars and the building of roads. The conventional wisdom, established in the United States (the first country in which they became part of the everyday lives of millions) is that cars created the demand for roads. First came the dissemination of the new technology, then the demand for the infrastructure suitable to that technology. In the case of the United States, the new technology came in the shape of the Model T, which brought motorization to millions before there were decent roads on which the millions could drive their motor cars. Then, so the story goes, the political and economic pressure was created for the vast expenditure required to develop a modern highway network free of mud and dust. But was it? Even in the United States there was pressure for good roads long before the arrival of the Model T. During the 1880s the 'Good Roads Movement' attempted, with some success, to galvanize American state legislatures into action, and by the 1890s organizations of urban bicyclists were agitating nationwide for better roads, and in 1892 the bicyclists' national umbrella organization of cyclists' clubs, the 'League of American Wheelmen' began its magazine *Good Roads*, the aim of which was to press for road improvements. The first 'Good Roads Association' was formed in Missouri in 1891; the first State Highway Commission was established in Massachusetts in 1894; and during the 1890s the US Federal government was taking an increased interest in the condition of the country's roads (*America's Highways*, 1976, pp.41–52).

That bicyclists should have figured so large in the pressure for better roads in the United States is revealing. During the 1890s there was a boom in bicycle production and ownership, as prices dropped for what was essentially a new product. Two developments were significant, and both originated in Britain: the introduction of the safety bicycle with rear-wheel chain drive, the Rover safety cycle produced in Coventry in 1885, and the introduction of the pneumatic tyre by J.B. Dunlop three years later (Bagwell, 1974, p.150). The result was a more comfortable, safer means of transport, attractive to women as well as men, and eagerly bought by the urban middle classes – the people who campaigned for road improvements in the United States in the 1890s. Bicycles also came to be widely used by working people to get to and from work in Britain and elsewhere; however, widespread practical use of the bicycle in the United States probably was cut short somewhat by the fact that the motor car came within reach of ordinary people so quickly.

There is evidence to suggest that, at least with regard to road improvement, the initiative was as much political in origin as it was technological. American city governments, for example, often put money into road improvements in advance of widespread car ownership. Thus Eric Monkkonen, examining American urban developments around the turn of the century, notes that 'the age of hard surfaced roads preceded the age of the automobile' (Monkkonen, forthcoming, chapter 6). Even more telling were developments in inter-war Germany. There, as we have seen, the political initiative for massive road improvements did not follow a widespread dissemination of the new transport technology among the population. The German paradox is that the country which pioneered the motorway was one of the most backward with regard to the spread of private motor transport. In Germany the autobahns, together with the Volkswagen project, were designed to stimulate the spread of private motor transport, not respond to it. The impetus for improving the German road network was political and economic (for the autobahn building programme was designed also to combat the mass unemployment which faced the Nazi government in 1933).

A technological-determinist approach often underpins explanations of spatial relationships, in particular of why cities have taken the shapes they have. We have observed that the 'walking city' differed physically quite considerably from subsequent urban development, for example, as electric tram systems were expanding; and the urban developments of the late nineteenth century differed again from those built when large numbers of people had their own cars. Different modes of transport made possible different commercial, residential and commuting patterns. This type of argument is made particularly frequently with reference to the effects of the motor vehicle, perhaps because of the increasingly critical attention which the consequences of mass car ownership and the shift of goods from rail to road has received recently. Consider how the influential American urban historian, Sam Bass Warner, evaluates the (admittedly profound) consequences of the growth of the road-freight industry from the First World War:

> The change in the costs of short-haul transportation was probably the single most important factor to influence the dispersal of job locations within the modern metropolis. Intra-city freight movement had formerly been dependant on men and boys who carried parcels in handcarts or on horse-drawn wagons, and its slow pace and high costs had restricted business users of freight service to rail locations in the manufacturing sectors or near the central terminals of the inner city . . . the truck and automobile loosened and broke these constraints. (Warner, 1972, p.117)

As Warner sees it, the spread of new transport technology promoted decentralization and changed the commercial framework, and thus the structures within which millions of people lived their everyday lives. No one would deny that changes in transport technology had profound consequences. But, as our short discussion of road building suggests, the impetus for change did not necessarily spring from the technology by itself.

Explanations of urban and transport development often are coloured by a certain hostility towards cars and the world they have made and towards the 'decline of transit' which they (and the interests which profited by them) have brought about (Yago, 1984). Back in the good old days people were able to take public transport, in the form of trams, to get where they needed to go in (by today's standards) relatively compact cities. Present-day urban geography, and a fairly ugly geography in many cases, is determined largely by the car – with plans for residential and commercial development (shopping centres, industrial parks) assuming access by private automobile transport. Leaving aside debates about the benefits of contemporary development, we can see that this picture is historically questionable. We should be wary of applying present-day dislike of cars retrospectively, and thus creating a skewed picture of how and why the motor car spread so rapidly during the first half of the twentieth century. For rail did not provide a real day-to-day alternative to walking for most people eighty years ago. The alternative which provided vastly increased mobility was the motor car, whether we like it or not.

6.3 TRANSPORT TAKES TO THE AIR

Today millions of people have flown; air transport has almost completely supplanted the railway as the chief means of long-distance travel in the United States and ocean liners as the chief means of intercontinental travel; and in some areas of the world (for example, in Siberia) air travel provides the only link between major settlements and the outside world. Although air transport had only begun to affect large numbers of people by the end of our period, the ways in which it did so proved to be important harbingers for the future. Further, more than any other means of transport developed between 1870 and 1950, air travel owed a tremendous amount to the military and the demands of war.

In terms of public fascination, few technological developments could compete with air transport during the early decades of the twentieth century. Stunt flyers regularly attracted large crowds; the 'air aces' of the First World War (two of the more famous were Baron von Richthofen and Hermann Goering) became well-known public figures; and the feats of Charles Lindbergh (who flew the first solo flight across the Atlantic in 1927) made front-page news across the world. Not even the Soviet Union was immune: at the height of the purge trials of 1936 and 1937 Soviet newspapers were filled with accounts of the exploits of Soviet pilots ('Bolshevik knights of culture and progress', 'Stalin's falcons'), exploits that included the first landing on the North Pole in May 1937 and a non-stop popular flight from Moscow to the United States one month later. According to L.M. Kaganovich, a member of the Politburo of the Soviet Communist Party at the time, 'Aviation is the highest expression of our achievements' (Bailes, 1978, pp.388–93).

Manned flight is not a new thing. The first person to go aloft did so in a Montgolfier balloon in 1783; the first successful human-carrying glider took flight in 1809; and the first trip in a motor-powered lighter-than-air craft was made near Paris in 1852, with a steam engine driving an airship. But the development of air transport into something that could alter people's everyday lives came much later, and was dependent on technological advances elsewhere. Already by the middle of the nineteenth century a great deal was known about aerodynamics; the problem was how to power a flying machine. What was required was a powerful but relatively lightweight engine – one that had a sufficient power-to-weight ratio to drive an aircraft without adding so much weight as to prevent it from getting and remaining aloft. As with the motor car, the solution was the petrol-powered internal combustion engine developed in the 1880s by Gottlieb Daimler. Indeed, this development proved even more decisive for air transport than for motorized road transport, for unlike the case of motor cars (which also have been powered by steam and electricity), mechanically-powered air travel in heavier-than-air machines would have been impossible without the development of some form of reliable internal combustion engine.

The first controlled and sustained flight of a heavier-than-air craft was made at Kitty Hawk, North Carolina, in December 1903 by the brothers Wilbur and Orville Wright. The Wright brothers and other early aviation pioneers powered their flying machines with engines similar to those that powered the cars of the time. However, petrol engines were adapted fairly soon to the purpose of powering propeller-driven aeroplanes: air-cooling began to be used as well as water-cooling (the Wrights' engine had been water-cooled), and rotary engines were designed with the cylinders arranged around a stationary crankshaft. Even so, despite some attempts to use aeroplanes to deliver goods and post before the First World War, air transport generally remained a rather exotic technological curiosity. It was not until the war that aeroplanes were put extensively to practical uses, such as surveillance, machine-gunning ground troops and bombing. The war contributed greatly to the technological development of aeroplanes, with multi-engined craft with enclosed fuselages, and stimulated a vast increase in aircraft manufacture. In 1914, there were only about 5,000 aeroplanes in the entire world; by the time the war ended the United States alone had production facilities capable of producing 21,000 aircraft per year; in Britain, which had had no aircraft industry before the war, at the time of the Armistice 112,000 people were working to build aeroplanes in what had become the world's largest aircraft manufacturing industry. By the time the war ended, aircraft had developed to a point where they had become sufficiently safe and reliable to be considered for civilian uses.

When the First World War ended there were thousands of aircraft left behind which had been built for the military as well as considerable facilities for building aircraft for which there was no more demand. The need to use this spare capacity lay behind the inauguration of the first regular international air service, between Paris and London, started in 1919. During the first half of 1919 the Royal Air Force ran a regular air service between Hendon and Le Bourget, which often was used by those involved in the peace negotiations underway near the French capital. Then, after civil aviation was permitted once again, a Paris–London service was continued by George Holt Thomas's 'Air Transport and Travel' company, which used converted light bombers for what was the world's first scheduled daily international air service. Holt Thomas's business group, which included Airco, had emerged from the First World War as the largest aircraft manufacturing company in the world, and needed new ventures to stimulate continued demand for aeroplanes once war production ceased. Holt's attempts to restructure were a failure, however, and the Paris–London operation ceased in 1920: military planes were not comfortable enough to serve civilian passenger needs, and the British could not compete with the French, whose government subsidized air services.

During the early post-war years most aircraft in civil use were adapted military planes, and it was not until the late 1920s that aircraft specifically designed for civilian uses began to appear. Increased interest was shown in the use of aeroplanes for the transport of mail (although Britain lagged behind in this regard, with the first domestic airmail service only established in 1934), and during the 1920s air passenger services developed. In Britain, for example, a number of airline companies were established in the 1920s, the most important of which was Imperial Airways – an amalgamation in 1924 of a number of existing companies, enjoying a monopoly of government subsidies for air services. However, the capacities of the available aircraft were limited, with room for only about six passengers on average in the early 1920s; the range of the aircraft was quite limited; safety records left a lot to be desired; night flying was impossible; and flights frequently were cancelled because of bad weather. Even in the mid-1930s only about 60 per cent of scheduled flights actually were carried out in winter, and as late as 1938 only three civil aerodromes in Britain had equipment to assist landings in bad weather (Aldcroft, 1974, p.213). Generally air services were expensive and most operated at a considerable financial loss; civil aviation required government subsidy to keep going.

The two countries that took a clear lead in civil aeronautics during the inter-war period were Germany and the United States. Despite their early lead at the end of the First World War and despite the increase in British air passengers carried during the 1920s and 1930s, the British fell behind. One indication of this is that on the eve of the Second World War the German Deutsche Luft Hansa owned more than three times as many aircraft as did Imperial Airways (220 to 71), which meant that British aircraft manufacturers lacked a sufficiently large market to develop successful, large civil aeroplanes. Whereas German civil aviation benefited from the attentions of a government which had been prohibited from developing military aviation, the lead of the United States stemmed from different sources. The United States did not have a state airline, but because of its vast size there was a large potential market for airmail and passenger services where air travel held clear benefits over cheaper rail travel. For this reason private airlines were able to expand rapidly, and in turn provided the demand for the development of new, larger, twin-engined, all-metal passenger aeroplanes. Large American air carriers were in a position to place orders for new aircraft (with Boeing, Douglas and Lockheed) which could exceed anything British aircraft makers might hope for.

During the inter-war period a number of developments made air transport generally a much more widespread and viable proposition. In the first place, the aircraft available became faster, more reliable and capable of carrying a much greater payload. For example, during the early 1930s some Imperial Airways' planes were able to carry as many as thirty-eight passengers (Bagwell, 1974, p.290). The most famous and successful aeroplane of the

Figure 6.9
A Lufthansa Fokker-Grulich is loaded at Berlin's Tempelhof airport in the late 1920s. (Lufthansa Archives)

Figure 6.10
The Junkers F13, the world's first all-metal transport plane. (Lufthansa Archives)

1930s, the reliable American Douglas DC-3, could carry between twenty and thirty passengers; and the DC-4 could carry twice as many. This meant that it became possible to run at a profit air services which previously required government subsidy. The use of metal propellers, metal frames and cladding with strong and lightweight aluminium alloys, stressed-skin construction, electric engine starters, retractable undercarriages, and (on the eve of the Second World War) pressurized cabins (allowing flight at higher and more economic altitudes, above dangerous bad weather) revolutionized the passenger aeroplane.

There were important changes on the ground as well. Hitherto, landing fields had been few and far between and rather makeshift. Britain in particular lagged behind in the building of civilian airfields: at the end of the 1920s Britain had only four municipal airports; Germany – which had been forbidden from developing military aviation and therefore devoted much resources (from both municipal and national government) to extending civil aviation – had twenty times that number. (One consequence was that in 1927 German aircraft carried 151,000 passengers, while the British carriers flew a mere 19,000.) But a concerted campaign for better facilities brought results: by 1932 there were twelve municipal and forty-three other aerodromes in Britain, and by 1939 the number of municipal aerodromes alone totalled thirty-eight; during the 1930s a network of weather stations and radio control towers were put into operation, although it was not until 1938 that the British government began to channel money into providing night-lighting equipment for airports (Bagwell, 1974, pp.287–92; Myerscough, 1985). In the United States the major push forward came from Secretary of Commerce (and later President), Herbert Hoover. Hoover, who had an engineering background, was the first great technocrat to rise to the pinnacle of American government. In 1926 he pressed the American Congress to pass the Air Commerce Act giving the US Department of Commerce extensive powers over commercial aviation. At Hoover's initiative, a nationwide campaign was set in motion to build and improve municipal airports, provide radio beacons, weather stations, emergency landing fields and the like; and lucrative contracts for carrying airmail (which the US Post Office had done itself, with its own pilots, in the early 1920s) were given to commercial airlines. (By contrast, when the British Post Office began to give mail contracts to British airlines in the 1930s, 'the practice was to accept the lowest tender for short-term contracts which usually meant that the companies could only carry them out at a loss' – Aldcroft, 1974, pp.216–17). By 1929 American industry was producing 7,500 aeroplanes annually, and in 1931 the number of passengers carried by America's airlines exceeded half a million (Hicks, 1960, pp.176–77).

This short sketch illustrates that the growth of air transport during the inter-war period was a result not only, or even necessarily primarily, of new technological developments in aeronautics, but also of other causes: commercial considerations (in particular state help – whether this was in the form of direct aid to state-owned airlines as on the European continent, state subsidies to private airlines as in Britain, or the granting to private airlines of lucrative postal contracts as in the United States), and technological developments in other fields (for example, in radio transmission). By the time the Second World War broke out, however, air travel and transport still had not touched the lives of most people, even in the United States. Not until the war itself, and its immediate aftermath, did air transport really affect the everyday lives of millions of people, and then in ways rather different from those envisaged by optimistic airline entrepreneurs during the 1930s: not as a means of passenger travel, but as delivery systems, for supplies and for bombs.

The Second World War, like the First, stimulated advances in the technologies of air transport. Aircraft became faster, with longer ranges and greater capacities. This in turn vastly increased the potential of aircraft as long-distance bombers, bringing warfare to civilian populations far from the front. The increased capacities allowed bombers to carry many more and heavier bombs, and the increased range allowed bombers to bring destruction to cities and towns hundreds of miles from the front lines. German bombers managed to inflict damage on cities such as Rotterdam, Coventry, Southampton, Plymouth and London during the early stages of the Second World War, but the full force of airborne bombing was felt by the German (and then Japanese) civilian populations from 1942.

On the night of 31 May 1942 the Royal Air Force launched the first 'thousand bomber' raid, on the western German city of Cologne. In the space of two hours Royal Air Force planes dropped 864 explosive bombs and 111,044 incendiary bombs; of Cologne's housing stock of 68,582 residential buildings, 12,840 were damaged and 3,340 completely destroyed – which meant the loss of 13,010 flats, which had housed 45,132 people; large numbers of bakeries, butchers' shops, restaurants and grocery stores were shut, and the food distribution system within the city was brought to a standstill (only shipments from the surrounding region saved it from complete collapse); and where once there had been a normal city landscape there now were streets filled with rubble, emergency kitchens and shops, shells of buildings and dangling electricity leads for the city's trams (Hege, 1981, pp.30–31). Worse followed. On 29 June 1943 an even larger raid killed over 4,000 people, and thereafter Cologne experienced repeated bombing raids, the last of which, on 2 March 1945 (just four days before the US First Army occupied the city), sent 80,000 people fleeing the city for safety. By the end of the war Cologne had suffered 262 air raids, during which 1.5 million bombs were dropped, 20,000 people were killed and more than half a million evacuated; almost 90 per cent of the city had been destroyed, leaving over 30 million cubic metres of rubble to clean up.

Cologne's fate also befell other major German cities. During the series of air attacks on Hamburg in July and August 1943, 250,000 flats were completely destroyed – roughly half of the area's entire housing stock; water, gas and electricity networks were paralysed; and of a population of 1.4 million people over 600,000 either left the city or had been killed (Recker, 1979, pp.408–12). In Berlin roughly 730,000 dwellings were destroyed, in Germany as a whole between 3.5 and 4 million – or one-fifth of the country's entire housing stock. Millions of people were evacuated from the cities or put up in makeshift emergency mass quarters; and transport on the ground was severely disrupted as rail track, tram lines, rolling stock and roads were blown up. For the first time, it had been possible to destroy large cities almost at a stroke.

However, the possibilities for transforming people's lives created by the development of air transport were not all destructive. Germany had been the target of the first successful attempts to destroy large cities, and Germany also witnessed the first successful attempt to supply a major city from the air. The city was West Berlin. On 24 June 1948 the Soviet occupation authorities in the eastern zone of Germany reacted against the western decision to establish a new West German currency (effectively dividing the country economically) and to introduce it in West Berlin: they blocked passenger and goods transport over land and water routes from the western occupation zones to the western sectors of Berlin. Overnight West Berlin was cut off from its supplies of food, coal and electricity. The Western Allies responded first by announcing a counter-blockade of shipments of coal and steel to the Soviet zone, and then by organizing an airlift to supply the beleaguered city. The Berlin airlift lasted for almost eleven months, until 12 May 1949, when both the Berlin blockade and the western counter-blockade

6Science, technology and everyday life 1870–1950

were lifted. During that period, food, fuel and clothing for a city of roughly 2 million inhabitants was airlifted on a daily basis; even massive turbines, urgently required for a new electricity-generating station, were brought by air. American and British aircraft flew round the clock into the newly extended Tegal airfield in the French sector, sometimes more than 900 planes carrying over 6,000 tonnes of goods flew in on a single day. Altogether 1.5 million tonnes of goods were airlifted to Berlin. For the first time in the history of the world, a major city had been supplied entirely from the air.

Thus the greatest development and impact of air transport upon people's everyday lives was in large measure a result of political and military considerations. Even where commercial demands were influential – as with air passenger transport between the world wars – this was only within the framework of state intervention and military considerations: the need both to keep a viable aircraft-manufacturing industry and to develop a network of airports was never far off-stage. More than with any other mode of transport, in air transport technological developments required large amounts of capital, larger than market demand could justify, and this, combined with the increasing need for regulation for the sake of safety, meant air transport evolved with a greater degree of state involvement than any other mode of transport had done. By 1950 the state had come to take a leading role in determining how new transport technologies were to affect people's everyday lives.

6.4 CONCLUSION

Transport technologies have affected people's lives in many ways and for various reasons: commercial, political, military and – of course – as a result of the development of the technology itself. Technologies do not have lives of their own; they do not simply present themselves but need to be sold, to meet commercial or political needs, to benefit from the necessary financial or technological infrastructure in order to become widely established. There would have been little incentive to develop motor cars had there been no one with enough cash to buy them, or to build large-scale urban tramway or underground networks if the necessary labour and capital were not readily available. No less important has been the role of the state both in creating the fiscal and legal framework within which transport technologies have developed and in taking a direct role in that development. Road building, the taxation and regulation of motor vehicles, and the building of public transport systems all involved the state; state subsidies and intervention were central to the development and spread of air-transport technology. All this underlines that technological change is neither a 'natural' nor an autonomous process.

Because transport technologies so often determine the way we view our world (from the window of a car, or laid out on a road map), it is easy to assume that transport technologies structured the world we are looking at. No doubt to some extent this is true, but the ways in which transport technologies have structured our world are also a function of the economic and social context in which they have been introduced. For developing a new car model or aircraft, or investigating the possible applications of a new technology, involves economic, political and social decisions as well as the requisite scientific and technological knowledge.

The history of transport developments from 1870 is in large measure a history of the selling of technology. Not only did technological innovations in the transport field have to promise a respectable return on the capital invested (which, for example, was one of the main reasons for the success of electric traction around the turn of the century); they also had to be sold to the consumer. In part this meant meeting social and economic needs; but it also meant creating new perceived needs and arousing interest in technological 'progress'. This is well illustrated by the troubles of Henry Ford during the late 1920s. His Model T had satisfied real social and economic needs, but the cars rolling off the General Motors assembly lines did more than that: they created new perceived needs, and exploited the desire to be 'up-to-date' and in possession of the latest products of the new technology. Technology often has been regarded as a good in itself; public identification with the latest technology is something sought not only by the marketing divisions of manufacturing industries but also by politicians. It is a commonplace that transport technology also has symbolic importance for its users. For example, motor cars mean a lot more to many of their owners than just a means for getting from A to B, or even as embodiments of technological progress. They also embody symbolic values. Thus the decision of many Americans during the Depression 'to give up everything in the world but their car' was not just a reflection of practical needs. But the symbolic values attributed to pieces of technology do not arise from that technology itself; they often are reflections of deeper cultural values which shape people's lives.

To end with a particularly grotesque expression of such values: in May 1943 Viktor Lutze, the leader ('Chief of Staff') of the Nazi storm-troopers organization (the SA, *Sturmabteilungen*) died as a result of injuries suffered in a car crash. In the memorial service at the Reich Chancellory, Hitler solemnly intoned:

> My Chief of Staff of the SA, Viktor Lutze, was a soldier throughout his lifetime. I could not fulfill his burning desire . . . to be allowed to go to the front. Now he nevertheless has met a death which brings his National Socialist life to a manly conclusion. (Quoted in Glaser, 1986, p.32)

REFERENCES   Aldcroft, D.H. (1974) 'Britain's internal airways: the pioneer stage of the 1930s' in Aldcroft, D.H. (ed.) *Studies in British Transport History 1870–1970*, David & Charles.

Aldcroft, D.H. (1976) 'A new chapter in transport history: the twentieth century revolution', *The Journal of Transport History*, III, No.3 (new series).

America's Highways 1776–1976. A History of the Federal-Aid Program (1976) US Department of Transportation, Federal Highway Administration.

Bagwell, P.S. (1974) *The Transport Revolution from 1770*, Batsford.

Bailes, K.E. (1978) *Technology and Society under Lenin and Stalin. Origins of the Soviet Technical Intelligentsia, 1917–1941*, Princeton University Press.

Barker, T.C. (1985) 'The international history of motor transport', *Journal of Contemporary History*, XX.

Barker, T.C. and Robbins, M. (1974) *A History of London Transport. Passenger Travel and the Development of the Metropolis. Vol.II. The Twentieth Century to 1970*, Allen & Unwin.

Barker, T.C. and Savage, C.I. (1976) *An Economic History of Transport in Britain*, third edition, Hutchinson.

Barrett, P. (1983) *The Automobile and Urban Transit. The Formation of Public Policy in Chicago, 1900–1930*, Temple University Press.

Blackbourn, D. (1984) 'Peasants and politics in Germany, 1871–1914', *European History Quarterly*, XIV.

Bryant, L. (1974) 'The origin of the automobile engine' in Scientific American (ed.) *Scientific Technology and Social Change*, Freeman.

Burnett, J. (1980) *A Social History of Housing 1815–1970*, Methuen.

Cudahy, B. (1979) *Under the Sidewalks of New York. The Story of the Greatest Subway System in the World*, The Stephen Greene Press.

Desai, A.V. (1969) *Real Wages in Germany 1871–1913*, Oxford University Press.

Fearon, P. (1978) 'The growth of aviation in Britain', *Journal of Modern History*, XX.

Fearon, P. (1979) 'Aircraft manufacturing' in Buxton, N.K. and Aldcroft, D.H. (eds.) *British Industry between the Wars. Instability and Industrial Development 1919–1939*, Scholar Press.

Fuguitt, G.V. (1978) 'The city and countryside' in Rodefeld, R. et al., *Change in Rural America. Causes, Consequences and Alternatives*, Mosby.

Glaser, H. (1986) *Das Automobil. Eine Kulturgeschichte in Bildern*, Verlag C.H. Beck.

Hege, I. (1981) 'Köln am Ende der Weimarer Republik und Während der Herrschaft des Nationalsozialismus' in Dahn, O. (ed.) *Köln nach dem Nationalsozialismus. Der Beginn des gesellschaftlichen und politischen Lebens in den Jahren 1945/46*, Peter Hammer Verlag.

Hicks, J.D. (1960) *Republican Ascendancy, 1921–1933*, Harper & Row.

Hilton, G.W. (1969) 'Transport technology and the urban pattern', *Journal of Contemporary History*, IV, No.3.

Hohorst, G., Kocka, J. and Ritter, G.A. (1978) *Sozialgeschichtliches Arbeitsbuch. Materialien zur Statistik des Kaiserreichs 1870–1914*, Verlag C.H. Beck.

Hounshell, D. (1984) *From the American System to Mass Production 1800–1932*, Johns Hopkins University Press.

Kellett, J.R. (1969) *The Impact of Railways on Victorian Cities*, Routledge & Kegan Paul.

Lynd, R.S. and Lynd, H.M. (1929) *Middletown – A Study in American Culture*, Harcourt, Brace & Co.

Lynd, R.S. and Lynd, H.M. (1937) *Middletown in Transition – A Study in Cultural Conflicts*, Harcourt, Brace & Co.

McKay, J.P. (1976) *Tramways and Trolleys. The Rise of Urban Mass Transport in Europe*, Princeton University Press.

Miller, M. and Church, R.A. (1979) 'Motor manufacturing' in Buxton, N.K. and Aldcroft, D.H. (eds.) *British Industry between the Wars. Instability and Industrial Development 1919–1939*, Scolar Press.

Monkkonen, E. (forthcoming) *The New World City: The Evolution of American Cities and Towns, 1780–1980* (Chapter 9 'Transportation: from animal to automobile').

Lord Montagu of Beaulieu (1986) 'The early days of motoring', *History Today*, XXXVI, October.

Myerscough, J. (1985) 'Airport provision in the inter-war years', *Journal of Contemporary History*, XX.

Olson, D.J. (1979) *The Growth of Victorian London*, Penguin.

Overy, R.J. (1975) 'Cars, roads and economic recovery in Germany, 1932–8', *The Economic History Review*, second series, XXVIII.

Pettifer, J. and Turner, N. (1984) *Automania. Man and the Motor Car*, Collins.

Plowden, W. (1971) *The Motor Car and Politics 1896–1970*, Bodley Head.

Recker, M. (1979) 'Wohnen und Bombardierung im Zweiten Weltkrieg' in Neithammer, L. (ed.) *Wohnen im Wandel. Beiträge zur Geschichte des Alltags in der bürgerlichen Gesellschaft*, Peter Hammer Verlag.

Rhys, D.G. (1972) *The Motor Industry: An Economic Survey*, Butterworths.

Rostow, W.W. (1971) *The Stages of Economic Growth. A Non-Communist Manifesto*, second edition, Cambridge University Press.

Schievelbusch, W. (1979) *Geschichte der Eisenbahnreise. Zur Industrialisierung von Raum und Zeit im 19. Jahrhundert*, Ullstein.

Statistisches Jahrbuch für das Deutsche Reich 1928, Verlag von Reimar Hobbing.

Statistisches Jahrbuch für das Deutsche Reich 1938, Verlag für Sozialpolitik, Wirtschaft und Statistik Paul Schmidt.

Treue, W. (1975) *Gesellschaft, Wirtschaft und Technik Deutschlands im 19. Jahrhundert*, Deutscher Taschenbuch Verlag.

Warner, S.B. (1962) *Streetcar Suburbs: The Process of Growth in Boston, 1870–1900*, Harvard University Press.

Warner, S. B. (1972) *The Urban Wilderness. A History of the American City*, Harper & Row.

Weber, E. (1976) *Peasants into Frenchmen. The Modernization of Rural France, 1870–1914*, Stanford University Press.

Wilder, L.I. (1956) *Little House in the Big Woods*, Methuen.

Williams, T.I. (1982) *A Short History of Twentieth-Century Technology c.1900–1950*, Oxford University Press.

Yago, G. (1984) *The Decline of Transit. Urban Transportation in German and US Cities 1900–1970*, Cambridge University Press.

Zunz, O. (1982) *The Changing Face of Inequality. Urbanization, Industrial Development and Immigrants in Detroit, 1880–1920*, The University of Chicago Press.

Figure 6.11
Leisure on wheels. A drive-in cinema in California in 1939. (Motor Vehicle Manufacturers Association of the United States Inc., Detroit)

7 COMMUNICATIONS

James R. Moore

> These are the days of miracle and wonder
> This is the long distance call
> The way the camera follows us in slo-mo
> The way we look to us all . . .
>
> ('The Boy in the Bubble', *Graceland*, Warner Bros. Records)

So accustomed have we become to modern methods of communication that this memorable refrain from Paul Simon's best-selling album may read like 1980s nostalgia for an age of technological innocence. Half a century has passed since science popularizers celebrated the 'wonders' of the telephone and photography (Hall, 1936; Hawks, 1939). Hardly anyone today devotes a book on 'how everyday things work' to the radio, the gramophone, and the typewriter (Anon, 1948). We have got used to these things, even if we still do not understand their principles. Other things now preoccupy us, such as 'How does a nuclear breeder reactor work?' 'How much radiation can the body safely receive?', 'What is cancer?' and 'Do animals ever commit mass suicide?' Or so we are led to believe by a popular book published in 1980 by an American engineer who spent his career in radio research with the Bendix Corporation. As his title suggests, these are the questions now considered to be vital for understanding *Science in Everyday Life* (Vergara, 1980). In the book no discussion of modern communications is to be found.

But in fact Paul Simon's technological lyric is subtler and more timely than might at first appear. In its original setting the tribute to 'miracle and wonder' follows the news of a terrorist explosion – 'The bomb in the baby carriage/ Was wired to the radio' – and this manifest irony turns sardonic after a subsequent verse:

> These are the days of lasers in the jungle
> Lasers in the jungle somewhere
> Staccato signals of constant information
> A loose affiliation of millionaires
> And billionaires . . .

No nostalgia here. What this new refrain offers is a sharp commentary on modern communications, which is itself communicated through the modern medium of sound recording, with its 'millionaires and billionaires'. The miracles and wonders celebrated by our ancestors are turned against them, just as their technologies have been turned against ourselves. Now these may confront us as black magic. The popular artist would impress us that communications remain an urgent problem of science in everyday life.

The object of this essay is not to survey communication methods at the end of the twentieth century or even to discuss the recent development of these methods, since the age when the telephone, photography and wireless could be marvelled at innocently. Nor, on the contrary, is the object simply to analyse historic technologies 'for their own sake', without reference to present-day concerns. Instead, starting from divergent contemporary views on the relative importance of communications in everyday life, this essay aims to give a historical overview of the subject, from the advent of mass circulation periodicals to the beginnings of commercial television, which emphasizes the problems and paradoxes of communication technologies as well as their possibilities. In this way the essay addresses the concerns of a pop artist rather than a radio engineer.

7.1
A CRITICAL
STANDPOINT

Communications in everyday life need to be studied critically in at least three respects. Firstly, in the most general sense, communication is the *matrix* of all human activities, political, economic and personal; it is the means by which we apprehend the world. There would be no teaching or learning, describing or understanding, without the exchange of symbolic messages (Williams, 1976, chapter 1). In the past century we have come to accept that reliable communication in this sense can be established with places and even – via sound recording and cinematography – with times that are increasingly remote from personal experience. The scope of reality for most of us has been enlarged, but at a risk. Reality as we conceive it is now largely formed and mediated to us by distant messages rather than encountered in person. We absorb these messages and trust them, on the whole, almost as if they originated from our own senses, when in fact they may colour and distort remote events as well as alter our immediate perceptions. Plainly, if the world as we conceive it is to approximate to the world as it really exists, the communications matrix of everyday life must be viewed in a critical light (Schlesinger, 1978; Bennett, 1982).

Secondly, in a more conventional sense, communications refers to the *methods* employed by people to send messages to each other: daily newspapers, hourly radio bulletins, the telephone, and so on. These methods themselves may contribute to the distortion of our sense of reality, which they have helped to enlarge, and so must be examined critically as well. Yet in attempting this we are conditioned by our tacit dependence on the very methods we seek to comprehend; we risk superficiality. The last things we are apt to analyse in depth are those fixtures in everyday life that seem most 'natural' or that we can least do without. Newspapers, radio and the telephone are our artificial limbs: they enable us to 'keep in touch'. We rely on them day-by-day, accepting their messages as adjuncts of our nervous system. For this reason a critical analysis of communication methods will also of necessity be historical. We need to understand where our addictions came from. If our ancestors regarded communication technologies as solemn 'wonders', we, in our turn, are prone to underestimate their impact, as though the methods we now depend on had always been taken for granted. This minimizing attitude originates in over-familiarity with current technology. It demonstrates an ahistoric bias that may itself be the chief impact of modern communication methods on everyday life.

Finally, the study of communications in everyday life embraces a technical *model* of the communication process, a model that has furnished a conceptual apparatus for understanding both the human matrix and the technological methods of communication. For example, a standard speech text, *Communication in Everyday Use* (Andersch *et al.*, 1969), and a Rand Corporation research study, *A Taxonomy of Communication Media* (Bretz, 1971), both couch their analyses in the same technical jargon. We ourselves sometimes use this jargon in ordinary conversation: terms such as 'media' and 'feedback', as well as 'encoding' and 'decoding', 'transmitting' and 'receiving', 'information', 'channels' and 'noise'. It needs to be emphasized, however, that this terminology belongs to the subject under investigation. Most of it derives from a basic model of signalling that originated in electronic engineering and developed through military research on the behaviour of self-regulatory systems into a comprehensive science of control and communication, which in 1948 Norbert Wiener called 'cybernetics'. Thereafter, drawing on collateral research funded by the Rockefeller Foundation and the United States Army into the effects of propaganda, various 'communication theories' were elaborated, and the study of communications became a science in its own right, allied to social psychology (Dechert, 1967; Gerbner, 1967; McLeod, 1967). History was extruded from this new field except in so far as it could be used during the Cold War to exhibit the liberatory aspects of communications technology and its potential for building political 'consensus' (Carey, 1983). Needless to say, while a critical approach to any subject will resist taking its terms of reference from the subject itself, a historical overview of everyday communications, which also aims to be critical, must necessarily assume a different standpoint.

The standpoint adopted in this essay has been influenced by recent radical sociological studies of the media (Gardner, 1979; Gurevitch *et al.*, 1982) and by the tradition of interdisciplinary analysis inaugurated a generation ago by the Canadian scholar, Harold Innis, and now pursued by communications historians such as James W. Carey. Although the sociologists and historians concerned may belong to different intellectual traditions, their views on the three aspects of everyday communications discussed above are strikingly compatible. It will be convenient to summarize them here.

Firstly, the matrix of communication, consisting of symbolic messages, is the seedbed of ideology. There reality as we conceive it is 'produced, maintained, repaired, and transformed' on behalf of social interests (Carey, 1975, p.10). The so-called 'mass media' in particular serve to generate consent in their audiences by representing the real world in ways that confer legitimacy on the social order in which they subsist. Secondly, the methods of communication, consisting of technologies, do not simply convey 'reality' in the form of symbolic messages, but also effect a reality of their own. The electric telegraph, for example, divorced communication from transportation and reduced space instantaneously to the service of commercial interests, leaving time as the last frontier to be invaded and controlled (see section 1.3.2). Mass circulation periodicals and radio broadcasting have eroded people's capacity for oral discourse and have 'transformed the reading and listening public into a reading and listening audience' (Carey, 1981, p.87). Some communication methods introduced in the past century have blurred the distinction between public and private life, while others have accentuated the latter.

These themes will be resumed and embellished in the following pages. The third aspect of everyday communications discussed above, its technical model, falls outside the scope of this essay. But it is well to be reminded that models are not simply dispensable. We cannot investigate communication adequately unless we have some idea or representation of what it is, or at least what it was taken to be in a historical period. Carey (1975, pp.2–10) stresses this point and proposes a model derived from the religious background of the idea of communication during the nineteenth and twentieth centuries. Although this background has been largely obliterated, especially in European cultures, the dual-aspect model of communication, as transmission and as ritual, still survives in secular forms.

Communication, seen as *transmission*, is the sending and distribution of messages through space to influence people and events; it takes place after the manner in which the Word of God was sent into the world and the apostles, in turn, were commissioned to take the Gospel to every creature. This view, suitably secularized, remains predominant in the industrialized world, and its moral character is apparent. Communication becomes the extension through space of benign influence, whether in the form of commerce, government or 'civilization'. The *ritual* aspect of communication, by contrast, has been less emphasized; its picture of people as religious communicants, united by a common cup of meanings, is incongruous with the individuating and expansionary forces of modern life. But Carey suggests that this view also holds relevance for understanding how everyday communication actually works. Communication, seen as ritual, is the representation of shared beliefs through common experience. It is not directed to the extension of messages in space but to the intensification of a particular view of the world that gives life coherence and tone. Reading a newspaper, watching a movie or listening to the radio are like attending a mass – 'mass communications', as it were. On the one side, reality is presented in an ideological form; on the other, little if anything new is learned and the recipients feel grateful and blessed (Chaney, 1986).

Everyday communication cannot be reduced simply to its 'transmission' and 'ritual' aspects – this essay does not attempt to do so. But in conjunction with recent perspectives on the matrix and the methods of communication, the religious model offers the prospect of understanding communications both critically and historically, in sympathy with our ancestors who wondered at what we now take for granted, if not exactly from their standpoint. The essay is divided into three sections, each of which will deal with issues raised in these introductory paragraphs: section 7.2 discusses printing technology and mass circulation newspapers and magazines; 7.3 focuses on pictures rather than printed words, chiefly cinematography; 7.4 features audible communication at-a-distance by telephone and radio.

7.2
MAKING NEWS:
WORDS IN PRINT

Communication may be the matrix of everyday life but the methods employed depend very much on the circumstances. Both natural and social barriers constrain the methods available for a given group and time. With children the spoken word predominates, among deaf-mutes sign language. Caste or class-based cultures regulate and differentiate the forms of address. An entire history of communication could be written, not as a story of technological 'breakthroughs', but as the history of the barriers that remain unbroken because they have shifted, strengthened, or just emerged. Communication in its broadest sense is not only about who is talking to whom, and how; it is also about who is *not* talking to whom, and why.

In the early nineteenth century there were numerous barriers to communication by printed word. Technical know-how did not stand in the way – methods had already been devised to print more things faster and less expensively than ever before. The main constraints were social and economic (Smith, 1979, chapters 4–5). A large proportion of people in Europe could not read until the 1860s. Those who could often found the cheapest source of information available, the newspaper, beyond their means. The press was not 'free' in any sense of the word. What government censorship, libel and licensing laws, and the threat of heavy fines failed to achieve could be safely left to a rigged market. In Britain, for example, paper was dear, with a high rag content, and subject to duty besides; printing equipment was expensive; and newspapers (interpreted very broadly) were taxed on every copy. The net effect was to restrict 'intelligence' – the news – to the respectable classes, who could afford to print and buy it. The lower-class majority, left to their well-thumbed Sunday scandal sheets and cheap subsidized religious and educational magazines, were kept in relative ignorance. This scheme of economic censorship did not always work of course, and the history of the radical, 'unstamped' press in Britain, and of efforts elsewhere – notably in France – to free the printed word, contains as many breakthroughs, or apparent breakthroughs, as the history of contemporary printing technology (R. Williams, 1978, 1979).

Between 1860 and 1880 most of the social and economic barriers to mass circulation newspapers were removed. Most people in industrialized countries could now read; censorship and 'taxes on knowledge' were being curtailed or abolished while real incomes rose. The bourgeois revolution, now entering its final phase, had brought an intellectual 'free market'. Europeans began to experience the kind of liberties that in America had long since acquired the force of law (Desmond, 1978). More people could now afford a newspaper. More people could vote and thus take an active interest in politics. More people lived in reach of railways and postal services that brought the latest news to their door. Some people also began to enjoy the liberty of making a market of the rest. For the irony of press freedom on both sides of the Atlantic was that, while the few who owned the presses retained the freedom to speak to everyone, the many who could only afford the product became in some ways less free to inform themselves. The first mass medium had been born.

**7.2.1
Printing, typesetting and process**

The basic technology to print newspapers rapidly in bulk was already in place by the time the constraints on newspaper publishing began to fall, but there was little incentive to develop and perfect the technology without the clear prospect of large circulations leading to handsome profits. This may help to explain why many of the requisite innovations originated in the United States, where the greatest measure of press freedom was found. Consider four crucial, interrelated developments: (1) rotary printing on (2) both sides simultaneously of (3) inexpensive paper fed from a (4) continuous roll.

Traditional 'flat-bed' printing was inherently slow. The paper, placed on a bed of type, moved horizontally in a reciprocating motion beneath a cylinder that gave the impression. Rotary printing permitted continuous motion and was the precondition of speed. This was achieved by Robert Hoe and Company of New York (later of London) in the mid-1840s. The Hoe presses were the first to print full pages by using an impression cylinder to hold individual sheets against a rapidly moving printing cylinder, the type being locked round its circumference. *The Times* of London purchased two of these machines, each adapted to print ten sheets at once, 20,000 per hour (Jacobi, 1911). They were still, however, not 'perfecting' presses, which delivered sheets printed on both sides. Each sheet had to pass through the press a second time. Nor was the paper yet inexpensive. Both these technical obstacles to rapid bulk printing were overcome in America with the fillip given to newspapers by the Civil War. Since 1854 paper consisting of wood-pulp and rag had been available, but by 1867 Henry Pagenstecher succeeded in manufacturing paper entirely from woodpulp. This cheap newsprint, prepared on a continuous roll, or 'web', was then used to full advantage in the perfecting press developed at Philadelphia by William A. Bullock (Figure 7.1). In this machine the paper passed in turn between two pairs of cylinders, one carrying the type, the other giving the impression, each pair printing the web on a single side. Knives cut the web automatically into sheets, and these were delivered by metal fingers fixed to endless belts (Jacobi, 1911; Brown, 1928; A. Smith, 1979, pp.108–09).

*Figure 7.1
William Bullock's rotary press of 1865, introduced at the* Philadelphia Enquirer, *from a contemporary engraving. (Reproduced from Geoffrey A. Glaister, second edition 1979,* Glaister's Glossary of the Book, *Allen and Unwin, by permission of the publishers)*

Bullock incorporated into his press a device of the utmost importance for economizing and accelerating newspaper production. In this respect it was he rather than the French inventors, Claude Genoux and Nicolas Serrière, who realized its full potential. Publishers had found that lead type became worn with frequent use, especially at higher press speeds. Replacement was expensive. It was also expensive to invest in the extra type required to print the same page or many pages on separate machines simultaneously. The obvious answer was to economize on type by finding a cheap substitute, and this is what Genoux and Serrière contributed in 1852. Using papier-mâché, they made page-moulds, or 'flongs', from type already set, so that printing could take place from multiple cheap casts of these moulds, or 'stereotypes', and the original type could be redistributed. The flongs, moreover, had the advantage of being flexible; a curved stereotype plate could be prepared and fitted to the printing cylinder of a rotary press (Figure 7.2). Bullock adopted this technique but he did not live to see it perfected. In 1867 he was caught in the drivebelt of one of his presses and killed (Jacobi, 1911, pp.353–56; Eilert, 1928, pp.183–84; A. Smith, 1979, p.109).

*Figure 7.2
Curved stereotype plate 1857. (Science Museum, London)*

By 1871, when a Bullock machine first achieved commercial success, the web perfecting press, developed in conjunction with cheap newsprint and the stereotype, had emerged as the printing technology of the mass circulation

Figure 7.3
Hoe's Double Octuple Rotary machine, probably the latest development in rotary technique, erected in 1908 to print Lloyd's Weekly, *the largest circulation newspaper in Britain. 'These presses print from eight different reels of the double width, four placed at each end of the machine, the delivery being in the centre, and from eight sets of plates, four pages on each type cylinder, making a total of thirty-two pages in all. Each press produces of that number of pages 50,000 copies per hour, printed both sides, cut, folded and counted off in quires complete; by increasing the sets of stereotype pages the same machine will produce 100,000 copies per hour of sixteen pages, and by duplicating the folding and delivery apparatus, 200,000 copies of eight pages of the same size. . . The paper is fed from reels placed at the two ends in decks, one above the other, each reel containing about five miles of paper, and weighing about fourteen hundredweight. The process of unwinding these long reels of paper in the course of printing takes only half an hour; they are arranged on a revolving stand so that directly they are spent the stand is turned half way round, and four other full reels already in position are presented ready to be run into the press'.*
(From Encyclopaedia Britannica, *eleventh edition 1910–11, Cambridge University Press, Vol.22, p.357)*

newspaper. Circulation merely depended on the number of presses in use. Electricity replaced steam as the driving force by about 1900, and for several decades afterwards the chief improvements to the press dealt with component parts, automatic controls, and ancillary operations such as splicing, folding and wrapping. All were geared to the increase of operating efficiency and speed. Presses also expanded to incorporate multiple units, such as Hoe's four-decked 'double octuple' machine (Figure 7.3), which entered service early in the century. Printing, however, was only the most visible and dramatic aspect of newspaper production. The clattering behemoths devoured copy at a prodigious rate. Ways had to be found to feed them more efficiently. In the background a quieter revolution went on. Traditional labour-intensive methods of manual typesetting and illustration by hand-engraving were rapidly displaced. Mass circulation newspapers demanded mechanized typesetting and photoengraving, or 'process'.

Up to 1886 practically all typesetting was done as it had been for 400 years. Many attempts had been made to mechanize the work but no one had succeeded in producing a machine that both arranged type in lines and 'justified' them by altering the space between words. Where mechanization had been achieved, it affected only the first of these operations; justification was always done by hand as the lines were set into the printing frame, or 'forme'. It was skilled work. Hand compositors had to be able to read type upside down and back to front with a sharp eye for detail. They had to be able to calculate the spacing of words and lines according to the printer's standard. Their job was to design and lay out the page and lock the type, illustration blocks, and lead spacers into the forme in readiness for stereo-typing or the press. Working with lead in this way, and often carrying the completed formes, required strength and stamina, which was one reason given why, in mixed-sex print shops, women were excluded from typesetting. Another reason was that men controlled the trade and guarded it jealously against 'cheap labour'. Women were left the tedious, unskilled task of distributing the type from the forme into hoppers for re-use. Then in 1886 a machine appeared that eliminated the distributing operation and produced lines that were justified automatically. Anxious for their jobs, the hand compositors commandeered it. Women all but vanished from newspaper print shops until the present day (Cockburn, 1981, 1983).

This composing machine was invented by a German named Ottmar Mergenthaler, who had fled to America to avoid military service. It used a keyboard operation in principle like that of the typewriter. Now the typewriter had been on sale since 1874 from Remington, the firearms company, which had diversified out of weapons after the American Civil War. A wide variety of firms were soon manufacturing the machine, and it took some years for Remington's QWERTY keyboard to become the industry standard.

Figure 7.4
Typewriter demonstrated in
1876 at the American
Centennial Exhibition in
Philadelphia. 'Typing then
was a muscular activity',
recalled J.B. Priestley (1934,
p.123). 'You could ache after
it. If you were not familiar
with these vast keyboards, your
hand wandered over them like
a child lost in a wood. The
noise might have been that of
a shipyard on the Clyde.'
(Bettmann Archive, New
York. Reproduced in B.
Partridge and O. Bettmann,
1946, As We Were, *McGraw*
Hill)

Furthermore, the early typewriters were massive contraptions; operating them required considerable strength and stamina (Figure 7.4). Typists had to master the keyboard as well as learn it. None of this, however, proved a deterrent to women, although fears were raised as to the suitability of the female constitution when in 1881 a six-month typing course was advertised by the New York City YWCA (Stern, 1937, p.49; Moran, 1978, pp.1270–71). By the First World War the female typist had become a fixture of working life in industrial centres across Europe and North America, and there seems to have been no reason, apart from entrenched masculine power, why women who had distributed type so well could not have learned to set it on the large, non-standard keyboard of Mergenthaler's composer (Figure 7.5).

What made the machine distinctive is indicated by its brand name. The 'Linotype' produced a solid line of type, or 'slug', rather than individual type that had to be justified by hand. As the keyboard was operated a series of type matrices fell into place automatically with the correct spacing to form the mould of a line. The mould was filled with molten lead, then cooled and ejected from the machine – the slug – ready for the forme. When printing was finished all the slugs could be melted down and the metal re-used. Operating on similar principles, a 'Monotype' composer became available in 1894, so-called by its American inventor, Tolbert Lanston, because it cast individual type and spaces. The keyboard prepared a punched tape that controlled a separate caster. The cast type and spaces assembled in a channel to form justified lines, which were then arranged in long frames, or 'galleys'. (Here women had access to the keyboard but the caster was strictly reserved for men – Cockburn, 1981, p.133.) This system had the advantage that corrections could be incorporated without remaking an entire line. It was used most advantageously in printing books and magazines (Eilert, 1928, pp.181–83; Moran, 1978, pp.1272–73).

Between them, the linotype and monotype machines ended the intolerable bottleneck between composing room and press. A skilled linotype operator could do the work of five or six average hand compositors. By the 1940s, after improvements to the machine, this amounted to upwards of 900 lines per hour. But there was another bottleneck, this one between composing room and studio. If typesetting was mechanized to feed a hungry press, artwork also had to be expedited. Electrotyping and photography had been known since the 1840s; coloured inks proliferated after 1856 with the discovery of aniline dyes. While Mergenthaler and Lanston worked on their new composers others were developing the techniques of process.

'Process' is an imprecise term that by the last quarter of the nineteenth century had come to stand for the various photo-mechanical methods by which illustrations were reproduced in printing. Before this period all kinds of illustration were prepared by hand engravers: either professionals, whose fastidious work was time-consuming and dear, or skilled artistic hacks, who churned out cheap impressions to publishers' deadlines. Newspapers and most magazines employed the latter individuals; their engravings were usually prepared in 'relief'. The engraver inscribed lines and dots, varying in thickness and proximity, into a hard surface from which a cast or 'electrotype' – a stereotype prepared by electrolytic deposition of metal on the surface – could be made. This plate, its printing surface raised above the surrounding area in the manner of ordinary type, was then mounted on a block for locking up in the forme. Despite its relative cheapness, however, hand engraving by job lot was slow and costly in relation to the increased efficiency of typesetting. The end-product was at best an inferior interpretation of reality (Bale, 1911, pp.408–09).

Figure 7.5
Early Linotype composing
machine. (Science Museum
collection, London)

Photography dispossessed the hand engravers with chemists and mechanics. The trick was, as usual in photography, to get light to cause a chemical reaction that left a permanent record of its intensity. For the purposes of printing, the record had to be left on a metal plate rather than on transparent film. This was done by coating the plate with a light-sensitive emulsion and exposing it through a negative. If the negative represented a photograph with subtle 'half-tones', intermediate between black and white, it was prepared behind a cross-ruled glass screen, so that the image consisted of minute dots varying in size inversely as the intensity of the light (Figure 7.6). When light passed through the negative on to the plate, it fixed and hardened the light-sensitive substance wherever it impinged. After the unexposed residue had been washed off, the plate was baked and etched to reveal a relief surface suitable for the press. Photographs printed from the plate were called 'half-tones'. For thirty years English, German and French experimenters worked on aspects of the half-tone process, but it was perfected only in the 1880s by Frederic Ives and Max Levy in the United States. Indeed, as early as 1881 Ives, using ruled screens and light filters, prepared the first half-tone blocks for three-colour printing (Gamble, 1901; Bale, 1911, pp.410–12). By the turn of the century black-and-white half-tones had become commonplace in newspapers and magazines; colour half-tones were limited to artistic reproductions.

Process techniques became extremely sophisticated over the next thirty years, particularly those involving colour. While newspapers generally stuck to half-tones, many magazines and a few newspapers that published supplementary sections eventually adopted the superior methods of photolithography and photogravure. Photolithography, used chiefly by magazines in the early part of the twentieth century, was a method of 'offset' rather than relief printing. A thin metal plate was treated photographically to hold ink only on those surfaces that formed the image. When the plate had been inked and washed, the remaining image could be 'set off' on to a rubber pad against which the paper was impressed. Soft and subtle colour effects

Figure 7.6
Enlargement of half-tone newspaper illustration. (Reproduced from Open House, *November 1987).*

were achieved by this method, but the usual colour process used by newspapers in the twentieth century was photogravure. The term, a generic one, stood for a method of inverse relief, or 'intaglio', printing by which the image was photochemically etched into the plate. The ink collected at different depths beneath the level of the surrounding surface to give continuous shading on the impression. A half-tone screen could be used to achieve the shading effect in etching the heavier plates needed for rotary work, or 'rotogravure'. This system, first used in England by wallpaper and calico manufacturers, became common in Europe before the First World War and in America soon afterwards (Fishenden, 1910; Bale, 1911, pp.412–13; Moran, 1978, pp.171–72). Unlike the half-tone process, it offered near-facsimile reproduction and could print colour on cheaper stock, including newsprint. Colour supplements, comic strips and quality advertising immediately became selling points of the mass circulation newspaper (Eilert, 1928, pp.186–87; Giegengack, 1937, pp.243–44).

7.2.2 Readership and advertising

The rapid dissemination of new printing technology after 1870, the gradual displacement of traditional craft skills from the trade, and the dramatic growth of newspaper titles and circulations were integral developments. They could be paralleled again and again in other sectors of capitalist industry at the time. It is often impossible to assign the exact priority of events. Did new technology bring about increased circulations or did increased demand elicit the technology? Were savings on skilled labour translated directly into lower cover prices, thereby stimulating demand, or were the savings ploughed back into cost-efficient machinery? In any case, this much at least seems clear: new technology was developed, almost without exception, both by and for the printing industry as a lucrative investment. The effort and expense found sanction in the prospect of untold sales following the removal of social and economic disincentives to publication. Newspapers, far from retaining a privileged readership, were now to be mass produced. Newspaper content was to be shaped and altered to capture the wider market. Newspaper publishing was set to become big business.

Statistics may never tell their own story but at this point they seem relevant. By far the majority of daily newspapers throughout the period were published in Western Europe and North America. In the 1880s this amounted to almost 90 per cent of the titles then known. The national leaders were the United States, Germany, the United Kingdom and France. In 1900 these alone accounted for 80 per cent of the titles, with the United States publishing no less than five times as many as the runner up, Germany, or fully 50 per cent of newspaper titles worldwide. Measured against population, the United States was still distinctly in the lead: in 1886 there were on average about 7,000 readers for every title as compared with 20,000 in France and the United Kingdom and 30,000 in Germany ('Newspapers', *EB*, 1911). These figures obviously reflect the fact that in a large federated nation such as the United States many more newspapers came into existence to address the interests of local and regional groups. But the figures nevertheless obscure as much as they reveal, and relate only to the period of dramatic newspaper growth that culminated in the First World War. Consider, for example, that from 1850 to 1914 roughly the same number of daily newspapers were published in the United Kingdom and the United States, a rise from about 400 to around 2,500 titles. Yet in 1900, when somewhat over 2,000 dailies were appearing in each country, the total number of newspaper titles published in the United States was about 16,000, in comparison to some 3,000 in the United Kingdom. Evidently other kinds of newspaper, including what might also be called magazines – the weekly, fortnightly and monthly press – assumed a greater role in one country than in the other ('Newspapers', *EB*, 1911; Schramm, 1960, p.195; Lee, 1978, p.121).

But even these clear-cut figures obscure a good deal. Although daily newspapers were about equal in number, circulations differed widely, and the same was true of the non-daily press. In 1900 the total daily newspaper circulation in the United States was about 15 million copies. This began to level off at a little over twice that figure in the 1920s. Joseph Pulitzer's New York *World* achieved a circulation of a quarter of a million by 1887, a national record repeatedly broken in a degrading competition with William Randolph Hearst's sensationalistic *New York Journal* (Figure 7.7), which in 1898 capitalized on the threat of war with Spain to sell as many as 1.25 million copies in a day (Melville and Brande, 1922; Agee *et al.*, 1976, pp.57–59; Davison *et al.*, 1976, pp.10–13). In Britain, by contrast, the total daily newspaper circulation did not reach 15 million until the 1930s. The first paper to reach a steady million-plus circulation was Lord Northcliffe's *Daily Mirror* (1903). This occurred in the run-up to the First World War. But long before then the weeklies had broken all records and become the real forerunners of the 'mass' press that only emerged much later. Cheap Sunday papers such as *Reynolds's News* and *Lloyd's Weekly* enjoyed national circulations of 350,000 as early as the mid-1860s. The latter topped the million mark in 1896, the year the much-vaunted halfpenny *Daily Mail* was launched (Lee, 1978; Murdock and Golding, 1978).

These comparative statistics can be interpreted variously, but one thing they point to is the diverse prospects for a national press. Once mass circulation newspapers became established in metropolitan centres throughout the United Kingdom, economies of scale combined with the relative ease of nationwide distribution enabled them to annex the readership of the provincial press and, by the 1930s, to become national dailies. In the United States, where the population was spread out across an entire continent, the provincial press could easily retain its independence; the readership for mass circulation newspapers lay in metropolitan areas. A national press could not be achieved on a daily basis but rather less frequently – weekly, fortnightly or monthly. Thus the American counterpart of *Reynolds's News*, *Lloyd's Weekly*, and 'class' or 'trade' papers such as *Tit-Bits*, with their popular mass readership, were national magazines.

These first appeared in the 1880s, after the enactment of advantageous postal rates. Their heyday came between the wars, when in Britain the dailies and their 'press barons' – the *Mail* and Lord Rothermere, the *Express* (1900) and Lord Beaverbrook, and the *Herald* (1912) and Lord Southwood – were

Figure 7.7
Front page headline, New York Journal, *17 February 1898, on the occasion of the destruction of the USS Maine during the Spanish–American conflict. (Photograph by courtesy of the Newspaper Library, New York Public Library)*

fighting each other with promotional gimmicks to reach the magical circulation mark of two million (Boyce, 1987). The *Ladies Home Journal* (1883) sold a million copies before the turn of the century, *Munsey's Magazine* (1893) a half million. *Cosmopolitan* (1886) and *McClure's Magazine* (1893) had by then begun to achieve fabulous if short-lived circulations for their exposure of corruption, or 'muckraking'. After the First World War, when muckraking became passé, glitzy new or refurbished journals vied to capture the national mood. The *Saturday Evening Post*, appealing to all classes, soon broke the 2 million mark. By the mid-1920s two dozen magazines, each with a circulation of a million or more, 'had a combined impact that compared favourably with that of newspapers, since their circulation amounted to more than 40 million in a country of fewer than 30 million households' (Davison *et al.*, 1976, p.21).

Mass circulation newspapers and magazines purveyed a wide variety of information, ranging from slushy entertainment to stock-market prices. On the whole the newspapers stuck to news; the magazines dealt with the lighter side of things, although *McClure's* and later *Time* (1923) and *Life* (1936) contained serious journalism. Both were the instigators as well as the beneficiaries of the new technology that could print bulk orders of two, three and (latterly) four-colour issues to tight production schedules. News reporting was considerably enhanced by half-tone illustrations. Fiction, fashion, and the myriad other items of human interest in magazines acquired a new dimension through colour process. But the main impact of the new technology was felt through advertising.

Classified advertising had always been a staple, if not the chief, source of revenue for newspapers in the nineteenth century. Most of it originated with small businesses and private individuals seeking local custom. Modern 'display' advertising, which developed earlier in Great Britain and the United States than elsewhere, originated in the needs of highly capitalized industries, geared for large-scale production, both to create and to control consumption in a broadly based market (A. Smith, 1979, pp.145–47; Beniger, 1986, chapter 8). Given a national infrastructure of roads and railways, serviceable in conjunction with a national postal system, the problems of demand-management and distribution tended to merge. The question became: How to use the channels of communication (broadly conceived) to maximum effect? In this context, clearly, what was good for industries where commercial success depended on maintaining regular supplies, whether of goods or information, was also good for newspapers and magazines. Untold revenue could be won from well-heeled clients by those who advertised their products most widely and effectively. This revenue would enable them to print larger issues, expand circulation, increase their revenue, and so on. Thus the efflorescence of national brand-name consumer goods – foods and medicines for the most part – in the 1880s and 1890s bore the closest relationship to the emergence of mass circulation periodicals. Indeed, the same technology served them both. The goods were wrapped in paper made cheap by the same processes that gave rise to the halfpenny newspaper. The press that printed the newspaper could also print the paper in which the goods were wrapped. The trademark on the wrapper came from the same stereotype mould that supplied the press (Figure 7.8).

During the First World War government propaganda showed how effective advertising could be, even without an obvious commercial motive. Afterwards, when paper was no longer rationed, a consumer boom took place in those economies that had escaped the worst of the devastation. In the United States the boom was led by twice the volume of advertising in periodicals that had been obtained just five years before. Newspapers cashed in with rotogravure sections and picture tabloids. Magazines, now recognized to be 'the premier national advertising medium', burst into colour (Brown, 1928, pp.220–24).

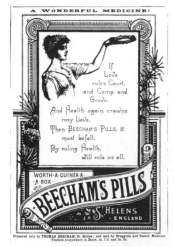

Figure 7.8
A brand-name product:
*Beecham's pills. (*Illustrated London News, *31 June 1890)*

Here as in much else the United States set the trend. The object was to advertise style rather than price. People would pay more for things they thought were fashionable – so advertising agents argued. Colour was fashionable, the technology was available to print it, and editors were happy to oblige. Only the manufacturers needed to be won over. The agents therefore set about persuading them that colour could do wonders for ordinary utilitarian objects, from fountain pens to automobiles and even domestic furnaces. One manufacturer who did not listen was Henry Ford. His monochrome Model T – 'any colour as long as it's black' – cost him dearly after General Motors introduced multiple colours in its 1924 models and used colour magazine advertisements to associate them with high fashion. But by 1927, when at last the new Model A appeared in several hues, Ford had joined the large and increasing number of American manufacturers who were convinced, as the advertising trade journal *Printer's Ink* put it, that colour was 'the sex appeal of business' (in Marchand, 1985, pp.120–24). Clearly, without new technology this collective seduction could not have occurred, but the decisive factor was certainly economic. Magazines did not embrace colour wholeheartedly until advertising made it pay. Manufacturers did not pursue it until persuaded by successful advertising that it would sell. Consumers had the final word.

7.2.3 Industry and ideology

The web-perfecting press, linotype and monotype, half-tone and colour process – all these and many subsidiary elements of the new printing technology that emerged in the decades after 1870 were designed and built to service the needs of mass circulation periodicals. How then was the human matrix of communication affected? What was the ideological impact of the new technology as achieved through the printed page? In what ways was everyday 'reality' altered? Can a single model of communication be said to accommodate the process?

These are large and difficult questions that cannot be dealt with fully here. Several points, however, can be made suggesting the direction in which answers may be found. Firstly, the salient feature in the history of mass circulation periodicals is the *industrialization* of the press. This can be seen most clearly in the case of newspapers. Formerly newspapers, on the whole, were owned by families and a scattering of well-to-do individuals. They were creatures of party and class. Although expensive to run on a large scale, they were not beyond the means of like-minded people with an interest in portraying the world congenially to a body of more or less faithful readers. But with the removal of publishing disabilities and, in many places, the enfranchisement of vast sectors of a newly literate populace, newspapers had to face for the first time a relatively free competitive market. Survival depended, as it did elsewhere in industrialized economies, on efficient production and distribution leading to quantity sales. Three things followed from this: newspapers had to invest in new technology; they had to find additional revenue; and they had to change their basis of appeal. New technology would keep production up and prices down. New revenue would pay for the technology and, if necessary, subsidize prices. A new basis of appeal would attract the wider readership to make it all worthwhile.

New technology was, needless to say, expensive. Other production costs, including additional staff and 'newsgathering' facilities, added to the bill. And as competition drove prices down, the circulation level newspapers needed to reach before they broke even became progressively higher. This meant that as time went on more and more capital was required to establish a paper in the mass competitive market. By the 1880s provincial papers in Britain needed £20,000 or £30,000 working capital; a London daily could not be kept going with less than £100,000. Northcliffe in the 1890s is estimated to have spent half a million pounds on plant and machinery when setting up the *Daily Mail*. Many British newspapers were formed as joint-stock companies, it is true, but this made them susceptible to take-over by competitors, followed often by amalgamation or closure. By the end of the First World War the pattern of concentrating ownership was well established. Year by year fewer papers with larger circulations were owned by fewer people, so that by 1948 the three leading companies controlled 43 per cent of the daily market. In the United States 'chain journalism' – multiple ownership by one publisher or corporation of titles in different cities – operated to much the same effect, the foremost example being the coast-to-coast empire built up by the swashbuckling populist William Randolph Hearst. In Germany it was the stranglehold on the provincial press and wire services achieved by Alfred Hugenberg, formerly chairman of Krupp munitions at Essen, that helped to stifle democracy in the late 1920s and bring the Nazis to power (Brown, 1928, pp.214–16, 224–25; Curran, 1978, p.68; Lee, 1978, p.119; Murdock and Golding, 1978, p.135; A. Smith, 1979, p.177).

New revenue was not just available from wealthy investors though. Commercial advertisers, as we have seen, also offered their custom. By the early twentieth century mass circulation newspapers had become major industries in their own right, integral cogs of the great corporate machine of which consumption was the motor. Having contrived successfully to sell themselves, they now were paid as never before to undertake on behalf of others. This is the second point to be made in relation to the ideological impact of the new printing technology. Capital expenditure in the newspaper industry had come to depend to an unprecedented extent on revenue from advertising. Without this income, no investment; no investment, no market for the likes of Hoe and Mergenthaler; no market, no research and development – quite possibly no new technology. Advertising, in other words, was the corollary of innovation. In the United States daily newspapers depended on advertising for about 40 per cent of their income in 1879. By 1919 the figure had risen to nearly two-thirds, although this fell back about eight or nine percentage points in the next decade because of competition from commercial radio. Meanwhile in Britain, where commercial broadcasting did not begin until the 1950s, the press remained 'solidly dependent on advertising revenue, which provided up to three-quarters of the income of a national daily' right through the Second World War (Murdock and Golding, 1978, p.131; Beniger, 1986, p.361; Curran, 1986).

Clearly, advertising could make or break a mass circulation newspaper, and there is evidence that discriminatory practices by agents on behalf of their business clients had something like this effect. George Lansbury, editor of the left-wing *Daily Herald* during the 1920s, complained, 'The more copies we sold, the more money we lost'. Crippled by lack of advertising, and without the capital resources needed to establish it in the mass market, the paper could not survive, even by doubling its cover price, and it was forced to moderate its line (Curran, 1978, p.70). Other newspapers, however, adapted more readily to the *consumerization* of the press. This occurred especially in countries such as the United States, where differentiation of readership by social class was less pronounced. Content, layout and editorial policy were consciously tailored to the needs of advertisers; surveys were conducted to entice advertisers with information about readership attitudes and trends (Brown, 1928, p.223; A. Smith, 1979, p.147). The new appeal of newspapers tended to be mass-based rather than class-based. Cynicism and stunts, comic strips and crusades, flourished in the popular press; the 'serious' press, also heavily dependent on advertising revenue, tended to debate politics within each paper rather than among them. The 'new journalism', lively, topical and meliorist, was geared to maximizing its readership for commercial gain by 'massifying' its audience on behalf of commercial sponsors. 'Mass industry, requiring a corresponding mass individual . . . hoped to create an "individual" who could locate his needs and frustrations in terms of the consumption of goods' rather than in the quality and content of everyday working life (Ewen, 1976, pp.42–43). Before the advent of commercial television, mass circulation newspapers and magazines were the most effective means for achieving this ideological task.

But newspapers contained a good deal more than advertising, even though they depended inordinately on it and adapted themselves to its requirements. Ostensibly newspapers had 'news' to 'report'. To most readers this news described the world more or less as it really existed, when in fact what they exposed themselves to was a particular version of events. The new printing technology not only enabled newspapers to reproduce and dispense this 'reality' on an unprecedented scale; it also provided individuals with the opportunity to update themselves on a daily basis at a price they could afford. The ideological consequences of this have not yet been fully studied, but several features may be discerned.

Firstly, the *re-temporalization* of events: newspapers, fed continuously by wire services with reports measured against global or national standard time (see section 1.3.2), collapsed these into issues produced locally on a daily cycle. The temporal relations between events, particularly those on the boundaries of the cycle, easily disappeared. The seamless web of history was reconstituted as a patchwork to conform with production schedules. Henry Justin Smith, editor of the old Chicago *Daily News*, made the point colourfully if unintentionally in his account of 'The Day':

> Throughout the newspaper plant a finely-timed engine, deftly blended of the human and mechanical, is turning. Everything must move: the grotesque arms of the linotypes, the lumpishly-moving tables of the stereotypers, the gigantic glistening coils of the presses, the rolling sidewalks upon which the finished papers slide towards the delivery wagons. All must turn with the clock-tick. It makes no difference whether the day be dull or thrilling. The relentless machinery waits for its injections of human intelligence. The world waits for the news. And always, among these men in the newsroom, there is a dim sense of the mechanisms forever at work below them, a tinge of fear lest, through some fault, there be a break in the process, a dreadful pause in the endless tune. (H. J. Smith, 1922, pp.145–46)

What never reached the press or what fell, as it were, between the cogs was lost. The machine ground on relentlessly, cutting time, as Harold Innis remarked (in Carey, 1981, p.85), 'into pieces the length of a day's newspaper'. For staff and mass readership alike, history itself was thus subjected to the clockwork routine that characterized everyday life under industrial capitalism.

Other ideological effects of the new printing technology were achieved through the *privatization* of news exposure. With the advent of cheap dailies everyone could update their purchase on reality in isolation. The image of the tramcar full of silent commuters, each with his or her nose stuck in a morning paper, immediately comes to mind. No longer was news to be mediated primarily through personal intercourse and public debate. News by word-of-mouth was now considered on a par with hearsay evidence, as unreliable as home-grown produce bought in a general store. Local news-sheets were little better, while only 'backward' cultures posted their papers in public for all to read and discuss. Cheap, plentiful newspapers now meant that everyone could have a private window on the world. Each individual had direct personal access to the purveyors of reality as a more-or-less standardized product. In so far as people became habitually dependent on this form of news exposure, it may be argued, they became its captives.

Removed from alternative sources of discussion they became in effect less free to inform themselves.

Lastly, the basis of trust between a newspaper and its readership: the *objectification* of news reporting. Although this resulted largely from the demands placed upon reporters by the electric telegraph (see section 1.3.2), it was inseparable from the overall industrialization of the press, particularly in the United States. With the advent of new printing technology the newspaper became a fully manufactured product. Design, layout, headline display, and even newsworthiness were to be judged by their commercial effects. Packaging, in other words, became paramount. One element of the package was the news report. To capture and hold a politically heterogeneous mass audience the newspaper literally could not afford to print purely partisan stories. Even where the paper appealed to a more or less committed readership, conspicuous evenhandedness was required to stay competitive. Journalists therefore had to cultivate 'objectivity' (Carey, 1969, pp.31–37). Their traditional roles as critics, commentators and advocates had to be pigeon-holed. Now they were to be for the most part simply reporters, presenting the 'facts' according to professionally established criteria. Journalism, a creative 'symbolic stragegy' for organizing social experience, thus became what James Carey calls an 'industrial art':

> Stylistic devices such as, for example, the inverted pyramid, the 5 W lead, and associated techniques are as much a product of industrialization as tin cans. The methods, procedures and canons of journalism were developed not only to satisfy the demands of the profession but to meet the needs of industry to turn out a mass produced commodity. (Carey, 1974, p.5)

In this view the technology of news reporting kept pace with that of printing. Neither was merely neutral. Together they promoted an 'essentially utilitarian-capitalist-scientific orientation toward events', a slant which perhaps more than any other single factor, except advertising, conditioned the 'reality' to which newspaper readers were exposed (Carey, 1969, p.36).

In daily obeisance to this reality through deep devotion to share prices and the sublime pursuit of bargain advertisements, people lent credence to the idea of communication as ritual. The idea of communication as transmission is applicable enough to circulation 'wars' and other competitive claims to have subdued and bound space over through printed words to private commercial interests. We hardly need consider it. The ritualistic view of mass circulation periodicals, especially newspapers, is, however, particularly useful for understanding how a new reality afforded by new printing technology got a hold on people. In this view 'news' was not merely information conveyed nor just manufactured reports; it was ideological drama (Carey, 1975, pp.7–10). Day-by-day, individually but en masse, people rejoined themselves through the printed page to a world portrayed 'objectively' as an arena of contending forces, a moving *mise en scène* in which, though spectators, they could also somehow feel themselves to be participants. Disconcerting it might occasionally be, but reassuring on the whole, to have a great man with whom to identify, a great cause to support, a view of life confirmed (Figure 7.9). In an era of religious pluralism and secularization the press became the main repository of the distinctive icons and shibboleths of nation, economy and class, the patriotisms and consumerisms to which lip-service had to be paid, even if their origins and implications remained opaque (Curran, 1978, p.72). While the printed page has always to some extent served as a political means of grace, never it might be said, since the time of Gutenberg, the high noon of the Holy Roman Empire, has a *deus* so powerful for good or ill had so many devotees as the one that appeared *ex machina* in the mass periodical press.

THE PIONEER SPIRIT STILL SURVIVES
From the *Tribune* © (Chicago, Illinóis)

Figure 7.9
The meaning of Charles Lindbergh's non-stop solo flight from New York City to Paris in May 1927, according to the Chicago Tribune *and the* Columbus Dispatch *(Ohio). 'Lindbergh gave the American people a glimpse of what they liked to think themselves to be at a time when they feared they had deserted their own vision of themselves.' But they were also 'deeply torn between conflicting interpretations of their own experience. By calling Lindbergh a pioneer, the people could read into American history the necessity of turning back to a frontier past. Yet the people could also read American history in terms of progress into the industrial future. They could do this by emphasizing the machine which was involved in Lindbergh's flight' (Ward, 1958, pp.5–6, 12–13). ('The pioneer spirit still survives'. Reproduced by courtesy of the* Chicago Tribune. 'It's a big relief...' Columbus Dispatch, *May 1927)*

IT IS A BIG RELIEF TO BE LOOKING UP INSTEAD OF DOWN
—Ireland in the Columbus *Dispatch.*

7.3
MAKING FACES: PICTURES ON FILM

The Judaeo-Christian prohibition of idolatry, to make no 'graven image', could reasonably have been invoked against the daily cult of the printed page, perhaps especially against Sunday papers. But it is in fact to the history of photography that we must turn to find collective observances so profane as to call forth righteous remonstrance. With the Bible widely familiar not only in vulgar translation but also in great illustrated editions, the devout, too, had come to identify ultimate reality with its static representations. 'Bibliolatry', as it was called, revered truth as fixed in print. Truth set in motion, reality artificially animated, and particularly depictions of human flesh shown among strangers in darkened rooms, were held, on the contrary, to be uniquely corrupting and idolatrous, regardless of the subject matter. 'You come straight home', a pious mother admonished her teenage son, bound for a lantern slide exhibition at the local church, 'if them pictures start to wiggle'. (The son, the late Arnold T. Olson, president of the Evangelical Free Churches of America, told the story in the author's hearing some twenty years ago.)

This primitive assertion of the non-neutrality of technology, although perhaps more typical of the midwestern United States than elsewhere in the early twentieth century, was nevertheless an understandable reaction to certain prognostications being made for cinematography at the time. For instance:

> It is the crown and flower of the nineteenth century magic, the crystallization of eons of groping enchantments. In its wholesome, sunny, and accessible laws are possibilities undreamt of by the occult lore of the East . . . It is the earnest of the coming age, when the great potentialities of life shall no longer be in the keeping of cloister and college, of money bag, but shall overflow to the nethermost portions of the earth at the command of the humblest heir of the divine intelligence.

So wrote William Dickson in 1896, reflecting on his development of the kinetoscope (in Hays, 1928, p.533). Dickson had worked on the machine at the laboratory in Orange, New Jersey where Thomas Edison, who got the credit for inventing it, had re-established his prototypal research and development organization. The optimism and populism of Dickson's assessment were entirely typical of the laboratory, and indeed of the larger social forces that brought it into existence. Cinematography had no single inventor – not Dickson, nor the Lumière brothers and E.J. Marey in France, nor even William Friese-Greene in England – but, rightly or wrongly, it became so associated with the name of Edison, and through him with American commercial culture, that an account of the invention may usefully start with the life and times of a gifted young man on the make.

7.3.1
Edison, inventor for
investors

Thomas Alva Edison, a self-taught individualist of the first order, rose from humble circumstances to become America's most respected inventor. His scientific career followed a trajectory more familiar from the Horatio Alger stories and the lives of the capitalist 'robber barons'. While still a teenager in the 1860s he published his own three-cent newspaper and distributed it singlehandedly by rail to capitalize on the news of the Civil War. Had he not familiarized himself in the process with the electric telegraph and attempted to start his own local business he might well have become a tabloid journalist to rival Hearst. When the business failed Edison became a 'tramp operator' for Western Union. To make time for tinkering on the job he invented a revolving disc repeater that took down signals in a volute spiral, which he could then decipher at leisure. Eventually the tinkering and tramping brought the lad himself by a circuitous route from his native Michigan to the political and financial heartland of the east coast. There in 1868, at the age of twenty-one, he first saw the real prospects for technologies that promoted the American way of life.

Edison obtained his first patent for an electric vote recorder. After trying unsuccessfully to have it adopted by the House of Representatives in Washington, he immediately devised a stock ticker for registering share quotations by telegraph. His experience supervising the central transmitter of gold prices on the New York exchange during the panic of 1869 taught him the power of electrical instruments on American business, just as his successive enterprises had already instilled in him the democratic spirit of self-help. In about 1870, therefore, he set himself up as an inventor for American investors, probably the first person expressly to subordinate the creation of patented products to the demands of capitalist commerce. Soon, with forty-six patents for improvements in stock tickers to his name, as well as a host of other telegraphic inventions, he took charge of his own laboratory at Menlo Park, New Jersey. Economical with truth, complacent about money, Edison became a cigar-smoking wheeler-dealer who knew how to get things done by chicanery and hard work. His business amounted to a sort of technological racket. 'He bossed a gang engaged in blackmailing nature. He oppressed the facts of science until he squeezed inventions out of them'. He devised brilliant experimental attacks for his henchmen to carry out (Crowther, 1937, p.21). The laboratory began to specialize in forestalling piracy and destroying monopolies by creating inventions to order. In Edison's hands for the first time research and development became a commercial strategy with the patent as its weapon.

More than one thousand patents eventually came to Edison, conferring intellectual property rights that, when sold or licensed, brought in fabulous revenues for reinvestment in the patent-making business. After Bell's invention of the telephone in 1876, Edison made it practicable with his carbon button transmitter. A year later he patented his most original invention, a lineal descendant of the revolving disc repeater: the phonograph. In 1879 he perfected the carbon-filament incandescent lamp using a process developed by J.W. Swan in England. Within three years it became a commercial success in conjunction with Edison's far-sighted but ill-fated direct current supply system. The mid-eighties saw two patents of great significance for the future of radio: an aerial system for wireless telegraphy by electrostatic induction, which Edison sold to the Marconi Company in 1903; and the 'Edison effect' in incandescent bulbs, which led J.A. Fleming in 1904 to develop the diode valve.

By 1887, when Edison opened a new and vastly enlarged laboratory at Orange, New Jersey, he was looking for a product that would do for the eye what the phonograph did for the ear. The phonograph had not been developed for a business client or as part of a competitive research programme, yet it had emerged directly from Edison's telephone and telegraph work, drawing on his expertise in the design of commercial precision instruments. The device operated like a lathe, using a clockwork mechanism to turn a horizontal brass cylinder, scored with a continuous spiral groove, beneath a sharp needle fixed to a membrane that was vibrated by sound. By covering the cylinder with tinfoil and causing the vibrating needle to press it into the groove as the cylinder turned, a record of the sound was made as a continuous series of indentations in the foil. The sound could then be reproduced through the membrane by returning the needle to its initial position on the foil and setting the cylinder in motion.

Edison made several improvements to the phonograph in its first decade, chiefly by substituting an electrically driven wax cylinder, a more sensitive membrane, and a sapphire stylus ('Phonograph', *EB*, 1911). Its basic operating principle, however, remained the same – information stored on a revolving cylinder – and although the mechanism at first proved too awkward for use in business as a robot stenographer, Edison found that it appealed to children of all ages as a sophisticated toy. Deaf since youth, he now had a daughter, Dot, and a son, Dash, to help him see – or rather hear – the commercial possibilities of mechanically reproduced sound entertainment (Figure 7.10). The question was whether such possibilities existed for visual entertainment as well.

With Dickson's expert assistance, Edison went to work in 1888 adapting the phonograph mechanism to display moving images. He replaced the spiral groove with a series of discrete micro-images on the cylinder, the vibrating membrane and stylus with a magnifying eyepiece. To move the cylinder from

*Figure 7.10
Marketing entertainment, or
the commercialization of
leisure, in the* Illustrated
London News, *30 December
1899. The rights to Edison's
'Improved Phonograph' and
to Alexander Graham Bell's
'Graphophone' of 1887
became vested in a single
company, headed by Edison,
which sold machines directly to
the public. 'By the end of the
1890s the manufacturers . . .
were making healthy profits.
The recordings themselves
had improved greatly in
quality, and sales – albeit in
side-street cycle shops and
hardware stores – were
steadily increasing. The
pioneering days were over; the
machine was about to become
a true musical medium'
(Daly, 1980, pp.12–13).
(Photo: Mansell Collection)*

image to image and operate the shutter on the eyepiece he borrowed a ratchet wheel, an electrical switch, and two sets of solenoids from his telegraph instruments. The analogy between phonograph and kinetoscope, acoustic and visual reproduction, seemed set to be fairly close. But Edison and Dickson ran into problems. Photographic images were difficult to fix on a metal cylinder and needed to be flat for undistorted viewing. A polygonal cylinder was therefore substituted and Edison considered ways of projecting the images on a screen.

Then in mid-1889 the cylinder was abandoned. Edison had attended the Paris exhibition in the summer and met European experimenters such as Marey, who had been among the first a few years earlier to expose paper film in rolls from a hand-cranked camera. Immediately on returning to his laboratory, Edison knew what had to be done. The kinetoscope was not to resemble the phonograph after all. Within a month he undertook to patent a viewing system employing perforated roll film fed from reel-to-reel by sprocket wheels before a continuous light source and a revolving shutter. Henceforth motion picture apparatus would resemble Edison's devices for printing on sprocket-fed rolls of paper tape. Like the phonograph, it had not been developed for a commercial client; its analogy had nevertheless become the stock ticker (Jenkins, 1975, pp.264–67; Jenkins, 1987, pp.48–55).

7.3.2
Eastman the entrepreneur

When Edison sent Dickson up to Rochester, New York, in the autumn of 1889 to obtain a sample of George Eastman's new celluloid film for the kinetoscope, he established a permanent link between motion pictures and mass commercial culture. Eastman had just brought out his 'Kodak' camera, which did for photography what Wedgwood had done for dining and what Ford would do for transport. Now motion pictures were destined to have a comparable impact on entertainment.

Photography had long remained in the hands of the middle classes and of those who serviced their requirements. It was a relatively democratized and affordable means of self-representation in comparison with the oil paintings commissioned by aristocratic élites. The most common form of photograph became the *carte de visite*, although portraits and pictorial scenes appeared with increasing frequency on Victorian parlour walls (Open University, 1982). Photographic apparatus and techniques were, however, another matter. Only specialists could understand and use them. They were complex and expensive. From the early-nineteenth century, when photography was treated as a novelty, a range of chemical processes were devised for making permanent records of images. Industries sprang up to exploit them on both sides of the Atlantic. 'Heliographie' (1827) and the 'daguerreotype' process (from 1839), originating in France, printed images on metal plates. The 'calotype' (1841), patented in England by William Fox Talbot, was a direct reproduction made on paper by a process used subsequently to print from negatives prepared on glass plates by the collodion (from 1850) and collodion emulsion (from 1864) processes. Although exposure times were reduced in turn by each of these techniques, from hours to mere seconds, and the quality of images was much improved, the main constraints on the photographic industry were still technological. Its sophisticated products still went to specialists who prepared photographs for the better-off. Simpler and cheaper methods had to be found for recording images if the potential market for photography was to be tapped (Abney *et al.*, 1911; Open University, 1982).

The changeover began in the late 1870s, when gelatin-coated dry glass plates became available from British manufacturers. Collodion process plates were wet and perishable; they had to be specially prepared for each photographic session. Gelatin dry plates were ready to use from the box and, although at first dearer, they were considerably more sensitive, requiring exposures of as little as one-fifteenth of a second. Eastman was among the first to manufacture gelatin dry plates in the United States, and by 1884 he and his colleague, William Walker, had devised a machine that made ready-to-use photographic paper as well. Previously the sheets had to be sensitized just before printing. The new machine produced pre-sensitized paper on a continuous roll, coating it with the same gelatin bromide emulsion used on the glass negative plates. Photography had thus been twice simplified by becoming dependent on prepared commercial products when Eastman, a shrewd entrepreneur, conceived the final decisive step that would 'deliver the entire photographic market into his hands' (Jenkins, 1975, p.98).

The glass plates had to go. They were an expensive encumbrance: heavy, bulky and breakable. A new system of photography had to be devised around gelatin coated flexible film on a roll. Eastman would invent the film; Walker would design the camera roll holder; together they would create the film-making machinery along the lines adopted for manufacturing sensitized paper. Labour costs fell by 95 per cent, materials by one-half, and by the end of 1884 the system was ready. But it did not sell. The negative film had to be printed through the paper, giving grainy or faded results. 'Stripping film', subsequently introduced, required five separate operations to remove the photosensitive emulsion from its paper base and prepare it for printing. Serious photographers continued to prefer the gelatin dry plates. In 1887 Eastman therefore turned to the general public. His business had survived on sales of photographic paper and income from factory printing and enlarging. Now he proposed to extend these services and create a market for his principal product. Ordinary people would buy his roll film if it were already installed in a simple, inexpensive camera that they could use and return with a modest payment to his factory in exchange for reloading and their prints. 'You press the button, we do the rest', became Eastman's pitch. It was 'the most revolutionary moment in the history of photography' (Jenkins, 1975, p.112; Chanan, 1980, chapter 7).

The Kodak camera – so named as a unique trademark that could not be mispronounced – went on sale in 1888. It cost twenty-five dollars, which was not cheap. The factory reload and 100 prints cost ten dollars each time. Eastman advertised in all the national magazines and distributed through department stores and druggists (Figure 7.11). Sales mushroomed everywhere, costs and prices fell. Walker, in London, was supervising agencies all over Europe and the British Empire within a year. A new and improved camera was introduced, and Eastman continued his policy of acquiring a monopoly on all patents related to his products. Meanwhile the search went on for a lightweight, flexible, tough material, inert to photographic chemicals, that would replace the paper substrate in roll film. Nitrocellulose compounds had been available since the 1860s; one of these that fitted the bill, celluloid, had been used in photographic experiments on both sides of the Atlantic during the 1870s and 1880s. In 1888 Eastman first considered it with his chemist Henry Reichenbach. Their experiments met with such success that in April 1889 they applied for patents to protect the manufacture of celluloid film. Secret production began in a new factory and by the end of the summer the film was put on sale. Epitomizing his commercial strategy, Eastman exclaimed, 'The field for it is immense . . . If we can *fully* control it I would not trade it for the telephone. There is more millions in it than anything else because the patents are young and the field won't require 8 or 10 years to develop it and introduce it' (in Jenkins, 1975, p.131).

Nothing used up celluloid film faster than motion pictures: about forty-six frames per second in Edison's kinetoscope, 165,000 frames per hour. By 1911 cinematographic film had become 'the largest sector of sales (and, no doubt, profits)' for the Eastman Kodak company. The American market alone was buying at the rate of 91 million feet – over 17,000 miles – per year (Jenkins, 1975, pp.278, 288). Two decades earlier even Eastman in his enthusiasm had not anticipated this, but Edison had in effect. Gelatin dry emulsion and continuous roll film were not introduced with cinematography in mind. Even celluloid film was devised merely to simplify processing. Each of these developments, however, had originated in a strategy to achieve market dominance, a strategy that Edison was pursuing elsewhere along his own lines. The conjunction of these strategies, the intersection of patented celluloid film with patented stock ticker mechanisms, occurred in a laboratory already geared to realizing the commercial possibilities of the phonograph. When Edison first demonstrated the kinetoscope in public, to the National Federation of Women's Clubs during their visit to his laboratory in 1891, it marked the start of the biggest entertainment industry the world had ever seen.

Figure 7.11
Kodak camera and film advertisement c.1900. (Photo: Aaron Scharf)

7.3.3
The celluloid shell

The kinetoscope made its commercial debut on Broadway, New York City, in April 1894. It was a smash hit. Under a contract with Edison the Kinetoscope Company, founded by two speculators with the likely names of Raff and Gammon, thereafter supplied the machines to a chain of parlours in major cities across the country. Everywhere people jostled and queued to drop a coin in the slot and peer in amazement for a few seconds at a crude flickering representation of a prize fight or a dance (Figure 7.12). From this all else followed. Money was to be made and the changes began to ring on this familiar theme. Inventors tried to circumvent Edison's early patents; manufacturers of peep-show apparatus openly infringed them. In Europe, where Edison and others had neglected to file patent applications, the kinetoscope soon had numerous competitors, and by Christmas 1894 the Lumière family in France had developed the first cinema projector. Others followed in quick succession – R.W. Paul in England, the Skladanowsky brothers in Germany, Woodville Latham and Thomas Armat in the United States. The Lumières in Paris and Latham in New York held demonstrations of their equipment early in 1895. Armat exhibited his projector in September, whereupon Raff and Gammon pounced on it and persuaded Armat 'that in order to secure the largest profit in the shortest time it is necessary that we attach Mr. Edison's name to this new machine' (in Czitrom, 1982, p.39). They christened it the 'Edison Vitascope' and introduced it to the public on 23 April 1896 as the last act of the evening at Koster and Bial's Music Hall on lower Broadway. The timing was prophetic, the effect portentous. Edison observed from the audience. People leapt from their seats in the front rows to escape the surf they saw breaking on the screen. Soon Vitascope shows were touring all over the country. Curious citizens paid in their thousands to watch Edison's latest wonder. The music hall had seen its day (Hays, 1928, pp.509–12; Sharp, 1969, chapter 2; Jenkins, 1975, pp.268–76).

Meanwhile, with the market for motion pictures firmly established by the kinetoscope, technical improvements proceeded apace. Shutter, light source and feed mechanisms were repeatedly modified. New celluloid films became available, adapted to new machines. Edison's encounter with Eastman's film was a brief though decisive one, and he turned to other sources for heavier

Figure 7.12
Charles Urban's kinetoscope and phonograph parlour, Detroit, 1895. (Photo: Science Museum, London)

stock that would endure being pulled repeatedly through the kinetoscope on sprockets. After 1896, however, Eastman Kodak recaptured the American market; and with the introduction of continuous production methods in 1900, splice-free film of any length became available and the company's dominance of world sales was assured. Bayer and Agfa, the German chemical giants, learned too late how to manufacture cine film; Austin-Edwards of England and Gevaert of Belgium together could not match the quality for price achieved by their New York competitor. The Lumières' company remained competitive for a time, but their film lacked uniformity and producers rejected it for Eastman Kodak's superior product. By 1910 the firm controlled over 90 per cent of the world market for cine film (Jenkins, 1975, pp.266, 278).

As Eastman Kodak grew larger and cine film became cheaper the motion picture industry began to assume its modern form. The big manufacturers of projection apparatus such as Edison and Biograph in the United States, Pathé in France, and Messter in Germany, produced and sold motion pictures by the foot to enhance their sales. But with the initial market for projectors limited by the number of cinemas, it quickly became clear that the real money was to be made by controlling the film. Unlike other commodities, cine film did not have to pass physically into the hands of customers for its value to be realized. The value lay in the viewing; admission prices determined income. This explains in part why the early cinema was dominated by travelling showmen who had purchased their own stock (Sharp, 1969, chapter 3). Market saturation resulted if an exhibitor stayed in one place; therefore, quite literally, the show had to go on. Cine film did not, however, have to pass into the ownership of exhibitors either. It could be rented from distributors who purchased their stock from the manufacturer-producers. Distribution, though more risky than exhibition, promised to be extremely lucrative as well. Thus the manufacturer-producers faced the problem of controlling both these operations to assure a 'steady flow of profits' (Jenkins, 1975, pp.282–86; Chanan, 1980, chapter 15).

The problem was compounded in the United States by litigation over patent infringements among the manufacturer-producers and competition from small producers who did not manufacture projection apparatus. While the industry leaders fought among themselves, in other words, they also had to contend with outsiders who could sell motion pictures more cheaply because they did not have to mark up prices to compensate for loss of royalties. But a way out of this impasse lay close at hand. What everyone needed to do business was Eastman Kodak film. The big companies seized on it as a lever to restructure and reorganize the industry in their own interests. George Eastman and the executives of Edison's manufacturing company, the principal patent-holder, took the lead. Access to the film would be restricted to manufacturers and producers who agreed to submit their patents and pay appropriate royalties to a licensing organization founded specially for the purpose in 1908, the Motion Picture Patents Company. The Company would apportion the royalties to its members, including Eastman Kodak; the extra costs would be passed on to distributors and exhibitors. The larger firms in the United States and nearly all the European participants in the American market had little choice but to accept these terms.

Within a year the strategy began to come unstuck. The reason was quite simple. Distributors and exhibitors, now forced to bear the producers' extra costs, were also made an offer by Motion Picture Patents that they could hardly refuse. Motion pictures originating from companies in the patent pool would be made available to them only on condition that they paid licence fees themselves. Some distributors rebelled and began organizing as 'independent' producers. Motion Picture Patents responded in 1910 by organizing almost all the distributors into the General Film Company, making it nearly impossible for independent producers to distribute through traditional channels. The independents countered by forming their own production and distribution company, using the inferior Lumière stock. They met with qualified success, and by 1912 the company had expanded to become Universal Film (Jenkins, 1975, pp.286–88).

Eastman Kodak were worried. Perhaps the celluloid shell in which the industry leaders had sought to protect themselves could be exploded after all. But the company had one additional advantage. Nitrocellulose film was indeed highly flammable, particularly when displayed before an electric arc in a projector driven, as some were, by a petrol engine. A series of disastrous fires had made this a matter of public concern, particularly in Europe. Non-inflammable acetate-cellulose film had, however, been developed by Eastman Kodak in efforts to forestall government safety restrictions and keep ahead of their European competitors. And when the firm had entered into the agreement with the Motion Picture Patents Company in 1908, this new product was 'seen as a means of raising even higher the entry barriers to independents' (Jenkins, 1975, p.289). It only remained to convince state and municipal authorities to pass legislation requiring exhibitors to use only non-inflammable film.

But the political campaign failed, the trade remained indifferent to the new film even after its initial defects were removed, and Eastman Kodak did not introduce it successfully into Europe. Acetate-cellulose film was abandoned and in 1911 Eastman himself, now seeing the company's interests best served by marketing to the new independent producers, renegotiated his contract with Motion Picture Patents. This signalled 'the ultimate failure of the first attempt at the rationalization of the cinematographic industry' in the United States (Jenkins, 1975, p.291).

7.3.4
Integration and the
coming of sound

In the aftermath the American motion picture industry rapidly assumed its familiar characteristics. Concentrating now on technical and patent control, Motion Picture Patents set off a barrage of lawsuits that drove Universal Film offshore to Cuba. There, free from the American courts, the independents from New York and Chicago found an environment so suitable for motion picture production that on returning to the mainland their attention was drawn to sunny southern California. Beginning in 1911 many of them moved their production facilities into the vicinity of a place called Hollywood. As the historic migration continued, in 1915, Universal and other independents won their greatest victory with a successful anti-trust petition against Motion Picture Patents for its attempt both to control production and distribution and to license exhibition. The company immediately went out of business and most of its constituent firms soon vanished (Jenkins, 1975, p.292).

But the days of Motion Picture Patents had been numbered in any case. The independents had already adopted a successful counter-strategy in the market. Eastman doubtless recognized this when he agreed to sell them film. Motion Picture Patents, representing chiefly the dominant interests of big manufacturer-producers and distributors, had lost touch with exhibitors. They continued to sell short, bland, undifferentiated motion pictures by the foot when their up-and-coming rivals were struggling more creatively to capture audiences. 'Instead of conceiving motion pictures as single-reel standardized products with anonymous actors, actresses, and directors, the new leaders of the industry regarded them as highly differentiated products of feature length (at least five reels) with known plays and famous or well-known actors, actresses, and directors' (Jenkins, 1975, p.292). Universal's 'Biograph girl', Florence Lawrence, was introduced in 1909–10. Soon the Famous Player's Company combined the 'star system' with the feature film, offering the first full evening's entertainment in the four-reel picture, *Queen*

Elizabeth, with Sarah Bernhardt in the title-role. In 1915, as the independents gained their final legal triumph, *The Birth of a Nation* by D.W. Griffiths, an American epic complete with specially composed musical score, opened a record-breaking run on Broadway (Hays, 1928, pp.516–19; Ramsaye, 1947, pp.31–33; Jenkins, 1975, pp.292–93).

Unsurprisingly, the independents now set about achieving what Motion Picture Patents had failed to do. Having combined production and distribution, they swallowed each other up and set their sights on exhibition. Oligopolistic control of the motion picture industry by fully integrated corporate giants was finally within reach.

When films first became available for hire about 1905, exhibitors no longer required initial capital to purchase a working stock. Also, given a wide choice of titles, they could keep their show in one place. Immediately the motion picture business was opened up to every two-bit entrepreneur and flimflam artist who could afford a second-hand projector and set up a 'nickelodeon' or 'penny gaff' in a storefront. Then, as popular films became longer and more complex, these premises had to be enlarged. Fewer showings of more expensive films meant that larger audiences had to be accommodated for exhibitors to break even. Thus, before the First World War the nickelodeon was in terminal decline, and hundreds of bright new 'picture palaces' had emerged, attracting crowds as much by their ornate ambiance as by the entertainment they provided (Sharp, 1969, chapters 4–5).

Here lay the real gold mine in motion pictures and in America the big independent production companies exploited it. Film sales were abolished; cinemas were classified on the basis of their size, location and potential audience; rental rates were differentiated accordingly, and in respect of a film's quality, cost and date of release. Nationwide distribution was co-ordinated to maximize exposure and return, while 'block booking' ensured that independent exhibitors took lower quality pictures with the best, thereby repaying each of the producers' investments. Some exhibitors, in response, combined to negotiate favourable rates, and the First National Exhibitor's Circuit eventually branched out into production. But the main thrust towards integration came from the production houses, which progressively annexed the cinemas. By the mid-1920s the industry had become dominated by a handful of giants whose names were household words: firstly Paramount, followed by Fox and Loew, with Universal and Warner Brothers in a tertiary position (Jenkins, 1975, pp.293–96).

Eastman Kodak, another household word, had perfected cellulose acetate for coating the fabric skin of military aircraft during the war. None too soon, the company now began supplying 'safety' film for exhibition in the colossal movie houses that sprang up across the United States in the twenties and in Europe a little later. It was not, however, safety considerations or even primarily centralized ownership and control that permitted the boom in cinema building. For just when radio had begun to attract listeners on a massive scale, keeping audiences at home, the silent movie was rescued by sound (Sharp, 1969, chapter 7; Jenkins, 1975, pp.295–98).

'Talking pictures' had been a reality ever since Edison installed a synchronized phonograph in one of his early kinetoscopes. The difficulty lay in making the sound available to a cinema audience. This awaited developments in the telecommunications industry, chiefly the thermionic valve, the loudspeaker and the photoelectric cell. After electronic amplification had been achieved from a phonographic stylus, it was simply a matter of time before someone installed one of the mass produced 'gramophone' discs invented by Émile Berliner – Edison's cylinders, difficult to mould, had been superseded – in a film projector and synchronized the motor with the turntable. Western Electric devised such a system using centre-start, one-sided gramophone records, sixteen inches in diameter, rotating at thirty-three and one-third

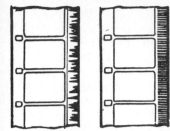

Figure 7.13
Types of optical sound track.
Left: variable area records
sound impulses as a wavy
image spreading across the
track. Right: variable density
track records sound impulses
as variations in density along
the track. (Reproduced from
The Focal Encyclopedia of
Photography, *1956, Focal*
Press. Reproduced by
permission of the publishers)

revolutions per minute. Each record carried the sound for a single reel of film. Warner Brothers snapped up this 'Vitaphone' and in October 1927 introduced Al Jolson in *The Jazz Singer*, the first sound motion picture. The rest of the industry, witnessing the movie's huge success, went over to sound within two or three years, although by then Warner Brothers had bought up and equipped hundreds of cinemas, consolidating a major leadership position for the first time (Sharp, 1969, chapter 7; Jenkins, 1975, pp.297–98; Thomas and Ward, 1978, pp.1309–10).

But the Vitaphone had drawbacks, one of which was the procedure to be followed if the film broke in mid-reel. After it was mended, either the reel had to be run again from the beginning to synchronize with the sound or the remaining portion of the film had to be shown as a 'silent' (Hall, 1936, pp.254–55). Clearly, a better way of achieving perfect synchronization was needed. The technique perfected from the turn of the century by researchers on both sides of the Atlantic was to print the sound on the film (Figure 7.13). A separate track, adjacent to the frames, carried a continuous pattern of exposure varying either in density or in width. The track was laid down by electronically modulating a light source with the original sound and projecting this light onto the side of the film as it passed before the camera lens. A visual pattern resulted, locked to the image. This pattern was then decoded on the printed film, as it passed before the projector lens, by simultaneously projecting a beam of light through the sound track on to an appliance made of a photoconductive material such as selenium. As the pattern caused the beam to vary rapidly and continuously, this photoelectric cell converted the light into a fluctuating current which, when amplified, drove a loudspeaker to reproduce the original sound (Figure 7.14).

Figure 7.14
'Appallingly complicated
apparatus, of a sensitive
delicacy entirely beyond the
comprehension of ordinary
mortals' (Hall, 1936,
pp.252–53): a hybrid
projector, or
'cinematograph',
incorporating both sound-on-
disc and sound-on-film
methods of reproduction. The
light originates from an
electric arc focused by a mirror
(A) and passes through the
condenser (B) to the film at the
light gate (C), where it
proceeds through the
projection lens (D). Both light
intensity and sound
amplification are adjusted at
the control panel (F). The
gramophone (E) is connected
to the projector motor
through a clutch (G). The film
sound track passes at the
sound gate (I) between the
exciter lamp (L), focused by a
condenser (K) and lens (J),
and the photocell (H), where
it is decoded. (Reproduced
from Cyril Hall, 1936,
Everyday Science, *Blackie)*

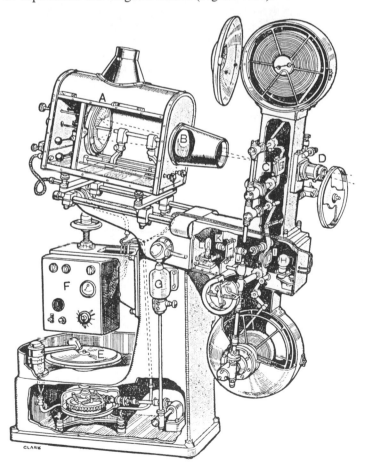

As early as 1926 the Fox organization invested in a sound-on-film system developed by Tri-Ergon in Germany. When Warner Brothers backed the Vitaphone, Fox quickly produced their much improved alternative, which was the first system to lend newsreels the immediacy of sound in the famous 'Movietone' news. Within a few years the Vitaphone proved to be a technological dead-end, and just in time for the momentous events of the 1930s, cinemas across the world were rewired and refurbished to accommodate synchronized sound-on-film projection. No longer could projectors simply be speeded up to reduce flicker or to accommodate more showings. Projectors had to match the camera's constant speed to preserve audio fidelity. In consequence reality was dispensed more realistically than ever before. Not even the coming of Technicolor in 1932 at the hands of an Eastman Kodak rival could match the impact of the 'talkies' (Sharp, 1969, chapter 7; Jenkins, 1975, pp.297–98; Thomas and Ward, 1978, pp.1312–13).

7.3.5
Empire and ideology

Cinematography affected everyday life in a multitude of ways, from sound systems to the star system, from the advent of home movies in the 1920s to the proliferation of 'drive-ins' across the United States after the Second World War. The new technology of Edison, Eastman and a host of other inventor-entrepreneurs was the precondition for this varied impact. Quality film, as we have seen, was deemed so essential to the mass exploitation of cinematography that an attempt was made to monopolize it. When the attempt had failed and the film became readily available from Eastman Kodak (and eventually from several European competitors), the cine camera emerged as the essential prerequisite of motion pictures. This artefact, too, would repay study as a technology of demarcation and control, access to which differentiated between producers and consumers, between the makers and the members of an audience. But the salient feature in the history of cinematography as it bore on everyday life was, like that of contemporary newspaper and magazine history, the *industrialization* of the medium. The conjunction of Eastman's commercial strategy with Edison's in the late 1880s marked the direction events would take. Manufacture and control of motion pictures and ownership of the means of mass exposure passed quickly into the hand of a few large and (in the event) highly financed corporations. The largest and most influential of these were based in the United States. By the end of the First World War it was their success above all that had made the cinema 'the most popular form of commercialized amusement throughout the world' (Croy, 1922, p.694).

It is worthwhile being reminded just how popular the cinema was in a world without television. Literacy did not limit the audience as long as the pictures told the story, which they did largely until the sound track replaced captions. Anyone who was not partially sighted could enjoy a film. And since everyone was curious and exhibitors relied on audience turnover for their daily bread, admission prices stayed relatively low and cinemas opened up as fast as distributors could supply them. Nickelodeons appeared by the thousand almost overnight, beginning in 1905. By 1920 there were 40,000 cinemas worldwide, with at least 17,000 in the United States, 5,000 in Great Britain, 3,200 in Germany, 2,700 in France, and over 1,000 in Italy. New York City alone had 400 cinemas, Buenos Aires had 131, and even Bangkok had 9. In the United States cinema attendance after the First World War was running at 10 million a day, a figure that rose to at least 80 million per week and perhaps as high as 100 million – equivalent to three-quarters of the population – in the golden years from 1925 to 1945. In Britain over the same period the starting point was a number equal to about half the population in attendance twice each week, or an equivalent daily attendance of 6 million – proportionately much higher than the initial American figure. By 1947 it has been estimated that up to 80,000 cinemas around the world hosted audiences of some 235 million each week (Croy, 1922, p.694; Hays, 1928, p.530; Ramsaye, 1947, p.24; Schramm, 1960, p.197; Czitrom, 1982, pp.41–42).

What most of the people saw most of the time throughout the period were motion pictures that originated in the United States. The major European countries developed notable industries of their own, but after the Great War they were unable to compete effectively against gigantic integrated empires, which by 1935 were releasing on average two feature films every day (Schramm, 1960, p.197). The war decimated the Europeans; Hollywood went from strength to strength. Audiences could be had for the taking, so the Americans simply made extra prints of films intended for domestic consumption and shipped them across the Atlantic. By 1925 Hollywood had captured 95 per cent of the British market and 70 per cent of the French. In the smaller countries the situation was much the same. The Americans' grasp was solidified with the coming of sound, which both required substantial investment and demanded that it be amortized quickly through widespread distribution. Meanwhile the European companies, with their very considerable talents, found the enormous American market almost impenetrable. There, in contrast to Europe,

> . . . the structure of the industry was based upon the mass production of films exploited profitably in company-owned theatres and block booked into independent houses. To introduce foreign films would have meant disrupting the production-distribution-exhibition chain and voluntarily giving away a portion of the box office to foreign producers. In monopolizing the home market, American companies were following the dictates of economic self-interest. (Guback, 1969, p.69)

The American dominance of the cinema industry had important consequences not only for foreign production companies but for foreign audiences as well. The United States became the best known, if not the best loved, nation in the world; the values that had shaped its civilization were introduced insensibly everywhere through images of cowboys, gangsters, and slapstick comedians. But perhaps the most general and significant change brought about by cinematography under the aegis of American business lay in the intensified *commercialization of leisure* (Jones, 1986, chapters 2–3).

The cinema in its early years belonged primarily to urban street culture, where vaudeville and burlesque theatre competed for custom alongside pool rooms and dance parlours. People entertained each other for a price, and the entertainment was always live. Then gradually the cinema simplified the environment, marginalizing the rest. Where people had thronged to eat, drink and make merry, they now began crowding together anonymously in darkened halls, sitting more or less in silence, side-by-side, row upon row, in awe of the spectacle that unfolded mechanically before them. Their recreation was turned to amusement and they became an audience. The personal immediacy and conviviality of the stage or the dance floor gave way to a celluloid substitute, although, as F. Sherwood Taylor recalled (1952, pp.226–27), the cinema did afford the British 'what . . . winter had never before possessed – a place for lovers to sit together'. Indeed, for the great majority who never attended an indoor concert or a play, the only experience comparable to the cinema was attendance at church. Little wonder that cultural traditionalists, who looked down on the cinema and its associations, berated them as 'worshippers of the silver screen'.

Cultural traditionalists not only objected to the commercial crassness of the early cinema; they also condemned the values that it disseminated, especially among the lower classes and the young. Profanity, sedition and sexual licence, purveyed in multiple copies and viewed for a few pennies,

Figure 7.15
Palace Cinema, Kentish Town, north London, 1913.
(Reproduced by permission of the Royal Commission on the
Historical Monuments of England)

threatened to corrupt society on an unprecedented scale. The industry, fearful of political interference, responded by cleaning up their act. Survival meant nothing less than conformity to the dominant standards of civic virtue. The cinema therefore began to lose its tawdry, proletarian image. The picture palace was as much an effort to accommodate bourgeois values as a means of accommodating larger audiences (Figure 7.15). And the *institutionalization of censorship* before the First World War was the industry's own answer to the problem of attracting these audiences from every class of society.

In Great Britain and the United States the effects of self-censorship were particularly pronounced, for there the industry had to demonstrate its rectitude in competition with local and municipal authorities who retained the power to ban individual films. The British Board of Film Censors, established in 1912, had a list of forty-three rules by which indecorous, indecent and illicit scenes were to be judged. The list was frequently refined and elaborated to take account of changing circumstances. Their principal client, however, made it easy for them. The American industry subjected itself in 1909 to the National Board of Censorship of Motion Pictures, in 1922 to the 'active policy of betterment' promoted by the Motion Picture Producers and Distributors of America, and in 1930 to the infamous 'Hays code', whose draconian restrictions sought to ensure that worldwide audiences would be exposed to nothing inconsistent with 'common decency and American mores' (Ramsaye, 1947, p.36; Chanan, 1980, pp.256–57; Czitrom, 1982, pp.53–54). As the eponymous Will H. Hays, America's titular 'czar of the movies', interpreted these developments, the corporate custodians of the cinema had awakened fully to their 'responsibilities'. 'From a business standpoint, the motion picture industry has settled down and is operating along the sound, common sense lines which govern other American industries' (Hays, 1928, p.522).

But the impact of motion pictures was not always so market oriented as the foregoing accounts of censorship and the commercialization of leisure would suggest. Both of these trends depended significantly on the industrialization of the medium and marched to the beat of the American production houses. Less commercial at first, but no less influential on the cinema-going public, were the creative techniques adopted by cinematographers, especially in Europe, to achieve the *revisualization of events*. In these lay the overwhelming power of the motion picture, which in turn made it ripe for commercial exploitation.

Founded on 'persistence of vision', the illusion that twenty-four images seen in sequence each second constitute a continuous motion, the film was the medium par excellence for bending and reshaping reality. Through flashbacks, close-ups, montage, and complex cutting, cinematographers could recreate the world countless times before an audience with all the apparent realism of photography and the seeming objectivity of the lens. Time could be moved backward or forward at different speeds; space could be expanded or contracted at will; causality could be made a nonsense. The cinema screen, presenting itself as a window, in fact became a mask; and in cultures where 'I see' was used habitually to mean 'I understand', the temptation to suspend disbelief for the duration of a film and impute ultimate reality to it could be irresistible. The cinema thus became an infallible means of escape from harsher realities in everyday life. By the same token, just because the cinema was known to offer a powerful emotional experience, it could also become difficult to convince a seasoned audience that the reality portrayed in a film had not been wholly contrived – that the screen was not *merely* a mask. Taylor recalled (1952, p.228), for example, the family who had seen a film about the French Revolution and believed the events they had witnessed to be based purely on fiction. The ambivalent capacity of the motion picture to impart reality to events whether or not they had actually occurred was exploited to the full in the newsreels that remained on cinema programmes from the turn of the century until the 1960s. Here, on the whole, the escapist mentality prevailed. 'Despite a history spotted with fakes and fictionalizing, news film maintained its credibility because people believed their eyes' (Davison *et al.*, 1976, p.25).

The ideological potential of the newsreel made cinematography the preeminent instrument of political propaganda for a quarter century, beginning in the 1930s (Aldgate, 1987). Commercial advertisers meanwhile buttressed their ideology of consumption with the knowledge that the 'matinee crowd' valued 'opportunities for illusion and escape above all else'; and advertisements featuring glamour photos and dramatic tableaux soon appeared in periodicals (Marchand, 1985, pp.61–63). Perhaps, however, the most general ideological impact of cinematography was achieved, not through what it portrayed, but through what it omitted; not by distorting the real world or representing bourgeois values on film, but by concealing the antecedents and conditions of film production.

The cinema was the site of the first mass encounter with what later would be called 'high technology' (Biddiss, 1977, pp.287–88). Telephones were still relatively expensive in the early decades of the cinema; aeroplanes appeared only occasionally at a great altitude. Few people listened to the wireless and fewer still had ever seen a modern printing press. The private automobile was rapidly becoming a fixture of everyday life in the United States, but before the 1920s, and in some places until much later, fewer people had experienced it as an exemplar of modern innovation than had viewed a motion picture. As late as 1934 Cyril Hall reminded the popular readers of his *Everyday Science* (p.248),

> If it fell to our lot to explain to an ignorant but intelligent savage the meaning and purpose of science, the best thing we could do would be to take him to the cinema. No other single roof covers so much concentrated science as the up-to-date 'talkie' house, except a science museum or a science laboratory. The cinema is so chock-full of science that we are apt to forget science is there at all!

Just so. The reason why people were 'apt to forget' is that the 'science' could not be seen. Outside the projection booth, in the curtained darkness, the process of mechanical reproduction was invisible. Only the mesmeric images (and later sound) impinged upon the senses. And behind these images, beyond the film that bore them, lay a vast complex of other processes – shooting, processing, printing, editing – that remained mysteriously hidden from the audience. The wonderful 'reality' conjured by the film was marked by a constant absence of the labour process and the scientific and technological 'wonders' that made it possible. In the cinema, therefore, some things became not only invisible but, for that reason, less thinkable as well; and this is a characteristic effect of ideology. Cinematography in its commercial development contributed directly to the *mystification of science and technology* in everyday life (Chanan, 1980, pp.191–95, 286).

7.4
MAKING WAVES:
VOICES IN THE AIR

Electrical communication had been mystified to some extent ever since wires and undersea cables first netted nations together and held out the millennial prospect of universal understanding. Information was to lead to co-operation, and co-operation to peace (Carey and Quirk, 1970). That telegraph technology served the very military and industrial policies it was supposed to prevent did not always register with its devotees. The mythos held sway powerfully, fortified by the hope that human beings might one day not merely signal, but actually *speak* peace to each other. In parts of Africa, it was known, people communicated by 'talking drums', which imitated the tones of their voice. Europeans mystified even this technology, believing that 'Africans could speak to one another across their continent by the throbbing of tom-toms in the night' (Headrick, 1981, p.207). Such was their obsession with long-range communication and the efficacy of speech, particularly in the hands of subjugated peoples. One day soon the subjugators must have talking drums themselves.

Telephony – literally, voice at a distance – was a phenomenon of the great electrical age that began in the nineteenth century. Its methods were two. The first depended on electromagnetic principles made familiar by the operation of the electric telegraph. Here the sound was confined along a wire in the form of a fluctuating current. The second method depended on the entirely new principle of electromagnetic radiation, which had merely been predicted in theoretical physics. In this case the sound was released into the atmosphere in the form of electromagnetic waves. Both methods of telephony enabled people to speak directly to each other, but only in certain ways. Wire telephony, or the telephone, was generally a method of private communication. Wireless telephony, or radio, made communication public. Although the telephone and radio were linked together in vast intercontinental communications systems by the early decades of the twentieth century, the characteristic features of these technologies and the industries that sponsored them are best examined in the order of their origination.

7.4.1
Telephone monopolies

'If I can get a mechanism', Alexander Graham Bell is reported to have said in 1875, 'which will make a current of electricity vary in intensity, as the air varies in density when a sound is passing through it, I can telegraph any sound, even the sound of speech' (in Marland, 1964, p.187). Many researchers worked on practical wire telephony from the mid-1850s, but Bell, a Scottish-born inventor who emigrated to the United States in 1871, was the first to patent a simple, reliable instrument. Between 1874 and 1876, when the patent was granted, he experimented with devices using, so to speak, an electromagnet operating in reverse. These devices, skilfully constructed by his assistant Thomas A. Watson, each comprised a flexible diaphragm, an electromagnet, and a battery (Figure 7.16). The diaphragm

*Figure 7.16
Bell's earliest telephone.
Probably one of the original
pair made for Alexander
Graham Bell in 1875. (Science
Museum, London)*

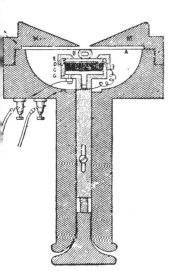

*Figure 7.17
Schematic cross-section of
Edison's carbon-button
transmitter. The diaphragm
(A) held in place by the mouth
piece (M) transmits vibrations
through a piece of rubber
tubing (B) to the disc covering
the cell filled with carbon
powder. (From*
Encyclopaedia Britannica, *
eleventh edition 1910–11,
Cambridge University Press,
Vol.26)*

was mounted so that it could vibrate freely and pass the vibrations through a mechanical linkage to the armature of the electromagnet. The coil of the electromagnet was energized by the battery, but not strongly enough to close the armature. When someone spoke into the transmitter diaphragm the armature vibrated in the vicinity of the coil, and this 'induced' fluctuations in the current passing through it – 'electromagnetic induction'. This current proceeded through wires to another electromagnet at a distance and set up identical fluctuations in its armature, which in turn was coupled to a receiver diaphragm that reproduced the original vibrations, and so a facsimile of the original voice.

Bell went on to construct a 'voice-powered' instrument that used a permanent magnet. This design was subsequently retained in the ear-piece, or receiver, of most telephones, while Bell's original transmitter was replaced everywhere by devices bearing a family resemblance to an invention patented by Edison in 1877 (Figure 7.17). Edison found that a vibrating diaphragm, pressed against a small button-shaped cell filled with carbon powder, caused the electrical resistance of the cell to fluctuate with the vibrations. If a large enough current passed through the cell it could carry the fluctuations to a distance and reproduce the vibrations through a magnetic receiver. In 1878 the English electrician D.E. Hughes, investigating the variable resistance phenomenon, coined the word by which the voice transmitter would thereafter be known: the microphone.

No sooner had the feasibility of the telephone been demonstrated than the rush began to wire up subscribers to the service through local 'exchanges'. The first of these interconnecting points opened for commercial service at New Haven, Connecticut, in January 1878. The first exchange in Britain, located at Coleman Street in London, entered service in August 1879 (Tucker, 1978, pp.1222–25). From the outset the business on both sides of the Atlantic was dominated by Edison and Bell. Each had patented an instrument that was indispensable for wire telephony and in Britain each started his own company to exploit it. In the United States, however, the rights to Edison's microphone belonged to Western Union, the telegraph giant, which had commissioned its development; Bell's patent was vested in the National Bell Telephone Company. With Edison's help Western Union sought to enter the telephone business. National Bell threatened litigation, and in 1879 Western Union withdrew unconditionally in exchange for a fixed royalty on its various patents. The National Bell Company was now reorganized as American Bell; in Britain the Edison and Bell interests amalgamated to form the United Telephone Company (Chandler, 1977, pp.200–01). In 1880 the firms had an equal start in the race to set up a national network.

But their chances of success were very unequal. In Britain, as in many other countries, communication by telegraph had become a state monopoly. This in itself was no bad thing. Since 1868, when the Post Office took over the telegraph companies, American engineers had come to practise in Britain, thereby escaping the stifling influence of Western Union, which discouraged innovation by monopolizing important patents. But the Post Office brooked no challenge to its supremacy in the field of electrical communications. In 1880, faced with the prospect of competition from the American-owned United Telephone Company, it went to court and had the telephone declared a telegraph, effectively bringing the company under state control. Thereafter for many years the development of wire telephony in Britain was frustrated at every turn. Applications to lay underground wires were repeatedly refused. Attempts to establish an inter-urban network of 'trunk' lines were first prohibited, then tolerated on the condition that a royalty was paid to the state. The Post Office dabbled in the business, licensed competing companies, and generally dragged its feet when it was not compelled to change its policies by successive governments. Local authorities were obstructive as well. In 1889 the competing firms amalgamated to form the National Telephone Company. The government failed to exercise its option to buy out the firms but it compelled them to sell their trunk lines to the Post Office instead. The dithering went on until 1905, when the government finally contracted to nationalize the telephone service. By 1912 only a handful of municipal systems remained outside the Post Office monopoly (Garcke, 1911).

Although the telephone in Britain remained inefficient and expensive on account of nearsighted political interference, the scope of the network outstripped that of nearly all the rest of Europe. In 1906 there were more working telephones in the United Kingdom, with its population of 42 million, than in the eleven countries of Austria, Hungary, Belgium, Denmark, Holland, Italy, Norway, Portugal, Russia, Sweden and Switzerland, with their combined population of 288 million. Only France, Germany and Switzerland had more working telephones than there were in metropolitan London. Between 1910 and 1920 the Scandinavian countries had the largest number of telephones in relation to population, but only Germany, with as many as three telephones per 100 people, had a consistently larger number of subscribers than in Britain, where less than 2 per cent of the population had telephones at any time (Garcke, 1911; 'Telephone', *EB*, 1922).

Bright as the prospects for wire telephony were in Britain, relatively speaking, the contrast with the United States could hardly have been more complete. By 1885 American Bell, with a flourishing inter-urban network, had ten times as many subscribers as *all* the Post Office-licensed companies in the United Kingdom. Thereafter, when these companies were able to open trunk lines, the American lead did not abate. At no time between 1910 and 1920 did the United States have fewer than ten times as many working telephones as there were in Britain, or about six times as many telephones per 100 population. In 1920 this amounted to twelve times the number of telephones per 100 population in all of Europe – over 60 per cent of the telephones in the world ('Telephone', *EB*, 1922). What made wire telephony in the United States feasible on an unequalled scale was not, however, merely the democratic impulse to send messages beyond class barriers, nor the communications needs of entrepreneurs, nor even the reluctance of state and Federal governments to interfere with private commerce. It was above all the monopolistic strategy of American Bell under the leadership of Theodore N. Vail (Garnet, 1985).

Like his contemporaries Edison and Eastman, Vail determined to make the Bell Company invincible through institutionalized research and development geared to the creation of patented products. He also sought to dominate the telephone market by the purchase of competing companies and the control of long-distance traffic. Western Electric, founded in 1881, the Bell Company's manufacturing subsidiary, became a centre of industrial research; American Telephone and Telegraph (AT&T), founded in 1885, also pursued research in conjunction with its role as the Bell subsidiary in charge of building and operating long-distance lines. The two research organizations would merge in 1925 as the famous Bell Telephone Laboratories. In 1900 AT&T became the parent company for the Bell system as a whole and, with Vail in charge, established a centralized administration that covered the United States. Standardization and optimization of both service and equipment could now be imposed on the remaining local independent companies, for AT&T owned and controlled the long-distance lines by which they were forced to interconnect (Chandler, 1977, pp.202–03; Noble, 1977, pp.91–92).

By the First World War, when the Post Office in Britain was just picking up the pieces into which the national network had been allowed to fragment by decades of indecision, the Bell system had become an efficient private monopoly. Forty-four per cent of Americans, on average, made a telephone call each day (Craven *et al.*, 1937, p.218). The corporate leadership at AT&T attributed their success, and rightly so, to 'the exercise of foresight'. America's 'great industrial nervous system' owed its existence to the 'centralized development of telephone equipment' (Jewett, 1928, p.461; G.D. Smith, 1985). Already among the 9,255 patents the company would secure in its first fifty years were the rights to Michael Pupin's 'loading coils', which vastly improved the quality of long-distance calls, and to Lee De Forest's 'audion', the three-element vacuum valve soon known as the 'triode'. This device served to generate the high-frequency currents needed for sending numerous conversations on the same line, or 'multiplexing', and formed the heart of the telephone amplifier, or 'repeater', which, in conjunction with loading coils, made transcontinental telephony practicable by 1915. It also proved to be the key to popular radio.

7.4.2
The control of radio

Beginning in 1887 Heinrich Hertz demonstrated publicly what his colleagues in theoretical physics had known for over twenty years: that the electromagnetic forces in and around a wire could be released into space as waves travelling at the speed of light – 'electromagnetic radiation'. Soon experimenters everywhere were trying it. Their trick was to produce a rapidly alternating disturbance in an electrical circuit by means of a high-voltage spark from a storage jar or induction coil. The main frequency of the disturbance depended on the dimensions of the circuit. Waves emitted at this frequency were detected by constructing another circuit at a distance and adjusting its dimensions, or 'tuning' it. This circuit usually contained a device known as a 'coherer' that conducted an electric current when energized by electromagnetic waves. A current passing through the coherer could be used to operate an ordinary telegraph instrument that gave a record of incoming signals. By 1896 electromagnetic waves were being sent and received from experimental 'spark-gap' transmitters in England, France, Germany, Russia, Italy, India and the United States. The radio age had begun.

In the early years, of course, it was always called 'wireless telegraphy'. The term took on significance as one or the other word was stressed. First, in communication that was truly *wireless*, no one owned the medium. Electromagnetic waves travelled through the 'ether' of space, the invisible, intangible fluid with which space was thought to be filled. And since the ether was everywhere and belonged to everyone and no one, communication could now, in principle, be opened up to all. Indeed, some believed that, with a better understanding of the mysterious ether, direct telepathy might prove to be the ultimate form of wireless. In the second place, though, the only means of wireless signalling known at the turn of the century was *telegraphy*. Wireless telegraphy appeared to be at best an adjunct of existing land-based telegraphs, which would enable them to reach over water to islands and ships at sea. At worst it loomed as a competitor for inland and cable communications, although the telephone at least was not thought to be under threat (Figure 7.18). But in neither case, whether wireless telegraphy was seen as the precursor of free and democratic interchange or as the province of vested interests, did its real potential become apparent. Not even the man whose name is most often associated with the early history of radio, the Italian inventor Guglielmo Marconi, foresaw what the industry he started would become.

The young Marconi, having failed to interest his own government in wireless telegraphy, arrived in Britain in 1896 with a practical spark-gap apparatus workable over several kilometres. He filed for a patent and contacted the Post Office and the Admiralty, offering his apparatus as a solution to their communication problems. The Post Office, charged with inland telegraphs, had tinkered for years with methods of improving the service to coastal regions and lightships in the interests of maritime safety. The Royal Navy,

GIVING THEM WARNING.

Electricity (to Submarine Cable and Land Telegraph). " I DON'T LIKE TO GET RID OF OLD AND VALUABLE SERVANTS, BUT I'M AFRAID I SHALL NOT BE ABLE TO KEEP EITHER OF YOU MUCH LONGER."

Figure 7.18 Prospects for the wireless industry. After Marconi achieved reliable coastal and cross-channel communication at the beginning of 1899, his company's shares rose in value six-fold. Punch's comment on 8 February 1899 illustrates the mystique with which wireless was then invested.

charged with protecting imperial trade routes, had already set up a secret laboratory to investigate wireless telegraphy as a solution to the problems of ship-to-ship and ship-to-shore communication. Confronted now with successful demonstrations of the Marconi apparatus, the organizations responded predictably. The Post Office under its chief engineer William Preece played for time, equivocated, misunderstood the physical principle involved, and passed up the chance to acquire the rights to Marconi's patent. The Royal Navy, advised by their chief wireless experimenter, Captain Henry Jackson, welcomed Marconi aboard. After July 1897, when Marconi vested his patent in the Wireless Telegraph and Signal Company, which was set up by his mother's family, the Jameson's of Irish whiskey fame, the naval engineers stayed closely in touch with him, exchanging notes and generally ensuring that his main lines of research were directed to meeting Admiralty needs. In 1900 a contract arrived to equip the Royal Navy for wireless communication. The Marconi Company, as it was now called, became the sole supplier of wireless apparatus to the largest fleet in the world. With its marine subsidiary, which equipped civilian shore stations, and American Marconi in the United States, the organization dominated the emerging global radio industry until the First World War (Pocock, 1988).

Not even the sustaining influence of a prototypal 'military–industrial complex' could, however, ward off commercial conservatism. Marconi apparatus in its improved form was robust and reliable. By spanning the Atlantic in 1901–02 and especially through vital service in a series of maritime disasters, it acquired an unmatched reputation and made the inventor's name a household word (Figure 7.19). But the spark-gap method it employed was messy and inefficient. Despite 'selective tuning', introduced in the early 1900s, the signal from a Marconi transmitter occupied many frequencies because it originated in a rapid series of decaying electrical pulses. This meant that it interfered with other transmitters and distributed its electromagnetic energy across the spectrum. To concentrate the energy and so keep transmitters from interfering and make them more efficient, it was necessary to generate a 'continuous wave' at a single frequency. Moreover, as a few engineers had urged, without continuous wave transmission there was no prospect for wireless telephony.

Marconi was not among them. While his organization continued to supply spark-gap equipment of increasing sophistication, the incentive to develop the technology for wireless telephony became strongest in the United States. There were two main reasons for this. Firstly, the Marconi Company, an arm of British imperialism, dominated international telecommunications by only leasing its equipment and refusing to permit intercommunication between its stations and those of other systems. Secondly, AT&T, the largest private monopoly in the United States, dominated domestic telecommunications by controlling the long-distance lines. Wireless telephony promised

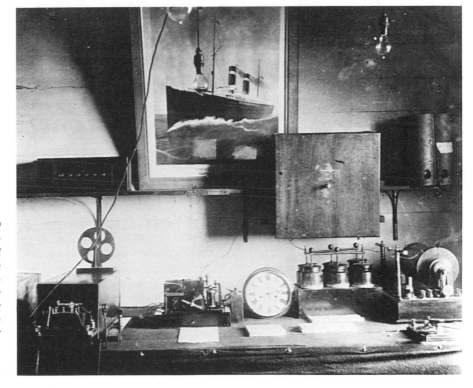

Figure 7.19
The Marconi Company's station at the Lizard around the turn of the century. The induction coil and spark gap are at the right, behind the telegraph key. The coherer mechanisms are immediately to the left of the clock. Further left are the recording devices. (Photo: Science Museum, London)

to give its users a competitive advantage over both industrial giants. It would restore control of transoceanic radio to the Federal government via the US Navy and thereby serve the national interest. It would also provide point-to-point communication more cheaply by dispensing with the enormous fixed costs of a wired network. From the turn of the century, therefore, American venture capital poured into projects for constructing a continuous wave transmitter.

Three methods had been devised by 1914. The 'arc generator', patented in 1903 by the Danish engineer Valdemar Poulsen, produced a pure high-frequency oscillation across the terminals of an electric arc operating in a gas-filled chamber subjected to a magnetic field. It was perfected by the Federal Telegraph Company of California under a contract to the United States Navy. In 1918 the Navy purchased the company's patents. The second method, the 'high-frequency alternator', a sophisticated dynamo, generated an alternating current at a single frequency when driven at high speed by a motor. It was developed simultaneously in France and Germany, and in the United States, where the main work was carried out by the company into which Edison's manufacturing interests had merged, General Electric (GE). In 1919 the Navy again acted in the national interest by blocking the Marconi Company's belated attempt to acquire continuous-wave technology by purchasing alternators from GE. Arc generators and high-frequency alternators had proved their worth during the First World War, when they provided reliable transatlantic communication. The military wanted to control them (Aitken, 1985, chapters 2–3, 5).

The third method of generating a continuous wave was the wave of the future. And it proved difficult to control. Arcs and alternators were large, expensive, and sometimes temperamental. They ran continuously at high power, using prodigious amounts of energy. As technologies for wireless telephony, they were more appropriate for governments than for would-be competitors with AT&T. But in 1906 De Forest had patented the triode valve as a device for amplifying weak currents; by 1913 this little glass bulb had been wired up with a few simple components to generate a high-frequency continuous wave (Figure 7.20). It was a turning point in the history of radio. Voices could now be transmitted using relatively inexpensive equipment of modest proportions. Reception of wireless signals was also much improved. Fleming's diode valve had already replaced the coherer as a detector of electromagnetic waves. The triode's role was to take the incoming signal currents and not only to amplify them, but, working as a 'superheterodyne' oscillator, to shift their frequency to one at which greater discrimination between signals, or 'selectivity', could be achieved (Tucker, 1978, pp.237–38; Aitken, 1985, chapter 4).

All these developments were spurred by military needs during the Great War, when the United States government promoted mass production of valves and wireless apparatus by assuming responsibility for patent infringements among manufacturers. In the aftermath a completely new situation obtained. For AT&T, anticipating in its chief engineer's words, 'a dominating influence in the art of wireless telephony' (in Noble, 1977, p.96), had purchased the rights to De Forest's patent. The triode was hostage to the company's ambition to extend its network. Other electrical giants, each with its own patents to protect, were still geared up to wartime production but helpless now to exploit the crucial device in the interests of point-to-point communication. GE, stymied in its bid to sell alternators to Marconi, bought out the company's American branch and formed the Radio Corporation of America (RCA) to take over its assets. RCA and GE negotiated a cross-licensing deal with AT&T, which the electrical manufacturer, Westinghouse, was subsequently invited to join. By 1921 each party to the agreement had 'got what it desired and what it thought it deserved' (Reich, 1977, p.218).

Figure 7.20
Lee De Forest audion valve in 1907. (Photo: Science Museum, London)

The triode had been freed. GE, RCA and Westinghouse could exploit it in the field of wireless communication. In this they were protected from their only apparent rival, AT&T, which in turn gained the security to use the triode in pursuing a monopoly over wire telephony.

But just as the industry was getting down to business as usual, the wireless group of companies made a discovery. No one, from Marconi to the mandarins at AT&T, had foreseen it. Everybody wanted to listen in. In November 1920 Westinghouse began regular broadcasting in Pittsburgh to stimulate sales of receivers. The result was a surge of orders – and requests to buy transmitters as well. Only AT&T, however, could *sell* transmitters as part of communication systems by the terms of the cross-licensing agreement. And only the wireless group of companies, which were free to build and operate their own transmitters, had the right to engage in the much more lucrative business of manufacturing and selling general coverage broadcast receivers to the public. Therefore AT&T decided to flex its monopoly muscles and get a share of the listening market. First the company sought to dominate demand by putting up the price of its transmitters and prohibiting the other companies from using its telephone lines for outside broadcasts – a formidable threat. Then in mid-1922 it undertook to do what it forbad in purchasers of AT&T transmitters: to sell air-time on the equipment. America's first radio commercial was broadcast in August that year from an AT&T station in New York City. Finally, in 1924, faced with mounting opposition to its policies, AT&T decided to crack the receiver market directly by selling fixed frequency sets of superior design, tuned to AT&T broadcast stations. One found its way into the White House, a deed that caused consternation at RCA (Reich, 1977, p.225).

None of these ploys quite worked, but they forced GE, RCA and Westinghouse to seek arbitration. At first it seemed that AT&T had good grounds for its behaviour. The company's patents gave it a secure foothold in the radio business. But in 1925 a pre-war lawsuit over the improved, 'high-vacuum valve' was finally settled in favour of RCA. The implications were that AT&T could no longer produce fixed frequency receivers entirely under its own patents, nor could it even sell broadcast transmitters. The high-vacuum valve was essential to them all. In 1926, therefore, AT&T and the wireless group of companies came to terms. The industry was carved up again. AT&T agreed to stay out of broadcast radio and obtained increased monopoly powers as a consolation prize, including control of two-way ship-to-shore and transoceanic radiotelephony. RCA and the other companies got what they wanted all along: domination of the radio receiver market and the right to use telephone lines as an adjunct to broadcasting for hire. The commercialization of American radio was now in principle complete (Reich, 1977, 1985).

7.4.3
The control of
broadcasting

Radio was the first method of instantaneous mass communication. It began with experimenters and engineers who wanted to extend the scope of conventional telegraphy and telephony as a means of point-to-point and person-to-person interchange. It enlisted the skills and enthusiasm of countless 'amateurs' who freely built and operated their own apparatus before the First World War and afterwards 'provided the original seed capital and audience' for the broadcasting manufacturers (Czitrom, 1982, p.73). Finally, through a complex series of licensing schemes and regulatory agreements during the 1920s and 1930s, radio became the domain of large-scale commercial and political organizations. Newspapers and cinematography were also progressively industrialized over the same period but the control of radio of necessity acquired a political dimension beyond the obvious need for censorship. Print and film were elastic media, limited only by the availability of woodpulp or celluloid. Radio, operating in a universal medium, was nevertheless constrained by its inherent physical property, the finite number of frequencies at which electromagnetic signals could be transmitted and received without interfering with each other. The frequency spectrum for practicable radio communication was greatly enlarged by 1950, while 'beam' transmitting aerials and enhanced selectivity in receivers made its use more efficient. But to allot space equitably and to protect a whole range of essential communications services that had become dependent on radio, national and international regulation was needed. Governments inevitably got involved.

In the United States the organization and finance of radio broadcasting was based from the outset on private enterprise. The Federal government merely licensed individual stations, assigned their frequencies of operation, and policed the radio frequency spectrum. A station could be purchased by almost anyone with the money, which in effect made its channel private property. Manufacturers, newspapers, department stores, and even churches went on the air – 600 stations by 1930, 900 by 1945 (Schramm, 1960, p.196). Most of the more powerful stations were linked up by AT&T's long-distance lines on a subscriber basis into a few vast corporate 'networks' that covered the country. The government promoted and protected this network oligopoly as a means of bringing order and stability to radio (Rosen, 1980). RCA established the National Broadcasting Company (NBC) in 1926, which incorporated its own 'Blue' network and a 'Red' network, consisting of stations acquired from AT&T. A year later a prominent phonograph firm backed the Columbia Phonograph Broadcasting System, later known as CBS. In 1934 a group of privately owned stations combined to form the Mutual Broadcasting System, and in 1943 the millionaire candy man Edward J. Noble, maker of 'Lifesavers', bought NBC's Blue network and turned it into the American Broadcasting Company (ABC). Each of the major networks, and numerous regional groupings besides, derived their income partly from subscribers' fees but mainly from the sale of air-time for advertising and the commercial sponsorship of programmes (Barnouw, 1966–68). This was a bonanza for business and represented 'a substantial victory for the ideology of consumption in American life'. Radio could penetrate the nation's homes like a prowler – 'through doors and windows, no matter how tightly barred', crowed NBC's director of development. It brought the message of happiness and fulfilment through the purchase to each family in their vulnerable moments of relaxation (in Czitrom, 1982, pp.76, 77; Marchand, 1985, chapter 4).

But the American government's weak administrative regulation of the triple alliance of broadcasters, networks and advertisers was far from typical of radio broadcasting worldwide. Most countries developed very different systems of control by 1950. In Europe the only private commercial station to survive from an early period until after the Second World War was Radio Luxembourg, which went on the air in 1931. State-operated broadcasting became the norm in Russia and latterly across Eastern Europe. Private corporations in which the state held a controlling interest undertook broadcasting in Italy, Sweden and Switzerland. Public corporations or authorities, independent of the state, but over which the state exercised final control, were appointed in Germany, the Netherlands and the United Kingdom. In France and Belgium mixed systems of commercial and state or public broadcasting existed until the Second World War, when public corporations took over. Almost every country in Europe elected to subsidize broadcasting with a licence fee for each household or receiver. A few systems derived their income from commercial advertising, although this took the form of paid announcements rather than wholesale programme sponsorship as practised in the United States (Paulu, 1967, chapters 3–4).

British broadcasting, perhaps most of all, prided itself on freedom from crass commercialism. This is reflected in the apt titles of the British and

American national histories of broadcasting from the 1930s, Erik Barnouw's *The Golden Web*, referring to the lucrative network business in the United States, and Asa Briggs's *The Golden Age of Wireless*, evoking the classical bias within Britain's paternalistic service (Elliott and Matthews, 1987). The bias was epitomized in the person of John Reith, the paterfamilias and first director-general of the BBC. Set up in 1922 amid characteristic dithering by the Post Office, which granted its licence, the British Broadcasting Company was owned by the big radio manufacturers, led by Marconi, and operated on their behalf in the 'public interest' to avoid the competitive chaos into which American broadcasting was seen to have fallen. Reith, still in his thirties, shepherded the Company through its early difficulties and presided over its divorce from commercial backing and reorganization in 1926 under independent governors as a public corporation (Briggs, 1985, chapters 1–2). At no time was the American experience far from his mind. In 1931, when he travelled to the United States on behalf of the BBC, Reith heard for himself what his broadcasting monopoly had averted.

A programme about valvolene. The announcer read a dozen lines of puff, turned on an outsize record of a jazz band; in the middle of it the conductor of the band gave his opinion of valvolene. After the record the announcer had another dozen lines to say about valvolene; listeners were urged to note the same time next week for another jolly twenty valvolene minutes. The sporting editor of the newspaper [which owned the station] was then to have interviewed some athletes attending a convention . . . He failed to appear but four husky individuals carried on without him; interviewed each other; played the fool generally; quite enjoyed themselves. (Reith, 1949, p.150)

In vain Reith remonstrated with the Americans about the mediocrity of their competitive commercial system. Talk of right-minded men, impelled by the 'ideal of public service', who would be the guardians of radio who 'guarded themselves' and made democracy 'safe for the world', was listened to but politely. Americans disliked public monopoly and cherished individualism. 'Any considerable central control' of radio was to them anathema. President Hoover told him so at the White House (Reith, 1949, pp.144–48). For his part, the President might equally have remonstrated with Reith about radio's authoritarian role in Britain (Figure 7.21).

Figure 7.21 Cartoon by David Low during the General Strike of 1926. John (later Lord) Reith wrote in his diary on 11 May: '. . . we are not going to be commandeered. The cabinet decision is really a negative one. They want to be able to say that they did not commandeer us, but they know that they can trust us not to be really impartial' (Stuart, 1975, p.96). (Reproduced by permission of the David Low Estate/Solo Syndication)

7.4.4
Radio and other media in everyday life

The power of mass communications to inculcate commercial and civic values has been a central theme of this essay. Radio, like print and film, acquired this power chiefly through the concentration of property rights and productive capacity in a relatively small number of large communications firms. These firms shared with other enterprises an interest in controlling consumption; they shared with their governments a concern to influence and regulate political behaviour. Their patronage and growth may thus be attributed primarily to their message-making function. But in many cases the power of the communications combines also derived from their role in the manufacture and distribution of radio apparatus. For whoever supplied the apparatus had a large say in who communicated with whom, and how. The early relations of the Marconi Company with the Royal Navy and the BBC illustrate this to some extent. The emergence of NBC from RCA, and RCA from GE, is a better example. It suggests how the ethos of American broadcasting may be traced back through the GE laboratories to the individualism and commercialism of Edison. The mass media were never merely neutral channels of communication, and Edison would probably have been the first to agree (Beniger, 1986, chapter 8; Garnham, 1986).

But while the *industrialization* of radio and, as we have seen, its *consumerization* in the United States allied it with print and film as promoters of mass conformity, its impact on everyday life differed in certain respects. In the first place, newspapers, periodicals and motion pictures were difficult and expensive to produce and almost impossible to distribute widely without the resources of a large organization. Radio signals, on the other hand, could be generated easily and cheaply; distribution took place instantaneously through a medium that nobody owned. The popular potential of radio was obvious. Hundreds of amateurs got on the air for next to nothing in the early days and exchanged as many messages as they liked free-of-charge. After the First World War, when manufactured components became readily available and prices began to fall, a radio craze swept Europe and North America. Transmitting was now for the most part closely regulated, but anyone with a little money and a little know-how gleaned from one of the local radio clubs or the hobbyist magazines that blossomed everywhere, could wire up a valve or two and listen to the broadcasters. Indeed, such was the interest in home construction in Britain that the collective demand for royalties from the 'Big Six' manufacturers (Figure 7.22), including Marconi, Metropolitan Vickers, and GEC, came to naught, and the Post Office was forced in 1924 to abandon the royalty system on manufactured equipment and issue Constructors' Licences (Pegg, 1983, pp.41–43).

Thus it would appear that the early decades of radio saw a partial *democratization* of mass communication, accompanied and eventually succeeded by a partial *demystification* of its technology. Neither of these effects was then notable in the printing and cinematography fields. Until governments and international conventions intervened to parcel out the electromagnetic spectrum, ordinary people could communicate via wireless with impunity. In doing so they built their own equipment and operated it under conditions that would have dispelled any lingering mythos about the efficacy of electrical communication. During the 1920s, when only broadcasters and bona fide experimenters were allowed on the air, people got their fingers dirty in radio cabinets as never before or since. The sets went out of order as fast as they went out of date, and this called for do-it-yourself repairs. These intrepid tinkerers, and thousands more who came home clutching a box of components and a precious triode valve to brave constructing their own receivers, were rapidly disabused of the notion, still put about by engineers to popular audiences, that the radio was a 'magic box', full of the 'wizardry of science' (Ewing, 1932, p.349). Even the religious admirers of wireless technology had to acknowledge its inherent limitations (Figure 7.23).

Figure 7.22
Stamp used by the British Broadcasting Company, 1922–24, indicating that the royalty on a set bearing the stamp had been paid to the company. Listeners were obliged to obtain a licence as well. (Reproduced by courtesy of the BBC)

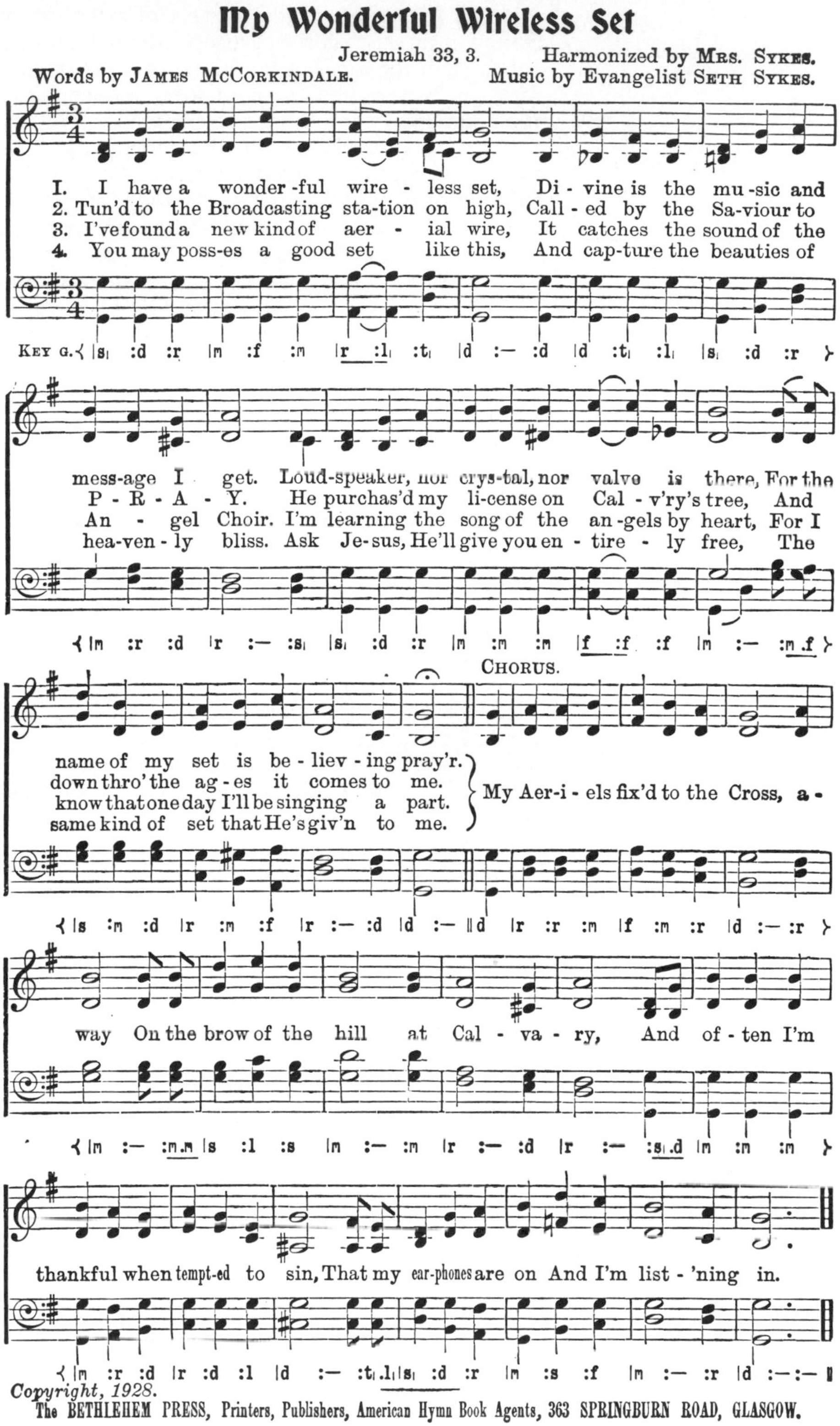
My Wonderful Wireless Set
Jeremiah 33, 3.
Harmonized by MRS. SYKES.
Words by JAMES McCORKINDALE.
Music by Evangelist SETH SYKES.
1. I have a wonder-ful wire - less set, Di-vine is the mu-sic and mess-age I get. Loud-speaker, nor crys-tal, nor valve is there, For the name of my set is be-liev-ing pray'r.
2. Tun'd to the Broadcasting sta-tion on high, Call-ed by the Sa-viour to P-R-A-Y. He purchas'd my li-cense on Cal-v'ry's tree, And down thro' the ag-es it comes to me.
3. I've found a new kind of aer-ial wire, It catches the sound of the An-gel Choir. I'm learning the song of the an-gels by heart, For I know that one day I'll be singing a part.
4. You may poss-es a good set like this, And cap-ture the beauties of hea-ven-ly bliss. Ask Je-sus, He'll give you en-tire-ly free, The same kind of set that He's giv'n to me.
KEY G.
CHORUS.
My Aer-i-els fix'd to the Cross, a-way On the brow of the hill at Cal-va-ry, And of-ten I'm thankful when tempt-ed to sin, That my ear-phones are on And I'm list-'ning in.
Copyright, 1928.
The BETHLEHEM PRESS, Printers, Publishers, American Hymn Book Agents, 363 SPRINGBURN ROAD, GLASGOW.

Figure 7.23
Wireless without wires: evangelical religion à la *radio.* (*From* Living Gospel Songs and Choruses by Mr and Mrs Seth Sykes, *1944, The Bethlehem Press*)

In the second place, the impact of radio on everyday life differed from that of print and film because, although the medium was pervasive and unbounded, the locus of public exposure to its messages was generally more confined. Newspapers, sold on street corners and in shops, could be carried about and read anywhere. The cinema required its audiences to assemble in public rooms. Radios could, theoretically, be installed wherever one liked and be overheard by whoever was in the vicinity, but in practice the great majority of people listened *en famille* in the comfort of their homes. There were practical reasons for this. The earliest broadcast receivers needed space for batteries, a permanent aerial, and assorted cables. They were anything but 'wireless'. When loudspeakers became generally available in the mid-1920s they sat alongside the set and trailed their connecting lead. The sound quality was thin at best, requiring constant hushed attention. By the time integral aerials and improved loudspeakers had appeared, and a 'B-eliminator', or power supply, could be purchased to run sets off mains electricity, the listening pattern was established. The *domestication* of mass communication had been achieved. In 1924 one in every ten households in Britain was licensed for wireless reception. By 1930 the figure had trebled, and in 1934 fully half the population had a loudspeaker at their fingertips. In Germany and the United States a similar boom took place. Germany saw the total number of receiving licences more than treble on average every year from 1924 to 1930. The United States in 1930 had a radio installed in 40 per cent of households. Ten years later there was a radio on average in almost every one (Schramm, 1960, p.196; Landes, 1969, p.427; Pegg, 1983, pp.7–8).

The telephone, it might be thought, would have affected everyday life in a manner similar to radio, tending to make the home a self-sufficient locus of communication. But the opposite seems to have occurred. By supplanting correspondence as the ordinary means of communication at-a-distance, the telephone promoted both more frequent and more personal exchanges of messages. Children, the illiterate, and the disabled could also keep in touch. Furthermore, by putting people directly and immediately in contact, the telephone helped break through the isolation of the rural family; it assisted the formation of 'psychological neighbourhoods' in anonymous urban areas; and, like the cinema, it added a new dimension to courtship (Aronson, 1971). The wider communication facilitated by the telephone was, of course, mostly casual and perfunctory. It did not entertain; it performed a service. Most telephone companies accordingly did not anticipate that their instruments could confer status and identity, becoming objects of desire. AT&T, for example, offered home extensions in 1929 but did not advertise coloured telephones until the late-1950s. Here the contrast with radio was especially telling. The very design of the electrical appliances indicated their domestic roles. After 1925 broadcast receivers rapidly evolved into imposing parlour pieces, built to please the entire family. Self-contained sets with generous loudspeakers mounted in acoustically shaped wooden cabinets made for easy listening from armchair and settee. Large illuminated push-button dials replaced the crude and complex controls of just a few years before, turning consumer choice into child's play. The radio, unlike the telephone, became the pride and chattel of every well-equipped household (Czitrom, 1982, pp.78–79; Marchand, 1985, pp.88–94, 105–10, 117–20; Sparke, 1986, pp.27–28).

As a source of domestic entertainment and information radio affected everyday life in ways already familiar from the study of print and film. For example, people began to use their leisure hours differently. During the American radio boom, between 1927 and 1932, annual sales of phonograph records fell from 104 million to just 6 million, an effect also partly attributable to the talkies. In Britain, as Taylor recalled a little later, it had been nine years since he had 'heard a private person sit down at a piano and sing' (Gammond, 1980, p.28; Taylor, 1952, p.230; Frith, 1987). Like the cinema, radio detracted from participatory recreation and fostered passive amusement.

People also received more news of the world, or at least received it more frequently. The fact that broadcasters depended on the press and its main news source, the wire services, for information did not, however, encourage diversity of reporting, whatever audiences may have believed. By the eve of the Second World War, according to a reputable survey, '70 per cent of Americans relied on the radio as their prime source of news and 58 per cent thought it more accurate than that supplied by the press'. This was at a time when around one-third of all radio stations in the United States were owned by newspapers (Czitrom, 1982, p.86; Beniger, 1986, p.369). Thus people became subject as never before, in the security of their own homes, to mass produced versions of reality.

'Ideological broadcasting' was pioneered between 1929 and 1935 by the Soviet Union, followed by Germany and Italy, with Vatican Radio and an American missionary station in Ecuador adding their voices to the war of words (Browne, 1982, chapter 2). 'No more rapid perversion of an invention has hitherto been recorded in human history', declared those of the contrary part, dismissing the broadcasts as 'propaganda' (Casson, 1937, p.265). But whether one considers Reith's aims for the BBC, or Trotsky's hopes for radio in the Soviet Union, or the rhetoric of broadcasting magnates in America, the message was much the same: radio performed an ideological task and propaganda was its weapon. Reith congratulated himself with the thought, 'If there had been broadcasting at the time of the French Revolution there might have been no French Revolution'. Trotsky believed radio was an essential tool of 'economic and cultural communication', building socialism through 'the transformation of the country into a single whole'. The Americans contrasted the 'European system' of broadcasting unfavourably with their own, arguing that only the latter 'produced national unity, prevented disintegration of the populace into classes, and cemented the country by common sources of entertainment, economic interests, ideals, problems, and dangers' (Reith, 1949, p.109; Trotsky, 1927, p.260; Rosen, 1980, pp.180–81).

But although radio in the home perpetuated or intensified certain trends already discernible in the effects of mass communication on patterns of leisure and news exposure, its overall impact differed significantly from that of print and film in one last respect. Newspapers habituated readers to a daily assemblage of events; the cinema tore time apart and reassembled events for emotional effect on the viewers. In both cases, in reading and in viewing, the experience of temporality was limited and discrete. One read the morning paper; one went to the pictures on Saturday afternoon. Radio brought a different experience: the *regimentation of time*. It did this by simultaneously filling time up and organizing it.

Broadcasting ran to a strict schedule, particularly on American networks, where time was money. And by 1950, with the advent of FM (or VHF) broadcasting, a multitude of stations could stay on the air for twenty-four hours. Listeners had their choice of scores of programmes throughout the day, punctuated by news bulletins and trails for future programmes. Many scheduled their lives around these events in the same way that they waited for trains. Others let the programmes run continuously, the sounds following them from room to room, whatever their activities, and at night in bed when they were too tired for anything else. Radio engineers helped ensure there was no escape by developing broadcast receivers that could be operated outside the home. By 1951, when almost every household in America had at least one receiver, half the automobiles did as well. Three years later, when the mass marketing of transistor radios began, no niche was left in daily routine that broadcasting could not fill (Carey, 1981, pp.88–89; Beniger, 1986, pp.368–69).

The telephone's ubiquitous ringing as an accompaniment to daily life has been likened to 'the ever present tolling of church bells in a Medieval village or *bourg*' (Aronson, 1971, p.273). Since, however, the bells rang at regular intervals whereas the telephone issues its peremptory summonses without warning, the comparison could be more apt. Perhaps it might have found a modern semblance in the familiar tones and time signals by which radio marked the days and seasons for half of humankind in the mid-twentieth century. For here civic ritual made its closest approximation to bygone religiosity. If the daily newspaper stood in place of morning mass; if the Saturday matinee offered congregations a secular sabbath; then the radio broadcast saw the nation united each day in its homes, families gathered about the electronic altar, thinking one thought, hoping one hope, paying devotion to the Queen, the Lone Ranger, or Colgate toothpaste (Chaney, 1986). Like true religion, moreover, radio held special meaning for the less well-off, whose principal diversion it became. For them 'listening to certain programmes assumed almost a ritual character' (Landes, 1969, p.428). Only television, by combining sound and moving image, the immediacy of radio with the mass appeal of illustrated periodicals and the cinema, would have greater liturgical power. Only a world war could resist it (Briggs, 1969, p.46).

'When to the spoken word is added the living image, the effect is to magnify the potential dangers of a machine which can subtly instil ideas, strong beliefs, profound disgusts, and affections'. So wrote an American government spokesman in 1937, peering into what he believed would be the immediate future. 'Technology', he added, 'has provided the power to enrich the leisure hours, to promote family solidarity by bringing the theatre into the home, to develop national uniformity and unity at the cost of provincialism, and to widen man's knowledge of the world in which he lives.' All these the spokesman imagined to be unmitigated blessings. But one question remained, 'a fundamental question of national policy': 'What ideas, whose ideas, shall be mass-communicated? Who shall control television? . . . Whatever body wields such power might conceivably be able in time to undermine all opposition to its power' (Gilfillan, 1937, pp.32–33). The answer was close at hand. It had been practically decided. People made their own communication methods but they did not make them under circumstances of their choosing. If the history of communications has anything to say it is this. In the press room, at the cinema, on the air – it had always been a question of power. And in the electronic age, power, though widely dispersed, was distributed very unequally. Television, like radio, the cinema, and mass circulation periodicals, would therefore become dominated by Paul Simon's 'loose affiliation of millionaires and billionaires'. Fifty years later the miracle and wonder is that they still have not managed to 'undermine all opposition'.

REFERENCES   Items recommended for further reading are preceded by an asterisk.

EB, followed by volume and page numbers, refers to *The Encyclopaedia Britannica*, 11th edition, volumes 1–29; 12th edition, volumes 30–32 (1910–22) Encyclopaedia Britannica Co.

Abney, W. de W., Waterhouse, J. and Hinton, A.H. (1911) 'Photography' in *EB*, 21, pp.485–523.

Agee, W.K., Ault, P.H. and Emery, E. (1976) *Mass Communications*, 5th edition, Harper & Row.

*Aitken, H.G.J. (1985) *The Continuous Wave: Technology and American Radio, 1900–1932*, Princeton University Press.

Aldgate, T. (1987) 'The newsreels, public order, and the projection of Britain' in Curran *et al.* (1987) op.cit.

Andersch, E.G., Staats, L.C. and Bostrom, R.N. (1969) *Communication in Everyday Use*, 3rd edition, Rinehart.

Anon (1948) *How and Why It Works: How Everyday Things Work in the Home, Office, Industry, and Transport*, Odhams.

Aronson, S.H. (1971) 'The sociology of the telephone' in Gumpert, G. and Cathcart, R. (eds.) (1982) *Inter/Media: Interpersonal Communication in a Media World*, 2nd edition, Oxford University Press, pp.272–83.

Bale, E. (1911) 'Process' in *EB*, 22, pp.408–14.

Barnouw, E. (1966–68) *A History of Broadcasting in the United States*: vol.1 *A Tower in Babel*; vol.2 *The Golden Web*, Oxford University Press.

*Beniger, J.R. (1986) *The Control Revolution: Technological and Economic Origins of the Information Society*, Harvard University Press.

Bennett, T. (1982) 'Media, "reality", signification' in Gurevitch *et al.*, op.cit., pp.287–308.

Biddiss, M.D. (1977) *The Age of the Masses: Ideas and Society in Europe since 1870*, Penguin.

Boyce, D.G. (1987) 'Crusaders without chains: power and the press barons, 1896–1951' in Curran *et al.*, op.cit., pp.97–112.

Boyce, G., Curran, J. and Wingate, P. (eds.) (1978) *Newspaper History from the Seventeenth Century to the Present Day*, Constable.

Bretz, R. (1971) *A Taxonomy of Communication Media*, Educational Technology Publications.

Briggs, A. (1961–65) *The History of Broadcasting in the United Kingdom*: vol.1 *The Birth of Broadcasting*; vol.2 *The Golden Age of Wireless*, Oxford University Press.

Briggs, A. (1969) 'Prediction and control: historical perspectives', *Sociological Review Monograph*, no.13, pp.39–52.

*Briggs, A. (1985) *The BBC: The First Fifty Years*, Oxford University Press.

Brown, J.W. (1928) 'Journalism and publishing' in Wile, op.cit., pp.198–228.

Browne, D.R. (1982) *International Broadcasting: The Limits of the Limitless Medium*, Praeger.

Carey, J.W. (1969) 'The communications revolution and the professional communicator', *Sociological Review Monograph*, no.13, pp.22–38.

Carey, J.W. (1974) 'The problem of journalism history', *Journalism History*, 1, pp.3–5, 27.

Carey, J.W. (1975) 'A cultural approach to communication', *Communication*, 2, pp.1–22.

Carey, J.W. (1981) 'Culture, geography, and communications: the work of Harold Innis in an American context' in Melody, W.H., Salter, L. and Heyer, P. (eds.) (1981) *Culture, Communication, and Dependency: The Tradition of H.A. Innis*, Ablex, pp.73–91.

Carey, J.W. (1983) 'The origins of radical discourse on cultural studies in the United States', *Journal of Communication*, 33, pp.311–13.

Carey, J.W. and Quirk, J.J. (1970) 'The mythos of the electronic revolution' *American Scholar*, 39, pp.219–41, 395–424.

Casson, S. (1937) *Progress and Catastrophe: An Anatomy of Human Adventure*, Hamish Hamilton.

*Chanan, M. (1980) *The Dream That Kicks: The Prehistory and Early Years of Cinema in Britain*, Routledge & Kegan Paul.

Chandler, A.D., Jr. (1977) *The Visible Hand: The Managerial Revolution in American Business*, Harvard University Press.

Chaney, D. (1986) 'A symbolic mirror of ourselves: civic ritual in mass society' in Collins *et al.*, op.cit., pp.247–63.

*Cockburn, C. (1981) 'The material of male power' in Mackenzie, D. and Wajcman, J. (eds.) (1985) *The Social Shaping of Technology: How the Refrigerator Got Its Hum*, Open University Press, pp.125–46.

Cockburn, C. (1983) *Brothers: Male Dominance and Technological Change*, Pluto.

Collins, R., Curran, J., Garnham, N., Scannell, P., Schlesinger, P. and Sparks, C. (eds.) (1986) *Media, Culture and Society: A Critical Reader*, Sage.

Craven, T.A.M., *et al.* (1937) 'Communication' in National Resources Committee, op.cit., pp.210–33.

Crowther, J.G. (1937) 'Thomas Alva Edison, 1847–1931' in *Famous American Men of Science*, vol.2, reprinted Penguin, 1944, pp.7–94.

Croy, H. (1922) 'Cinematograph or motion pictures' in *EB*, 30, pp.694–700.

Curran, J. (1978) 'The press as an agent of social control: an historical perspective' in Boyce *et al.*, op.cit., pp.51–75.

Curran, J. (1986) 'The impact of advertising on the British mass media' in Collins *et al.*, op.cit., pp.309–35.

Curran, J., Smith, A. and Wingate, P. (eds.) (1987) *Impacts and Influences: Essays on Media Power in the Twentieth Century*, Methuen.

*Czitrom, D.J. (1982) *Media and the American Mind: From Morse to McLuhan*, University of North Carolina Press.

Daly, K. (1980) ' "Your Marvellous Invention": the early history of recording' in Gammond and Horricks, op.cit., pp.1–23.

Dance, F.E.X. (ed.) (1967) *Human Communication Theory: Original Essays*, Holt, Rinehart and Winston.

Davison, W.P., Boylan, J. and Yu, F.T.C. (1976) *Mass Media: Systems and Effects*, Praeger.

Dechert, C.R. (1967) 'The development of cybernetics' in Dechert, C.R. (ed.) (1967) *The Social Impact of Cybernetics*, Simon & Schuster, pp.11–37.

Desmond, R.W. (1978) *The Information Process: World News Reporting to the Twentieth Century*, University of Iowa Press.

Eilert, E.F. (1928) 'A century of progress in the printing industry' in Wile, op.cit., pp.178–97.

Elliott, P. and Matthews, G. (1987) 'Broadcasting culture: innovation, accommodation, and routinization in the early BBC' in Curran *et al.*, op.cit., pp.235–58.

*Ewen, S. (1976) *Captains of Consciousness: Advertising and the Social Roots of the Consumer Culture*, McGraw-Hill.

Ewing, A. (1932) 'An engineer's outlook', *Nature*, 130, pp.341–50.

Fishenden, R.B. (1910) 'Some experiments towards rotary intaglio printing' in Moran, op.cit., pp.100–03.

Frith, S. (1987) 'The making of the British record industry, 1920–64' in Curran *et al.*, op.cit., pp.278–90.

[Gamble, W.] (1901) 'A wonderful process' in Moran, op.cit., pp.85–96.

Gammond, P. (1980) 'Coming of age: recording in the LP era' in Gammond and Horricks, op.cit., pp.24–47.

Gammond, P. and Horricks, R. (eds.) (1980) *The Music Goes Round and Round: A Cool Look at the Record Industry*, Quartet.

Garcke, E. (1911) 'Telephone' in *EB*, 26, pp.547–57.

Gardner, C. (ed.) (1979) *Media, Politics, and Culture: A Socialist View*, Macmillan.

Garnet, R.W. (1985) *The Telephone Enterprise: The Evolution of the Bell System's Horizontal Structure, 1876–1909*, Johns Hopkins University Press.

Garnham, N. (1986) 'Contribution to a political economy of mass-communication' in Collins *et al.*, op.cit., pp.29–32.

Gerbner, G. (1967) 'Mass media and human communication theory' in Dance, op.cit., pp.40–60.

Gernsheim, H. (1978) 'Photography' in Williams, T.I, op.cit., pp.1281–301.

Giegengack, A.E. (1937) 'Communication by printing and photography' in National Resources Committee, op. cit., pp.234–47.

Gilfillan, S.C. (1937) 'Social effects of inventions' in National Resources Committee, op.cit., pp.24–38.

Guback, T.H. (1969) *The International Film Industry: Western Europe and America since 1945*, Indiana University Press.

Gurevitch, M., Bennett, T., Curran, J. and Woollacott, J. (eds.) (1982) *Culture, Society, and the Media*, Methuen.

Hall, C. [1936] *Everyday Science*, new edition, Blackie.

Hawks, E. [1939] *How it Works and How It's Done*, Odhams.

Hays, W.H. (1928) 'Motion pictures' in Wile, op.cit., pp.504–33.

Headrick, D.R. (1981) *The Tools of Empire: Technology and European Imperialism in the Nineteenth Century*, Oxford University Press.

Jacobi, C.T. (1911) 'Printing' in *EB*, 22, pp.350–59.

*Jenkins, R.V. (1975) *Images and Enterprise: Technology and the American Photographic Industry, 1839 to 1925*, Johns Hopkins University Press.

Jenkins, R.V. (1987) 'Words, images, artifacts and sound: documents for the history of technology', *British Journal for the History of Science*, 20, pp.39–56.

Jewett, F.B. (1928) 'Telegraphy and telephony' in Wile, op.cit., pp.445–63.

Jones, S.G. (1986) *Workers at Play: A Social and Economic History of Leisure, 1918–1939*, Routledge & Kegan Paul.

Landes, D.S. (1969) *The Unbound Prometheus: Technological Change and Industrial Development in Western Europe from 1750 to the Present*, Cambridge University Press.

Lee, A. (1978) 'The structure, ownership and control of the press, 1855–1914' in Boyce *et al.*, op.cit.

McLeod, J.M. (1967) 'The contribution of psychology to human communication theory' in Dance, op.cit., pp.203–35.

Marchand, R. (1985) *Advertising the American Dream: Making Way for Modernity, 1920–1940*, University of California Press.

Marland, E.A. (1964) *Early Electrical Communication*, Abelard-Schuman.

Melville, L. and Brande, H. (1922) 'Newspapers' in *EB*, 31, pp.1105–14.

Moran, J. (ed.) (1974) *Printing in the Twentieth Century*, Northwood.

Moran, J. (1978) 'Printing' in Williams, T.I., op.cit., pp.1268–80.

Murdock, G. and Golding, P. (1978) 'The structure, ownership and control of the press, 1914–76' in Boyce *et al.*, op.cit.

National Resources Committee (Subcommittee on Technology) (1937) *Technological Trends and National Policy, Including the Social Implications of New Inventions*, Government Printing Office.

'Newspapers' (1911) *EB*, 19, pp.544–81.

*Noble, D.F. (1977) *America by Design: Science, Technology, and the Rise of Corporate Capitalism*, new edition, 1979, Oxford University Press.

Open University, The (1982) U203 *Popular Culture*, Block 6 Unit 25 *The image and mass reproduction*, The Open University Press.

Paulu, B. (1967) *Radio and Television Broadcasting on the European Continent*, University of Minnesota Press.

Pegg, M. (1983) *Broadcasting and Society, 1918–1939*, Croom Helm.

'Phonograph' (1911) *EB*, 21, pp.467–71.

Pocock, R.F. (1988) *The Early British Radio Industry*, Manchester University Press.

Priestley, J.B. (1934) *English Journey*, Heinemann.

Ramsaye, T. (1947) 'The rise and place of the motion picture' in Schramm, op.cit., pp.24–38.

Reich, L.S. (1977) 'Research, patents, and the struggle to control radio: a study of big business and the uses of industrial research', *Business History Review*, 51, pp.208–35.

Reich, L.S. (1985) *The Making of American Industrial Research: Science and Business at GE and Bell, 1876–1926*, Cambridge University Press.

Reith, J.C.W. (1949) *Into the Wind*, Hodder and Stoughton.

Rosen, P.T. (1980) *The modern stentors: radio broadcasters and the federal government, 1920–1934*, Greenwood Press.

Schlesinger, P. (1978) *Putting 'Reality' Together: BBC News*, Constable.

Schramm, W. (ed.) (1960) *Mass Communications: A Book of Readings*, new edition, University of Illinois Press.

Sharp, D. (1969) *The Picture Palace and Other Buildings for the Movies*, Hugh Evelyn.

*Smith, A. (1979) *The Newspaper: An International History*, Thames and Hudson.

Smith, G.D. (1985) *The Anatomy of a Business Strategy: Bell, Western Electric, and the Origins of the American Telephone Industry*, Johns Hopkins University Press.

Smith, H.J. (1922) 'The day' in Schramm, op.cit., pp.141–53.

Sparke, P. (1986) *An Introduction to Design and Culture in the Twentieth Century*, Allen & Unwin.

Stern, B.J. (1937) 'Resistances to the adoption of technological innovation' in National Resources Committee, op. cit., pp.39–66.

Stuart, C. (ed.) (1975) *The Reith Diaries*, Collins.

Taylor, F.S. (1952) *The Century of Science*, 3rd edition, Heinemann.

'Telephone' (1922) in *EB*, 32, pp.706–14.

Thomas, D.B. and Ward, J.P. (1978) 'Cinematography' in Williams, T.I., op.cit., pp.1302–16.

Trotsky, L. (1927) 'Radio, science, technology, and society' in *Problems of Everyday Life and Other Writings on Culture and Science*, reprinted Monad, 1973, pp.250–63.

Tucker, D.G. (1978) 'Electrical communication' in Williams, T.I., op.cit., pp.1220–67.

Vergara, W.C. (1980) *Science in Everyday Life*, new edition 1982, Sphere.

Ward, J.W. (1958) 'The meaning of Lindbergh's flight', *American Quarterly*, 10, pp.3–16.

Wile, F.W. (ed.) (1928) *A Century of Industrial Progress*, Doubleday, Doran & Co.

*Williams, R. (1976) *Communications*, 3rd edition, Penguin.

Williams, R. (1978) 'The press and popular culture: an historical perspective' in Boyce *et al.*, op.cit., pp.41–50.

Williams, R. (1979) 'The growth and role of the mass media' in Gardner, op.cit., pp.14–24.

Williams, T.I. (ed.) (1978) *A History of Technology*, vol.7, *The Twentieth Century c. 1900 to c. 1950*, part 2, Clarendon Press.

8 FOOD

Gerrylynn K. Roberts

From farm to table, the production, processing, distribution and consumption of food are processes of economic and social life in which science and technology play a considerable part – to the extent that our current habits have been characterized as 'technological eating' on an international scale (Pyke, 1972). For not only is our food technologically produced, processed and distributed, but the social and economic circumstances under which that is achieved in order to fulfil our requirements for consumption are in turn affected.

Looking at the cases of Britain and the United States, a number of factors interacted to create a rising demand for a greater quantity and a greater variety of foodstuffs over the period 1870 to 1950. Chapter 1 pointed out that an important feature in both Britain and the United States during the nineteenth century was population growth accompanied by urbanization. Feeding the growing urban and industrial populations was a major task for agriculture. However, sheer numbers alone do not account for the pattern of development. In Britain, the consolidation of industrialization brought rising average real wages from 1850 and falling food prices, especially from 1875, with a consequent rising standard of living for many in the working classes from the 1880s onwards. While such a generalization obscures the brutal poverty and hardship (including undernourishment) persistently suffered by many sections of the population, none the less basic food prices did decline both absolutely and relative to average real incomes during the final quarter of the nineteenth century. Not only were the basics more cheaply available, but rising incomes were used by wage-earners to fund more varied diets. Although this trend was checked somewhat by sharply rising prices in the early years of the twentieth century, the overall pattern in Britain and America during our period was toward foodstuffs requiring an ever smaller proportion of family incomes (Johnston, 1977, chapter 1).

Our concern in this chapter is with the role of science and technology in this changing pattern of everyday life. We shall discuss briefly in turn developments in various aspects of the overall movement of food from farms to consumers' tables, looking also at scientific and technological change in relation to some particular foodstuffs. It was over the period 1870 to 1950 that the production, processing and distribution of food became industrialized for mass consumption. By 1870, agriculture was becoming mechanized and gradually more science-based in Britain, parts of Europe, and the United States, while some food processing, such as canning and meat packing, was already done on a factory level. Changes in transport and marketing practices during the following decades greatly affected the availability of food to consumers. At the turn of the twentieth century, however, much food was still processed if not in the home, then locally on a small scale. But by 1950, centralized mass production had become the norm. Although our discussion in this chapter will concentrate on developments in certain sections of the food industry, it should become clear especially when we touch on questions of consumption, that the food industry interacts with a much wider range of social, economic and political circumstances.

8.1
FOOD PRODUCTION:
AGRICULTURE

For Britain, despite the withdrawal of tariff protection from 1846, the period 1850–1875 was one of agricultural prosperity. This was the period of 'high farming'; investment was heavy and output was increased by bringing newly drained additional land under cultivation, by the application of artificial fertilizers, by the use of purchased feedstuffs, and by mechanization. However, so technically intensive a system was still vulnerable to the vagaries of the weather, and a series of disastrous grain harvests in the late 1870s started off the process by which free-trading Britain, long an importer of some foreign grain especially from Eastern Europe, became ever more dependent on grain imported now cheaply from America as well.

America's ability to export grain from the 1870s and meat from the 1880s rested on a number of developments. Over the last forty years of the nineteenth century, cultivated American acreage was increased by an amount more than ten times the land area of England and Wales. The expansion was accompanied by mechanization which made the handling of large areas at the pressure times of ploughing and harvesting feasible, despite scarce labour which was made even more expensive by the Civil War of the early 1860s. Furthermore, the extension of railways across the American continent made possible the cheap and rapid transport of bulk commodities to more distant markets. Rail links to the great shipping ports and rapid steam-powered, screw-propelled journeys in larger, steel-hulled ships completed the chain cheaply. Between 1870 and 1900, the cost of transporting grain from Chicago to Liverpool dropped by two-thirds (Chambers and Mingay, 1966, chapter 7).

Once refrigerated transport was feasible from the 1880s, meat as well as grain could be exported cheaply. Refrigerated and frozen meat imports from South America, Australia and New Zealand as well as the United States also displaced British production. Because of a marked increase in the demand for meat, this was not so disastrous as the drop in the grain price. However, unable to recover its competitive position in grain and bulk meat, Britain and other European countries entered a period of agricultural depression, when such farming profits as there were came not from grain, but from a shift into dairying, market gardening, and premium beef and mutton (Chambers and Mingay, 1966, p.181). Denmark and Holland were, for example, important high-value meat and dairy produce exporters. Some continental countries took steps to increase production of diversified goods for home consumption behind tariff barriers. But by 1900, when American exports reached a peak, the grain growing acreage of still free-trading Britain had contracted by almost 30 per cent.

8.1.1 Mechanization

Although this brief discussion has tied the changing fortunes of British and American agriculture to broad economic and other changes, technological and scientific changes within farming practice itself were also important. We have already mentioned mechanization in passing. Many agricultural machines had been developed and introduced gradually before the start of our period. By the 1870s, steam-powered threshing was all but universal in both countries, while mechanical drills and horse hoes had become the norm. By then, roughly three-quarters of American cereals and up to two-thirds of British ones were cut by horse-drawn mechanical harvesters. The features of these were improved continually during the final decades of the nineteenth century. Continental agriculturists too began to adopt them, though both Germany and France had a large unmechanized agricultural sector until well into the twentieth century.

On the large fields of America, the early years of the twentieth century saw the combine harvester come into widespread use. These huge machines 'combined' into one operation the cutting, threshing and dressing of the grain which had previously been done as separate stages by the horse-drawn reaper and steam thresher. At the same time, the combines eliminated a number of intermediate processes which had previously required a great deal of manhandling. In Europe, the combine was most readily adopted for the huge fields on the large collective farms of inter-war Soviet Russia, with, of course, state finance. The combine harvester was adopted rather later in Britain (there were only 100 in 1939) because of its high capital cost in a country with decreasing corn acreage and depressed agriculture, and because of mechanical problems of adjusting its proportions to smaller British fields. After the Second World War, with a return to agricultural prosperity and revival of cereal growing, combines were adopted more readily there and effort was put into solving the technical problems (Collins, 1969, p.42).

Apart from the introduction of electricity to farming (chapter 3), perhaps the major innovation in twentieth-century agricultural mechanization to 1950 was the adoption of a new form of motive power. Nineteenth-century farming mechanization had brought a big increase in the horse population which peaked in the early years of the twentieth century. However, then the internal combustion engine in the form of tractors and lorries began to replace horse-traction in the United States particularly, where the tractor was already in mass production by 1920. The agricultural horse population of the United States fell from roughly 18 million in 1920 to 5 million in 1953. There, it was often a case of direct substitution of automotive for animal power. Already in 1920, there was ten times more automotive than animal horsepower across the economy as a whole in the United States, and by 1940 there was twenty times as much (Barker, 1983, pp.106–07).

In Europe as a whole, animals still provided three-quarters of draughting power in 1950. In Britain, the agricultural horse population fell from 1.1 million in 1910 to 650,000 in 1939. At that time, horses accounted for about half the available British draughting power but two-thirds of the total work done. Surprisingly though, Britain had about 20 per cent more tractors per 1,000 acres of arable land than the United States at this time. Rather than direct substitution as in America, tractor power in Britain was used to complement horsepower on individual farms. Tractors were only used to about one-third of their capacity before the Second World War. Effectively, the horse remained the cheaper unit of power during the inter-war years, and was used accordingly. It was steam power, rather than animal power, for which the tractor substituted (Collins, 1986, pp.23, 41–43). The demand for increased production, and hence for more draughting power, during the Second World War led to a dramatic increase in the number of tractors, which the government supported. It was simply not possible to increase the horse population as quickly as the number of tractors. By 1948, potential tractor draughting power was more than ten times as much as animal draughting power (Holmes, 1985, p.16). And greater post-war farming prosperity made capital investment more widely feasible so that by 1955, the number of agricultural horses in Britain had fallen to 161,000 (Barker, 1983, p.109). In addition to consuming no energy when not in use, the tractor enabled the farmer to achieve an increase in speed at various crucial times of the year. This made it possible to slip in an extra cycle of crops.

8.1.2
Agricultural science

Direct scientific input was also important for boosting agricultural productivity during the period of the course. In the United States, federal funding was given as early as the 1860s to provide technical 'land grant' colleges for improving agriculture (among other things) in the expanding areas. In Britain, various private institutions were set up in the nineteenth century for training farmers and carrying out field trials. On the continent too, many research projects arose out of agricultural questions. Plant and animal breeding in particular brought new strains of wheat and strains of animal that were suitable for the premium market. Those segments of the population who could afford meat would have noticed a shift to more compact, leaner varieties. After the First World War, an elaborate state-supported agricultural research network was set up deliberately to foster agricultural development in Britain with the Board of Agriculture, County Councils, and universities playing an important role.

Another major area of innovation where science played a direct role was in the use of fertilizers. Manufactured phosphatic fertilizers were applied from the 1840s after the discoveries of German, French and British chemists. Their manufacture became an important part of the chemical industry in the nineteenth century. Furthermore, the import of nitrogenous fertilizers to Europe became big business. The intensive farming practices in parts of Germany and Holland made those two countries the largest consumers per acre of fertilizers. In the early years of the twentieth century, important processes were devised, first in Germany then in England, for making nitrogen-based products artificially, starting from the gaseous nitrogen of the air. Pest control too was the subject of scientific research. Before the Second World War, most pesticides were either plant derived or were traditional chemical mixtures. Synthetic insecticides (including DDT) and selective hormonal weedkillers were developments of the 1940s, and soon came into widespread use (Holmes, 1985, p.18).

8.2
FOOD PROCESSING
The industrialization of food processing technology during the period 1870 to 1950 also contributed to an increase in food output and a lowering of its price. Until the middle years of the nineteenth century, many foodstuffs were consumed near their point of production. At that time, the principal methods of food processing for purposes of preservation were the centuries-old ones derived from natural processes: drying or baking, fermentation (including pickling), salting, freezing (in northern climates), smoking and adding sugar (after the discovery of the New World). There were no radically new food processing methods until the nineteenth-century development of canning. Mechanical refrigeration also became important on an industrial scale during this period. Aimed initially at preservation for longer term and longer distance distribution of foodstuffs, the new methods also had the eventual dietary effect of making a wide range of foods available for a much longer period of the year.

8.2.1
Canning
The principle of canning was originated in France around the turn of the nineteenth century, as the result of a Napoleonic competition seeking a reliable source of food for revolutionary armies travelling far from home sources of supply. The original method was to place food in loosely sealed glass containers, immerse them in boiling water to expel the air, and then to seal the containers tightly. 'Canning' became the appropriate English term for this process in about 1810, after the use of tin-plated iron (later steel) cans was introduced. The process was not properly understood until the implications of Pasteur's bacteriological work of the 1860s were realized by research at the Massachusetts Institute of Technology during the 1890s: the thorough heating was necessary to destroy harmful enzymes and bacteria in the food, the air-tight seal was necessary to prevent their re-entry. Despite some spectacular instances of 'poisoning', when the process worked, it worked well, enabling the military and merchant navies to have much broader, less monotonous diets. Their demand was sufficient to sustain modest industries in Britain, but mainly in the United States, which developed a number of improvements.

One line of improvement was the gradual mechanization of the slow process of making the cans themselves. The modern open-topped can, with which we are now familiar, did not come into general use until after an 1897 American patent for a rubber sealing composition was widely taken up, guaranteeing a reliable seal. The new can made possible the speeding up of the canning process both by providing a larger aperture for the filling operation, and by not requiring any soldering as the ends could be mechanically crimped on against the rubber seals. Can making was then fully automatic and for the most part done by specialist manufacturers; cans could be produced at the rate of 35,000 per day by 1910 and 18,000 per hour by 1930. An important improvement in can design of the 1920s was the enamel lining. Neutral to foods which had previously absorbed discolouring or flavour altering tin salts from tin-lined cans, enamel linings made possible the canning of foods such as grapefruit and sweet corn. From the inter-war years, Norwegian can manufacturers began to use cheap aluminium.

Sound cans were of course essential to one side of the bacteriological safety issue articulated in the 1890s. The other, the proper heating of their contents, was also an area of development in the nineteenth century, although at the time of development the issue was speed and productivity rather than quality *per se*. In Britain, from the middle of the nineteenth century, a bath of boiling calcium chloride solution was used by some canners. This boils at a higher temperature than water (240 versus 212 degrees F.), so the cooking process was speeded up considerably, from a capacity of 2,500 to 20,000 cans per day (Hampe and Wittenberg, 1964, p.117). At the same time, the higher processing temperature had the then inadvertent effect of killing certain micro-organisms which survived the boiling point of water (Williams, 1982, p.206). This method was adopted in America from 1860, and was crucial in meeting the demand for canned food from the armies of both sides in the American Civil War. An alternative method, heating in an autoclave, was employed from the 1870s. (The auto-clave is essentially a pressure cooker – the application of pressure in the vessel raises the boiling point of water.) This reduced cooking times still further, gave very accurate control over temperatures and, by equalizing the pressures inside and outside the heating cans, avoided the considerable nuisance of cans exploding during processing.

Once the processing phases of canning were made swifter, the many hand-based preparative stages became the slow steps. These were streamlined and mechanized during the decade around the turn of the twentieth century. By the 1920s, continuous processing from raw crop to labelled cans packed in cases for distribution, using conveyor belts developed for the purpose, had become the norm in the United States. To guarantee supplies, canners moved their interests to an even earlier stage in the process. They developed a system of contracting with farmers for crops of certain varieties, quality and quantity, often even providing seeds. Furthermore, rather than just canning primary products, some canners diversified into new ranges of prepared foods – what we would now call convenience foods. Items such as beans in tomato sauce and condensed soups are inventions of the 1890s.

The American canning industry grew rapidly. However, a British canning industry was slow to develop. It was not that the public was unfamiliar with canned goods (or antipathetic like the French). Canned milk, meat, fish and certain fruits had long been imported from the United States and elsewhere, and the amount of imports grew substantially after the First World War (Johnston, 1976, p.173), though American canners were not impressed by the post-war European uptake of their war-boosted production (Hampe and Wittenberg, 1964, p.125). In the mid 1920s, the Ministry of Agriculture and Fisheries, hoping both to help a very depressed agricultural sector and to limit imports, organized a meeting of canners, financiers, tin-box manufacturers, growers and scientists to discuss the British industry. One outcome was to designate the Fruit and Vegetable Research Station in Chipping Camden, Gloucestershire, as a centre of technological problem solving for the industry. It worked on a variety of matters, such as preserving greenness, and it developed the 'processed pea', later an important feature of the British industry.

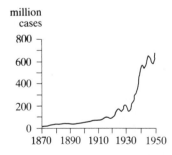

million
cases

*Figure 8.1
Canned food production,
1870–1950. (Reproduced by
permission of the National
Food Processors Association,
Washington)*

The industry grew rapidly in the 1920s but the majority of canned foods was still imported in the thirties. The reasons for this were not just technological. Britain lacked the food surpluses, and British farmers preferred to take their chances selling their output in the open produce markets rather than on fixed contracts to processors. The canners therefore lacked reliable supplies for processing which made their output expensive.

8.2.2
Refrigeration and freezing

While canning was a process totally new in principle, the idea of chilling foodstuffs artificially derives, of course, from a natural process. In the first half of the nineteenth century, harvesting, storing and transporting natural ice became a big business for the northern United States, aided in 1827 by the invention of a more efficient ice house which reduced melting by 60 per cent. However, already before 1850, there were numerous patents for cooling and ice-making machines. For the most part they all made use of the fact that when liquids become gases (or vaporize), they absorb heat, and when gases become liquids (or condense), they give off heat. The key to mechanical refrigeration was the control of this process so that a liquid 'refrigerant' would remove heat from one place, taking it to another – removing it from the closed space of a cooling box to the outside, for example. Among the first commercial ice-making plants were those built in Australia in the middle years of the century. As a result brewing could take place successfully even in hot weather.

Refrigeration played a key role in the development of the American meat-packing industry. For much of the period up to 1870, meat moved on the hoof to a place quite near its point of consumption. In Europe, for indigenously produced meat, this largely remained the case. However, in America, where the circumstances of production were totally different, an elaborate meat-packing industry was developed. It was the existence of the huge grazing plains, distant from centres of population, which led to the early processing of meat by factory methods. Initially, it was more a question of factory methods of organization than mechanization *per se*. Though hand methods of slaughtering and butchering were used in the large Cincinnati pork industry, from the 1830s, assembly-line procedures governed the passage of carcasses hooked onto conveyor belts through the works. Before refrigeration, processing to the point of salting (the common method of preservation) had to be done extremely rapidly; so to cope with the vast quantities, very detailed division of labour was practised.

These basic assembly-line processes were mechanized further and integrated in the Chicago meat-packing industry from the 1860s. The famous Chicago stockyards were built in 1865 where ten rail lines converged. The City became a clearing house for western animals which rode to market instead of walking there. Initially, animals were shipped live for slaughtering in the Eastern cities or abroad. This was profitable for railways and shipping companies, but not for the meat industry since long journeys severely affected the quality of the beasts (Perren, 1971, p.433; Horst, ˮ ˮ4, pp.9–10). Refrigeration transformed the industry. First of all refrigerated store rooms, using ice initially, helped extend the meat-processing season. However, Chicago could not consume everything it produced; meat had to be exported to the rest of the urban United States or abroad. Canning was one way of preserving meat for travel. Corned beef, for example, was developed in the 1870s. Another means of preservation developed at this time was the refrigeration of fresh meat. This had the advantage of providing the consumer with a familiar product. Various experimental refrigerated rail cars were tried in the late 1860s. While refrigerated shipping relied on mechanical methods, the refrigerated rail car carried ice in special insulated tanks. The famous meat-packing barons, Gustavus Swift and Philip Armour, made their initial fortunes not in packing, but in refrigerated transport from the mid 1870s.

This was used not only for meat but also for transporting perishable fruit and vegetables from warmer areas to the industrial north. It was not simply a matter of having the technology available, but of establishing an integrated, technologically compatible distribution network between the packing houses and points of sale to the consumer (Giedion, 1948, pp.213–46; Anderson, 1953, chapters 8 and 10).

The first successful shipment of meat between Australia and England took place in 1880, when forty tons of frozen Australian beef were landed in London. A shipment of frozen mutton had made it from Argentina to Le Havre with the aid of mechanical refrigeration in 1877. A chilled, as opposed to frozen, beef trade was begun from the United States to London using salted ice as early as 1870, but it really took off after 1879 with mechanical refrigeration. The relative shortness of the voyage made the transport of unfrozen beef possible, and this came to dominate the British import market. From the turn of the century, when domestic American demand made trans-atlantic shipping less competitive, the South American trade became predominant, especially after improvements in refrigeration techniques made it possible to ship chilled (not frozen) meat across the Equator from about 1909 (Perren, 1971, p.443). Another contribution to the rise of South American, at the expense of US, trade with Europe was the investment by American meat-packing firms in South American plant (Horst, 1974, p.34).

Imported chilled meat was preferred to frozen meat in Britain as the techniques of freezing and thawing altered the quality of meat, making it not unsafe, but certainly less palatable. The damage was caused by the large ice crystals formed during the slow freezing process at about the temperature of ice (−2 degrees C.). Impressed by the quality of 'naturally' frozen food during a wartime government expedition to Labrador, Clarence Birdseye developed during the 1920s a fast freezing process using lower temperatures which formed smaller ice crystals and preserved quality. Importantly from the manufacturing point of view, since canning already was a continuous process, Birdseye's freezing process was a continuous one. Packeted food was squeezed between two endless, moving belts which were continuously sprayed with a brine solution at 40 degrees below zero Fahrenheit. Very quickly, the canning industry practice of buying up crops before they were even planted was adopted. But despite general consumer satisfaction with the quality of its output, the frozen foods industry grew very slowly.

8.3 FOOD DISTRIBUTION

During the period 1870 to 1950, the farmer's experience of selling and the consumer's experience of buying changed considerably in the United States and Britain, as did various steps in the systems in between.

8.3.1 From the farm

In nineteenth-century America, the goods that farmers did not sell directly to local customers were sold in local markets to agents, who then sold the crops on to central markets for distribution to wholesalers, then retailers. Rail became the main means of transport, there and in Britain, extending the range from which perishable products such as liquid milk and vegetables could reach urban markets. Especially in Britain, the telegraph played a key role in keeping farmers in touch with markets. The coming of both radio and personal motor transport in the early 1920s altered the way American farmers marketed their goods. The Department of Agriculture began to broadcast day-to-day market information. Knowing prices in a number of markets, and having independent transport to get to the optimum one, farmers began to enjoy flexibility in marketing. In America, the truck-load came to be a unit of negotiation for crops.

Indeed, from the 1920s, the lorry in the United States began to take the custom of bulk goods away from rail for distribution generally. Lorries were able to offer flexible door-to-door services, eliminating costly and time-consuming transhipment at terminals. Rail remained competitive for long hauls, but not for shorter journeys. Lorries also took over the task of delivery to and from railheads. Furthermore, given the size of the units, an extraordinary range of specialized lorry equipment was developed for carrying particular loads. To save space, given the smaller size of a lorry when compared with a railway car, mechanical refrigeration was developed. This gave very precise temperature control and was later important in the transport of frozen goods. In 1921, with 1.2 million in service in the United States, lorries carried less than 1 per cent of the freight while rail carried 84 per cent. By 1950, some 8.5 million lorries carried 16 per cent of US freight as compared with 56 per cent on the railways (Hampe and Wittenberg, 1964, p.238). As chapter 6 indicates, road transport was less developed in this period in Britain and on the continent. However, in Britain too the motor lorry affected the geographical pattern of production after 1920, enabling farmers distant from railways to market perishable items.

8.3.2
From the food
manufacturer

As Swift and Armour perceived, mass production without appropriate distribution mechanisms led nowhere. Not only did they run refrigerated packing plants and railroad cars, but they also constructed refrigerated depots in the eastern cities from which meat would be distributed directly to retailers. During the nineteenth century, when a market for canned food had to be created, canners themselves functioned as salesmen sometimes selling door-to-door in homes, but also bringing their goods to retailers. Subsequently, some firms, such as the soup company, Campbells, operated through brokers who would promote their goods to wholesalers and retailers. Other firms such as Heinz opted to have their own marketing and distribution networks, the financing of which required large-scale sales.

From the very beginning of the canning industry, advertising of brand names was crucial to successful distribution. People had to be convinced, and timing had to be right. The first launch of baked beans in the north of England in 1905 flopped. Canned foods were not within the financial reach of working-class housewives, and the baked bean was a complete unknown. Launched again in the south of England some twenty years later accompanied by a massive advertising campaign, the product quickly became a staple.

Frozen foods were even more difficult for they required investment in special handling and storage equipment. For this reason, well into the 1940s, most frozen food in America was sold to further processors, bakers and institutions. Only 10 per cent was sold through the approximately 13,500 retail stores with frozen food cabinets. Indeed, it was only in America that a frozen food market developed on any scale at all before 1950. In Britain, for example, refrigerators were uncommon, let alone freezers, and there was hostility from the struggling canning industry. To encourage retailers in the early years, frozen food companies themselves provided a full service to retailers, renting them cabinets and stocking the foods at fixed prices. Retailers then tended to stock only one brand, so building up a customer following.

Both the amount of frozen food produced and the number of retailers handling it doubled in the United States during the Second World War because cans were needed to feed distant armies. Waxpaper-wrapped frozen foods stayed at home. Quite apart from the retailers' storage problems, the home freezer was not marketed until the early 1950s. Initially these were marketed on the basis of encouraging housewives to do their own freezing for the sake of economy and convenience. Stocking up with manufactured products would have been an expensive luxury even for those who could afford the freezers (Strasser, 1982, p.274). Later sales of freezers and frozen foods came to be mutually reinforcing. In the early years, however, frozen foods had to be purchased fairly close to home and consumed on the same day. Fruits, vegetables and juices made up the vast majority of frozen food sales until 1950, when frozen poultry and meats became more prominent, though frozen prepared dinners appeared from the 1940s. And of course, advertising aimed largely at women was fundamental to the lot. Well tuned to promoting the ideology of housework (chapter 3), advertising promised uniformity, reliability, convenience, ease and pleasure – the prospect of fresh fruit and vegetables all year round.

8.3.3
Retailing

Chapter 6 opened with a reminiscence of a big event in the lives of two young girls living in rural America in the 1880s – a rare trip to the general store in a small Wisconsin town. Apart from some sweets, the only foodstuffs their parents acquired were a pound of tea and a small packet of store sugar. Otherwise, they were self-sufficient for food. The store sugar was not really necessary; it was a delicacy, a treat in contrast to daily home-made maple sugar (Wilder, 1932, chapter 9). A few years later, having moved further West to the frontier and gone over to growing cash crops, the family still found it exciting to visit the local general store, but they had become far more dependent on store-bought foodstuffs, especially the staples of flour, corn meal, beans, salt and sugar (Wilder, 1953, chapter 30). During one particularly harsh winter, the family was brought to the point of starvation and freezing because their railway link with food and fuel supplies from more easterly depots was cut off (Wilder, 1940, chapter 21).

Any individual's reminiscences of childhood can only be indicative of important historical changes. Over the same period a rural English child might have noted the gradual displacement of itinerant traders, and the complementing of local markets by the spread of village shops carrying branded goods. The shopping experience of Laura Ingalls' urban contemporaries would have been quite different again. In Britain and the United States, until the 1860s, urban food retailing was accomplished for the most part through small independent shops – butchers, grocers, bakers and so on – which established personal relations with their customers, offering credit, delivery services and a very wide range of goods. The urban working classes tended to buy food more cheaply either from markets or street traders. However, such outlets could handle only relatively small quantities of goods, amounts inadequate to cope with either the increasing demand or the increasing supply of cheap foodstuffs. From the 1870s, the implications of mass production and mass consumption were realized in relation to the business of selling food.

It was dealing with this problem in relation to feeding the working classes that led to the development of a completely new form of retailing. In Britain, working-class co-operative societies were early to appreciate the problem. By 1863, co-op membership numbered more than 100,000. Members grouped together to buy food wholesale, and then divided the profits among themselves. Initially aimed at eliminating adulteration and exploitation, the co-ops developed a policy of reliable quality and fixed prices. Local societies grouped together into wholesaling and producing organizations, and were able to handle vast amounts of food through their numerous retail outlets. By 1914, with some 3 million members, co-ops accounted for more than 15 per cent of UK food sales. By 1939, the movement had 8.5 million members and accounted for 20 per cent of national grocery trade, 25 per cent of the milk trade, 15 per cent of bread, and 10 per cent of the meat trade (Johnston, 1977, pp.76, 83).

Private enterprise developed a similar form of organization: multiple-shop retailing. Individual entrepreneurs began buying bulk quantities of particular foodstuffs which they marketed through a network of branch shops. The economies of scale, and the relatively small number of items handled initially, on the basis of cash sales and rapid turnover, meant that prices could be kept low. Standardized, packaged foods were developed in the context of these outlets, which were ideal for handling the new processed foods. The consumer came to know what to expect and a number of the chains became national in scope. The creation of branded goods and store identity was fundamental to such a strategy. Advertising and all the gimmicks of promotions were widely deployed to create the mass demand that would warrant such bulk distribution.

During the inter-war years, the nature of retailing in Britain began to change further, as demand for ready-to-eat manufactured foods increased with rising incomes and changing domestic habits. Since ever more branded, standardized goods were sought, competition between the big multiples shifted from being price based to being service based. Ironically, they reintroduced, but on a larger scale, some of the practices of their Victorian middle-class grocer forebears. This, of course, also gave scope for small independents to continue to compete, and in 1939 they handled about half of the British food trade.

In America, the pattern was broadly similar in the nineteenth century. The A&P food chain opened its first shops in 1859, run on much the same basis as the British multiple-shop retail outlets would be, though initially they allowed credit and offered delivery. From 1912, the already vast A&P chain offered economy, no frills shopping, cut profit margins to the minimum, but greatly pushed up volume as a consequence. Direct buying from processors made this policy possible and tight managerial control, including the monitoring of consumer response, was essential to the success of the enterprise. In America too, advertising and in-store promotions, often in collaboration with food processors, played a major role. The idea proved popular, and by 1928, there were 315 food chains operating in the United States, accounting for almost a third of the grocery trade (Hampe & Wittenberg, 1964, p.278). So successful were the chains that independents fought back via their state legislatures and also sought federal anti-trust action. Others combined forces into wholesaling groups, and thereby managed to compete successfully with the chains while maintaining independent ownership. In 1950, chains accounted for 36 per cent of US grocery trade and groups of retail owners for 33 per cent.

The retailing innovation that we all associate with America is, of course, the supermarket. The self-service idea, with stores especially designed to accommodate customers, originated in the early years of the First World War. During the 1920s, added to the idea of self-service was that of the combination store, one that carried produce, meat, dairy products and baked goods, as well as groceries. The idea of the supermarket brought together the concepts of self-service, combination stores, and the chain-store concept of low margin/high volume marketing. Relying on the mobility and carrying capacity of the automobile, which was spreading rapidly in 1930s America, and increasing disposable incomes, the supermarket created a new form of consumerism, encouraging customers to buy more by making more available at prices even lower than the chains because of their huge capacity. This was mass merchandising for a mass market.

A whole support industry of supermarket equipment manufacturing, aimed at marshalling the consumer 'efficiently' through the store, developed. Pre-packaging and pre-pricing, even of meats once a clear cellophane wrap was devised (chapter 4), gave the customer direct access to every item. Check-out stations with improved cash registers were positioned so as to ease the flow through the stores. The now familiar shopping cart dates from the 1930s. It too encouraged greater volumes of purchases. No longer did the customer define a shopping trip by the capacity of a hand-carried basket, nor was this necessary if the customer had arrived by car. The supermarket too met

*Figure 8.2
Early Big Bear supermarket,
Elizabeth, New Jersey
c.1932–33. (Photograph by
courtesy of* Progressive
Grocer)

with attempts at legislative opposition from chain store and independent competitors, but consumers so obviously responded to the low-price lure of the supermarket concept, that chains and independents began also to adopt supermarket practices. By 1950, just over 4 per cent of US stores were supermarkets, but these accounted for 40 per cent of grocery store sales (Hampe and Wittenberg, 1964, p.332). In America, the demands of the supermarkets came to determine the nature of the food industry as a whole as farmers and food processors adapted their output to suit the circumstances of supermarket retailing.

Free parking was a feature of such stores, and even the early ventures in New Jersey in the 1930s attracted customers from up to fifty miles around. The supermarket idea particularly fitted with the growth of American suburbia. Refrigeration too played a role, both in the stores and in homes. Doing a 'big shop' only made sense if domestic storage facilities were available: the greater distances could then be balanced against less frequent trips. Shopping became depersonalized, but an ever greater part of the housewife's role. No longer was the butcher or baker available as advisor. She had to learn to be an expert consumer in order to be an efficient household manager (see chapter 3). Advertising was her medium of consumer education. Helping to create demand while seeking to constrain choice, it was a cornerstone of mass merchandising and a determinant of the mass market (Strasser, 1982, pp.259–61).

8.4 FOODSTUFFS

So far, we have been looking at broad changes in the way that food moved from farm to table over the period of the course, focusing on the various stages of that movement. In this section, we will shift our focus to particular foodstuffs.

8.4.1 Bread

For centuries a mainstay of the human diet, bread remained an important source of both protein and energy throughout our period, although the way it was produced and distributed changed considerably: from being home produced, bread became the product of small-scale local bakeries and then a standardized factory product. Not only did baking become mechanized over this period, but the method of producing flour, and hence the nature of the main raw material, altered significantly as well. Over the same period, apart from exceptional wartime circumstances, *per capita* consumption of bread declined as real incomes rose (Johnston, 1977, p.23).

The milling of grain into flour was one of the most important traditional food processing technologies. Generally wind or water powered, mills extracted flour from grain by grinding it between two stones. 'Low milling', where the stones were kept close together throughout the process, was the favoured English technique. This gave a coarse, non-white flour (and bread). The more costly continental technique of 'high milling', where the stones were brought together in stages during the process, was used for the more brittle Eastern European grains. Because stone grinding effectively crushed the oily part of the grain into the flour derived from other parts, such flour did not have good keeping properties. Furthermore, because of public taste for whiter breads, which were regarded as socially superior products, harmful adulterants were often added to meet public requirements cheaply. From the middle of the nineteenth century, better flour sifting methods made a whiter loaf possible, and brown bread become virtually extinct in Britain (Collins, 1976, p.29).

Mechanization   It was the process of roller milling, however, which made possible the large-scale production of very much whiter and finer flour. Developed in Hungary, the centre of the Eastern European trade, and simultaneously in the United States, roller milling substituted rollers for the stones in the high milling system. The grain was squeezed through a series of spirally fluted rollers and then plain rollers. This broke it into its various fragments which could be separated. The process was repeated several times, with sieving in between each stage, so that several grades of flour could be produced from the same wheat. Roller milling was trebly economical – in extracting more flour from the grain than stone milling, in the flour's having better keeping properties, and in the flour's better absorption of water hence more economical use. When American grains began to be imported into Britain in large quantities, the technique of roller milling came as well; the harder grains required it. Large mills were set up at ports of entry to produce a range of standardized flours.

Milling was by definition a flow process, organized by the early nineteenth century into a system of continuous production. The introduction of rollers improved speed and quality and brought the transition to mass production. Bread baking, a complicated craft process with several stages each requiring quality judgements, was not so straightforwardly suited to continuous production. Throughout the nineteenth century, mechanical devices were introduced for various stages of the bread-baking process. Clearly beyond domestic scope, such devices were developed by the growing number of small-scale bakers who came to supply the urban loaf during the later years of the nineteenth century. Thus mixers, ovens, belting systems, and so on, were developed piecemeal. Reliably uniform roller-milled flour fitted this level of mechanization as it helped guarantee a predictable product to the consumer. It was not until the 1920s that bread making was automated on any scale. The invention of the high-speed dough mixer, brought into use in the United States from the mid 1920s, was the step which made full automation 'worthwhile'. Not only was it very fast, but it did a very thorough job, making for a more uniform and an even whiter bread (Giedion, 1948, p.173). Automatic slicing and wrapping machines were introduced in the 1930s, again requiring a very uniform loaf of quite precise qualities so that the slicer could function.

The effects of   What automation made possible was a tremendous increase in volume rather
mechanization   than speed of production (Giedion, 1948, p.195). Such volume, of course, required access to, and the ability to exploit, a huge market. In the United States, the plant bakery quickly became dominant, accounting in money terms for twenty-five times more output than small units by 1939 (Giedion,

1948, p.192). In Britain, the move was more gradual, but none the less pronounced, with about 12 per cent of national bread production done in plant bakeries in 1937 and some 35 to 40 per cent in 1953 (Collins, 1976, p.27).

Writing an appeal for the restoration of the human element in mechanized society in 1948, Siegfried Giedion was in no doubt about the deleterious effects of mechanization on the quality of bread.

> The bread of full mechanization has the resiliency of a rubber sponge. When squeezed it returns to its former shape. The loaf becomes constantly whiter, more elastic and frothier. This is not the result of mechanization alone. With the increasingly more complex machinery and greater capital outlays, new ways of pushing consumption had to be devised. (p.198)

So, extra shortening, milk and sugar were added to make it more cake-like in texture and to give it a more lustrous, visually appealing crust. Furthermore, as mechanized bread became softer, freshness became an issue, since freshly baked bread is softer. In addition, thin-crusted, soft bread made of finely milled flour bakes faster, and can therefore be produced more quickly. So planned obsolescence was, according to Giedion, also a feature of automated bread production.

Not only did Giedion dislike manufactured bread, he was also part of a long line of commentators who argued that roller milled flour was less healthy than stone ground.

> Mechanization of the milling process yielded a brilliant façade and a more or less artificial product. The oleaginous germ that formerly made the flour somewhat greasy to the touch, and which contains the most valuable elements, has been rigorously excluded. More recently, we have seen attempts to make good the values removed from the flour by vitamin reinforcements added to the yeast or the dough. The whiteness of the flour remains unspotted. But such measures remind one of a dentist who extracts good natural teeth, filling the void with a bright and handsome set of artificial ones. (Giedion, 1948, p.190)

As early as 1880, the Bread and Food Reform League had begun campaigning in Britain for a return to wholemeal bread on then rather unsupported nutritional grounds. The high wheat-germ content Hovis flour was patented later in that decade, getting its name after a national competition from the Latin 'hominis vis', strength of man. By 1896, there was a move to make Hovis a national product; successful intensive and extensive advertising campaigns were mounted to make Hovis a household word, synonymous with good health and good sense. Even in the pre-wrapper days, Hovis was not an anonymous bread, for the company provided bakers with tins which would leave 'Hovis' embossed on the side of every loaf. Yet its market share was never greater than 5 per cent in our period (Collins, 1976, pp.29–31).

Skirmishes between champions of white and brown bread flourished from time to time. The discovery of vitamins favoured the brown bread cause. A rather coarse wartime British national loaf, however, gave it a bad reputation. White bread suffered from concerns in the 1920s about the bleaching agents used, but the white bread troops retaliated with a mid 1920s survey of a thousand doctors arguing that white bread was nutritious *in a mixed diet*. A report published in 1954 on some post-war feeding experiments carried out with German children seemed to indicate that unenriched white bread was as valuable as wholemeal bread in their diets. In the early 1950s, it none the less became required in Britain that flour above a specified level of refining should be enriched.

Figure 8.3
Wonder Bread. Advertisement
for sliced and wrapped bread,
1944. (Reproduced in
Siegfried Giedion, 1948,
Mechanization Takes
Command, *Oxford University*
Press)

Clearly views at any one time were as likely to arise out of preconceptions as out of scientific evidence. Giedion, for example, felt that mechanization had gone too far; white bread was a great waste in his view. To others, the 'scientific enrichment' of their bread was a great attraction. Advertising campaigns aimed at newly vitamin-conscious Americans in the 1940s boasted that white bread could contain all the vitamins and minerals of natural whole wheat. Magazine publicity on enrichment reached over 30 million readers in 1941, 50,000 news items on enriched bread were published over a six-month period during the same year in the daily press. On the other hand, the British Ministry of Health, reporting favourably on the value of white bread in the 1920s, noted that there was a demand for white bread and that the use of bleaching agents had helped the British miller in competition with overseas suppliers (Johnston, 1977, pp.27–31). It may be fruitful to consider some of the motives for the vogue of brown and home-baked breads in some circles in our own high-tech day.

8.4.2 Butter and margarine

Whatever the public's view of the qualities of manufactured bread, it was still broadly the same traditional foodstuff. Margarine, by contrast, was a completely new foodstuff developed in the nineteenth century as a substitute for a traditional one, butter.

Butter production changed little in the nineteenth century. For the most part, it was done on a domestic scale for home consumption, surpluses being sold at local markets though rail transport made longer distance marketing feasible. Broadly, there were three stages: cream was separated from the milk by setting overnight in an open pan; the separated cream was allowed to ripen for two days; then it was churned into butter. The by-product of churning, skimmed milk, was fed to pigs, or calves. The main 'industrial' innovation during this period was the centrifugal cream separator, invented in 1877. Only of use to the new-style larger dairies because of its cost, this device both sped up the process of separating cream from milk and took up much less space than the traditional open 'setting' pans. The centrifugal separator was a key invention in the shifting of dairy production to the factory which was to take place in the inter-war years. However, in the closing decades of the nineteenth century, the amount of butter produced, and the price at which it was produced, could not fulfil the requirements of the ever larger urban populations for dietary fats.

Margarine is another invention resulting from a government sponsored French competition, this time for a cheap nutritive fat. The motives for this particular competition are variously suggested as needing to feed the military and wishing to promote a healthy workforce. Nutritional research, and especially research on fats, was well established in France. A consulting chemist who had worked on various foodstuffs, Hippolyte Mège Mouriès, noted that fasting cows did not produce butterfat, the fragment of cows' milk which forms cream. Concluding therefore that butterfat derived from cows' body fat, he devised a process for extracting the oily fragment (oleo) from beef suet. Churning this with skimmed milk gave an edible fat.

When margarine was invented in 1869, Dutch butter merchants, whose main market was a seemingly insatiable Britain largely dependent on imports, moved into margarine manufacture and launched it at the low income end of the British butter market. At roughly half the price of butter initially, it became widely used in urban working-class households (Wilson, 1954, chapter 3; Hoffman, 1969, pp.14–15). Within a decade it was manufactured in most of the butter producing countries of Europe – Holland, Germany, Austria and Norway – as well as in the United States. During the 1880s, Sweden, Denmark and England joined the list of producers.

The introduction of this substitute foodstuff did not go unopposed. In Britain, the initial name under which margarine was marketed, 'butterine', was outlawed from 1887 on the grounds that consumers should be able to distinguish clearly between the two products. It was not in fact in direct competition with butter there because it was bought by sections of the population which could not afford butter in the first place. Indeed, butter remained the preferred product, and the profits of the margarine industry fluctuated wildly with the price of butter. When butter was low, margarine sales fell off dramatically. In the United States, the small farmers' lobby was particularly powerful. By the mid 1880s, twenty-two states had restrictive legislation regarding margarine, including New Jersey's law that margarine should be coloured pink. A federal law of 1886, over-rode such state legislation, but imposed high taxes. Further legislation in 1902 forbade margarine being coloured, forcing it to be sold in its 'natural' state, an unpalatable white at the time. Ingeniously, margarine was subsequently sold with little capsules of yellow dye which the user could work in. It was not until 1950 that the opposition to margarine from dairy farming eased in the United States (Stuyvenberg, 1969, pp.283–90; 304–08).

Ironically, margarine manufacture had been taken up most quickly in butter producing countries because skimmed milk, one of the principal raw materials for margarine, was so readily available as a by-product of butter making. In the early years of the European industry, the main source of the other raw material, fat, was the mid-Western US meat packing industry. Margarine manufacture provided an outlet for what would otherwise have been a waste product, and large amounts of animal fat were shipped across the Atlantic. When an indigenous US industry started competing for this raw material, vegetable oils were sought as a substitute. However, it was not until the development of the process of catalytic hydrogenation in the early years of the twentieth century that liquid vegetable oils could be 'hardened' for use in margarine manufacture. Once that was possible, and refining processes were developed, the source of fat shifted to transoceanic colonies and a large new seed-crushing industry developed at various European ports. Initially, naturally growing materials were harvested, but eventually special plantations were developed by large manufacturers. The vast European demand for vegetable oils had considerable political, economic and social impact on the lives of natives in the various colonial countries (Pyke, 1972).

Vegetable oils had a number of advantages. In addition to broadening the resource base, the oil industry had other outlets in animal feedstuff manufacture and in soap manufacture. This integration with other industries helped to keep supplies in balance when demand for margarine was down. In relation to margarine itself, some vegetable oils 'naturally' produced a yellow margarine. However, they lacked the vitamins which made animal-based margarine and butter nutritious products. Once vitamins were understood, from the 1920s, margarine too was fortified with vitamins A and D.

As with every foodstuff we have mentioned, margarine had to be sold. Initially, it filled a slot which butter could not fill, a cheap fat for the working-class urban population. Like butter, it was first sold unbranded to wholesalers in large units which would be prepared for the customer by shopkeepers. Eventually, the technique of selling branded goods directly to the new retail shop groups was also adopted. Some margarine manufacturers even bought in to shop chains. Advertising created followings for specific brands, especially for the better quality varieties.

8.4.3 Milk

The production of butter is, of course, closely linked with the production of its chief raw material, milk. Until the advent of rail transport, milk was a locally consumed product, seldom reaching more than ten miles from the farm. Major towns had cow-keepers who sold milk directly to consumers. The only way in which milk travelled more widely was in the form of condensed milk, which was developed by Gail Borden in the United States from the 1830s. He evaporated milk in a vacuum, and then, from the 1850s, canned it with sugar as a preservative. In Britain this proved very popular, especially in working-class households. In dilution, it was cheaper than ordinary liquid milk; its sweetness was attractive; and in the pre-refrigeration era, it kept well. It was particularly used as an infant food, since it was a reliable source of 'clean' milk.

Local consumption in urban areas gave way from the 1860s in Britain after a severe outbreak of cattle plague. Rail transport of liquid milk from farms to town centres, already established in the 1850s, expanded. It was the invention of the milk cooler which made distances of up to 100 miles feasible. The device was very simple in principle. Soon after collecting, the milk was passed over a metal construction containing cold water, which looked rather like a modern radiator, before being placed into churns for shipment to urban retailers. Cooling also made it possible to send milk from farms to creameries for processing into butter or cheese.

Though chilling improved the keeping qualities of milk, it was no guarantee of quality when standards of bovine health and farm hygiene were uncertain. Pasteur's bacteriological work showed the way to purer milk supplies. During the early years of the twentieth century, pasteurization (controlled heating for a prescribed period to kill harmful bacteria) began to be employed by some large milk distributors. This retarded souring, but pasteurized milk still required refrigeration or quick consumption. In the north of England, sterilization was preferred. This killed all bacteria and gave a longer shelf life. Over the same period, following the nineteenth-century isolation of bacteria causing tuberculosis, tuberculin tests were introduced which revealed a high number of unhealthy herds. Enforcement of regulations regarding clean milk supplies was hindered by apathy and ignorance plus the administrative complexity of a borough by borough system of responsibility. Any particular retailer might deliver to several London boroughs and receive his supplies in yet another.

Such high-profile 'scientific' activity was important for creating public confidence in liquid milk, a foodstuff with a deservedly dangerous reputation in the nineteenth century. Medical opinion was however divided on the best way to proceed. Some experts were concerned that heat treatment would destroy nutritional quality. Many argued that a policy of pasteurization would allow farmers to ignore requirements for bovine health and hygiene, and

Figure 8.4
Milk cooler and 17 gallon churn. Ingram-Fowler Country Life Museum, Cricket St Thomas, Dorset. (Photograph from Arthur Ingram, Dairying Bygones, *Shire Publications by permission of publisher and author)*

consequently opposed it (Whetham, 1976, p.69). Furthermore, the capital expense of pasteurization plant put it beyond the reach of individual farmers, making them more dependent on wholesalers and milk depots. The fortifying of milk with additional vitamins, which became common in the inter-war years, also favoured the larger establishments. Milk production became industrialized.

During the First World War, a milk shortage developed in London. The four major wholesalers, who by this time controlled the London trade, pooled resources in order to economize on horses, dairies, equipment and roundsmen, and to control the margins on the milk that they distributed. The resulting firm, United Dairies, was scrutinized as a monopoly by the government. Indeed, for a time the Ministry of Food took control of milk distribution, and proposed nationalization. Such plans evaporated after the war and the United Dairies combine remained in existence. From the early 1920s it sold only pasteurized milk. For extra protection to the consumer, the company moved to distributing it in sealed glass bottles instead of open churns. By 1925 almost all London milk was pasteurized. However, the debate between proponents of pasteurization and of clean herds carried on throughout the inter-war years, which were generally bad for farming anyway. There was too still the worry about affecting the trade of the smaller farmer, especially since a shift to road transport during the 1930s meant that many more farmers came within reach of the urban markets.

The Milk Marketing Board was set up in 1933 to meet an immediate crisis of over-production and falling incomes in dairy farming. All milk was to be sold in the first instance to the Board by farmers; the Board would then negotiate with the industry over milk pricing and the distribution of the raw material over the various sectors of the industry. The upshot was that 24 per cent more milk was sold over the Board's first four years and the number of producers increased dramatically (Miles, 1978, p.62). Much of the Board's early work was educational and promotional. From 1934 it administered the Milk in Schools Scheme. If all 5 million schoolchildren were reached, 45 million gallons of milk per year would be disposed of. The argument was put in terms of public health, but such a boost in consumption would clearly be a great help to dairy farmers. More importantly, the children would become accustomed to milk as a normal part of their diet. Milk supplied under the scheme had to be pasteurized. This was resented by many smaller farmers, who saw it as a device to force pasteurization when they considered the issue to be as yet unresolved (Hurt, 1985, p.190; n.27). The issue of how (or whether) to judge nutritional deficiency and therefore who should receive free or subsidized milk was, of course, highly political, especially in an era when the state of the nation's health was under debate by nutritionists of various persuasions.

**8.5
CONCLUSION**

**8.5.1
Food consumption**

Because of our focus on changes in science and technology in relation to everyday life, this discussion has concentrated on the United States and Britain. The particular combinations of population growth, urbanization, industrialization, government attitudes and social, cultural and economic values in these two countries provided the conditions for large-scale, eventually mass, consumption of technologically produced foods there. This is not to imply that developments in other countries were irrelevant, but that diverse social, cultural, political and economic contexts resulted in diverse experiences of consumption and, indeed, diverse nutritional experiences.

Think for a moment of the number of times that French innovations have been mentioned above – canning, margarine, pasteurization. There were also French developments in freezing and refrigeration in the 1870s. In chapter 3 we noted French reluctance, for social and cultural reasons, regarding refrigeration. However, when processed food made sense for financial reasons, it was used: canned American beef was welcomed in the late 1870s because it was so much cheaper than local meat. A small French canning industry did emerge around the turn of the twentieth century, but the bulk of its output was sardines for export. In order to explain the French antipathy to canned food, it has been argued that high costs in a low-volume industry may have been significant. And further that

> . . . either food producers preferred to stick to traditional methods of adulteration, which were all well developed, in order to reduce the cost of food . . . or else that profits in the retail grocery trade were so high that there was little inducement to try new methods; or finally that the preserving of food by the housewife in the home was an established alternative. (Zeldin, 1980, p.391)

France, which was industrializing gradually over the period of the course (chapter 1), remained remarkably traditional, regional and small-scale with regard to food. Indeed, some historians have used the gradual abandonment of peasant cuisine in France as a rough index of modernization. This traditional fare lasted until the 1950s (Zeldin, 1980, pp.381–82). On the other hand, and on another social level, the French fame for gastronomy was developing from the nineteenth century. The contrast with the United States and Britain is of course striking.

> England's prosperity may in fact have been excessive [as regards encouraging good cooking]: ample supplies of good meat may have made skilful preparation unnecessary – which was certainly what happened in the USA. England also preferred to devote its attention more to the elaboration of sweet dishes; it consumed three times more sugar than France . . . [T]he English, precisely because they were rich enough to entertain at home, therefore ate out less, and there were far fewer restaurants in England as a result. The restaurant was an essential cause of France's competitiveness in cooking . . . when the English aristocracy lost their predominance, the grand style of life vanished with it. In France, by contrast, the tastes of the aristocracy were spread by their cooks who opened restaurants, and upper- rather than lower-class ideals became the most widespread in matters of food. The prosperous English worker kept his tastes even when he moved into the middle class; but the French peasant who ended up as a bourgeois sought to become, at least in eating habits, a minor seigneur. (Zeldin, 1980, pp.406–07)

Looking at other cultures and social systems, such as Eastern Europe and the Soviet Union, would throw up still other points of contrast.

**8.5.2
The effects of war**

The two twentieth-century world wars caused major dislocations in international agriculture and food supply. In Britain and Europe during the First World War, demand for overseas imports increased dramatically, as well as demand for domestic production. Attempts to meet these demands created a severe problem of post-war over-production and consequent falling prices, which coincided with the broader economic collapse to undermine agriculture generally in the industrialized countries. Tariffs were imposed throughout Europe (even in Britain in 1932) and efforts were made to increase home production behind the new barriers. Governments of various political persuasions began to intervene in the control of agriculture. There was, throughout Europe, a movement for land reform, with a view to breaking up large estates and getting more people on to the land. On the technical side, land reclamation projects provided inter-war showpieces for the contrasting governments of Italy and Holland. Greece and Germany (in Schleswig) also had reclamation projects. In other countries, farmers were offered incentives for improved cultivation techniques, the use of fertilizers, and new varieties of seed. However, almost no European country achieved self-sufficiency in foodstuffs. By 1937, Italy produced 95 per cent of food consumed, France and Germany (1934 borders) produced 83 per cent, the Netherlands 67 per cent, and Britain 25 per cent (Clough and Cole, 1967, p.783). Many would argue that it was not until after the Second World War that British agriculture was able to recover properly. The Agriculture Act of 1947 provided a government price floor for farm products in an effort to balance farmers' needs for income with consumers' needs for cheap food. However, Britain had remained heavily dependent on imports of essential foodstuffs right through the inter-war years. Meanwhile, American agriculture too entered a prolonged period of crisis led by over-production from the twenties, when the markets for its exports collapsed. This was compounded by a series of droughts and the world economic problems of the thirties. Federal legislation, totally inimical to the principles of many independent small farmers, sought ways of easing the distress with devices such as subsidies, loans, market quotas, storage of surpluses, paying for non-production and soil conservation programmes. Not until the United States entered the Second World War did farm prices recover.

The coming of the Second World War again greatly increased the world demand for food, causing disruption and dislocation in an already meagrely fed world. In practice, it was only the most developed countries with the most efficient agriculture that were able to be flexible enough to marshal the political and technical resources needed to adjust production to meet wartime requirements (Milward, 1977, p.251).

> In spite, therefore, of the inherent tendency of war to raise both the output and the productivity of agriculture, the complicated realities of the war reduced both. One result of the Second World War was to reduce the world's total available food supply and make it difficult for world agriculture to regain its former output levels. Of the main products of agriculture only grains were still produced in quantities close to pre-war levels. The devastation of battles, the deterioration of capital equipment, the loss of labour (for large numbers of former agriculture workers were either unable or did not choose to return to their previous employment), the loss of draught animals and the delays in retooling factories to produce agricultural machinery all played their part. And even in countries where output had gone up, a certain percentage of this rise had been due to concentration on short-term gains which, because of soil exhaustion, could not be sustained in peacetime.
>
> As incomes improved and people's expectations rose it became clear that the war had been the turning point between the apparent food surpluses of the 1930s and a new situation in which, in terms of human expectations, food shortage was to become a permanent feature of the post-war world. (Milward, 1977, p.293)

8.5.3
Technological eating

There are many other influences on questions of consumption which space does not permit us to explore. Dietary expectations and the changing state of nutritional knowledge, on the part of consumers and producers, were also important.

> The American diet underwent marked changes after the First World War. Some of the old staples [such as potatoes] lost favor . . . But the consumption of dairy products, citrus fruits, tomatoes and leafy, green, and yellow vegetables grew astonishingly. Among the factors responsible were the

increasingly sedentary nature of our lives, which diminished both our need and our desire for the heavy foods of our fathers, and dietary indoctrination, which was undertaken sometimes in the interest of public health and sometimes in the interest of a particular product. (Anderson, 1953, p.272)

Despite persistent regional differences (Allen, 1968, chapter 9), the British diet too changed considerably between 1870 and 1950, and partly for the similar reason of a changing profile of daily work (chapter 1). In both countries, a transition to the consumption of primarily processed food was all but completed over this period. The scientific, technological, economic and social changes we have been discussing resulted in 'technological eating'. That this could occur in certain countries while starvation was still common elsewhere is among the saddest of the ironies of technological progress.

REFERENCES   Allen, D.E. (1968) *British Tastes An Enquiry into the Likes and Dislikes of the Regional Consumer*, Hutchinson.

Anderson, O.E. (1953) *Refrigeration in America: A History of a New Technology and its Impact*, Princeton University Press.

Barker, T.C. (1983) 'The delayed decline of the horse in the twentieth century' in Thompson, F.M.L. (ed.) *Horses in European Economic History: A Preliminary Canter*, British Agricultural History Society.

Chambers, J.D. and Mingay, G.E. (1966) *The Agricultural Revolution, 1750–1880*, Batsford, paperback reprint, 1978.

Clough, S.B. and Cole, C.W. (1967) *Economic History of Europe*, third edition, D.C. Heath.

Collins, E.J.T. (1969) *Sickle to Combine: A Review of Harvest Techniques from 1800 to the Present Day*, Museum of English Rural Life.

Collins, E.J.T. (1976) 'The "consumer revolution" and the growth of factory foods: changing patterns of bread and cereal-eating in Britain in the twentieth century' in Miller, D. and Oddy, D. (eds.) (1976) op.cit.

Collins, E.J.T. (1986) 'The agricultural tractor in Britain, 1900–1940' in Winkel, H. and Hermann, K. (eds.) *The Development of Agricultural Technology in the 19th and 20th Centuries*, Scripta Mercaturae Verlag.

Giedion, S. (1948) *Mechanization Takes Command: A Contribution to Anonymous History*, Oxford University Press, reprint Norton, 1969.

Hampe, E.C. and Wittenberg, M. (1964) *The Lifeline of America: Development of the Food Industry*, McGraw Hill.

Hoffmann, W.G. (1969) '100 years of the margarine industry' in Stuyvenberg, J.H. van, *Margarine: An Economic, Social and Scientific History, 1869–1969*, Liverpool University Press.

Holmes, C. (1985) 'Science and practice in arable farming, 1910–1950' in Miller, D. and Oddy, D. (eds.) (1985) op.cit.

Horst, T. (1974) *At Home Abroad: A Study of the Domestic and Foreign Operations of the American Food-Processing Industry*, Ballinger.

Hurt, J. (1985) 'Feeding the hungry school child in the first half of the twentieth century' in Miller, D. and Oddy, D. (eds.) (1985) op.cit.

Johnston, J.P. (1976) 'The development of the food canning industry in Britain during the inter-war period' in Oddy, D. and Miller, D. (eds.) (1976) op.cit.

Miller, D. and Oddy, D. (eds.) (1976) *The Making of the Modern British Diet*, Croom Helm.

Miller, D. and Oddy, D. (eds.) (1985) *Diet and Health in Modern Britain*, Croom Helm.

Johnston, J.P. (1977) *A Hundred Years of Eating: Food, Drink and the Daily Diet in Britain since the Late Nineteenth Century*, Gill and Macmillan.

Miles, S.G. (1978) 'The British dairy industry' in The Open University (1978) T273 *Food Production Systems*, Units 12 and 13 *Organizational Frameworks (The Rural Web)*, The Open University Press.

Milward, A.S. (1977) *War, Economy and Society, 1939–1945*, Allen Lane.

Perren, R. (1971) 'The North American beef and cattle trade with Great Britain, 1870–1914', *Economic History Review*, 24, pp.430–44.

Pyke, M. (1972) *Technological Eating or Where Does the Fish-finger Point?*, John Murray.

Strasser, S. (1982) *Never Done: A History of American Housework*, Pantheon.

Stuyvenberg, J.H. van (1969) 'Aspects of Government Intervention' in *Margarine: An Economic, Social and Scientific History, 1869–1969*, Liverpool University Press.

Whetham, E.H. (1976) 'The London milk trade 1900–1930' in Miller, D. and Oddy, D. (eds.) (1976) op.cit.

Wilder, L.I. (1932) *Little House in the Big Woods*, Puffin, paperback reprint, 1981.

Wilder, L.I. (1940) *The Long Winter*, Puffin, paperback reprint, 1981.

Wilder, L.I. (1953) *On the Banks of Plum Creek*, Puffin, paperback reprint, 1982.

Williams, T.I. (1982) *A Short History of Technology from c. 1900 to c. 1950*, Clarendon Press.

Wilson, C. (1954) *The History of Unilever: A Study in Economic Growth and Social Change*, Cassell, paperback edition, 1970.

Zeldin, T. (1980) *France 1848–1945: Taste and Corruption*, Oxford University Press.

9 FROM SANITARY REFORM TO SOCIAL WELFARE

Noel Coley

This essay is concerned with the ways in which community activity to prevent disease and promote health developed in Britain between 1870 and 1950, with some comparisons with other countries, especially Germany and America. Active concern for public health in Britain dates from the 1840s, though it was not until the 1870s that the applications of science and technology to public-health problems began to be significant. Most public-health measures since then have been based on an amalgam of preventive medicine and public hygiene with varying emphasis, but their implementation has often been limited by technological feasibility. There is also dichotomy and sometimes conflict between the reasonable demands which can be made of local authorities and central government for the provision of health care and preventive measures, and those precautions which individuals can fairly be expected to take for themselves. Thus, while local authorities provide adequate clean water supplies and sewerage systems, clean the streets, remove refuse, control local markets and investigate 'nuisances', individuals should endeavour to protect themselves as far as possible against preventable diseases. These aspects of public health are obviously linked.

In 1870 it was generally thought that the solution of public-health problems depended on improved sanitation provided by large-scale civil engineering projects. Later, science and medicine began to play an ever increasing part. With the rise of bacteriology following the discoveries of Pasteur and Koch in the 1880s, the germ theory assumed importance in the fight against communicable diseases. There was a revival of interest in aspects of the urban environment such as cleanliness, good housing, fresh air and open spaces. The isolation and care of the sick was seen to be an essential protective measure for rich and poor alike, since all classes present a common front to the threat of infection. Moreover the social aspects of public-health measures were slowly realized. Wage levels, housing, nutrition and conditions in the home and at work, all play a part in determining the general health of a community. These points were re-emphasized at the beginning of the present century, and the evolution of public health from basic sanitary measures to environmental health and the wider concerns of social medicine can be seen in all the major Western countries (especially in Scandinavia) during our period.

While public-health measures protect the population as a whole, social medicine seeks to teach vulnerable individuals the art of healthy living both for their own benefit and as a means of protecting other members of the community. Experience showed it was easier to enforce preventive measures than to train individual patients with chronic communicable diseases to conduct themselves so that they did not constitute a health hazard. This was particularly necessary for tubercular patients who had to be shown how best to avoid infecting others. Mortality from tuberculosis was already falling in the 1850s, at least thirty years earlier than for other major infections (Figure 9.1). From the late nineteenth century clinics were set up where tubercular patients could receive help and advice, sanatoria where they could be treated and centres for re-training and employment. Tuberculosis, a scourge of the industrial era, was one of the first diseases to receive such attention, but it was slowly realized that patients with certain non-communicable conditions like rheumatism, cancer and heart disease also needed support.

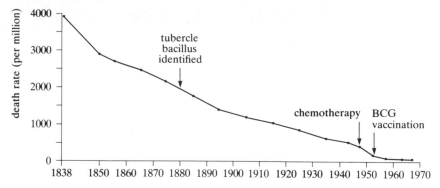

Figure 9.1
Respiratory tuberculosis –
mean annual death rate:
England and Wales.
(Reproduced from
T. McKeown and
C.R. Blackwell, 1974, An
Introduction to Social
Medicine, *Blackwell by*
permission of the publishers)

Between 1870 and 1950 too, infant mortality was reduced as a result of improved sanitation and medical care, while child welfare clinics were established where mothers were helped and advised. In addition to these medical concerns, advocates of social medicine also recognized the need to alleviate poverty by providing financial assistance. At first this depended on the generosity of wealthy philanthropists and charities, but from the beginning of the twentieth century it became part of public welfare.

Hospitals also underwent a marked change during our period. In 1870 most hospitals were charitable institutions supported by the community and served by local doctors. Often they were dirty, the patients were poorly cared for and the death-rate from gangrene and septicaemia in surgical cases was high. Improvements had begun already in the 1840s with the discovery of anaesthetics, while in Britain Lister introduced the use of antiseptics from about 1865 and Florence Nightingale began the training and organization of nurses about 1860. But before these improvements, surgical operations were very dangerous and even when successful the chances of survival were usually low. Listerism not only increased the prospects of recovery after operations to correct compound fractures and other necessary surgery, but it also allowed surgical intervention in cases which had previously been beyond such help. The introduction of anaesthetics coupled with Listerism made relatively safe extended surgery possible. However, this required expensive special equipment so that in Britain, especially after the introduction of the National Health Insurance scheme in 1911, hospitals were increasingly financed by and brought under the control of local health authorities. Medical work in hospitals became divorced from general practice and hospital doctors specialized in treating particular medical conditions – an important and controversial development in medical practice.

9.1 THE SANITARIAN APPROACH

The rapid growth of towns such as Manchester, Liverpool and Glasgow in nineteenth-century Britain created a vast complex of problems, while the cholera epidemics of 1831 and 1848–49 caused public concern about the health of the urban environment. Overcrowding coupled with *laissez-faire* policies, lethargy and lack of will by local authorities in the face of apparently insuperable technical difficulties and inadequate financial resources compounded the difficulties. In this daunting situation the question of which problem to attack first seemed almost unanswerable. Better housing, sanitation, street paving and cleansing were all needed together with provision for the removal of domestic and industrial waste. The sanitarians urged large-scale efforts to clean up the urban environment in the belief that public-health problems would prove amenable to technical solutions. The first priorities were to provide improved sewage disposal and a safe water supply, and in Britain a start was made on some of these problems in the 1840s as a result of pressure for reform from men like J.P. Kay in Manchester and

Edwin Chadwick in London. Chadwick, who was neither a sanitary engineer nor a medical man, accepted the prevailing *miasma* theory of the origins of disease, which said that infectious diseases were caused by bad smells from the drains or from putrefying organic matter in the streets. Chadwick argued that the control of public-health facilities should be in the hands of professionals, who besides organizing the environmental clean-up would also investigate nuisances caused by tanneries, abattoirs and similar establishments.

Chadwick's proposed reforms arose out of his work as a Commissioner for the 1834 Poor Law Amendment Act, which had convinced him of the direct links between an insanitary environment, poor living and working conditions and health. He realized that cleanliness was impossible while water supplies remained so defective. Yet, since wealth and prosperity afforded no immunity from the attacks of epidemic disease, it was in the interests of the rich to pay attention to improvements in the living conditions of the poor. It is doubtful if Chadwick realized the enormous scale of the administrative and technological problems involved in the reforms he proposed. Nevertheless in the three decades following his *Report on the Sanitary Conditions of the Labouring Population of Great Britain* (1842), a start was made on some of his proposals in many of the larger towns, so that by the 1870s improvements in the urban environment were already evident, although there were still too many low-quality dwellings and the services provided were inadequate and patchy. Moreover, while Chadwick's idea of removing human and domestic waste in currents of water undoubtedly cleaned up many towns in Britain, and made an important contribution to improving environmental hygiene, the sewage so produced still required treatment to make it safe. At first this was not done and the sewage flowed untreated into rivers and the sea. This soon became unacceptable and methods of treating the sewage were introduced later in the nineteenth century as chemical and bacteriological techniques improved.

In many towns in 1870 water supplies were inadequate. The urban poor, living in overcrowded conditions in courts or back-to-back houses, had access to running water only at a standpipe in the cellar, or in the court outside, and even then the supply was often intermittent. While by 1870 many of the old privies had been replaced by water closets, it was often the case that large numbers of poor people were forced to share their use. Houses were still built too close together with inadequate access to light and fresh air, often lacking a proper damp-course. Even after cholera, typhoid, typhus and other endemic diseases had been tackled, there was still the silent scourge of the nineteenth century, tuberculosis. Of course this disease was not confined to the working class, nor was it found only in the towns. Nevertheless, inadequate diet combined with long working hours in factory or mill and the adverse effects of damp, ill-ventilated homes, certainly helped to spread it among the workers.

Improvements needed to raise the standards of sanitation and hygiene in the environment are always costly, but in mid-nineteenth-century Britain the magnitude of the problem was immense. Since the majority of working people were too poor to make any but the most token contribution, the major cost of any improvements fell on factory owners, employers and the upper classes generally. Realizing this and that the only arguments likely to impress those prominent on local councils were economic ones, Chadwick pointed out that expenditure on the pauper and the cost of preventing disease were two sides of a single problem and he reiterated this in his efforts to promote public-health reforms. But sound as many of his proposals were, they had the drawback of being influenced by the dominant ideas of the Poor Law. To be poor was regarded as an avoidable offence caused by some inadequacy in the victim which could be cured by harsh treatment. Thus, the nineteenth-century workhouse in Britain was a place of last resort designed as a deterrent to prevent people from applying for help.

The 1870s in Britain saw the introduction of several important public-health measures. In 1871 the Local Government Board was established with responsibility for Poor Law operation as well as public-health control, and in the following year the country was divided into sanitary areas which later became urban and rural districts each under the control of its own local council. Then in 1875 came the Public Health Act, a comprehensive charter for environmental hygiene bringing together all the reforms of the preceding forty years. Its main objectives were to secure wholesome and sufficient water supplies, provide sewerage systems, regulate streets and new buildings, control the health of existing dwellings, remove nuisances, regulate markets, inspect food and provide sanitary burial. The control of public health under central legislation and the codification of nineteenth-century sanitarian ideals were embodied in this Act. But the passing of laws was only the first step; their translation into action was in the hands of local authorities with wide powers of discretion. The success with which the laws were implemented was a result of the administrative ability of men like John Simon, Medical Officer of Health for the City of London from 1848 to 1855 and later MO to the Privy Council until 1876. Characteristically, Simon recognized the value of civil engineers in designing and constructing urban sanitary improvements and he admitted that their work in this area was as important as that of the medical profession.

While these developments were occurring in Britain, Max von Pettenkofer, professor of hygiene in Munich from 1865, studied the relationships between the health of the urban community and the influence of the environment. He investigated the effects of soil, ground water and the atmosphere on health, noting especially conditions which favoured the incidence of cholera. Like Chadwick, Pettenkofer tried to convince reluctant authorities of the need for reform on economic grounds. He founded an Institute of Hygiene in Munich in 1866 and six years later gave two popular lectures on 'The value of health to a city' which influenced sanitary reform in Munich. In these lectures he outlined the material losses caused by disease and the savings which health measures could bring. Unfortunately, Pettenkofer's reputation was marred among his contemporaries because he refused to accept the germ theory and the role of micro-organisms in disease. Despite this, Pettenkofer was by far the most influential health expert of the late nineteenth century. He introduced the term 'social hygiene', though he used it to mean public health.

The first textbook of social hygiene was published in France in 1888 by Jules Rochard who wrote, 'Hygiene is pre-eminent among the social sciences. It is directly associated with all the problems which concern the life of the people . . . health and prosperity go hand in hand . . . Any expenditure incurred in the name of health is money well-spent' (Rochard, 1888, quoted in Sand, pp.207–08).

Rochard was writing some forty or fifty years after his fellow-countryman Louis Villermé had studied the health of workers in the textile mills at Mulhouse near the German border, which led about 1850 to one of the first industrial housing developments in Europe financed by the employers. At the World Exhibition of 1889 in Paris, part of the social economy section was devoted to aspects of social hygiene.

These developments were quickly followed in Germany where social hygiene was often interpreted in public-health terms. In 1890 Max Rubner, professor of hygiene in Berlin, vigorously condemned slum housing, malnutrition, overwork and inadequate wages. In Germany the increasing interest in social hygiene was also connected with growing concern about falling birth-rates.

In America public-health reforms were pioneered by Lemuel Shattuck, a bookseller and publisher in the small town of Concord, Massachusetts, who had a keen interest in social welfare, demographic statistics and health problems. In 1845, at the request of the town council, he made a fuller census of the town than anything previously attempted. This work alerted him to the need for improvements in public health and he later became a member of the sanitary commission appointed to survey the entire state. In 1850 Shattuck published the results of this survey of the sanitary conditions of Massachusetts in a report which was as much a landmark for public health in America as Chadwick's was for Britain. It recommended the revision of sanitary legislation, together with the appointment of a Central Board and local Boards of Health which would conduct investigations, publish annual reports, organize land drainage, sewerage, control road paving and cleansing, issue building licences and establish cemeteries. Shattuck's report contained fifty recommendations based on sanitarian principles. The era of sanitary reform brought in by Chadwick and Shattuck called for engineers, architects, chemists and administrators, and as sanitary science became an increasingly specialized subject, doctors gradually lost interest.

While Massachusetts pioneered advances in American public health, other states lagged behind, but from 1857 onwards public health in the United States was promoted by the National Sanitary Convention inaugurated by William Jewell of Philadelphia. Like the Health of Towns Association in Britain this provided a forum for doctors and non-medical workers. In 1872 the American Public Health Association was founded and Shattuck's work was continued by others who brought about the acceptance and implementation of the sanitary programme. As bacteriology assumed greater importance a state laboratory for Massachusetts was founded in 1895 under the control of Theobald Smith, a leading American bacteriologist who directed the preparation of large quantities of diphtheria antitoxin and vaccine lymph ready for use in an emergency. He also supervised many bacteriological tests at a time when these were novel and so made some important discoveries.

**9.2
WATER SUPPLY**

The provision of a safe water supply is essential to any satisfactory system of public-health control. In most primitive systems and places lacking surface or ground water sources, rainwater was collected from the roofs of buildings or specially paved areas. The water was stored in closed containers, but no matter how carefully the collecting surfaces and storage vessels were maintained, the water would not be safe for drinking without treatment. Rivers were also often used as sources of water supply in the nineteenth century, but here too pollution with dissolved and foreign matter was an ever-increasing problem. In many large towns the same river was used both as a means of sewage and industrial waste disposal and as a source of drinking water. For greater safety water had to be collected from such rivers at points well above the town as near to the source of the river as possible. This often meant constructing a dam to impound water in a man-made reservoir. In the 1850s and 1860s this was done at several places in the Pennines to collect water for towns such as Sheffield and Huddersfield. Unfortunately, the techniques used to construct these dams were the same as those used by eighteenth-century canal engineers to build very much smaller reservoirs to maintain water levels in canals. These dams consisted of earthworks with a puddled clay interior and they had insufficient strength to withstand the pressures exerted upon them by the large volumes of water in the new reservoirs. There were some tragic accidents in the 1860s and it became clear that much stronger masonry dams were needed, as for instance at lake Vyrnwy in Wales, completed in 1892. The dams had to be constructed in mountainous areas usually far distant from the towns for which the water supply was intended (for example, Vyrnwy was built to supply Liverpool, about thirty miles away) so that miles of aqueducts and pipelines were required, involving costly large-scale civil-engineering projects.

In towns built on sandstone, gravel or limestone, water could be obtained by sinking wells or boreholes, sometimes to considerable depths. Such water is usually very pure, although it often has to be pumped to the surface. Natural springs have also been used as sources of water supply. They occur where ground water is brought to the surface at the junction of pervious and impervious strata and as the water has filtered through the rocks it is often quite pure, although the yield may be small and in any case varies with the seasons. All of these sources were already in use in various towns by the late nineteenth century, but before water could be used safely for drinking it always needed treatment. Already in the eighteenth century it had been found that if water was allowed to stand it became brighter in appearance as sediment was deposited. For water pumped from wells or taken from natural springs it was necessary to store it for a few days in covered settling tanks, but for water from reservoirs this settling process would have occurred naturally. In some cases a better result was achieved by adding small quantities of coagulants such as aluminium sulphate, which improved the settling process by removing even the finest particles of suspended matter.

After settling the water was clear and bright but it was possible to improve its appearance still further by passing it through filter beds consisting of layers of sand supported on graded gravel over a system of brick, tile or concrete drains. The sand filter was first introduced in 1828 by James Simpson, water engineer to the Chelsea Water Company in London. After the discovery of the germ theory in the 1880s, it was found that in addition to suspended matter many micro-organisms were also removed by the sand layer. In the top 10–25 millimetres a slimy coating of bacteria, algae, worms and insect larvae collects and these living organisms oxidize organic matter and remove germs. The surface layer gradually thickens and begins to retard the flow of water through the filter so that it is necessary to scrape it off and begin again. The slow sand filter was thorough in action, but as demand for good quality water grew in the late nineteenth century, and especially as domestic demand rose with the installation of bathrooms in private houses from the 1920s (earlier in America), it was necessary to speed up the filtration process by applying pressure to force the water through the sand layer. This led to the invention of a new type of sand filter enclosed in a metal container and much smaller than the older gravity-fed filter. For the rapid sand filter to work efficiently it was necessary to add coagulants and the flocculent precipitate which these formed replaced to some extent the action of the biological layer in the slow sand filter. But, though the rapid filter could be made to treat much larger quantities of water under pressure, it was far less efficient in removing germs.

From the beginning of the twentieth century, to ensure the safety of water filtered through rapid sand filters, chlorine or one of its compounds has been used as a germicide. At first this was applied in the form of bleaching powder (chloride of lime), but gaseous chlorine was introduced after about 1905. The quantity of chlorine to be added was measured and adjusted to the rate of flow of the water. The chlorinated water was then passed into the water main at such a rate that a period of half an hour would elapse before it was dechlorinated by passing in the exact amount of sulphur dioxide needed to neutralize the chlorine. As a result, although sulphates were formed in the water, it was left with no unpleasant taste. Another germicide, which was used mainly in France until quite recently, was ozone. Although more expensive than chlorine, ozone rapidly decomposes to oxygen and this has commended the method to those who do not like the idea of drinking 'medicated water'.

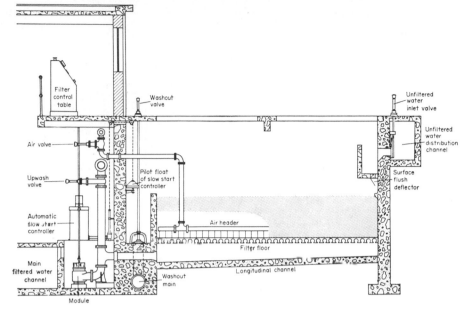

Figure 9.2
Section of a rapid gravity sand filter. In this design the filter bed consists of 0.7m of sand on 0.3m graded gravel. The water level is about 1.4m above the sand during filtration. To wash the filter, the water is lowered to the level of the weir to the left of the bed. Compressed air is admitted to the underdrains and produces intense agitation of the sand. This is followed by an upward flow of water to carry the dirt away through the washout main. (Courtesy of Paterson Candy International Ltd. Reproduced from V. Robson, 1979, The Theory and Practice of Public Health, *Oxford University Press by permission of the publishers)*

After treatment, water must be distributed to consumers through a network of pipes. Throughout our period the pipes laid in the ground conveying water to individual homes (water mains) were made of cast-iron, but domestic water pipes inside the houses were made chiefly of lead. It is of course this use of lead piping in domestic water supply which gave rise to the term 'plumber'. Lead was chosen for its resistance to corrosion and ease of working, but as a toxic substance the use of lead for water pipes was highly dangerous. Indeed, it was only possible because public water supplies were usually hard. That is, they contained dissolved calcium and magnesium salts which would react with the inner surfaces of the pipes coating them with a protective layer of insoluble lead salts. Most of the houses built to the end of the 1930s were fitted with lead water pipes, but after 1945 lead was superseded by copper piping which, besides giving a neater appearance, withstands the force of expansion exerted by the water when it freezes in the pipes during cold weather. While the hardness of the public water supply was a useful safeguard against lead poisoning, it was a nuisance in other respects. Hard water wastes soap by forming scum which sticks to fabrics during laundering and consequently hard water is not very satisfactory in the laundry. Also, when boiled hard water deposits scale in kettles, boilers and hot-water pipes, this wastes fuel and makes hot-water systems inefficient. More seriously it may lead to explosions caused by uneven heating of boilers or the complete clogging of pipes. In the 1930s soap began to be replaced for laundry purposes by synthetic detergents which do not react with the calcium and magnesium salts in hard water, while domestic water softeners depending on ion-exchange processes also became available.

From the first all the pipes carrying the water supply were made to run completely full under pressure, and in nineteenth-century Britain there were many arguments about the feasibility and especially the cost of establishing such a supply of treated water continuously under pressure. The supply was often cut off for many hours during each day, but this was found merely to cause inconvenience without leading to any significant financial savings. In any case, until after the First World War it was the exception rather than the rule for dwellings in the poorer districts to have running water. A standpipe in the cellar or outside in the court was usually considered sufficient.

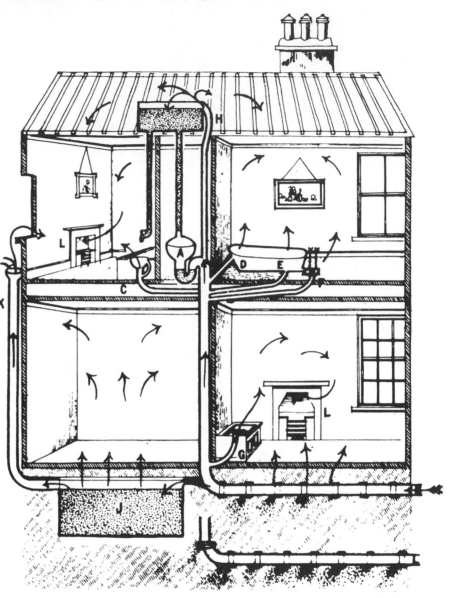

Figure 9.3
'Every sanitary arrangement faulty.' (A) Water-closet in the centre of the house. (B) House drain under floor of a room. (C) Waste-pipe of lavatory – untrapped and passing into soil-pipe of WC, thus allowing a direct channel for sewer gas to be drawn by the fires (LL) into the house. (D) Over-flow pipe of bath untrapped and passing into soil-pipe. (F) Save-all tray below taps untrapped and passing into soil-pipe. (G) Kitchen sink untrapped and passing into soil-pipe. (H) Water-closet cistern with over-flow into soil-pipe of WC, thus ventilating the drain into the roof, polluting the air of the house, and polluting the water in the cistern, which also forms the water-supply of the house for drinking and washing. (J) Rain-water tank under floor, with over-flow into drain. (K) Fall-pipe conducting foul air from tank fouled by drain gas, and delivering it just below a window. (L) Drain under house with uncemented joints leaking; also a defective junction of vertical soil-pipe with horizontal drain; the drain laid without proper fall. (From T.P. Teale, 1879, Dangers to Health. A Pictorial Guide to Domestic Sanitary Defects, J.A. Churchill)

Domestic hot water for washing or the bath was obtained by heating water in pots and pans over the fire or in a 'copper', a large hemispherical cast-iron container set into a brick stove in the basement or outhouse. Already by the 1850s gas had begun to be used for heating water in the home and many attempts were made to devise safe domestic gas heaters. More common was the hot-water boiler built into the kitchen range. Some early forms of gas heaters for bath water used the bath itself as the water vessel with the gas jets beneath it, but about 1868 the gas geyser was invented. At first this was a dangerous device and there were many accidents before it was made safe enough for ordinary domestic use. Nevertheless the performance of some of these early gas geysers compares well with modern standards. The flush toilet also evolved to more or less its modern form during the nineteenth century, especially after 1870 when methods of providing an adequate water-flush and an efficient trap to prevent bad air seeping into the house from the sewers were introduced. If not installed efficiently, plumbing could have significant ill effects on health – a fact pointed out by the surgeon T.P. Teale in his *Pictorial Guide to Domestic Sanitary Defects* (1879). The evolution of a safe system of domestic plumbing for hot and cold water, bath, wash-basin and flush toilet was slow, but by the turn of the century internal plumbing had become common in the homes of the upper classes.

Soon after the First World War very large numbers of enamelled baths and wash-basins were being manufactured to be installed not only in newly-built houses, but also in existing properties. Town houses had been built from the 1860s with the idea of dependence on the domestic servant in mind, but life styles changed as a result of the war and in the 1920s it was no longer easy to find domestic servants willing to toil up and down the stairs with buckets of coal, cans of water or trays of food (Wright, 1960, p.258). Other arrangements for running the home were needed. Properly plumbed bathrooms were available, but it was often impossible to fit them neatly into existing houses without major alterations or additional building and many houses remained without. In any case, as little space as possible seems generally to have been allocated to the bathroom; portable baths were often used instead. Even as late as 1958 a housing survey in Morley, Yorkshire showed that 50 per cent of older houses built before 1920 had no fixed bath and 30 per cent shared a lavatory, while in the Gorbals in Glasgow less than one house in four had a lavatory and only one in thirty a bath. In the same year a report by the inspectors of the West German Baths Society showed that in 200 homes surveyed there were only three fixed baths. In America by contrast, about 80 per cent of all homes had a bath by 1958 (Wright, 1960, p.263).

(a)

(b)

(c)

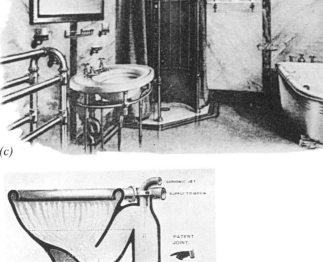

(d)

Figure 9.4
Contemporary illustrations from Lawrence Wright, 1960, Clean and Decent, *Routledge by permission of the publishers:*
(a) washstand, 1895; (b) improved spray bath, 1882; (c) 'model bathroom', 1902; (d) syphonic 'Closet of the Century', 1900.

**9.3
SEWERAGE**

While the provision of a safe water supply was one achievement of the Sanitarian Movement, Chadwick had seen this as an essential complement to an adequate system of sewerage. As urbanization rapidly developed, there was at first no other available solution to the problem of human waste disposal than the cesspit which, while perhaps less obnoxious in the country where the population density was relatively low, was at best a very primitive expedient. Together with the many open sewers and drains in the towns, cesspits or middens constituted a serious health hazard, especially where they were placed too near to a well from which water for washing and drinking was drawn. From the early years of the nineteenth century, large urban centres such as London had possessed some primitive underground sewers, but most of these were brick built, poorly designed and little more hygienic than the thousands of cesspits with which the towns were riddled. Chadwick had emphasized the importance of removing human and domestic waste in currents of water running in self-cleansing sewers. From the 1850s such sewerage systems were adopted by many towns in Britain after the exposure of disgraceful urban conditions in so many places in the Report of the Town Commissioners about 1847.

Most nineteenth-century sewerage systems were intended to carry not only domestic waste but also rainwater run-off from the streets, including flood-water thrown down suddenly during heavy rain and storms. The volumes of foul water carried by the sewers in such combined systems therefore varied enormously, but as the whole was disposed of untreated such variations were relatively unimportant. In fact these early sewerage systems merely succeeded in transferring the problem of pollution from the urban environment to the rivers and coastal waters of the sea. It had not been sufficiently realized that the initial removal of sewage from the vicinity of dwellings was only the first stage of the sanitary process and one that would cause immense pollution problems elsewhere unless it was complemented by methods of treating the sewage to make it safe. Even in Bazalgette's monumental drainage scheme for London, completed about 1866, the sewage was discharged untreated into the sea, but before the construction of this system was complete it became clear that the sewage would have to be rendered harmless if it were not to prove a health hazard, and in the last two decades of the nineteenth century bacteriological methods of sewage treatment began to be developed.

In one early form of sewage disposal, the sewerage farm, the liquid effluent was run over the surface of agricultural land. This purified the sewage to some extent by the oxidizing action of aerobic bacteria while providing water and organic nutrients for growing plants. Stringent precautions were necessary and the method, which had been advocated by Chadwick, required very large areas of land. As the quantities of sewage to be treated increased attempts were made to concentrate the method of land treatment in carefully selected smaller areas. In the late 1880s continuous biological filtration through coarse gravel was introduced, a method which now shares the field of aerobic sewage treatment with the activated sludge process. Both depend on the oxidation of organic matter by aerobic bacteria. In the biological filtration process the bacteria form a layer on the surface of the small stones over which the sewage percolates continuously, while in the activated sludge process, introduced in 1914, the bacteria are kept suspended by continuous agitation within the liquid. This process yields higher quality effluents than percolating filters; it also needs less space, but being more mechanized its operators require more skill.

Standards of purity for the effluents from sewage works were laid down in 1912 by a Royal Commission on Sewage Disposal and these have served as a guide in Britain ever since. In cases where a large sewage works discharged its effluent into a relatively small stream, however, further purification was often necessary. In this respect the activated sludge process was found to be more successful than the percolating filter method, but it was less able to cope with sudden influxes of *industrial* effluents. This has been a growing problem throughout our period. One difficulty was caused in the 1940s and 1950s by the growing use of synthetic detergents in industry, laundries and the home. These substances dissolve readily in water while reducing the solubility of oxygen so that the action of aerobic bacteria is inhibited. It therefore became necessary to modify the chemical structures of these detergents so that they would not affect the operation of sewage works. Since the treatment of effluents involved biological methods affecting organic matter, mineral impurities such as metal salts passed through without change and where these were poisonous, as for example mercury salts, they constituted a serious health risk. It was necessary to ensure that effluents from sewage works were safe, and in this respect the chemical analyst played a most important role in maintaining the safety of the public.

9.4 URBAN WASTE DISPOSAL

Street cleansing and the removal of domestic waste from the urban environment was also advocated by the sanitarians and has been practised in towns and cities since the mid-nineteenth century. Collected at first in open carts often by private contractors acting on behalf of the local authorities, this material was tipped on to suitable sites where it was used to build up the land.

(a)

(b)

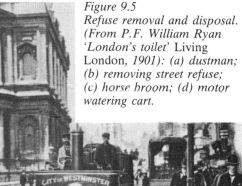

Figure 9.5
*Refuse removal and disposal.
(From P.F. William Ryan
'London's toilet' Living
London, 1901): (a) dustman;
(b) removing street refuse;
(c) horse broom; (d) motor
watering cart.*

(c)   (d)

But in addition to such public services there have always been individuals who have earned a living by scavenging. The value of waste materials has often allowed the 'rag-and-bone man', the gypsy and the tinker, to scratch a living from collecting scrap metal, old clothes and other domestic rubbish.

In urban refuse collection the main technological developments have been in the design of hygienic waste collection vehicles and in the treatment of waste at collection depots. Methods of tipping in a controlled manner known as 'sanitary land-fill' were developed to avoid unsightliness and nuisance; to reduce the risk of fire and to discourage rats and flies. Sometimes waste was incinerated and pulverized before tipping, but in Britain since the end of the nineteenth century about 80 per cent of all refuse has been tipped directly on to the land without previous treatment. Experience has shown that properly controlled refuse tipping may be neither offensive nor unsightly while being useful in reclaiming low-lying or irregular areas of land for agriculture, playing fields, parks and even for house building. During the period between 1870 and 1950 the content of urban domestic waste changed significantly. At first it consisted largely of ashes from domestic coal-fires with some vegetable and animal matter. Up to the 1930s street cleansing involved the removal of large quantities of horse dung but after the Second World War this declined sharply with the increased use of motor vehicles. On the other hand the quantities of glass and metal in the form of bottles, jars and food cans steadily increased, as did the amount of paper and other packaging material including plastic wrappers and containers which have proved particularly troublesome. The trend has therefore been to separate out these items mechanically or by hand for special treatment or re-cycling. Economic arguments have always been at least as persuasive as social and medical ones in securing sanitary improvements. It was important to find profitable uses for domestic waste products so as to reduce the cost to the community of essential sanitary services. The balancing of costs and benefits in this field has always been a matter of prime concern.

**9.5
HOUSING**

Perhaps the most important of all public-health measures relate to the standards applied to house building. These include the density of housing, provision of sanitation, adequate light and air and minimum standards of quality for all aspects of the builder's craft which can be inspected and controlled by local authorities with legal powers of enforcement. In many countries, notably Germany, Britain and America, doctors, health experts and philanthropists joined forces to undertake investigations mainly concerned with the problem of tuberculosis. Efforts were made to educate public opinion, stimulate the authorities and generally promote improved public-health provision in their areas. It was widely realized that housing exerts an important influence on morality, family life and the education and future prospects of the young as well as on health. Bad housing may be defective for many reasons. It may be poorly situated so that the inhabitants get too little light and air and too much smoke, dust, wind, industrial pollution or noise. It may be badly built, inadequately equipped or unhealthy because of age or lack of repair. It may be overcrowded or situated in an unhealthy district. All of these conditions existed in various parts of almost every major town or city in the industrialized world in 1870.

The housing policies which were a feature of the period were always co-ordinated with sanitary measures. In Britain the Artisans Dwellings Act of 1875 laid down standards for working-class houses and made provision for the condemnation of sub-standard housing, but too often nothing was done even when houses had been condemned because there were too many local authorities to be consulted before effective action could be taken. The Housing of the Working Classes Act of 1890 simplified the procedures, required MOHs to report on insanitary houses and gave local authorities powers, with appeal to the courts, of demolition and closure as well as the right to build council housing for rent. One of the earliest public housing schemes was started in 1890 by the LCC with its Boundary Street Estate in Bethnal Green. But besides such public-housing developments in all parts of Britain throughout the remainder of our period, there were also some important company housing schemes. Of these Bournville in Birmingham, founded by George Cadbury, the chocolate manufacturer, for his workers in 1879, is still cited as a model of town planning, while Port Sunlight near Liverpool, a model village complete with an Art Gallery, was established in 1888 for the workers in Lever Brothers soap factory. In 1911, of almost 9 million houses in Britain, 89 per cent were rented from private landlords, 10 per cent were owner-occupied and only 1 per cent were rented from councils or new town corporations. Forty years later in 1951 there were almost 14 million houses and the relevant proportions were 52.5 per cent, 29.5 per cent and 18 per cent respectively.

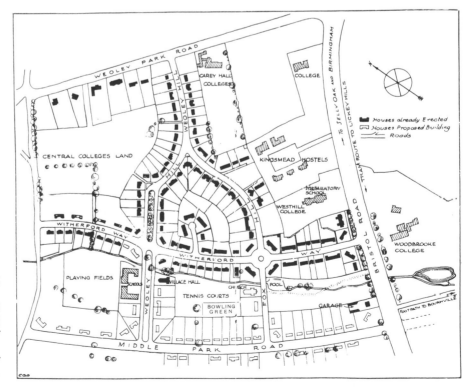

*Figure 9.6
Bournville Estate,
Birmingham: Weoley Hill
Estate: junction of Fox Hill
and Weoley Hill; plan of
Weoley Hill Estate.
(Reproduced by permission of
the Bournville Village Trust)*

Figure 9.7
Air pollution: Southwark area
of London 1914. Note the
atmospheric pollution caused
by the emission of coal smoke
from hundreds of domestic
chimneys in this densely
populated area. (Photo:
Greater London Record
Office)

In Germany at Essen, where Krupps also provided workers' housing, one motive was to reconcile their employees to their social status by welfare policies. In the 1880s pioneering legislation was brought in for medical and accident insurance as well as invalid and old age pensions (Bohme, 1978, p.81).

Sadly there were many places where serious faults in housing were still uncorrected in 1950, despite the fact that standards were laid down time and again by national and international bodies, including the League of Nations Health Organisation and the International Labour Office in the period between the wars. While the standards proposed differed according to climate, national customs and life styles, natural resources, the prosperity of the regions for which they were intended and the urban, industrial or rural character of the locality, they all took account of a set of basic requirements. These were governed by the need to secure adequate light and air as well as labour-saving arrangements inside the dwellings for heating, lighting, cooking, washing, cleaning and the storage of food. Sanitary and safety regulations were laid down along with provisions for adequate space and facilities for family life in pleasant surroundings, including a garden or proximity to a park. In the period between the wars some 3 million houses were built in Germany largely by public enterprises; by contrast, in Britain 4 million were built mainly by private concerns. This brought about a rise in the general quality of workers' housing with some reduction in rents, but little was done to solve the problems of the slums. It was necessary to force local authorities to survey slums in their areas and submit plans for demolition and reconstruction. This activity was brought to a halt at the outbreak of war in 1939 and many problem areas remained untouched apart from bomb damage, until long after the war had ended.

At the end of the nineteenth century social reformers focused attention on improving the living and working conditions of ordinary people. In Britain early surveys were made by Charles Booth in a massive seventeen-volume study of the *Life and Labour of the People of London* (1899–1903), and by Seebohm Rowntree in his study of conditions in York entitled *Poverty, a Study of Town Life* (1901). These works made clear that housing was not merely a question of providing reasonably priced, sanitary living accommodation, desirable as that was. It should also be made possible for the occupants to enjoy all the advantages of community life and for that an integrated plan was required. This marked the beginning of the study of town planning and urban development. The idea of the garden city was proposed by Ebeneezer Howard in 1898. He suggested the planning of complete towns on open sites wholly owned by the town council with full control over the distribution of land between agriculture, urban development, transport, industry and other uses, co-ordinated in the most rational and pleasing manner. The first such new town to be built was begun at Letchworth in 1902 and in the same year Howard's book, *Garden Cities of Tomorrow*, was published. This was translated into many languages, and societies for encouraging the building of garden cities were established in various European countries and in America. Often developments were restricted to 'garden suburbs' attached to existing towns, an idea quite different from Howard's vision, but the town of Radburn in New Jersey was built on Howard's plan with the added advantage of being specially designed to minimize the danger and inconvenience caused by the problem of motor traffic mingling with pedestrians. In Britain between the wars Howard's ideas were invoked as a means of controlling the rapid and apparently unlimited growth of London by establishing satellite towns on the outskirts, but such planned development remained the exception rather than the rule. In general little control was exerted over the purchase of land or the planning of streets and houses, although each successive building control Act introduced improvements to the regulations controlling house design and construction. Thus, after the 1936 Housing Act houses built in Britain were required to have adequate toilet facilities including a water closet. To comply with this regulation while at the same time satisfying growing public demand most local authorities thereafter built houses for rent which included a bathroom as a standard feature.

9.6 POLLUTION OF THE ATMOSPHERE

Pollution of the environment was an inevitable consequence of crowding people and industry into limited space in nineteenth-century towns and most important public-health measures arose from the need to control it. In the first half of the century pollution of water and of the urban environment by human domestic and industrial waste constituted some of the chief problems, as we have already seen, but there was also a massive amount of atmospheric pollution. In the 'Black Country' north of Birmingham for instance, iron and steel furnaces belched out vast clouds of thick smoke contaminating the atmosphere with soot and dust; further north the same was true of the many pottery kilns. Similar problems were common wherever industry developed. They are found in Saxony from the 1840s and later in the Ruhr, or near Cleveland in America. After 1830 in Britain, and later in Europe and America, the railways also added their quota of smoke and atmospheric pollution, while in the crowded urban areas domestic coal-fires poured out smoke and sulphurous gases. In Britain the Railway Clauses Act of 1845 and Town Improvement Act of 1847 required locomotives and furnaces to consume their own smoke, and these requirements were written into the Public Health Act of 1875 with some practical results. Until 1926 the emission of smoke from industrial chimneys was controlled by the provisions of the 1875 Act, although more stringent regulations were introduced for London in 1891.

In 1926 modifications concerned with industrial smoke abatement were introduced in Britain but did not apply to domestic fires. One reason for this was that supplies of smokeless domestic fuels were inadequate. This situation continued until the mid-twentieth century.

The commonest domestic fuels up to about 1950 were wood, coal and peat. In America oil was also used. At the temperatures reached in domestic burners the combustion of these fuels was not complete and large amounts of solid carbon were emitted as smoke and soot. By contrast, in properly stoked industrial furnaces combustion was more complete, although the quantities of gaseous combustion products such as the oxides of carbon and

sulphur, were greater. Much of this material escaped into the atmosphere to
be dispersed over the surrounding area either as soot or in the form of
acidified rain. During the winter months especially, when every house in the
town was emitting these products, a dirty atmosphere was created giving rise
to fog and causing or aggravating bronchial diseases among the people. The
London 'smog' of 1952, intensified by these atmospheric pollutants is said to
have caused about 3,000 deaths (Table 9.1) and comparable increases in
mortality have been recorded in other cases. Bronchitic and related diseases
have always been more common in towns than in the country.

**Table 9.1 Deaths registered in London Administrative County for the smog episode
of 1952**

Cause of death	Number of deaths		Ratio a/b
	(a) Week of smog	(b) Week before smog	
Bronchitis	704	74	9.3
Respiratory tuberculosis	77	14	5.5
Influenza and pneumonia	192	47	4.1
Other respiratory diseases	52	9	4.8
Coronary disease and myocardial degeneration	525	206	2.6
All other conditions	934	595	1.6
Total	2,484	945	2.6

(Source: McKeown and Lowe, 1974, p.166)

Buildings in towns showed the effects of atmospheric pollution as they
became dirty and the acid rain caused damage over long periods of time.
The scale of this problem was considerable and increased throughout the
period. The idea of the 'smokeless zone' was introduced in some residential
areas in Britain as early as 1927, but it was not until 1956 that the first Clean
Air Act prohibited the emission of dark smoke entirely in areas designated
as smokeless zones. It must also be remembered that the technologies
concerned with the manufacture and use of smokeless fuels in the domestic
situation had to be developed before smokeless zones could be successfully
established and enforced. Advocates of smoke abatement strongly favoured
electricity as a clean fuel, but unfortunately in Britain the cost of electricity
for domestic purposes remained high and its use was therefore restricted.

In America there was agitation for the control of smoke emission from
the last quarter of the nineteenth century, especially in the Midwest where
the main fuel was a highly volatile, bituminous coal which produced large
amounts of sulphurous smoke and soot. In Chicago in 1881 an ordinance
was passed which stated that the emission of dense black smoke from the
smokestack of any boat or locomotive or from any chimney anywhere within
the city would be considered a public nuisance. The penalty for violation
was to be a fine of up to $50. This was the first attempt to control smoke
emissions in the United States but within a few years similar ordinances were
adopted by several other cities. Early in the twentieth century a survey was
made in Pittsburgh to estimate the damage caused by smoke and its cost to
the people. The results showed that the annual cost of smoke to each resident
of Pittsburgh amounted to $15–$20. This included waste of fuel, the cost of
laundry and cleaning, damage to clothing, furnishings and the merchandise
in stores, the cost of extra artificial lighting and of the repair of damage to
the exterior of buildings. The latter was caused mainly by 'acid rain' formed

when the sulphuric acid produced from the burning of sulphur and its compounds in the coal was washed out of the atmosphere by rain. In the 1920s and 1930s there was more agitation for stricter controls over the emission of soot, fly ash and cinders, and towards the end of 1939 the American Society of Mechanical Engineers set up a model smoke-law committee which deliberated for a decade until at last in 1949, some recommendations were published which were used as a guide by many cities in revising their smoke abatement ordinances. Despite all this activity, however, the first Federal air pollution control programme was not introduced in the United States until 1955, just one year before the Clean Air Act in Britain.

**9.7
THE RISE OF THE
PUBLIC ANALYST**

While the need to clean up the urban environment and provide more sanitary living conditions was clear by the mid-nineteenth century, there were other ways in which the town dweller could be at a serious disadvantage. Take diet for example. Since most forms of manual work were heavy and laborious, workers needed good food to maintain health and vigour. The quantity of meat available to the urban worker in nineteenth-century Britain has been discussed by economic historians but the real problem concerned its quality. Meat was sold in several grades of which the poorer urban workers could afford only the lowest, cheap offal and sometimes even diseased meat. Until 1912, street vendors of food, unlike other market and street traders, were not licensed and so there was no effective control of the quality of foods, including meat, offered for sale. In the 1860s, after the introduction of legislation to control the situation, the number of prosecutions for selling bad or diseased meat increased. In 1865–66, for example, large quantities of diseased meat were seized in London following an outbreak of cattle plague. However, the fines permitted when an offender was successfully prosecuted were not heavy enough to discourage the trade in sub-standard foodstuffs, and the quantities of bad meat as well as fish, vegetables, fruit and poultry on sale in the markets were enormous in spite of efforts to control the situation. By the early years of the present century market traders were being prosecuted for selling bad meat but the prosecutor was required to produce the whole diseased carcase, whereas usually only parts of any one carcase were displayed on traders' stalls. This made the successful prosecution of offenders extremely difficult.

In nineteenth-century Britain bacon was the meat most commonly eaten by the working class and the poor because it could be bought in small quantities and, being cured, it kept better than other meats. The pig was an important source of meat for the town dweller, who often kept one to fatten up on domestic scraps and slaughter privately. Butchers too, would keep them in their slaughter yards to consume offal which they could not sell. Though pigs were especially prone to anthrax this does not appear to have prevented the consumption of their meat. Food poisoning was not uncommon in Britain and in view of the fact that bacon would still be eaten when it had begun to smell, or showed black spots because of anthrax, it was fortunate that this meat was generally used as a flavouring and not as a main course. When a sample of meat had become putrid, or otherwise unfit to eat, it would often be boiled or converted into some form of cooked meat such as brawn in the belief that heat-treatment would render the meat safe.

From the 1860s in America the processing of meat for human consumption began to be mechanized; factory farming techniques were introduced to produce meat on the hoof at a sufficient rate for the mechanized slaughter houses working on a conveyor-belt system. Poorer quality meat was sent to be canned while better cuts were frozen and packed for export. The centre for this trade in America was Chicago. In the 1880s frozen beef from the

Argentine began to appear in the shops in Britain, but like canned meat from Australia this was not cheap and remained relatively unpopular.

Bread was another item of diet which varied widely in quality. The adulteration of bread began with the flour to which rice flour, oatmeal, barley meal and even sawdust was added. Bakers also traditionally added alum to whiten the loaf. It was commonly thought that the cheaper the bread the more alum it contained, but Dr John Snow showed that this was not so and that the fashionable Regent Street shops sold a very white bread which contained over an ounce of alum in each loaf. In the 1850s Arthur Hill Hassall showed how the microscope could be used to detect adulteration and his methods were incorporated into the Sale of Food and Drugs Act of 1875, but chemical and microscopical analysis were still far from incontestable and clever counsel were adept at finding loopholes which would get their clients acquitted. After 1875 in Britain, alum and sawdust were no longer used in bread, a fact which may be regarded as a triumph for public-health legislation, but bread was still baked in unhygienic conditions and that sold to the poor was often only three-quarters cooked so that it would retain as much of its moisture as possible to add to the weight.

Other items of diet were also suspect. Until 1875 the Chinese 'improved' the appearance of their tea by colouring it with prussian blue (ferric ferrocyanide) which, poison though it was, pleased foreign buyers, including English tea drinkers, with expensive tastes. Cheap tea had often been mixed with hawthorn and elm leaves and even dried *used* tea leaves were also added, but after 1875 tea was tested by the customs department, and by that time most imported tea was genuine although adulteration by retailers was still a possibility. Pickles were often treated with copper salts to give them a brighter green colour. Children's sweets were coloured with copper carbonate, lead carbonate, copper arsenite and lead chromate, while chocolate was often treated with Venetian red (red iron oxide). All these adulterants are, of course, poisonous.

The first law to prevent the adulteration of food and drink was passed in 1860 but it was not effective and a second Adulteration Act was passed two years later which provided for the appointment by local authorities of public analysts, allowed the collection of samples for testing and the establishment of separate policing. In the absence of an unambiguous definition of the meaning of adulteration however, it is not surprising that there were complaints about unjustified prosecutions, and a Select Committee in 1874 proposed that public analysts should meet to discuss the problems of definition and analysis. This meeting was held on 7 August 1874 when the Society of Public Analysts was formed with Theophilus Redwood, professor of chemistry and pharmacy at the Pharmaceutical Society in London, as chairman. But the formation of a learned society did not solve the practical problems, although it did provide a forum for discussion and the possibility of a united voice.

The greatest difficulties in 1875 were that the chemical reagents used in tests were not absolutely pure, while the tests themselves were clumsy and not very reliable. It was to improving these things that the Society of Public Analysts first turned its attention. Two years later in 1877, the Institute of Chemistry was established with the application of chemistry to public-health problems, especially the chemical and microscopical analysis of water, food and drugs, among its stated aims. From the beginning the Institute intended to ensure that those who practised as consulting or analytical chemists would be professionally qualified and it later became the qualifying body for these categories through its grades of Associateship and Fellowship. Eventually in 1899, the Local Government Board agreed to accept the Institute's Certificate in the analysis of water, food and drugs, together with therapeutics, pharmacology and microscopy as a qualification for the many new public analysts' posts which were to be set up under the revised Sale of Food and Drugs Act of 1900. Thus the profession of the public analyst was established and the inspection and testing of food, water samples and drugs became routine practice in public-health laboratories in all the larger towns in Britain.

**9.8
THE DEVELOPMENT
OF SOCIAL MEDICINE**

In 1904 as a result of the investigation of the low standard of physical fitness among army recruits during the Boer War, measures were brought in to protect the health of expectant mothers, infants and schoolchildren by medical examination. These moves strengthened the growing belief in the importance of personal health care as a counterpart to environmental hygiene. Thereafter public-health activities in Britain turned increasingly to the field of social medicine with emphasis on the individual rather than on the community as a whole. Advice centres and antenatal clinics for working-class mothers and children were opened, while nurses were trained for home visiting. These functions were taken on with varying success by the new county and county borough councils set up in 1888. In the early years of the twentieth century more responsibility for health care was devolved to the local councils. In 1902 they began to supervise midwifery services under the Midwives Act, and five years later the larger authorities were made responsible for the school health service which provided for regular medical and dental examination of schoolchildren as well as frequent checks for general cleanliness such as the absence of headlice. In 1908 further controls were placed on the employment of children in factories. Between 1912 and 1918 measures for the control and treatment of tuberculosis and venereal diseases were introduced, while the registration and care of the mentally handicapped was made mandatory as was the registration of all births.

There was also widespread concern about the falling birth-rate at the beginning of the twentieth century. In Germany efforts were made to encourage the healthiest to increase their families so as to improve the race, while in America tens of thousands of 'subnormal' people were compulsorily sterilized to avoid the risk of their producing subnormal children. Such methods have never been accepted in Britain.

Another new approach to social medicine which was intended to make medical treatment available for all working people, and in which many medical practitioners in Britain would become involved, was first introduced by Lloyd George in 1911 in the form of a National Health Insurance scheme. This provided medical, sickness, maternity, disablement and sanatorium benefits for some 16 million workers. There was great dissatisfaction with the Local Government Board because some undesirable aspects of Poor Law legislation still prevailed, but under the new scheme medical practitioners would be able to seek out adverse social and environmental factors. After the introduction of National Health Insurance no worker who had been properly covered by the scheme need become destitute as a consequence of illness. After 1945, public health was swallowed up in the flood of social legislation which led to the welfare state. This affected the lives, financial security and prospects of every individual in Britain. With the establishment of the welfare state there was a change in the pattern of resource allocation and the emphasis of public-health legislation shifted towards the social results of disease. This was accelerated by the transfer of hospitals to a new authority and the provision of comprehensive medical care for all.

In the United States and Canada, as in Britain, public health came to include social and preventive medicine. From the 1870s in the United States, public-health legislation increased steadily at local, state and national levels. Local health services covered the inspection, supervision and sanitary control of water supply, sewage disposal, milk production and distribution and food-handling establishments, garbage collection and street cleansing. Many local health boards also set up laboratories to identify sources of infection in epidemics, to develop and supply vaccines and carry out immunizations, blood tests and other forms of medical screening as preventive measures. By 1930 many towns provided free clinics for such tests and treatments together with free or cheap treatment for venereal disease, tuberculosis and other conditions. In the following two decades local health services were greatly expanded and many more functions were added: clinics for mothers and children, a public-health nursing service, community hospitals and nursing homes, community-health planning and the control of communicable diseases along with campaigns for public-health education and the provision of information. Schoolchildren were required to be vaccinated against smallpox and later the school-health programme was extended to include free eye, ear, dental and physical examinations, while concern over malnutrition led some communities to provide free milk and even free lunches in schools.

The Federal government also expanded its public-health services, although it was only in 1935 with the introduction of the Federal Social Security Act which dealt with pensions, that a beginning was made to co-ordinate a comprehensive Federal health and welfare programme. Direct individual medical assistance to civilians came in the United States by way of a long-standing programme of aid to veterans of the armed services, one of the largest state health-care systems in the world. It was in 1833 that the Federal government first established a pension scheme for the relief of disabled veterans. This was followed in 1865 by the establishment of the National Home for Disabled Volunteer Soldiers and Sailors, which by 1930 had eleven branches known familiarly as 'old soldiers' homes'. In 1890 Federal pensions were extended to all disabled veterans regardless of whether or not the disability was incurred in the services, and in 1904 the pensions were extended to all veterans over sixty-two years of age regardless of disability. Then in 1917 further developments occurred by which the US Health Service took on the operation of the veterans' hospitals with their large staffs of doctors, nurses and technicians. Since 1917 hundreds of thousands of former service personnel have been treated in veterans' hospitals and the veterans' medical service is still the nearest approach to social medicine in the United States.

In Germany social medicine became important from the early years of the twentieth century, after the introduction of social insurance had shown what a heavy burden sickness placed upon the nation. The insurance authorities, trying to reduce their expenses, took preventive as well as curative measures, recognized tuberculosis as a social disease and led a campaign for peoples' sanatoria. The first courses in social medicine began about 1902, and in the years preceding the First World War a number of manuals by medical authors were published. But social medicine met with opposition from the hygienists who had themselves only just begun to gain recognition. Max Rubner, whose work has already been mentioned, refused to admit that socio-medical factors constituted a separate branch of study, and it was not until 1920 that a chair of social medicine was established in Berlin under the Prussian socialist government. Academies of social medicine were also founded at the same time in Düsseldorf and Breslau but they were all closed in 1933 by the Hitler regime. In Austria, however, the study of social medicine continued at Graz and Innsbruck, while Julius Tandler, a city magistrate in Vienna, contributed in practical ways to the development of social medicine among the working class there in the 1920s.

9.9 CONCLUSION By now it will be clear that public health is an extremely wide topic which touches upon many aspects of modern life. It involves science and technology as well as medicine and the social sciences in a very complex manner. It developed rapidly, as we have seen. But besides the issues we have already discussed it must be remembered that many new medical techniques were first introduced during the period 1870–1950 based on scientific and technological advances. New drugs became available; methods for screening large numbers of people such as mass X-radiography were introduced; methods of preventing diseases such as poliomyelitis by inoculation were advocated together with new forms of treatment. There were also advances in industrial medicine, improvements in the conditions of health and safety at work, encouraged by insurance companies and enforced by legislation. In these and many other ways the public-health picture in Britain and other industrialized countries changed quite fundamentally during the period.

Striking evidence of the effectiveness of these improvements can be seen in the fact that the expectation of life in Britain rose from 30 to 40 years in the 1870s to 60 to 70 years at the end of the period. At the same time both the death-rate and the birth-rate declined (Figure 9.10). The age distribution of the population also changed. In the 1850s, for example, of every 1,000 persons, 66 were aged 65 years and over, while about 340 were children under 15. In 1953, on the other hand, the proportions were 113 old persons and 224 children per thousand.

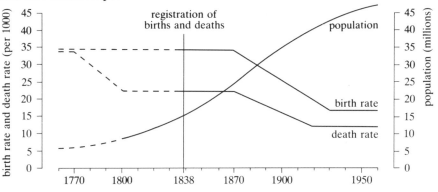

Figure 9.8 Population, birth-rate and death-rate: England and Wales. (Reproduced from T. McKeown and C.R. Blackwell (1974) An Introduction to Social Medicine, *Blackwell, by permission of the publishers)*

The incidence of infectious diseases such as cholera and typhoid fever declined sharply and although the number of tuberculosis cases declined from 3,000 to 200 per million of the population during the century from 1850 to 1950, it nevertheless remained a major menace. As a cause of death its greatest incidence changed from the young female factory worker to those over 45 years of age (Table 9.2).

Infant mortality also declined markedly between the 1840s and the mid-1950s so that while in 1840 64 per cent of all deaths were among children under five years of age, by 1953 this proportion had fallen to just 4 per cent. These statistics convey some impression of the degree of success achieved by improvements in public health. By the 1950s 90 per cent of all deaths were in persons over 40, 75 per cent in those over 60 and 50 per cent in those over 70; half of all deaths were caused by diseases of the circulatory system. By the 1950s infectious diseases, while not the cause of high mortality, still gave rise to much notifiable illness and loss of working days. Over 25 per cent of absences from work in 1952, for instance, were caused by influenza, bronchitis, pneumonia, tonsillitis and the common cold, all conditions which arise from viral infections.

A large proportion of absenteeism from industry was also caused by mental illness arising from neuroses or psychosomatic diseases. This indicates the changing causes of stress in the urban community and is an area of growing concern in social medicine. While these statistics indicate improvement for Britain, similar figures could be quoted for other Western countries, though in many cases the developments came somewhat later.

Perhaps the most important general development of the period 1870–1950, often regarded as a second industrial revolution, was the increased use of

Table 9.2 Mean annual mortality rates per million living (standardized*) caused by certain communicable diseases in decennia 1851–60 and 1891–1900

Cause	1851–60 (a)	1891–1900 (b)	Difference (a)–(b)	Difference per cent of total difference (a–b) 100 / 3,085	
Tuberculosis – respiratory	2,772	1,418	1,354	43.9	} 47.2
Tuberculosis – other forms	706	603	103	3.3	
Typhus, enteric fever, simple continued fever	891	184	707	22.9	
Scarlet fever	779	152	627	20.3	
Diarrhoea, dysentery, cholera	990	715	275	8.9	
Smallpox	202	13	189	6.1	
Whooping cough	433	363	70	2.3	
Measles	357	398	−41	−1.3	
Diphtheria	99	254	−155	−5.0	
Other causes	13,980	14,024	−44	−1.4	
Total	21,209	18,124	3,085	100	

*Standardized to age and sex distribution of 1901 population.
(Source: McKeown and Lowe, 1974, p.9)

science, no less marked in medicine and public health than in industry and other aspects of life. New diseases have called for new methods of diagnosis and treatment both in medicine itself and in the appraisal of public-health problems. As the nineteenth century advanced, as workers became more unionized and more vocal, especially after the First World War, public demand increased for better standards of housing, better domestic and public sanitation, more varied food, improved health care and better urban services in general. All of this meant that the purpose of public-health legislation and practice changed from the basic aims of the early sanitarians to the more sophisticated objectives of social medicine. As we have seen this has been the direction which public health has taken during the period, and the changes occurred not only in Britain but also in other Western countries as the examples from Germany and America show.

REFERENCES   Bach, W. (1972) *Atmospheric Pollution*, McGraw-Hill.

Binnie, G.M. (1981) *Early Victorian Water Engineers*, Thomas Telford.

Bohme, H. (1978) *An Introduction to the Social and Economic History of Germany*, Blackwell.

Burnett, J. (1983) *Plenty and Want (A Social History of Diet from 1815 to the Present Day)*, Methuen.

Burnett, J. (1986) *A Social History of Housing, 1815–1985*, Methuen.

Butler, S. *et al.* (1986) *The Social History of the Microscope*, Whipple Museum of the History of Science.

Chadwick, Sir Edwin (1842) *Report on the Sanitary Condition of the Labouring Population of Great Britain* (edited with an introduction by Flinn, M.W., 1965), Edinburgh University Press.

Checkland, O. and Lamb, M. (1982) *Health Care as Social History. The Glasgow Case*, Aberdeen University Press.

Dyer, B. (1932) *The Society of Public Analysts and Other Analytical Chemists: Some Reminiscences of its First Fifty Years*, Heffer.

Gauldie, E. (1974) *Cruel Habitations: A History of Working-Class Housing 1780–1918*, George Allen & Unwin.

Hanham, H.J. (1976) *Bibliography of British History 1851–1914* (sections on social welfare and medicine), Oxford University Press.

Harley Williams, J.H. (1932) *A Century of Public Health in Britain, 1832–1929*, A & C Black.

Hassall, A.H. (1857) *Adulterations Detected; or Plain Instructions for the Discovery of Frauds in Food and Medicine*, London.

Hobson, V. (1979) *The Theory and Practice of Public Health*, Oxford University Press.

Hodgkinson, R. (ed.) (1973) *Public Health in the Victorian Age: Debates on the Issue from Nineteenth-century Critical Journals*, Gregg.

James, G.V. (1971) *Water Treatment*, Technical Press.

Jones, G. (1986) *Social Hygiene in Twentieth Century Britain*, Croom Helm.

Katz, A.H. and Spencer, J. (eds.) (1965) *Readings in the Philosophy and Sciences of Public Health*, Free Press.

Lewis, R.A. (1952) *Edwin Chadwick and the Public Health Movement 1832–1848*, Longman.

McKeown, T. and Lowe, C.R. (1974) *An Introduction to Social Medicine*, Blackwell.

Newman, Sir George (1932) *The Rise of Preventive Medicine*, Oxford University Press.

Pickstone, J.V. (1985) *Medicine and Industrial Society: A History of Hospital Development in Manchester and its Region 1752–1946*, Manchester University Press.

Pope, R., Pratt, A. and Hoyle, B. (1986) *Social Welfare in Britain, 1885–1985*, Croom Helm.

Purdon, P.W. (1971) *Environmental Health*, Academic Press.

Rochard, J. (1888) 'Traite d'hygiene sociale et de prophylaxie sanitaire' in Sand, R. (1952) *The Advance to Social Medicine*, Staples.

Rolt, L.T.C. (1979) *The People's Health, 1830–1910*, Croom Helm.

Russell, C.A., Coley, N.G. and Roberts, G.K. (1977) *Chemists by Profession: The Origins and Rise of the Royal Institute of Chemistry*, Open University Press.

Ryder, J. and Silver, H. (1970) *Modern English Society: History and Structure, 1850–1970*, Methuen.

Simon, Sir John (1890) *English Sanitary Institutions*, Cassell.

Smith, F.B. (1979) *The People's Health, 1830–1910*, Croom Helm.

Snow, J. (1936) *Snow on Cholera, with a Biographical Memoir by B.V. Richardson*, Commonwealth Fund.

Sproll, W.T. (1970) *Air Pollution and its Control*, New York.

Teale, T.P. (1879) *Dangers to Health. Pictorial Guide to Domestic Sanitary Defects*, J. & A. Churchill.

Treble, J.H. (1983) *Urban Poverty in Britain 1830–1914*, Methuen.

Wohl, A.S. (1984) *Endangered Lives: Public Health in Victorian Britain*, Methuen.

Wright, L. (1960) *Clean and Decent*, Routledge.

10 MEDICINE AND SCIENCE

Franz-Josef Brüggemeier

The history of medicine in the years 1870 to 1950 can be described in very different, often contradictory, terms. On the one hand it embodies the successes and advances of modern science. In 1876 for instance, at the beginning of the period we are studying, Robert Koch, a German doctor, proved for the first time that micro-organisms could cause disease. His discovery was a turning point for modern medicine and eventually led to the discovery of antibiotics, the most famous of which, penicillin, is said to have influenced decisively the battle for Italy in the Second World War, at the end of our period.

In other areas too, dramatic changes took place. The general standard of health improved, most obviously in the case of babies. In 1880, as many as 20 per cent of babies did not survive their first year, while in 1950 this number had sunk to less than 3 per cent. For most of the nineteenth century surgery was very risky and extremely painful, abdominal surgery was almost certainly fatal; at the end of our period, it had become a matter of routine to carry out operations unheard of before.

While these advances undoubtedly took place, the overall contribution of modern medicine is analysed critically. It is hotly debated whether the improvement in the general standard of health is to be attributed to medicine or whether it is a result mainly of better nutrition, housing and hygiene. It can be shown, for example, that most infectious diseases started to decline long before antibiotics were introduced. Furthermore, it can be argued that advances, especially in modern surgery, have not been prudently used but have, on the contrary, led to countless unnecessary operations. At the same time it seems that the treatment of rheumatism and chronic, degenerative diseases in general hardly improved at all.

Another criticism is that the health system has become much too expensive and is heading in the wrong direction, restricting itself to the microscopic view of isolated organs and laboratory results, at the expense of a holistic approach that looks at the patient as a person. It is argued that an ever-increasing machinery leaves no room for patients, for their self-help, responsibilities and abilities. Rather, doctors and the medical infrastructure have tried to push aside the contribution of popular knowledge and especially of women, who traditionally formed the backbone of lay medicine. (For an outspoken criticism see Illich, 1976.)

The picture is rather complicated. Certainly, there was an improvement in the general standard of health between 1870 and 1950, but the reasons for this are not clear. Medicine played a part, but its contribution may have been of secondary importance. It is very difficult to come to clear-cut answers, not the least because it is not easy to say what the term 'medicine' means. We have laboratories, where chemical and physiological processes are analysed using modern scientific methods; then, there is the complex structure of hospitals, with all their machinery for diagnosis and treatment and their hierarchy of patients, nurses and doctors; and we have the different aspects of alternative and/or lay medicine, which were of great importance during the period under consideration, and are still important now.

It would be very difficult to identify the particular contribution of these different elements precisely, and, generally speaking, in medicine it would be even more difficult to distinguish neatly between science, technology and everyday life; it would be especially wrong to overstate the status of laboratories as an area of pure science, set apart from mere applied medicine. On the contrary, it is in medical practice that theories and treatments must prove themselves. If they fail to do so, they must be discarded regardless of their theoretical standing. Diseases can not be understood by relying solely on the parameters and quantifications of laboratories, nor can they be reduced to somatic processes. Rather, they originate and are defined in a complex process, shaped by environmental and social conditions, by the everyday lives we all live.

Given such a complex situation, it is understandable that in the area of medicine different points of view co-exist, leading to the contradictory judgements cited above. This chapter will try to deal with them. Out of the vast number of possible topics, it will concentrate on the following aspects:

- developments in modern medicine and their scientific base;
- the question of how medical advances have changed everyday life, giving special emphasis to the experience of women;
- the problem of the definition of disease using eugenics and hysteria as an example;
- the rise of medicine as a profession, an important process over the last 100 years, which was, however, not unopposed by lay medicine.

The aim, however, is not to explain away the contradictions mentioned or to offer easy answers. Rather, it should be stressed that they are to a large degree inevitable since our understanding of medicine, that is, of our bodies and ourselves, is shaped by social processes, which by their very nature are characterized by different positions and contradictions.

10.1 DEVELOPMENTS IN MODERN MEDICINE

For two reasons, 1870 serves as a convenient starting point for a survey of the history of modern medicine. Around this time the rate of mortality began to fall decisively and important developments began to take place in medicine. In fact, it is no exaggeration to claim that it was in the second half of the nineteenth century that the transition to modern medicine occurred. It is not at all clear, however, how these two trends were interrelated.

The crude death rate in 1870 stood at about 22 per 1,000 (see Figure 10.1) as against approximately 30 in 1680. While this decrease took some 200 years, the situation after 1870 changed radically within a short span of time. In the words of the social historian J.M. Winter (1982, p.100): 'In roughly three generations, crude death rates (deaths per 1,000 population per year) were halved, infant mortality rates were reduced by 80 per cent, and at all ages mortality due to infectious diseases was reduced by approximately 90 per cent.'

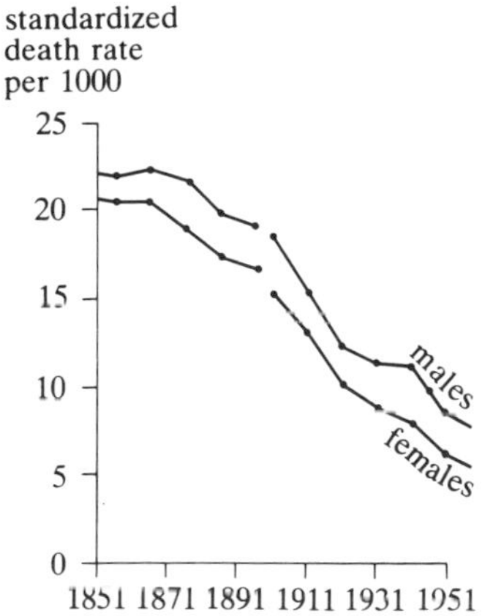

In medicine, too, important changes came about on different levels and in different areas at about the same time. Some of them were spectacular: the introduction of anaesthetics or the discovery of bacteria and, later, anti-biotics. Others took a long time to develop and were hardly noticed by the general public, but their consequences, in the field of pathological anatomy, for example, were far-reaching.

The changes, which laid the basis for modern medicine, resulted from several factors. Hospitals gained a new importance and allowed a more systematic study of patients and diseases as well as treatments on an unprecedented scale; autopsies were performed in great numbers, so that clinical diagnoses could be controlled. With microscopes, the description and analysis of bodily processes became much more precise, leading to the investigation of even smaller units. Contributions from chemistry and physiology brought about an understanding of the complex processes within the body and the use of sophisticated statistical techniques established connections previously unknown or only assumed. All these combined to shape our understanding of medicine to such a degree that the current situation appears normal. In order to understand how far reaching and how recent the changes actually were, we have to look at the years before 1870.

standardized death rate per 1000

Figure 10.1 Death rates in England and Wales, 1841–1971. (Reproduced from T. McKeown, 1979, The Role of Medicine. Dream, Mirage or Nemesis, *Blackwell)*

In the nineteenth and early years of the twentieth century hospitals were unpleasant places, where the poor, the old, and other people were looked after – if they had nowhere else to go. Whoever could, avoided hospitals like the plague; indeed, they were no less dangerous. The rate of infection was high and the treatment often harsh (Waddington, 1973, pp.211–24). As late as 1880–1889 there were 9 deaths per 1,000 births due to sepsis in hospitals, while the rate for home-births was 3.5. Before the introduction of asepsis the ratio was even higher. It is no surprise, therefore, that hospitals were unpopular.

Until well into the nineteenth century, medicine was a science based upon what the eyes could see and what words could describe. The processes within the body were generally unknown; diseases, consequently, were defined according to what could be seen on the outside. Definitions were rather arbitrary and the number of diseases very great because of the enormous variation observed. At the same time, distinctions between diseases were oversimplified by reducing them to general categories, the most important being 'fever' and the 'plague'. Systematic observation in new hospitals, autopsies, and especially the increasing use of microscopes, all contributed to changing the situation: it became possible to reduce the seemingly unlimited number of observed variations to a few elements. Where the eye saw colours, muscles, blood, sweat and vessels in an endless number of combinations, the microscope saw nothing but cells. It could be shown, furthermore, that the differences between types of cells were only apparent. A muscle-cell and a liver-cell looked different, but they were basically the same. The German physician Rudolf Virchow summed it up in the 1850s and 1860s when he proclaimed 'omnis cellula e cellula': each cell originates from another cell. Cells, therefore, were the basis of all processes, the starting point for all investigations (Cartwright, 1977, pp.136–37).

At the same time, advances in physiology and chemistry allowed a better understanding of the processes. The view through the microscope is static; even where it can describe variation, it cannot detect or explain the physiological and chemical processes. Here, too, the nineteenth century witnessed important breakthroughs, even though their therapeutical consequences often were not realized until the end of our period. Slowly, however, a better understanding of diseases developed as well as more effective ways of dealing with them (see for example, Shyrock, 1947; Singer and Ashworth Underwood, 1962). This can be shown most clearly in the fields of bacteriology, surgery and hygiene.

The introduction of anaesthetics in 1846 fundamentally changed surgery in two respects: the new medicaments (ether first, then chloroform) effectively suppressed the pain and gave surgeons more time. While before speed mattered more than anything else because of the pain suffered, doctors now had much more time at their disposal and, therefore, could proceed more carefully. With new techniques, surgery became constructive; instead of amputations, which had prevailed until then, repairs of hernias and reconstructions of diseased joints or displaced bones developed into routine procedure, greatly increasing the status of surgeons, who until then rarely had an academic background. Previously the medical profession had tended to leave surgery to, for example, barbers or bone-setters, some of whom developed a considerable expertise.

The new operations, however, still carried a great risk, because infection could not be controlled. During the Franco-German War of 1871, for example, French doctors carried out some 13,000 amputations, 10,000 of which proved fatal, largely because of infection. In hospitals, the situation was rather better, the operative death rate being around 10 per cent in the 1860s, but since many more operations were carried out than before, the total number of deaths also was much higher. It was only after antisepsis was introduced by Lister in the 1860s that the rate of infection fell: Lister used carbolic impregnated lint to cover injuries or the part of the body on which he wanted to operate. Later, he soaked his hands and the instruments as well, and filled the room with carbolic mist. He was able to reduce infection, but initially many surgeons did not follow his example. In fact, there was strong opposition to his suggestions, because carbolic had side-effects and because Lister's proposals depended upon the so-called germ-theory, which remained controversial (Cartwright, 1977, pp.143–46).

As already mentioned, the definitions used for disease until the end of the nineteenth century were not always precise, reflecting the poor state of knowledge. This was especially true for infectious diseases, for which causes, mechanisms of transmission and treatment remained unknown. One theory was based upon the notion of miasma, that is a gas produced through the fermentation of filthy water, excrement and general dirt. In 1864, the King of Saxony visited one of his cities. His arrival was unexpected and the mayor had only fifteen minutes to prepare. Unfortunately, although the streets had just been swept, there were small heaps of dirt everywhere and a disquieting smell began to spread, from which the dreaded miasma threatened to arise: 'The suggestion of a councillor came to his relief. All the prisoners and vagabonds were immediately taken out of prison and custody and ordered to line up around the heaps. There, they were ordered to inhale the smell by rhythmically opening and closing their nostrils' (quoted in Göckenjan, 1985, p.114).

This report may be exaggerated, but the underlying theory was widely shared. It was opposed by another theory that explained diseases as arising through direct personal contact, possibly via germs. In some cases this had been demonstrated, but no proof existed for diseases such as cholera, yellow-fever and typhus until the 1880s and 1890s. None the less, protection was sought by avoiding personal contact: sick people were isolated, quarantine imposed and borders closed. These were drastic measures and were criticized for medical, political and economic reasons. The imposition of quarantine greatly upset trade, which had become more important than ever before (Ackerknecht, 1948, pp.562–92).

Lister was influenced by the work of Louis Pasteur, who had demonstrated in 1864 that a flask of milk he had had sterilized and kept airtight for some months did not show any signs of life. Consequently, he argued that air must be filled with germs creating both life and infection. His demonstration, however, did not settle the problem because he could not establish a definite link between germs and disease (Cartwright, 1977, pp.137–38). Twelve years later, in 1876, Koch proved that anthrax, a disease affecting mainly animals, was caused by the anthrax bacillus. In quick succession other bacteria were discovered and, for the first time, it was possible to prove beyond doubt the connection between disease and a particular cause, thereby establishing a model to explain other diseases.

For quite a time, however, the breakthrough in bacteriology did not have immediate therapeutic consequences. The first antibiotic, salvarsan, was developed by Paul Ehrlich in 1908. It proved quite effective, mainly against syphilis, but it had many side effects; it remained, however, the only means of curing acute infection until the time of the Second World War. The modern era of antibiotics began in the late 1930s, when sulphanilamides were discovered; more importantly penicillin was introduced during the Second World War. It can be argued, therefore, that 'had a great epidemic occurred in Western Europe at any time before 1939, physicians would have been as helpless to cure their patients as were doctors in the Black Death. They could only have assisted the patient's own resistance to infection' (Cartwright, 1977, p.147).

However, the (belated) development of antibiotics was not the only consequence of the work of Lister and Koch. Surgery became much safer, although the reason was not properly understood. Lister's contribution is a good case in point. Though his assumptions concerning the transmission of germs were inadequate, the procedures he proposed were of lasting value. After initial resistance they were widely adopted and further improved: antisepsis was replaced by asepsis; surgeons began to wear rubber gloves, and instruments, clothes and other equipment were sterilized. The activity of germs was not just suppressed; rather, the aim was to have the operating theatre as germ-free as possible. Consequently the mortality rate from surgery fell decisively; it is assumed to have been at about 3.5 per cent at the turn of the twentieth century and decreased further thereafter. The introduction of antibiotics brought about another sharp drop, although this came into effect fully only after our period (Cartwright, 1977, p.146). These figures do not tell the whole story, since many more operations were undertaken, including those that were avoided previously as being too dangerous. For example, it became a matter of routine to open the abdomen to remove the appendix, gall-bladder or all or parts of the stomach. Simultaneously, however, there developed a tendency to perform operations too often.

The public-health movement, too, benefited from the emphasis on hygiene and the bacteriological breakthrough, although the picture here is rather complicated. It is known that Edwin Chadwick (for a long time a leading figure in this movement) had little respect for the medical profession of his day. Furthermore, well after the discovery of bacteria, leading public-health reformers did not accept the new theories and their demands were largely based on the miasma-notion. Though this theory did not survive the age of bacteriology, its stress upon clean water, clean air and a general improvement in hygiene contributed enormously to healthier living conditions (Wohl, 1983, p.142ff). For some physicians, housing conditions and other factors had to be improved as well. The more radical minded of them stressed the importance of social conditions and favoured social and political reforms, although the breakthrough of bacteriology made their arguments sound less convincing. Reforms, however, were introduced over almost all of Europe at the same time, and because the link between environmental factors in the form of bacteria and disease had been proved beyond doubt, it became more difficult to refuse the money to pay for them.

The development of the public-health movement shows that the contribution of modern medicine and doctors in shaping everyday life cannot easily be defined. It can be shown for example that most infectious diseases started to recede long before effective treatments in the form of antibiotics became available, as is shown for tuberculosis in Figure 9.1 on page 272. It would be misleading, however, to neglect the efforts for healthier living conditions and better hygiene and to restrict the influence of modern medicine to surgery, hospitals or the development of new and effective pills, though it must be stressed that the changes were most obvious in the first two areas. Not only the mortality rate after operations fell; hospitals in general became safer places and began to attract the middle classes. After the turn of the century hospitals had lost most of their bad reputation, helped by the fact that infections were less threatening and that many of the new methods and treatments were concentrated there. The number of hospital beds grew markedly as Table 10.1 shows.

The greater efficiency of hospitals, however, had disadvantages, too. Patients were no longer treated in their everyday surroundings; rather, they were taken to the artificial world of an institution. Here doctors tended to rely on laboratory results rather than observation of the patients themselves. Furthermore, there was a growing process of specialization. While at the beginning of our period doctors were still expected to cover most fields of

Table 10.1   Beds in English hospitals (excluding asylums), 1861–1938

Year	Beds in public hospitals Number	Rate*	Beds in voluntary hospitals Number	Rate*	Total Number	Rate*
1861	50 000	2.6	11 000	0.6	61 000	3.2
1891	83 000	2.9	29 000	1.0	113 000	3.9
1911	154 000	4.3	43 000	1.2	197 000	5.5
1921	172 000	4.6	57 000	1.5	229 000	6.1
1938	176 000	4.3	87 000	2.1	263 000	6.4

*Rate = Number of beds per thousand population.
(Source: based on Abel-Smith, 1964, pp.46, 152, 200, 353, 382–5)

medicine, towards the end of it we find specialists for almost every part of the human body. This process of specialization has been criticized constantly, not least from within the profession. Doctors too complained about it, partly because they could not cope with the process, and partly because they thought that, as a result, medicine would lose contact with the patient as a person (Honigsbaum, 1979, and Ehrenreich and English, 1978, pp.84–88).

10.1.3 Everyday medical practice

Very little is known about the daily routine of doctors and what ordinary people did when they fell ill. Here, we can only put forward some tentative arguments. It can be assumed that in the 1940s people had more contact with doctors than was the case in the 1870s. This was because of an improved service from the doctors, and the spread of health insurance. Germany was the first country to introduce a comprehensive state system; others followed suit, with the notable exception of the United States, where no state system exists even today. In Britain, the number of people protected by the National Health Insurance (NHI) Act of 1911

> . . . rose from about 15 million in 1913 to 25 million in 1942, thereby increasing the proportion of the population covered from one-third to one-half. Nevertheless, it still left out the dependents of insured workers – their non-working wives and children – as well as most of those who were unemployed or who were engaged in non-manual occupations. The Act was thus one designed specifically for employed members of the working classes. (Honigsbaum, 1979, p.9)

Before the introduction of widespread health insurance, it was expensive to consult a physician, and rarely considered worth it, given the poor standard of treatment. A doctor's anatomical or biological knowledge may have been superior to that of herbalists, bone-setters or midwives, but that was not necessarily true of his practical skills. Consequently patients tried a variety of treatments before deciding what to accept (Woodward and Richards, 1977; Peterson, 1978).

At first glance, one could assume that by the 1940s the importance of non-academically trained people practising medicine had declined. This was most certainly true for injuries and acute diseases, especially where surgery was required. The state health insurance systems favoured the official medical sector since, with very few exceptions, they only covered costs that arose when academically trained doctors were consulted. The position of qualified doctors was further strengthened because only they could certify sick leave.

The support given by the emerging insurance systems was perhaps the single most important factor in establishing the strong position of the medical profession at the end of our period. This argument becomes even more convincing if one looks at the effectiveness of treatments in areas other than surgery. The discoveries and improvements described above only affected some aspects of health and medicine, mainly in the field of acute diseases. The treatment of chronic diseases, on the other hand, and of a great variety of minor and major complaints such as bronchitis, pneumonia and heart disease, did not undergo such dramatic changes. Here, the model of specific causes as established in bacteriology did not (and still does not) apply to the same degree; rather, a combination of different factors has to be taken into account, making it much more difficult to develop effective cures. It is not surprising, therefore, that in these areas we get a very confusing picture.

On the one hand, therapeutical scepticism existed; at the same time there was a never-ending stream of promises and wonder pills. In the 1890s, for example, Koch assumed that he had discovered a treatment for tuberculosis and – being a prominent scientist by now – caused an enormous uproar. Hundreds of thousands of people wanted to be treated with the new drug; frenzy broke out and doctors from all over the world asked for more information, only to be bitterly disappointed. It turned out that Koch had not discovered a potent drug; he had discovered a test to find out whether a person had already had tuberculosis.

It has often been stressed that right up to the end of our period (and even beyond) modern medicine has been found wanting in the fields of therapy and medicaments. The contraceptive pill is a product of the 1950s and 60s, as were drugs such as tranquillizers, which have come under much criticism lately. Many of them are definitely prescribed and used much too widely, while others were – and still are – of great value in the treatment of psychiatric disorders. Until the 1950s, there had been little treatment for the mentally ill. Psychoanalysis was developed around the turn of the century, as were other theories still with us today, but most of the mentally ill were shut up in lunatic asylums. These institutions may not have been brutal by nineteenth-century standards; but they grew so large that they sometimes housed several thousand patients, for whom there was little hope of recovery. The new drugs, introduced just after our period, did not offer a cure either, but they made it possible to release patients from asylums and treat them as out-patients, because violent outbursts, for example, could largely be suppressed. As a result, families could cope with the mentally ill in a way that may have existed in former times, but which had definitely receded in the years 1870–1950. Between 1830 and 1930 the average size of British asylums increased more than tenfold, from just over 100 patients to more than 1,000; in the United States some institutions had as many as 15,000 patients. (For a more general discussion see Scull, 1979.)

In our period, too, new drugs were introduced, though the effects rarely were as far-reaching. Apart from the use of ether and chloroform as anaesthetics, the greatest impact was possibly made by aspirin, which was introduced in 1899; at about the same time also, hormone deficiencies began to be treated. Vaccination also developed, and in 1922 a vaccine against tuberculosis was introduced. It did not offer a cure, but it did substantially reduce the threat; it was only in 1952 that an effective antibiotic treatment became available.

But in many areas of medicine no decisive changes took place in our period, a fact resented by GPs. They had the closest contact with the everyday worries and diseases of ordinary patients, some of whom felt let down by their doctors and turned to traditional or alternative therapies, even if they had to pay for these. It is quite plausible, therefore, that non-professional medicine also expanded in our period, although on a more modest scale than the 'official' medical sector (Armstrong, 1982, pp.109–22).

The term 'non-professional medicine' is vague and can cover a wide range of activities. It is sometimes inaccurately applied to widely respected alternative therapies such as homoeopathy and acupuncture, and at the same time, to wonder cures advertised by quacks. The term 'quack' is often used to

Figure 10.2
Patent medicine advertised
c.1900: Carter's Little Liver
*Pills (*Illustrated London
News, *December 1899)*

denigrate anyone practising medicine who is not academically qualified. During our period there were those who deserved this name, for selling a variety of pills and medicine of often dubious value. In between the poles of respected alternatives and quackery, an enormous variety of therapies and theories existed, which are difficult to describe precisely. Very little research has been done in this area and in contrast to orthodox medicine, which more or less adheres to a common school of thought, popular theories and treatments are often characterized imprecisely. They contain elements of orthodox medicine, folklore and simply of superstition. A recent study from a German village has shown that among the elderly even until today there exists a widespread conviction that people develop cancer because of sins committed in their youth. In London, too, it was found a few years ago that popular beliefs about health and disease are still shaped by traditional thinking, such as the old notion of humoral theory and the belief in attack by malign spirits (Helman, 1984, pp.10–16).

This is not intended to denigrate popular medicine or to minimize its contribution; rather it emphasizes a need for more knowledge of its workings before its contribution can be judged. We cannot go into this problem much further here. Instead we will look more closely at one aspect which is often discussed today: the notion of a holistic approach to medicine taking social conditions and other factors into account – usually positively set apart from a science-oriented approach that concentrates predominantly on isolated aspects. Looking closely at our period, however, the picture gets somewhat blurred.

10.1.4
Holistic approaches:
the case of social medicine

Shortly before our period many prominent doctors were advocating radical reforms to improve the social conditions thought to contribute a great deal to the poor state of health of the poorer parts of the population. One of them was Virchow who – as has already been mentioned – became a world-famous pathologist, and whose work symbolizes the breakthrough of scientific medicine, but who did not lose sight of a wider perspective.

In 1847, at the age of twenty-six, Virchow was asked by the Prussian government to study a typhus epidemic in Silesia. His investigation of the epidemic was based upon a close observation of the geographical conditions, the climate and, above all, the social and political context. He came to the conclusion that the problem was not primarily a medical one: a solution could only be found if democracy, freedom and education were to prevail over the autocratic and backward character of the Prussian state (Acker-knecht, 1953). Doctors throughout Europe made similar demands: the English doctor Julian Hunter, who had studied the role of social conditions thoroughly, wrote in 1849: 'If other causes have slain their thousands, poverty has slain its tens of thousands', and he continued: 'The relation of poverty to disease is so great and so inseparable that it is astonishing legislators should not ere now have acknowledged it' (quoted in Wohl, 1983, p.46).

Some years later, rather different arguments were put forward. The link between poverty and disease was accepted, but it was argued that the poor themselves were to blame for not spending their money wisely, drinking too much alcohol, neglecting their families and not working hard enough, so that disease became inevitable.

In the wake of the debate about Social Darwinism, the argument took another turn. Around the middle of the nineteenth century Charles Darwin had developed a theory of evolution, based among other things on the notion of the survival of the fittest. This notion – derived from observation of nature and animal life – was misinterpreted and transformed into Social Darwinism, which asserted that Darwin's theories could also be used to explain processes in human societies. It was argued that the fittest, that is, the strongest, should survive at the expense of weaker members of the human race who were no longer to be protected. Reforms to alleviate the situation of the poor were therefore not just too expensive and ineffective; they were declared to be harmful. Where earlier only the fittest had survived, welfare measures – it was argued – helped the poor to survive to have too many children. They had four or even more children per family, while the middle classes very often had just two. Haycroft argued in 1894: 'I do not see how we can shirk the fact that preventive medicine and civilisation between them have already deteriorated in a marked degree the healthy vigour of our race . . . Preventive medicine is trying a unique experiment, and the effect is already discernible – race-decay' (quoted in Wohl, 1983, p.334).

Opinions such as this were widely voiced far beyond the medical world, shared by conservatives and ardent socialists, who not only wanted to improve society by doing away with capitalists, but also wanted to reduce the so-called asocial elements by birth control or even enforced sterilization (eugenics). Feminists too, fighting for the right of women to control their number of children, used such arguments as Haycroft's, thus hoping possibly to overcome the widespread hostility to their demands (Gordon, 1978, pp.144–84; Ludmerer, 1972).

These ideas gained great influence, particularly in Germany, with terrible results between 1933 and 1945. The mass-murder in the concentration camps cannot be regarded as the inevitable result of racist or Social Darwinist theories, and one should not draw a strict line from Haycroft to Mengele, who performed barbaric experiments on his victims. But Mengele, too, saw himself first and foremost as a scientist, and anti-semitism was for him based on scientific argument. In the 1880s Virchow tried to show that racist theories could not be justified by scientific arguments. He had 6.7 million schoolchildren examined to find out whether the notion of the Aryan German race was justified. The colour of their eyes, their hair and their skins was registered. The result showed that only 31.8 per cent corresponded with the Aryan ideal; among Jews the number was no less than 11.17 per cent. Virchow came to the conclusion that each nationality, for example, the

German or the Slav, is of a mixed character, and nobody can tell for certain which tribe the individual developed from (Virchow, 1886).

In Germany, attempts to fight racist theories were not successful. There are many explanations for the rise of Nazism, mainly economic, social and political ones, but it cannot be said that National Socialism was mere propaganda or ideology. It had many followers among students and professors, who based their support on scientific convictions. They also registered the colour of the skin, the hair and the eyes, and measured skulls and heads to justify their claims; today we know that they have no scientific basis. Elsewhere such theories were not so influential and the consequences not as terrible. But in France, England, the United States and other countries, similar theories were put forward and held widely across the whole political and scientific spectrum.

Medicine in Nazi Germany not only upheld racist theories: holistic notions and popular medicine gained in official status, too. Popular medicine prospered because herbalist cures were cheaper than the treatments usually prescribed by doctors; but there was more to it than that. Folklore was highly esteemed, as were traditional customs, practices and beliefs; the notion of community was also prized. Modern medicine was compared unfavourably with it, accused of concentrating on isolated medical symptoms, and thereby neglecting the concept of community and especially *Volk*. Here again it can be argued that the National Socialists perverted traditional thinking. To a degree they did, but it can be shown that many adherents of holistic concepts were willing to support National Socialist ideology and policy, and their proposals were far removed from those of Virchow. Indeed, Virchow was attacked fiercely during the Third Reich, and his son went to great lengths to prove that his father was not Jewish: anti-semitism was used to attack the scientific approaches established in the latter half of the nineteenth century (Wuttke-Groneberg, 1982; Schreiber, 1973).

10.2 MEDICINE AND WOMEN

As the preceding sections have shown, it is almost impossible to come to a firm conclusion about the precise role of medicine in society, partly because a lot of research still has to be done, but mainly because so many different factors have to be taken into account. To get a clearer picture of the contribution and ambiguity of modern medicine we shall consider the experience of women.

At the turn of the century women did not necessarily look forward to the birth of a new child. Their anxieties sometimes were so great that the very thought of pregnancy could put an enormous strain on their married life. Marie Stopes, who, in 1921, founded the United Kingdom's first instructional clinic for birth control, remembers one of her women clients: 'She could hardly bear to hear an amiable note in her husband's voice for fear it should lead to sex indulgence, when she was at the mercy of his all too unreliable "self-control" ' (quoted in Stopes, 1925, p.47).

Such fears are understandable, especially for working-class women, very few of whom enjoyed financial security; but it was not just material considerations that accounted for the women's anxieties. Pregnancy could be a difficult time and birth painful. Anaesthetics had been introduced in the mid-nineteenth century and were widely used, though occasionally it was argued that the pain was God-given and should not be interfered with. In any case, even today anaesthetics cannot be used indiscriminately because of the risk to both mother and child. The rate of infection, too, had been markedly reduced by the end of the nineteenth century, but still the mortality for mothers was around 4 per 1,000 births in 1903, compared with 0.9 in 1950. For children the mortality rate was higher: stillbirths and neonatal deaths (covering deaths that occur in the first four weeks of life) amounted to 70

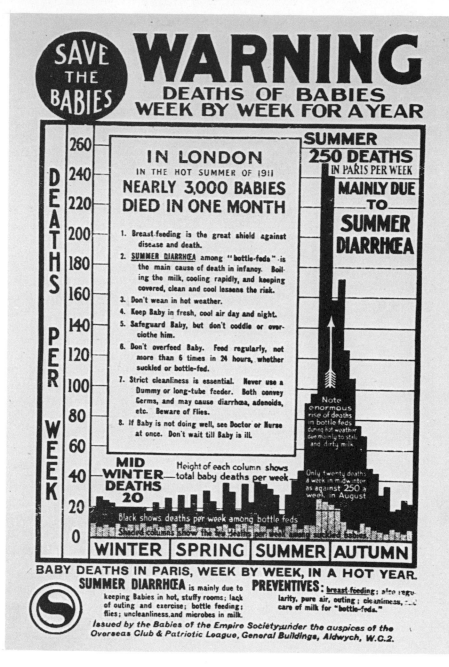

*Figure 10.3
Warning of infantile mortality
c.1918. (Photo: Wellcome
Institute of the History of
Medicine)*

per 1,000 births in 1928, the first year for which we have exact statistics (Gilliat, 1954, pp.257–93; for reluctance to use anaesthetics see Shorter, 1982).

In 1899, 163 babies per 1,000 did not survive their first year. Thereafter this number started to decline slowly, but in 1917, the 'cost of infant mortality was driven home with some force. No less than 1,000 babies still died each week, a rate that exceeded even the heavy war toll: for every 9 soldiers killed in the trenches, 12 babies died at home'. It was, as the leaders of the infant mortality movement put it, 'more dangerous to be a baby in England than a soldier in France' (Honigsbaum, 1979, p.23).

If the child was safely born, however, the worries did not stop; it had to be fed, clothed and nurtured, a task mainly left to mothers, who, as a

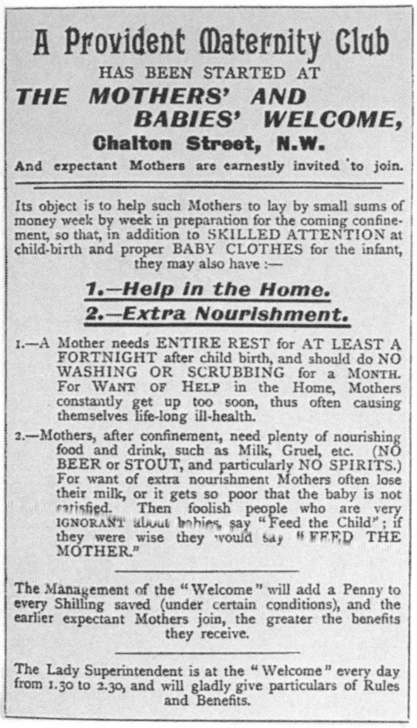

(a)

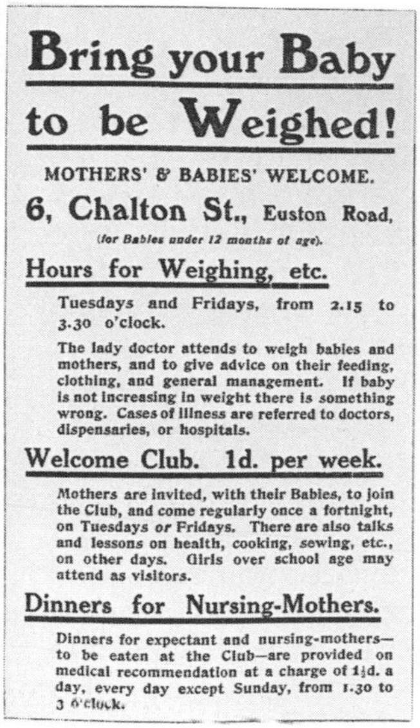

(b)

Figure 10.4
Help for nursing mothers c.1907: (a) Advertisement for a Provident Maternity Club; (b) Bring your baby to be weighed. (Photos: Wellcome Institute of the History of Medicine)

consequence, were restricted to family life. Working-class wives in Germany who had married before 1905 still gave birth, on average, to five children, so that the period of childbearing was frequently more than fifteen years, a greater part of their active adult life, given the fact that after the age of forty men and women of the working classes were worn out; for them old age began much earlier than today (Spree, 1981, p.180). Standards of nutrition, housing and clothing were barely adequate and the extra burden of a new child often proved too much. Both women and children suffered, and the children bore the consequences all their lives. They remained small, were prone to infection and disease. At the turn of the century, the infant death rate for British working-class babies was as high as 20 to 30 per cent, approximately double that of the middle classes (Wohl, 1983, pp.10–42).

It is therefore understandable that there were many methods of contraception and inducing abortion. However, the contraceptive methods were not always effective, and abortions were dangerous. Popular medicine offered many herbs and applications to prevent conception, but they were unreliable. At least they were not harmful, and in an age of risky and often fatal treatment, this was not something to be taken for granted. There was much speculation on how these methods worked, but hardly any firm knowledge. Lactation was a natural contraceptive, but was not very reliable; poverty and malnutrition also contributed to reducing pregnancies by interfering with the menstrual cycle. Nevertheless, the number of children in poor families remained higher than average (Gordon, 1976; Himes, 1963; Shorter, 1982).

Coitus interruptus was a rather obvious way to prevent pregnancy which, until recently, was condemned by many doctors as damaging to health. A variety of theories supported this claim; the best known of them argued that imbecility and spinal consumption could result from it. Medical advice was often not very helpful: until the 1880s, for example, it was assumed that menstruation indicated the fertile period, and it was only in the 1920s that the rhythm method was given a scientific rationale (Tietze, 1965, pp.69–85).

More effective and easier to use were condoms, which came into widespread use at the turn of the century, although mainly in big cities and non-Roman Catholic regions. The church's opposition to contraception was shared by elements of the public and the medical profession, who were afraid that the declining birthrate would weaken the supposedly superior European race. Some prominent leaders of the German Social Democrats, on the other hand, encouraged more children, because they wanted class-conscious children to outnumber and overwhelm the capitalists (Neumann, 1978, pp.408–28). Another method of contraception was the Dutch cap, or vaginal diaphragm, introduced in the 1870s. It was fairly safe and without notable side-effects, but it was expensive and difficult to use. Condoms were expensive too, so that for working-class women the prevention of conception was a much greater problem than for the middle classes. As the birth-control movement pointed out, those who needed contraceptives most were least able to afford them.

For a long time, the birth-control movement encountered a hostile reaction from the medical profession, partly on moral grounds, but also because doctors did not play an important part in it; on the contrary, doctors were afraid of lay-people interfering in areas they regarded as theirs. Feminists were prominent in advocating birth control, although many of them were reluctant to take up the issue, because its sexual overtones could have made their struggle even more difficult (Harrison, 1981, p.64ff). The association with eugenics (see chapter 11) brought the movement into closer contact with doctors, but wider acceptance within the profession only came about in the 1930s, when the birth-control movement in both Britain and the United States made it their policy to win over 'key figures in the medical profession and to cultivate important links with government' (Harrison, 1981, p.68).

This collaborative approach contrasted sharply with late-Victorian radical crusades. Recently this conversion to collaboration (and to eugenics) has been characterized as a 'desertion of feminism', and a failure, because its feminist convictions were not deep enough (Gordon, 1976, p.172). While this may be a debatable position today, it cannot be assumed that feminism as we now understand it existed then, nor can it be argued that something like 'true feminism' exists, which can be used to analyse, let alone judge, historical processes. It is striking (and so far unexplained) that in Britain, as well as in Germany and the United States, the birth-control movement, including its feminist elements, turned to eugenics.

Abortion attracted even more hostility. It was illegal, and remained so well after the period under discussion, except in cases of serious threat to the health of the pregnant woman. But given the low reliability of contraceptive methods abortions were of greater significance before the age of the contraceptive pill. Popular medicine had many ways of inducing abortions, but they were no more effective than women's attempts to miscarry by taking strenuous physical activity, hot baths, and so on. In the last resort, women had to use various methods to irritate or injure the uterus, either with needles, injections or other mechanisms (Shorter, 1982, pp.177–224). These methods were effective but dangerous. Anatomical knowledge was often inadequate and conditions were germ-ridden. Infections were the rule rather than the exception. Risks were reduced if abortions were carried out by midwives or other experienced women; doctors more often than not increased the risk. Although theoretically they were more competent, only a few doctors were willing to carry out abortions, so they lacked the practical experience. Nonetheless, doctors were responsible, if indirectly, for the improvements in safety of this operation, by their improvements in surgery and hygiene; at the same time, new instruments were developed which were easier to handle.

The new methods were so effective and easy to use that women were able to help each other, by-passing not just doctors but any professional help. A French judge declared in 1907 that: 'The technique of abortion has nowadays become so simple, that it is no longer necessary to have recourse to professionals. It suffices to have an understanding girl friend and to procure . . . the famous cannula. I have always been struck at how easy they are to obtain' (quoted in Shorter, 1982, p.202). It is not surprising, therefore, that the rate of abortion was high. In Germany, it was estimated that during the first decades of the twentieth century, one in four pregnancies ended in an illegal abortion. Sometimes doctors helped out by liberally performing D and C (dilatation and curettage) – normally used in cases of irregular menstruation or imminent miscarriage. They could, for example, take a cough as a sign of tuberculosis and thereby justify the operation. Some doctors performed these operations for financial reasons, but whatever the motives, it can safely be assumed that there existed more co-operation between doctors and women than official statements from the profession imply (Shorter, 1982, pp.202–03).

There were also advances in other areas of gynaecology: developments in anaesthetics and disinfection made surgery less risky and for the first time it became safe to perform a caesarean section; the technique was known before but in most cases resulted in the death of both mother and child. By the 1940s almost 3 per cent of all hospital births in the United States were caesarean sections and the mortality rate had dropped to 0.9 per cent, while the number of hospital births had increased to approximately 80 per cent (see Table 10.2).

The proliferation of caesarean sections, however, underlines that the changes could be a mixed blessing: by the end of our period this operation had become almost a matter of routine. Hysterectomy was even more contro-

Table 10.2   Percentage of hospital births in Germany and the United States in the nineteenth and twentieth centuries

	Year	Percentage
Germany	1877	less than 1%
	1891	1
	1924	9
	1936	27
	1952	46
	1962	72
	1970	95
	1973	98
United States	1935	37
	1945	79
	1955	94
	1977	99

(Source: Shorter, 1982, Table 7.1, p.157)

versial. In 1945 Norman Miller, an American gynaecologist, gave a lecture on 'Hysterectomy: therapeutic necessity or surgical racket?' In it he argued that some of his colleagues performed hysterectomies too frequently and suggested that their motive was financial. Feminist scholars have argued that hysterectomies have been and still are carried out too often by a male-dominated profession. Undoubtedly there is some truth in this assertion, but more recent data are ambiguous (Daly, 1979; The Open University (1985), Book II, pp.59–72).

While many women who have been operated upon complain about negative results, others talk positively about their experience. Furthermore, hysterectomy appears to lengthen the average woman's life, if only by a few months. It can also be argued that the tendency to operate too frequently was not restricted to women. In surgery in general reduced risks contributed to a 'knife-happy' attitude among surgeons, while the cell-theory developed by Virchow encouraged a strain of medical thinking that localized diseases, so that, in the case of tumours for example, it seemed sensible to cut out the affected part. In other areas, however, not least in gynaecology, this approach has turned out to be of doubtful value. Hysteria is a good example.

10.2.1
Defining disease and the role of women: the case of hysteria

In the nineteenth and early twentieth century hysteria was prominent among women. It had existed before, 'but between 1870 and World War I – the "golden age" of hysteria – it assumed a peculiarly central role in psychiatric discourse, and in definitions of femininity and female sexuality' (Showalter, 1987, p.129). It was everywhere and nowhere; it was obvious, well known, and eluded a precise definition. Mood and temper of the women supposed to suffer from it could change abruptly, depression alternated with hyper-activity, frigidity was diagnosed as well as nymphomaniac behaviour. In an age where the majority of doctors believed all complaints to be physically based, no such basis could be found for hysteria. Innumerable attempts were made to find an anatomical reason for hysteria, often with catastrophic consequences. The uterus was held responsible and removed, with no success. The same happened with ovaries. In the United States thousands of women had their ovaries removed and were thus castrated, but hysteria remained (Smith-Rosenberg, 1972, pp.652–78).

Recent research suggests that the symptoms have to be explained largely by the status of middle-class women in their families as well as in society at large. As the nineteenth century came to a close, many women were no longer content with their role as housewives and mothers, not least since the demands on them were rather contradictory. They were expected to be well educated, but were not allowed to follow a career. They had to look after the household and the children almost alone, but their skills were not to be employed outside the home, except for social duties. To develop signs of hysteria was, if we follow this argument, one way to escape the contradictory demands.

The medical profession was among the most outspoken opponents of emancipation. Doctors offered 'vigorous intellectual resistance to the campaign for women's suffrage [and] used their votes and influence to exclude women from Oxford, Cambridge, Edinburgh and other universities' (Harrison, 1981, pp.26–27). The idea of women working was anathema to the majority of doctors. When bourgeois women began to take up careers or to pursue interests outside the home, doctors denounced their aspirations as 'unnatural', and a cause of hysteria.

The question of whether women working contributed to a higher infant mortality rate raised a fierce controversy. Examples were taken from working-class districts, but the discussion was fundamentally about the role of women in society.

To account for the high mortality rate of new-born babies, some doctors and health reformers stressed the connection between poverty and illness, but another view prevailed. John Simon, director of the General Board of Health, wrote in 1890:

> . . . that in proportion as adult women were taking part in factory labour or agriculture, the mortality of their infants rapidly increased; that in various registration districts which had such employment within them the district death-rate of infants under one year of age has been from two and a quarter to nearly three times as high as in our standard districts; and that in some of the districts more than a few of the infants were dying of ill-treatment which was almost murderous . . . (Quoted in Wohl, 1983, p.26)

Undoubtedly there was neglect and ill-treatment, but Simon's argument is more widely based: he does not complain about individual cases; it is working women in general who arouse his wrath. There were numerous surveys to prove the same point, and they were believed. More scrupulous investigators could not establish such a relationship and argued that the main factor in infant mortality was poverty, which drove working-class women to factories. After years of studying the problem, Arthur Newsholme, a Medical Officer of Health, stated in 1913 that many other factors were important: 'Poverty, uncleanliness, overcrowding, alcoholic indulgence and disease are closely inter-related . . .' (quoted in Wohl, 1983, p.27). It was suggested that the income of working women might actually improve infants' chances, since parents could then afford better food, housing, clothes and heating. But this remained a minority position, and was not seriously taken up, in contrast to the great number of attempts to establish a link between women's working and infant death rate.

These arguments were part of a wider discussion about the family and the role of women, amid fears that the alleged disintegration of family life diagnosed in the working classes would also reach into the middle and upper classes. It was, however, not easy for women to escape their traditional roles. It seems that for some developing symptoms of hysteria brought rewards, even if they were not consciously sought. Hysteria guaranteed attention and possibly even affection. Women were looked after and excused if, for example, they fainted or fell ill. Doctors, however, profited too. They were the experts who dealt with the illness, and gained a reputation as professionals. At the same time they gained moral authority: in their opinion it was women's behaviour which lay at the root of it all – women were reading too many books, which caused nervousness and overagitation, and they were no longer content to stay at home but sought pleasure or, worse, jobs.

Developing hysteria might have had its rewards, but it did not solve women's problems. On the contrary, some women suffered from operations or other treatments tried on them, and the medical definition contributed to perpetuating the problem. By excusing their changing moods, their fainting and other symptoms, medical opinion kept them in a weak position. At the same time, all 'abnormal' activity was stigmatized, so that it became almost impossible to escape the contradictions and to develop self-respect (Schaps, 1982, pp.130–38; Showalter, 1987, pp.145–64).

Today it could be doubted whether hysteria was an illness at all. This, however, is a tricky problem. If we accept the argument that most diseases and especially the definitions of diseases are socially conditioned, then hysteria as defined here was certainly an illness. It is important to analyse the causes of an illness, but it does not make much sense to grade illnesses as more or less 'real', depending upon the relative influence of somatic, psychic or social factors. In this case, there can be no doubt that women suffered, and their symptoms existed.

The theory that hysteria was closely connected to female biological peculiarities received a decisive blow during the First World War, when a great number of soldiers suffered from it – better known as shell shock. In Britain alone some 80,000 cases passed through army medical facilities. At first it was assumed that the noise of shells exploding at close range had caused the symptoms, but it soon became clear that this was not necessarily the case. Some of the patients had 'never been near an exploding shell, had not been under fire for months, or had not come under fire at all' (Showalter, 1987, p.168). Here, too, organic causes could not be found and neither could concussion, nor changes in atmospheric pressure, nor carbon-monoxide poisoning be held responsible. Gradually

> . . . most military psychologists and medical personnel, if not generals, came to agree that the real cause of shell shock was the emotional disturbance produced by warfare itself, by chronic conditions of fear, tension, horror, disgust, and grief; and that war neurosis was 'an escape from an intolerable situation', a compromise negotiated by the psyche between the instinct of self-preservation and the prohibitions against deception or flight, which were 'rendered impossible by ideals of duty, patriotism and honor'. (Quoted in Showalter, 1987, p.170)

The constriction of the trenches, Sandra Gilbert suggests, was analogous to the domestic, vocational and sexual restraints on nineteenth-century women: 'Paradoxically, in fact, the war to which so many men had gone in hope of becoming heroes, ended up emasculating them . . . confining them as closely as Victorian women had been confined' (Gilbert, 1983, pp.422–50, quoted in Showalter, 1987, p.174).

To sum up, the developments between 1870 and 1950 were very contradictory, many of them for the better, others of doubtful value or even for the worse. By and large, it can be argued that women benefited from them: their general standard of health improved, the birth rate declined (as did the mortality rate after birth), pregnancies became safer. Other changes, especially in the field of surgery, caused suffering, while old prejudices lingered on. Brian Harrison values the medical contribution highly and argues that it 'amounts to a major liberation of women and perhaps deserves more attention than the legal, educational and political dimension of women's emancipation which have hitherto dominated the textbooks' (Harrison, 1981, p.16).

While Harrison is right to stress the importance of the medical contribution, it is pointless to argue which of the different factors was of more importance; furthermore, it is questionable whether it makes sense to distinguish too clearly between them, particularly as many of the activists bringing about the changes were engaged in legal, political, educational and medical issues at the same time. It can be stated, however, that modern medicine contributed to the emancipation of women. It cannot be stated with the same conviction though that the majority of doctors welcomed this emancipation or even deliberately promoted it; rather, the opposite is true. As the example of abortion shows, the contribution of modern medicine was not always deliberate. In the end, doctors could not prevent their discoveries being appropriated and bringing results they originally did not have in mind.

10.3 SCIENCE, PROFESSIONALIZATION AND EVERYDAY LIFE

Perhaps the most striking change in modern medicine is not to be found in therapy, gynaecology or physiology; rather it is a fundamental change in the status of doctors. At the end of our period they enjoyed a high level of prestige and a good income. While there were other people offering medical services, professional doctors and academic medicine were, and still are, in a class of their own. This was not always the case; in fact it is a rather recent development which occurred to a large degree in the years between 1870 and 1950.

A Hungarian physician arriving in New York in the 1870s observed:

As I soon found out, physicians in America were more concerned with establishing a feeling of confidence and trust, than were our colleagues abroad. To a great extent, this was a natural consequence of the difference between the status of the physician in the United States and in Europe. Abroad, the medical degree *per se* invested the physician with a social standing and authority unknown in America, where, in 1874, the meager educational requirements made it easy to secure a diploma after 'two sessions of so many weeks in a year'. With some exceptions, the rank and file of the profession were – as far as general education went – little, if any, above the level of their *clientele*. And the *clientele* not only felt this but knew it. Hence the medical man had to be more modest; he had to be circumspect, even deferential, in facing ignorance, absurd pretensions, and ill manners – especially where they abound most, among a certain class of the self-made, uncultured wealthy. (Quoted in Starr, 1982, pp.80–81)

Compared with their American colleagues, European physicians may have had a higher standing, but their position was far from secure. During most of the nineteenth century we find countless guides for doctors, the aim of which was to help them win the respect of their patients. The recipes for success were not necessarily concerned with medical knowledge; at least as important were refined manners, cultivated behaviour and amiability. In short, a doctor had to be a man of the world in order to succeed (Huerkamp, 1985; Brand, 1965; Rothstein, 1972; Parry, 1976).

While it often helps to have good manners, for doctors at that time it was of vital importance as, to put it crudely, they had little else to offer. They had a good knowledge of anatomy, could use a microscope and had profited from the advances in chemistry, physiology and other subjects which contributed to the rise of modern medicine. But in that area in which patients were most interested – therapy – the advances were not nearly as impressive. Around the turn of the century disillusion had set in, since the important discoveries that held such promise had as yet hardly influenced daily practice. Nor was the position of doctors improved by the patients' traditional habit of seeking the advice of those who were not academically trained. Midwives, herbalists and others were called in, and their suggestions could turn out to be more effective than those of the doctor – which did nothing for the standing of doctors in the community. Doctors lived in a highly competitive world. Some were successful and became famous, but this did not generally hold for the profession as a whole. For many ordinary physicians, medicine was a profession of limited scope.

Towards the end of our period the situation had changed considerably. Doctors had undergone a process of upward social mobility; they had gained prestige and a level of income unknown before and envied by other professions even today. It is, however, very difficult to explain this change. For a long time it was assumed that the better standing of doctors was the logical consequence of advances in medicine, that their superior status was the result of their providing a vastly improved service. This argument is not altogether wrong, but it needs to be qualified. Firstly, the practical results of the scientific approach left much to be desired and, furthermore, doctors had begun to acquire special status and privileges long before scientific medicine became established, though the situation differed considerably from country to country. Generally speaking, it was very important for doctors to get the state to support their demands.

In France, for example, doctors managed to secure a professional monopoly at the beginning of the nineteenth century; in the United States on the other hand, a bitter rivalry existed between academically trained doctors and a great variety of other medical practitioners until well into this century (Ramsey, 1984, pp.225–305). In Germany and England, doctors could not establish a professional *monopoly* in the field of medicine, but they did manage to secure a privileged position for those who had been to university and whose names were officially registered. In England, for example, the Medical Act of 1858 established that it was not illegal to practise medicine without being listed in the official Medical Register, but those practitioners whose names did not appear in the list were at a considerable disadvantage.

> They could not call themselves "physician", "surgeon", "apothecary", or "doctor", they could not serve as military officers or hold appointments in the poor or sanitary administrations or any similar government office; they could not sue for fees. Only the registered could deliver legal attestations; only they would be exempt from ordinary military, community, and jury duties. The law prescribed a penalty for falsely assuming a title or falsely claiming to be listed in the Register and a much stiffer penalty for securing a place in the Register through fraud. This was the essence of the definitive model: all practitioners must identify themselves correctly. The government would be free to choose its official physicians, and it would choose the certified. (Ramsey, 1984, p.248)

New official status made it much easier to maintain a position of authority, but it did not immediately change the relationship between doctors and patients. Patients were still free to consult whomever they saw fit, and here the national insurance systems proved of decisive importance; with minor exceptions they only covered services provided by registered doctors and patients had to pay to consult other experts. At the end of the nineteenth and into the early twentieth century, the situation was rather complicated and again there were great differences between countries. The national insurance systems mainly covered the working classes, while the middle classes either paid the fees themselves or were privately insured and so had greater freedom in whom they could consult. Furthermore, the lines between official and alternative medicine were not altogether clearly drawn: some doctors practised homoeopathy (mainly in the United States) or acupuncture (especially

*Figure 10.5
Poster encouraging medical
consultation c.1918. (Photo:
Wellcome Institute of the
History of Medicine)*

in France). These approaches, however, fell gradually into disrepute among the profession, for whom hospital-centred medicine became the symbol of their professional expertise. Hospitals stood for medical progress and were proof that academic medicine was superior to rival practice, which did not have access to hospitals.

Doctors' attempts to establish a privileged position did not go unchallenged. While traditional healers were not able to mount an effective opposition, there existed among the middle classes a widespread rationalistic and libertarian scepticism about the doctor's art. Privileges and professional monopolies ran counter to the principle of *laissez-faire* which greatly influenced nineteenth-century political and social thinking. The Thomsonian botanical medical sect, for example, which had a great following in nineteenth-century America, wanted to make 'every man his own physician' (Ramsey, 1984, p.252), and the temperance movement in England was characterized by the notion that each individual is the best guardian of his or her own health. Florence Nightingale stated in 1860 that 'instead of wishing to see more Doctors made by women joining what there are, I wish to see as few Doctors, either male or female as possible' (quoted in Harrison, 1981, p.36).

A great variety of groups combined to oppose professional privileges for doctors, as Brian Harrison describes:

> The medical dissenters and anti-vaccinationist laymen, whose interference the doctors so feared, were as ready to associate with feminists as with any other type of reformer. Temperance reformers dabbled in hydropathy and phrenology; anti-vivisectionists hobnobbed with homeopaths; and the anti-vivisectionist doctor tended to be a Chadwickian pioneer of public health who expected medical progress to arise only from sanitary measures which would bring man into closer harmony with the divine order – not from grovelling in the entrails of animals. (Quoted in Harrison, 1981, pp.31–33)

Doctors felt particularly threatened by feminists, who aimed 'to emancipate themselves from the male doctor, and perhaps from doctors altogether' (Harrison, 1981, p.38). The birth-control movement is a good case in point.

*Figure 10.6
Professionalization—an effect
of the British Midwives Act of
1902. The old 'handywoman'
on the left was replaced by the
new, smarter, better-trained
licensed midwife. (Photo:
Royal Society of Medicine)*

It was largely run by lay people, and women were at the forefront; the movement opened its own clinics and gave advice on a variety of medical topics, thereby arousing deeply felt hostility within the male-dominated profession. The profession was afraid that its recently won and still precarious position might be jeopardized. For most of our period, therefore, feminists and the medical profession were at loggerheads.

In many ways, the medical establishment tried to restrict the role of women. The medical business greatly expanded and women were, for example, allowed to work in hospitals, as nurses who had to carry out doctors' orders; they could work as midwives, but here, too, doctors were their superiors. Nursing and midwifery were reformed in our period and this undoubtedly resulted in better training. Furthermore, it opened up a wide range of opportunities, though doctors made sure there would be no threat to their own position.

The attitude of the medical profession towards women's emancipation influenced not just the organization and distribution of jobs in the expanding medical business; it also influenced medical thinking and theories, as is obvious in the case of hysteria described above. It was not just doctors, however, who wanted women to stay at home; these notions were widely shared among the (male) public. And it was not just in medicine that daily experiences and prejudices influenced scientific thinking and theories. The same can be shown to have existed – and to still exist – in other branches of science, too. Science and everyday life are not completely set apart, but rather are closely interrelated.

I would argue that scientific hypotheses and arguments do not differ fundamentally from everyday assumptions, but that scientific hypotheses are systematically tested, and undergo a process of constant criticism from colleagues so that eventually the results are obtained rationally. If, however, the assumptions influencing the hypotheses are widely shared, it can happen that these assumptions themselves are not discussed critically, and even meticulous research can come to unjustified conclusions, as the examples of hysteria and eugenics demonstrate.

In our period, the concept of hysteria was not so much disproved by scientific debate; rather, it lost ground since the continuing process of emancipation made it clear that in almost all areas of business, science, sport, and so on, women are as capable as men. In eugenics, too, it was not scientific debate but rather everyday experience that disproved the concept. The economic crisis of the 1920s and 30s made clear that anybody could become unemployed, even those from the middle classes. They realized that it could be difficult to survive in the capitalist market and that it was not just the urban poor who failed. Social Darwinism and eugenics, stressing the survival of the fittest, were therefore shown to be of doubtful value. Finally, the rise of Nazi Germany, where some of the theories were put into practice, discredited eugenic and racist theories.

To conclude, everyday life, medicine and science are closely interrelated. They influence each other. Scientific arguments and everyday assumptions can be very much alike, the main difference being that in science arguments are more systematically tested and criticized. This is no minor difference, but all the same it does not necessarily prevent science from being characterized by prejudices which sometimes are only belatedly detected. Contradictions, therefore, are signs of a continuing scientific debate, while their absence can point to a deceptive unanimity.

REFERENCES

Abel-Smith, B. (1964) *The Hospitals, 1800–1948*, Heinemann.

Ackerknecht, E.H. (1948) 'Anticontagionism between 1821 and 1864', *Journal of the History of Medicine and Allied Sciences*, 22.

Ackerknecht, E.H. (1953) *Rudolf Virchow, Doctor, Statesman, Anthropologist*, University of Wisconsin Press.

Armstrong, D. (1982) 'The doctor-patient relationship: 1930–1980' in Wright, P. and Treacher, A. (eds.) *The Problem of Medical Knowledge. Explaining the Social Construction of Medicine*, Edinburgh University Press.

Brand, J.L. (1965) *Doctors and the State. The British Medical Profession and Government Action in Public Health, 1870–1912*, Johns Hopkins University Press.

Cartwright, F.F. (1977) *A Social History of Medicine*, Longman.

Daly, M. (1979) *Gyn/ecology: The Metaethics of Radical Feminism*, The Women's Press.

Ehrenreich, B. and English, D. (1978) *For Her Own Good. 150 Years of the Experts' Advice to Women*, Anchor Press.

Gilliat, W. (1954) 'Maternal mortality – still-birth and neonatal mortality' in Kerr, J.M.M., Johnstone, R.W. and Phillips, M.H. (eds.) *Historical Review of British Obstetrics and Gynaecology, 1800–1950*, E. & J. Livingstone.

Göckenjan, G. (1985) *Kurieren und Staat machen. Gesundheit und Medizin in der bürgerlichen Welt*, Suhrkamp.

Gordon, L. (1976) *Woman's Body, Woman's Right: A Social History of Birth Control in America*, Grossman.

Gordon, L. (1978) 'The politics of birth control, 1920–1940. The impact of the professionals' in Ehrenreich, J. (ed.) *The Cultural Crisis of Modern Medicine*, Monthly Review Press.

Harrison, B. (1981) 'Women's health and the women's movement in Britain, 1840–1940' in Webster, C. (ed.) *Biology, Medicine and Society 1840–1940*, Cambridge University Press.

Helman, C. (1984) 'Feed a cold, starve a fever' in Black, N., *et al.*, *Health and Disease: A Reader*, Open University Press.

Himes, N.E. (1963) *Medical History of Contraception*, USA National Committee on Maternal Health.

Honigsbaum, F. (1979) *The Division in British Medicine. A History of the Separation of General Practice from Hospital Care 1911–1968*, Kogan Page.

Huerkamp, C. (1985) *Der Aufstieg der Ärzte im 19. Jahrhundert. Vom gelehrten Stand zum professionellen Experten: Das Beispiel Preussens*, Vandenhoeck & Ruprecht.

Illich, I. (1976) *Limits to Medicine: Medical Nemesis, the Expropriation of Health*, Boyars.

Ludmerer, K.M. (1972) *Genetics and American Society: A Historical Appraisal*, Johns Hopkins University Press.

McKeown, T. (1979) *The Role of Medicine. Dream, Mirage or Nemesis*, Blackwell.

Miller, N.F. (1946) 'Hysterectomy: therapeutic necessity or surgical racket?', *American Journal of Obstetrics and Gynaecology*, 51.

The Open University (1985) U205 *Health and Disease*, The Open University Press.

Parry, N. and J. (1976) *The Rise of the Medical Profession. A Study of Collective Social Mobility*, Croom Helm.

Peterson, M.J. (1978) *The Medical Profession in Mid-Victorian London*, University of California Press.

Ramsey, M. (1984) 'The politics of professional monopoly in nineteenth-century medicine: the French model and its rivals' in Geison, G.L. (ed.) *Professions and the French State 1700–1900*, University of North Carolina Press.

Rothstein, W.G. (1972) *American Physicians in the Nineteenth Century: From Sects to Science*, Johns Hopkins University Press.

Schaps, R. (1982) *Hysterie und Weiblichkeit. Wissenschaftsmythen über die Frau*, Campus.

Schreiber, B. (1973) *The Men Behind Hitler. A German Warning to the World*, H.P. Tadeuss.

Scull, A.T. (1979) *Museums of Madness: The Social Organisation of Insanity in Nineteenth-century England*, Allen Lane.

Shorter, E. (1982) *A History of Women's Bodies*, Allen Lane.

Showalter, E. (1987) *The Female Malady. Women, Madness and English Culture, 1830–1980*, Virago.

Shyrock, R.H. (1947) *The Development of Modern Medicine*, Hafner.

Singer, C.S. and Ashworth Underwood, E. (1962) *A Short History of Medicine*, Oxford University Press.

Smith-Rosenberg, C. (1972) 'The hysterical woman: sex roles in nineteenth-century America', *Social Research*, 39.

Spree, R. (1981) *Soziale Ungleichheit vor Krankheit und Tod*, Vandenhoeck & Ruprecht.

Starr, P. (1982) *The Social Transformation of American Medicine. The Rise of a Sovereign Profession and the Making of a Vast Industry*, Basic.

Stopes, M. (1925) *'The First Five Thousand'. Being the First Report of 'The Mothers' Clinic' for Constructive Birth Control*, John Bale & Co.

Tietze, C. (1965) 'History of contraceptive methods', *Journal of Sex Research*, 1.

Virchow, R. (1886) 'Gesamtbericht über die von der deutschen anthropologischen Gesellschaft veranlassten Erhebungen über die Farbe der Haut, der Haare und der Augen der Schulkinder in Deutschland', *Archiv für Anthropologie*, 16.

Waddington, I. (1973) 'The role of the hospital in the development of modern medicine: a sociological analysis', *Sociology*, 7.

Winter, J.M. (1982) 'The decline of mortality in Britain, 1870–1950' in Barker, T. and Drake, M. (eds.) *Population and Society in Britain, 1850–1950*, Batsford.

Wohl, A.S. (1983) *Endangered Lives. Public Health in Victorian Britain*, Dent.

Woodward, J. and Richards, D. (eds.) (1977) *Health Care and Popular Medicine in Nineteenth Century England. Essays in the Social History of Medicine*, Croom Helm.

Wuttke-Groneberg, W. (1982) *Medizin im Nationalsozialismus. Ein Arbeitsbuch*, Schwäbische Verlags-gesellschaft.

11 SOCIAL AND HUMAN ENGINEERING

Bernard Waites

PART 1 SCIENTIFIC MANAGEMENT AND INDUSTRIAL PSYCHOLOGY

The ambition to reform society by turning the methods and findings of the natural sciences upon human affairs is one we can trace back to Francis Bacon and the seventeenth-century scientific revolution. This remained a speculative, utopian project until unplanned industrialization began a new phase of social development in the early nineteenth century. Industrialism, with its substitution of mechanical for human power, its sub-division and specialization of labour, and factory system, brought enormous gains in productivity and the prospect of hitherto unimaginable material progress. Yet the social consequences of industrialism subverted that prospect by creating class divisions and conflicts which threatened hierarchies of rank and deference. The desire to reconcile progress with order by implementing a 'science' of society modelled upon the natural sciences inspired Henri de Saint-Simon (1760–1825) and Auguste Comte (1798–1857), joint founders of modern sociology and the diffuse intellectual movement known as 'positivism'. This term resists precise definition, for it embraces rather more than the doctrines of its author, Comte. The most salient features of positivist thought have been empiricism and phenomenalism (the belief that 'reality' consists in sense-impressions); an aversion to metaphysics; an inductivist model of scientific discovery; and commitment to the continuity of the natural and social sciences – the idea that they share logical and methodological foundations and that there are 'natural laws' of social processes (Giddens, 1977, pp.29–89). Comte avoided the fatalism implicit in this last tenet with the maxim that knowledge gives the power to foresee and intervene in human affairs; both he and Saint-Simon promoted the idea of a technocracy of socially disinterested experts as the new ruling class of industrial society.

'Human' and 'social' engineering were two tributaries of positivist thought, for, though not always directly affiliated with Saint-Simon and Comte, they flowed from a scientistic and technocratic world-view which these two thinkers had done much to form. In this essay, I have reserved the term 'human' engineering for political projects derived from the life sciences which sought to control the selection of (and thereby improve) the human species itself.

The term 'social' engineering can refer to several, distinct features of the development of the advanced societies. Its most extensive reference indicates the remodelling of a whole society according to a systematic plan in which the allocation of labour and material resources, the control of prices, the prioritization of production as between capital and consumer goods, and the forecasting of output are all centrally co-ordinated and rationalized. The 'model' for this most extensive form of social engineering is provided by the industrialization of the Soviet Union during its first Five Year Plan (1928–1933). For its admirers in the West, such as Sidney and Beatrice Webb, the form of 'social engineering' practised by Soviet Communism was the acme of a rationality which was simultaneously social and scientific. Here, they thought, was 'a new civilization' which counted on 'a vast and unfathomable advance of science in every field' and in place of 'merely traditional beliefs and postulates about man and the universe' was creating a living philosophy of 'scientific humanism' (Webbs, 1941, pp.xxix–xxx).

Soviet 'social engineering' accomplished the swiftest, most complete transformation of a nation's way of life in history: the urban population rose from 28.7 million in 1929 to 63.1 million in 1940, the non-agricultural workforce increased from 10 million to 45 million between 1926 and 1955 (Lane, 1970, pp.65–66; see also chapter 12, pp.365,376–7). Applied science and technology were critical instruments of this transformation, the central feature of which was the massive development of the capital goods industries, but its dominating agency was the single-party state. The human costs, which involved the compulsory collectivization of agriculture and the liquidation of 'richer' peasants or kulaks, were appalling. We might well call this 'engineering' *societal*, to distinguish it from the more piecemeal developments in capitalist societies where, although the state has 'commanded' the economy in wartime, the market has a fundamental role in determining investment, prices (including the price of labour), the level of employment and the changing sectoral balance of the economy. The relative decline of manufacturing industry and the growth of the tertiary sector in Western societies, for example, have been overwhelmingly determined by market forces.

This essay will say very little about the impact of 'societal' engineering on the Soviet model on everyday life in state socialist societies. It will concentrate, instead, on the origins and diffusion of a type of 'social engineering', the dominating agency of which has been the corporate capitalist enterprise, and the chief effects of which have been felt in the everyday working lives of modern factory workers and business office employees. 'Social engineering' in this limited sense refers to the organization and control of labour in managerial capitalism. In practice, this will mean analysing American innovations in 'scientific management' and business organization and tracing their adoption by European firms. This is not to say that European societies in the late nineteenth and early twentieth century did not have their own traditions of applying so-called scientific principles to the organization of industry and commerce; France, in the person of Henri Fayol (1841–1925), possessed a leading theorist of scientific administration; Germany, through the work of Hugo Münsterberg, pioneered applied industrial psychology. However, by 1920 the economic preponderance of America, won by her domination of the mass-production and science-based industries (electrical, chemicals, radio), meant that her example profoundly influenced European industrialists, politicians and ideologues as they strove to 'recast' bourgeois Europe in the aftermath of the First World War (Maier, 1970 and 1975).

Indeed, the prodigious technological efficiency of American industry was admired even by the revolutionaries in the Soviet Union dedicated to the overthrow of capitalism and bourgeois society. When Lenin set out 'The Immediate Tasks of Soviet Government' in April 1918, he defined F.W. Taylor's system of scientific management as

> . . . a combination of the subtle brutality of bourgeois exploitation and a number of [capitalism's] greatest scientific achievements in the field of analysing mechanical motions during work, the elimination of superfluous and awkward motions, the working out of correct methods of work, the introduction of the best system of accounting and control, etc. The Soviet Government must at all costs adopt all that is valuable in the achievements of science and technology in this field . . . We must organize in Russia the study and teaching of the Taylor system and systematically try it out and adapt it to our purposes. (Cited in Maier, 1970, p.51)

11.1
TAYLORISM IN ITS
CONTEXT

In some respects, Lenin and more recent Marxist writers on Taylor (1856–1915) have heaped on his name a bouquet of undeserved compliments. Many of his work-study methods were arbitrary and can scarcely be dignified as scientific achievements. The notoriety of his 'labour reforms' disguised the fact that his most substantial innovations lay in the technical field of machine and tool design (most notably the development of high-speed tool steel), and factory layout and organization. These had far more impact than his labour measures, which were introduced *in toto* in only a handful of firms in his lifetime (Nelson, 1980, p.x). It is a mistake to identify him too closely with the modern bureaucratic corporation – an institution Taylor generally distrusted – or to credit him with an overall strategy for managerial capitalism, for he was neglectful of the larger organizational and financial aspects of business administration (Nelson, 1980, p.103). More fundamentally, the invocation of his name in an elastic notion of 'Taylorism' (often stretching to practices for which he was not responsible) leads to an excessively personalized view of history. Unquestionably, Taylor was at the forefront of early twentieth-century 'social engineers', but the significance of his work derived from and has to be understood in the context of complex changes in capitalist organization, in the relationship of science and the scientific professions to industry, and in factory technology and organization.

11.1.1
Managerial capitalism

The most important change in capitalist organization was the emergence of the modern business enterprise, containing many distinct operating units, and employing a hierarchy of middle- and top-salaried managers to supervise them. This form of business organization did not exist before 1840. In America, it evolved first in the large railroad companies when they outgrew the capacity of a single superintendent. The needs for the internal co-ordination of the companies' different functions and the external regulations of competition, as well as external co-operation over track and rolling stock, led to hierarchies of professional managers. Top-level managers came to share, with representatives of investment banks, the strategic decisions with respect to the construction of new lines and the allocation of resources. This form of organization was copied by steamship, urban transport and utility companies, and the communications monopolies, Western Union and American Telephone and Telegraph. It spread next to distribution, where mass retailing by firms like Sears and Roebuck required complex management structures to co-ordinate the flow of goods from producers to customers. It was adopted in production when manufacturers who had developed large-batch and continuous process technology for low-price goods (such as soap), or who were processors of perishable products for national markets, or who were selling mass-produced machines to the consumer market, integrated forward with their own mass distribution networks. American Tobacco, Procter and Gamble, Eastman Kodak – all large-batch, continuous-process producers – created such marketing organizations in the 1880s. In the next decade the large meat packers and brewers began to build national and often international networks of branch houses with refrigerated warehouses and distribution facilities, as well as fleets of temperature-controlled railroad cars and ships. The Singer Sewing Machine Company went into retailing, while the agricultural implement manufacturers relied on franchise dealers whom they supported with wholesale organizations. The impetus to the spread of managerial hierarchies in other sectors of American business was given by the great merger boom of 1898 to 1903. Many mergers were speculative ventures on the part of financial 'tycoons' and did not last. To profit from the economies of scale provided by merger, firms had to integrate vertically (thus gaining control of supplies and distribution) and create a hierarchy of management to co-ordinate operations. By 1917, large corporations dominated those areas of manufacturing which were capital-intensive, relied on

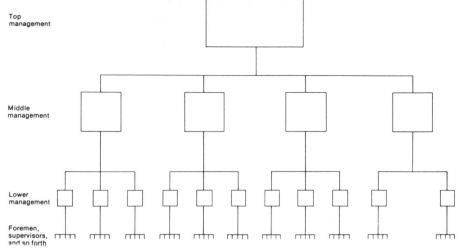

Top
management

Middle
management

Lower
management

Foremen,
supervisors,
and so forth

Figure 11.1
The basic hierarchical
structure of modern business
enterprise (each box represents
an office). (Reproduced from
Alfred D. Chandler, 1977,
The Visible Hand. The
Managerial Revolution in
American Business, *Harvard*
University Press, by
permission of the publishers)

continuous- or large-batch technology, and were capable of standardized production for mass markets. These firms internalized functions which had been previously co-ordinated by market and price mechanisms, and in more traditional business sectors remained so (Chandler, in Chandler and Daems, 1980, pp.9–29; Chandler, 1977).

For several reasons, the managerial capitalism of the giant firm evolved more slowly in the European national economies. The size of the American market was critically important. Significant, too, were her legal traditions which forbade 'trusts' or cartels as conspiracies against the public interest (because they reduced competition) and so encouraged growth through merger. In Germany, America's chief industrial rival by 1900, cartelization was legal, and this was the chief form of business consolidation until outlawed under heavy American pressure after 1945. Giant firms did develop in the German producers' goods industries (notably in chemicals and electrical engineering) and as in America these integrated production with distribution. They also integrated production with basic scientific research by creating cadres of technically- and scientifically-qualified, salaried managers and industrial research laboratories. In some instances, technically trained directors of research departments took over managerial functions and became part of the firm's leadership. The emergence of technically-qualified, salaried managers meant that scientific and technical expertise increasingly substituted for personal and familial authority in the routines of business, and greatly reinforced trends towards professionalism and scientific management in industry (Kocka, in Chandler and Daems, 1980, pp.92–97). In Britain, industrial concentration and the emergence of a stratum of salaried managers were delayed until the 1920s, partly because British manufacturers had tended to specialize in non-standardized products (such as marine engines) for export. After 1916, however, there was a pronounced tendency towards concentration and the next fifteen years saw the creation of such industrial giants as ICI, Unilever and English Electric. France lagged still further behind in the development of multi-divisional, professionally-managed firms. Medium-sized family enterprises characterized the French economy until after the Second World War, and informal business practices tended to restrict competition, maintain prices and preserve the existence of many independent firms. There were notable exceptions to this, such as the automobile industry, in which Louis Renault and Andre Citroën dominated the market and were instrumental in introducing assembly methods and scientific management. Even here, however, personal ownership and the strategic direction of the company remained vested in the same individual.

**11.1.2
Science-based industry**

The growth of big firms staffed by technically-qualified managers was closely associated with the exploitation of science in production. The two industries in which the large-scale, direct exploitation of scientific experiment and invention took off were chemicals and electrical (with its subsidiary, tele-communications). Up to the 1880s, Britain was the dominant chemicals producer, but her industrial leadership was based upon the older-established heavy inorganic chemicals and acid and alkali production. In these branches of the industry, she continued to be fairly competitive. However, in organic chemicals – which had a different 'knowledge-base' – the locus of innovation shifted from about 1870 to Germany which developed, in an extraordinarily short space of time, the world's leading synthetic dyestuffs industry, accounting for 90 per cent of world production by 1900. 'In technical virtuosity and aggressive enterprise, this leap to hegemony, almost monopoly has no parallel. It was Imperial Germany's greatest industrial achievement' (Landes, 1969, p.276). Germany's predominance was aided by her highly-developed system of technical education, which provided industry with trained cadres, and the large-scale operations of her coal-tar firms which enabled them to carry a profitable and diversified range of products and to finance research and development costs (Kocka, 1980, p.96; Richardson, 1968, p.286). Germany's lead in dyestuffs over America was facilitated by American patent laws which enabled German firms to patent chemical products, even when manufactured by methods over which they had no patent rights. For this reason, although America was the leading processor of sulphuric acid and superphosphates, she had no synthetic dyestuffs industry to speak of before the US government stripped the German firms of their patent rights during the First World War and issued them to American companies. This was the real beginning of a science-based American chemicals industry, in which a few giant firms (Du Pont being the best known) dominated production and industrial research (Noble, 1977, pp.12–13).

Meanwhile, a pattern had emerged in the American electrical industry whereby a very small number of firms came to control the market because of their monopolies of certain crucial scientific patents. Patent control was the most important impetus behind the formation of the General Electrical Company (GEC) in 1892 (the forerunner of General Electric). The two companies that merged into GEC each controlled patents necessary for the other to develop its lighting, railway and power equipment business without fear of infringement suits and injunctions. The enormous business opportunities provided by the development of electrically-powered urban transport at this time encouraged the two rivals to overcome this difficulty by merging (see section 6.1). Similarly, the Bell industrial organization was able to achieve a commanding position in communications by monopoly control of the original telephone patents and by creating a research and development department charged with patenting new devices to strengthen the company's position (Noble, 1977, pp.6–10). Once established, these industrial giants integrated forward and made the capital threshold for entry into the business so high as to prohibit competition. Since the protection afforded by patent control was only temporary, the newly integrated industrial empires also shifted to a dependence on the output of their specialized research departments to help maintain their dominant positions. By the first decade of the twentieth century giants like General Electric, Westinghouse and Du Pont all had extensive departments where salaried scientifically-trained managers and technicians spent their careers improving products and processes (Chandler, 1977, pp.374–75).

The emergence of science-based corporations had profound consequences for the professions of electrical, chemical and mechanical engineering. These professions grew extraordinarily rapidly between 1880 and 1920 (from 7,000 to 136,000 members in the United States), the golden age for the application of science to American industry (Layton, 1971, p.3). At the same time, the locus of professional practice for the great majority shifted from independent consultancy to salaried corporate employment. Engineers became acutely conscious of their social role and not uncommonly saw themselves as the builders of a new civilization of unparalleled material abundance and leisure (Layton, 1971, p.59). There was, potentially, a conflict of interest between the engineers' technical rationality, their demand for professional autonomy and colleagual control, and a competitive economic system based on private ownership and the profit motive. In practice, the engineers subordinated their professional interests to those of the corporate economy. This was not just a matter of individual beliefs and values: the engineers' professional societies (such as the American Society of Mechanical Engineers, founded in 1880, and the American Institute of Electrical Engineers, 1884) became closely allied with and financially dependent on business interests. Business corporations exerted an increasing influence on engineering education. Moreover, the typical career pattern for an engineer involved an upwards movement to management after about fifteen years in industry. A survey conducted in the 1920s indicated that 60 per cent of all engineers made this shift eventually (Layton, 1971, p.13). By mid-century, almost one in five of the managerial élite of company presidents and board chairmen were engineers by training. The career expectations of engineers reinforced their commitment to a professional practice guided by the interests of the companies that employed them. In designing machinery, for example, the need to minimize both the cost and autonomy of skilled labour was as imperative as the desire to harness the potentials of matter and energy (Noble, 1977, p.34). The dollar became the final term in every engineering equation.

11.1.3
The factory 'revolution', c.1880–1920

The emergence of the giant corporation in America was much publicized, and the fear that these new huge organizations would corrupt democratic processes prompted 'progressive' political demands for greater control by the federal and state governments over industry and commerce. The parallel developments in factory organization attracted less publicity, although their impact on working lives, on patterns of authority at the workplace and industrial conflict were much greater. The cumulative changes in plant size and layout, in technology and the use of electric power, in the sub-division of labour and the adoption of continuous 'flow' production, in the growth of managerial functions and the de-skilling of large parts of the labour force were sufficiently momentous to speak of a 'factory revolution' between 1880 and 1920. Ford's Highland Park plant – constructed in 1908–10, converted to assembly-line production by 1914 – was the quintessential material result of this revolution, Taylor its most representative figure.

Before 1880, the typical American factory outside the textiles sector was witness to the birth of industrialization in the craftsman's workshop. Factories were commonly congeries of shops rather than the closely integrated enterprises that we know today (Nelson, 1975, p.4). Construction methods then in use allowed for only limited natural lighting and reliance on steam power necessitated a maze of transmission shafts and belts. In highly mechanized industries, machines were grouped generically rather than according to their place in the sequence of production, and gangs of unskilled labourers manhandled semi-finished products and components from shop to shop. Skilled tasks were carried out by functionally autonomous craftsmen who often fixed their own output quota or 'stint', and whose ethical code demanded a 'manly' bearing towards the boss and a high degree of mutual solidarity (Montgomery, 1979, pp.12–16). Frequently, craftsmen were organized in gangs under a contractor who negotiated a price for the job with management and then paid the men according to skill and seniority out of this sum. Contractors were independent businessmen within the factory. Iron and steel manufacture and tin-plate rolling were almost universally carried on under the contract system, as was machine and locomotive building in New England. Where the contract system did not prevail, managerial functions were concentrated in the foreman: he often accounted for labour and material costs, acted as timekeeper, hired, supervised and disciplined workers (Nelson, 1975, p.40).

The physical environment of the factory was transformed by the use of new materials, such as structural steel and reinforced concrete, in its construction (see sections 5.5 and 5.6). These were much stronger than traditional building materials and allowed for far more natural lighting, as did too the adoption of the saw-tooth roof. The replacement of gas and oil lamps by arc and then incandescent bulbs from the early 1880s made for more efficient artificial lighting, and spurred owners and managers to introduce electricity for other purposes (see section 3.4). Where they were adopted, electrically-powered hoists, cranes and conveyors eliminated much unskilled manual labour and facilitated the co-ordination of different shops and departments. The use of electricity to drive machine tools followed more slowly and, often, the costs of electrification meant that this took place in newly-built factories. When tools became individually motorized, factory designers were able to eliminate shafts and belts and evolve new forms of plant layout, designed to ease the flow of work between departments. The new factories were much larger than the preceding generation, but less constrained by the technologies of construction and the labour process. 'Steel and brick or reinforced concrete construction and electrical power permitted far more flexibility in arranging the plant and manufacturing process than progressive engineers and manufacturers of the previous generation had ever imagined possible' (Nelson, 1975, p.23). Despite their greater size, the new factories permitted closer managerial surveillance and control.

11.2 TAYLORISM IN THE UNITED STATES

11.2.1 The man and his work

Taylor's career as works manager, consultant 'efficiency' engineer and publicist exemplified the 'factory revolution' and was dedicated to maximizing the productivity of the factory as a complete unit and centralizing its control within management. After training as a skilled machinist and qualifying as a mechanical engineer, he quickly rose during the 1880s to the position of shop superintendent at the Midvale Steel Company, Philadelphia. The impetus towards the labour control measures for which he became notorious stemmed, in a large measure, from his enormous technical creativity. His inventions included a tool grinder and a machine-tool table, and he was responsible for a prolonged series of metal-cutting experiments out of which was perfected high-speed chromium steel. These experiments are now regarded as the beginnings of scientific management, for Taylor found that the exploitation of their resulting technical advances demanded organizational innovations of comparable significance. Faster cutting times meant potentially greater output from the machine and the machinist, and this in turn had implications for production and stock controls (Nelson, 1980, pp.36–37). If production was to be 'speeded up', then the whole factory had to be integrated into a more closely co-ordinated system. In particular, the human input into production – labour – had to be treated in the same manner as inputs of materials and energy. Work was analysed so that it could be sub-divided into basic tasks and the amount of labour necessary for any task measured. Hence, the most characteristic of Taylorism's methods: the use of the stop-watch for time study. Workmen were instructed in the most economic ways of performing tasks and optimal times calculated for their performance. To discourage 'soldiering' or the restriction of output sanctioned by the skilled workers' ethical code, an incentive wage and differential

piece rate were introduced which rewarded workers who achieved a calculated production target and penalized those who did not. To co-ordinate
operations, Taylor created a planning department with responsibility for
issuing detailed daily instruction cards to the workmen.

Taylor's labour measures were put forward within a larger framework
of systematic management which included cost-accounting procedures, the
standardization of tools and machines, the relocating of machines and belts
to facilitate the flow of production, and the introduction of functional foremanship. The last meant that the varied responsibilities of the old-style
general foreman were broken down into specific functions and these re-
allocated among a number of functional foremen. In Taylor's experience,
'almost all shops are under-officered . . . [and] the foreman's duties are in no
way clearly circumscribed' (Taylor, 1947, pp.94–95). Foremen, he proposed,
should (no less than workmen and gang bosses) be entirely relieved of
planning and clerical duties and be responsible only for executing decisions
made in the planning room. By the same token contractors and independent
businessmen had to be eliminated from the internal economy of the factory.
Nor did Taylor's proposed reforms stop short within the factory: they
included the reorganization of sales and purchasing with a view to broadening
and stabilizing the market for its products (Hoxie, 1915, p.22).

After retiring from consultancy work, Taylor codified his system in *Shop
Management* (1903) and *The Principles of Scientific Management* (1911), and
built up a school of disciples to spread the gospel among industrialists,
corporate leaders and politicians. In this last phase of his career, Taylor was
attempting to address a national audience in the belief that 'the fundamental
principles of scientific management are applicable to all kinds of human
activities' (Taylor, 1947, p.7). Scientific management was put forward as a
Saint-Simonian ideology of the 'industrial classes' and much of its appeal lay
in its vulgar positivism and scientism. The system was supposed to display
the 'natural laws' of the labour process and its experts were to present capital
and labour with the unimpeachable 'facts' of work. Even the most mundane
tasks – such as pig-iron handling – had, according to Taylor, their 'science',
the laws of which were revealed only to the experts.

Taylor's theories became linked with the wider cult of 'efficiency' and were
taken up by Louis Brandeis, a leading 'progressive' jurist, in a celebrated
suit brought against the New Haven railroad company. Brandeis submitted
that the grossly incompetent company management was abusing the public
with its high tariffs, and called a succession of scientific management experts
to testify that freight costs could be radically reduced under an efficient
management. Taylor received less favourable publicity from the strike which
followed the 'Taylorization' of the national arsenal at Watertown, Massachusetts, and from the testimony of representatives of the American Federation
of Labor to the US Commission on Industrial Relations: that his methods
led to 'driving', the degradation of craft skills through the excessive sub-
division and specialization of labour, rate-cutting, and divisive competition
among workers. Taylor and his disciples were bluntly opposed to organized
labour: they assumed that collective bargaining was inimical to scientific
management and sympathized with the drive to exclude it from the industrial
relations of heavy industry led by US Steel in the 1900s (Nadworny, 1955).
The craft unions reciprocated this deep-seated distrust. Though they were
largely powerless to oppose Taylorism in private enterprise, they did succeed
in persuading Congress to prohibit time study and the premium bonus system
in government establishments (Nadworny, 1955, p.103).

Taylor's own propagandist writings, and the good and bad odours that
clung to his name, obscured the real material effects that his system (and its
imitations) had had on workers' lives and factory regimes where they had
been introduced. The ideological programme of Taylorism was, and has been

since, mistaken for its achievement. In fact, Taylor experienced a number of setbacks in his career, particularly with his attempts to extend managerial control over the labour process and impose his much vaunted 'task idea' on workers. During his time at Midvale, he found that rate-setting for skilled machinists was a complex task made more difficult by the shop-floor solidarity and defensive unionism of craft workers. Factory and yard labourers, usually unorganized, of ethnic stock and often poorly conversant in English, and competing in a labour market glutted by new waves of migration, were a much easier target (Nelson, 1980, pp.42–43). Taylor had much the same experience as a consultant at the Bethlehem Iron Company, between 1898 and 1901, where he was forced to look to the yard labourers to demonstrate the efficiency of his methods, and he was unable to elicit greater output from the skilled workers who really mattered (Nelson, 1980, pp.91 and 98). Moreover, many of Taylor's methods did not long outlive his (or his associates') departure from a consultancy position in a factory, and they could not compensate for business difficulties encountered because of general movements of the economy into recession. Taylor's methods promised lower unit costs, not lower costs as such. They were expensive to introduce in their full panoply and the reward for a factory's greater efficiency and labour productivity was dependent on a buoyant market for its products.

**11.2.2
Diffusion and
rapprochement with
organized labour**

By the time of Taylor's death, about 180 American factories had been Taylorized and several thousands of plants had introduced elements of scientific management while ignoring such key features of Taylor's system as formal planning departments, and the use of detailed instruction cards and functional foremanship. An investigation by R.F. Hoxie, for the US Commission on Industrial Relations, indicated that even the establishments with a claim to be following Taylor's system varied considerably in their practices and fidelity to his ideas. Among the shops Hoxie visited, there was no general uniformity in the steps taken to standardize tools and machinery and improve layout (which Taylor regarded as prerequisites for his labour 'reforms'). Sometimes the task and bonus system or differential piece rates were the only features of Taylorism seriously implemented. Relatively few scientifically managed shops employed a full system of functional foremanship. Even fewer had adopted Taylor's proposals for the 'scientific' selection of workers. Standard written instruction cards had similarly made little permanent impact on the factory regime: in the case of simpler, routine jobs the written card had tended to degenerate into a mere order to do so much work in so much time for so much pay; where the work required exceptional judgement, then the card lost its significance and utility (Hoxie, 1915, p.37).

Even with respect to the most characteristic feature of Taylor's system – time study – Hoxie found its methods and results to be 'the special sport of individual judgement and opinion, subject to all the possibilities of diversity, inaccuracy and injustice that arise from human ignorance and prejudice' (Hoxie, 1915, p.40). Time study originally had a two-fold purpose: firstly, to improve and standardize working methods by eliminating wasteful movement, co-ordinating sequences in the industrial process, and so on; secondly, to establish an optimal time for a task *after* the first purpose had been achieved. Most scientific management employers were neglecting the first, or not even recognizing the distinction between the two. Times were being set by quite arbitrary methods, and it was not uncommon to establish the necessary time for a job simply by reference to the company records for other jobs or other shops. These would record the time allowed for specific sub-operations, some of which would be common to the new job. A clerk would total up the relevant times; time study had become an office process (Hoxie, 1915, p.51). Times established by this procedure ignored variations between shops and variations in the way any operations related to each other in different jobs. Both materially affected the real time it took a worker to fulfil different tasks. In Taylor's system, time study was supposed to arrive at objective and unarguable facts which precluded the informal bargaining between craftsmen and foremen over times and rates which had taken place under the old factory system. Theoretically, it was a crucial part of the centralization of the knowledge of the industrial process in management for which Taylor strove. In practice, time study was delegated to low-paid, low-status white-collar workers, inaccurate, and often the source of industrial grievance. Among other drawbacks, task setting by the time-study methods Hoxie encountered often failed to discriminate between genuine differences in skill among workers and eroded the differentials between craftsmen and semi-skilled machinists.

In the final, propagandist phase of his career, Taylor had presented scientific management as a solution to the 'labour problem'. The vast gains in productivity that would follow from the universal application of his system would, he claimed, so increase the social product that labour and capital would cease to quarrel over increasing their respective shares. 'Scientific management will mean, for the employers and workmen who adopt it . . . the elimination of almost all causes for dispute and disagreement between them . . . the great increase in wages which accomplishes this type of management will largely eliminate the wage question as a source of dispute' (Taylor, 1947, p.143). The effect of the various wage systems introduced in scientifically managed shops had scarcely fulfilled this promise. They tended – especially in shops where the character of the product varied greatly and production was for specific orders rather than stock – to undermine the stability and continuity of earnings and employment. Not only was there a strong tendency to weed out less efficient workers, there was also a disposition to 'hustle' workers while orders lasted, and then lay them off or put them on low-paid day work while orders were slack. 'In the one case, continuity of employment is sacrificed, in the other, stability of income' (Hoxie, 1915, p.83).

This catalogue of discrepancies between the theory and ideology of scientific management and actual practices in shops which had employed consultants to overhaul and rationalize them is, partly, explained by the relative novelty of the movement. Businessmen, as well as craftsmen, had an understandable tendency to conserve existing practices and plant because of the capital and expertise embodied in them. It was by no means obvious that all Taylor's innovations would meet the capitalist's rational criterion of profit maximization, and the temptation to exploit only those that were clearly and immediately profitable was a strong one. Generally, in fact, America's industrialists took from Taylorism two interrelated principles which had been familiar features of her industrialization since its beginning: a commitment to the division and specialization of labour and the substitution of machines for skill. By 1915, scientifically-managed shops had universally carried specialization of labour to its most feasible limits and had abandoned the apprenticeship system except for the training of a few beginners destined for managerial positions. All were substituting the one-job or machine specialist for the all-round workman (Hoxie, 1915, pp.38 and 123–26). These developments had a profound influence on twentieth-century American industrial labour, encouraging as they did what has been called 'the degradation of work' (Braverman, 1974). It was not the case, however, that with the lapse of time industrialists moved beyond these admittedly fundamental principles to embrace each and every other of Taylor's precepts. Functional foremanship did not, on the whole, replace the 'military style' of line management; nor did task setting become the universal basis of industrial remuneration linked with productivity. On the contrary, the sophisticated incentive-pay schemes promoted by scientific management made little progress outside the metal-working industries. A survey of factory wages undertaken in 1924 showed that 56 per cent of workers were still on hourly wages, 37 per cent on piece work, and only 7 per cent on premium or bonus plans (Montgomery, 1979, p.38).

Equally, the novelty of scientific management will partly explain its virtual confinement, in 1915, to the capital-intensive machinery industries whose direction was dominated by mechanical engineers. Though there was an impressive range of industrial concerns in those listed as scientifically managed by 1915 (it included printing, textiles, construction and footwear), the notion of scientific management's extensive influence beyond the machine shops was illusory. Fully scientifically-managed firms were isolated exceptions in the sprawling empire of American industry. The constantly replenished supply of immigrant and farm labour meant that some large concerns relied on brute muscle rather than machine power: manual labour was so abundant on the New York docks, for example, that not a single pier had even installed a moving crane before 1914 (Montgomery, 1979, p.36). Migrants entering American industry – including the science-based oil, chemical and rubber industries – were highly unlikely to encounter anything like Taylor's rational ideal of labour selection and control, and incentive wages. On the contrary, often as not they met 'with arbitrary, petty tyranny wielded by gang leaders, skilled workmen, and hiring bosses' (ibid, p.36). Common labour rates – which scientific management theorists condemned for indiscriminately paying 'positions' not people – were the norm for manual workers.

One important obstacle to the diffusion of scientific management was removed by the striking change in relations between organized labour and the management movement. During the First World War, their mutual antipathy waned as a result of the collaboration of employers' organizations and trade unions in the war economy and the growing influence within the Taylor Society (the leading management organization) of a more 'consensual' approach to industrial relations. By the early 1920s, a remarkable rapprochement between organized labour and scientific management had taken place. Most of Taylor's disciples now acknowledged that his system had to be 'humanized'; they accepted collective bargaining and unionism as necessary features of the industrial system, and advocated union participation in the introduction of scientific management. The craft unions who dominated the American Federation of Labor (AFL), and who were motivated far more by fear of the mass of unorganized, unskilled workers than of labour solidarity, were now convinced that their interests lay in increasing production. As one contemporary put it, whereas 'The old rough-and-ready trade unionism battled over the division of the product . . . the new suave discreet unionism talks the language of the efficiency engineer and busies itself about ways and means of increasing output' (quoted in Nadworny, 1955, p.150). Scientific management-union co-operation was evinced in the reorganization of the Baltimore-Ohio railroad workshops under the aegis of joint committees of managers and labour authorized to discuss job analysis, scheduling and routing of work, the hiring of new men, and improving tools and equipment. This administrative method and its results were copied in other railroad shops (pp.124–25). Public acknowledgement of organized labour's willingness to accommodate itself with scientific management was made by William Green, president of the AFL, in the major address to a joint meeting of the Taylor Society and the Management Division of the American Society of Mechanical Engineers in December 1925. This reconciliation of the unions and 'efficiency' experts contrasted very markedly with the persistent hostility of the great majority of employers (and the Federal government in the early 1920s) to collective bargaining and independent trade unionism. Rather ironically, the employers and their organizations – with their company unions, individualist approach to bargaining and constant resort to the courts for anti-union injunctions – were considered by Taylor's heirs a more serious obstacle to scientific management than organized labour in the late 1920s.

**11.3
FORD AND MASS
PRODUCTION**

Taylor's system of scientific management has not uncommonly been seen as influencing, even inspiring, the first fully-developed system of mass production of a multicomponent consumer durable, at Ford's Highland Park factory (for example, Giedion, 1948, pp.115–16 and 121). More recent studies have failed to uncover any direct contact between Ford officials and the scientific management movement. While several of the innovations adopted by Ford (such as the use of work study to eliminate wasteful movement, the creation of a central planning department which arrogated the mental labour of production) were also features of Taylor's system, there is reason to doubt that Taylorism contributed significantly to the new assembly line at Highland Park (Hounshell, 1984, p.250). A fundamental difference between Fordism and Taylorism lay in their approaches to the co-ordination of labour and technological hardware: Ford, in his approach, sought to eliminate labour by machinery, not, as the Taylorites customarily did, to take a given production process and improve the efficiency of the workers. Although Taylor had regarded the standardization of machines and their optimal location as indispensable steps in scientific management, he had basically taken the production hardware as a given and sought revisions in the labour process and the organization of work. Ford engineers took a much more radical approach to the production hardware: before the introduction of the Highland Park assembly line, the company scrapped much of its existing technology and made a huge capital investment in specially designed machine tools. Having mechanized its work processes, it then sought a stable workforce to feed and tend its machines (Hounshell, 1984, pp.252–53; Meyer, 1981, p.24).

Before the introduction of the assembly line, the majority of Highland Park's workers were skilled men who worked in groups at sub-assembly points in the factory. With the growing demand for the Model T, much was done to rationalize the labour process by, for example, locating component bins so that workers would no longer have to fetch and carry from the stores. Later, gravity chutes and conveyors were introduced to move components. Increasing output to match the demand led to the rapid growth of the labour force – Ford employed 450 workers in 1908 and 14,000 in 1913 – and a dilution of skilled labour as the concentration on the standardized design of one product led to the specialization and routinization of machine and work processes. The decision to adopt true assembly-line manufacture – first used experimentally in April 1913 to assemble magneto fly-wheels – was only one aspect of the innovations in the industrial process of mass production. The progressive production of sub-assembly units in the machine shop presented formidable technical difficulties which were overcome by the sequential placing of machines and the use of gravity work-slides and rollways to ensure the constant and continuous movement of raw materials, parts and components through the factory. These innovations resulted in extraordinary reductions in assembly times: a chassis which had originally taken twelve and a half hours to assemble took one hour thirty-three minutes after the reorganization of Highland Park (Meyer, 1981, pp.29–35).

The Ford Company's huge success in raising the output of the Model T was achieved at the expense of the skill, happiness and stability of its workforce. As the labour force grew in size, the proportion of skilled native-born Americans declined; by 1914, three-quarters of workers were foreign born. Before assembly-line production came into full force, a series of measures had degraded assembly work; after its introduction, the 'deskilled specialist' (or the man who performed a single machine operation) became the principal occupational type in the factory. Ninety per cent of Ford jobs required no formal training and a contemporary management authority was to remark: 'The Ford Motor Company has no use for experience, in the working ranks anyway. It desires and prefers machine-tool operators who have nothing to

*Figure 11.2
Ford's model T moving
assembly line, Highland Park,
Michigan c.1913.
(Photograph from the
collections of the Henry Ford
Museum and Greenfield
Village, Dearborn, Michigan)*

unlearn, who have no theories of current surface speeds for metal finishing, and who will do what they are told, over and over again, from bell-time to bell-time' (H.L. Arnold, quoted in Meyer, 1981, p.52). Ford workers, a veteran later recalled, 'cease to be human beings as soon as they enter the gates of the shop. They become automatons and cease to think. They move their arms spontaneously to and fro, stopping long enough to eat in order to keep the human machinery in working order for the next four hours exploitation' (quoted in Meyer, 1981, p.40). With the assembly line, Ford had introduced a uniform pay-rate of $2.34 a day and a strict supervision of work that was essential for sequentially arranged, synchronized production processes. The number of foremen greatly increased – in 1914, one foreman supervised fifty-three workers, in 1917, fifteen – and the foreman's duties were circumscribed on the lines of Taylor's conception of functional fore-manship (pp. 54–56). The workers reacted to these highly regimented, degraded and alienated conditions of labour by leaving the factory in droves: in 1913, the annual labour turnover was 370 per cent; most left voluntarily. Absenteeism and stress-related sickness were chronic problems. 'Blue Monday' disrupted the output of the working week.

Ford responded to this labour crisis by doubling the money a worker could earn at Highland Park, instituting a series of welfare reforms and creating a network of social controls which extended the authority and influence of the company over its employees beyond the bounds of the factory and the confines of the working day. The $5 day inaugurated in early 1914 was, strictly speaking, a profit-sharing plan under which the 'profit' element in the worker's wage was withheld if he failed to conform to certain norms of industrial and social behaviour. As the company advised its workforce, 'to secure these exceptional earnings . . . conformity with its general plan for the betterment of its employees' was required (quoted in Meyer, 1981, p.117). Workers were expected not only to be conscientious time-keepers and obedient employees, but sober, prudent family men. Men known to gamble, drink heavily or frequent brothels were denied the profit element in their pay until they mended their ways. To ascertain the moral state of his labour force outside working hours, Ford created a Sociological Department charged with investigating the everyday lives of the workers and, where necessary, reforming their manners. Investigators would descend on working-class streets instructed (as Ford told a reporter) 'to learn the nationality, the religion, the bank savings, whether the man owns or is buying property, how he amuses himself, the district he selects to live in – this and much else is tabulated' (quoted in Meyer, 1981, p.116).

The activities of the Sociological Department developed and refined a tradition of industrial paternalism which was to be found in the labour relations of all capitalist societies of the time. Contrary to the expectations of social critics such as Mill and Marx, industrialism did not create a class of 'atomized' workers bound to their employers only by the cash nexus. The mid-nineteenth century factory in the industrial north of Britain was often a moral and deferential community where the worker depended on his 'master' not just for a wage, but for housing, a Sunday School for his children, a library, a brass band, and religious and political leadership. Exceptionally, nineteenth-century British industrial paternalism left social and institutional legacies which survive to this day: the Bournville Village Trust, for example, created by the chocolate manufacturer George Cadbury, still controls the development of an extensive acreage to the south and west of his Birmingham factory, purchased to provide inexpensive housing, with ample room for gardens and recreations, mainly for his workers. American employers, often persuaded that industrial 'betterment' and 'welfare' would ameliorate the rancour and violence of late nineteenth-century labour relations, were responsible for similar measures. W.H. Tolman catalogued – in a study which first gave the term 'social engineering' wide circulation – about twenty 'model' schemes for the provision of low-cost employees' housing undertaken by American companies which included the Colorado Fuel and Iron Company, the Westinghouse Air Brake Company and the Ludlow Manufacturers Associates. Such firms were also providing educational facilities and supplementing those of the public schools attended by the children of their employees by, for example, furnishing textbooks free of charge (Tolman, 1909, chapters 8 and 9). These schemes were often linked with such measures of welfare capitalism as the promotion of employee savings associations, profit-sharing schemes and employee benefit funds. They were evidence that 'our American industrialists are beginning to realize that an intelligent regard and a tactful care for the labour part of the business is not only right, but a large factor in industrial peace and contentment' (Tolman, 1909, p.49).

The activities of the Ford Sociological Department fell within this wider movement for industrial 'betterment'. It was responsible for the provision of extensive recreational facilities, set up a Medical Department and an Employees' Savings and Loan Association and provided language instruction at the Ford English School. Many of its educational functions were consciously directed towards the 'Americanization' of immigrant workers whose values and ways of living, as well as their native language, were foreign to those of the Protestant middle-class host community. Workers were expected to conform to that community's norms, and the profit-sharing element in the $5 day was used as a blunt instrument in the struggle for conformity. For example, wives of Ford workers had to observe middle-class ideals of domesticity. A Sociological Department instruction to its investigator made it clear that if a man wanted to remain a profit sharer, then his wife would have to stay at home and assume the obligations she undertook when she married (Meyer, 1981, p.141).

The inquisitorial methods of the Sociological Department were deeply resented in the communities where Ford workers lived and encountered the suspicion, if not hostility, of a wider public sensitive to personal liberty and privacy. In the event, the industrial strategy of high wages and close moral controls Ford had initiated proved short-lived. Rapid inflation during the First World War eroded the value of the $5 day and the competitive edge of Ford in a tight labour market. In 1919, the company introduced a $6 day in an effort to retain its advantage and the monetary inducement for its employees to stomach its welfare supervision. Meanwhile, changes in the wider society of wartime America – such as the growing demand for Prohibition and the nationalist hysteria for 'Americanism' – meant that some of the moral aims of the Sociological Department were being undertaken by other, more legitimate, agencies. In the post-war period, when America was obsessed by the threat of Bolshevism, the regime of welfare paternalism within the Ford factories gave way to a harsher system of control designed to crush the growing Auto Workers Union and speed up production still further. Management spies were infiltrated into the labour force, union activists expelled and 'goons' hired to break strikes. During 1920–21, the profit-sharing scheme was wound up and the Sociological Department dismantled. In its place, the company recruited a private army – euphemistically known as the Ford Service Department – to impose a rigid internal discipline on the workforce. A former Ford employee wrote, of the new River Rouge plant, 'Once you're on the bridge at Ford Rouge (the doorway to HELL) you lose your freedom and become a slave to Fordism under the rules of his service men, or shall I call them rats, jailbirds and crooks' (given in Auerbach, 1969, p.289). The chief consolation for the worker was that the end of the Sociological Department signalled the failure to control the 'private sphere' of everyday life. This was symptomatic of a general trend in social relations. The autonomy of the family has generally, in twentieth-century capitalist societies, been preserved against the type of industrial paternalism that Ford briefly espoused.

The technical advances in assembly-line production which Ford perfected had a far greater impact. Because the company was very open about its methods, and sought to publicize them extensively, their diffusion among other sectors of American industry was rapid. Within a decade, many household appliances such as vacuum sweepers and radios were being assembled on conveyor systems. There was a widespread sense that a new human era of 'Mass Production' was beginning; an *Encyclopaedia Britannica* supplement article of 1925 – nominally penned by Ford – led to the common use of the term that superseded 'Fordism' (Hounshell, 1984, pp.2 and 260–61).

There were, however, quite definite limits to mass production as Ford conceived it. In certain sectors of industry mass-production methods failed because they could not be correlated with mass consumption. Only 4,500 customers were found for the mass-produced houses of Foster Gunnison, and it is to be doubted whether mass-production methods would, even in the most favourable market circumstances, have resulted in significant cost reductions. More surprising was the failure of mass-production methods to penetrate the furniture industry. The technical obstacles were trifling, but the nature of furniture consumption as a deeply personal statement of one's taste and personality and the relatively lengthy possession of furniture by a consumer worked decisively against the introduction of mass production (Hounshell, 1984, p.315). In a sense, too, there was a definite historical limit to Ford's conception of mass production: he had saturated the American market with the lowest-priced utilitarian automobile, and by 1925 the future of the car industry lay with a more flexible system of mass production geared to regularly re-styling and up-dating the product (see chapter 6, pp.177–79). In the newly emerging car market, Ford (with its specially designed machine tools) was disadvantaged as compared with competitors using standard or general purpose machinery which could accommodate change more easily. Moreover, in these new market conditions, the producers had to 'engineer' mass consumption by providing credit finance for their customers, creating franchises for retailers, using market research and advertising to ascertain and construct consumer tastes.

**11.4
THE INTERNATIONAL
DIFFUSION OF
TAYLORISM AND
FORDISM: FRANCE**

We have already noted the spread of Taylorism *qua* ideology to Europe after 1914 when it seemed to offer a solution to class conflict and political schism in a 'non-zero sum' world in which classes no longer prospered at each others' expense (p.317 above; Maier, 1970). But scientific management can also claim to be a *technology*, and as with other technologies the speed of its international diffusion, and the conditions for and obstacles to its implementation by foreign entrepreneurs, constitute a major area of enquiry. The process of technological diffusion was necessarily more complex than the ideological borrowings Maier describes, since it involved thousands of investment decisions (or decisions not to invest) by capitalists and managers calculating uncertain profits during a period of exceptional political and economic instability in most European countries. Although most states recovered economically during the later 1920s, none enjoyed the exceptional prosperity of America, nor the advantages of her huge internal market, and none had benefited in quite the way she had done from the 'war boom' of 1915–18. These American macro-economic conditions were clearly highly favourable for the type of investment made by Ford and other manufacturers and for the 'Taylorization' of factories. Such investment decisions could only be undertaken with a high degree of probability of long-term profitability. European manufacturers were still living in the later 1920s with the economic consequences of the First World War, which had overthrown the world's multilateral trading system and removed a major economic power, Russia, from the capitalist orbit. Many major industries – coal, steel, shipbuilding, heavy engineering – in inter-war Europe faced a chronic problem of spare capacity and excess labour. Even before the economic blizzard of 1931, scientific management meant, for many entrepreneurs, the 'rationalization' of industry to limit capacity and injurious competition.

These remarks should suggest why the material effects of scientific management in Europe appear, from the detailed studies available, disproportionately small compared to the ideological clamour American industrialism aroused. My discussion will be brief and concentrate on France where scientific management developed furthest in inter-war Europe. A tradition of research in applied industrial science and an indigenous school of scientific administration associated with Fayol created a receptivity to Taylorism. The demonstration at the 1900 Paris exhibition of high-speed steel familiarized French engineers with Taylor's technical accomplishments, although French factories were slow to introduce it into the production process and in 1909 only the Renault factories were making general use of high-speed steel. In 1910 this motor manufacturer became the first French industrialist to introduce scientific management at his Billancourt works, where one of his young engineers made use of time study to fix piece-rate prices and experimented with Taylor's innovations in the fabrication and maintenance of tools. Not all Taylor's technical prescriptions were adaptable to French conditions, mainly because French steels were softer than American. None the less, the savings in labour costs achieved by time study and the introduction of piece work were highly gratifying to their author. While engineers at other auto works, such as Panhard and Levassor, made some use of Taylor's methods, they stopped far short of 'Taylorization', chiefly because the owners would not sanction thorough-going reorganization. This caution was due more to doubts about cost effectiveness and fear of labour troubles than technical conservatism. In newly-built plant of the pre-war period, French car manufacturers showed an awareness of problems of machine layout and factory design which made their works technically superior to many American counterparts. The Lorraine-Dietrich factory at Argenteuil was organized in an approximation to assembly-line production, with sequentially placed machines, and a conveyor belt supplemented by strategically located stacks of components. The chief constraint on technological modernization was the limited market for what long remained in Europe a luxury product. No manufacturer could contemplate mass production of a low-cost vehicle, and car makers were to be frequently reminded of the dangers of over-production.

After 1910, the pace of the diffusion of Taylorism in France picked up, chiefly because of the strong resurgence of economic growth which persuaded manufacturers to increase production while seeking to lower their costs in order to meet new competition, chiefly American (Moutet, 1975, p.31). Scientific management began to spread beyond its foothold in the car industry to mines, glassworks, shipyards and other enterprises, although the number of works affected by 1913 was tiny. Renault extended time study to all his factories as he sought, by lower costs, to regain the position he had lost in the English market as a result of the setting up of a Ford assembling plant at Manchester. But his peremptory demand that the management introduce piece work, without taking preliminary measures with respect to the standard-ization of machines and tools, was considered by the workers to be a piece of crude 'driving' that would not guarantee them a living wage. Though the Renault factories were not union strongholds and workers had no previous reputation for militancy, the 'crash programme' of scientific management led to two strikes in the winter of 1912–13.

The disputes brought the issue of scientific management before a far wider public than hitherto, familiarizing employers with its potential and organized labour with its threat. One worker wrote that Renault could 'boast of having delivered the Taylor system a body blow . . . It's now certain that in no matter which automobile firm they attempt to introduce time-study, it will be badly received by the workers, even if the industrialist has the best of intentions' (cited in Moutet, 1975, p.41). In the French craftsman's resistance to scientific management there was fear of technological unemployment and anxiety that it would deny older, less productive workers a minimum wage, but also the psychology of the independent producer whose social ideal was syndicalism or workers' self-government in industry.

The Renault strikes abruptly checked the spread of Taylorism in France, but the outbreak of war in August 1914 gave it a new, massive impetus. The measures taken by all combatants to institute 'war economies' when the duration, and human and material costs, of modern warfare became clear made imperative the adoption of managerial techniques which would augment the production of *matériel*. By early 1915, all the combatants had exhausted their shell stocks and faced critical shortages of skilled labour in their engineering and metal-working industries. All took a similar range of measures to overcome these problems: skilled labour was 'diluted' by an influx of less skilled workers to undertake the repetitive, machine-minding operations in industry, while the craftsman's talents were reserved for the toolroom and setting-up machines; mass-production methods were, wherever feasible, introduced into munitions making; piece work – to encourage output – was much more extensively used and time study to calculate prices became more general; and, finally, managers and state functionaries were compelled to assess objectively the relationships between hours of labour, output and fatigue. The psycho-physiology of work – which Taylor and his associates had almost entirely neglected – was much encouraged by the need to conserve labour for the great armaments drives. In France, the *union sacrée* disposed trade unionists to accept managerial changes they would have resisted in peacetime. Some of the most notable applications of scientific-management methods took place in the French armaments industry and they were not confined to establishments engaged in large-batch or mass production. The military's central automobile repair shop was reorganized and a system of routeing vehicles through the works, greatly akin to Taylor's recommend-ations, introduced. Sophisticated job cards were adopted and the work of gang leaders and foremen 'carefully arranged beforehand so as to strengthen labour discipline and ensure the regular distribution of work' (ILO/Devinat, 1927, p.235). The shipbuilding yards at Penhoët had been crippled by the mobilization of skilled workers and similar methods of work organization were introduced.

While such steps were being taken to strengthen managerial control of the labour process and the costs of production, some French industrialists, with the encouragement of the wartime state, were adopting the technical advances of Ford's system of mass production. Assembly lines were introduced for the manufacture of aircraft engines at Renault's Billancourt works in 1915 and for the production of tanks in 1918. The lorry manufacturer, Maurice Berliet, adopted Ford's methods when he built a new factory at Vénissieux. The integrated production of shells was carried furthest at Citroën's new plant in Paris. But though in these instances the war gave a clear-cut stimulus to technological diffusion, it may have retarded the spread of assembly-line methods to other sectors of the economy. Military needs often led to the refinement and diversification of products which militated against mass-production techniques (Fridenson, 1978, p.162).

In the post-war world French automobile manufacturers took the lead in adopting the assembly line for peacetime production. Citroën started a line for its first post-war model in 1919, Berliet in 1920, and Renault and Peugeot in the next two or three years. They were somewhat in advance of their German, Italian and Czech rivals and more than a decade ahead of Morris, the leading British manufacturer, who did not install a moving assembly line at Cowley until the factory was rebuilt in 1934 (Fridenson, 1978, p.162). The attractions of assembly-line manufacture lay in its potential to save labour (notably expensive skilled labour) and to offer closer control over the flow of production; and these were all the greater because the war had led organized workers throughout Europe to demand the eight-hour day and to press for workers' controls.

After 1919, managements were looking to the techniques of American industries to raise productivity and reassert control. In France, the coming of the assembly line was closely associated with the wider use of Taylor's

Figure 11.3 Citroën (Javel) body assembly line 1931. (Photo: Boyer-Viollet, Paris)

methods. At Berliet's works in Lyons, for example, these were applied in their entirety, including the introduction of functional foremanship (ILO/ Devinat, 1927, p.238). The consequences for the labour force of the French car industry were highly similar to those experienced by Ford's workers. The engineer responsible for the adoption of the assembly line by the Renault company remarked:

> Skilled workers demand high wages. So they cannot be committed any more to assembly work . . . The new methods care very little for the workers' technical ingenuity . . . Thus, most skilled workers have been eliminated. From now on each worker always does the same job, and . . . it is easy for him to reach the [required] dexterity . . . He is now able to work almost by reflex, automatically, and to the maximum extent of his powers. (Cited in Fridenson, 1978, p.166)

The similarities went further in that unskilled and semi-skilled workers on the line were often migrants of rural or foreign origin (at the Citroën factories in the late 1920s they included Arabs, Africans, Chinese and Vietnamese) and poorly organized. What was lacking in the European context was Ford's commitment to high wages and working-class mass consumption. At the most, French manufacturers could hope to extend their market to petit bourgeois strata. The big firms strove to do so by market research, to such effect that the 'liaison between [their] technical and commercial departments . . . is considered in France as one of the best results of industrial rationaliz- ation' (ILO/Devinat, 1927, p.239).

It is difficult to arrive at an overall assessment of the economic and social consequences of French scientific management. It seems to have contributed substantially to the rapid development and international competitiveness of her mechanical industries in the 1920s when French industrial growth was the fastest in Europe. In 1929, the peak inter-war year for global private motor-car production, France was the leading European manufacturer, turning out 248,000 vehicles, as compared with Britain's 182,000 and Germany's 128,000. But these figures pale into insignificance beside Amer- ica's production of 5,358 million vehicles; the United States exported more cars (excluding parts exported for assembly abroad) than Europe produced in aggregate. Furthermore, the innovativeness of the French mechanical industries did very little to protect the French economy overall from the ravages of the 1930s Depression. In 1937, whereas Britain and Germany had substantially increased their industrial output above 1929 levels, French output was more than a quarter below (Landes, 1969, p.391). French recep- tivity to the methods of American industrialism had – it would appear – created isolated pockets of proficiency in a conservative society. A large peasant agricultural sector and the low purchasing power of urban workers held back the mass production of consumer goods. In the late 1930s, the price of a new French car was twice a worker's annual wage. In spite of the promotion of hire-purchase and second-hand dealing, ownership was extremely restricted in France (as in other European countries) until the later 1950s. In 1954, only 11 per cent of French townspeople owned a car, and it was calculated that, until about that date, there were families with sufficient disposable income to increase the number of possible purchasers by only one-fifth (Zeldin, 1980, pp.281 and 294). When 'mass consumption society' did arrive, as a result of sustained post-war economic growth, a new form of scientific management was partly responsible for it. This was 'indicative' national planning by a technological élite of senior civil servants in 'voluntary collusion' with leading industrialists and corporate managers (Schonfield, 1969 edition, p.128). Scientific management in capitalist society had found its highest and, perhaps, most effective level.

**11.5
SCIENTIFIC
MANAGEMENT AND
INDUSTRIAL
PSYCHOLOGY IN
BRITAIN**

In illustrating the diffusion of scientific management by reference to France, other distinct national developments have been neglected and can be mentioned only briefly. In Britain the work of the physiologists and psychologists on the problems of fatigue and labour turnover during the First World War led firstly to the establishment of the Industrial Fatigue Research Board in 1918, under the joint auspices of the Department of Scientific and Industrial Research and Health of Munition Workers' committee, and secondly, to the founding of a private body, the National Institute of Industrial Psychology, in 1921. The Board was genuinely independent of management, although its report on such subjects as the effects of different shift systems in industry and the causes of industrial accidents were meant to promote industrial efficiency and could be indirectly beneficial to businesses. NIIP, on the other hand, was set up principally to carry out investigations at the request of individual firms, and although partly supported by the Carnegie UK Trust and private donations, its income came mainly from consultancy fees. In choosing a title for the new organization, its creator, Charles Myers (formerly Director of Cambridge University Psychological Laboratory), deliberately eschewed the terms 'efficiency engineering' and 'scientific management'. These were now so firmly associated with 'speeding-up' and the degradation of craft skills that they would have immediately drawn on the Institute the hostility of organized labour.

Myers believed that Taylor's conception of management was *un*scientific in that it rested on the discredited mechanistic psychology which postulated that human motivations were reducible to a calculus of pleasure and pain. Myers hoped to place at the service of industry both the experience gained with civilian labour in wartime, and the insights he had derived from his position as a leading army psychologist with a responsibility for treating 'shell shock' casualties. The incidence of functional neurotic disorders in the trenches was a massive demonstration of the force of instinct and non-rational drives in the human psyche. By tendentious reasoning, these psychic drives could be regarded as the dynamics of industrial and social conflicts and industrial psychology as their appropriate therapy. A colleague of Myers at NIIP wrote in 1929: '. . . the human sciences of psychology and physiology have now entered the industrial field to ensure that the physical and mental energies of man are used to the best economic effect . . . If further psychological study results in a better understanding of those mental disorders known as strikes and lockouts, it may well serve the economic life of the nation' (F.W. Lawe in Myers, 1929, pp.216–17).

The Institute's work tended to divide between empirical studies of time and motion, and of workers' responses to improved ventilation and other alterations of their physical environment; advising employers on 'scientific' vocational selection and devising standardized tests for aptitudes and abilities; and educating the public on the virtues of psychologically-informed personnel management. The evidence does not suggest that in any of these tasks it made great headway in its founder's purpose of placing psychology at the service of industry. Though deriving quite a considerable income from consultancy fees by the 1930s (about £20,000 in 1938), this was less than its expenses and indicates only a modest level of interest in industrial psychology among businessmen. Many activities of the Institute's early years, which promised to be of great benefit to employers, never moved beyond the experimental stage: for example, between 1922 and 1924 Cyril Burt was employed half-time in the Institute's Vocational Research and Guidance Section and investigated the use of standardized tests for clerical occupations. In spite of the predictive value claimed for these tests, there is no indication that they came into widespread use. Trainee clerical workers were selected on their school records and educational attainments. Again, tests were devised and used experimentally in the selection of engineering apprentices;

in practice, the great majority of engineering apprentices were taken on by the time-honoured methods of personal recommendation and knowing the foreman. It is true that the work of the Institute diversified after 1930 into studies of vocational guidance on behalf of local educational authorities and into consumer psychology, but its clientele was small and its financial situation always precarious.

Applied psychology had promised a reformation of the social relations of industry because of its unique insight into the 'human factor'. In a wireless broadcast of 1923, Myers prophesied that the twentieth century would be an age of industrial 'humanism' as opposed to the 'mechanism' of the nineteenth century which Taylor embodied (*NIIP Journal*, Vol.1, No.8, October 1923). The bitter industrial strife of the 1920s belied the prophecy – has it ever been fulfilled? Psychology and personnel management brought a new dimension to the industrial welfare work of a few employers, but the 'institutional structure of trade unions and employers' organisations and the vicissitudes of the British economy were . . . far more important in determining the character of industrial relations' (Briggs, 1954, p.38).

11.6 INDUSTRIAL PSYCHOLOGY AND 'HUMAN RELATIONS' IN AMERICA

Whereas in Britain, industrial psychology made little headway against the indifference of employers, in America it enjoyed a considerable vogue in the management practices of leading corporations after the First World War, only to have its pretentions cruelly exposed by the experiments carried out at GE's Hawthorne (Chicago) works by Elton Mayo between 1924 and 1927. During the war psychologists were employed to administer standardized tests of intelligence and other aptitudes to 1.7 million US Army recruits. This demonstration of the utility of testing encouraged the nascent industrial psychology movement to extend the method to vocational selection, and after 1917 a great number of establishments introduced testing into their personnel departments. The tests were broadly of three types: trade tests of acquired skills; tests of supposedly inherent aptitudes (such as sensitivity of touch); and tests of general intelligence. The latter two were scientifically controversial in their claim to measure innate characteristics and putatively of great value to employers in selecting labour and assigning workers to tasks appropriate to their abilities. Research undertaken for the Winchester Repeating Arms Company popularized tests of motor and perceptual abilities for selecting factory workers. Tests of general intelligence were being adopted in the educational system at the same time as industrial corporations began to make use of them. In an excellent study of American labour, the Frenchman André Philip told how he had met these tests in such large establishments as the Scovill Manufacturing Company, Cheney Brothers and GE. He found them regularly used in universities in place of conventional exams to select students (Philip, 1927, pp.110–11). Philip even found tests being used to measure an individual's virtue by his ability to rank, in order of gravity, a number of moral failings, such as not paying one's tram fares, telling a dirty story and working on Sundays.

The testing movement endeavoured to measure individual abilities and match them with occupational requirements. The futility of much of its work was shown when Mayo observed that the output of groups of workers could be raised by quite arbitrary and apparently contradictory ways, such as altering shift times, enforcing rest periods (which both increased output) and then reverting to the old working pattern (which increased it still further). What became evident was that workers were responding simply to being subjects of the experiment and that the primary group, rather than the individual, was what counted in determining output. The performance of workers bore little relationship to measured ability and Mayo concluded that 'The belief that the behaviour of an individual within the factory can be predicted before employment upon the basis of a laborious and minute examination by tests of his mechanical and other capacities is mainly, if not wholly mistaken' (cited in Braverman, 1974, p.145).

Mayo was influenced by the French sociologist Émile Durkheim and the Chicago school of sociology and believed that *anomie* (or the absence of common, integrative norms) was a chronic ill of industrial society. To counter this, he proposed a 'Human Relations' style of management which would 'humanize' the working environment, and foster the solidarity of groups within the workplace and loyalty of groups to the factory. The tone and focus of this style of management were clearly different from the confrontational attitude of Taylorism which approached the workforce as a mere aggregate of individuals. Whether the 'Human Relations' school was any less a servant of capitalist power is to be doubted. For a start, Mayo completely ignored those groups such as trade union locals, which were actually or potentially hostile to management. GE spent considerable sums on industrial espionage (as well as employing Mayo as a consultant) for the purpose of weeding out union activists. 'Human Relations' in industry was tolerable to the company only on condition that it decided what 'groups' were to be recognized. Like other American employers it had to be forced to recognize unions and bargain collectively by New Deal legislation. Moreover, under Mayo's style of management, questions of the paratechnical division of labour and the control of work were left entirely to production engineers. 'Human Relations' could scarcely escape the charge of merely habituating the workers to a labour regime entirely controlled by others. Finally, Mayo's research was posited on assumptions that were fundamental to the spirit of capitalist enterprise; as one critic, Daniel Bell, wrote, Mayo and his associates 'uncritically adopt industry's own conception of workers as *means* to be manipulated or adjusted to impersonal ends'. Bell added, 'The social science of the factory researchers is not a science of man, but a cow-sociology' (cited in Brown, 1954, p.93).

**11.7
CONCLUSIONS TO
PART 1**

It seems appropriate to conclude this examination of 'social engineering' by asking: what does modern management owe to Taylorism? Answers to this diverge markedly. In his brief, but perceptibly sympathetic essay on management, Glenn Porter concludes that the spread throughout the capitalist world since 1945 of the multi-unit enterprise has brought a number of new directions both to the practice and teaching of management:

> The older Tayloresque emphasis on the internal administration of factories persists in the study of production, but modern business is a vastly more complex phenomenon than the one-product, one-factory world assumed by . . . the analysts of . . . scientific management. The fields of finance and marketing and the areas of international and general management have eclipsed production as the most intricate and pressing challenges for twentieth-century executives. (Porter, 1978, p.89)

Older definitions of management have, he argues, become increasingly irrelevant to contemporary business analysis which draws more and more on psychology, sociology, economics, mathematics, statistics and organization theory. Porter has little doubt that the sophistication of the practice and study of management have greatly benefited everyday lives: '. . . the improvements in our understanding of management have contributed to our ability to improve the level of material existence in technically advanced societies. They represent a significant part of the "software" of twentieth-century technology' (Porter, 1978, pp.89–90).

In his highly influential study of *Labor and Monopoly Capital* (1974), the American Marxist, Harry Braverman, reached very different conclusions. For him, the extraction of surplus value by the wage labour system remains fundamental to capitalist accumulation, and control of the labour process is, therefore, critical to the economic system based on private ownership of the means of production. Braverman argues that the popular notions that Taylorism has been 'superseded' by later management schools (such as Mayo's), or that it is outmoded because specific features of Taylor's system (such as functional foremanship and incentive wages) have been discarded, are erroneous. Taylor's successors, he maintains, are to be found in engineering and work design, and top management; Mayo's in personnel departments. 'Work itself is organised according to Taylorian principles, while personnel departments and academics have busied themselves with the selection, training, manipulation, pacification and adjustment of the "manpower" so organised. Taylorism dominates the world of production; the practitioners of "human relations" and "industrial psychology" are the maintenance crew for the human machinery' (Braverman, 1974, p.87).

Braverman's arguments have been criticized by – interestingly – a Marxist economist, Andrew Friedman, in a study partly devoted to the Coventry motor-car industry (Friedman, 1977). This, like other industries, has been organized between 'central' firms who enjoy a near monopoly position in the market (they are able to dictate prices), and those working for the 'peripheral' firms, where market conditions are extremely competitive and businessmen have to take prices. This divide tends to coincide with a division between highly organized, well-paid labour at the 'centre', and badly paid, under-organized workers on the 'periphery', and to it can be traced the persistent pockets of poverty in certain regions and cities.

Friedman argues that the 'central firms' have been able to adopt more flexible approaches both to profit-making and control of the labour process. Top managers have, for example, been able to forego high, short-term profits in favour of lower, but stable, long-term profits. The strategic choices open to them in this respect have conditioned their managerial policies: where firms are highly competitive management strives for direct control of the labour force in order to maximize productivity and profits. But 'central' firms are imperfectly competitive and they can contemplate and practise other strategies in order, for example, to retain workers in tight labour markets or avoid the disruption of production and loss of sales which can follow strikes, go-slows and other forms of resistance to direct control. Generally, 'central' firms have been able to concede higher wages, but they have also negotiated complex procedural agreements with trade unions over manning levels and other working conditions and they have, in certain circumstances, granted some degree of autonomy to groups of factory workers. These concessions testify to the effectiveness of workers' collective resistance to managerial power – a factor that is strangely absent from Braverman's account.

Friedman illustrates these theses by reference to the Coventry motor-car industry in the post-war period. As a result of the destruction of continental rivals during the Second World War, the continued protection of the home market, and Government assistance to manufacturers to export, the post-war car industry enjoyed a considerable boom. By 1950, the United Kingdom was the world's largest car exporter. Labour was in short supply, and competition for workers was especially fierce in Coventry, where the industry was most concentrated. The local engineering shop stewards' organization was very powerful, having flourished under government approval when national and local labour leaders were co-opted for the wartime productivity drives. At Standard Motors, then the second largest employer in Coventry after Rootes, workers were able to impose on management a system of 'gang' labour under which the 'ganger' would negotiate a 'contract' (usually unwritten) with top managers to produce a given output. The ganger – who was elected by the gang and responsible to its members – would then keep track of work and money to try to ensure that each gang member kept up his workload. The system 'increased workers' direct control over productive activity, increased their job security, increased their security against other forms of disciplinary action and improved their working relations with each other' (Friedman, 1977, p.213). Those factories that adopted the system tended to have fewer stoppages, to pay better, offer more pleasant working conditions and a faster work pace. They also employed fewer administrative, technical and clerical workers.

The 'gang' system was a victim of the concentration of Britain's motor-car industry (in 1961, Standard was taken over by Leyland and merged into the British Leyland Motor Corporation in 1968) and the response of top management to keener foreign and multinational competition (particularly from Ford). There is no compelling evidence that the 'gang' system was the cause of the commercial problems of those firms that used it – these seem to have been rooted in under-investment in new capital assets – and successful companies like Volvo have adopted it in diluted form in order to 'enrich' jobs and retain workers. There are three reasons for discussing 'gang' labour in these concluding remarks: firstly, it illustrates a strategy of 'responsible autonomy' to which managers have, in certain circumstances, resorted as an alternative to the direct control propounded by Taylor. In identifying Taylorism with the fundamental practice of modern management Braverman confused one particular strategy for exercising managerial authority with managerial authority itself (Friedman, 1977, p.80). Secondly, the history of the 'gang' system belies the notion that a particular form of managerial authority must *inevitably* follow from a given technology. Technology alone does not determine the social relations of production (although it must *set limits* to what they can possibly be; we can scarcely envisage volume motor-car production under a domestic system of manufacture). Thirdly, these relations have been much affected by conflict and negotiation at the workplace.

These remarks, have, I think, a more general relevance to the way we think about the interaction between science, technology and everyday life. Technological determinism is – as one of its most effective critics remarked – 'an immensely powerful and now largely orthodox view of the nature of social change' (Williams, 1974, p.19). It is an attractively simple view; even Marx succumbed to the notion that 'The hand mill gives you society with the feudal lord; the steam mill society with the industrial capitalist.' As Williams goes on to argue, the basic flaw of technological determinism (and, indeed, of the opposite view which sees technology as merely symptomatic of other social forces) is the abstraction of technology from the structure of power in which it develops.

PART 2   HUMAN ENGINEERING: EUGENICS, MENTAL MEASUREMENT AND SOCIAL POLICY

The forms of social engineering that have been discussed up to this point took the human material of the factory or office as a given and attempted to alter the social relations of production in order to increase output and efficiency. We will now turn to a form of 'engineering' which projected the control and improvement of the human material itself. Strictly speaking, this form of engineering – known as eugenics from the Greek for healthy breeding – was also 'social', for it envisaged the improvement of society (or the race or the nation) through an intervention in human reproduction, but the focus on the biological organism justifies the adjective 'human' and distinguishes it from the social engineering of scientific management.

I will examine here the ideological use made of certain developments in later nineteenth-century evolutionary biology, mathematical statistics and differential psychology in Britain and America, and the consequences of this ideological 'presence' for the social policies of the two societies. The areas of social policy I will discuss are, with respect to America, the restriction of immigration in 1924 to exclude people considered to be of 'inferior stock', the introduction of legislation empowering states to sterilize the feebleminded and the delinquent in public custody, and the use of psychological testing in the public-school system. With respect to Britain I will examine the use of mental measurement to identify the educationally sub-normal and to select children for scholarships at the state-supported secondary schools. It is, I believe, by looking at the implications of human engineering for social policy that we can best explore the connections between 'science and technology' and 'everyday life', for ordinary lives in twentieth-century advanced societies have, increasingly, been both enhanced and circumscribed by the state. The state has become the chief sponsor of science and in its organizations and functions embodies many of the rationalistic characteristics of our scientific and technological culture. State institutions (such as the health service and the educational system) form a major nexus between 'science and technology' and 'everyday life'.

It is far from my contention that even in the areas selected for discussion the ideological use of science has been a decisive factor in social policy change and development. Any major legislative change in policy results from complex, multiple determinations among which scientific (or pseudo-scientific) arguments and nostrums often serve only as background rationaliz-ations. It can easily be established from the early twentieth-century pronouncements of individual human engineers that they saw in the tech-niques of mental measurement and the knowledge of human genetics the possibilities of truly Orwellian social selection and control. (Some are cited below.) But these possibilities were almost entirely unrealized by mid century. The influence of geneticists, psychologists and scientistic ideologues in shaping everyday life had been modest. The geneticist J.B.S. Haldane, who was an effective critic of the ideological abuse of his science, wrote in the early 1960s: 'The plain fact is that human genetics is a very difficult branch of science, and has only been developing on scientific lines for about sixty years. So far [in Britain] it has only saved a few thousand lives and prevented the birth of a few thousand defectives' (Goldsmith and Mackay, 1964, p.156).

The one state in which eugenically-motivated policies had had widespread and horrendous consequences was Nazi Germany, where the 'Euthanasia Action' of 1939–41 led to the mass-murder by gassing of 70,000 mental patients and others and approximately a quarter of a million forcible steriliz-ations. That the Euthanasia Action was a precedent for the 'Final Solution', and that both had common ideological roots in hereditarian racist science is unquestionable, but it would be a shallow historical analysis which traced a simple progression from hereditarian science to the gas chambers and concluded that one led straightforwardly to the other. In Weimar Germany, eugenic proposals had been put forward by the Left as well as the racist Right (just as eugenics had had an important following in the Soviet Union in the 1920s). (See Graham, 1977.) There was no necessary connection between eugenics and anti-semitism; indeed, Jewish communities were often admired by eugenists because of their respect for heredity and judicious breeding. The political conditions of a one party state, which had violated civil society, and was governed by irresponsible and competing bureaucracies bound only by the *Führerprinzip*, were clearly more significant than the rationalizations of eugenic ideology in bringing about the 'Euthanasia Action' and genocide.

One last point by way of introduction: I have already referred to the ideological use and 'presence' of science and this demands some glossing because the demarcation between science and ideology has been widely debated in modern philosophy since the appearance of Karl Popper's *Logic of Scientific Discovery* (first published in German in 1934). I think it is possible to argue that 'science' and 'ideology' are not mutually exclusive terms without questioning the validity of the epistemological criteria put forward to demarcate between them (though these have, in fact, been matters of considerable dispute).

I find the critique of science and technology *as ideology* advanced by the Frankfurt School persuasive. This asserts that with the fusion of science and technology to the state and the extension of rational decision-making to more and more areas of social life, technocratic consciousness has displaced traditional legitimations of power and become the dominant ideology of advanced society. This consciousness entails an unacknowledged form of domination derived from modern science's capacity for the technical control and exploitation of nature. Intrinsic to this capacity is an objectifying outlook on the world whose only measures of the 'good' are utility and efficiency. There is no place in science for ethical questions of what ought to be for the social good, and the peculiar ideological effect of technocratic consciousness is that it models itself on science by turning ethical questions for the community into matters of technical control. As Habermas puts it: 'Technocratic consciousness reflects not the sundering of an ethical situation but the repression of "ethics" as such as a category of life.' Where this consciousness is the dominant ideology 'the reified models of the sciences migrate into the socio-cultural life-world and gain objective power over the latter's self-understanding'. Using the term 'practical' to describe reasoning about the social good by dialogue within the community, Habermas concludes that 'The ideological nucleus of [technocratic] consciousness is the elimination of the distinction between the practical and the technical' (Habermas, 1971, pp.81–113).

This analysis of science and technology as ideology has a striking pertinence to the atomic age in which technocratic criteria of cost effectiveness and the potential for technical control dominate such public issues as energy, defence and transport. But the analysis is relevant to earlier phases of social rationalization: the early twentieth-century vogue for 'efficiency' in America and Britain displayed a specific historical form of technocratic consciousness. Eugenics, the pursuit of biological efficiency, has been illuminatingly called 'scientific management of the race', a phrase that sums up the desire to reduce social to biological development and subject it to scientific authority. Associated with eugenics was the reifying procedure characteristic of scientific method, for eugenists were obsessed with objectifying and measuring human qualities which would allow them to compare individual 'fitness' for procreation.

**11.8
THE SCIENTIFIC AND
INTELLECTUAL
BACKGROUND TO
HUMAN ENGINEERING**

The notion that 'man' could consciously breed better 'men' is an ancient one, advocated by Plato for the Guardians of his Republic. As the language implies, the idea entails a chattel status for women as the matrices of male perfectibility; it could only arise where sexual relations and human reproduction were interlaced with social domination and power. In modern times, conscious improvement of this kind was first practised by the Bible Communists or Perfectionists of Oneida, New York, under the leadership of John Humphrey Noyes. The community believed that conventional morality was for the unregenerate and that those, like themselves, who had attained perfection in Christ were above the moral code. They adopted a system of 'complex marriage' barely distinguishable from free love, and in 1869 pledged themselves to participate in an experiment to breed better Perfectionists by matching those most advanced in health and perfection (Haller, 1963, pp.37–38). The experiment was ephemeral, on the margins of society and its inspiration was religious rather than scientific.

For human engineering to be seriously entertained by intellectual opinion and proposed as a policy for society as a whole, it had to arise from secular and scientific consciousness. The progenitor of human engineering in these terms was the remarkable Victorian gentleman of science, Francis Galton (1822–1911), who made important contributions to statistics, psychology, biology and anthropology, and in 1883 coined the term 'eugenics' to designate the science of racial improvement by healthy breeding. Galton's chief inspiration for eugenics was his reading of Darwin's *The Origin of Species* (1859) and his projected science could be summarily described as the attempt to turn scientific knowledge of evolution back upon society and humankind, to substitute 'human' for natural selection. When Galton first adumbrated his new science in the 1860s (he then called it 'stirpiculture'), liberal intellectuals tended to emphasize the plasticity of human nature and the role of the cultural environment in producing observed differences within and between societies. Galton was already disposed to an hereditarian account of racial differences as a result of his explorations in Africa where he had encountered supposedly 'lower' races doomed, as he saw it, to extinction in an irreversible process of evolution which it would be foolish to oppose or even deplore. Hereditarian racism of this kind predated the Darwinian revolution and had both inspired and been reinforced by the rise of physical and cultural anthropology. Galton's reading of Darwin convinced him of the importance of heredity in determining variations or differences *within* ethnically homogeneous populations.

The study of pedigrees of distinguished families demonstrated to his satisfaction that intellectual abilities were largely inherited for outstanding scientists, lawyers, statesmen and others had among their forebears and descendants many relatives of only slightly less distinction. The frequency of 'genius' within families was, he argued, far greater than chance and could only be explained by biological inheritance (Galton, 1869). Henceforth, Galton made the scientific study of the sources of individual variation his life's work and the methodology he and his successors brought to bear upon it was vital statistics (or biometrics). Hitherto, breeders and natural scientists had worked with very imperfect descriptions of likeness and difference when comparing biologically related plants and animals. Galton developed the correlation coefficient to measure variation accurately. Earlier statisticians, notably Gauss and Quetelet, had observed that the physical characteristics of populations – such as height – are distributed in such a way that when the frequency of different heights is plotted on a curve it forms the famous 'bell shape' which represents statistical normality. Galton's basic project was to determine the respective contribution of heredity and the environment to deviation from the norm and he was the first to see the value of studying monozygotic or identical twins for this purpose. (They have a common biological inheritance and should they be separated in infancy and brought up in different environments then the role of heredity in determining likeness and difference can, theoretically, be established.) Galton also proposed to extend the study of differences from physical to mental traits – which he assumed to be normally distributed – and advocated mental measurement and the correlation of mental abilities. Though he had no systematic theory of mind, and his experimental work in the study of 'lower' mental processes was amateurish, his insights undoubtedly contributed handsomely to the rise of an experimental psychology closely related to the evolutionary life sciences, and having as one of its major problems the explanation of individual psychological differences.

Now, it is clear that mental and symbolic abilities are what distinguish human and social from other forms of life. The study of the role of heredity in determining how individuals differed in their abilities offered a compelling opportunity for synthesizing biological and social theory, though we will have to take something of a detour to see why that synthesis, with its policy prescriptions, was not really firmly established until the 1900s.

Biological differences between organisms of the same species played a crucial part in the Darwinian theory of evolution through natural selection, but the mechanism by which differences were transmitted from the parental to the filial generation were not understood, and Darwin (together with many contemporaries) accepted the hypothesis that advantageous, acquired characteristics were heritable. This theory – usually known as Lamarckianism – buttressed the type of 'optimistic' *laissez-faire* social evolutionism expounded by Herbert Spencer (1820–1909), who argued that the prevailing tendency of society led the fittest to be selected in the struggle for survival and that it was the business of sociology to instruct men in the folly of intervening in this ineluctable process. If the characteristics acquired by the fit could be transmitted to their progeny, then the trajectory of civilized development could, plausibly, be construed as the gradual, cumulative selection of individuals inherently better fitted for survival. Ameliorative social policies which helped sustain the weaker members of society (and their children) stood, no less plausibly, condemned as anti-evolutionary and anti-progressive. Spencerian nostrums enjoyed an extraordinary vogue in post-bellum America, where they served as a blatant legitimation for the cut-throat capitalism, and minimal government intervention in the economy, of the era. Clearly, they could not serve to rationalize a project of human engineering which, to be carried out on a social scale, demanded strong, interventionalist government in affairs which prevailing sentiment deemed private.

The testing and apparent refutation of Lamarckianism by the German biologist August Weismann (1834–1914) was extremely important both in discrediting beneficent *laissez-faire* social evolutionism and creating intellectual receptivity to the idea of engineering human reproduction. The experimental breeding of mice, over many generations, from parents who had had their tails amputated showed that this 'acquired' mutilation was not heritable and demonstrated what Weismann termed 'the continuity of the germ cells'. Furthermore, Weismann observed (as had Galton) that under laboratory breeding conditions, where the force of natural selection was suspended and all organisms were equally free to propagate, then there was a tendency for the measurable characteristics of offspring to revert to the mean or average of the population. It appeared that without the pressures of natural selection, species would, in a qualitative sense, be declining. Weismann's findings quickly became biological orthodoxy, although the Lamarckian heresy had a number of twentieth-century proponents (most notably the Soviet agronomist T. Lysenko). Weismann's findings were almost as quickly incorporated into social evolutionary doctrines, especially by the influential British Social Darwinist, Benjamin Kidd. Kidd remarked that:

. . . nothing tends to exhibit more strikingly the extent to which the study of our social phenomena must in future be based on the biological sciences, than the fact that the technical controversy now being waged by biologists as to the transmission or non-transmission to offspring of qualities acquired during the lifetime of the parent, is one which, if decided in the latter sense, must produce the most revolutionary effect through the whole domain of social and political philosophy. If the old view is correct, and the effects of use and education *are* transmitted by inheritance, then the Utopian dreams of philosophy in the past are undoubtedly possible of realisation. If the individual tends to inherit in his own person at birth the result of the education and mental and moral culture of past generations, then we may venture to anticipate a future society which will not deteriorate, but which may continue to make progress, even though the struggle for existence be suspended, the population regulated exactly to the means of subsistence, and the antagonism between the individual and the social organism extinguished, even as Mr Herbert Spencer has anticipated. But if, as the writer believes, the views of the Weismann party are in the main correct; if there can be no progress except by the accumulation of congenital variations above the average to the exclusion of others below; if, without the constant stress of selection which this involves, the tendency of every higher form of life is *actually retrograde*; then is the whole human race caught in the toils of that struggle and rivalry of life which has been in progress from beginning. (Kidd, 1894, pp.203–4. Original emphasis)

American contemporaries drew remarkably similar implications for social evolution from Weismann's theory; as one of them put it, 'our only hope for the permanent improvement of the human stock would . . . seem to be through exercising an influence upon the selective process', and there can be little doubt that the discrediting of Lamarckianism was a condition for the spread of eugenical ideas among scientific communities and the establishment of eugenics on an institutional basis in the 1900s. (See Haller, 1963, p.60; Ludmerer, 1972, p.91.) A further condition was the rediscovery in 1900 of Gregor Mendel's paper of 1865 in which he set out the simple ratios of inheritance he derived from the experimental crossbreeding of varieties of pea. Mendel's postulates are now recognized as the foundations of modern genetics and his name was given to a new paradigm of heredity theory. Hitherto, an individual's biological inheritance was assumed to involve the blending of parental endowments and Galton had formulated a Law of Ancestry setting out the fractions in which previous generations contributed to an individual's heredity. A 'blending' theory accorded well with the continuous variation which we do, in fact, observe with some characteristics (such as height) but not with others (such as gender, which is either male or female, and never a 'blend' of the two). Mendel's work indicated that the way heredity determines gender typifies the mechanism of biological inheritance: in other words, we receive it in discrete particles; either we inherit a genetically determined characteristic or we do not.

In Britain, the Galtonian school of biometricians, led by the statistician Karl Pearson, quarrelled furiously with the Mendelians, led by the botanist William Bateson – a scientific controversy which seriously divided the infant eugenics movement of the 1900s. Not until 1918 did R.A. Fisher demonstrate conclusively that the appearance of continuous variation is reconcilable with the Mendelian conception of heredity if we assume that many characteristics are polygenically determined. This controversy was far less significant in America, which quickly became the stronghold of Mendelism and where the theory allied itself to existing hereditarian accounts of feeblemindedness, criminality, drunkenness and other forms of social deviation to constitute a powerful movement for 'negative' eugenics (or the prohibition of the procreation of the 'unfit'). Human genetics developed rapidly in the first decade of the century and many bodily human characteristics were found to obey Mendel's laws. From the start, genetic research was intimately related with eugenics: the two most important research bodies were the Committee of Eugenics of the American Breeders' Association and the Eugenics Record

Office, both headed by the biologist Charles Davenport. The eugenics movement was carried forward on a mixture of scientifically valid work into genetically related disorders (such as deaf-mutism), amateur genealogical field studies and the clamour for legislation which would protect the future of white, Anglo-Saxon America against further contamination by degenerate 'stocks'.

**11.9
AMERICAN EUGENICS:
THE STERILIZATION
OF THE 'UNFIT' AND
THE CONTROL OF
IMMIGRATION**

The account so far has stressed the scientific conditions for the rise of eugenics and has, no doubt, given an excessively 'rationalistic' impression of the origins of the movement and ideology. Unquestionably there were political, social and demographic conditions for the emergence of eugenics and its interlacing with the interests of, broadly, the professional middle classes. These extra-scientific conditions were very different in America and Britain, and go far to explaining why eugenics was a predominantly racist ideology in the former and a class ideology in the latter. They also explain why eugenically-inspired legislation found its way on to the codes of many states, whereas in Britain the influence of eugenics on legislation was confined to the Mental Deficiency Act of 1913.

It is a commonplace that racism has deep historical roots in America. Until the passing of the Thirteenth Amendment under the duress of 'the Civil War, the Constitutional right of southern states to maintain the 'peculiar institution' of slavery was universally recognized throughout the American Union. This prizing of the white's right to property over the black person's right to freedom was embedded in a political conception of possessive individualism, and reinforced from the early nineteenth century by racist notions of the inherent inferiority of blacks which disqualified them from the status of property-owning citizenship and legitimized the master/slave relationship. The abolition of slavery did not end the political and cultural assumptions with which the institution was entangled, and their legislative consequences were to be felt after 1881 in a string of state laws disenfranchising blacks, segregating public institutions and forbidding miscegenation. These laws were upheld by a Supreme Court dominated by northerners and endorsed by most white opinion throughout the Union. Early twentieth-century reform organizations – such as the Woman Suffrage movement and the Progressive Party – accepted the racist assumptions of the segregated south, and even proposed to extend the legal framework built upon them to the north.

Blacks were the most prominent, but not the only victims of racism and 'caste consciousness'. Aboriginal Americans had been enslaved, massacred and confined without political rights to reservations. Irish Catholic immigrants in the mid-nineteenth century had encountered a Protestant 'nativism' which sought to eliminate the foreigner as a political force, although not to restrict the flow of immigration. In 1882, the Chinese became the first victims of racially-discriminating immigration control. After 1890, the 'new' mass migration from Southern and Eastern Europe inspired a racist demand for the restriction of immigration which, though pre-dating eugenics, grew in strength with the new science. There took place, in fact, a marriage of 'mutual attraction' between racism and eugenics:

> Many eugenists, already predisposed to nativism, found in the powerful and popular movement to restrict immigration a forum for placing eugenic attitudes before the public as well as an opportunity to strike a blow against what they believed to be degeneration of American stock . . . Racists and restrictionists, at the same time, found in eugenics the scientific reassurances they needed that heredity shaped man's destiny and that their assumptions rested on biological facts. (Haller, 1963, p.144)

Leaders of the Immigration Restriction League were instrumental in setting up restrictionist committees within the Eugenics Section of the American Breeders Association and the American Genetic Association. Both the *Journal of Heredity* and *Eugenical News*, official organs of the eugenics organizations, became 'avidly racist and restrictionist' (Haller, 1963, p.144).

The eugenic rationale for the restriction of immigration almost invariably began with the claim that modern science held heredity to be the dominant factor in shaping personal and cultural traits. The refutation of the inheritance of acquired characteristics enabled racists to deny that American institutions could mould the immigrants or their children to the American pattern. Hence the exclusion of 'inferior' races had the same justification as 'negative' eugenics directed against those in custodial care. As a leading restrictionist explained in 1910: 'The same arguments which induce us to segregate criminals and feebleminded and thus prevent their breeding apply to excluding from our borders individuals whose multiplying here is likely to lower the average of our people' (quoted in Haller, 1963, p.146). Not uncommonly, the restrictionist argument then went on to claim that Europeans were divided in three broad racial streams: the 'Mediterraneans', the 'Alpines' and the 'Nordics', of whom the last were taken to be endowed with the racial characteristics of 'love of organization, of law and military efficiency, as well as the ideals of family life, loyalty and truth' which had created the civilization of Protestant America. Madison Grant, who advanced these fantastic claims for Nordic superiority in *The Passing of the Great Race* (1916), used modern genetic notions to defend a conservative, aristocratic vision of America. His writings, and those of his protégé Lorthrop Stoddard, were often anti-semitic and in their hands eugenics came close to the *Völkisch* racism of National Socialism. Despite their inconsistencies and absurdities, they won a good measure of approval among scientific communities where egalitarian ideas were widely regarded as sentimental nonsense and notions of rule by a technocratic élite were much in vogue. However, the racist case for restriction was not just advanced by élitist social conservatives. E.A. Ross, the liberal, progressive sociologist (but also avid eugenist), indulged in the same kind of ethnic and racial stereotyping when he portrayed the danger of the new immigration to American stock in *The Old World in the New* (1912). The labour aristocrats organized in the American Federation of Labor, who perceived a threat to their high wages and craft status in the waves of Slav and Italian migrants, also allied themselves to the restrictionist movement and adopted many of its racist assumptions.

Before America entered the First World War the restrictionist case had won considerable Congressional support, and the chief means to impose discriminatory emigration which the legislature hit upon was the literacy test which favoured migrants from Northern and Western Europe with effective national educational systems. Hitherto, America had only excluded (apart from Asiatics) the sick, mental defectives and anarchists. Literacy test laws were opposed three times by the Presidential veto on the grounds (as Woodrow Wilson put it) that they represented 'a radical change in the policy of the Nation' by imposing tests whose object was 'restriction, not selection' (quoted in Degler, 1984, p.327). Literacy tests became mandatory in 1917, though as it happened the European war had already effected a great reduction in emigration. America's participation in the war strengthened the restrictionist case because it created a climate of zenophobic nationalism and sanctioned the curtailment of civil liberties. Prohibition, an illiberal measure sponsored chiefly by Protestant agrarian and middle-class America and directed mainly against the new migration, became national policy as a result of the war's impact on public opinion. (Rather oddly, prohibition was often advocated on eugenical grounds.) Furthermore, the massive use of group mental tests by psychologists employed by the US Army provided apparently scientific (and consequently highly persuasive) data to strengthen the eugenical case for restriction. Tests were used to screen out the mentally unfit from the army and help select officer trainees. They were supposedly culture free and provided the first important data on the relative intelligence of ethnic and racial groups. Their analysis by C.C. Brigham, who had helped direct the Army testing, produced results which accorded very nicely with the existing racist case for restriction: blacks performed on average worse than any white group, and among the foreign-born, immigrants from North-Western Europe were found to have mental ages significantly higher than those from Southern and Eastern Europe. (The fact that test scores were positively correlated with length of stay in America, which strongly suggested a relationship between culturation and test performance, was more or less ignored.) Brigham concluded:

> Our data . . . indicate that the Alpine Slav . . . is intellectually inferior to the Nordic type . . . We must now frankly admit the undesirable results which would ensue from a cross of the Nordic in this country with the Alpine Slav, with the degenerate hybrid Mediterranean, or with the negro . . . The steps that should be taken to preserve or increase our intellectual capacity must of course be dictated by science and not by political expediency. Immigration should not only be restrictive but highly selective. (Brigham, 1923, pp.203–10)

In the aftermath of war, America faced a renewed wave of immigration from a Europe ravaged by war, disease and revolution. The 'Red Scare', prompted by the Bolshevik revolution, and fear that the new migrants were the fodder for political and industrial radicalism, abetted the paranoia of middle America. Unrestricted immigration had few influential defenders and the restrictionists were demanding much more stringent controls than the literacy tests. The legislative result of the nativism of the war and post-war period was the Immigration Restriction Act of 1924. It both reduced the total volume of immigration and altered the ethnic balance of what remained by introducing national quotas based on the 1890 census, taken before the great influx from Eastern and Southern Europe and, therefore, discriminating against immigrants from these areas. By the early 1920s there were irresistible social and political pressures for ending the 'open-door policy', irrespective of the scientific and pseudo-scientific arguments for restriction, but eugenics was powerfully represented before the House Committee on Immigration and Naturalization which framed the 1924 Act. Testimony submitted by the biologist, H.H. Laughlin – credited as an 'Expert Eugenics Agent' – was considered of such influence as to form the principal basis of the Act (R.L. Garis, *Immigration Restriction*, 1927, quoted in Samelson, 1975, p.472).

How important the expert evidence of psychologists and the Army testing results were in the passage of the Act is a matter of some dispute. Leon Kamin, a devastating critic of IQ research, has argued that 'the science of mental testing may claim substantial credit' for the new law (Kamin, 1974, p.46). A more thorough examination of the evidence does not substantiate this· not one of the three reports submitted by the House Immigration Committee in support of the new law made any mention of psychological testing and there was very little reference to the Army tests in congressional debates. Test data formed a very small part of the total body of evidence considered in committee. It may be – as Franz Samelson has suggested – that the really puzzling question arising from a scrutiny of the evidence is 'why, *in spite of* the efforts by some psychologists, so *little* use was made of the presumably relevant scientific evidence of psychology?' (Samelson, 1975, p.474). There was a broad coalition for restriction long before the First World War put intelligence testing 'on the map' and if Samelson's assessment is right, the IQ psychologists provided only minor confirmatory arguments for a demand being pressed on economic, political and racist grounds (p.476). Though it would appear mistaken to attach much responsibility to the mental testers for the ending of 'open-door' immigration, eugenists can rightly be seen as orchestrating and legitimizing the demand. Most looked upon it as *the* legislative triumph of eugenics.

The United States has not been alone in imposing immigration controls inspired by racist and ethnic prejudice and compared with the British Dominions in this period was rather liberal: Australia and New Zealand rigidly excluded Asiatic immigration, and the latter's Undesirable Immigrants Exclusion Act of 1919 prohibited the landing of any person not of British birth and parentage, unless in possession of a special permit. America's immigration policy, however, had a significance not only for her own but for world history which dwarfed that of the other areas of extra-European white settlement. For more than a century she had been a huge magnet freely attracting migrants from Europe, and in the two decades before 1914 was the destination of the greatest unplanned shift in population in modern history. Going to America – not necessarily permanently – had been a common expectation of millions of Europeans; migration was part of the moving pattern of everyday life. About 6 million Italians migrated permanently between 1901–13, the majority going to the United States; the exodus from Poland, other parts of Eastern Europe and Greece was on a similar scale. The conscious decision to stop this demographic flow was a momentous instance of the 'political' shaping the 'quotidian,' one in which scientistic ideology played no small part.

We have already noted that the second major area of 'negative' eugenic influence on social policy – the sterilization of the 'unfit' – rested upon the same basic rationalization as the restriction of immigration, and it is noteworthy that H.H. Laughlin, 'Expert Eugenics Agent,' was a vigorous proponent of both. Legally-sanctioned eugenic sterilizations of people in public institutions reached a cumulative total of 61,000 by 1960, which is a not inconsiderable intervention in biological destiny (although in a far briefer period Nazi Germany sterilized about five times that number) (figures given in Reilly, 1977, p.126). The issue was subject to judicial argument – for many sterilization laws were challenged in the courts – and public debate. For much of the period the judiciary and the laity were remarkably insensitive to the human rights issues involved in sterilization. In according the state the right to violate bodily integrity in this fundamental way, the judicial consensus allowed the scientific claims for the heritability of feeblemindedness, criminality and other conditions to decide the ethical issues of who is 'fit' for parenthood and why future generations should conform to a biological 'norm'. That these are matters for moral reasoning – 'practical rationality' as Habermas calls it – escaped judicial attention until the 1940s. There may well be, of course, a moral case to be made for prohibiting the procreation of people with genetic diseases and disorders, but the case cannot be made in scientific discourse. In allowing science (often immature science) to settle the issue, the ethics of sterilization were repressed.

The origins of sterilization for eugenic purposes date back in America to the last decades of the nineteenth century when superintendents of asylums and doctors responsible for the insane became increasingly pessimistic about the curative effects of institutional care. In this period expert opinion came to accept that most mental disorders were congenital in character and that mental subnormality was far more extensive than the numbers in institutions would suggest. Many were persuaded by Lombroso that criminality was a hereditary trait linked with subnormality. Psychologists began identifying more subtle gradations of mental deficiency than they had done in the past and commonly ascribed a hereditary component to 'higher grade' defectives.

The belief that they were naturally prolific, prone to criminality and immorality, and that their progeny would be a huge burden on the public purse was encouraged by such genealogical studies as Richard Dugdale's *The Jukes* and Henry Goddard's *The Kallikak Family*. Fear of being 'swamped' by the feebleminded, later associated with the belief in the inexorable decline in average national intelligence, led to recurrent panics about the mentally subnormal. The eugenic argument for the custodial care of such people was greatly strengthened when it appeared that psychologists had found in the intelligence test an appropriate technology for their identification. Lewis Terman, who introduced into the United States the tests first devised by Simon and Binet in France, argued that:

> . . . in the near future intelligence tests will bring tens of thousands of these high-grade defectives under the surveillance and protection of society. This will ultimately result in curtailing the reproduction of feeble-mindedness and in the elimination of an enormous amount of crime, pauperism and industrial inefficiency. It is hardly necessary to emphasize that the high-grade cases, of the type now so frequently overlooked, are precisely the ones whose guardianship it is most important for the State to assume. (Terman, 1919, p.6)

The eugenic argument for sterilization was often justified by Mendelian concepts of genetic 'dominance' and 'recession'. The linking of certain mental disorders with a 'recessive' gene had a particular ideological potency because it suggested that unless eugenic measures were taken, then certain hereditary conditions would lurk in the shadows of posterity, ready to catch the future unawares.

Isolated cases of sterilization preceded the creation of an institutionalized eugenics movement or even the widespread use of the term eugenics. In 1897 a bill calling for the asexualization of the feebleminded and certain criminals was introduced in the Michigan state legislature, but ultimately defeated. About the same time, the castration of forty-four boys and fourteen girls in the Kansas State Institution for Feebleminded Children was carried out by a resident physician, before the public outcry forced him to stop (Haller, 1963, p.48; Ludmerer, 1972, p.91). Castration has major endocrinal and hormonal effects on the body and was considered intolerable in a society whose Constitution forbad 'cruel and unnatural punishments'. Public acceptability of sterilization for punitive and therapeutic, as well as eugenic, purposes was really conditional on the perfection of the operation of vasectomy for men and salpingectomy for women. In 1899, Dr Harry Sharp of the Indiana Reformatory introduced the vasectomy operation to curb the excessive masturbation of an inmate (who had, apparently, requested his own castration). Masturbation was then considered by medical opinion as a prime cause of physical and spiritual degeneracy, and the success of the operation in this case – which is a bit puzzling because vasectomy has no physiological effect on libidinal drive – opened up such a therapeutic vista that by the end of the year Sharp had operated on seventy-six youths. It then occurred to him that (in his own words) 'this would be a good method of preventing procreation in the defective and physically unfit', and he became an insistent advocate of sterilization for eugenic reasons. In 1907, he was instrumental in persuading the Indiana State legislature to pass an act making sterilization mandatory for confirmed criminals, idiots, imbeciles and rapists in state institutions when recommended by a board of experts (Haller, 1963, pp.48–49).

During the next five years, Indiana's example was followed by fourteen other states, although the laws were not always used and were in a number of cases struck down when challenged in the chief appeal court of the individual state. Some of these laws were directed against classes of malefactors (such as 'drug fiends' and 'drunkards') whose offences had nothing to do with heredity, and several laws assumed a heredity cause behind diseases and disorders about which scientifically-qualified eugenists like Davenport were themselves sceptical. Because they feared the discredit that would fall on eugenics from badly framed, ill-informed legislation, and were sensitive to the hostility of the Catholic Church, many eugenists did not support the sterilization campaign. But their most prominent publicist emphatically did. Madison Grant argued for asexualization on a scale which would have genetically 'purified' the nation:

> The individual himself can be nourished, educated and protected by the community during his lifetime, but the state through sterilization must see to it that his line stops with him, or else future generations will be cursed with an ever increasing load of victims of misguided sentimentalism. This is a practical, merciful and inevitable solution to the whole problem, and can be applied to an ever widening circle of social discards, beginning always with the criminal, the diseased and the insane and extending gradually to types which may be called weaklings rather than defectives and perhaps ultimately to worthless race types. (Quoted in Reilly, 1977, p.124)

While legislation was being challenged in the state courts, and before the constitutionality of sterilization had been adjudged by the Supreme Court, an effective eugenical programme was not a serious political possibility. The judgement of the Supreme Court in 1927 – written by Justice Oliver Wendell Holmes, a eugenics sympathizer – upholding a Virginia sterilization law on the grounds that it fell within the police power[1] of the state, was extremely important in encouraging a fresh wave of legislation which physicians felt confident of using. Holmes argued that:

> We have seen more than once that the public welfare may call upon the best citizens for their lives. It would be strange if it could not call upon those who already sap the strength of the state [in this instance an unmarried mother in the Virginia State Colony for Epileptics and Feebleminded] for these lesser sacrifices, often not felt to be such by those concerned, in order to prevent our being swamped by incompetence. It is better for all the world, if instead of waiting for their imbecility, society can prevent those who are manifestly unfit from continuing their kind . . . Three generations of imbeciles are enough . . .

There is no more striking confirmation of the immaturity (not to say infantilism) of the science on which the case for sterilization rested than the fact that the daughter of the appellant in this case had been tested at one month and diagnosed feebleminded; she turned out to be of above average intelligence (Haller, 1963, p.139; Reilly, 1977, p.125).

In the decade following the Supreme Court Judgement, sterilization laws were adopted in twenty states and enforced in others where they had been unused. Although legislation was enacted in all regions of the Union, the mid- and far-western states implemented it more energetically than others. Despite the fact that scientific research was undermining earlier genetic theories of retardation, alcoholism and epilepsy which eugenists had advanced, the total number of sterilizations climbed steeply. It would seem quite likely that the crumbling eugenic rationale was of little concern to many of the administrative authorities who ordered the sterilization of people in

---

[1]Police power is a technical term in American legal parlance meaning the strictly limited power of government to regulate society in the interests of public welfare.

their custody. The operation could – it would seem – serve as a blunt instrument of social control: in the 1930s, girls and boys at the Kansas State Industrial Schools were being routinely sterilized as a punishment for misbehaviour (according to *The Washington Post*, 24 October 1937). The Chairman of the Board of Administration of the Kansas reformatories reportedly said: 'Girls have been sterilised who were obstreperous, fighting or perverts. In our opinion we did not exceed the law and we do not believe the girls we sterilised were fit for motherhood' (from the account in the British *Daily Worker*, 25 October 1937). When a new Democratic state administration stopped the practice in 1937, sixty-two recent victims had been under sixteen. There were sufficient instances of such flagrantly punitive sterilizations for critics of eugenics in the later 1930s to point to the American democracy rather than Nazi Germany when warning of the danger of the political abuse of science.

Even among the democracies, however, the United States was by no means alone in making sterilization an important instrument of social policy: two Canadian provinces and all the Scandinavian countries introduced statutory measures in the late 1920s and early 30s. In Britain, eugenists campaigned determinedly for the legalization of voluntary sterilization for mental defectives and for the 'Social Problem Group' of large families in long-term unemployment. Their campaign was unsuccessful, largely because of the hostility of the medical profession and the Catholic Church, and the National Government's unwillingness to bring in contentious legislation (Searle, 1979, pp.159–69).

Assessing the impact of compulsory sterilization on everyday life in America is by no means easy. At the first blush, it might appear an issue of fundamental ethical importance but trivial social significance, for the total numbers sterilized were but a small fraction of the categories to which the various laws applied, and only in California were sterilizations so frequent as to be described as routine. Most historical accounts do, in fact, treat it as a symbolic issue which has been confined to the past by revulsion from the atrocities of Nazi 'race science' and a greater judicial sensitivity to human and civil rights. The obituaries of eugenics now seem slightly premature: since the 1960s there have been recurrent attempts in the United States to revive sterilization as an instrument of social policy by making it a condition for the receipt of welfare under the Aid to Families with Dependent Children programme, and a number of distinguished scientists have argued that people of low IQ should be paid to undergo sterilization. More fundamentally, it does seem to me that sterilization has a *symptomatic* significance for the relations of the power and authority which permeate everyday life in modern society. In some brilliant passages of his *History of Sexuality*, Michel Foucault argued that modernization has transformed the nature of power in our society and that the biological notion of human life, at both the individual and species level, has become the object of an array of technologies of power which seek to 'normalize' and whose legitimacy is derived from the statistical concept of the norm. Power in the *ancien régime*, Foucault argues, was epitomized by the sovereign's right to decide life and death; its symbol was the sword. This negative power to take life remains, but alongside it has grown a positive power 'to administer, optimize and multiply [life], subjecting it to precise controls and comprehensive regulations'. This power over life was manifested in two basic ways: what Foucault calls the 'disciplines' (of physical pedagogy, drill) which worked on the individual body, and the regulatory controls of the population or social body. These 'constituted the two poles around which the organization of power over life was deployed' (Foucault, 1979, pp.135–45). Around these two poles clustered forms of knowledge (such as physical anthropology and demography) directed at the measurement of humankind and employing the concept of the norm to assess deviation. These new forms of knowledge both constituted an intellectual authority for the administration and management of human life and allowed for a dispersal of power to new 'expert' professions (of psychology, social work, psychiatry) with the competence to measure 'fitness' for education, employment, even procreation. If we are to follow Foucault's argument, therefore, sterilization of the 'unfit' is not a shocking, but marginal abuse of modern surgery: rather, it was a particular outcome of the dual transformation of power and the construction of human life as an object of knowledge and power which was a central process in the formation of modern societies. My feeling is that this has a relevance for any analysis of everyday life which goes beyond a trivializing compendium of facts.

Clearly, Foucault provokes objections, as well as compelling admiration. His argument illuminates the 'Malthusian' politics of population of the early nineteenth century, the rise of varieties of Social Darwinism and eugenics in the later nineteenth century, the concern for the biological 'fitness' of the nation in an era of imperial competition which we find in movements for 'National Efficiency', the racist policies of National Socialism as well as immigration and sterilization in twentieth-century America. What it fails to do is to explain specific national differences in the politics of human life and procreation: why, for example, should two liberal democracies, Britain and America, have adopted very different judicial and social attitudes to sterilization? This is the sort of question that falls through the mesh of Foucault's metahistorical net and can only be answered by a close comparative analysis of the relationships between law, ideology and political institutions which is outside the scope of this essay.

11.10 MENTAL MEASUREMENT, SOCIAL STRATIFICATION AND SOCIAL SELECTION

We have already had reason to notice the intellectual connection between eugenics and psychologists in the demand for immigration restriction. Here, I shall outline a theory of social stratification derived from Galton's work and perfected by IQ psychologists in Britain and America, and explore the extent to which this theory has shaped processes of social selection through its implementation in public educational systems.

In aristocratic societies – such as Britain remained until late in the nineteenth century – wealth, prestige and power were the birthright of a hereditary élite for whom descent alone legitimized their status. To this conservative élitism, Galton opposed a liberal élitism whereby social position would correspond to innate individual worth. His ideal society was a meritocracy and it was in the intellectual professions that he regarded its principles as best realized. While this aspect of his thought made him critical of the existing social order of the 1860s, 70s and 80s, his belief in innate inequality separated him from near contemporaries – such as J.S. Mill – whose egalitarianism inclined them towards socialism. Galton was convinced that the innate talent necessary for success in a meritocratic society (which he first dubbed 'natural ability', later 'civic worth') was normally distributed: in a seminal lecture on 'The Possible Improvement of the Human Breed under the Existing Conditions of Law and Sentiment' he put forward a notional eight-fold classification of the population according to the distribution of 'civic worth', and suggested that this could be compared with the actual distribution of the population into socio-economic classes made by Charles Booth in his epochal survey of London's *Life and Labour*. The implication of the comparison was that the distribution of 'civic worth' corresponded with the hierarchy of social stratification. Indeed, the nearer society actually came to Galton's meritocratic ideal the closer the correspondence would be, and the more innate 'civic worth' would be acting as a cause of social inequality.

It was the case, of course, that with social emancipation and industrialization, many men (though far fewer women) of humble birth 'rose through

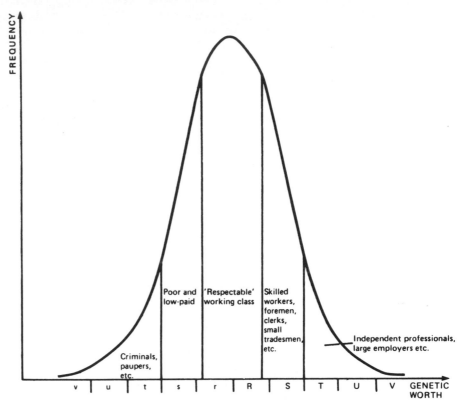

Figure 11.4
Galton's view of British social structure, relating the 'bell-shape' curve of statistical probability to late Victorian social stratification. (From D.M. MacKenzie 'Eugenics in Britain', Social Studies in Science *6, 1976, p.514, by permission of Sage Publications, London)*

the ranks' to positions of wealth and/or intellectual eminence. As a liberal individualist, Galton approved of this occupational and social mobility and believed he had found a natural cause for it in the phenomenon of regression to the mean. If 'civic worth' was distributed and inherited like height, then the tiny upper-middle class of highly educated professionals most endowed with this quality would not have enough children of equivalent native talent to reproduce that class in the next generation. Most new members of the class would be born into strata immediately below it, although the lower down the pyramid of social stratification one went, the less the relative frequency of social promotions would be. In other words, the chance of a son of an upper-middle class professional remaining at that status was far greater than that of a lower-middle class boy ascending to it.

Galton was advancing on biological and psychological grounds a theory of 'the circulation of élites' (such as we find in the writings of the Italian sociologist Vilfredo Pareto) which could serve as a defence against egalitarian critiques of class inequality. This theory has had powerful exponents in Britain and America, notably Sir Cyril Burt (1883–1971) and the Harvard psychologist Richard Herrnstein, whose *IQ in the Meritocracy* (1971) is a recent and sophisticated statement of the Galtonian position. When Galton sketched out his view of the relationship between the distribution of innate qualities and social stratification, the ill-defined, unmeasurable nature of 'civic worth' was a serious difficulty in the way of implementing the 'positive' eugenic proposals with which the concept was linked. Galton hoped 'to improve our race' by granting diplomas to the 'worthiest' young men and women, encouraging their intermarriage and 'by promoting [through dowries] the early marriage of girls of that high class' so that they would bear more children. One suspects that this genial flight of fancy was certain to float like a bubble over the marital and childbearing practices of the professional middle classes.

The development, in the work of the British psychologist Charles Spearman (1863–1945), of a theory of general intelligence brought it somewhat closer to the ground. From the statistical analysis of motor-sensory tests he had administered to children, and a comparison of independent assessments of their intellectual ranking by their teachers, Spearman postulated that two factors were involved in all higher mental processes, a general or common factor, which he called (g), and special factors (s's) which were specific to particular operations. Here, Spearman claimed, was a theoretical basis for the heterogeneous tests Binet was using to assess mental age in France. Binet had found that the most useful diagnostic tool was a 'hotchpotch' of tasks and problems, graded according to age and teachers' independent assessments of an average child's performance. Thus at five a child would be expected to compare two weights, copy a square, count four coins and so on. A child able to perform slightly more advanced tasks was reckoned to have a 'mental age' in excess of five, and in a revised edition of his tests Binet published an age scale. In Spearman's view, Binet had fortuitously stumbled on a suitable method for assessing general intelligence, for the very heterogeneity of the items in Binet's battery meant that the individual s's cancelled each other out so that *in toto* the battery was an adequate test of g.

Spearman had strong eugenic sympathies and was predisposed to believe that g was largely determined by heredity and fixed at birth; if such was the case it could prove an invaluable instrument of social selection. In 1912, Spearman anticipated the day when the measured intelligence of every child throughout the kingdom would go into a yearly official registration of the 'intellective index' which might enable every child's education to be properly graded according to his or her capacity. Possibly the index could be used to match young workers to professions really suited to their capacities. One could even conceive, thought Spearman, of the 'establishment of a minimum index to qualify for the parliamentary vote, and above all for the right to have offspring' (Spearman and Hart, 1912). Evidence that general intelligence was determined by heredity came from Burt's first academic paper of 1909. He, too, had strong eugenic sympathies and prefaced his discussion with a statement of how important the question of the inheritance of intelligence was to the 'possible improvement of the human breed' (Burt, 1909). Like Spearman, he saw in the measurement of intelligence a remarkable opportunity for social control, suggesting in a 1918 lecture to London social workers that:

> Eventually a complete 'psychogram' of every school child might be compiled. Each, as it left school, would be the subject of a special *dossier*, passed on, like the school leaving form, to some juvenile advisory. In such a *dossier* innate abilities, both general and specific, would be noted according to some comparable quantitative scheme . . . Everybody might be thus indexed according to their mental powers . . .

He then sketched out how psychologists could institute scientific vocational selection by assessing the abilities required for particular occupations and matching young workers to jobs on the basis of innate individual abilities: 'The key . . . to social efficiency is vocational fitness – a place for every man, and every man in his place' (Burt, 1918).

Burt's interest in scientific vocational selection led him to participate in the National Institute of Industrial Psychology, and thus establish a bridge between the 'social' engineering stemming from Taylorism and the 'human' engineering from eugenics and individual psychology. An address on 'The Principles of Vocational Guidance' at the Seventh International Congress of Psychology of 1923 gave Burt the opportunity to publicize the Galtonian theory of social stratification. Burt claimed that material gathered in his capacity as an educational psychologist working for the London County Council enabled him to estimate the distribution of the population into eight grades of measured intelligence, starting at Grade 1 with the tiny percentage of the population with IQs of 150+, moving down through the populous grades which clustered round the mean, and tailing off with the small imbecile grade at the end of the distribution. He then arranged the occupation of adults, by strata, in a corresponding series, using (so he claimed) US Army and NIIP data and information gathered by the British Civil Service when testing new entryists. He thus produced an eight-fold occupational classification, with each class grouped about an average IQ. (The accompanying illustration, taken – with acknowledgements to Burt – from a widely used manual on education and psychology for trainee teachers – will clarify the two tables Burt had constructed.) There was a tolerable symmetry, but not a perfect correspondence, between the two series and the purpose of scientific vocational selection was to align them as closely as possible, to produce a society where the social friction of individual misfits was minimized.

On Galton's foundations, Burt had created an impressive intellectual edifice which provided a rational, 'naturalized' model for the hierarchy of occupational inequality and indicated how it could best be reproduced and conserved. The model had the great attraction of dynamic stability, for it

Intelligence Quotient.	*Vocational Category.*
Over 150	*Highest professional*, e.g. lawyer, physician, university teacher, architect.
130-150	*Lower professional*, e.g. teacher, secretary, surveyor, engineer.
115-130	*Clerical and highly skilled*, e.g. book-keeper, electrician, compositor, hospital nurse.
100-115	*Skilled*, e.g. tailor, cabinet-maker, bus-driver, routine typist.
85-100	*Semi-skilled*, e.g. barber, laundry worker, domestic servant, miner.
70-85	*Unskilled*, e.g. packer, labeller, farmhand, sweep.

I.Q.	*Educational Category.*	*Percentage in the Population.*
50 and below	Ineducable idiots ; occupation centres.	0·2
50-70	Mentally-defective pupils ; special schools.	2
70-85	Dull and backward pupils ; "C" classes in senior schools.	10
85-115	Normal pupils ; "B" and "A" classes in senior schools.	76
115-130	Bright pupils ; selective central schools.	10
130-150	Scholarship pupils ; secondary schools.	2
150 and above	Scholarship pupils ; secondary schools, ultimately university honours.	0·2

*Figure 11.5
Burt's tables purporting to show mean IQ levels in the different social classes. (From A.G. Hughes and E.H. Hughes, 1937,* Learning and Teaching, *London, Longman)*

required the selection and movement of individuals within a social structure of constant shape. In subsequent publications, Burt drew on the work of Fisher on population genetics to refine the model, and in a famous paper of 1961 on intelligence and social mobility put forward data which confirmed (apparently) the values for regression which Fisher's theory predicted. Burt concluded: 'Of the various causal factors affecting the individual's rise or fall in occupational status, differences in intelligence and motivation appear to be the most influential. Differences in home background and in education seem to exercise a secondary or supplementary influence, but without the basis of the first two they are of little effect' (quoted in Norton, 1981, p.312). Burt's data have conclusively been shown to be fraudulent. Indeed, from the very beginning of his career his papers show slipshod, poorly reported research, sometimes more suggestive of farce than science (like the claim to have administered camouflaged intelligence tests to London grandparents). His studies of the correlations of intelligence between twins separated at birth contained impossible consistencies which ought to have exposed them as fraudulent when they were published. Their faults notwithstanding, they provided, until the early 1970s, the major evidence for the predominant role of heredity in determining IQ, and had an important bearing on social policy because they were cited to criticize educational policies designed to discriminate positively in favour of the environmentally disadvantaged. A clear example of a hereditarian intervention relying heavily on Burt's work was the article by the American psychometrician A.R. Jensen 'How much can we boost IQ and scholastic achievement?', which appeared in the 1969 *Harvard Educational Review*. This sought to question the 'Headstart' programme of compensatory education for (mainly black) ghetto children on the grounds that genetical determination of average IQ differences between social classes and between blacks and whites meant that these differences could not be eliminated by 'interventionist' educational reforms.

We must now ask how this model of social selection and the technology of intelligence testing has influenced educational practices in Britain. There is compelling evidence that psychometricians won the respectful attention of opinion close to government during the inter-war years, for from 1924 the Consultative Committee of the Board of Education sought their advice when reporting on elementary and secondary education. Burt contributed substantially to its 1924 *Report on Psychological Tests of Educable Capacity*, and his lightly disguised views were given great prominence in the Spens Report of 1938 on Secondary Education. Here, the theory of innate general intelligence, which was purportedly the central governing factor in a child's development and when measured accurately predicted the ultimate level of his or her intellectual powers, was used to justify selective secondary education at eleven. The Report was not exactly a statement of official policy, and was to some extent rationalizing educational developments already taking place 'on the ground'. It can, notwithstanding, be seen as a blueprint for the rigid system of tripartite secondary education established in England as a result of the 1944 Education Act. The use of intelligence tests in the 11+ examination played a significant and highly controversial role in this post-war system. Critics claimed that intelligence testing led to many individual cases of injustice, warped the curricula of primary schools, and discriminated against working-class children because test questions contained a cultural bias favouring a child from a middle-class home. There was little substance to the last charge, at least, for research showed that where intelligence tests were removed from the 11+, the proportion of scholarship winners from working-class homes actually declined. Many were prepared to defend intelligence tests on the pragmatic grounds that, if selection had to be made, then intelligence tests were the least culturally biased, most successful predictors of later educational attainment around. The most substantial charge against

IQ theory – it seems to me – is that it was used in an attempt to exclude from the political agenda alternative forms of post-primary education (such as multilateral and comprehensive schooling) and to provide a 'natural science' legitimation for the élitist grammar schools. In the public acrimony over comprehensive reform in the 1960s, the mental testers adopted the technocratic strategy of arguing that while selective secondary education was the only system concordant with the psychometric 'facts', their critics' proposals were founded on utopian ideology. Progressive educational principles and practices, wrote Burt in 1969, 'are advocated – as they always have been – not on the basis of experimental trial or factual evidence, but as deductions from certain ideological theories' (Burt, 1969). Which, given subsequent revelations, is painfully comic.

To many, it seemed that Burt's own 'ideological theory' had had a malign influence on the educational system since he first caught the ear of the Board of Education's Consultative Committee in the early 1920s. Brian Simon, the leading Marxist educational historian, has argued that 'the doctrine of mental testing' both legitimized and provided the technology for a crude educational functionalism which aspired to do no more than match the school system to the social order and 'turn out children at appropriate ages for available levels of employment' (Simon, 1974, pp.240–50). Unfortunately, Simon assumes – as others have – that the favour mental measurement found with the Board of Education officials and the Board's semi-official advisers meant that mass intelligence testing for streaming and selection at eleven was an accomplished fact by the 1930s. Reality was far more complicated: English local educational authorities could decide for themselves what methods they used to select children from the public elementary schools for the Free and Special Places in grant-aided secondary schools. Rather more than half did at some time use something they called an intelligence test in their 11+ examination, but many used them only intermittently, and others used 'homegrown' tests which did not meet the technical requirements of standardization demanded by specialists. A substantial number of authorities simply took no notice of the official advice to incorporate intelligence tests into their selection procedures; the 11+ examination in these areas tended to be culturally biased tests of English which discriminated against working-class children in overcrowded local primary schools. The small minority of authorities who used the testing services of Moray House – headed by the psychologist Godfrey Thompson – benefited from a punctilious attention to the contents and standardization of tests designed to ensure the maximum fairness in dealing with 11+ candidates whatever their class or family background (Sutherland, 1984, pp.188–90 and 213–18). Thompson was no hereditarian and a major critic of Spearman's *g* theory, yet he did more than anyone else to spread the technology of testing, with the intention of liberalizing secondary education opportunities for working-class children. The consequences of his work appear to have been altogether benign.

The patchy and uneven understanding of mental measurement in interwar England contrasts strikingly with the enthusiasm with which this technology was adopted in the United States. There, the powerful corporate foundations (such as the Carnegie Foundation for the Advancement of Teaching) financed a testing movement which, though non-profit making, grew into a multi-million dollar business (Karier, 1977, pp.339–64). The foundations exercised a considerable influence on public policy at a state (rather than a national) level. Their usual *modus operandi* was to initiate projects which, when they had gathered momentum, would be taken over as permanent programmes by the local school board, the state education authority, or a university's own budget (Karier, 1977, p.341). The foundations furthered the interests of the corporate wealth on which they were built by promoting policies of meritocratic efficiency which would stabilize the distribution of wealth and power in America and legitimize it in the eyes of the masses. Their officers and the psychologists who worked with them were not conspirators: the belief in capitalist democracy, regulated by scientific expertise and an enlightened bureaucracy, was a public commitment which linked them with the pre-war Progressive movement. Mental testing was obviously given a huge shot in the arm by the First World War, but the reasons for its rapid permeation through the public-school system lie deeper in the structure and ethos of American society. America's incredibly heterogeneous and mobile population constituted an administrative problem of classification: everyday teachers were faced by Italian, Russian and other foreign-speaking children, and the non-verbal group tests were an appropriate technology for initial assessment and streaming. The content of the verbal tests also suggests that testing was a subliminal form of 'Americanization', for success in them required a cultural competence in dominant American values. Furthermore, the American commitment to a functionalist philosophy of education meant that teachers and administrators were much more receptive to the testing procedure than the grammar-school élite of the English teaching profession whose humanistic conceptions of learning were deeply ingrained. A standard text on American public school administration opined that:

> Our schools are, in a sense, factories in which the raw products (children) are to be shaped and fashioned into products to meet the various demands of life. The specifications for manufacturing come from the demands of twentieth century civilisation, and it is the business of the school to build its pupils according to the specifications laid down. This demands good tools, specialised machinery, continuous measurement of production to see if it is according to specifications, the elimination of waste in manufacture, and a large variety in the output. (Quoted in Karier, 1977, p.344)

Given this concept of the school, the mental testers had a ready-made role as the 'progress chasers' and quality controllers of education.

**11.11
CONCLUSIONS**

The two parts of this essay have tried to trace the working out of an (intellectually misguided) endeavour to extend the method and logic of natural science to society. After positivism, its historical antecedent, broke up as a movement this endeavour was always fragmented among different professional organizations, scientific communities and technical cadres, and it cut across conventional divisions between left and right, revolution and reaction. It is impossible to offer an authoritative judgement on the extent to which the joint project of 'human' and 'social' engineering has carried out its own programme: the subject is too vast for easy summary. We can say with some confidence that the everyday world of work in modern societies has been shaped by the technocratic impulse that has been described here, although that impulse has met sharp resistance and often been deflected from its original purposes. Social administration has been, in certain societies and in certain circumstances, responsive to what we could call 'bio-politics' or political programmes seeking to control life itself. But social administration has, frequently, resisted pro-natalism and selection on eugenic grounds. The extent to which eugenics was a largely ineffective movement in democratic societies needs to be stressed for it helps put into perspective aspects of daily life which have (thankfully) not become subject to technocratic despotism.

REFERENCES   Aldcroft, D.H. (ed.) (1968) *The Development of British Industry and Foreign Competition, 1875–1914*, Allen & Unwin.

Auerbach, J.S. (ed.) (1969) *American Labor: The Twentieth Century*, Bobbs-Merrill.

Block, N. and Dworkin, G. (eds.) (1977) *The IQ Controversy*, Quartet.

Braverman, H. (1974) *Labor and Monopoly Capital*, Monthly Review Press.

Brigham, C.C. (1923) *A Study of American Intelligence*, Princeton University Press.

Briggs, A. (1954) 'Social background' in Flanders, A. and Clegg, H.A. (eds.) *The System of Industrial Relations in Great Britain*, Blackwell.

Brown, J.A.C. (1954) *The Social Psychology of Industry*, Penguin.

Burnham, J. (1941) *The Managerial Revolution*, Penguin.

Burt, C. (1909) 'Experimental tests of general intelligence', *British Journal of Psychology*, 3, pp.94–177.

Burt, C. (1918) 'Individual psychology and social work', *Charity Organisation Review*, 252, new series (January).

Burt, C. (1969) 'The mental differences between children' in Cox, C.B. and Dyson, A.E. (eds.) *Black Paper 2*, The Critical Quarterly Society.

Chandler, A.D. (1977) *The Visible Hand: the Managerial Revolution in American Business*, Harvard University Press.

Chandler, A.D. (1980) 'The United States: seedbed of managerial capitalism' in Chandler and Daems, op.cit.

Chandler, A.D. and Daems, H. (eds.) (1980) *Managerial Hierarchies*, Harvard University Press.

Degler, C. (1984) *Out of Our Past* (third edition), Harper.

Evans, B. and Waites, B. (1981) *IQ and Mental Testing*, Macmillan.

Forrest, D.W. (1974) *Francis Galton: the Life and Work of a Victorian Genius*, Elek.

Foucault, M. (1979) *The History of Sexuality*, Allen Lane.

Fridenson, P. (1972) *Histoire des usines Renault, 1898–1939*, Seuil.

Fridenson, P. (1978) 'The coming of the assembly line to Europe' in Krohn, Layton and Weingart, op.cit.

Friedman, A.L. (1977) *Industry and Labour*, Macmillan.

Galton, F. (1869) *Hereditary Genius*, reprinted Fontana 1962.

Giddens, A. (1977) 'Positivism and its critics', *Studies in Social and Political Theory*, Hutchinson.

Giedion, S. (1948) *Mechanization takes Command. A Contribution to Anonymous History*, Oxford University Press.

Goldsmith, M. and Mackay, A. (eds.) (1964) *The Science of Science*, Souvenir Press.

Graham, L.R. (1977) 'Science and values: the Eugenics Movement in Germany and Russia in the 1920s', *American Historical Review*, 82, pp.113–1164

Habermas, J. (1971) 'Technology and science as "ideology" ' in *Toward a Rational Society*, Heinemann.

Haldane, J.B.S. (1964) 'The proper social application of the knowledge of human genetics' in Goldsmith and Mackay, op.cit.

Haller, M. (1963) *Eugenics*, Rutgers University Press.

Hearnshaw, L.S. (1979) *Cyril Burt*, Hodder and Stoughton.

Hounshell, D.A. (1984) *From the American System to Mass Production, 1800–1932: The Development of Manufacturing Technology in the United States*, Johns Hopkins University Press.

Hoxie, R.F. (1915) *Scientific Management and Labor*, Appleton.

ILO/Devinat (1927) *Scientific Management in Europe*, ILO Studies and Reports, Series B (Economic Conditions), No.17, prepared by Devinat, P.

Kamin, L.J. (1974) *The Science and Politics of IQ*, Erlbaum.

Karier, C.J. (1977) 'Testing for order and control in the corporate liberal state' in Block and Dworkin, op.cit.

Kidd, B. (1894) *Social Evolution*, Macmillan.

Kocka, J. (1980) 'The rise of the modern industrial enterprise in Germany' in Chandler and Daems, op.cit., and Krohn, Layton and Weingart, op.cit.

Krohn, W., Layton, E.T. and Weingart, P. (eds.) (1978) *The Dynamics of Science and Technology, Sociology of the Sciences, Vol.2*, Reidel.

Landes, D. (1969) *The Unbound Prometheus*, Cambridge University Press.

Lane, D. (1970) *Politics and Society in the USSR*, Weidenfeld.

Layton, E.T. (1971) *The Revolt of the Engineers*, Case Western Reserve University Press.

Layton, E.T. (1976) 'American ideologies of science and engineering', *Technology and Culture*, 17, October.

Ludmerer, K.M. (1972) *Genetics and American Society*, Johns Hopkins University Press.

MacKenzie, D.M. (1976) 'Eugenics in Britain', *Social Studies in Science*, 6, pp.499–532.

Maier, C. (1970) 'Between Taylorism and technocracy: European ideologies and the vision of industrial productivity in the 1920s', *Journal of Contemporary History*, 5, April.

Maier, C. (1975) *Recasting Bourgeois Europe: Stabilization in France, Germany and Italy in the Decade after World War I*, Princeton University Press.

Meyer, S. (1981) *The $5 Day: Labor Management and Social Control in the Ford Motor Company, 1908–1921*, State University of New York Press.

Montgomery, D. (1979) *Workers' Control in America*, Cambridge University Press.

Moutet, A. (1975) 'Les origines du système de Taylor en France: le point de vue patronal (1907–1914)', *Le Mouvement Social*, 93, October–December.

Myers, C.S. (1926) *Industrial Psychology in Britain*, Cape.

Myers, C.S. (ed.) (1929) *Industrial Psychology*, Cape.

Nadworny, M.J. (1955) *Scientific Management and the Unions, 1900–1932*, Harvard University Press.

Nelson, D. (1975) *Managers and Workers*, University of Wisconsin Press.

Nelson, D. (1980) *F.W. Taylor and the Rise of Scientific Management*, University of Wisconsin Press.

Noble, D. (1977) *America by Design: Science, Technology and the Rise of Corporate Capitalism*, Knopf.

Norton, B. (1981) 'Psychologists and class' in Webster, op.cit.

Philip, A. (1927) *Le problème ouvrier aux Etats-Units*, Alcan.

Porter, G. (1978) 'Management' in Williams, T.I. (ed.) *A History of Technology, Vol.6 The Twentieth Century, 1900–1950*, Clarendon Press.

Reilly, P. (1977) *Genetics, Law and Social Policy*, Harvard University Press.

Richardson, H.W. (1968) 'Chemicals' in Aldcroft, op.cit.

Samelson, F. (1975) 'On the science and politics of the IQ', *Social Research*, 42, No.3, pp.467–88.

Schonfield, A. (1965) *Modern Capitalism*, Royal Institute for International Affairs/Oxford University Press, reprinted in paperback 1969.

Searle, G.R. (1976) *Eugenics and Politics in Britain 1900–1914*, Noordhof.

Searle, G.R. (1979) 'Eugenics and politics in Britain in the 1930s', *Annals of Science*, 36, pp.159–69.

Simon, B. (1974) *The Politics of Educational Reform 1920–1940*, Lawrence and Wishart.

Spearman, C. and Hart, B. (1912) 'General ability, its existence and nature', *British Journal of Psychology*, 5, March.

Sutherland, G. (1984) *Ability, Merit and Measurement: Mental Testing and English Education 1880–1940*, Clarendon Press.

Taylor, F.W. (1947) *Scientific Management* (comprising *Shop Management, The Principles of Scientific Management* and Taylor's testimony before the Special House Committee), Greenwood Press.

Terman, L.M. (1919) *The Measurement of Intelligence*, Harrap.

Tolman, W.H. (1909) *Social Engineering*, McGraw.

Webb, B. and S. (1941) *Soviet Communism: A New Civilisation*, Longman.

Webster, C. (ed.) (1981) *Biology, Medicine and Society 1840–1940*, Cambridge University Press.

Williams, R. (1974) *Television: Technology and Cultural Form*, Fontana.

Zeldin, T. (1980) *France 1848–1945: Taste and Corruption*, Oxford University Press.

12 RUSSIA: TECHNOLOGY TRANSFER AND SOCIAL CHANGE

Colin Chant

In this final chapter, we seek a broader perspective by considering, for the first time in any detail (though see chapter 1 and section 11.1.1), the relations of science, technology and everyday life in Russia, which emerged from the Second World War and its aftermath as a world power second only to the United States. The contexts in which science, technology and daily life met in these countries could hardly contrast more. The Russian setting gives us an opportunity to reconsider some of our main themes: above all, the role of the state and of ideology in bringing science-based technologies to bear on daily life (sections 1.2 and 1.3). These issues lead logically to one of our major theoretical concerns: the status of technology as an agent of historical change. Do the contrasting American and Russian experiences demonstrate, for example, the non-neutrality of mass-production techniques (section 2.3), and generally make nonsense of Ellul's doctrine of 'autonomous technology' (section 2.2)? Or do superficial historical contingencies conceal an underlying, homogenizing trend, as modern societies, of whatever political complexion, increasingly march to the drum of scientific technology?

Not all of these big questions can be addressed directly, let alone answered definitively; some unsubstantiated generalizations, as well as drastic selectivity, are unavoidable. It should also be stressed that the detailed consideration of particular technologies in limited arenas of everyday life undertaken in the preceding chapters can hardly be emulated here. The focus will be on the wholesale *transfer* of much of the Western technology already discussed, and on certain broad social changes of the sort surveyed in section 1.1: above all occupational change bound up with the dual process of urbanization and industrialization.

The essay has two main sections, dealing with the two main convulsions of Russian society under the onslaught of forced industrialization: the first under the Romanov Tsars, the second under Stalin. The first section dwells longest on the everyday world of work, and extends the discussions in chapters 5 and 11. The second says something about communications and ideology, thereby complementing chapter 7.

12.1 TECHNOLOGY UNDER THE TSARS

12.1.1 The Witte System

Bernard Waites' distinction (section 11.1) between 'social engineering' in the United States and 'societal engineering' in the Soviet Union is an important one for our purposes, but we should remember that for most of our period, Russia continued to be ruled by the Romanov Tsars. Following the invasion by Napoleon's armies in 1812, the Tsarist autocracy struck a hostile and defensive posture towards the West, fearing the potentially revolutionary consequences of industrialization. But counterbalancing fears about the security, internal and external, of the vast Russian Empire were raised by Russia's military humiliation in the Crimean War (1853–56). The feudal institution of serfdom, or forced agricultural labour, was finally abolished in 1861 by Alexander II; and grudging and half-hearted as the emancipation measure was, it nevertheless marked a new point of departure for capitalist enterprise based on wage labour.

Soviet and Western scholars are sharply divided over the timing of Russia's industrial take-off. There was some manufacturing in pre-reform Russia, but although its eighteenth-century iron industry had been the largest in the

world, from the beginning of the nineteenth century it retreated and stagnated behind tariff barriers in the face of England's new coal-based technology (section 5.1). Soviet scholars attach more significance to a spon-
taneous spurt in light industry from the 1830s, mainly in cotton textiles, in
which 'free' wage labour was employed – or more accurately, serfs whose
obligation to their owners was measured in money rather than days of agricultural labour. Western scholars have accepted that growth in certain industries
should qualify portrayals of Russia at the time of the Crimean War and the
Emancipation as languishing in feudal backwardness and stagnation. The
consensus is, however, that this growth could not have exerted the industrial
'multiplier' effect ascribed to textiles growth in late eighteenth-century
England. Foremost among the reasons given are the textile industries'
reliance on imported machinery, and the absence of a large domestic market
for consumer goods, partly because of the very low incomes of most peasants,
and partly because of very ill-developed internal communications. But it was
not the economic penalty of poor communications which alarmed the Tsars
so much as the effect on their capacity to police the growing millions of their
enthralled subjects, and to defend the Empire's lengthening boundaries. This
was the dilemma which eventually impaled the Romanov dynasty: in order
to combat the revolutionary contagion of the industrialized West and reassert
Russia's international prestige, some measure of industrialization was
required, if only to finance the modernization of the military, and ensure its
efficient deployment.

Russia's belated industrialization followed the European pattern in being
railway-led. Between 1869 and 1874, a spurt of construction by private operators more than doubled the embryonic network. The initial growth was
almost entirely dependent upon imports of coal, rails and locomotives from
Britain, in the absence of any decisive policy on industrialization. Systematic
state involvement began in the 1880s, when successive ministers of finance
managed to convince their rulers – Alexander III (1881–1894) and Nicholas II
(1894–1917) – that Russia's great power status hinged on the rapid development of its own heavy industry. From that point, railway construction was
directly organized by the state, which by 1914 owned and operated more
than two-thirds of the system (Falkus, 1972, pp.54–55).

The outstanding proponent of forced industrialization was Count Sergei
Witte, a former railway manager, and Minister of Finance from 1892 to 1903.
Continuing his predecessors' policies of high tariffs, high taxation and strict
fiscal control, he added much greater reliance on foreign investment, such
that Russia became the world's largest debtor nation by the end of the
century (Rogger, 1983, p.103). Witte's gamble on Russia's behalf was that
massive state and foreign investment in heavy industry, especially railways,
would eventually pay dividends: not least in opening up European and Asian
markets for the export of raw materials, above all grain; but more indirectly,
too, by creating a chain reaction of domestic demand which would eventually
stimulate agriculture, and justify the bleeding of the tax-ridden peasantry.
This was a policy in large measure imposed by the absence of any significant
domestic capital or of any entrepreneurial tradition (Russian merchants were
notoriously conservative, and dependent on the Tsar for their monopolies
and protective tariffs). The policy was so reliant on punitive taxation and
the squeezing of domestic demand that it is hard to see how the later stages
of Witte's vision could have been realized.

The first stage of Witte's programme was nevertheless on the face of it a
spectacular success. Industrial growth between 1860–1913 averaged a credi-
table 5 per cent per annum, but in the 1890s this jumped to around 8 per
cent. Textiles, mining, metallurgy, mechanical engineering and oil led the
way in this unprecedented surge. During the decade 1890–1900, coal
production rose from 6 to more than 16 million tonnes, iron ore from 1.7 to

6 million tonnes, and oil from nearly 4 to over 10 million tonnes (Falkus, 1972, p.67). In the same period, foreign (mostly French and Belgian) investment in Russian enterprise rose from 214 to 911 million roubles, about a half of joint-stock company investment (p.70). The mainspring of expansion was the extension of the railway to the rich mineral resources of the South. In the Ukraine, the Yekateranin railway (opened in 1885) linked the abundant iron ore at Krivoy Rog with the coal deposits of the Donets Basin. The resultant steel industry was based on the most up-to-date foreign technique and expertise, and soon outproduced the labour-intensive traditional Urals iron industry. A railway was opened in 1883 linking the Caspian with the Black Sea, and the Caucasus oil industry, pioneered in the 1870s around Baku by the Nobel brothers, began the explosive growth (supplying kerosene for lighting) which enabled it briefly to overtake the United States in the 1890s.

Characteristic of the industrialization of the 1890s were government sponsorship, substantial reliance on foreign capital, and an emphasis on heavy industry. Direct state investment was largely confined to the railways, the social significance of which Witte outlined in terms redolent of technological determinism: 'The railroad is like a leaven, which creates a cultural fermentation among the population. Even if it passed through an absolutely wild people along its way, it would raise them in a short time to the level prerequisite for its operation' (quoted in von Laue, 1969, p.191). Witte's most prestigious project was the 5,400-mile Trans-Siberian railroad, built between 1891 and 1901, although many more rails were laid in European Russia in the same period.

The greatest beneficiaries of the consequent demand for materials were the largely French and Belgian entrepreneurs whose up-to-date plant transformed the southern steppes: 'Western engineers almost invariably acted as if they believed that their advanced industrial technology could be transplanted to Russia in its highly developed form without significant modification . . . Advanced technology was a given, and there was simply a right way and a wrong way of doing things' (McKay, 1970, pp.107–08). The South Russian steel companies stood comparison with their West European parents on many counts, such as the capacity of blast furnaces, Bessemer converters and open hearths, and the electrification of rolling mills. Only American blast furnaces were more productive than Russian blast furnaces in 1900; not that Russian plant was actually *superior* to West European at this time – rather, Krivoy Rog ore was much richer. The poorer performance of inexperienced Russian labour in the South made comparisons less favourable the more finished the product: refined steel from the best Russian mills was less than 10 per cent dearer than Belgian steel, but rails could be nearly half as much again in price. By 1900, southern steelworks were over 5 times more productive than the traditional charcoal-based Urals ironworks, and 10 times more by 1909 (McKay, 1970, pp.122–35). Because the Urals industry was overtaken by modern technology at another corner of the Empire, Russia missed – with one or two isolated exceptions – the transition from wrought iron to bulk-steel manufacture within one and the same group of workers (section 5.3).

Geography and timing lent other distinctive aspects to the technology of the 1890s 'big spurt'. By comparison with the West, the most striking general feature was the commingled transfer of the technologies of the First and Second Industrial Revolutions. Thus even in cotton textiles, where peasant entrepreneurs had imported English spinning machines in the 1840s, and factory workers had begun to outnumber domestic outworkers by the 1870s, it was only in the 1890s that mechanization produced notable gains throughout the industry: by then, factory looms had started to outproduce domestic hand weavers (Gatrell, 1986, p.160). In the coal industry, the small peasant mines which predominated in 1890 quickly gave way to large, deep-level mines with modern coke-making facilities, mostly owned by French and Belgian entrepreneurs. Hand- and horse-powered windlasses were replaced by steam- and electric-powered hoists, though the pick and shovel remained the principal means of extraction (McKay, 1970, pp.148–54).

The foreign investors, who were profiting from Russia's attempt to catch up on the First Industrial Revolution, also saw opportunities to exploit more recent innovations. AEG, Siemens and the Nobel brothers were among the pioneers of the large-scale manufacture of electrical equipment in St Petersburg, beginning in the late 1890s, a time which also saw the first industrial applications of electric motors and diesel engines. Belgian streetcar companies were active in South Russia from the early 1880s, and in 1892, the first electric tramway was built in Kiev, capital of the Ukraine. It was not until 1907 that the electric tram began to expel the horse-drawn trams of St Petersburg to the periphery. But even though public transport trips averaged 150 per inhabitant in 1912, this was still fewer than in most American and European cities; and for the average factory worker, St Petersburg was still a walking city (Bater, 1976, pp.268–77, 284).

The industrialization drive, and Witte's ministry, were terminated by economic depression. There followed a disastrous war with Japan (1904–05), and serious labour unrest in 1905, culminating in armed revolt and the concession of some representative institutions. These difficult years saw the emergence of large syndicates of employers controlling prices in entire industries, somewhat analogous to the United States merger boom of 1898–1903 (section 11.1.1). There was a further period of sustained growth between 1907–13, this time less marked by government investment and foreign capital. Just as the growth of industrial syndicates has been interpreted by Marxist-Leninist historians as a sign of the maturity of Russian capitalism, and of the imminence of socialist revolution, so this phase of growth has been seen by some Western historians as evidence that Russia was set to follow a Western liberal economic path, only to be diverted from it by the exceptional circumstances of a World War.

The first view underestimates the general poverty of the Russian economy in the period of industrialization. Even though Russia had become the fourth largest industrial nation in Europe by 1913, per capita income remained among the lowest, with overall annual economic growth in the period 1860–1914 below 2 per cent, and factory workers by one estimate still no more than 5 per cent of the active population (Crisp, 1978, p.309). The second view underestimates the peculiar conditions of Russian industrialization, and the strains on a still almost feudal agrarian social structure imposed by such rapid, forced and localized growth. Thus, although the proportion of urban dwellers in the rapidly reproducing population at large rose from 10 to only 15 per cent in European Russia between 1863 and 1913, this in fact amounted to a trebling of the urban population, from 6.1 to 18.6 million, as against an overall doubling, from 61.2 to 121.8 million (Falkus, 1972, p.34). Growth in several cities was even sharper, notably in the two principal cities, Moscow and St Petersburg, and in the new southern industrial areas, where Kiev, the capital of the Ukraine, grew sevenfold, and Ekaterinoslav (iron and steel) and Baku (oil) increased ten times and more (Rogger, 1983, p.126).

12.1.2
The transformation of Russian society

It is arguable that the most decisive element in the revolutionary transformation of the Tsarist social structure was the transfer of Western technology, in that it served to *concentrate* the opposition which would inevitably intensify as Russia was drawn into international conflict with technologically superior foes. Industrial concentration was more marked in Russia than anywhere else in the industrial world. By 1914, some 41 per cent of industrial workers were to be found in plants employing in excess of 1,000, more than double the figure for American industry (Rogger, 1983, p.113). The explanations are various: the scarcity of foreign managers, the low productivity of Russian workers, as well as the installation of the latest Western technology. The consequences were surely momentous, as these factories became finishing schools in socialism.

Here I must hang back from attempting to explain the Russian Revolution, and be content with describing the broad social change which most would accept as at least a prerequisite to the events of 1917. The hallmark of Russian society at the time of the Emancipation was dependence on the state, personified in the autocrat. Peter the Great (1682–1725) consummated his Muscovite predecessors' efforts in subordinating the Church and landowning aristocracy to the autocracy, and created a society in which noble status was contingent upon position in a hierarchy of state service (open to plebeians), and rewarded with ownership of land and 'souls' (serfs). By the first half of the nineteenth century, a distinct social pyramid of estates (*sosloviya*) had been defined, the most prominent being, in descending order, the nobility (*dvoryane*), the clergy, the merchants (*kuptsy*), the townspeople (*meshchane*) – artisans, shopkeepers, and so on – and the peasantry.

Acquisition of noble status was a rich prize indeed by the nineteenth century: it brought with it exemption from poll tax and corporal punishment, and from the *obligation* to do military or bureaucratic state service – though in practice, state service remained the prime means of social advancement, rather than farming, so generally low were agricultural yields. For this reason, there was no tradition of local politics based on landed wealth to balance the power of the crown, as there was, for example, in England. Instead, the socially ambitious gravitated towards the court and the two capitals, St Petersburg and Moscow. An analogous lack of independence among the mercantile class has already been noted; this too was reinforced by the prospect of noble status. In this case, the characteristic aspirations of the richest Russian merchants – ennoblement, and the cultivation of a lifestyle based on country estates, scholarship or patronage of the arts (Rogger, 1983, p.124) – were more reminiscent of those of British industrialists in late nineteenth-century Britain.

Freeze (1986) has argued that the estate structure was less fixed and better able to accommodate social change than either Western or Soviet historians have allowed. But even his revised picture shows the ultimate incompatibility of this agrarian hierarchy with social change accelerated by forced industrialization. This was partly because, as the nobility retrenched, and the government took fright at the social unrest which greeted the Emancipation, 'the state's commitment to the *soslovie* system became increasingly intense – and ideological – after 1870' (p.27). The most anomalous groups were the new educated professions and working class. Although established professions, such as doctors, were recognized as legal estates, and allowed to have their own organizations, such privileges were not extended to newer groups, such as teachers, journalists, engineers, statisticians and agronomists. There were some half a million professionals at the time of the 1897 census, and it was this social group, discontented as it was with lack of recognition and limited rights of organization, which voiced a liberal critique of the estate system, rather than the largely complacent business community.

Professionals were prominent in the liberal political groupings which dominated the largely ineffectual post-1905 elected assemblies (Dumas), and the Provisional Government which replaced the autocracy after the February Revolution of 1917. If historians are largely agreed in portraying the liberals as hopelessly ill-based to buffer the countervailing forces of autocratic repression and worker and peasant unrest, there is a contrasting lack of unanimity in explanations of the part of industrial workers in these revolu-

tionary years. Depictions of the working class are inevitably informed by the
historian's commitment either to the necessity, or the contingency, of the
Bolshevik Revolution of October 1917. Soviet scholars have seen in the rapid
industrialization of Russia a recapitulation of capitalism along Marxist lines,
and in particular the birth of a class-conscious hereditary proletariat able to
take the lead in a genuine socialist revolution. There is less unanimity among
Western historians on the causes of Russian industrial workers' militancy;
some stress their recent peasant origins, others their newly acquired skills.
They generally agree, however, that the October Revolution was the
outcome of a peculiarly Russian interplay of policy and social structure, with
no obvious export potential.

The value of this debate for our purposes is that it has focused increasing
scholarly attention on the details of everyday working life in pre-revolutionary urban Russia. It is clear that the Russian working class was in many
respects as heterogeneous as its Western counterparts (section 1.1). Divisions
of skill, occupation, gender and nationality existed, but in differing degrees
and mixes according to the industrial region. At the turn of the century, the
Moscow region, for example, was notable for the relative lack of state
involvement in its industry, and greater reliance on indigenous capital and
management. The major industry was textiles, which employed low-paid,
semiskilled and unskilled labour, 44 per cent of which was female. In St
Petersburg, the picture was much more representative of Russian industrialization as a whole: much greater reliance on state sponsorship and foreign
investment, with the emphasis on heavy industry, the main branches of which
were munitions, shipbuilding, railway construction, mechanical engineering,
and electrical engineering. In contrast with textiles, 80 per cent of metalworkers were skilled, and almost all male (Bonnell, 1983a, pp.34–35).

There were metalworkers and textile workers in both major cities, and
differences were keenly felt, as the recollections of a St Petersburg metalworker suggest:

> Metalworkers considered themselves aristocrats among other workers.
> Their occupations demanded more training and skill, and therefore they
> looked down on other workers, such as weavers and the like, as an inferior
> category, as country bumpkins; today he will be at the mill, but tomorrow
> he will be poking at the earth with his wooden plough. The superiority of
> the metalworker and everything that it implied was appreciated by all.
> (Quoted in Bonnell, 1983b, p.11)

Metalworkers, then, took themselves seriously as skilled workers (*master-
ovye*) and patronized the semiskilled and unskilled workers (*rabochie*). The
difference was reflected in their appearance, as metalworkers would affect
urban styles of dress – suits and patent leather shoes – while the unskilled
retained their peasant beards, blouses and boots. The skilled were also less
drawn to the urban industrial subculture of heavy drinking and gambling,
and instead went to clubs and theatres, and read books and newspapers: 73
per cent of St Petersburg metalworkers were literate in 1897, compared with
44 per cent of textile workers, and 52 per cent of the Russian working
population as a whole (Bonnell, 1983b, p.26).

The skilled urban worker – a category including patternmakers, metalfitters, lathe operators, smelters and tinsmiths in the metalworking industries,
fabric cutters in the garment industry, engravers, chromolithographers, type-
setters and press operators in printing houses – was a recent Russian social
phenomenon standing outside the traditional agrarian *soslovie* structure.
These workers had acquired a new social identity based on craft or occupation, and nurtured by several years of apprenticeship and urban residency.
By 1902, 42 per cent of factory workers and 46 per cent of artisanal workers

in Moscow had either been born there, or been resident for more than ten years; and in general between one third and two thirds of all those working in factories, mines and railways were following in their father's footsteps (Bonnell, 1983a, p.44; Rogger, 1983, p.113). All this suggests the existence by then of a hereditary urban proletariat; but at the same time, some 90 per cent of urban workers held internal passports declaring their continued membership of the peasant estate (*soslovie*).

The recent peasant origins and continuing rural ties of the new urban workers in Russia mark them off from their West European counterparts, though there are parallels in the links East European immigrant workers in the United States maintained with their native country (section 5.3). Because of the low productivity of much Russian agricultural land, there was already a long tradition of peasant cottage industry, and then of seasonal migration, especially to textiles and food-processing factories, involving some 4 million peasants at the turn of the century (Rogger, 1983, p.112). Seasonal migration often involved the temporary disruption of families, and many permanent urban workers who remained members of their village commune left their families behind, living as cheaply as possible in overcrowded and insanitary company barracks or rented accommodation. The powers of the commune had been strengthened by the Great Reform of 1861, partly to prevent the emergence of a Western style landless proletariat. The migrant peasant worker was obliged to pay taxes to the commune to obtain the passport necessary for movement within the Empire. This was a nuisance for the better-off skilled workers, but for the rest it was a form of social security: the piece of land or property tended for them by relatives would support them in the event of unemployment, old age or infirmity. A study of Moscow workers in the late nineteenth century argues for the two-way movement between village and factory of even the apparently 'hereditary' worker: 'The typical worker had one foot in the village and one in the factory but showed little inclination to commit himself irrevocably to either alternative' (Johnson, 1979, p.50).

It might be argued that Johnson's conclusion would be less applicable to St Petersburg or to the Ukraine, where heavy industry predominated. It might also be added that the power of the commune was much diminished in 1906–07, when another modernizing minister, Stolypin, enacted land reforms intended to stimulate free enterprise in agriculture, measures that also released another wave of young peasants into the urban milieu. Johnson's interpretation is clearly aimed against attempts to make the Russian case fit the orthodox Marxian sequence, requiring the maturation of a capitalist economy and the emergence within it of a class-conscious urban proletariat. But it is also aimed at explanations ascribing Russian labour militancy in general to the disorientation of young peasant migrants lacking any craft traditions; and in particular at the thesis that the militancy immediately before the Revolution was caused by the outnumbering of workers with experience of the 1905 Revolution by the mass of young workers released by the Stolypin reforms (notably Haimson, 1964, 1965). Johnson agrees in attaching importance to urban workers' peasant ties, but argues instead that it was not disorientation and inexperience that led to revolutionary activism, but rather the tradition of peasant revolt against a harsh rural regime made more potent in an urban context: 'the fusion of urban and rural discontents and propensities produced an especially explosive mix' (p.158).

More recent Western studies, based on statistical analyses of strikes and other forms of worker activism in the revolutionary years, have more directly opposed the Haimson thesis, and furnished evidence that skilled workers, especially those in the metalworking industries, were disproportionately active. Bonnell (1983a, p.67) attributes the leadership of the skilled metal-workers to the control most of them experienced in the small workshops into

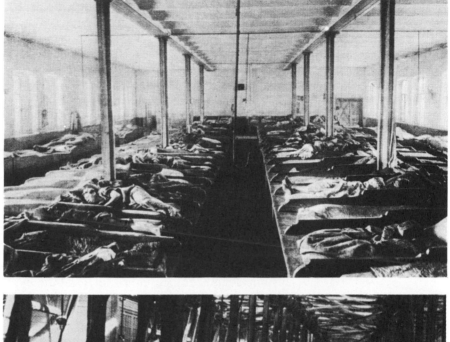

*Figure 12.1
Factory barracks at
Prokhorovskaya
Trekhgornaya textile mill,
Moscow, in early 1890s.
(From* Istoriya Moskvy,
*1955, Vol.5, p.63. Photo:
British Library by permission
of the publishers Akademiya
Nauk)*

*Figure 12.2
'Factory artisans' in the shell
shop at the Putilov works, St
Petersburg, in early 1900s.
(From* Istoriya rabochikh
Leningrada, *1972, Vol.1,
following p.480. Reproduced
by permission of the Main
Archive Administration of the
USSR)*

which even the largest factories were usually divided, and argues that this
contributed to their combined readiness to press for more control over other
facets of the workplace. Her case is that, although there was some mechanization and division of labour in Bessemer and open-hearth departments, in
general this was not so: the peculiarity of the Russian situation was the
propinquity of 'factory artisans' in large plants such as the Putilov works in
St Petersburg, which employed 12,000 mostly skilled metalworkers at the
turn of the century. Labour activism was thus led by skilled craftsmen subject
to minimal division of labour.

Koenker and Rosenberg (1986) have largely confirmed Bonnell's emphasis:
skilled workers had market power, translated into relatively favourable
wages, hours and conditions, which along with their literacy, favoured organization; they had a measure of workplace autonomy to defend, and being
almost all male, were less vulnerable to repression. Their figures on strike
participation during 1917 further reinforce the leading part of metalworkers:
'In terms of workers on strike, metalists were disproportionately active: our

figures suggest that the equivalent of 75 per cent of the metalist labor force engaged in strikes during the year, second only to leather workers in this measure of strike intensity' (p.618). There is, however, an uncertainty in Koenker and Rosenberg's argument. They identify between the ranks of the skilled and unskilled, a growing group of semiskilled workers associated with the introduction of new technology: these workers 'staffed assembly lines, worked with interchangeable parts, or labored as operatives in mechanized plants (such as in textiles, tobacco or shoe production), doing jobs which required some training but little of the discretion and personal talent characteristic of their skilled comrades' (p.608). They even concede that their statistical evidence 'adds up to a suggestion that it was semiskilled rather than skilled workers who dominated the strike movement, numerically and proportionally' (p.611). This was unarguably true of the crucial months of September and October, when the great majority of strikers were semiskilled; but Koenker and Rosenberg prefer to conclude that by the autumn of 1917, skilled workers had lost faith in the strategic value of strikes, and now looked to radical political change (p.615).

It must be said that the recent efflorescence of works by American and British historians on the pre-revolutionary Russian worker is strong on social-historical methodology and sociological theory, but generally light on history of science and technology. An exception is the work of Heather Hogan (1983) on the influence of Taylorism and scientific management in Russian industry. These ideas played no part in the explosive growth of the 1890s; that was a notably inefficient but nevertheless profitable combination of imported capital equipment and very cheap and abundant indigenous labour. From 1900, economic recession and growing labour unrest forced manufacturers to look more carefully at costs and productivity. Russian managers, relying as they did on foreign capital, expertise and training, were naturally *au fait* with scientific management. From 1905 onwards, many plants fell under a typical regime of time study, 'progressive' wage incentive schemes, worksheets and automatic timeclocks, collection of production-line data, refined accounting methods, and revised factory layout. The 'American system' or *amerikanka* soon became a worker bugbear; Taylorism and the 'factory revolution' were subjects of debate in the labour press. Hogan depicts the skilled worker as increasingly compressed between the expansion of technical personnel above, and of semiskilled and unskilled labour below. She presents evidence of lowering wage rates despite rising output in the metal industries, a trend reflecting the replacement of male adult skilled workers by women or adolescents, and supporting Haimson's point about the growing number of inexperienced workers following the Stolypin reforms, even in metalworking – indeed, Hogan sees herself as building on Haimson's thesis.

Hogan is at pains to stress that the process of industrial rationalization was only just beginning, and was no more than a contributory factor in the breakdown of Russian social relations in 1917. We should keep in mind that it played no part in the 1905 Revolution, and that the actors in the 1917 revolutions included not only metalworkers, but other factory workers, artisans, professionals, intellectuals, peasants, and army and navy mutineers. There is a quite different argument that the decisive element was 'decay in the apparatus of repression', and that twentieth-century revolutions have more to do with the state of the army than of the working class (Moore, 1978, pp.368, 375), though it is not obvious that military indiscipline and working-class unrest should be viewed other than as aspects of the same social phenomenon.

We are in no position to adjudicate between the various interpretations of the revolutionary transformation of Russian society thus far canvassed. But Hogan's emphasis does raise the question of the possible role of technological innovation as one of the main determinants, and the answer is somewhat different for each interpretation. Hogan herself, and Koenker and Rosenberg, give different weight to the de-skilling characteristic of the Second Industrial Revolution. Barrington Moore, with his emphasis on the inadequacy of the railway system to support the Tsarist regime during the crisis of war, points to an incomplete transfer of the technology of the First Industrial Revolution (p.364). Bonnell's picture of the skilled metalworker as proud 'factory artisan' also has more to do with the First Industrial Revolution, with the critical Russian peculiarity that it was spatially concentrated in large enterprises. The inference here is that the radicalization of this section of the new working class rested on the general absence of the de-skilling and arguably de-politicizing effects of the managerial revolution already well under way in the West, as well as on the peculiar interplay of Western technology and the distinctive Russian social and economic structure.

The distinction between First and Second Industrial Revolutions can only be invoked for comparative purposes; in the Russian context alone it makes little sense, as the mechanization of textiles, railway and machine construction, bulk steelmaking, scientific management, and a measure of electrification followed hard upon each other. In her account of the revolutionary orientation of the St Petersburg and Moscow trade unions, Bonnell sets great store by the peculiar 'conflation of stages' in Russia, stages that occurred sequentially in Western societies undergoing the transition from an agrarian to an industrial economy: thus Russian industrial workers joined the labour movement at the same time as artisans, and as a result craft and industrial unions, and craft and class consciousness, developed almost synchronously and without the divisive antagonisms of the United States labour movement (Bonnell, 1983a, p.446; section 5.3). There is surely parallel with this phenomenon a corresponding Russian 'conflation of technologies' under the special conditions of rapid, state-led industrialization. Can a technological-determinist construction be placed on these peculiarly Russian conflations? On the face of it, if Western technology was associated with the revolutionary transformation of Russian society, but not of American or other European societies at the time, then technology itself cannot be the prime determinant of arguably the greatest social change of the century. Soviet scholars, working from a 'technicist' reading of Marx (section 2.2), ascribe to Western technology a fundamental role in the reconstruction of the economic base; but the fact that Russia achieved socialism ahead of other industrial nations can scarcely be attributed to the greater development of its productive forces, as we have seen.

It would be more plausible, surely, to highlight the non-technological peculiarities of the Russian situation. Looking at the United States at this time, we find a society relatively unscathed by the First World War, and one in which many workers, having left behind the worst social ills of industrialization, had some hopes of upward social mobility. In St Petersburg, the number of people per apartment persisted at around seven throughout the capital's half-century of industrialization before the 1917 revolutions, and in 1900, a third of its inhabitants were still without running water or water closets. Throughout the period, it was the unhealthiest of all European and American cities, perpetuating the familiar dismal story of early, unregulated industrialization: overcrowded and insanitary accommodation, polluted drinking water, fearful mortality rates from infectious diseases, including cholera and typhus. In 1908 (a year of cholera epidemic), 47 per cent of all deaths were caused by infectious diseases, but no steps were taken to improve the city's water supply and drainage systems until 1914 (Bater, 1976, pp.326–53).

The American working class was also less internally cohesive, riven as it was by ethnic, religious and craft divisions. Russian workers were generally less divided along these lines. There were great national mixes in the south, where in the oil industry, for example, Russians worked alongside Armenians, Persians and Tartars; but in Moscow, the catchment area for migrant peasants was relatively limited, and overwhelmingly Russian-speaking and Orthodox. St Petersburg was rather more cosmopolitan, but residential segregation along religious or ethnic lines was generally weak, with one or two exceptions, notably the persecuted Jewish community (Lyashchenko, 1949, p.747; Johnson, 1979, pp.31–32; Bater, 1976, pp.375–77). Not only was there less division among Russian industrial workers, but it was clearer to them what was to blame for their undeniable miseries: so closely identified were foreign capitalists, native entrepreneurs and the Tsarist bureaucracy, that labour unrest was arguably bound to make the entire social system its target, especially at a time of acute economic crisis brought about by the First World War.

The comparison with the United States reflects this section's deliberate concentration on Russian workers. If space permitted, further social, economic, political and ideological contrasts between Russia and the United States could readily be made, and the rout completed of any simple-minded technological determinism. A more resourceful defence of that position might, however, appeal to the marked disparity in the technological development of both nations. Could it be Russia's unique technological configuration (concentrated, but skill-based) which detonated its unique social revolution? Such an argument is open to all the standard objections considered in section 2.2; most obviously, that however decisive the presence of advanced technology may have been in the backward Russian context, it was surely not 'autonomous'. Quite the reverse: it was a deliberate and calculated decision by the government, gladly backed by foreign finance, to unleash the forces of Western technology in Russian society. But the argument need not end there: clearly Witte's gamble failed to pay off. Was the Russian regime now at the mercy of 'technics-out-of-control'? Either immediately, as its own social structure was weakened at vital points by the emergence of powerful new groups; or failing that argument, mediately, as it fed its young soldiers to the technologically superior firepower of its Western enemies from 1914?

Was there in any case any real choice for the Tsars, following the exposure of Russia's technological backwardness during the Crimean War? An Ellul might argue that the industrialization of Europe and the United States would sooner or later have forced the Russian autocracy down the same path if it were to ensure its external and internal security. There was no policy option devoid of great risk, and this is reflected in the vacillation and internal conflict within the government throughout the period. The Ministry of Finance was continually at odds with the Ministry of the Interior, the one trying to balance the state budget, the other fearful of the effects of economic change on public order. One upshot of this contradictory stance was a violently see-sawing policy on labour organization. The first unions were actually set up by the police as a stabilizing measure – the so-called Zubatov associations of 1902 – and then fired upon by troops in 1905; independent unions were legalized in 1906, and then quickly suppressed. Government indecision, it might be argued, is fully consistent with the autonomy of technology, even supportive of it. But it is unlikely that a 'progressive' technological determinist like Ellul – one whose argument is that industrial society is progressively more governed by technique – would stake his case on a backward country like Tsarist Russia, in which there was no prevailing ethos of technical rationality. More support for Ellul's version of technological determinism may be found in Russia after the Revolution, when the official ideology of 'autocracy, Orthodoxy and nationality' was supplanted by a 'technicist' reading of Marx.

**12.2
SCIENCE,
TECHNOLOGY AND
SOCIAL CHANGE IN
THE SOVIET UNION**

No attempt can be made here to chronicle the extraordinary daily experiences of the Russian people from the outbreak of the First World War until the death of Stalin in 1953. 'Everyday life' seems an inapplicable term in a period when countless millions perished, whether at the Eastern Front in the First World War, in the Allied intervention and civil war which followed the (relatively bloodless) 1917 revolutions, in the famine resulting from the forced collectivization of agriculture from 1929, in the wretched conditions of the forced labour camps, in the terror visited on all the upper echelons of Soviet society by the secret police (NKVD) in the middle thirties, and worst of all, in the slaughter following Hitler's invasion of 1941. There were more lives lost by the Russians in the 900-day siege of Leningrad, than by the Americans and British combined during the entire Second World War – one measure of the seemingly divergent trajectories of the Soviet Union and United States in the period; trajectories which set them on a collision course by 1950 as the two main nuclear powers.

The main aim of this section is to look (somewhat dispassionately, it must be said) at the main features of social change which can be discerned in this desperate story, and to relate them to the new regime's investment in science and technology. This gives us a basis to consider a hypothesis consistent with the 'progressive' technological determinism identified with Ellul, Marcuse and Habermas: that in their increasing obeisance to a scientific-technical rationality, the Soviet Union and the United States were following convergent paths. The discussion, as ever, must be highly selective. Briefly covered will be the commitment of the new Soviet regime to science and technology; the massive industrialization programme of the first Five-Year Plans; the rise of the technical intelligentsia; and the importance of communications media to the regime's stability.

**12.2.1
Science and technology:
theory and practice**

Under the Tsars, very little attempt was made to nurture a home-grown scientific technology; this could always be bought ready-made from the West. Neither government nor industry was prepared to heed the calls of its engineers and university scientists for an emulation of the industrial research laboratories, and private and state research institutes which had mushroomed in the United States and Western Europe since the 1890s. The most that was done was to ensure, through an established, though limited, tradition of technical education, that there were trained indigenous officials and managers, who would oversee the implementation of foreign technique. The government was jolted out of its complacency by the outbreak of the First World War, with the consequent loss of its supply of German technique; it started to support, through its War Industry Committees, research on military projects. A Commission for the Study of the Natural Productive Forces of Russia (KEPS), set up in 1915, laid the basis of a system of state-funded research institutes, though no funds were made available until after the October Revolution.

The founding of thirty-three research institutes in 1918 and 1919 was symptomatic of the new Soviet government's infinitely greater ideological and practical commitment to science and technology; though in fact the severe economic strain of the civil war and Allied intervention reduced the science budget below even its pre-war level in the early years (Lewis, 1979, p.7). The Soviet leadership's ideological commitment to science doubtless reflects the 'scientific' pretensions of Marxism-Leninism to explain all phenomena, natural, social and psychological, by recourse to one set of dialectical natural laws; but their faith in scientific research as the source of desirable technological innovations is hardly ideologically specific in our period. Lenin's own commitment found expression in 1918 in this generalization about the relations of science, technology and socialism: 'Socialism is inconceivable without large-scale capitalist engineering based on the latest

*Figure 12.3
'Electrification and counter-
revolution', poster signifying
the political investment in
electrification by the Soviet
leadership. (Reproduced
from Peter Kenez, 1985, Birth
of the Propaganda State.
Soviet Methods of Mass
Mobilization 1917–1929,
Cambridge University Press
by permission of the
publishers)*

discoveries of modern science. It is inconceivable without planned state organization, which keeps tens of millions of people to the strictest observance of a unified standard in production and distribution' (Lenin, 1960–70, Vol.27, p.339).

In chapter 11, Bernard Waites cited Lenin's qualified endorsement of Taylor's ideas on scientific management; his enthusiasm for electrification was quite unalloyed. In December 1920, he declared to the Eighth All-Russia Congress of Soviets: '*Communism is Soviet power plus the electrification of the whole country* . . . only when the country has been electrified, and industry, agriculture and transport have been placed on the technical basis of modern large-scale industry, only then shall we be fully victorious' (Lenin, 1960–70, Vol.31, p.516, original emphasis). Lenin regarded the plan of the State Commission for the Electrification of Russia (GOELRO), published in 1920, as 'the second programme of our Party', second, that is, to its political programme (p.514). He often conceded that the plan might take ten years to implement. In the event, the proportional consumption of electric power in production was never more than average by world standards in our period, reaching some 11 per cent in 1961; and GOELRO's target of electrifying 3,500 kilometres of railway line within fifteen years was not achieved until after the Second World War (Hutchings, 1976, p.96). Lenin's faith in scientific technology is nevertheless a persistent Soviet theme, with minor variations only, as Khrushchev's reworking in 1963 indicates: 'Communism means Soviet power plus the electrification of the whole country, plus the chemicalization of the economy' (Hutchings, 1976, p.118).

Despite its uncertain beginnings, Soviet expenditure on scientific research grew rapidly from 1924, and reached a peak in the mid-1930s (before Stalin's purge of the scientific élite) of some 0.6 per cent of National Income, compared with 0.35 per cent in the United States. Investment in industrial research grew less quickly to begin with, but rocketed from 1928, the start of Stalin's forced industrialization programme. For a while in the 1930s the numbers employed in Soviet state industrial research institutions exceeded those in American industrial research laboratories: some 40,000, as against 30,000, in 1934 (Lewis, 1979, pp.17, 29). In practice, the productivity of these fledgling institutions was low. By the toughest Western estimates, there was little other than the development of synthetic rubber to show for all this investment in R & D in our period (Sutton, 1968–73, Vol.2, p.346). The engine of industrialization remained the 'massive importation of foreign plant and technical know-how', now mediated by state 'project organizations' such as Gipromez, the State Institute for Projecting New Metallurgical Factories. There seems to have been little contact between these organizations and the domestic research network (Lewis, 1979, pp.24, 146).

The research network, whatever its shortcomings, demonstrates the Soviet regime's practical and ideological commitment to scientific technology (*nauchnaya tekhnika*). All the participants in the struggle for leadership following Lenin's death in 1924 – Stalin, Trotsky, Bukharin, Kamenev and Zinoviev – looked to the power of science and technology in their shared aim of catching up the advanced capitalist countries. The leadership struggle took place against the ideological backdrop of a prolonged debate over industrialization, occasioned by the violent swings of economic policy as the regime fought for survival. The immediate aftermath of the October Revolution saw a wholesale breakdown of traditional authority, with officers being elected in the army, and worker control established in the factory. But in the emergency of the civil war, these measures were reversed, with strict, hierarchical discipline restored in the Red Army and industry, and forced requisitioning of grain visited on the peasantry. The effectiveness of these policies, now dubbed 'War Communism', persuaded Trotsky, Bukharin and Lenin to persist with them, until strikes, peasant unrest, and a major revolt of sailors and workers at Kronstadt in 1921, precipitated a further reversal. The New Economic Policy (NEP) conceded some private trading to the peasants, and although public ownership of major enterprises persisted, they were left to respond to market forces.

By the mid-1920s, post-war production levels in agriculture and industry had been restored. But with industrial prices rising, and agricultural prices falling, the small peasant producers were reluctant to sell their surplus, and output began to decline again. With capital equipment in industry in sore need of replacement, faith in NEP began to wane. Bukharin persisted in seeing NEP as the way forward, advocating a balance between agriculture, light and heavy industry, based on an alliance (*smychka*) with the peasantry. But the Bolsheviks were first and foremost a party of the industrial workers, and many of the 'Left Opposition' saw in NEP too many concessions to capitalism and to the richer peasants (kulaks). Trotsky, Kamenev and Zinoviev became their leading spokesmen, but were unable to contend with Stalin's growing power as General Secretary of the Party, based on his control of key appointments. A temporary alliance with Bukharin led in 1927 to the expulsion of the Left Opposition, or 'super-industrializers'. But by now, Stalin was ready to swim with the leftward tide and back the State Planning Commission's first Five-Year Plan, and indeed to step up its targets for the growth of heavy industry beyond anything envisaged by his Left Opponents. Having finally brought about the removal of Bukharin and the 'Right Opposition', Stalin was by the end of 1928 empowered to embark upon a 'programme of social engineering without precedent in human history' (Acton, 1986, p.217).

12.2.2
The Plan Era   The period of the first three Five-Year Plans (1928–41 – the Third was cut short by the German invasion) saw social and economic change even more breathtaking in its rapidity than the industrialization of the 1890s, or the years of revolution. Stalin's exhortation to the first conference of workers in Moscow in 1931 is typically urgent, as well as uncannily prophetic: 'We are fifty or a hundred years behind the advanced countries. We must make good this distance in ten years. Either we do this or they will crush us' (quoted in McCauley, 1981, p.73).

There were many fluctuations and setbacks in the plan era, and much disagreement exists among Western and Soviet analysts over the scale and efficiency of the industrialization process. Western estimates give an almost threefold growth in industrial output between 1928 and 1940, compared with a fivefold growth on Soviet figures; the Western figure for annual growth is about 10 per cent (Blackwell, 1970, p.134). As in the 1890s, the emphasis was on mining, metallurgy and machine building, an industrialization model by then seen as the 'American option', with less priority accorded to the electrical and chemical industries (Bailes, 1978, p.342). The effort was divided between established centres (Leningrad, Moscow and the Donets Basin), and completely new ones, notably the vast Urals-Kuznets Basin complex, in which an industrial city, Magnitogorsk, was created out of nothing. New plant like this underlay a quadrupling of coal and steel output in the period, by one estimate, and a number of large dams, such as the Dnieper Dam, helped boost electricity generation tenfold (Acton, 1986, p.218). As in the pre-war industrialization drive, Western technology and expertise was essential. Thus in 1929 the Ford Motor Company contracted to supply a new automobile plant at Gorky, based on the River Rouge plant; General Electric assisted in the manufacture of turbines, electric motors, electric locomotives and a range of electrical equipment; RCA was involved in radio installations; and the Magnitogorsk steelworks was designed by the McKee Corporation of Cleveland as a replica of US Steel's Gary, Indiana plant, then the largest in the world (Sutton, 1968–73, Vol.1, pp.246–9, Vol.2, pp.74–7, 158–65).

A major difference between the two industrialization drives was the absence in the Soviet case of direct foreign investment. Somehow, all the imported technology had to be paid for by the state, as the sole owner of large-scale industry. As we saw, the operation of the market under NEP led to a conjunction of rising industrial and falling agricultural prices, known at one stage as the 'scissors crisis'; peasants reacted by consuming their own surplus, and cutting back on production. Stalin was unprepared to base his massive industrialization policy on the economic rationality of the peasantry; his solution was to bring the full force of state power to bear on the economy. It was a fiercer, more thorough and uncompromising revival of War Communism, overlaid with distinctly Tsarist methods of compulsion: the forced requisitioning of grain, heavy taxation, compulsory state labour, convict labour, increased working hours for industrial workers, the restriction of their movement by internal passports.

The brunt of forced industrialization was borne, as ever, by the peasants. The Party was determined that the fate of its policy should not rest in the hands of the small peasant producers, and on what they chose to do with their surplus. From now on, the state would exact its requirements in cash and kind first. The industrialization drive must therefore be considered in conjunction with the momentous decision in 1929 to collectivize agriculture. A fundamental inefficiency in this sector stemmed from the Revolution itself, and the rapid disintegration of erstwhile noble estates into some 24 million small subsistence farms (Blackwell, 1970, p.83). Stalin confronted the problem by making a scapegoat of the better-off peasant farmers (kulaks), dispossessing them and deporting them to some of the most inhospitable parts of Asiatic Russia. In this way the elimination of the kulaks as a class was brought about in 1930 – estimates of the numbers involved range between 5, and Stalin's own figure of 10 millions (Blackwell, 1970, p.99, McCauley, 1981, p.75). Those who were left were obliged to merge their smallholdings into a self-financing collective farm (*kolkhoz*), or find employment as wage labourers on a state farm (*sovkhoz*), usually a large, mechanized 'grain

Figure 12.4
Mastering technology, poster
depicting female industrial
workers, by V. Serov, 1934.
(Reproduced by permission
of the Society for Cultural
Relations with the USSR,
London)

Figure 12.5
Political poster from early
1930s urging women to study
and work in industry.
(Reproduced from Kendall
E. Bailes, 1978, Technology
and Society under Lenin and
Stalin, *Princeton University*
Press by permission of the
publishers)

factory' established on land not presently cultivated by peasants. By 1937, kolkhozes and sovkhozes accounted for almost all cultivated land.

There was, it need hardly be said, violent opposition to the collectivization, including destruction of implements and livestock. Agricultural output fell by a fifth during the first Five-Year Plan, and in 1933 a terrible famine claimed millions of lives. The Party was forced to relent, at least to the extent of granting each peasant family the right to profit from a small amount of land and livestock. It was indeed the private sector that contributed most of the nation's meat, dairy products, eggs, fruit and vegetables, while the socialist sector provided the grain, cotton, sugar beet and flax. In this mixed way, the agricultural sector was able to recover from the early disastrous years. This was as well for the government, since its economic policy rested largely on the diversion of agricultural surplus into heavy industry: 'In the final analysis, through a system of direct taxes and outright requisitions, high prices for goods and services and exceedingly low or even nominal prices for agricultural produce, the government was able to extract about a quarter of the wealth of the Russian peasantry' (Blackwell, 1970, p.103).

But the suffering was not confined to those who stayed on the land. One effect of collectivization was to release another flood of peasant workers into the towns and cities, in far greater numbers than had been envisaged in the first Five-Year Plan. Russia's urban population increased by some 25 million during the first ten years of the plan era. Existing housing was simply inadequate to accommodate these numbers, and many had to make do with tents, underground dugouts, mud and scrap hovels, or barracks. Even in 1950, there were on average four individuals to a room. Inadequate housing was only one aspect of a decline in urban standards of living. Real industrial wages were halved between 1928 and 1931, and remained below the original level until the 1950s (Blackwell, 1970, pp.108–10). There was no preferring of the urban dweller in the overall policy of restricting domestic consumption in favour of investment in heavy industry: in the urban context this was effected largely by the suppression of real wages and by heavy indirect taxation. What relative growth there was in the consumer goods industries in the mid-thirties was extinguished by the growing threat of Nazi Germany: defence spending grew from 3.4 per cent of total expenditure in 1933 to 32.6 per cent in 1940 (McCauley, 1981, p.76).

In some ways, the new Soviet workers were worse off than their pre-revolutionary forebears. Living conditions were as bad, strikes were suppressed, their trade unions were absorbed into the Party structure and were now partly responsible for the administration of a harsh industrial discipline – a discipline, moreover, that owed much to F.W. Taylor's ideas on scientific management. There were some aspects of industrial life which improved upon the Tsarist days, such as state provision of educational and medical services, and age and sickness benefits. The decline in real wages was partly offset by increased employment opportunities for women: the proportion of women workers rose from 28.8 per cent to 43 per cent in 1940 (Lewin, 1985, p.251). Industrial workers also had priority over peasants when it came to the allocation of scarce food, and certainly over the millions who worked, and frequently died, in the secret police's forced labour camps. The existence of these camps, administered by GULAG, a branch of NKVD, the secret police, is on the face of it a political phenomenon, a drastic way of dealing with opposition to collectivization and industrialization; but their economic role in providing unpaid labour – estimated at 8 or 9 million in 1938 and 1939 (Blackwell, 1970, p.113) – and in taking consumers out of the market may have supplied part of the rationale for the mass arrests of the Great Terror (1936–38).

12.2.3
The technical intelligentsia

The plan era was evidently a time of radical social change associated with the transfer of Western technology. This change was admittedly more directly the result of the chosen means of transfer, than of the technology itself; but the means were arguably those of an administration besotted with technical rationality. It may be questioned whether this social change was actually the most fundamental of the Soviet era. What could be more profound than the virtual elimination of the landowning and business classes, and the social demotion of the clergy, in the first months of Soviet rule? There is, however, a further aspect of social change consummated in the plan era, which has persisted in Soviet society, and which is grist to the technological determinist's mill. This is the rise of the 'technical intelligentsia', a social group defined as 'intellectual workers closely concerned with production' (Lampert, 1979, p.7), or, more specifically, as 'engineers, agronomists, technicians, and applied scientists, that is, scientists directly tied to material production' (Bailes, 1978, p.4).

It might be expected that the major beneficiary of the October Revolution would have been not the engineer, but the industrial worker; there were however only two moments when 'the dictatorship of the proletariat' neared a description of reality. The first was the immediate post-revolutionary establishment of worker control in the factories, soon terminated under War Communism by the introduction of 'one-man management' and the rehabilitation of 'bourgeois specialists'. The effect of the civil war was in any case a remarkable reversal of much pre-war industrialization, as conscription, death, and a mass return to the countryside more than halved the working class – the populations of Moscow and Petrograd (formerly St Petersburg) dropped by a half and two-thirds respectively (Lewin, 1985, pp.211–12). The second occasion was the incredible turmoil of the first Five-Year Plan (1928–32), two complementary elements of which were 'proletarianization' – the preferential drafting of workers into higher education and administration – and 'specialist baiting' (*spetseedstvo*).

The new regime's dependence on non-Bolshevik, 'bourgeois' specialists in the administration, industry and the army had been a bitter pill to swallow. Essentially, these were the new educated professionals thrown up alongside the proletariat by the Tsarist industrialization, a largely liberal group which had always trimmed its political demands for fear of mass revolution beneath them, but which had struck in large numbers in protest at the Bolshevik seizure of power. Their attitude of political neutrality was unacceptable to Stalin, who demanded absolute submission to the state, and he set about replacing them with a new politically reliable intelligentsia drawn from the workers. The campaign began with a heavily-publicized trial in May–July 1928 of fifty-three engineers and technicians, accused of sabotage in the coal mines of the Shakhty district of the Donets Basin. Later linked with an alleged international counter-revolutionary plot, most received prison sentences, and five were shot (Lampert, 1979, p.39). The hunt for 'wreckers' spread throughout industry and into the central administration, and culminated in further widely publicized show trials in 1930 and 1931, in one of which a group of high-ranking engineers, known as the 'Industrial Party', was accused of a technocratic conspiracy to take over the Soviet government. The charge was not entirely baseless, as there was a 'technocratic trend' among the old technical intelligentsia at the heart of the economic administration which foresaw that 'the future belongs to managing-engineers and engineering-managers' (Bailes, 1978, p.108).

Stalin may arguably have identified the germs of a new counter-revolutionary political élite, but he could not stamp it out and at the same time hope to sustain the industrialization drive:

The First Five-Year Plan not only marked a stage in Russia's first industrial revolution – that is, the development of railroads, metallurgy, mining, textiles, and so forth – but also marked the Soviet Union's fuller entry into the second industrial revolution, including the development of electrification, a chemical industry, and wide application of the internal combustion engine. All these industries require well trained and competent specialists for their proper functioning, the second cluster of industries even more than the first. (Bailes, 1978, p.118)

In order to resolve this contradiction, an attempt was made to create a new intelligentsia by requiring higher technical education to admit a quota of 65 per cent of students with a working-class background, soon raised to 70 per cent. The original quota was almost achieved in 1933 and 1934, a sharp rise over the 1928 figure of 38 per cent. But in 1935, the quotas were abolished, and by the late thirties, the proportion of working-class engineering students had fallen back to 44 per cent (Bailes, 1978, p.196).

The abolition of quotas was in fact one of the last measures in the retreat from a 'cultural revolution' intended to eradicate all 'bourgeois' vestiges from the intelligentsia (that is, non-manual workers with higher education). Faced with the threatened collapse of their industrialization and collectivization policies, the leadership called a halt to specialist-baiting and proletarianization. In 1931, Stalin spoke out against 'petty-bourgeois egalitarianism', and wage differentials were widened, at first within the working class, and then between the manual workers and the growing white-collar occupations. The technical intelligentsia was rehabilitated, and granted the privileged access to food, housing and education formerly reserved for workers. After 1932, many of the newly recruited working-class Party members were purged, and the Party increasingly came to represent non-manual workers: by the end of Stalin's rule, 75 per cent of members had white-collar occupations (Acton, 1986, p.272). Because of the emphasis on heavy industry, the technical intelligentsia benefited most from this trend. The total number of engineers with higher education rose from 47,000 in 1928 to 289,900 in 1941: no other professional occupation grew as fast. By 1941, the technical intelligentsia as a whole represented 39.6 per cent of professionals employed in the national economy. Many engineers left direct production and joined the Party administration or the secret police. About 70 per cent of Party recruits between 1939 and 1941 came from the technical or administrative intelligentsia (Bailes, 1978, pp.218–19, 335).

The technical intelligentsia became one of the most prominent élites in Soviet society. Of the full members of the Party's Central Committee in 1966, about 65 per cent had a higher technical education (Bailes, 1978, p.6). It must be stressed that this burgeoning social substratum was increasingly far removed from the old technocratic technical intelligentsia which, apart from its humiliation in the show trials of 1928–31, was numerically swamped during the thirties by 'red specialists', products of a distinctly Soviet educational system. The ascendancy of a more and more hereditary scientific-technical élite over the working class was, however, an inevitable feature of a society in which the leadership invested so much in science and technology as the basis of its survival. How indeed did it survive? How did it avoid the terminally destabilizing effects of the Tsarist industrialization? The two drives have much in common: a forced transfer of Western technology, accompanied by harsh discipline and privation among workers and peasants, and by the squalor and hardship of rapid urban growth, culminating moreover in the strains and sacrifices of war with Germany. Lewin (1985, p.222) attributes Soviet stability to the sheer unhinging or 'destructuring' of all social classes under the impact of the first Five-Year Plan, leaving the field free for the state and its institutions. The thirties was indeed a period of massive labour turnover, as well as the mobilization of millions of deportees, prisoners and labour conscripts. Unions had been assimilated into the party structure, and there was no organized focus of discontent as there was in the pre-revolutionary years, especially as the most able and articulate workers were recruited by the Party. A vital consideration is the differential effect of war with Germany: in the First World War, demoralization quickly set in at the Eastern Front within an army in which the social divisions of Tsarist Russia were simply magnified. But the effect of Hitler's invasion in most parts of the Soviet Union was to unite the people in a sense of shared suffering.

What role may be attributed to technology itself in these comparisons? The quotation above from Bailes points out the greater role in Stalin's industrialization of the technology of the Second Industrial Revolution. Some of the consequent de-skilling of the working class may have abetted its 'destructuring'; and some de-skilling may lie behind a notable increase in work specialities between 1930 and 1939 among metalfitters, lathe operators and electricians: from 12 to 176, 10 to 109 and 3 to 188 respectively (Bailes, 1978, p.250). Technology, especially the modernization of the transport system, undoubtedly strengthened the hand of the state and its security organs, so that the means of repression and social control were far more effective than in Tsarist times.

12.2.4 Communications and ideology

State exploitation of modern technology is nowhere more evident than in the use of mass communications, above all the press, for propaganda purposes. The publicity attending the show trials of bourgeois specialists has been mentioned. Another celebrated propaganda exercise, associated with the introduction of wage incentives to boost labour productivity, was the nationwide publicity given to Aleksey Stakhanov, a Donets Basin coalminer, who in 1935 reportedly extracted the equivalent of fourteen norms of coal in one shift. Numerous other prodigious Stakhanovite feats were henceforth recorded, and output norms duly upgraded.

The press had always played a vital part in the Bolsheviks' pre-revolutionary activity; indeed, it was the closure of their newspapers by the Provisional Government which sparked their seizure of power on 24 October 1917. At that time, they had seventy-five publications, twenty-five of which were dailies, with a combined circulation of 600,000 (Kenez, 1985, p.35). Lenin was quite clear on the ideological function of the press, regarding it as 'the centre and foundation of political organization'. He discouraged political debate in newspapers, seeing them instead as a means of educating the masses. A framework was quickly established for the control of the press. A department of agitation and propaganda (*Agitprop*) was set up in 1920, and a branch of it soon directed specifically at the press. Newspaper content was further controlled by Party press departments, and by the chief censorship agency *Glavlit*, established in 1922. Further measures provided for state monopolies of printing-houses, advertising and distribution, but not all were enforced under NEP: in 1923, of 678 existing printing plants, 233 were in private hands (Hopkins, 1970, p.73). The exclusive right to gather national and international news was vested from 1918 in the Russian Telegraph Agency (ROSTA), which was absorbed by a new all-Union Telegraph Agency (TASS) in 1925.

Absolute control of newspapers was established by Stalin, incensed by the publication of factionalist views during the power struggle. Editors and journalists were purged if they failed to toe the Party line, and henceforth the press was dedicated to promoting the industrialization drive, and the cult of Lenin and Stalin, and suppressing any evidence of opposition or hardship. The vital role of press propaganda may be inferred from a dramatic rise in

Figure 12.6
A striking ideological use for modern technology: slide portrait of Stalin projected on to a cloud over Red Square, Moscow, during celebrations to mark Stalin's 70th birthday, 21 December 1949. (Reproduced from Edward Acton, 1986, Russia, Longman, source unknown)

circulation figures. In 1913, there had been 1,005 newspapers with a circulation of 3.3 million; these figures fell in the aftermath of the Revolution, though by 1928 there were 1,197 newspapers with a circulation of 9.4 million. But by the end of the first Five-Year Plan in 1932, the number of newspapers (comprising national, provincial and many more localized titles, often aimed at distinct groups, such as workers, peasants, the army, non-Russian-speaking nationalities, and so on) had reached 7,536, with a circulation of 35.5 million (Hopkins, 1970, p.93).

The printed word – newspapers, and to a much lesser extent, magazines – was the main instrument of Stalinist ideology. Until after the Second World War, radio played a lesser role, largely because of the absence of electricity in rural areas (where, ironically, illiteracy was highest, and radio would have had most ideological impact). In 1920, Lenin had predicted a time when 'we will have hundreds of radio receivers, and all of Russia will be able to listen to a newspaper read in Moscow' (Hopkins, 1970, p.90). Regular broadcasting began in Moscow in 1924. By 1928 there were only 70,000 radio receivers, and 22,000 loudspeakers, connected to a sending station by telephone wires. By 1940, the figures were 1.1 million and 5.8 million, respectively. The loudspeakers were often mounted in clubs and meeting halls, and along streets, but it is estimated that broadcasting reached less than a third of the population, mostly in cities (Hopkins, 1970, pp.90, 246, 248).

It is fitting to end the section on the Soviet Union with a brief discussion of mass communications, since there could hardly be a greater contrast between the Soviet Union and the United States in this area: on the one hand, a crushing monolith imposing an ideology of production, and on the other, an often sensationalist miscellany purveying an ideology of consumption (section 7.2.3). It would have been instructive, had space and competence allowed, to juxtapose the Hollywood dream factory (imported products of which were popular with Russian audiences in the 1920s but banned by Stalin) and the Soviet fare in the thirties of historical costume dramas, and optimistic tales of women textile workers getting to meet Stalin by overfulfulling their norms (Kenez, 1985, pp.258–59). Evidently, both nations during the thirties had a reality to escape, but it requires some considerable subtlety to detect underlying similarities beneath eye-catching contrasts.

That goes for the period as a whole. In almost every aspect of the relations of science, technology and everyday life, the American and Russian experiences look poles apart. By 1950, there is little evidence in the Soviet Union of the mass consumption which funded its chief opponent's military budget. The difference is best indicated by the near absence in Soviet towns and cities of the private automobile; starting with 50 in 1928, maximum output of passenger cars in the plan era was 27,000 in 1938 (*Great Soviet Encyclopedia*, 1973–1983, Vol.1, pp.508–09). The methods of delivery of scientific technology to the arenas of everyday life were fundamentally opposed: in the United States it was advertising, in the Soviet Union administration. We have already seen that the technological determinist has difficulty in coping with the differential social impact of the Tsarist and the Stalinist transfers of Western technology. Comparison beyond the Russian borders only reinforces this point, as Kendall Bailes concludes:

> Widespread adaptations of Western technology to fit Soviet conditions did not change the basically Western nature of most Soviet technology. Yet the evidence of this study also indicates that the social relations connected with the use of such technology were in key respects quite different from those in the West. A major implication of this is that similarities in technology adopted by industrial societies do not necessarily determine the kind of social relations that may emerge. Quite the contrary. Differing cultural traditions, ideological climate, and social structure at the time of adoption are crucial factors. A rigid technological determinism seems contradicted by the evidence of this study. (Bailes, 1978, p.408)

But not all technological determinisms are rigid; some are 'progressive'. An Ellul, presumably, would attribute the great disparities between American and Soviet society to technological lag. Two societies so dedicated in their own ways to scientific-technical rationality will surely end up following a similar path. Technical élites will grow more dominant in each administration, and the obvious differences of political and economic structure will count for less. This point is urged repeatedly in *The Technological Society*: for example, Ellul relates Stakhanovism to Taylorism, charges the Soviet regime with expropriating even more 'surplus value', or profit, from its workers than capitalists, and insists on the increasingly public nature of the capitalist corporation (Ellul, 1965, p.246). Ellul's dramatic thesis requires tendentious generalizations, but they are not entirely without basis. Although the ideological and political contexts of science, technology and everyday life in the Soviet Union and the United States seem utterly at odds, there is some common ground: the commitment to technological progress in both the 'technicist' reading of Marx and the American Ideology (sections 1.3 and 2.2) and the pursuit of technical progress through strict industrial discipline. The greatest disparity lies between the respective roles of the state and private enterprise, but some convergence can be argued here, in view of the US federal government's increasingly interventionist role in the decades of World War and Depression.

It is an odd coincidence that these concluding words are being written at a time (late 1987) of nervous Western optimism about *glasnost* and *perestroika* in the Soviet Union, and a plethora of news items and television documentaries, many originating from the Soviet Union itself (it should be noted that one of the meanings of *glasnost* is 'publicity'). Reports abound of Muscovite punk rockers, and of a new cultural significance for 'heavy metal'; ominously, the streets are now emblazoned with Pepsi-Cola vending machines, and there is Coke and McDonald's on the way. A Habermas or Marcuse would scarcely be taken aback at these developments; their full significance remains to be seen.

REFERENCES

Acton, E. (1986) *Russia*, Longman.

Bailes, K.E. (1978) *Technology and Society Under Lenin and Stalin: Origins of the Soviet Technical Intelligentsia, 1917–1941*, Princeton University Press.

Bater, J.H. (1976) *St. Petersburg: Industrialization and Change*, Edward Arnold.

Blackwell, W.L. (1970) *The Industrialization of Russia: An Historical Perspective*, AHM Publishing.

Bonnell, V.E. (1983a) *Roots of Rebellion: Workers' Politics and Organizations in St. Petersburg and Moscow, 1900–1914*, University of California Press.

Bonnell, V.E. (1983b) *The Russian Worker: Life and Labor Under the Tsarist Regime*, University of California Press.

Crisp, O. (1978) 'Labour and industrialization in Russia' in Mathias, P. and Postan, M.M. (eds.) *The Cambridge Economic History of Europe*, Vol.7, Part 2, pp.308–415, Cambridge University Press.

Ellul, J. (1965) *The Technological Society*, Jonathan Cape.

Falkus, M.E. (1972) *The Industrialization of Russia, 1700–1914*, Macmillan.

Freeze, G.L. (1986) 'The *soslovie* (estate) paradigm and Russian social history', *American Historical Review*, 91, pp.11–36.

Gatrell, P. (1986) *The Tsarist Economy 1850–1917*, Batsford.

Great Soviet Encyclopedia (1973–83) 31 volumes, Macmillan.

Haimson, L. (1964, 1965) 'The problem of social stability in urban Russia, 1905–1917', *Slavic Review*, 23, pp.619–42, 24, pp.1–23.

Hogan, H. (1983) 'Industrial rationalization and the roots of labor militance in the St. Petersburg metalworking industry, 1901–1914' *Russian Review*, 42, pp.163–90.

Hopkins, M.W. (1970) *Mass Media in the Soviet Union*, Pegasus.

Hutchings, R. (1976) *Soviet Science, Technology, Design: Interaction and Convergence*, Oxford University Press.

Johnson, R.E. (1979) *Peasant and Proletarian: The Working Class of Moscow in the Late Nineteenth Century*, Leicester University Press.

Kenez, P. (1985) *The Birth of the Propaganda State: Soviet Methods of Mass Mobilization*, Cambridge University Press.

Koenker, D. and Rosenberg, W.G. (1986) 'Skilled workers and the strike movement in revolutionary Russia', *Journal of Social History*, 19, pp.605–29.

Lampert, N. (1979) *The Technical Intelligentsia and the Soviet State: A Study of Soviet Managers and Technicians 1928–1935*, Macmillan.

Lenin, V.I. (1960–70) *Collected Works*, Progress Publishers.

Lewin, M. (1985) *The Making of the Soviet System: Essays in the Social History of Interwar Russia*, Methuen.

Lewis, R. (1979) *Science and Industrialization in the USSR: Industrial Research and Development 1917–1940*, Macmillan.

Lyashchenko, P.I. (1949) *History of the National Economy of Russia to the 1917 Revolution*, Macmillan.

McCauley, M. (1981) *The Soviet Union since 1917*, Longman.

McKay, J.P. (1970) *Pioneers for Profit: Foreign Entrepreneurs and Russian Industrialization 1885–1913*, University of Chicago Press.

Moore, B. Jr. (1978) *Injustice: The Social Bases of Obedience and Revolt*, Macmillan.

Rogger, H. (1983) *Russia in the Age of Modernization and Revolution 1881–1917*, Longman.

Sutton, A.C. (1968–73) *Western Technology and Soviet Economic Development*, 3 volumes, Hoover Institution.

Von Laue, T.H. (1969) *Sergei Witte and the Industrialization of Russia*, Atheneum.

INDEX

Compiled by Jackie McDermott

abortion, 305, 307, 310
acid rain, 286, 287
acupuncture, 300, 311–2
Adorno, T. W., 53
AdulterationActs, 288
advertisements: electrification and, 97–8, 102–4; film, 229; food, 258, 259, 262, 263, 265; newspaper, 208–11, 212, 214
agriculture, 15, 250 3: electrification, 108–9; collectivization of (Soviet Union), 317, 376–7
Agriculture Act (1947), 268
Air Commerce Act (1926), 194
air transport, 137, 191–6
aircraft industry, 17, 128
Alexander II, 362
Alexander III, 363
alienation (of labour), 52, 328
alkali industry, 80, 115–6, 320
alloy steel, 142, 149–50, 322
alternating current, 70, 71, 76–82, 168
alternative medicine, 300–1, 311–2
aluminium, 80, 109, 137, 159, 194, 254
Amalgamated Association of Iron and Steel Workers, 147
American Bell, 231–2, 320
American Breeders' Assocation, 344, 346
American Broadcasting Company (ABC), 238
American Federation of Labor, 326, 346
American Genetic Association, 346
American Ideology, 30–1, 34, 35–6, 49, 58–9, 383
American Institute of Electrical Engineers, 321
American Public Health Association, 275
American Society of Mechanical Engineers, 287, 321, 326
American Telephone and Telegraph (AT & T), 232–3, 235–8, 242, 318
'Americanization', 18, 358
anaesthetics, 272, 295, 296, 300, 303
anomie, 337
anthrax, 287, 297
anti-semitism, 302–3, 340, 346
antibiotics, 133, 294, 295, 297–8, 300
antiseptics, 272, 297, 298

applied science, 41, 42, 45, 47
apprenticeships, 12, 325, 335–6
arc generator, 236
arc light, 22, 72
Armat, Thomas, 221
Armour, Philip, 255, 257
Arnold, H. L., 328
Artisans Dwelling Act (1875), 282
aspirin (impact), 300
assembly lines, 150, 177, 319, 321–2, 327–34
asylums, 300, 348
atmospheric pollution, 285–7
autonomous technology, 35, 46, 52, 53–4, 55, 57, 149, 196, 362, 372

Bacon, Francis, 46, 316
bacteriology, 27, 275, 296–9
Badger, Daniel, 151
Baekeland, Leo, 127
Bailes, K. E., 382
bakelite (and other resins), 127–30
Barnes, Barry, 44
Bateson, William, 344
Bazalgette, Sir Joseph, 280
Beard, C. A., 34, 36
Beaverbrook, Lord, 209
Bell, Alexander Graham, 217, 230–2
Bell, Daniel, 337
Benz, Karl, 175
Berliet, Maurice, 333
Berlin Industrial Exhibition (1879), 166
Berlin International Automobile Exhibition (1939), 182
Berliner, Émile, 224
Bernal, J. D., 51
Bernhardt, Sarah, 224
Bessemer, Henry, 140–1
Bevan, E. J., 118, 122
Bible and Bibliolatry, 215–6
Bible Communists, 341
bicycle (development), 61–5
bicyclists (road improvements), 189–90
Bijker, Wiebe, 61–3, 65
Binet, Alfred, 349, 354
biometrician/Mendelian controversy, 344
Birch, A., 138
Birdseye, Clarence, 256
birth control, 300, 302, 303, 305–6, 312–3
birth rate, 13, 289, 291: infant mortality, 272, 291, 294, 295,

296, 303–4, 306, 308
Black, Max, 59
Bloor, D., 44
Bogardus, James, 151, 153
Bolshevik Revolution, 367, 375, 378
Bonnell, V. E., 368–9, 371
Booth, Charles, 20, 284, 352
Borden, Gail, 265
Bournville Village Trust, 329
Brandeis, Louis, 323
Braudel, Fernand, 10
Braverman, Harry, 337–9
bread, 260–3, 288
Brearley, Harry, 149
bricks and brickmaking, 158–9
Brigham, C. C., 347
British Broadcasting Corporation, 239, 240, 243
British Electrical Development Association, 97
British Empire Exhibition (1924–25), 127
broadcasting, 230–36: control, 237–9; and other media, 240–4
Brush, C. F., 72, 96
building materials, 158–60
Bukharin, N. I., 375
bulk steel, 137, 140–2, 149, 151
Bullock, William, 204
Burt, C., 335, 353, 354–7
Bury, J. B., 34–5
bus transport, 174, 183
butter, 263–5

Cadbury, George, 283, 329
caesarian section, 306
calcium carbide, 80, 126
canning industry, 253–5
capital goods industries, 317
capital investment, 23, 170
capitalism, 9, 20–1, 52, 60, 239, 302, 337–8: managerial, 317, 318–9, 371; Russian, 367
car industry, 86, 175–8, 183–5, 334, 338-9, 382: assembly line, 319, 321, 327–34; ownership trends, 21, 171–2, 174, 179–82, 186–90, 197, 334
carborundum, 80, 109
Cardwell, D. S. L., 45, 46
Carey, J. W., 32–3, 202, 213–4
Carnegie, Andrew, 143
Carothers, W. H., 122, 129
Carson, Rachel, *Silent Spring*, 117
cartels, 319
casein, 124